Computer Studies
for
BTEC

Second Edition

Geoffrey Knott BA (Open), AIB, Cert Ed
Nick Waites BSc, MSc, Cert Ed
Paul Callaghan BSc (Econ), MSc, MEd, Cert Ed, Cert I.R
John Ellison BA, MEd, Cert Ed

New College Durham

Illustrations And Graphics By
Trevor Moore and B. D. Wright
Flora Pearson, Caroline White and Nick Waites

Business Education Publishers Limited
1990

pg 99 Assignment after wit Mon

© GEOFFREY KNOTT, NICK WAITES,
PAUL CALLAGHAN and JOHN ELLISON 1990

ISBN 0 907679 36 6

First published in 1987
Reprinted 1988 (twice)
Reprinted 1989 (twice)
Second Edition 1990
Reprinted 1990
Reprinted 1991

Cover Design by Flora Pearson of Computer Design, Durham

Published in Great Britain by Business Education Publishers Limited
Leighton House 10 Grange Crescent Stockton Road Sunderland
Tyne and Wear SR2 7BN

Tel. 091 567 4963

Preface

This book has been written for BTEC National Courses in Computer Studies and covers:

Core Units

Information Systems

Introduction to Programming

Computer Systems

Quantitative Methods

Communication Skills

Programming Stream

Concepts and Practice Units

It provides students with all the necessary source material for each unit and the content of each chapter is developed through a series of realistic work-based assignments which form the basis of an active student centred learning programme. The book makes no assumptions about the student's previous knowledge and it has been written in a way which allows students to gain a fundamental understanding of the technical and applicational areas of computing.

The text is designed to be used in association with *Small Business Computer Systems for BTEC*, a book written for the unit of the same name by Geoffrey Knott and published by Business Education Publishers Limited.

Printed in Great Britain at the Alden Press, Oxford

Acknowledgements

The second edition of this book has been produced with the help of a number of people who deserve particular mention. Special thanks go to Jim Cox and Jim Morton of New College Durham who patiently read and commented upon much of the first draft of the material. Thanks also to the computer staff at Monkwearmouth College, Sunderland for their encouragement and support. Thanks are due to the administrative staff at Business Education Publishers including Sonia, Debra, Julie and particularly Lilias Smith and Sheila Callaghan for helping to ensure the success of the first edition. Trevor Moore and B.D. Wright interpreted our rough sketches to produce the excellent graphics for the first edition and Flora Pearson and Caroline White produced the equally attractive illustrations and graphics for the second edition. Flora also designed the cover with characteristic good taste. Moira Page and Caroline White were responsible for the production editing and managed this with their usual calm and good humour.

Most importantly we must thank our families, to whom this book is dedicated, for their continued sufferance through yet another book and without whose patience, understanding and encouragement it may never have been completed.

All errors and omissions should have been spotted. If they were not then they remain the responsibility of the authors.

Durham
June 1990

GK
NW
PC
JE

The Authors

Geoffrey Knott is Lecturer in Computing at New College Durham. He has had wide experience of teaching and developing BTEC courses and extensive practical experience in Computing and Information Technology before entering teaching. He is also the co-author of *Information Processing for BTEC* and the author of *Small Business Computer Systems for BTEC*.

Nick Waites is Senior Lecturer in Computing at New College Durham. He has taught Computing and Information Technology for many years and is currently responsible for staff development in computing and IT. His present research interests are in the area of computer graphics. He is the co-author of *Information Processing for BTEC*.

Paul Callaghan is Principal Lecturer and Director of Studies at New College Durham. His other books include *The Business Environment, The Organisation in its Environment, The Abbotsfield File - a business in action, Information Processing for BTEC* and *Core Studies for BTEC*. He has also had numerous articles published. He has edited several books on subjects including Travel and Tourism and Transferable Personal Skills. He has played a major role in developing relevant and practical teaching materials for BTEC courses.

John Ellison is a Senior Lecturer at New College Durham. He is the co-author of *The Business Environment, The Organisation in its Environment, The Abbotsfield File - a business in action, Core Studies for BTEC* and *Business Law for BTEC*. He has established a national reputation for his work in curriculum development and the production of business related texts.

Table of Contents

☐ Information Systems

☐ Introduction to Programming

☐ Computer Systems

☐ Quantitative Methods

☐ Communication Skills

☐ Programming Concepts and Practice

Chapter 34   Data Structures

Chapter 35   Sorting Techniques

Chapter 36   COBOL

Glossary

Index

Chapter 1

The Organization

The Formation of Organizations

The reasons why organizations are formed

The society in which we live is complex and sophisticated. As consumers we demand a variety of goods and services to enable us to maintain the quality of life we enjoy. In order to satisfy these demands, suppliers must produce the goods and services which the consumer wants by combining factors of production such as land, labour and capital in the most efficient manner. By this we mean producers must hire workers, rent or buy premises, perhaps invest in plant and machinery and purchase raw materials, and then organise the manufacture of the final product in such a way that they will make a profit. Society may also gain, as its scarce resources are being used in the way consumers wish rather than being wasted in producing things people do not need. Suppliers under such a system are known as commercial organizations. Many public sector organizations also provide goods and services to society and, in the same way as commercial organizations, these public sector bodies must employ staff, occupy premises and raise capital. The fundamental difference between these two types of organization lies in the objectives they seek to fulfil. We shall note later that the private sector tends to be motivated by profit, while public sector organizations will often have a much less mercenary motive, such as providing for the public good and improving the state of society.

If we wish to see society ordered and governed in such a way that individuals are free to express their demands and producers are able to meet such wants, it becomes necessary to form organizations to control and regulate society through a variety of administrative structures. These are the bodies which make up the organizations of the state. In the UK, these are Parliament, the Government and its Executive, the Civil Service, the Local Authorities and the Courts and justice system. These bodies are required to carry out legislative, administrative and judicial functions.

If you examine the nature and range of individual demands in an industrialised society you soon realise that most of them cannot be met other than by organizations. Individually we lack the knowledge, skills and physical resources to manufacture products that fulfil our needs, whether these are simple or sophisticated. It would be as difficult for us to make a biro or a floppy disk as it would a television or a computer.

Admittedly, some goods and services can be supplied by an individual working alone. A farmer may be able to grow sufficient food to satisfy himself and his family without any help from others. But what if he requires other goods and services? It is unlikely that the farmer will also have the ability or resources to produce his own combine-harvester or tractor. If he did not have such products which are manufactured by others, his life would be much simpler, but no doubt much harder.

A similar situation exists in the supply of services. A strong and resourceful individual may try to protect himself and his property from the dangers imposed by thieves or vandals. If he cannot, however, then he may turn to the state to demand protection. Recognising that a failure to respond to such demands from its citizens would lead to an anarchic system, the government must accept the responsibility and establish a legal system incorporating law enforcement agencies to provide the protection being sought.

How, then, are these goods and services produced? It is clear that individuals working independently would be unable to meet our complex physical and social needs. Therefore society has developed a system where people join together to form organizations. These bodies are extraordinarily diverse. They manufacture products, which they distribute and sell. They also provide all the services that we need. Thus the BBC is an organization producing a product in much the same way as the Ford Motor Company is.

Clearly, then, if individuals within society are to have all their various needs satisfied, there must be co-operation between workers. Each must specialise in a certain aspect of the supply process. These workers must be organised and allocated a specific role in which to perform co-ordinated tasks. These tasks are normally organised with the aim of producing a given product or service, although there are some organizations which do not specialise and which make an extremely diverse range of products. In the private sector of the economy, such businesses will usually have the objective of making a profit for their owners. Of course, this is just one example of an organization. As we have already noted, the state is another form of organization which is clearly more complex than a business, and it has a variety of objectives, such as increasing the wealth of citizens, improving their quality of life and protecting them if they are threatened. We are all members of organizations, some of which are formal while others are informal. Your family is an example of an informal organization, as is the group of friends you mix with. Other more formal organizations to which you may belong or may have belonged are the school you attended as a child, your employing body, or your trade union.

The tendency to form groups is a characteristic of human nature. Human beings are highly socialised, they need to 'belong' and will generally find it uncomfortable and disturbing if they cannot find 'acceptance' within a social group. An employee who is capable and confident in his or her job, and who is in turn regarded by the employer and the rest of the work force as a professional, gains a 'role' satisfaction through identifying as a vital part of the group. So organizations have an important role to fulfil in meeting the social needs of man. However, perhaps more important in the context of this course of study is the function of organizations as the satisfiers of needs. They allow individual workers to develop their specialist skills, and this in turn allows productive capacity to increase.

Since differing organizations concentrate on the supply of different goods and services, there must be a system established whereby products can be distributed to the consumers. Thus shops, wholesalers, transport companies and so on must all be involved. The fabric of the social and economic environment is based on a process whereby individuals form organizations which are dependent upon other organizations to survive. In just the same way as the needs of the individual cannot be met by that individual alone, so the same also holds true for organizations. They are interdependent. Organizational activity involves a perpetual interaction, one organization with another, as society steadily evolves in a direction that individually and collectively we try to guide. However, as we shall see, even though the overall aim of society is the advancement of our physical well-being, the methods for achieving this are the subject of much disagreement.

Characteristics common to all organizations

The specific reasons for the formation of organizations are many and varied, and may not, of course, always be clearly defined. Some are the result of the need for individuals to find company for a social or leisure reason, for example by forming a sporting or working-men's club. Others are formed with a more precise economic objective in mind, such as the desire to make a profit for the person who has established a business organization. Some, such as the organizations which make up the state and government, evolve as a result of the emergence of particular needs in society which require government intervention. For example, the Government established the National Health Service in 1946 to meet the needs of society for a high standard of free health care, available to all.

Nevertheless, most formal organizations have some common characteristics. These may be simply stated as follows:

(i) The establishment of an organization is usually for a specific purpose

For example, the Automobile Association was founded with the precise objective of promoting the interests of motorists within this country. Other organizations may be launched with one prime aim, but may later diversify in order to follow alternative causes or objectives. For instance, Guinness, the brewery company, was established to produce alcoholic drinks, but now has subsidiaries making a variety of products such as fishing tackle boxes and cassette cases. This illustrates how a business may try to evolve as the commercial environment changes and new commercial opportunities emerge.

(ii) Organizations usually have a distinct identity

People belonging to a specific organization can identify themselves as being part of a group either as a result of where they work or of what they do. A Manchester United footballer wears a red shirt to show he is part of the particular organization. A member of a trade union is given a membership card to signify he belongs to that union. Manufacturing companies promote their brand names through advertising. This sense of identity, which we have already seen is an important need for most people, can produce extreme loyalty to the organization.

(iii) Most organizations require some form of leadership

We have seen that organizations are normally formed for a specific purpose. In order to achieve this purpose, it is necessary to co-ordinate the efforts of the members of the organization. This requires management, or leadership. Formal organizations such as companies or a club have a specified management hierarchy which may be appointed by the owners of the organization. For instance, the shareholders of a company appoint the directors. Alternatively, the leadership may be elected, as in the case of a club or society where the members vote to have a chairman, secretary and committee. However, once appointed this management team has the responsibility for ensuring the organization achieves its objectives.

(iv) Organizations are accountable

Such accountability applies both to those the management team deals with and those it employs.

The objectives of organizations

The objectives of an organization are the targets it hopes to achieve. Clearly the objectives which are set will vary considerably between different types of organization. As we shall see later in this section, the objectives of commercial organizations will largely be based around the goal of profit. For organizations within the public sector, profit may not be the sole aim. Factors such as benefit to the community or the creation of jobs may also feature as targets for the public sector. It should be noted, however, that the profit motive is growing substantially in importance in the current economic and political climate.

The setting of objectives

The management of any organization, whether in the public or private sector, must ensure that its objectives are as clearly defined as possible. This is important because vague objectives cannot easily be achieved or quantified. The steps for setting an organization's objectives should be as follows:

(i) Identify clearly objectives for the organization

For instance, a local authority may wish to improve its provision of leisure facilities during the financial year.

(ii) Ensure objectives do not conflict

To use the same example, the authority may find that increasing its leisure facilities involves employing new staff at a time when central government is suggesting that staff levels should remain, at best, constant.

(iii) Determine the most appropriate means of achieving objectives

For example, the increase in leisure facilities may be attained by upgrading existing resources and redeploying staff, rather than by constructing an expensive new leisure centre.

(iv) Evaluate the success of the policy in achieving the objectives within a given time period

Check whether usage rates have improved over, for example, a comparable six-month period before the changes.

(v) Reassess the objectives

Examine again the objectives at regular intervals and decide whether or not they are still appropriate and/or achievable. If they are not, set new objectives.

The objectives of private sector organizations

For business organizations it is possible to distinguish between a number of differing objectives.

Primary objectives

The prime objective of any business organization is to survive. In order to achieve this it must make a profit. Maximum profit is not always the main goal of an organization. The level of profit regarded as satisfactory is often dependent on who is managing the business.

Secondary objectives

The organization may also make a profit through the achievement of what we may refer to as secondary objectives. These can be classified as:

> (i) economic

> (ii) social

Examples of economic objectives are increased productivity, reduced costs and increased sales. Social objectives may include promotion of a public image, the improvement of industrial relations, or the provision of better working conditions for employees.

When these secondary objectives are considered in detail, an underlying theme connects them all. This is to increase profit. So be wary when you consider the motives behind the actions of business organizations, as there is usually profit involved!

As an organization may have a variety of objectives, and not only one solitary aim, it is often necessary to rank these objectives in order of importance. So, for example, an organization may be faced with two problems: the need to increase revenue from sales, and the legal requirement to improve the safety conditions in the production area. It might see little improvement in profitability from tightening the safety procedures or spending money on fencing-in machines. Extra revenue from sales would help the organization's profit levels far more. However, when it is faced with possible sanctions from the Health and Safety Executive, such as the closure of dangerous production lines, safety becomes the prime objective. It is somewhat cynical to say that were it not for the law, business organizations would put profit before safety. However, the Health and Safety Executive has itself noted an increase in industrial accidents during periods of recession, which it has attributed to employers spending less on safety and employing more outside contractors. This may have short-term advantages for the employer, but in the longer run such cost cutting can prove more expensive, through loss of production occurring when vital staff are off sick, claims for compensation being made following accidents, and higher insurance premiums resulting.

1. Without defined objectives, there is a possibility that individuals or departments may act in such a way that they contribute nothing to the overall performance of the organization, or might even act in ways which conflict with actual aims.

2. If objectives are set quantitatively, for instance by specifying a certain target for the growth in sales as 20%, they can be measured reasonably accurately, enabling performance to be judged against them.

3. Objectives can only be set realistically by attempting to predict the future performance of the organization and possible changes in the factors which may affect its performance. Therefore we need to have some idea of how an increase or decrease in demand for the organization's product or service will affect sales. By attempting to forecast what is likely to happen, the company is in a better position to adapt to possible changes.

Non-profit maximising objectives

In the previous section we assumed that a business organization would normally have profit maximisation as its main objective. However, this is not so in all organizations. Even an individual trader is not always seeking the greatest level of profit, but simply enough profit to satisfy his or her particular wants or needs. This is sometimes referred to as satisfactory profit. An example may be a small shopkeeper who chooses to close the shop at 5.30pm in the evening instead of being 'open all hours'. This is because the shopkeeper will want to do other things, such as spending time with his or her family or enjoying a hobby or pastime. It is important to keep the running of a business in perspective. It is not a good idea to ruin your health or destroy your family life merely to gain ever-greater levels of profit.

We can also identify objectives other than profit in large organizations as well as small ones. Consider a large company and how different groups involved in its running will hold different objectives.

An important factor to recognise is that in the large organizations of today's business world there is a distinction between ownership and management and control. The owners are the shareholders who have bought a part of the company, and their degree of ownership is in proportion to the percentage of the shares they hold. In many organizations, the major shareholders are often large financial institutions such as insurance companies, pension funds and unit trust investment companies. Their objective is to earn the maximum return on their investment, and to do this the investment managers of these institutions will buy and sell shares in companies according to their assessment of the potential profitability of each organization. This means that a company must be sufficiently profitable to satisfy such institutional shareholders.

A second group who are involved in the company are the managers and executives. In small companies the managers are the owners. In the larger corporate bodies, in which there is a substantial share capital, ownership and management will invariably be in different hands, with the shareholders electing a board of directors as salaried, professional managers of the business. While the owners have ultimate control over the managers, with the power to dismiss them, the business could not be effectively carried on without permitting managers a broad degree of commercial freedom. Having this freedom they may pursue policies which are more personal than organizational. Some examples may illustrate this point.

A manager's power or salary is sometimes linked to the company's sales, and so he may prefer sales maximisation to profit maximisation. Executives may also regard the size of the business as a reflection of their power and so might encourage the growth of the company, even if this means a lower profit per share to the shareholders. Furthermore, the executive may wish to see any profit that the company does make reinvested in the company to encourage further growth and new developments. This may be at odds with the aims of the shareholders, who would rather see profits distributed to them in the form of dividends on their shares, so giving them an immediate return on their investment.

Such conflicts are rarely seen in public. Instead, the shareholders will put pressure on the managers in more discreet ways, such as by threatening to vote them out of control if they do not follow the shareholders' line. The success of such action depends on whether or not the directors can command the confidence of a majority, 51%, of all shareholders, and can therefore choose to ignore the wishes of blocks of shareholders who remain in the minority when it comes to the vote.

A final point to consider when looking at the objectives of managers is what are known as behavioural objectives. These are distinct from economic objectives and refer to a manager's desire to increase his or her power, status or work-force.

Behavioural objectives

As long as they are increasing the number of people working under them, many managers are happy. They feel that this increases their power. Conversely, managers may simply seek an 'easy life', resisting attempts to increase the size of their part of the company as this may bring with it extra stress or strain. Clearly, behavioural objectives depend upon the individual managers concerned. You can probably identify within your own experience the type of person who is a 'go-getter', and others who are perhaps more casual in their attitudes. It is therefore not an easy task for the shareholders to select management who are both competent and efficient and who will steer the fortunes of the business in a way which is compatible with the shareholders' objectives.

The objectives of public sector organizations

If we are to examine the objectives of public sector organizations, it is first necessary to distinguish between organizations which are established to provide a service such as health care or education and those which have been established to produce a product for sale to the general public. Whilst it is not always easy to categorise public sector organizations in this way, the distinction illustrates the importance of organizational type upon objectives.

Public sector service organizations

One of the objectives of the state which has evolved over the last century has been that of improving the welfare of its citizens. Collectively, the organizations which seek to achieve this are known as the 'welfare state'. They include:

- National Health Service
- Social Security system
- Education system
- Housing and Social Services departments of local authorities

Each of these is given the responsibility by government for ensuring that there is an acceptable level of provision of the services which they administer. When the National Health Service was established in 1946, its objective was to "secure improvement in the physical and mental health of the people of England and Wales and the prevention, diagnosis and treatment of illness". As you will realise, this is a very broad objective. The Act of Parliament which established the National Health Service did not go into specific detail. It did not say that all people who require a kidney transplant should be given one, or that all children should be inoculated against polio. The objective was phrased in such wide terms as to allow the administrators of the Health Service to determine where priorities and needs lay. It is therefore the responsibility of the Department of Health and Social Security, the Regional Health Authorities and, ultimately, individual hospitals and general practitioners to determine how best the health care of the nation should be provided. However, this does not mean that such decisions can be made only with needs of the patient in mind.

Unfortunately, the State has limited resources and the extent of the resources made available to the Health Service is determined by the overall evaluation of the competing demands of all aspects of the State by the central government. This involves a political judgement as to the amounts of taxation we as taxpayers are willing to pay and, also, judgement concerning the areas of expenditure to which this taxpayers' money will be allocated. No doubt we would all welcome substantial improvements in the standards of health care, education and social services, but we might not be willing to vote into power a government who proposed doubling taxation to finance such improvements. Obviously there are those who would accept higher taxation if this was accompanied by improved services, but politics does not operate in a way which presents the electorate with such straightforward choices. The political parties will only advocate that combination of taxes and services which they believe will gain them a parliamentary majority. Raising taxation is regarded by all of them as essentially unpopular. In fact, the Thatcher government has made the cutting of taxes a major plank in its policy. Such cuts must inevitably be accompanied by cuts in public services. Nevertheless, such a policy has found support from the electorate in the last three elections.

In this context, there is a yearly battle in cabinet, where the Chancellor of the Exchequer sets out the amount of revenue he thinks he can safely raise, and then the competing government departments each argue their case for a large share of the resulting expenditure.

These considerations give us some guidance as to the objectives of the public sector services. It is possible to define the objectives of those departments which provide a service as being twofold:

(i)   the provision of as wide-ranging a service as possible in meeting the needs of the population;

(ii)   the efficient and cost-effective use of the budget which they have managed to receive.

Public sector producer organizations

This group of organizations is sometimes referred to collectively as 'public enterprise', and it is a rapidly dwindling group. Included would be organizations such as British Coal, British Rail and the Electricity Generating Boards. These organizations all produce a product or service which is directly marketable to the general public. In other words, they sell what they make. Their objectives have certainly not remained constant over the period of their existence. Successive governments have used these Nationalised Industries to further various political aims. Many were taken into public ownership in the late 1940s by the post-war Labour government. Initially they had two main objectives:

(i)   to provide as wide a range of services as possible;

(ii)   to break even, taking one year with another.

These two objectives were not necessarily compatible, and for many years the major industries incurred substantial losses, safe in the knowledge that the government would cover any financial shortfall. The 1960s witnessed a change in government attitude towards public enterprise. The government encouraged these organizations to operate along 'commercial lines' as the main objective. Most of the industries underwent a process of 'rationalisation', resulting in the closure of many loss-making coal mines and unviable branch lines. Nevertheless, the government maintained as an objective the need to provide an acceptable level of output of these products to the public.

The coming to power of the Thatcher government in 1979 saw a further change of attitude to these organizations. Objectives were much more closely related to those of the private sector, with maximum profit becoming the main aim. The government, with its philosophy of non-intervention into the economy, set about a radical programme of privatisation - the sale of the nationalised industries to the private sector. Examples include British Telecom, British Gas and British Airways. Many others were 'prepared' for sale, as can be witnessed by the advertisements proclaiming a 'leaner, fitter' British Steel, and the substantial increases in the price of electricity, with the aim being to increase profitability, and therefore attractiveness to potential investors. The political justification behind the policy of privatisation is a complex argument, but the effect upon the objectives of public sector producer organizations certainly cannot be ignored.

The Structure and Operation of the Organization

In addition to the scale of an organization, two further important factors affect the suitability of an organization's communications system. These are:

(a)   the structure of the organization; and

(b)   its operating methods.

The structure of the organization

There are a number of overlapping structures in any organization. There is the financial structure, the legal structure and the organizational structure. Here we can simply note that all have implications for the communications system. For instance, the process of holding meetings in registered companies is regulated by statute, and thus such companies are obliged by their legal structure to conduct their business according to externally imposed rules.

The organizational structure of a business is concerned with the co-ordination and grouping of related activities to achieve the organization's objectives. The successful business will have divided its activities into a logical sequence and have allocated each such division sufficient resources to adequately perform its function. The responsibilities for each section of the business must be clearly defined and the authority to undertake such responsibilities must be delegated to the appropriate section. The overall organization must ensure that there is co-ordination between the various aspects of the business and that clear lines of communication have been established. However, the organizational structure must retain sufficient flexibility to allow it to adapt to change.

One important reason for a formal organization structure is to ensure that each individual is able to identify his or her position within the organization. Employees should be aware of their own responsibilities, to whom they are directly accountable and for whom they bear a managerial or supervisory role. A further advantage of a formal structure is that it should allow management to develop areas of specialism and expertise within the organization.

Almost certainly, informal structures will also develop within an organization as a result of personal relationships, work patterns and practical expediency. Such informal structures are to be encouraged unless they conflict with the efficient operation of the business.

The pyramid structure and communication flows

Most organizations have a pyramid structure in which authority and responsibility extend downwards in a hierarchical pattern. Senior management make the executive and policy decisions. They have the overall responsibility for the success or failure of such policies and have the authority vested in them to allow them to carry this out. As you move down the pyramid, status, responsibility and authority decreases.

However, the lower down the pyramid you descend, the larger the number of staff you are likely to find employed. Thus the pyramid represents both authority and quantity. An organization pyramid is illustrated below:

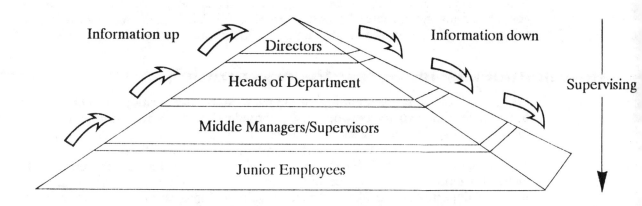

Information up and down

Within the pyramid information passes up and down. Policy decisions taken at board level by the directors are implemented by instructing the relevant departmental heads to see that the policy is carried out. They will then brief the middle managers for whom they are responsible, and the final stage in the process is the communication between middle managers and the junior staff. This may seem like a long winded process, but at each stage the staff involved not only get to know the decision made 'at the top' but are left to use their knowledge and initiative to best determine how to respond to the instructions they have been given. For instance, it may be that a supervisor needs only to speak to certain of his junior staff, and knowing them personally will choose the best time and method to inform them of changes to their working methods and practices. Thus a level of fine tuning is introduced which would probably be lost if the information came from higher up. In a sense what the pyramid reveals is that as organizations grow the need to delegate responsibilities increases. Someone who sets up their own business employing only two part-time staff can exercise full control over all aspects of the business. If in twenty years time the business has developed and now employs a hundred full time staff it will no longer be physically possible for the founder to manage the organization alone.

The information flow also passes from the bottom upwards. Staff provide feedback to their seniors. This may take many forms; it may involve monitoring shortages of materials, absences of staff, production problems, grievances, suggestions for improving work methods in the working environment. Anything which requires the authority or approval of someone further up the organizational hierarchy and which has been generated or identified below will pass back up the system. Only in extreme circumstances is it likely that an issue arising at the bottom of the pyramid will pass right back to the top for consideration and decision. For the most part an immediate senior is likely to possess sufficient authority to make a decision, but ultimately it is a question of the extent of the delegated responsibility held by senior employees that determines whether they can deal with the matter personally, or must pass it back to their own superiors. This in turn indicates just how much power the organization has vested in them. Clearly if a middle manager enjoys little autonomy to make decisions, but must in most cases refer back to the head of department, not only is the middle manager in the position of having a title without a corresponding authority, making his or her job virtually impossible, but it also means that the chain of communication is being unnecessarily extended. This is time wasting and expensive, for it defeats the purpose of creating a separate managerial tier, and may result in the senior employee carrying too heavy a workload.

As organizations grow bigger it is inevitable that communication flows, the messages passing within the organization, have much further to travel. This is not ideal since it is likely to take longer to transmit communications and there is a greater distancing between the giver and receiver, which can lead to a 'them and us' view of the organization by junior staff. However, it is clear that as the organization grows, so its communication system must become increasingly refined, for as we have seen the bigger the organization, the greater are the communication demands.

Information passing across the organization

Within each of the levels identified in the pyramid, communications also take place horizontally, that is to say, between staff of broadly the same status within the bands. Since most organizations consist of a number of component parts, usually referred to as departments (which are often further broken down into sections) these diagonal communications will invariably involve messages being transferred between departments, for most of the workforce will be attached to a particular department. Thus heads of department are likely to meet regularly. Junior staff may need to work together to deal with invoices, and in an organization engaged in production processes, production line workers, each with his or her own particular responsibility, will need to co-operate with fellow workers to ensure the smooth running of the line.

When horizontal communication is impaired serious damage can be caused to the entire enterprise, for each department is inevitably heavily dependant upon other departments if it is to function effectively. The interrelationship of departments and the significance of it for the communication system is examined in more detail below.

Information passing diagonally

This occurs when staff at different levels within the organization and who work in different departments, are involved in communicating with each other. For instance a Sales and Marketing Manager may request financial information from a financial assistant in the accounts department, or a junior employee in the production department may need personal details about a newly appointed employee to the department that is held by the Personnel Manager. Both in the case of diagonal communications, and those across the organization, care and tact are called for, since staff in one department are not accountable to staff in another department, thus it would generally be out of order for a senior member of department A to issue an instruction to an employee in department B, or seek to discipline someone in department C.

The diagram below illustrates communication flows within an organization, and indicates the types of communication that are likely to be involved.

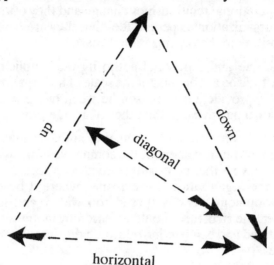

The direction of communications in an organization

Using the diagram above we can seek to identify the likely content of the communications involved.

Downwards communications will predominantly involve the issuing of (a) directives i.e., general orders such as a rule that no one below a certain level shall make long distance telephone calls before 1 p.m.; (b) specific orders, such as an instruction to prepare a report or clean a machine; and (c) requests. Additionally downwards communications will often involve the granting of authority to a subordinate, or confirmation of the action taken by a subordinate.

Upwards communications involve seeking information and advice and obtaining authority to act, and include suggestions and criticisms presented by subordinates to superiors.

Horizontal communications are essentially concerned with information exchange, for example, the giving and receiving of data between departments, and working on joint or group projects.

Diagonal communications are concerned, as we have seen, with requests for information and advice between staff of differing status located in different departments.

Organization charts

It is usually possible to identify two forms of authority in an organization:

(a)   line authority; and

(b)   functional authority.

Line authority is the direct relationship between a superior and his or her subordinates. It is shown on a organization chart by a vertical line indicating direct authority.

Functional authority indicates the responsibility for specialist functions in an organization. So, for example, the personnel department is responsible for that sphere of the organization's activities relating to the workforce in all of its departments. Organization charts are an attempt to record the formal structure of the business, showing some of the relationships, the downward flow of authority and responsibility and the main lines of communication. They have the advantage of forcing senior management to clearly define organizational relationships. They are a useful introduction to the organization for outsiders, particularly new employees, and they can form a starting point from which management can initiate change or evaluate the strengths and weaknesses of the operation. However, they can quickly become out of date as personnel and operational relationships change and they often introduce a degree of rigidity into the organization as people feel that they are constrained by the defined limits of their position in the organizational chart.

In terms of both line and functional authority the simplicity or complexity of the organization chart will be a reflection of the scale of the organization. The organization charts given below provide a comparison between two private sector organizations, one of a professional partnership, the other of a large private limited company.

Thus organization charts, by identifying lines of authority and responsibility, can be of great assistance in the improvement of the communications system by managers. They may, for example, reveal that an existing structure is such that it inhibits change and development in the organization, for example, where it becomes apparent that research and development work is spread too widely and is not co-ordinated. As mentioned earlier, the structure should be carefully monitored to ensure that it does not become outdated and begin to introduce rigidity into the roles and responsibilities of the workforce.

Organization charts are as valuable to public sector organizations as to those in the private sector. For instance, a newly elected councillor or full time employee of a local authority with a responsibility for servicing certain committees may find an organization chart of the kind shown below invaluable as a source of information.

The Sub-Units of Organizations

With growth in the size of an organization, responsibility for the various functions which are involved in the running of it will increasingly be handled by specialists, who will require their own suitably trained staff to support them. In the organization chart for the partnership, this process has already begun with its specialist accounts and administration departments. The process is further advanced for the limited company and the local authority. When organizations grow to this size it becomes possible to produce organization charts which focus purely upon the sub-units of the organization. For example, the organization chart for Southern Electronics could be presented department by department. In this way a picture can be gained of the whole organization in which all members of the workforce appear. It can also show more clearly how the different departments are organised, and in doing so may help to reveal why some are more difficult to operate than others. For instance, a production department is likely to employ far more people than a finance department, although both will encompass a wide range of specialist responsibilities.

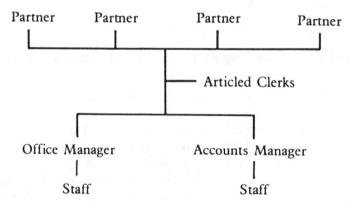

An organisation chart for a professional partnership

An organisation chart for a large private limited company *(Southern Electronics)*

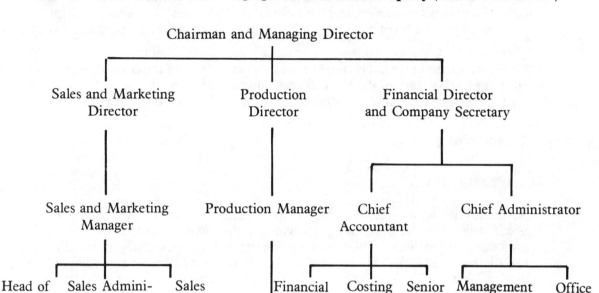

The value of an organization chart

The value of an organization chart is that:

(a) the task of preparing it enables the individual components of the organization to be brought under review;

(b) an assessment can be made of the relationship of each component part of the organization to the others;

(c) management must consider the authority required by individuals within the structure to carry out their responsibilities adequately;

(d) it assists staff in locating their role and status within the organization;

(e) it provides a simple picture of the organization.

The operating methods of the organization

The operating methods of an organization, that is the way in which it performs its work, should be carefully monitored to ensure that there are no barriers in the communication system which are inhibiting their effectiveness. While the structure may be clearly defined it does not follow that individuals are able to carry out their jobs effectively.

There may be physical and psychological barriers to communication preventing this. For instance, a personal assistant may be entirely clear about the nature of his or her role and status, but find that it is extremely difficult to liaise with the boss. The boss is never available when needed, and the assistant finds that the job cannot be adequately performed because he or she lacks authority to make decisions in the absence of the boss.

Particular attention should be paid to the support systems of the organization. These make up a sub-system of the broader communications network operating within the organization, and they include administrative, clerical and technical services.

Support systems

Administrative support

Administration is an aspect of management. A manager is essentially someone responsible for directing the workforce in carrying out their work so as to ensure that as far as possible the policies of the organization are being met. Managers usually have specific responsibilities, as can be seen in the company organization chart shown earlier. Without people to co-ordinate and control the work of the organization, it could not operate adequately. Not surprisingly administrators are a part of all medium and large scale organizations. They may even have a role in smaller ones as was seen in the partnership organization chart.

Technical support

In some large enterprises the scale of the activities enable it to maintain departments with highly specialised technical support functions. These will not only provide information but also assistance both to the organization as a whole, and to the individual staff within it. For instance, some organizations will have their own legal department, pension department and in-house travel agency.

Clerical support

Clerical support covers such jobs as filing, typing, handling mail, reproducing information, and switchboard work. All these tasks may be performed by a single office or department, usually called a General Administrative Office, or just a General Office. In practice this could be just a room or perhaps a suite of rooms or even various 'nooks and crannies' located in the building. When we think about 'the office' we all usually have some ideas about what activities are carried out there.

The major activity of all offices is to act as communication centres, places dealing with information. In larger organizations, staff working in such offices may be given titles which reflect their specific role such as a telephonist, receptionist, secretary, director of administration, filing clerk, clerical officer, reprographics operator, typist or clerk. In smaller organizations staff are usually engaged in the same type of work function, but often have to perform more than one of these tasks without being given a formal title. They may simply be described as 'office workers'.

Assignment

The Organization

Choose an organization with which you are familiar. This could be the organization you work for, or your local authority, or the college you are studying at.

Tasks

1.   Collect any available information that describes the structure of your chosen organization, and from this produce an organization chart displaying either the line authority within the organization or its committee structure.

2.   Investigate the operation of the communications system within your chosen organization, to enable you to produce an information sheet for distribution to all the staff of the organization, which describes:

   (a)   the method used by the organization for receiving and storing data;

   (b)   the system of administrative and clerical support it operates, and

   (c)   the method it uses for distributing information.

Developmental Task

Prepare some outline notes on the material you have produced under Task 2 that you could use to present a short talk. The talk would be given to other members of your group, and would:

   (a)   describe the administrative system operated by your organization; and

   (b)   introduce your ideas on how the system might be improved.

Chapter 2

The Functional Areas of the Organization

This chapter examines some of the procedures involved in the main functional areas of the organization. It would be impossible in a text such as this to cover every department in an organization so it is proposed to concentrate on the following departments.

(i) Purchasing;

(ii) Stock Control;

(iii) Production Control;

(iv) Wages and Salaries.

The final part of the chapter will outline the structure and operation of Management Information Services.

Purchasing

There are usually a number of distinct stages in the purchase of any goods or services by an organization and each of the stages requires the appropriate documentation. To illustrate these stages we will use the example of an accounts manager who wishes to buy a new micro computer for his section.

The Purchase Requisition

If the accounts manager has the authority to initiate such a purchase, he will issue a purchase order requisition. This is a request to the purchasing department asking for the piece of equipment which is required. At this stage the manager may have a particular make of machine in mind which will meet his requirements. If this is the case he should specify this on the requisition form. Alternatively he may have a specific task in mind that can be accomplished by any of a range of machines, such as the ability to handle spreadsheets, in which case he may not specify a particular model but allow the purchasing department to choose the best purchasing option available. The date when the machine is needed would also be shown on the requisition as this will give some indication to the purchasing department of the urgency of the purchasing procedure.

Placing the Order

When the buyer has examined all the potential offers to supply the product, he will select the most favourable and issue a purchase order. This is the organization's acceptance of the supplier's offer. It will have a separate purchase order number. The order will confirm the price, the delivery date required and any other terms or conditions which the buyer wishes to include in the contract. It will be signed by someone with sufficient authority to sanction the amount of money which is being spent. It is important that a copy of the order is forwarded to the accounts department for they will not pay the forthcoming invoice unless they can verify that an official order, which has an acceptable order number, has been placed.

The Acknowledgement

Most suppliers will immediately acknowledge the order and this will allow the buyer to confirm that the terms have been formally agreed. It will also act as a check that an order has been received by the supplier.

The Delivery Note

When the goods are delivered, a delivery note will be attached which has been made out by the supplier. This should clearly specify the goods which are being supplied. A copy is normally signed by the receiving organization and then retained by the carrier of the goods as proof that the goods have been delivered. Because of this it is important that the receiver checks the goods which are specified on the delivery note. Any discrepancy should be notified immediately to the buying department and on the delivery note itself.

The Goods Received Note

Once the goods have been checked it is normal procedure to produce a goods received note. This is an internal document which records the acceptance of the goods into the organization. A copy is held by the goods received department, a copy is passed to the purchasing department and a copy is sent to the accounts department. The goods can then be held in stock or as in the case of the micro computer we are considering, passed immediately into the user department.

The Invoice

The supplier will now bill the buyer using an invoice. This is the demand for payment for the goods supplied. The buyer will check the invoice against the original order form and the goods received note and, if all three tally, payment will be authorised. If there is a discrepancy the accounts department will usually ask the supplier to rectify the matter. If the buyer has been asked to pay too much the supplier will be required to issue a credit note which will allow the buyer to reclaim the difference either in the form of new goods or simply to pay the appropriate amount. If the buyer has been asked to pay too little then the supplier will issue a debit note to make up the difference.

The Statement

Many organizations will not pay for goods as they are bought but prefer to wait until the supplier issues a monthly statement which itemises all the purchases made in the month and requests payment of the total sum still owing. Payment on statement simplifies the number of financial transactions between the buyer and seller and is sometimes used to advantage by the buyer as it delays payment.

Stock Control

Most organizations need to carry stock. If the organization is involved in manufacturing it must hold stocks of components and raw materials. A retail organization must hold stocks of goods to meet consumer needs and even an organization in a service industry such as a local authority housing office or an insurance company must keep stocks of the stationery it uses.

The organization needs therefore to keep appropriate stock records which monitor not only the movement of stock into and out of the organization but also help to maintain minimum and maximum stock levels. This is usually achieved by the use of some form of stock record card. Movements into and out of the stock room are recorded on the card as they occur. Receipts are logged showing the date, the supplier and the invoice number. Issue of stock is shown with the appropriate requisition number and the department or section which has received the goods. With each transaction the balance of stock is adjusted and it is the responsibility of the stock control clerk to re-order once stocks are running close to the minimum stock level. The amount ordered should keep the stock held below the maximum stock level.

Production Control

If the organization is involved in manufacturing it will require some system to monitor and control production. Normally the activities of the production department are determined by the level of orders the organization has received or anticipates receiving. Production can be initiated from three sources:

    (i) a special individual order placed by a customer;

    (ii) anticipated demand leading the marketing department to initiate production;

    (iii) stock levels running low resulting in the stock controller requesting the production of additional stock.

If the organization has a regular level of sales in a stable market then it is likely that production will be maintained at a steady level with no fluctuation in activity rates. However some markets tend to be less stable and so the marketing department must work closely with production planning to adjust production to meet demand. It is the responsibility of the production planning section to co-ordinate production and to do this it must order sufficient materials either from the stores or from outside suppliers, through the purchasing department, to meet the production department's requirements. As some raw materials or components may need to be brought in, the production planning department must anticipate the necessary lead time required to place such orders. By 'lead time' we mean the time taken between initiating the orders and the delivery of the goods. Once the appropriate raw materials are assembled, the production department should ensure the production schedules are met. This requires the monitoring of progress and output and motivating the staff if necessary.

Wages and Salaries

Any employer must recognise that an efficient wages and salaries system is essential to maintain the continued co-operation of the workforce. They must be paid the appropriate amount due and also they must be paid on time. It is also the employer's responsibility to make the correct deductions from employees' wages of Pay As You Earn income tax and National Insurance Contributions. The first step is to determine the individual employee's gross pay. This may be fixed at the same level per week for a year or depend on the amount of overtime the worker has completed that week. Conversely there may be a reduction in gross pay for any time off work for which pay must be deducted. Many employers use a time card or a clock card system which records the employee's attendance at work. Other employers tend to leave it 'on trust' and accept the hours the employees claim. Once gross pay has been established the employer must calculate the tax and national insurance payments due and deduct them from gross pay. These are then forwarded to the Collector of Taxes who distributes them accordingly to the Inland Revenue and the Department of Health and Social Security. Employers are required by law to keep detailed records of all employees who are paid over the statutory minimum for national insurance contributions. Such records will provide a basis for wages and salaries analysis and also allow the employer to produce a P60 which is a statement given to each employee at the end of a tax year showing the amount of wages, tax and national insurance paid in the year. If an employee leaves for any reason before the end of the financial year the employer must provide a P45 which details tax and national insurance payments for the financial year up to the date at which the employee left.

Management Information Services

This section outlines the role and function of the Data Processing or Management Information Services Department. Some organizations still use the former title, but because of its changing role in producing management information as well as carrying out the routine data processing tasks, the latter title is used in this text. As its title implies, this department has a servicing function to the organization as a whole. Most such departments in large organizations have some centralized computer facility which carries out most of the computerized data processing. Smaller organizations may not have a central facility but instead have microcomputer systems in each department which uses a computer. In this context however, it is proposed to concentrate on the management information services of larger organizations.

Functions

Management Information Services has two principal functions:

(a)   To provide a facility to satisfy the *Operational* information needs of the main functional areas of the organization by computerized processing.

Each functional area has its own operational information needs. Examples are, the need for payroll details and payslips by Wages and Salaries and the need for customer invoices by Sales Order Processing. Here is a typical list of such routine operations:

(i) Keeping stock records;

(ii) Payment of suppliers;

(iii) General ledger, sales and purchase accounting;

(iv) Payroll;

(v) Invoicing;

(vi) Production of delivery notes;

(vii) Routine costing;

(viii) Filing of customer orders

This routine data processing work forms the bulk of the activity within Management Information Services, but there is an increasing demand for *management* information which introduces the second principal function.

(b)   To assist with operations which require management involvement and thinking but which can be partially automated or assisted by computers.

Examples of such functions include:

(i) Production planning;

(ii) Short term and long term forecasting;

(iii) The setting of budgets;

(iv) Decision making on financial policies;

(v) Marketing decisions;

(vi) Sales management;

(vii) Factory maintenance and management;

(viii) Price determination;

(ix) The selection of suppliers.

Although Management Information Services plays a central role, the advent of micro-computers and remote terminals (terminals connected to the computer by a telecommunications link) has meant that some of the above operations can be carried out by executive staff, with or without the use of the centralized facility.

Example

Consider the situation of a Sales Manager who is planning a sales strategy in terms of which geographical locations to increase sales representatives' visits. With the use of a microcomputer and database software package he or she could keep records of sales staff on 'floppy disk'. To obtain the required results, the Sales Manager may also need information stored with Management Information Services. Using a telecommunications link, he or she could call up the information from the central computer, combine it with the information on sales staff and use the database query facilities to obtain the required results. This example assumes that the organization uses a Database Management System which allows such enquiries. However, in this context it is not the particular methods of computer processing which are of interest. It is sufficient to know that such facilities exist. Database Management Systems are described more fully in Chapter 6.

Staffing

The following chart illustrates the staffing structure of a typical Management Information Services department.

Management Information Services

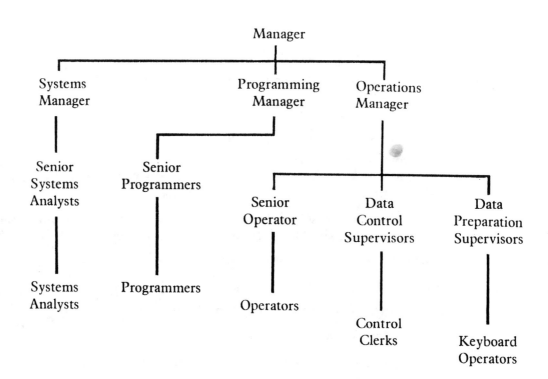

The department is normally headed by a Management Information Services Manager or Data Processing (DP) Manager. His or her major responsibility is to ensure that the department functions efficiently. He or she is responsible for ensuring that the information processing needs of the various functional areas and corporate management are met.

Beneath the control of the manager are staff involved in specialist areas of work within the department. There are broadly two areas of specialism:

(a)   Systems Development and Maintenance;

(b)   Operations.

Systems Development and Maintenance

The development of new computerized systems and the maintenance of existing systems involves specialist staff trained in Systems Analysis and Programming.

Systems analysis is concerned with the design of new computerized systems according to requirements laid down by corporate management. Prior to the design stage there is an investigative stage which necessitates close consultation with potential users in the various functional areas of the organization, to discover their information needs.

The result of the design stage is a System Specification which, rather like an architect's plans for a house, details all necessary materials and procedures to fulfil the specification. The specification will detail the clerical procedures necessary, the hardware required and most importantly what the computer has to produce for the users.

Once a system has been implemented it will require continual monitoring and modification as the information needs of the users change. The task of monitoring and modification remains with the systems analysts.

Programming is a task which perhaps lacks the creative element present in systems analysis and design. The programmer's job is concerned with coding the necessary computer instructions in a programming language such as COBOL or DbaseIV, in order to implement the requirements laid down by the systems analysts in the Program Specification (this forms part of the System Specification). Programmers involved in writing computer programs for user applications such as Invoicing or Payroll are known as Applications Programmers.

Operations

The Operations section is usually led by an Operations Manager and within his control are 3 sub-sections:

(i) Data Control;

(ii) Data Preparation;

(iii) Computer Operations.

Data Control

The staff in this section are responsible for the coordination and control of data flowing through the Operations section. The data received from, for example, Wages and Salaries, to enable the payroll master file to be updated and for payslips to be produced, has to be controlled to ensure its accuracy at all stages of processing. Chapter 8 describes the methods of control in detail.

Data Preparation

The work in this section involves the encoding of data from source documents such as customers' orders onto a 'machine-sensible' medium. Currently, this is usually magnetic tape or disk. Key-to-tape systems are dedicated, off-line devices, which allow data to be encoded directly onto cassette tape, without the use of a central computer. Prior to processing by computer, the cassettes from the magnetic tape encoders (it is likely that many will be in use) are gathered together and the data is merged onto a large reel for input to the computer. This form of encoding is rather outmoded and key-to-disk systems are generally more popular for large volume encoding. The latter system makes use of a minicomputer and a number of on-line keying stations. The processing power of the minicomputer allows much greater control, both in terms of verification and validation (Chapter 8 Systems Controls) of the data, than is possible with key-to-tape systems. The data entered via the keying stations is stored on magnetic disk and can be input to the main computer directly from there, or after transfer to magnetic tape.

Computer Operations

The staff in this section are essentially Computer Operators. They are responsible for the day-to-day running of the hardware, including the loading and unloading of input and output media, such as disk and tape. The computer hardware is under the control of software which constitutes the Operating System (which is discussed in Chapter 11), but the operator needs to communicate with the operating system regarding jobs to be processed and to deal with error conditions which may arise. Communication between the operator and the operating system software is effected through a terminal dedicated to that purpose.

Storage of Magnetic Tapes and Disks

Depending on the size of the organization, the tape or disk library (the cataloguing and storage area for computer file media) may be staffed by a librarian or by the operators. In any event it is vital that information files are properly indexed and kept in a *secure* environment. *Secure* means that the media need to be protected from physical hazards and unauthorized access. More detailed descriptions of *security* procedures are given in Chapter 8.

Assignment *Information for the Council*

Newborough County Council accommodates its various local authority departments in a purpose-built Civic Centre near the centre of Newborough. It uses a mainframe computer system for large volume processing tasks such as the payroll for local authority employees and the preparation of Community Charge demands.

Although some computing facilities are available in the various departments, through the use of microcomputer systems or on-line terminals, most of the processing is centralized. The large computer centre accommodates the mainframe computer and peripheral equipment and adjoining work rooms are used by the specialist staff working in the Management Information Services Department. Its staffing structure is illustrated in this chapter.

Task

You are employed as a Personnel Officer and the Personnel Manager has asked you to prepare a booklet outlining the role of Management Information Services in the Civic Centre and the jobs of the specialist staff who work there. The Department's manager is concerned that the work of the department as a servicing unit for the whole organization is recognized by other staff in the Civic Centre. It is intended that newly appointed staff are given a 'tour' of the various departments so that they can gain a wider view of the work of the council. The booklet of the work of Management Information Services seeks to support this aim.

Prepare the booklet.

Chapter 3

The Need for Information in Organizations

If you consider the organization you work for or the college you are studying at you will notice how as part of a constant process information is being generated, transferred, stored and retrieved. The task of handling this activity involves the establishment and maintenance of an information system within the organization. This chapter considers the nature and operation of information systems and goes on to examine the impact of information technology (IT) on modern business information systems.

Information Transfer

Any organization, whether it is a small business with only a few employees or a multi-national company with a staff of thousands, is involved in a continuous process of information transfer. This will include communication with outside individuals and organizations. Orders will be received, demands for payment made or letters of complaint received. There may be mail-shotting of customers, and so on. These are all examples of external information transfer. Internally, information is passed from superiors to subordinates and vice versa. Instructions are given, advice sought, tasks are allocated and worked on individually and in teams and praise and criticism handed out. In fact everywhere we look in an organization we see information transferred in a wide variety of forms: orally; in writing; electronically or even in the non verbal message conveyed by the shake of the head as the boss informs the supplicant worker that his pay rise has been refused. If this activity were to stop the organization would be unable to function, for information is as essential a resource as its workforce or its capital equipment. Denying it this information would be like restricting the flow of oxygen to the human brain: at first it works distortedly but finally it stops working altogether. For many organizations it is the information system itself which may produce this distorting effect. This is because the system does not function efficiently and thus creates a blurred picture to the 'brain' of the organization. In other words the individuals who manage it are not receiving the right information. Obviously it is of vital importance to the organization that such a situation is avoided at all costs. Later in this chapter we will be examining some of the symptoms which ineffective or inappropriate information systems reveal, and then considering how the causes can be dealt with. Our immediate task however is to examine the nature and scope of 'information transfer', in order to gain some idea of why this information transfer process is so vitally important. The first observation that can be made concerns the nature of the process, and involves us in looking at the functions of communications.

Why do we communicate?

If you reflect for a moment on the major aspects of your communications with others and examine what your reasons or motives are for communicating, you are likely to come up with a list that is longer than to simply to seek or to give information. For example it may be that you are merely being sociable, making an enquiry after someone's family, or it may be that you are providing psychological support to a friend or colleague who has a particular problem. Your communications could also have a more mercenary or commercial motive such as trying to persuade someone to buy your car. These then are only some of the purposes underlying our communications with others.

In a sense all of the examples given above have relevance to organizations. We can recognise that a workforce will be well motivated if its members enjoy satisfactory social relationships with each other. Furthermore if individual workers, in need of personal psychological support, are given it by the organization's personnel department to enable them to overcome their problems, then they may be able to achieve their full work potential once again. In the same way that you might try to sell your car, all commercial organizations are trying to sell their products or services and are thus in the business of persuading customers to buy. Furthermore within an organization managers may spend time trying to persuade staff to improve their timekeeping, change their working practices or increase their output. When the underlying purpose of a communication is social, psychological or persuasive it is not always easy to measure how successful it has been, for it does not necessarily have a tangible end product. Your friend may be pleased that you asked about her family, your colleague consoled by your words of help or the buyer persuaded to part with his money. But other factors may have played a part. The purchaser may have bought the car irrespective of your persuasion. However in the case of transferring information the success of the transfer process can be gauged by assessing whether the recipient has acquired the knowledge or information and it is expressed in such a way as to ensure it is understood. Thus the handbook for a personal computer will have failed if the user cannot follow the instructions to run a program, and an insurance salesperson will not be achieving potential sales targets where the 'sales pitch' he is exposing prospective customers to goes completely above their heads.

Next we need to consider why it is necessary to transfer the information in the first place. It is only by considering who is passing on the information, to whom it is directed and its nature that it is possible to decide whether the information transfer is necessary at all. For this purpose a distinction may be drawn between the internal and external communications of the organization.

The scope of information transfer

Internal communications

The structure of an organization refers not only to the physical environment in which the staff work but also to its social and psychological environment. By this is meant such factors as the respective positions and the authority and status of staff. It is the organization's structure which will influence the flow of information within it. For instance in a small organization with only one boss who likes to know everything that is going on , all the important information will be directed from or to that individual. In a large organization its functions will almost certainly be separated and dispersed. The managing director or chief executive will wish to be made aware only of information relating to major issues and will not normally be bothered to deal with every message of a trivial nature or to sign every letter that leaves the organization.

To determine the effectiveness of the process it is necessary to ascertain whether the right information gets to the right person at the right time or if there is some structural barrier to communication which needs to be identified and overcome. Appropriate organizational structures are those which recognise that information flows are necessary for the smooth running of the enterprise. Furthermore the processes used for satisfying the informational needs of the organization must be appropriate. For instance, when an accident occurs in the production process at work, there should be an existing procedure of which all staff are aware to cope with the situation. The procedure will involve not only the completion of an accident report form which is designed to enable all the information relevant to the incident to be recorded, but also to identify the departments of the organization which should receive a copy of the report. There is little point in circulating the report to all departments; the sales department would have little use for such information. Certainly for those departments that do require it, the report will have failed to do its job if the information it contains is ambiguous, unclear, or positively misleading.

External communications

It is important that the organization is alert to the communications it has with outsiders. The organization must be able to respond appropriately to information it receives and also be aware that the information it gives out will affect the value of its reputation with the outside world. Therefore such information needs to be transmitted intelligibly and in an appropriate format. Two examples may help to illustrate the significance of these aspects of the organization's external communications. Most organizations keep detailed computer records. They include lists of customers and their addresses, staffing records with previous employment histories, disciplinary action taken – perhaps even convictions. To cope with the danger that misuse of this information can cause to individuals the Data Protection Act 1984 was passed by Parliament with the support of the government. The Act obliges data users to register with the Data Protection Registrar if the data files they keep fall within the Act. Failure to do so can result in fines up to £2000. When an organization receives advance notification of such provisions, as information coming into the organization, it must have a system developed for passing the information, in an appropriate form, to the relevant personnel, so that they become aware of the change, and can meet it. Similarly information which has organization wide implications may come from other sources, such as Head office, the Inland Revenue, or the main trade union representing the workforce and will require distribution through a suitable system. Our second example relates to the output of information. Imagine the chaos and the damage to the reputation of a bus company whose published timetables contain inaccuracies about times, routes and destinations. Again there is a vital need to ensure that the organization communicates accurately and intelligibly to its recipients, using a suitable format.

An information process in practice

It is useful at this stage briefly to sketch an information process in practice. Let us take two familiar organizations, firstly your own local authority, and secondly the college at which you study, and examine how their information needs can be interlinked.

Your local authority will employ a workforce of many hundreds. It administers and performs the various duties and functions which by law the council must carry out. These operations are financed by grants provided from central government and income derived locally from the rates (or in future from the community charge), as well as from other sources such as council house rents. For this financial relationship to work there must be detailed flows of information between the local authority and central government to establish revenue needs. Thus it must provide central government with details of the number of children of school age, retired people and disabled citizens in its area. Furthermore there needs to be communication between the authority and its ratepayers to establish how much they will be required to contribute in charges for the coming financial year. This takes the form of a rate demand from the authority, containing information that tells the householder how much income the authority needs, where it is coming from, how it is calculated and how it is to be spent. The introduction of the community charge has altered the basis upon which rates are to be levied, but has not eliminated the need for local authorities to obtain information about the inhabitants in their areas.

Let us suppose that the authority is one obliged to provide education services. The education department will consist of administrators responsible for ensuring that school and college buildings are physically maintained and that staff are employed and paid for teaching in those institutions. The education department must therefore compile and maintain detailed records of the physical and human resources that it controls. It must ensure that it is regularly updates any changes to these resources and feeds back information to schools and colleges through head teachers and principals. This takes the form of education budgets. At the same time the schools and colleges themselves will be disseminating information in a variety of ways. They will be publishing prospectuses, listing the courses and subjects they offer, detailing examination results, and advertising extra mural activities. They will be informing new students and pupils of their timetables and gathering data about them using a variety of formats, such as enrolment forms and record cards. Your college will have a committee structure designed to enable it to operate efficiently and effectively. Committee members require notice of meetings and agendas; records will need to be kept of the meetings that are held and important decisions communicated to those who are affected by them. Information will be passed down from the college management to the teaching staff detailing changes in employment conditions, training opportunities and internal promotions. Information will be passed up through the committee structure from the staff to the management, identifying examination performance, reports of meetings and conferences attended.

Thus if you stop for a moment to consider the organization in which you work, the local authority whose area in which you live or the college at which you are studying, and examine the work it does, you may begin to appreciate the enormous amount of time and effort that is devoted to the business of giving and receiving information. It is very much like a production process. An organization can only function satisfactorily if its members operate together as a team, working together to meet the aims and objectives of that enterprise. It is inevitable that there must be information systems to assist the workforce in obtaining a clear view of what they need to know to do the job, whether it is in respect of the nature of their role, or simply whom to contact to obtain a particular file. If the system is deficient, the members of the organization are starved of the knowledge they require to perform their work. Like a computer controlled production process that has been incorrectly programmed there can be little hope that the end product will be what was originally intended. Data given or received which is inaccurate or incomplete, which arrives too late, is not actually needed, or is incomprehensible hinders rather than assists the achievement of overall business objectives.

An information system

Much of the business of managing an organization is directed towards ensuring that its policies are effectively implemented. The term 'policy' is very wide. In its broadest sense it refers to the general aims of the organization and is often framed in terms of organizational and individual objectives. Organizational objectives can be drawn in both economic and social terms. For example a business may establish a corporate policy to span the next five years, which indicates planned areas of expansion and anticipated levels of growth. Equally the policy may include more specific individual objectives set for personnel within the organization. These objectives may emerge out of a job description, or be a target or task set by a superior, such as a monthly sales target. Furthermore because of its underlying importance a general policy statement on communications is likely to emerge in any examination of the objectives of the organization. Such a statement will not be an end in itself, but simply the means by which the other objectives can be satisfactorily met. In arriving at this statement it is necessary to examine two related but nevertheless distinct aspects of the communications process: who communicates with whom and what is being communicated.

Who communicates with whom?

The larger an organization is, the more functionally sectionalised and departmentalised it becomes. In such circumstances there may be neither the time nor the need for individual employees to be aware of those activities of the organization which fall outside their own work responsibilities. However people in more senior posts acting in a controlling capacity need to take a much broader view. This is necessary to enable them to co-ordinate the work of the staff they are responsible for, and so achieve a satisfactory integration of this work with the activities of the rest of the organization in order that it operates as an integrated whole. Thus in larger organizations there will be lines of communication, paths along which information passes backwards and forwards. These lines of communication may be downwards (communications from a superior to a subordinate), upwards (subordinate to superior) or horizontal (communications between people of a similar status). Even an organization employing a small number of staff, such as a small retailer, is likely to have identifiable lines of communication which follows this pattern. How formal or informal these lines of communication are often depends upon the size and type of the organization. In a local authority for example, the range and complexity of work being carried out, together with the large number of employees performing it, leads to an essentially formal and clearly defined organizational and communications structure. It is unlikely that a junior clerical assistant will have direct access to the chief executive. This would be less likely in the case of a building site where a much more informal structure is appropriate to the type of team work the jobs involve.

What is being communicated?

The information content of an organization's internal communications is wide ranging and will vary according to the type of work being carried out. Nevertheless all organizations require basic systems dealing with such matters as financial records. The following list includes some common examples:

> Work rules; orders and instructions; grievance and disciplinary procedures; contracts of employment; accident reports; sales records; financial statements; statistical data, stock control records, and so on.

These examples are essentially related to the internal aspects of communications and fall within the expression 'control'; they are all control mechanisms in the hands of managers. Additionally there are the external communications of the organization, involving relationships with the outside world. This includes those it supplies or buys from, and those to whom it is responsible legally and economically. We have already seen that one of the aims of communications is to persuade. In practice the dissemination of information by an organization may often involve an attempt to convince the recipients that the company's product is worth buying or that the local authority is providing a valuable service to its ratepayers. In other words the information process often forms part of a marketing strategy. This is true not only for external communications but internal communications as well. When management inform the shop-floor workers that a fall in demand prevents the payment of a wage increase this year they will doubtless try to convince the workforce that there is no alternative. If the management's powers of persuasion are poor they may well face industrial unrest. As one aspect of its external information processes the organization will issue or receive communications that are purely informative, with no hidden persuasive component, such as invoices, rates demands, general correspondence, and a wide range of other documentation.

Having identified both the extent of the lines of communication and examples of the nature and content of the information being transferred it is finally possible to describe the information system or systems of an organization. However, whether or not the system operates as an effective and coherent whole can really only be answered by returning to our earlier discussion of objectives and determining how successfully these are being met. In practical terms the way to ensure that the organization's information transfer is satisfactory is by adopting appropriate formats. Thus it is important to bear in mind who the recipient is, what the information consists of and the purpose of the communication. But like any other system, regular monitoring is essential to prevent the existing system from losing its capacity to cope with demands that steadily change. If your organization is unaware that competitors are processing data ten times more quickly, it will soon find itself becoming uncompetitive through its lack of cost effectiveness. The reason why the competitors are able to process information more quickly may be that they have invested in an appropriate computer system while your organization has retained its traditional manual systems. Monitoring therefore is a way of recognising needs, by identifying operational problems or issues, and is vital in assessing how well or how poorly the information system is performing.

Processing information

The function of an office is to deal with information. Information passes to it and is passed from it, thus it acts as a focus of what we can call 'information flows'. In order to function effectively in performing this vital role offices in different types of business organizations will have information processing procedures specifically designed to meet the organizations own particular needs. These procedures will usually involve the following main tasks:

(a)   the receipt of incoming messages. These may arrive by post or courier, by telex or fax or over the telephone. Once received they must be passed on, 'routed', to the personnel to whom they are directed;

(b)   dealing with enquiries from clients, the general public or other parts of the organization, and processing them so that they are either dealt with straight away or are passed on to the appropriate staff for attention;

(c)   producing documents for staff. These may take the form of letters, memoranda, reports and minutes. It may be that originals are required, or that a copy or multiple copies of an existing document are needed;

(d)   operating an effective filing system. This may be electronic or manual but it must be coherent and accessible;

(e)   maintaining records about itself e.g. its staff and their personal details.

Since these activities are vital to the smooth running of a business let us consider certain aspects of them in greater detail.

The collection of source data

This involves the office collecting together information it has received from many different sources; both from outside the organization and from within it. At this stage all these separate pieces of information are termed the 'source data' because they have been merely received and nothing has yet happened to them. When source data is received into the office, staff need to register or reference the contents so that the appropriate action can be taken, where necessary. Registering all data is important so that there is always on hand, in permanent form, a record of data received. Once recorded, the information needs to be stored safely. This involves operating an appropriate storage system whereby data can be quickly accessed when and if it needs to be worked on.

The processing of source data

Data is accessed from storage so that it may be processed. 'Processing' is merely a term used to describe the kinds of operations which might then take place, before it becomes technically known as information.

The act of processing may involve merely sorting out data, or it may involve the need for some form of action to be taken. It may be that new data needs to be compared with old data, or that some kind of analysis has to be carried out. How the information is produced obviously depends upon what it is needed for. For example, data may be translated onto forms or documents, statistics may be required, reports or summaries may be needed. When data is already in the form of information it may be that it merely needs to be re-stored for reference purposes, or that a means of distribution is required so that further actions/decisions can be taken.

The distribution of information

Information (processed data) may need to be transmitted to a particular destination or destinations, either inside or outside the organization. Distribution involves the production of the information in written, typed, printed or electronic media in single or multiple copies.

Written material, and especially the use of forms are the focus of any organization's communications system. The advantage of using standard forms is that the information is collected in a uniform way, making it much easier to collate and compare.

The methods used by an office to carry out its information functions are dependent upon its nature and departmental structure. An organization may adopt exclusively manual systems which means that all these functions are operated by individuals using the minimal amount of machinery. When the organization receives data it is recorded, processed, stored and made ready for distribution and passed on from the office, all by hand. It is unusual for organizations to operate totally manual systems. In many smaller organizations it is common to find a combination of manual and mechanical procedures. This means that the organization operates using basic equipment such as typewriters, telephones, calculators and copying equipment. Other organizations, whether they are large and more forward thinking or simply because of necessity will have introduced electronic systems to aid information/communication flow. The enormous expansion of the use and applications of information technology in business since the 1970s has brought about a major revolution in office practices.

Storing and Recording Information

To operate efficiently an organization will need a suitable filing system. The system must ensure that:

(a)   there is a suitable place for the storage of records;

(b)   that these records are kept safely;

(c)   that data/information is easy to locate, select and retrieve.

If the recording and storage of data is considered in a wider context, it is important to recognise that an organization should adopt the system best suited to its individual needs. A wide variety of equipment is available on the market which is constantly being improved by manufacturers to meet both new demands and competition from rival suppliers.

It is a common myth that only 'old fashioned' businesses use manual systems; in many cases such systems work more than adequately and the introduction of new technology would represent an unnecessary expense and waste of time in setting up the new system and training staff.

Storage information and retrieval systems

In any filing system, whatever the methods and equipment used, it is essential that the system is simple to operate, so that the users can access relevant material quickly. It should be remembered, however, that a system which is simple to operate for those familiar with it may be difficult for the uninitiated to make sense of. Producing a filing manual may help to overcome this. An effective filing system should take account of the following points:

(a) Information should be easy to locate, select and retrieve. This means that attention must be paid to the way in which the material is collected for filing; the way it is examined to determine what heading it should be filed under (indexing); the need, if any, for cross-referencing; accurate filing, to avoid time wasted in futile searches.

(b) The storage of material to which no further reference is ever likely to be made simply wastes space, thus files often have a date after which they can be destroyed. Confidential waste should be shredded.

(c) There should be a suitable safe place for the storage of files. Files should be maintained in good physical condition. An inappropriate method of storage or heavy use of a file can cause deterioration. Access to files should be restricted to authorised staff.

(d) The system should incorporate a mechanism for ensuring that files or parts of files which are removed are charged out to the user, so that it is possible to trace a file that has not been returned.

Systems used for storing and retrieving information are:

(i) paper based;

(ii) photographic; or

(iii) electronic.

Paper-based filing systems

These rely on different types of filing equipment, and use a variety of methods for performing the filing work. Papers, letters, documents, plans and other types of material can be organised using alphabetic, numerical, geographical, subject and chronological arrangements, or any combination of these. For instance, an organization whose business is divided on a geographical basis may have a numeric filing reference for a particular type of correspondence, and within that file, the correspondence may be divided geographically according to district or area, the districts being arranged alphabetically. Within these sections of the file the correspondence would probably be arranged chronologically.

There are four basic physical methods of holding paper-based files: vertical filing, horizontal filing, lateral filing, and rotary filing.

Vertical filing

This normally uses filing cabinets, which contain files in drawers. It is common to find that each drawer uses a suspended file, which is a continuous chain of pockets running the length of the drawer. This system avoids individual files falling into the bottom of the drawer, and makes access easier if the drawer has not been over filled.

Horizontal filing

Cabinets with drawers which are shallow but wide are mainly used for storing drawings and plans.

Lateral or open shelf filing

The filing unit is usually similar to a bookcase, enabling files to be placed side by side along the shelves. This is useful for storing box files.

Rotary filing

A circular unit of varying height and circumference which can be rotated to gain quick and easy access to a file. The wedge-shaped spaces within these units make them ideal for storing book files and ring binders.

Photographic systems

Usually these involve photographing papers and documents and transferring them onto film (for example 8mm) using a microfilmer, hence this system is known as microfilming. The film is stored in round metal containers and can be accessed by viewing it through a scanner which can select individual frames. The scanner may be able to project a full-sized image onto a screen. In libraries, microfiche systems are used as a method of storing information, as an alternative to card indexing systems. A viewing machine is able to present the fiches (small plastic sheets containing closely printed and highly detailed information) on a screen, and the user is able to obtain information by scanning each individual fiche using a control lever across a reference grid. Microfiche has found applications in other areas as well as libraries. For instance, garages use such systems to locate individual parts for the repair of motor vehicles.

Electronic systems

These are being used increasingly as the most versatile and cost effective method of storing information, although the application of computer based information systems goes well beyond the mere storage of information. In an electronic office the item of equipment likely to create the greatest impact is the word processor. A word processing system contains five basic components:

> (a) a keyboard and display unit;
>
> (b) a printer, which can produce a printed copy of the information called 'hard copy';
>
> (c) the internal memory;
>
> (d) the text storage media; and
>
> (e) a processor or Central Processing Unit.

Modern computers are capable of dealing not only with the use of characters for storage or retrieval (i.e. words and numbers) but also all types of data for a range of processing purposes.

The applications of computer based information systems provide the clearest statement as to why they have revolutionised administrative and clerical work over the past few years. Using the system, standard letters and documents can be prepared, stored, retrieved and amended as necessary. No longer does a typist have to laboriously type over and over again the same letter or contract. In addition, enormous quantities of information can be stored as a 'database' in compact form on magnetic tape or disk. A database can be accessed rapidly and information extracted according to a wide variety of permutations or sequences. For example, suppose a database in a large organization contains details of thousands of people including their sex, age, date of birth, income, number of dependants and so on. Using a computer facility it becomes possible to obtain information on, say, the number of men between the ages of 40 and 45 who have more than two dependants and are earning less than £10,000 per year. Using traditional manual methods to extract this information would be very time consuming, but with the assistance of a computer database the task becomes relatively simple.

The communication system in operation – an example

We can conclude this examination of the relationship between the structure of an organization and the communication system operating in it by briefly tracing the process involved in employing staff and the implications this has for the communications network. Obviously employing people is only one of the many tasks involved in business operations, but it serves as a useful example because it provides a clear illustration of how far communications infiltrate processes. Large organizations, structured on functional lines, will have a personnel department responsible for all staffing matters. The communication aspects of the employment of a new member of staff are likely to emerge in the following sequence:

(i) a department identifies a vacancy and notifies the personnel officer of the details of the vacancy;

(ii) a job advertisement is prepared by the personnel department in accordance with the details provided. The advertisement probably follows a 'house style'. Decisions must be made on whether national or local advertisements are needed, and the possibility of approaching the local employment register and job centres to identify likely applicants who are available for work;

(iii) enquiries are received and application forms are sent out. Care should be taken in the design of the forms. They should be simple to understand, and provide the organization with the information it requires in advance to provide a short-list. Information about the organization, and a job description should accompany the application form. It may also be wise to provide details of conditions of service;

(iv) appropriate staff meet to produce a short-list. A representative of the appropriate department will be involved together with a representative of the personnel department;

(v) the short-listed applicants are notified of the time, date and place of the interview. Arrangements must be made to appoint and brief the interview panel;

(vi) the interviews are held. The panel should be aware of the social skills involved in conducting an interview. For example, interviewees should be put at their ease as far as possible, and the panel members should encourage interviewees to give of their best;

(vii) a decision is made on the basis of the interviews as to the appropriate interviewee for the job. The interviewees are notified of the outcome of the interviews;

(viii) the successful applicant is told when to start work and where and who to report to. A contract of employment is prepared and signed by both sides;

(ix) any additional information relevant to the new starter is provided - for instance details of an induction programme, health and safety procedures, and so on.

The effective integration of a suitable person for the job into the work of the organization depends on the quality of the above process.

The future shape of organizations

Change is something that we tend to take for granted. We live in a changing world and we are acutely aware that the pace of change is accelerating. Whilst change is a feature of our lives generally, we can apply the notion of change specifically to organizations. We may point to change in the size of organizations, their complexity and sophistication and to the increased use of information technology, as examples. There is another, more general feature that we shall consider under this idea of the changing 'shape' of the organization.

At present people generally 'go to work', that is they leave home to go to a building which has been designed to use labour in conjunction with capital (equipment and machinery etc.). There is much evidence to suggest that in the future more jobs will be capable of being done from home and transmitted by information technology to 'the organization'. Moreover this suggestion is supported by the belief that most new jobs to be created by the end of the century will need 'brain power' (not muscle) and will be essentially concerned with handling and processing information of a great variety. These kind of jobs which are sometimes referred to as 'cerebral' jobs can be done part-time or on short-term contracts, so that the existence of permanent, full-time employment in an organization will diminish. This more flexible approach to work and the organization could bring considerable changes to lifestyles in this country. A further example of the change dimension affecting organizations lies in the progress made towards establishing a single market within the territory of western Europe covered by the member states of the European Economic Community. In 1992 this process will have been completed, and organizations in the United Kingdom will find themselves competing in a single European market with a population in excess of 300 million people. In common with other aspects of change, the greater economic and social integration of the U.K. with the other states of the EEC presents both opportunities and threats.

Whether we like it or not change in one form or another is inevitable. We have briefly noted here some of the main dimensions of change currently influencing organizations and their employees. We can see that changes extend not only to the nature of the work being performed, but also to the ways in which it is performed and to the character of the economic and social environment in which business activities are conducted.

Assignment *The Property File*

McManus, Lorimer and Barnes is a firm of Estate Agents based in Portsmouth. The firm's junior partner, Peter Jones, believes that the service to clients could be improved by computerization or, at the very least, by some modification of the existing manual procedures. The firm's share of the Portsmouth area property market has been reduced by the increased competitiveness of other estate agencies in the area and Peter Jones suspects that the loss of business results from certain problems in the matching of prospective purchasers with properties for sale. A brief outline of the procedures involved in the process of property sales is described below.

1.   The initial request from a client wishing to sell a property is dealt with by one of the four partners. The partner then makes an appointment to visit the property and record the details of location, type, price range, number of rooms, etc.

2.   The property details are transcribed onto one of two standard forms, depending on whether the property is residential or used for business purposes. This task is carried out by staff in the Property Registration Section.

3.   A copy of the property registration form is passed to Property Sales Section, where staff categorize the property according to basic criteria, including property location, type, size, quality, number of rooms and price range. These basic details are transcribed onto record cards which are then used as the initial point of reference when a prospective purchaser makes an enquiry.

4.   In order to match prospective purchasers with properties for sale, a Purchase Clients File is maintained.Details of suitable properties are sent on a mailing list basis to each client.

Mr. Jones is preparing a report on the existing procedures to present to the senior partners. The firm will be approaching a Computer Software Consultancy, with a view to the possible computerization of the property and client recording procedures. The report will be used as a basis for the detailed analysis of the procedures, by the software consultancy.

Task

You are employed as a trainee office manager/ess by the estate agency. Mr. Jones has asked you to outline the procedures described above with the use of diagrammatic representations. He has suggested that these take the form of an Activity Table and Information Flow Diagram. The latter diagram should include both the firm's internal information flows and those between clients and the firm.

Developmental Task

Examine some of the estate agents' property advertisements in your local newspaper, in order to discover the criteria on which properties may be selected. Use the data collected to produce a simulation of the procedures and activities you described in your main task.

Chapter 4

Filing Information

This chapter deals with the ways in which information is stored, organized and processed by computer.

Files, Records and Data Items

In data processing, it is necessary to store information on particular subjects, for example, customers, suppliers or personnel and such information needs to be structured so that it is readily controllable and accessible to the user.

In traditional data processing systems, each of these 'topics' of information is allocated a *file*.

The figure below illustrates the structure of a typical Personnel File.

Works Number	Surname	Initial	Depart- ment	Grade	D.O.B.	Salary
357638	Watkins	P.	Sales	3	100755	9500
367462	Groves	L.	Marketing	4	170748	12800
388864	Harrison	F.	Sales	2	121066	6500
344772	Williams	J.L.	Production	4	010837	14700

A file consists of a collection of related *records*. The Personnel file which is shown above has a record for each employee. For example, the row containing information on P. Watkins is one individual *record*. The complete file would be made up of a number of such records, each one relating to a different employee.

Each record contains specific items of information relating to each employee. In the example, *Surname* is a *data item type* and listed in this column are *data item values* for each record shown. It is important to distinguish between data item type and data item value. The data item type refers to the category of information, in this case Works Number, Surname, Initial and so on. The data item value is the specific value that each individual record has for that type. Thus, the data item value of record 388864 for Department is 'Sales'. In other words F. Harrison works in the Sales department.

Fixed and Variable Length Records

The extent to which the information in a particular file can be standardized and categorized will determine whether each record in the file can be *fixed* or *variable* in *length*. The 'length' of the record is the number of 'character positions' allocated to it within the file. In the example shown above the file would probably contain *fixed length* records because:

(i) the number and types of data items required in this case are likely to be the same for each employee;

(ii) the number of character positions for each data item can be fixed or at least set to a maximum. For example, the Works Number is fixed at 6 character positions and Surname could be set to a maximum of 20, provided that no surnames exceeded this length.

Variable length records may be used in files which have storage requirements markedly different from those referred to above, for instance:

(i) Some records could have more data items than others. In a personnel file, for example, each record may contain details of previous jobs held. As the number of previous jobs may vary considerably from employee to employee, so the number of data items would be similarly varied;

Or

(ii) the number of character positions used for data item values within a data item type or types is variable. For example, in a library system each record may contain a data item which describes the subject of the book. The amount of text needed to adequately describe this may vary from book to book.

Listed below are some of the advantages of fixed length records:

(i) Fixed length records are simpler to process, in that the start and end point of each record can be readily identified by the number of character positions. For instance, if a record has a fixed length of 80 character positions, a program reading the file from the start will assume that the second record starts at the 81st character position, the third at the 161st character position and so on. Thus, programming for file handling operations is made easier;

(ii) Fixed length records allow an accurate estimation of file storage requirements. Therefore a file containing 1000 records, each of fixed 80 characters length, will take approximately 80000 characters of storage;

(iii) Where direct access files are being used, fixed length records can be readily updated 'in situ' (in other words the updated record overwrites the old version in the same position on the storage medium). As the new version will have the same number of characters as the old, any changes to a record will not change its physical length.

There are some instances when variable length records are more appropriate. For example:

(i) Where records in a file contain highly variable quantities of information, variable length records may be more economical of storage space;

(ii) When the saving in storage space makes the introduction of more complex file handling techniques worthwhile.

The Identification of Records - Primary and Secondary Keys

In most organisations, when an information system is operational it will be necessary to identify each record uniquely. In the Personnel File example given above, it might be thought that it is possible to identify each individual record simply by the employee's Surname. This would be satisfactory as long as no two had the same surname. In reality most organisations will of course have several employees with the same surnames. To ensure uniqueness therefore, each employee is assigned a unique Works Number. This is then used as the *primary key* in the file system. Each individual will have his or her unique Works Number and so a unique primary key.

There are certain circumstances when the primary key may be a *composite key,* that is made up of more than one data item. The example below shows how a pair of data items, which individually may not be unique, can be combined to provide a unique identifier.

The figure below shows an extract from a file which details suppliers' quotations for a number of different products. There is a need for a composite key because there may be a number of quotations from one supplier (in this case, supplier 41192) and a number of quotations for the same part (in this instance, part number A112).

Quotation File (extract)

Supplier-No	Part-No	Price	Delivery-Date
23783	A361	2.59	31/01/86
37643	B452	1.50	29/01/86
40923	A112	3.29	30/01/86
41192	A112	3.29	28/01/86
41192	C345	2.15	30/01/86

It is necessary, therefore to use both Supplier-No and Part-No to identify one quotation record uniquely.

Sometimes uniqueness is not always necessary. For example, if it is required to retrieve records which fulfil a criterion, or several criteria, *secondary* keys may be used. Thus, for example, in an information retrieval system on Personnel, the secondary key Department may be used to retrieve the records of all employees who work in, say, the Sales Department.

File Storage Media

There are basically two types of file storage media:

(a)   Serial Access Media;

(b)   Direct Access Media.

Serial Access Media

Serial access means that in order to identify and retrieve a particular record it is necessary to 'read' all the records which precede it in the relevant file. An example of such a storage medium is a normal cassette tape. One of the difficulties with such a storage medium is that there are no readily identifiable physical areas on the medium which can be *addressed* . In other words, it is not possible to give a name or code and refer this to a particular location. It is said to be *non-addressable.* To look for an individual record stored on such a medium requires the software to examine each *record key* in sequence from the beginning of the file until the required record is found.

Direct Access Media

Storage media such as floppy or hard disks allow *direct* access to individual records without reference to the rest of the relevant file. They have physical divisions which can be identified by computer software (and sometimes hardware) and are *addressable* so that particular locations can be referred to by a name or code to retrieve a record which is stored at that location. Looking for an individual record stored on such a medium is possible (depending on the way the file is organized) by specifying the relevant *record key,* thus providing the software with a means of finding and retrieving the specific individual record directly.

File Organization Methods

Another function of the primary key is to provide a value which can be used by computer software to assign a record to a particular position within a file. The file organization method chosen will dictate how individual records are assigned to particular *logical* positions within a file.

File Storage Media and File Organization Methods

Serial access media are limited in the file organization methods they permit because they are *non-addressable*. Direct access media are more versatile in that they allow a variety of file organization methods in addition to those allowed by serial access media. The different types of file storage media are discussed in some detail in the next chapter.

Assignment   *Sally's Wholefoods*

Sally's Wholefoods is a small, one woman business, with three shops in York. They each stock a wide range of vegetarian foods, some of which is ready-cooked and pre-packed. However, most of the food is sold loose and constitutes ingredients for home cooking. The business is extremely successful and attracts large numbers of academics and students from the university and colleges in York. The proprietor, Sally Henderson, employs two full-time assistants at each shop and occasionally employs one or two students during the summer vacation.

Although much of the stock consists of dried food items, freshness is important, so Ms. Henderson has to keep careful track of stocks held, outstanding orders from suppliers and orders made by her customers. She operates a home delivery service, which adds to the problem of control, since she keeps some stocks at home for this purpose. There are hundreds of different food items, some of which are seasonal, so the range of goods is not always the same. To keep tighter control of stock, orders from suppliers and customer orders, she has decided that a computer will be of service.

Task

You are employed by Ms. Henderson in a general accounting and clerical role and she has asked you to produce an informal report suggesting how best to structure the data files for a computerized system. The report should consider the following:

1. The design of suitable file structures for the stock, supplier and customer order files, with identification of the file, record and data item levels. Suggest appropriate data items for the unique identification of records in each file. Explain why uniqueness is necessary. It may also be useful to identify any secondary keys which may be helpful in the production of summary reports; explain the role of secondary keys.

2. The alternatives available for file storage. Give a reasoned recommendation as to which is needed for the applications in question.

Developmental Task

Research some of the operational characteristics of storage systems for micro-computers and draw up a table of comparisons. Include it as an appendix in your report to Ms. Henderson.

Chapter 5

File Storage Media

Magnetic Tape - a Serial Access Medium

Physical and Logical Records

Because of the physical characteristics of magnetic tape it is necessary, when processing a file, that the tape unit (the device onto which a tape is loaded for processing) starts to read the tape at the beginning of the reel. The 'takeup' spool receives the tape from the 'feed' spool via a 'read-write' head in the unit which can either record information onto or read information from the tape as it passes. As there are no specific physical locations on the tape which can be identified and referred to by the computer (except of course the beginning and end), the only way it can find a particular record is by 'reading' the whole file. Unless the whole tape is to be processed, it may only be necessary to read up to the point where the specific record it is seeking is found. There may well be more than one logical file on a tape but these will have to be read in the sequence that they appear on the tape. As the tape is read, the computer will compare the record key of each record which it comes to, with the specified key, until the required record is found. The following diagram illustrates the way in which a file is arranged on tape both *logically* and *physically*.

Illustration of how a file is stored on tape

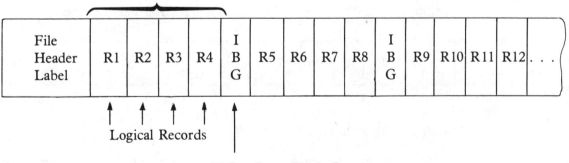

IBG = Inter Block Gap

You should note from the diagram that records R1,R2,R3 etc. are *logical* records. For example, if this were a stock file, each logical record would relate to one commodity held in stock. On the other hand each *block* or *physical* record consists, in this illustration, of 4 logical records. The reason for making the distinction between logical and physical records stems from the fact that data is transferred between the computer's internal memory and the tape storage medium in 'manageable chunks'. The optimum size of each 'chunk' (or to give it its proper name, *block*), will depend on factors such as the size of the computer's internal memory.

Each block of data is referred to as a physical record. Between each block transfer, the tape has to stop while the previous block is processed by the computer. In order to give the tape time to stop and then restart for the next block, there is an Inter Block Gap (IBG), a blank area of tape between each block. It is unlikely that the optimum block size will coincide with the actual length of a single logical record, so it is necessary to transfer a number of logical records between tape and internal memory at one time. Thus, a *physical* record or *block* will often consist of a number of *logical* records.

The example of a stock file is used again to illustrate this point further. Assume that each block contains 3 logical stock records (in other words three individual commodities). If the first record to be processed is stored in the fifth block, then the first four blocks have to be read in sequence into memory and each logical stock record examined for its record key, without any records actually being used. When the fifth block is eventually read into memory each of the three logical stock records is then examined for its record key until the required key is identified.

File Organization Methods Using Magnetic Tape

There are two ways in which a file can be organized on tape:

(i) Serially;

(ii) Sequentially.

This restriction stems from the fact that magnetic tape is a serial access medium. As is noted earlier, this means that it has no addressable locations and so records have to be traced by reading the file from beginning to end.

The processing of tape files can only be carried out satisfactorily if they are organized in the sequence of their record keys. This point is illustrated on the next page. This restriction applies to both master and transaction files. Serial files, which are out of sequence, are only useful as an interim measure, prior to processing.

Generally, when a transaction file is being created on tape, for example, when customer orders are received, they are written to tape in the order in which they are received. This creates a serial file. Before the master file can be updated, the transaction file has to be sorted by the computer to become a sequential file.

Serial and Sequential Files

Example 1 illustrating a transaction file which is serial and unsorted

R1	R2	R3	R4	R5	R6	R7 . . . . .

Master File - sequential

T3	T2	T1	T5	T7 . . . . .

Transaction File - serial and unsorted

Example 2 illustrating a transaction file which is sequential

Master File - sequential

R1	R2	R3	R4	R5	R6	R7 . . . . .

Transaction file - sequential

T1	T2	T3	T5	T6 . . . . .

Updating the Master File

When a tape file is updated, a new master file must be created on a new reel of tape. This is because the tape drive unit cannot guarantee to write an updated record to the exact position from which it was read. There is a danger, therefore, of adjacent records being corrupted or completely overwritten. The following procedures are followed during the update (assuming that no new records are to be inserted).

(i)   A transaction is read into memory.

(ii)   A master record is read into memory. If the record keys do not match, the master record is written, unchanged, to the new reel. Master records continue to be read, examined and written in the original sequence to the new reel until a match for the transaction is found.

(iii)   Once the match is found, the master record is updated in main memory and then written to the new reel.

These steps are repeated until all transactions have been processed and the complete updated master file has been written to the new reel.

Unless the transaction files are sorted into the same sequence as the master file, it is necessary to rewind the master file whenever a transaction requires a master record which has already passed through the system. Such rewinding would clearly be both inefficient and impractical.

The following Systems Flowchart illustrates the updating procedure:

Systems Flowchart - Magnetic Tape File Update

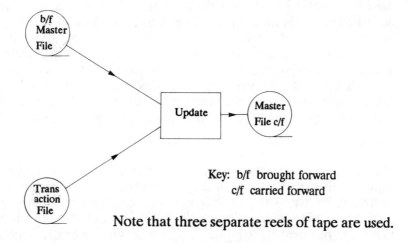

Key: b/f brought forward
      c/f carried forward

Note that three separate reels of tape are used.

Magnetic Disk - a Direct Access Medium

The Means of Addressing Magnetic Disk

Magnetic disk provides file storage facilities which are more flexible and powerful than those provided by magnetic tape. As an addressable medium, the surface of the disk is divided into physical locations which are illustrated in the figure below.

The Addressing Structure of a Magnetic Disk

The number of tracks and sectors vary with the system used.

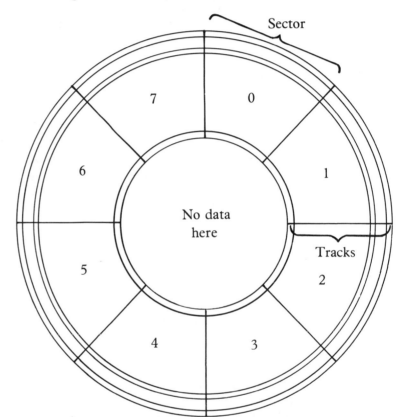

The *address* of any one physical location on a single disk incorporates a *track* number, and within that track, a *sector* number. Addressing in this way is rather like providing a street name (the track) and a house number (the sector). This addressable unit is the smallest physical area on the disk which can be addressed. Each of these addressable units is referred to as a *block* or *physical record*. (The meaning of this type of record is described earlier in the chapter). The size of the blocks is normally determined by the systems designer through the use of systems software, although some disk storage systems use *hard* sectoring; in other words, the block size cannot be altered. The number of logical records which can be accommodated in a particular block obviously depends upon the physical size of the block and the length of each logical record. Considerations regarding the determination of block size are beyond the scope of this text, but some of the design factors can be readily explained by the following example:

Example

If a disk's block size approximates to the storage of 500 characters and a stock file has logical records of a fixed length of 110 characters, then the maximum number of records which can be stored in a block is 4. To retrieve one logical stock record requires the software to address the relevant block and retrieve the physical record. This means that it will retrieve all the logical stock records in the block. Therefore, the larger the number of logical records stored in any specific block, the less selective the software can be in retrieving them but the faster the complete file is processed.

The Operation of Magnetic Disk

Although there are many variations in the capacities and sizes of disk that are available, there are certain physical characteristics which are common to all.

On smaller computer systems disks tend to be handled singly on individual disk drive units. On larger systems a number of disks may be mounted on a central spindle. This is shown in the figure below. To transfer data to or from the disk pack it is necessary to mount it on a disk drive unit which rotates the pack at high speed. Data is recorded magnetically on disk in a similar fashion to the recording on magnetic tape. Special 'read-write' heads are mounted on moveable arms within the disk drive unit in such a way that they move in synchronization across the disk surface. The software positions the heads for the writing or retrieval of records.

Section view of a Disk Pack showing read/write arms

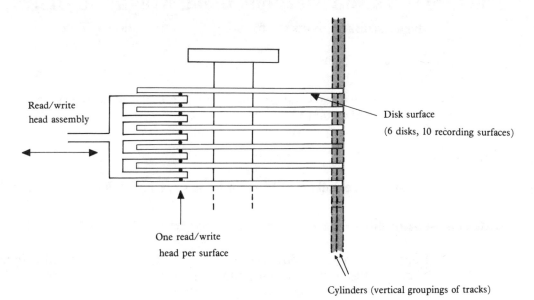

Further Disk Addressing Concepts: Cylinders and Buckets

Cylinders

If the two previous figures are considered together it can be seen that in a disk pack a specified Track on one disk (Track 0) is vertically above other tracks on lower disks which are also specified as Track 0. In other words, all the Track 0s are in the same vertical plane. Such a grouping is known as a *cylinder* or *seek area*. Similarly, all track 1s form another cylinder, as do track 2s and so on. It can be seen therefore, that there are as many cylinders as there are tracks on each disk surface.

The fastest way of reading or writing records on disks is by minimizing the movement of the read/write arms. This is achieved by positioning associated records, which are likely to needed as a group (they may form a complete file), into sequence (as a sequential file) on tracks in the same cylinder. Records are written to the disk pack, such that track 1 on surface 1 is filled first, followed by track 1 on surface 2 and so on, until all number 1 tracks are filled (the first cylinder). Then, if the file requires more than one cylinder, adjacent tracks are filled to form further cylinders, until the file is complete.

When access is required to the file it is quickest, in terms of keeping read/write head movement to a minimum, to deal with a cylinder of records at a time. Thus, a complete cylinder of records is processed before any head movement is required. A cylinder is also known as a 'seek area', because all records in a cylinder can be accessed by the read/write heads while they are positioned in that cylinder.

Buckets

The minimum amount of data which can be transferred between the backing store of the computer and its internal store is the *block*. However, there are occasions when a larger unit of transfer is required. On such occasions the concept of the *bucket* is used. Thus a number of blocks (up to the maximum of one track) may be given the same disk address (this is usually the address of the first block in the bucket) and any logical records held within such a bucket are retrieved when that disk address is used.

File Organization Methods using Magnetic Disk

Magnetic disk supports the following file organization methods:

Serial

As is the case for a serial tape file, records are placed onto disk one after the other in no particular sequence;

Sequential

As for a sequential tape file, records are stored on disk ordered by record key;

Indexed Sequential

Records are stored in sequence according to their record keys and an index is produced when the file is created. This allows the direct retrieval of individual records. The retrieval of records involves the software searching different levels of the index - the cylinder index, track index and the bucket or block index - before positioning the read/write heads to retrieve the block containing the required record.

The indexes may be structured as shown below, using a five-digit primary key in the range 00001 to 50000. The table represents an extract only.

CylinderIndex		Track Index for Cylinder 55		Sector/block Index for Track 3	
Cylinder	Highest Key	Track	Highest Key	Sector	Highest Key
1	00452	1	26000	1	26071
2	00940	2	26063	2	26076
3	01650	3	*26120*	3	26080
.	.	4	26185	4	26087
55	*26500*	5	26242	5	26095
56	27015	6	26320	6	26104
.	.	7	26426	7	26112
115	50000	8	*26500*	8	*26120*

The indexes are constructed as the records are written sequentially (according to the primary key) to the disk pack. As each sector is filled, the primary key of the last record to be placed in the sector (the highest key) is recorded in the Sector Index; once all sectors in a track are filled, the last key to be entered is added to the Track Index; the completion of a cylinder causes the highest key field in it to be recorded in the Cylinder Index. The process is repeated with subsequent cylinders until the file is complete. The retrieval of records requires a serial search to be made of the cylinder index, track index and sector index respectively, unless a complete track is to be read, in which case the sector index is not used. Referring to the previous table of indexes, suppose that the record with primary key 26085 is required; the indexes may be used as follows:

– a serial search of the cylinder index is made until a highest key entry is found which is equal to or greater than the required key. The entry which meets this requirement is 26500, indicating that a search of the track index for cylinder 55 is needed;

– a serial search of that track index, again looking for an entry greater than or equal to record key 26085, reveals that the record is to be found in track 3, where the highest key field is 26120;

– searching the sector index for track 3 returns the entry of 26087, the highest key field entry for sector 4.

Unless record 26085 has been placed in an overflow area, owing to a full sector, it can be retrieved by reading in the block of data occupying the address - sector 4, track 3, cylinder 55.

The cylinder index for a given file will normally be read into main memory when the file is first opened and held there until processing is complete. Each track index is normally held in the cylinder to which it relates and will be read into main memory as required. Similarly, the sector index is usually held within its relevant track.

The above procedures and mechanisms only illustrate the main principles of index construction and usage; the detail is likely to vary considerably from one system to another. To facilitate updating, space will normally be left in sectors, tracks and cylinders to allow for the insertion of new records. This method allows the efficient sequential processing of the file as well as direct retrieval of records using the indexes. Indexes can become quite large and the file may need to be reorganized periodically so that new records can be inserted in the correct sequence. Records which are marked for deletion need to be removed from the file and the indexes then have to be reconstructed. The frequency with which such reorganization is necessary depends on the level of file activity and the number of inserts and deletions. File reorganization is a *house-keeping* activity;

Random

This is a method which is impractical in any non-computerized situation. However, in a computerized system it is feasible to place records onto disk at random. The procedure for placing specific records in a particular position on disk uses a mathematical formula called an 'algorithm', which generates a disk address from the record key.

The algorithm operates on the primary keys within a given range to produce pseudo-random numbers which may then be used as bucket addresses to which the logical records are allocated. The aim of any randomizing or *hashing* algorithm is to achieve an even distribution of records over the disk space allocated to a file. Most random files allow more than one logical record to occupy a single bucket as any given algorithm will normally generate the same disk address from several different primary keys; these replicated addresses are known as *synonyms*. An uneven distribution of records means that some buckets overflow and cannot accommodate all the logical records allocated to them, whilst others remain empty or are seriously under-used. Excessive overflow slows the access time for any record which cannot be allocated to its *home* address.

To achieve a reasonably even spread, the selection of a particular algorithm requires consideration of the following factors:

(i) the pattern and range of the primary keys within the file;

(ii) the size of each bucket and the number available;

(iii) the average packing density required (number of records/total record capacity of the available buckets).

Example Algorithm

Prime Number Division

The primary key is divided by the largest prime number which is less than the number of available buckets. The remainder of this calculation is taken as the *relative* bucket number, that is the number of buckets after the first. For example:

available buckets		2000
prime number		1999
primary key		22316
22316/1999	=	11 remainder 327

The relative bucket number is thus 327.

The same mathematical formula is used to subsequently retrieve records. This is ideal in situations where random enquiries are the norm and there is little need for sequential processing. Randomly organized files can be processed sequentially but with less efficiency than sequentially organized files. An advantage of this method is the lack of large indexes which tend to take up considerable storage space on the disk.

Accessing Disk Files

Serial Files

As with magnetic tape, the only way to retrieve records is serially, in other words, one after the other.

Sequential Files

The addressing features of disk are not used and the method is the same as that for sequential tape files.

Indexed Sequential Files

There are 3 methods of retrieving such records:

Sequentially.   Transactions are sorted in to the same sequence as the master file. This is suitable when a large proportion of the records in the file are to be processed in one run, that is, when the *hit rate* is high. (The term 'hit rate' is explained in Chapter 7 Systems Development and Implementation). Minimal use is made of the index. The cylinder index and track index may be searched, then the whole track is read into memory, block by block, without reference to the sector index;

Selective or Skip Sequentially.   The transactions are sorted into master file sequence and the indexes are used, so that only those blocks containing master records for which there is a transaction are read into memory. This is suitable when the hit rate is low;

Randomly.   Transactions are not sorted. They are processed in the order in which they occur. The indexes are used to find the relevant master records as they are required. The read/write heads have to move back and forth through the file and so head movement is greater than with sequential methods of processing. This method is appropriate when records are updated immediately after the transaction occurs or, for example, when there is a need for random enquiries of a stock file.

Random Files

Records need not be in any logical sequence. Records are retrieved by generating the physical address from the record key. The software uses the same algorithm it used to assign the record to its address in the first place.

Assignment *Building a System*

Home Extensions Ltd is a building firm operating in the Swindon area. The two directors, Jim Atkinson and Arthur Haines, have bought a microcomputer system, primarily for job costing and control. It is envisaged that other applications will benefit from computerization in the future. The microcomputer system only has cassette tape storage. Generally, the firm has about thirty to forty jobs 'on the go' at one time and for each job, a record needs to be kept of the basic details, such as site location and the initial costings. Another record needs to be maintained to monitor spending on each job, as it progresses; this includes materials, labour and overheads. Jim Atkinson has attended a BASIC programming course and intends to write his own job costing package.

Task

Mr. Atkinson employs you as a trainee Site Manager and is aware that you have gained some computing knowledge during your studies. His knowledge of BASIC does not extend to the use of computer files and he does not seem to realise that the cassette tape system will be wholly inadequate for the application he has in mind. He does not want to spend any money consulting a specialist and has asked you to advise him of the need for a disk-based system. He would like to know the reasons behind any advice you give. To this end, Mr. Atkinson wishes you to provide him with some explanatory notes on the way files can be organized on magnetic tape and magnetic disk. Hopefully, by the time you have finished, he will see the sense of consulting a dealer and buying some packaged software, instead of writing his own programs.

Prepare some notes for Mr. Atkinson, explaining:

1. The file organization methods possible on magnetic tape and the reasons for its unsuitability for the above application;

2. The file organization and access methods possible on magnetic disk which make it appropriate for the above application.

Illustrate your notes with some sample data from building jobs.

Chapter 6

Computerized Information Systems

Information Needs

There are many different methods of processing information by computer. A wide range of computer hardware and software is available for such processing. The different types of hardware and software are considered in some detail in Chapters 18 and 10 respectively, but this chapter examines how the needs of an organization determine the hardware and software which will be used, as well as the methods of processing employed. It begins with a brief review of the computer systems available before considering the methods of processing appropriate to different computerized information systems.

Types of Computer

Broadly, computers fall into 3 main categories and although the divisions are not always absolutely clear, they provide convenient labels to identify different systems. These are:

(a)   Mainframe Computers

(b)   Mini Computers

(c)   Microcomputers

Each has particular features which will broadly identify a computer as belonging to one of the above types. However, computer technology is advancing so rapidly that some of the divisions between them begin to blur. For example, there are now powerful microcomputer systems (often referred to as super-micros) which far exceed the power and flexibility of earlier generation minicomputer systems.

Mainframe Computers

The mainframe computer has:

(i) Large main memory;

(ii) A very fast CPU and operating system software, which together allow many users and applications to be supported at apparently the same time;

(iii) Facilities for large numbers of both magnetic tape and magnetic disk storage units;

(iv) The capability of supporting a large number and variety of input and output devices.

Such computers are commonly used by large national and multi-national organizations such as banks, airlines and oil companies.

Mini Computers

The mini computer is technically very similar to the mainframe with the following differences:

(i) It usually only has magnetic disk storage;

(ii) The main input/output peripherals tend to be Visual Display Units (VDUs).

Medium-sized organizations may use minicomputers for their main processing applications. Larger organizations may apply them to Front End Processing (FEP). Employed in this way, a mini computer handles a mainframe's communications traffic with remote terminals or other computers, leaving the mainframe free to handle the main information processing tasks.

Microcomputers

The microcomputer is the smallest in the range and was first developed when the Intel Corporation succeeded in incorporating the main functional parts of a computer on a single 'chip' using Integrated Circuits (IC) on silicon. Subsequently, the technique of Large Scale Integration (LSI) further increased the number of electronic circuits which could be packed onto one 'chip'. LSI has been superseded by Very Large Scale Integration (VLSI) which packs even more circuitry onto a single chip, thus further increasing the power and storage capacity of microcomputers and computers generally. This type of computer storage is known as Metal Oxide Semiconductor storage (MOS) and has completely replaced the 'core store' used in earlier mainframe computers.

The miniaturization of the hardware, the vast increase in computer power and storage capacity, and the drastic reduction in cost make it possible for small organizations to afford computer facilities.

Microcomputers have the following characteristics:

(i) Microcomputers were initially stand-alone units allowing a single user to run a single application at one time;

(ii) Increasingly common is the multi-user system where a number of microcomputers can be linked together or *networked*. Such networks often share hard disk storage with a storage capacity measured in many millions of characters and allow different users to run different applications at the same time;

(iii) Generally the main input/output is carried out via a keyboard and monitor screen, although other devices such as light pens, mice, concept keyboards and graph plotters can be used.

The range of microcomputer software is now extremely wide and the quality generally very high. There are software packages available for most business applications. One area of recent rapid growth has been in the development of graphics-based applications and most popular applications software can now be operated via a graphical user interface and a 'mouse' (Chapter 18 Peripherals). Many microcomputers are now sufficiently powerful to allow extremely sophisticated Computer Aided Design (CAD) work, which until recently was only possible on a mini or mainframe computer system. Further classifications of computer systems are given in Chapter 17 (Computer Systems).

Methods of Processing

There are three main types of information processing systems:

(a) Batch Processing;

(b) On-Line Processing;

(c) Database systems.

Batch Processing Systems

Such systems process *batches* of data at regular intervals. The data is usually in large volumes and of identical type. Examples of such data are customer orders, current weekly payroll details and stock issues or receipts. Although associated with large organizations using mainframe or minicomputer systems, the technique can be used by a small business using a microcomputer.

The procedure can be illustrated with the example of payroll, which is a typical application for batch processing. Each pay date, whether it is every week or every month, the payroll details, such as hours worked, overtime earned or sickness days claimed, are gathered for each employee and processed in batches against the payroll master file. The computer then produces payslips for all employees in the company.

A major feature of this and similar applications is that a large percentage of the payroll records in the master file are processed during the payroll 'run'. This percentage is known as the *hit rate*. In general high 'hit rate' processing is suitable for batch processing. If, as is usual, the master file is organized sequentially, then the transaction file will be sorted into the same sequence as the master file. In Chapter 5 it is explained that the sorting of transactions is essential if the master file does not allow direct access (as is the case for magnetic tape files).

The batch processing method closely resembles manual methods of data processing, in that data on transactions is collected together into batches, sent to the computer centre, sorted into the order of the master file and processed. Such systems are known as 'traditional' data processing systems. There is normally an intermediate stage in the process when the data must be encoded *off-line*. This means that the data is transferred onto tape or disk. Such encoding may be carried out using another computer, such as in *key-to-disk* systems (Chapter 2 Management Information Services section), but the operation is carried out without the use of the main computer system.

A disadvantage of batch processing is the delay of often hours, or even days, between collecting the transactions and receiving the results of processing. This disadvantage has to be borne in mind when an organization is considering whether or not batch processing is suitable for a particular application.

Conversely batch processing has the advantage of providing many opportunities for controlling the accuracy of data and thus is commonly used when the immediate updating of files is not crucial.

The accuracy controls used in batch and other processing methods are explained in detail in Chapter 8.

On-Line Processing Systems

If a peripheral, such as a Visual Display Unit or keyboard, is *on-line*, it is under the control of the Central Processing Unit (CPU) of the computer.

On-line processing systems therefore, are those where all peripherals in use are connected to the CPU of the main computer. Transactions can be keyed in directly.

The main advantage of an on-line system is the reduction in time between the collection and processing of data.

It is important to note that on-line systems can also be used for batch processing, although the stages of intermediate encoding and sorting transactions are eliminated.

There are two main methods of on-line processing:

(i) Real-Time Processing;

(ii) Time- Share Processing.

Real-Time processing

Process Control in Real-time.   Real-time processing originally referred only to process control systems where, for example, the temperature of a gas furnace is monitored and controlled by a computer. The computer, via an appropriate sensing device, responds immediately to the boiler's variations outside pre-set temperature limits, by switching the boiler on and off to keep the temperature within those limits.

Real-time processing is now used in everyday consumer goods. This has come about because of the development of 'the computer on a chip', more properly called the microprocessor. An important example of the use of the microprocessor is the Engine Management System, which is now standard on an increasing range of cars. A car's engine performance can be monitored and controlled, by sensing and immediately responding to changes in such factors as air temperature, ignition timing or engine load. Further examples of the use of microprocessors can be found on the automated production lines of engineering works and car plants where operations requiring fine engineering control can be carried out by Computer Numerical Controlled (CNC) machines.

The important feature common to all these applications is that the speed of the computer allows almost immediate response to external changes.

Information Processing in Real-time

To be acceptable as a real-time information processing system, the *response-time* (that is the time between the entry of a transaction or enquiry at a VDU terminal,the processing of the data and the computer's response) must meet the needs of the user. The delay or response time may vary from a fraction of a second to 2-3 seconds depending on the nature of the transaction and the size of the computer. Any delay beyond these times would generally be unacceptable and would indicate the need for the system to be updated.

There are two types of information processing systems which can be operated in real-time. These are:

(i) Transaction Processing;

(ii) Information Storage/Retrieval

Transaction Processing. This type of system is one which handles clearly defined transactions one at a time. Each transaction is processed completely, including the updating of files, before the next transaction is dealt with. The amount of data input for each transaction is small and is usually entered on an *interactive* basis via a VDU. Interactive means that the user's communication with the computer is carried out by question and answer. In this way, the user can enter queries via the keyboard and receive a response, or the computer can display a prompt on the screen to which the user responds. Such 'conversations' are usually heavily structured and in a fixed format and so do not allow users to ask any question they wish.

A typical example of transaction processing is provided by an airline booking system. The following procedures describe a client's enquiry for a seat reservation:

(i) A prospective passenger provides the booking clerk with information regarding his/her flight requirements;

(ii) Following prompts on the screen, the clerk keys the details into the system so that a check can be made on the availability of seats;

(iii) Vacancies appear on the screen and the client can confirm the booking;

(iv) Confirmation of the reservation is keyed into the system, usually by a single key press and the flight seating records are immediately updated;

(v) Passenger details (such as name, address etc.) can now be entered.

Such a system needs to be real-time to avoid the possibility of two clients booking the same seat, on the same flight and at the same time, at different booking offices.

Information Storage/Retrieval. This type of system differs from transaction processing in that, although the information is updated in real-time, the number of updates and the number of sources of updating is relatively small.

Consider, for example, the medical records system in a hospital. A record is maintained for each patient currently undergoing treatment in the hospital. Medical staff require the patient's medical history to be available at any time and the system must also have a facility for entering new information as the patient undergoes treatment in hospital. Sources of information are likely to include a doctor, nurses and perhaps a surgeon and new entries probably do not number more than one or two per day.

This is an entirely different situation from an airline booking system where the number of entries for one flight record may be 200-300 and entries could be made from many different booking offices throughout the world.

Time-Share Processing

The term *time sharing* refers to the activity of the Central Processing Unit (CPU) in allocating *slices* of its time to a number of users who are given access to a central computer, normally via Visual Display Units (VDUs).

The aim of the system is to give each user a good 'response time' - no more than 2 seconds. These systems are commonly used where a number of users require computer time for different information processing tasks. The CPU *time slices* are allocated and controlled by a Time-share Operating System. The CPU is able to operate at such speed that, provided the system is not overloaded by too many users, each user has the impression that he or she is the sole user of the system.

A particular computer system will be designed to support a maximum number of user terminals. If the number is exceeded or the applications being run on the system are 'heavy' on CPU time the response time will become lengthy and unacceptable. Time-share systems are possible because of the extreme speed of the CPU in comparison with peripheral devices such as keyboards, VDU screens and printers. Most information processing tasks consist largely of input and output operations which do not occupy the CPU, leaving it free to do any processing required on other users' tasks.

Database Systems

Databases are based on the idea that a common 'pool' of data, with a minimum of duplicated data items, can be organized in such a way that all user requirements can be satisfied. Therefore, instead of each department or functional area within an organization keeping and maintaining its own files, where there are subjects of common interest, they are grouped to form a 'subject' database. Database systems are available for mainframe, mini and microcomputer systems.

The Physical and Logical Database

A database has to satisfy many users' differing information needs, generally through specially written applications programs. Because of this, it is often necessary to add further data items to satisfy changes in one or more user's needs. The software which controls the database must relate to the data at a data item level rather than at record level because one programmer's *logical* record requirements may contain some data items which are also required for another programmer's logical record description. The physical database must allow for both. It must be possible for data items to be connected into a variety of logical record forms.

Data Independence

In order that the physical database can be changed as necessary to accommodate user requirements, without the need to alter all applications programs (as is necessary with, for example, a COBOL program - if a file is changed, then any program accessing the file needs to be changed), the way the data is *physically* stored on the storage medium should be *independent* of the *logical* record structures required by applications programs.

Data Duplication

The fact that a database provides a common source of information for a number of user areas may suggest that each data item need only appear once. Although this is generally true, some data items need to be duplicated in order to establish necessary *logical* relationships between different records. Such limited duplication of data items is termed *controlled redundancy*.

A simple example will illustrate the need for some data duplication in a particular type of database system which is controlled by a Relational Database Management System.

Example of Logical Data Structures in a Relational Database

The data is set up in table form and the example shows two, one for *Job* and the other for *Employee*:

JOB

Job Ref	Job Title	Department	Grade	Salary
P23MIS	Programmer	MIS	2	12000
A32ACC	Accountant	Finance	3	13000
A14ACC	Accounts Clerk	Finance	1	6200
S24SAL	Sales Clerk	Sales	2	6700

EMPLOYEE

Employee Ref No.	Name	Address	Job Code
12345	Jones, P.	12 The Grove	P23MIS
32453	Wilkins, J.	13 Daly Street	A14ACC
23413	Herbert, R.	10 Dunn Avenue	P23MIS
15893	Fender, T.	6 Henley Close	S24SAL
56990	Harris, B.	5 Fairways Drive	A32ACC
99251	Parker, N.	123 Thompson Road	A14ACC

It can be seen that the Job Ref in *Job* and the Job Code in *Employee* are, in essence, the same data item type, except that they are given different names. These duplicate data items can be used by the programmer to establish relationships between the data in each table. To discover, for example, which employees hold grade 2 Programmer posts, the Job Ref P23MIS could be used to retrieve the information from the *Employee* table, namely Jones P., and Herbert R.

Creating the Database

A special language called a *Data Description Language* (DDL) allows the database to be created and changed and the logical data structures to be defined.

Manipulating the Database

A *Data Manipulation Language* (DML) enables the contents of the database to be altered by adding, updating or deleting records. This language is used by programmers to develop applications programs for users of the database.

Logical Views of Data

Different users may have different *logical* views of the same data. To illustrate this, consider the telephone number of a dentist. To his patients, the telephone number is that of their dentist. To the dentist's bank manager, it is the telephone number of a customer. It is the same data, but different people have different views of it.

To illustrate this idea further, here is another example. Consider the customer order form shown on the next page.

The first line (Item Code AB312) on the order form gives a quantity of 35 x Baked Beans 500g. The information may be required for different purposes by different users. In addition, each user department has a different 'key' to the information. The key will be one of the unique values which appear on the order form. They are:

Customer Account No. - which identifies the customer. Each customer is given a unique Account Number, so that it can be used to trace information on any orders relating to the customer in question;

Order No. - which identifies a particular order (each order must relate to only *one* customer);

Item Code. Each order will have a number of order lines but any item code will only appear *once* on an order.

HAWKINS SUPPLIES LTD.

Customer Order Form   Date: 3rd January 1987

Order No: 365746

Customer Name:
P. Jones Ltd
32 Slater Road
Newtown
NP3 4AS

Customer Account No: 13321

Item Code	Description	Quantity	Unit Price	Cost
AB312	Baked Beans 500g	35	0.20	7.00
AB316	Spaghetti 350g	20	0.25	5.00
				————
				12.00
			VAT 15%	1.80
				————
			Total	13.80

The information required is the Quantity (35) on the first order line of the order form. It may be required in the following ways:

(a)   The Sales department (which knows the Order No) needs the information because of a customer query.

(b)   The warehouse (which knows the Item Code) wishes to check stock issues.

(c)   The Accounts department (which knows the Customer Account No.) needs the information (together with the rest of the information on the order) to produce an invoice.

The data must be structured so that each stock item quantity may be easily accessed when any of these departments require it.

Accessing a Database with Applications Programs

Because different user departments have different information requirements, there is a need for different Applications Programs. These are written by programmers using a Data Manipulation Language (DML). Applications programs allow the computer to be used to process data for particular purposes, for example, the production of payslips, invoices etc..

The next diagram illustrates this in simplified form:

It should be noticed that two or more users may use the same application program.

An Overview of a Database System

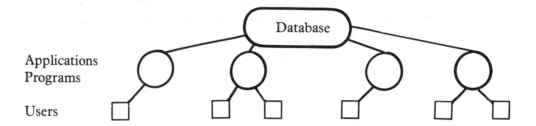

Database Storage

Because the database must allow for various user applications programs accessing it at the same time, direct access storage must be used. There are many ways of physically organizing the data which are beyond the scope of this text, but whatever method is used it must allow for any variety of logical structures needed by applications programs.

To illustrate the variations in logical file organization, consider a personnel file with the following data item types in each record.

Employee No	Name	Salary

The Salaries Department may require the file in the sequence of the Employee No., whereas the Personnel Department may require the records in alphabetical order by Name.

The applications programmer does not need to know how the data is physically stored. His knowledge of the data held in the database is restricted to the logical view he requires for the program.

The complete or global logical database is termed the *schema*.

The restricted or local logical views provided for different applications programs are *subschemas*. (see next page)

Database Management Systems (DBMS)

In order that each application program may only access the data which it needs for processing or retrieval (in other words that data which is defined in its subschema), a Database Management System (software) controls the database and prevents accidental or deliberate corruption of data by other applications programs.

An application program cannot access the database without the DBMS. The following diagram illustrates the relationship between users, application programs, the Database Management System and the database:

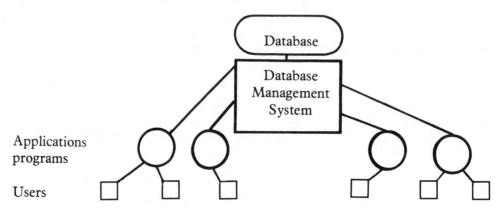

DIFFERING VIEWS OF DATA

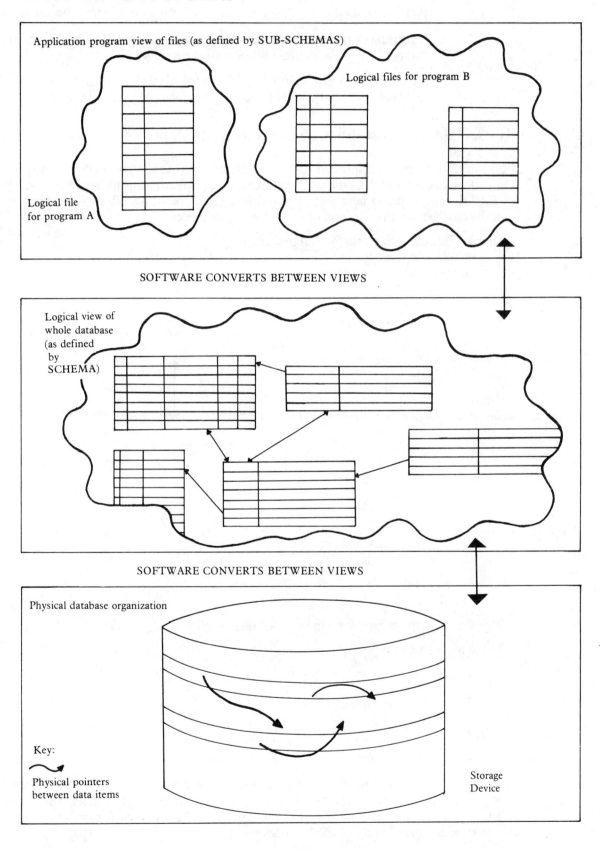

Application program view of files (as defined by SUB-SCHEMAS)

Logical files for program B

Logical file
for program A

SOFTWARE CONVERTS BETWEEN VIEWS

Logical view of
whole database
(as defined
by
SCHEMA)

SOFTWARE CONVERTS BETWEEN VIEWS

Physical database organization

Key:

Physical pointers
between data items

Storage
Device

A database management system, therefore, is a piece of software which has the following functions:

1.   It is the common link between all applications programs and the database.

2.   It facilitates the use and organization of a database, and protects the database from accidental or deliberate corruption.

3.   It restricts a programmer's logical view of the database to those items of data which are to be used in the applications program he is writing.

Case Study - CODASYL Database Management System

One of the alternative approaches to the Relational method is one based on *set* theory and developed by the Codasyl Committee, which also monitors standards in the COBOL programming language. The following diagram of a Codasyl logical *schema* serves to illustrate this method of database organization:

Codasyl Database Schema for Large Company

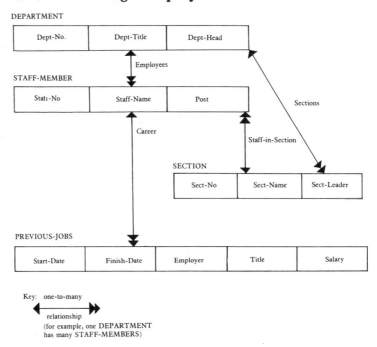

This schema can be explained in terms of *sets* as follows:

There are 4 record types:

1.   *Department*

2.   *Staff-member*

3.   *Section*

4.   *Previous-jobs*

Each of 1, 2 and 3 can be retrieved directly by its record key, Dept-No, Staff-No and Sect-No respectively. Record type 4 is only accessible via the *Staff-member* type record. This is reasonable as it would be unusual to search for a Previous-Jobs record without first knowing the identity of the Staff-Member.

There are 4 sets, each of which has an owner record and one or more member records. For example, one Department will have a number of Staff-Members (a one-to-many relationship). The sets are:

Employees (owner, *Department* / member, *Staff-member*)

Sections (owner, *Department* / member, *Section*)

Staff-in-Section (owner, *Section* / member, *Staff-member*)

Career (Owner, *Staff- Member*/member, *Previous-jobs*)

Diagrammatically, a set can be pictured as shown below.

For example, *Department* 4 as an owner record may have a number of *Section* member records.

Data Manipulation Language statements could be used to retrieve a Section record directly using its Sect-No or via its Sections Set (owned by Department Record). For example, if the section is in Department No 12:

1.   *move 12 to Dept-no*

2.   *find any Department*

3.   *show Section*

4.   *find next Section*

5.   *show Section*

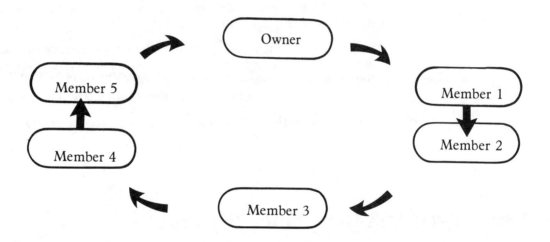

Steps 4 and 5 are repeated until the correct Section record is found or the end of set is reached. It should be noticed that a Previous-Jobs record can *only* be found via the Career set and the appropriate Staff-member record.

As with any database, a Codasyl DBMS organizes and accesses the *logical* database via the *schema* description. The logical organization is in terms of *sets*.

Query Languages

There are circumstances when the form of information needed from a database cannot be readily anticipated. Database management systems normally provide a specially designed language which allows a user who is trained in its use, to access a database without a specially-written applications program.

This type of language is called a *Query Language*.

An example of a Query Language can be illustrated by the following data held in a database:

Order No.	Supplier No.	Date	Quantity
6345	163	210482	135
6612	286	230582	310
6422	163	090382	155

To retrieve those orders for Supplier No 163 may require the following statement:

List Order No, Date, Quantity Where Supplier No = 163

This is an extremely simplified example and does not include all the necessary requirements in using a query language. It is not a simple alternative to applications programs but can be extremely useful for on-demand enquiries.

Advantages of Databases

(a)   Apart from Controlled Redundancy, there is no unnecessary duplication of data as occurs in traditional filing systems. Apart from the economic advantage, this means that transactions can update all affected areas of the database through a single input.

(b)   Because of the single input principle, there is less chance of inconsistency as may occur if the same transaction is keyed in several times to different files. Equally, of course, an incorrect entry will mean that all applications programs using the data will be working with the wrong data value.

(c)   The opportunities for obtaining comprehensive information are greatly improved with a central pool of data.

(d)   On-demand or ad hoc enquiries are possible through the use of a query language.

Centralized And Distributed Systems

Centralized Systems

In a centralized system, all processing is carried out by a central computer. Even when terminals are remote from the central computer and connected by telecommunications links, if they are dependent on the central computer for all processing, it is a centralized system.

Distributed Processing Systems

A distributed processing system allows some processing to be carried out at remote terminal sites. The terminals have their own computing power, some file storage and some programs. Limited database facilities may also exist at each site. Usually, before being transmitted to the central computer for updating of files, transaction data will require some *validation* and other accuracy checks (see Chapter 8) and this can be done at the terminal. Terminals with this facility are called *intelligent* terminals. Microcomputers equipped with suitable software are often used to emulate mainframe intelligent terminals, with the added advantage of being usable as stand-alone systems when not communicating with the mainframe.

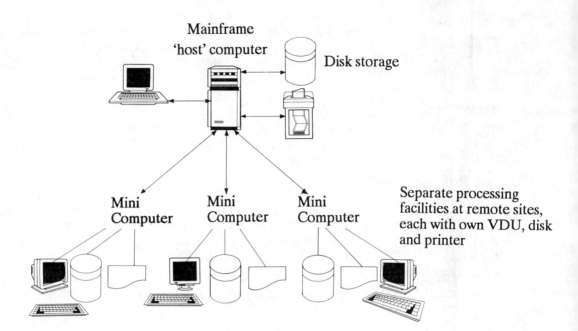

Mainframe 'host' computer

Disk storage

Mini Computer

Mini Computer

Mini Computer

Separate processing facilities at remote sites, each with own VDU, disk and printer

Reasons for Distributed Systems

Economy.   The transmission of data over telecommunications systems can be costly and local database storage and processing facilities can reduce such costs. Of course, to maintain such facilities at remote sites requires costly hardware, so the savings of distributed processing need to be set against the economies of scale provided by centralized systems. The radical reduction in computer hardware costs has favoured the expansion of distributed systems against centralized systems.

Minicomputers and Microcomputers.   The availability of minicomputer and micro-computer systems with data transmission facilities has made distributed processing economically favourable. An increasingly popular option in large, multi-sited organiz-ations, is to set up Local Area Networks of microcomputers at each site and connect them via communications networks to each other and-or to a central mainframe computer at the Head Office. This provides each site with the advantages of local processing power, local and inter-site communications through Electronic Mail and access to a central mainframe for the main filing and database systems.

Local Management Control.   It is not always convenient, particularly where an organization controls diverse activities, to have all information processing centralized. Local management control will mean that the information systems used will be developed by people with direct knowledge of their own information needs. Respon-sibility for the success or otherwise of their section of the organization may well be placed with local management so it is desirable that they have control over the accuracy and reliability of the data they use.

Electronic Office Systems

The concept of the electronic office aims to improve and partially automate office activities within an organization. Through the use of electronic equipment, changes can be introduced in 3 main ways:

a.   Document Preparation

–   by replacing, or at least supplementing the more traditional methods of recording information. At present, for example, preparation of documents such as an internal memorandum, may involve the office manager using a dictaphone (tape recorder for dictation and manager using a dictaphone (tape recorder for dictation and transcription) and the audio typist using a manual, electric or electronic typewriter. Additionally, documents with diagrams may involve an artist or draughtsman in their preparation.

b.   Document Storage and Retrieval

–   by improving the methods of storing and retrieving documented information. The existing methods may involve the use of indexed filing cabinets.

c.   Information Transmission

–   by improving the integration of office activities through more efficient information transmission. At present, for example, the main methods of communication may be by typed paper documents or the telephone.

The main components of an electronic office system consist of a variety of electronic products used in each area of activity listed above.

Document Preparation

Text Preparation

In text preparation, the main electronic component is the word processor. A word processor consists of a processor (CPU), memory, keyboard, screen, diskette storage and printer, together with appropriate software. The text appears on the screen where it can be manipulated and edited prior to printing or storing on diskette. The equipment also possesses many automatic features, including those for adjusting margins, tabulation points, headings and change of typeface (Chapter 11 Categories of Software).

Diagrams and other Graphical Material

Diagrams and other graphical representations can be included in the text in two ways:

(i)   The text layout can be left with gaps for insertion of graphical material at the printing stage, or

(ii)   Integrated software may allow the insertion of the graphical material while the text is still on the screen. In addition pictures from printed material can be reproduced within the document, through the use of a digitizer (hardware) connected to the computer and a graphics program. This is a technique now commonly used in newspaper production. The publishing industry now makes widespread use of Desk Top Publishing (DTP) systems, which are designed for the more powerful microcomputers. These systems make use of laser printers to produce the high speed, high quality output required by the publishing process.

Types of Word Processor

Dedicated Word Processor.   By dedicated, we mean that it is solely concerned with word processing and is programmed for that purpose only. A dedicated word processor provides a more sophisticated facility than a computer 'package'. Generally expensive, it can only be justified where there is a sufficient volume of text preparation to occupy a full-time operator. It may be linked to other equipment in the office, for example to the photocopier so that a number of copies of a document could be produced by a command from the word processor.

Computer with Word Processing Package.   Using a computer with a package such the computer is used for other applications as well. Apart from being less sophisticated than the dedicated word processor, it has the disadvantage of a general purpose computer keyboard without specialist word processing function keys. However, the programmable function keys (Chapter 18 Peripherals) are used by all word processing packages. Normally, a card or plastic template is provided, which fits over the function keys, thereby explaining the particular purpose of each key for that package. Some manufacturers of mini and mainframe computer systems will provide special keyboards to accompany the particular word processing package they sell.

Document Storage and Retrieval

The storage of documents with a high graphical content on computer storage is not particularly efficient, in that such documents occupy an excessive amount of computer memory. There are two main alternatives to computer storage available for the electronic office. They are:

(i) Microforms (microfilm and microfiche);

(ii) Optical disk (including Compact disk).

Microforms

As a celluloid medium, microform can store documentary information including graphical material. The structure of the microform can be either Microfilm (a continuous reel) or Microfiche (a grid pattern).

Microform reduces storage space requirements by approximately 95 per cent of that required by paper documentation.

There are two methods by which documentary information can be recorded on microform:

(i) by direct computer output (COM - computer output on microform). In this way, for example, text on screen could be recorded on microfilm using a microfilm recorder.

(ii) by photographic miniaturization.

To read information stored on microform, a special projector can be used to magnify the image and display it on a screen.

Retrieval of documents stored on microfiche can be made more efficient, particularly where large numbers are involved, by using a computer to locate and retrieve individual documents identified by unique codes. The computer will use indexing techniques to ensure an efficient search and retrieval process.

These document storage and retrieval techniques can be combined with computerized information systems used by other sections of an organization, to allow the combination of information from a variety of sources into a document.

Optical Disks

The optical disk uses laser beam technology to allow data to be recorded and read using bit-densities several times greater than a typical magnetic disk. Data are recorded as bit-patterns using high-intensity laser beams to burn tiny holes into the surface of the disk. The data can then be read from the disk using a laser beam of reduced intensity. A similar technology is used for Compact Disk (CD) digitized recordings of music and film. Its application in computing is still in the early stages of development but it is likely to have a profound impact on backing storage usage.

There are two main types of optical disk system presently available.

CD-ROM (Compact Disk-Read-Only Memory) Systems.   As the title suggests this type of disk only allows the computer to read data from the disk. The disk is pre-recorded by the manufacturer. It is of no use for the storage of data which require updating. Its main application is for Interactive Video Disk systems. A video disk can store text, images and audio signals and is of use in advertising, training and education. Sequences of film and sound can be retrieved under computer control.

WORM (Write Once, Read Many).   The large storage capacity of optical disks means that the writing facility can be used for a considerable period before all space is used up. Storage capacities are measured in gigabytes (thousands of millions of characters), which is way beyond the capacity of any magnetic disk system. Optical disk systems which provide an erase facility are available, but are still too expensive for most users.

Apart from its vast storage capacity, the optical disk is less prone to environmental hazards such as dust.

Information Transmission

Documents produced in the electronic office may be transmitted to those who should receive them by a variety of methods which all involve the conversion of text and graphical material into a digital form which a computer can handle. A global term for the variety of systems in use is *electronic mail*. The concept of electronic mail stems from its manual counterpart except that the medium of paper is made redundant during the transmission process and is not even essential if hard copy is not required by the receiver.

Until recently the standard methods of text transmission were:

> (i) Telex (teleprinter exchange);
>
> (ii) Facsimile Transmission.

Telex

Telex is a well established communications system which, rather like the public telephone network, allows subscribers to communicate with one another. There are over a million subscribers in this country at present.

Each subscriber is given a telex code (you will often see it at the top of business letter headings next to the telephone number) and must have a teleprinter which is a combination of keyboard and printer. There is no screen, so all messages sent or received are printed onto hard copy. The transmission rate of approximately 6 characters per second is slow compared with more modern telecommunications systems, but the limitations of keyboard entry and printer speed on the teleprinter, make any faster speed unnecessary.

The main benefit of telex is that a permanent record of communications is kept and the receiver does not have to be 'on the spot' when the message arrives.

Its main disadvantage is that there is no storage facility for messages. Any transmission has to be printed as soon as it is transmitted so that if the receiver is faulty, the system comes to a halt. However, systems now exist to allow Telex to be accessed via Prestel, using a microcomputer system with full word processing facilities.

Facsimile Transmission

This system can utilize either the telephone or telex networks to allow users to transmit an accurate copy of a document. The information (text or picture) is digitized by a facsimile machine which scans the page automatically to produce the required signals. Computer storage is used within the network so that signals can be queued if there is a hold-up in the system. Modern systems can transmit an A4 page in less than a minute.

Computer Networks

Networking or linking together computer systems has the effect of decentralizing computer processing and improving communication within an organisation. The topic of computer networks is discussed fully in Chapter 23 but their use for *electronic office* systems is described after the following brief outline of network features.

There are broadly two types of computer network:

Local Area Networks (LAN)

These are used to connect computers in a single room or within a building or buildings on one site. Its main feature is that, unlike Wide Area Networks, no special telecommunications hardware is necessary.

Wide Area Networks (WAN)

WAN are used to connect computers on different sites or even in different parts of the world. They make use of telecommunications systems (in this country the principal provider is British Telecom) including satellite links. These networks extend beyond the concept of the office as a single room or group of rooms. A user can be 'at the office' at home if he has the necessary terminal link. Organizations with offices abroad can benefit from the immediate communication facility normally available to people in the same room.

Computer networks provide several advantages for their users:

(i)   In local area networks there is the opportunity to share disk storage and possibly printer facilities. In all networks there is the facility for sharing information, perhaps in a central database.

(ii)   Improved communication facilities. Within a network a facility exists for terminal users to communicate with one another via the network. Therefore the results of processing, or perhaps a document prepared by word processing, could be immediately communicated to one or more of the other users on the system.

(iii)   Processing facilities can be provided for each user but an element of central control can still exist.

(iv)   The breakdown of one computer in the network does not effect the others in the system, except where a central *host* computer handles all communications. In the latter case, although some independent processing power may remain, inter-network communication is not possible. In a centralized system, if the central computer is 'down', all connected terminals lose their processing power.

Computer Networks for Communication

Three main electronic communication systems can be identified, although in practice they may be integrated. They are:

(a)   Electronic mail and message systems;

(b)   Electronic diaries and calendars;

(c)   Electronic notice boards.

Electronic Mail

Unlike telex and facsimile transmissions, which require paper for input and output, electronic mail systems based on computer networks are paper-less (except when a user requires hard copy). A major advantage is the facility for message storage if a destination terminal is busy, or has a temporary fault. When it is free, the message can be transmitted.

Certain basic features can be identified as being common to all electronic mail systems:

(i)   a terminal for preparing, entering and storing messages. The terminal will be *intelligent*, possibly a microcomputer, mainframe terminal or dedicated word processor. In any event, it should have some word processing or text editing facilities to allow messages to be changed on screen before transmission. A printer may also be available for printing out messages received over the system;

(ii)   an electronic communication link with other workstations in the network and with the central computer controlling the system;

(iii)   a directory containing the electronic addresses of all network users;

(iv)   a central mailbox facility (usually the controlling computer) for the storage of messages in transit or waiting to be retrieved.

Ideally, the following facilities are available to electronic mail users:

(i)   messages are automatically dated upon transmission;

(ii)   messages are automatically acknowledged as being received when the recipient first accesses it from the terminal;

(iii)   multiple addressing; that is the facility to address a message to an identified group, without addressing each member of the group individually;

(iv)   priority rating to allow messages to be allocated different priorities according to their importance.

Networks require two particular features in order to support electronic mail:

(i)   a message storage facility to allow messages to be forwarded when the recipient is available. This means that the recipient does not have to be using the system at the time the message is sent;

(ii)   compatibility with a wide range of manufacturers' equipment. Devices attached to a network have to be able to *talk* to the communications network using *protocols* or standards of communication. Network protocols are explained in Chapter 23.

Benefits of Electronic Mail

The following major benefits are generally claimed for electronic mail systems:

(i)   Savings in stationery and telephone costs;

(ii)   More rapid transmission than is possible with conventional mail;

(iii)   Electronic mail can be integrated with other computer-based systems used in an organization;

(iv)   All transmissions are recorded, so costs can be carefully controlled;

(v)   Electronic mail allows staff to 'telecommute', that is, to work from home via a terminal;

(vi)   The recipient does not have to be present when a message is sent. Messages can be retrieved from the central *mailbox* when convenient.

Electronic mail refers to communication over long, as well as short distances via Wide Area Networks, but internal office communication via a Local Area Network is referred to as Electronic Messaging.

Electronic Diaries and Calendars

An ordinary desk diary is generally used by managerial or executive staff to keep a check on important meetings and much of the time it is quite adequate for the purpose. A conventional calendar is usually pinned to a wall for staff to check the date. Electronic diaries and calendars do not attempt to replace these traditional facilities. To begin with, it would be extremely tedious if it were necessary to sit at a computer terminal simply to discover the date.

An electronic diary and calendar system may provide the following facilities:

Diary Entries

Entries are made under a particular date and can be retrieved using the relevant date. Used in this way, the system 'apes' the conventional diary by producing a list of entries for any date entered. At this level, it could be argued that a desk diary does the job just as well;

Search and Retrieval on Event

Instead of entering the date, the user requests a list of entries conforming to particular criteria. For example, a request for a list of Board meetings over the next six months would produce a list with the relevant dates. Similarly, for example, a request for a list of those supposed to be attending a Board meeting on a particular date would produce a list of attendees names;

Flexible Search and Retrieval

This facility can be used to produce a number of alternative strategies based on specified criteria. Suppose, for example, that a Board meeting has been called, but the exact date has not been set. The problem is to set a date which falls within the next three weeks and is convenient for all Board members. The search and retrieval facility allows the searching of each member's electronic diary for dates when all are available. The system may produce a number of possible dates. Such tasks can be extremely time-consuming to carry out manually.

At this point, it is important to note that the above examples assume a comprehensive diary system which is kept up to date. The system fails if, for example, one director's diary entries are incomplete.

Electronic Notice Boards

Electronic notice boards are essentially a localized version of the viewdata systems described in the next section. The system may be used by an organization to advertise staff promotions, training courses, new staff appointments and retirements.

Teletext and Viewdata Systems

The combination of the telecommunications and computer technologies has produced an 'information explosion' and there are now many services providing specialist information, which organizations can use either independently or in conjunction with their own computerized information systems.

Public Systems

Teletext

Teletext systems, such as Ceefax and Oracle, provide a public service based on a central computer database, which users can access via an ordinary television set with special adapter and keypad. The database consists of thousands of 'pages' or frames of information which are kept up to date by Information Providers. Pages can be accessed and displayed on the television screen through the use of the keypad, directly via page number or through a series of hierarchical indexes. Major subject areas include Sport, News, Business, Leisure and Entertainment, Finance and Travel. Pages are transmitted using spare bandwidth unused by television pictures, in 'carousels' or groups. The user may have to wait some time while the carousel containing the required page is transmitted.

Its major drawback is that communication is *one way*. The user cannot send messages to the database, only receive.

Viewdata or Videotex

The principle of a central database and frames of information forms the basis of viewdata systems. The major public viewdata system in the UK is Prestel. Each user requires a telephone, TV monitor or television set, electronic interface, a modem (for modifying computer signals for transmission over the telephone network), an auto-dialler (for contacting the database and identifying the terminal user) and an electronic device to generate the picture from the received data.

Its major benefit is that it provides an *interactive* system. Communication is *two way*. A user can transmit messages to the database.

Private Communications on Prestel

Prestel provides a facility for Closed User Groups (CUG) so that, for example, a group of estate agents could rent several pages which were for their own exclusive use and could not be accessed by ordinary users.

Access to other Databases via Prestel

A facility exists called Gateway which allows Prestel users to access their own bank's database, to carry out transactions on their personal or business accounts via the Prestel network. The user will register with their bank, pay an annual subscription and receive personal security details such as a password and sign-on code. The Bank of Scotland operate such a service called Home Banking.

Telex can now be accessed, from a microcomputer, through a Prestel gateway. LAN gateway products also exist to allow access to the Telex system by any user node on a LAN. Electronic mail facilities, such as those described in the previous section are not inherent in Telex. However, gateway software, such as Torus's Telex Gateway, can provide them instead. For example, incoming telex messages can be stored on disk at the gateway LAN station, be sent to any shared printer on the LAN if hard copy is required or, be distributed to other nodes electronically. Personal user directories can be set up and messages can be queued or assigned a particular time for transmission.

Assignment   *The Royal County*

The Royal County Hotel is situated in Princes Street, Edinburgh and has 350 rooms, each with en-suite shower and toilet facilities, colour television and video recorder. It has a reputation for haute cuisine and has an AA 5-star rating. It is not a member of any large hotel group, being the pride and joy of a self-made millionaire, Charles Pender, who started his career in the restaurant industry after some years as a chef with the Cunard shipping line. Mr. Pender has always tried to maintain a friendly but efficient service in the hotel and up to now has not made use of computer facilities for hotel administration. Recently, Mr. Pender has opened two new hotels of similar rating in Newcastle upon Tyne and Norwich. There are thirty administrative staff employed at the Edinburgh hotel, including a hotel manager, an assistant manager, a restaurant manager and three receptionists. The excessive workload on staff and the number of recent administrative errors affecting guests have persuaded Mr. Pender that computer facilities are needed.

You are currently employed as a trainee systems analyst by Datasoft, a software consultancy firm based in Edinburgh and the firm has been approached by Mr. Pender concerning the computerization of hotel office procedures. The idea is that hotel reception should be electronically 'part of' the main office, which is situated on the top floor of the building. In addition, inter-hotel communication would allow Mr. Pender to exert greater control over all three hotels. The use of 'electronic office' facilities would seem to be appropriate. The senior systems analyst, Judith Stewart, has asked you to visit the hotel and carry out a preliminary investigation of Mr. Pender's requirements. She has also asked you to provide a preliminary report on your findings for Mr. Pender.

Task

Prepare an informal report for Mr. Pender outlining the facilities which constitute an 'electronic office' and suggesting ways in which the facilities could be used in the hotels. Also explain, in simple terms, how the inter-hotel communication is to be accomplished.

Developmental Task

Research available software packages for hotel management, from hotel industry and computing magazines.

Assignment

Mr. Pender's Electronic Office

Referring to The Royal County Hotel case study on the previous page, identify the components which may be needed for the electronic office facilities.

Task

Produce a sample specification, detailing the components which may need to be purchased, their function within an electronic office system and the approximate costs.

Developmental Task

As a group effort, write to a number of manufacturers requesting a copy of their product catalogues. Alternatively, research the subject from computing and office machinery magazines. Try and organize a visit to an organization with a computer network and-or electronic office facilities.

Assignment   *Transaction or Batch*

Smith and Weston is a small plumbing and heating engineering firm, based in Scarborough. The partners, Ernie Smith and Brian Weston took over the business from Brian Weston's father in 1980 and are keen to expand it. The firm employs twenty five time-served plumbers and five apprentices. All employees are paid on the Friday each week. Ernie has been examining the possibility of computerizing a variety of the accounting tasks, including Sales Ledger and Wages. Much of the plumbing and heating work is carried on a sub-contracted basis for a number of larger contractors. About 60 per cent of the Sales Ledger accounts are updated on a weekly basis. Most of the available microcomputer software is designed for transaction processing, but some does have a batch processing facility.

Task

You are employed in a general clerical-office supervision role and currently carry out all the accounting tasks manually. Mr. Smith is unsure of the difference between batch and transaction processing and, being aware of your related studies at college, has asked you to explain the features of each method, pointing out the advantages and disadvantages of each to the firm.

1. Produce some notes to refer to when you explain the two methods of processing to Mr. Smith.

2. Role play an exercise in which you give an oral presentation to the lecturer of your explanations. Illustrate your talk with copies of documents (relevant to the business in question) used in batch processing. Make your own recommendations on the most appropriate processing method(s) for the applications mentioned above.

Chapter 7

Systems Development and Implementation

Introduction

When a new computer system is introduced, or an existing computerized information system is to be changed or modified, then a process of development and implementation should be followed. This process is known as the *System Life Cycle* and has a number of distinct stages.

An outline of this cycle can be illustrated as follows:

Initial Survey/Study
↓
Feasibility Study
↓
Systems Investigation and Analysis
↓
Systems Design
↓
Systems Implementation
↓
Maintenance and Review

The need for an application to be computerized or for an existing computerized system to be changed is often identified by the users. Such an initiative is described as being from the 'bottom-up'. Alternatively if the initiative stems from management it is described as being 'top-down'. However it is initiated, innovation or change requires close consultation between users and management, to consider its consequences and benefits and to decide the way it is to be introduced.

The system life cycle begins when a need for change or innovation is identified. The cycle may of course, be stopped at any stage if it is found that the change is not after all desirable. The specialist responsible for each stage in the cycle is the Systems Analyst whose broad responsibilities are described in Chapter 2 in the section on Management Information Services.

The activities within each stage of the system life cycle are described below:

Initial Survey/Study

Once a need for computerization has been identified, an initial survey is undertaken to decide whether or not such a need is justified and also to determine the objectives of the system.

To illustrate this, the following example gives the objectives of a stock control system:

Objectives of a stock control system

(i) to maintain levels of stock which will be sufficient to meet customer demand promptly;

(ii) to provide a mechanism which removes the need for excessively high safety margins of stock to cover customer demand. This is usually effected by setting minimum stock levels which the computer can use to warn users of variations outside these levels;

(iii) to provide automatic re-ordering of stock items which fall below minimum levels;

(iv) to provide management with up-to-date information on stock levels and values of stock held.

Before any single application can be computerized, it is necessary to establish its objectives clearly because users may have become so used to its procedures that they no longer question their purpose. It is self-evident that before any informed judgement can be made on the design of a computerized system, the objectives of the relevant application must first be clearly understood.

Feasibility Study

Having established that there exists the need for a new system, a feasibility study should provide sufficient information to either justify its computerization or make suggestions as to alternative methods for its operation. This is produced by a Study Team composed of systems analysts, users and management.

Such a study compares the costs and benefits of the existing system with the projected costs and benefits of a new system. Tangible savings , such as a reduction in staffing or, as is more likely, an increase in business without extra staffing, can be readily measured. The benefits of more accurate, up-to-date information and more management information however are less easy to quantify, yet they must nevertheless be taken into account when a comparison is made. Other tangible costs of the new system may include the costs of computer hardware, the costs of software which is either packaged or specially written, staff training and possibly specialist staff recruitment.

The social costs and benefits which relate to staff also have to be assessed. These may include training needs and changes in career prospects, salaries, job descriptions or job satisfaction. The feasibility study may well recommend that a particular manufacturer's computer system is purchased or that specific packaged software is employed. The end product of this stage of the cycle is a *Feasibility Report* for consideration by management. It should cover the following areas:

(i) A description of the application to be computerized, the overall business and individual system objectives which are to be satisfied and the position of the development in relation to the organization's overall computerization plans.

(ii) A description of the existing system, its good and bad features and the means by which the proposed system aims to improve on it. This area details the costs of the existing system to allow comparison with the proposed new system.

(iii) A description of the new system, its operation, costs and expected benefits.

(iv) Possible alternatives and recommendations. This is an important area, for should the recommendation be against the proposed system, then alternatives need to be presented.

(v) Costs of development and the timescale for development and implementation (if the recommended system is to be adopted).

It must be remembered that an application will not necessarily benefit from computerization and the study team may well recommend changes in the system which do not involve a computer. Increasingly however, reduction in costs of computer hardware and advances in software development which cover most applications have lessened the likelihood of this happening in most cases.

Systems Investigation and Analysis

If the feasibility report is favourable then a more detailed investigation begins. The information obtained should be analysed in terms of its bearing on the design and implementation of the new system. The objective of this stage is to produce a *Statement of User Requirements*. This is, in effect, a system proposal approved by the users. To design the most effective computerized system, the analyst needs first to gain a thorough knowledge of the operation of the existing system and then to analyse in detail the best solution for computerized working. This stage is a prerequisite of the detailed Systems Design stage.

The task of gathering such information may involve interviews with users, surveys by questionnaire, the examination of documents and procedure manuals and most importantly, the observation of users already operating the system. These various techniques are discussed later in this chapter. The systems analyst should produce a report which covers the following areas.

The Objectives and Scope of the Existing System

The objectives of a system describe its main functions and what it seeks to achieve. By the scope, we mean the boundaries of the system to be investigated. In this way, the limits of the investigation are established.

Input

Information on the source of the input data, the methods used to collect it, the volumes and the data items which comprise it, will allow the systems analyst to make design recommendations on computer methods of input. For example, it may be more efficient for users to enter data via visual display units, as part of an on-line processing system, than for data to be forwarded for batch encoding and input at a centralized computer centre.

The Files Used

Details of the master files to be used, the data items which will be included in each record, the sequence of organisation and the frequency of updating or access, will assist the systems analyst in the choice of computer storage media and the most appropriate file organization and access methods.

Processing Tasks

All the clerical and machine-assisted procedures which are necessary to achieve the desired output from the given input need to be identified. Identification of these procedures will allow the systems analyst to determine the role of the computer in the new system, the programs needed to take over certain processing stages and any necessary alterations to clerical procedures which precede and follow computer processing.

Output

Information on the form and content of outputs produced by the system will give guidance to the systems analyst on the objectives of the new system. In addition, it may be found that a computerized system may also produce additional outputs which cannot be produced efficiently at present.

Controls

The clerical procedures which control the accuracy and security of the data in the present system will provide a minimum standard for any new system. Of course, it would be hoped that a computerized system could improve such accuracy and security standards.

Management Information

The present system may already produce some management information, but generally, a computerized system can produce information which it is not practical to produce manually. Existing output should therefore be questioned. It may be that the management information currently produced is no longer necessary but continues to be produced through system inertia, in other words, because no one has realised that it is not really necessary or appropriate.

Problems and Difficulties

If the new system is to avoid the difficulties inherent in the existing system, then such difficulties must be clearly identified.

Methods of Gathering the Information

There are four main methods which a systems analyst can use to gather the information which has been discussed in the previous section. These are:

(i) Interviewing;

(ii) Questionnaires;

(iii) Examination of records and procedure manuals;

(iv) Observation.

The method or methods chosen will depend on the specific circumstances which relate to a system as each method has particular advantages and disadvantages.

Interviewing

This is probably the most commonly used method for collecting information even though the skills of interviewing are not easily acquired. The interviewer needs to know how to gain the confidence of the interviewee and ensure that the person feels that the information which is given will be of value in the design of the proposed new system. The questions need to be phrased unambiguously in order to obtain the desired information. Opinions, as well as facts, are valuable as they will tend to reveal the strengths and weaknesses of the present system.

It is important to ask the appropriate questions at the right level in the staff hierarchy within the organization. For example, the sales clerk would probably be the best person to ask about the completion of a customer order form.

For a check list of questions to be drawn up, the systems analyst needs to have prior knowledge of duties and responsibilities of staff who are to be interviewed.

Questionnaire

Questionnaires are useful when only a small amount of information is required from a large number of people. To provide accurate responses questions need to be unambiguous and precise. Questionnaires can be useful for gathering statistical information on, for example, volumes of sales transactions or customer enquiries at the different branches of a national organization.

Examination of Records and Procedure Manuals

If existing procedures are already well documented then the procedure manuals can provide a ready-made source of information on the way procedures should be carried out. However it is important to realise that the procedures detailed there may not accord with what actually happens. The examination of current records and the tracing of particular transactions from input to the production of the required output can be a method by which the systems analyst may discover how closely the set procedures are actually followed.

The use of special purpose records which may involve, for example, the ticking of a box when an activity has been completed, is another useful technique which does not significantly add to the work load of the staff involved.

Observation

It is most important to observe a procedure in action, so that irregularities and exceptional procedures are noticed. Observation should always be carried out with tact, and staff under observation should be made fully aware of its purpose to avoid suspicions of 'snooping'.

The following list details some of the features of office procedures and conditions which may be usefully observed by a trained person:

The Office Layout.   This may determine whether the positioning of desks, filing cabinets and other office equipment is convenient for staff and conducive to efficient working;

The Work Load.   This should indicate whether the volume of documents waiting to be processed is fairly constant or if there are peak periods during the week;

Delays.   These could show that there are some procedures which are continually behind schedule;

Methods of Working .   A trained observer can, through experience, recognize a slow, reasonable or quick pace of work and decide whether or not the method of working is efficient. It is important that such observations should be followed up by an interview to obtain the cooperation of the person under observation;

Office Conditions.   These should be examined as poor ventilation, inadequate or excessive temperatures or poor lighting can adversely effect staff efficiency.

Recording the Facts

During the investigation stage, the systems analyst is likely to accumulate a large volume of notes on all areas of the system. It is good practice, therefore, to organize these notes into sections according to the department or procedure to which they relate. A continuous narrative may be difficult and laborious to read and so wherever possible, use should be made of diagrammatic representations such as:

Organization Charts

Organization charts provide an overview of an organization's operations and show the relationships between people and the work for which they are responsible.

In attempting to discover how a current system functions, it is useful to know which individuals are responsible for each functional area. Organizations charts can be useful in this respect. An example is shown below.

A Formal Organization Chart

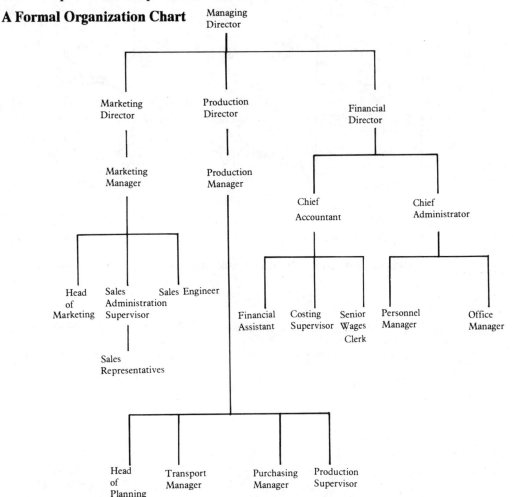

Information Interface or Flow Diagrams

Information interface diagrams provide a visual representation of information movement in an organization. They do not refer to specific hardware and are not, therefore, committing the systems analyst in this area. It is important that the systems analyst retains an 'open mind' in the early stages, so that improved hardware and software possibilities are not overlooked.

System Flowcharts

System flowcharts allow the systems analyst to plan the selection of hardware for the proposed system. It is a graphical representation of the procedures from input through to output, without any detail as to how processing is to be accomplished. Thus, the functions of a complete computer program may be represented by one symbol in the flowchart.

Basic System flowchart symbols

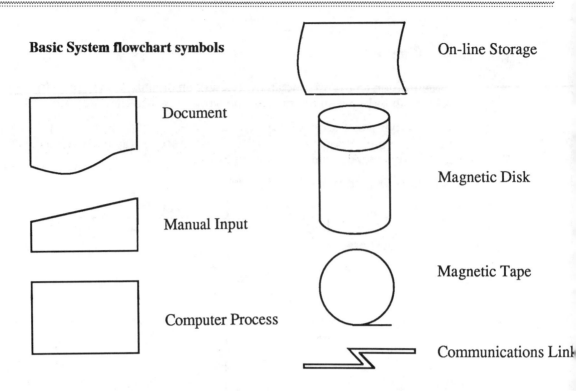

On-line Storage

Document

Magnetic Disk

Manual Input

Magnetic Tape

Computer Process

Communications Link

The following system flowchart illustrates a typical stock control system.

System Flowchart - Stock File Update Using Batch Processing

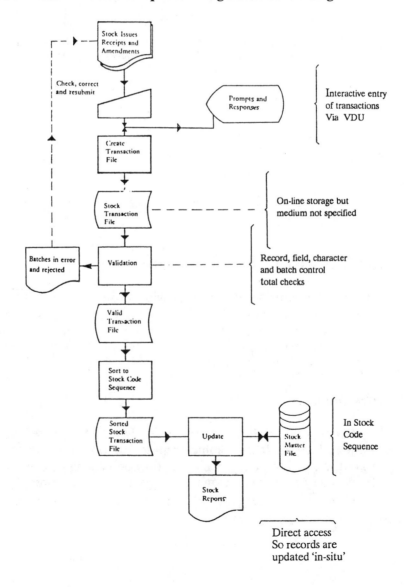

Analysis and Assessment of the System

Having gathered all the facts on the existing system, it then has to be analysed and assessed in terms of its objectives identified in the first stage of the investigation. Problems and difficulties which exist must be clearly pointed out so that any new proposals which the systems analyst puts forward will include, where appropriate, measures to overcome them. At the end of this stage, the resulting Statement of User Requirements will be discussed with all interested users and then used as a basis for the next stage of Systems Design.

Systems Design

Aims of Systems Design

The aims are to design a system which:

(i) satisfies the users' requirements as cost-effectively as possible;

(ii) is as flexible as possible. The system must be adaptable to changes in the information needs of the user. Such changes will not necessarily be radical but for example may simply be changes in the volumes of transactions being processed. In other words, growth and change should have been anticipated at the design stage;

(iii) processes data accurately so that users can be confident that the information stored on the master files is both accurate and up-to-date;

(iv) has the necessary controls to prevent accidental or deliberate damage to the system. This means that it should be secure against unauthorized access and sufficiently fool-proof in its operation to prevent a person's careless mistakes disorganizing the system;

(v) is secure against loss of data. Security measures should prevent the loss of information from files by a user error or physical damage to storage media;

(vi) is easy to use;

(vii) falls within the limits set by legal and other constraints. An example of a legal constraint is the requirement by the Companies Acts that all limited companies produce annual accounts which must be sent to Companies House in Cardiff and are available for public inspection. Other constraints may be set simply by custom and practice or by agreements with Trades Unions. A constraint which applies to all organizations is the requirement that accounting systems must be capable of being audited, so the systems analyst must consult with the organization's auditors to ascertain their requirements.

Stages of Systems Design

Before identifying the stages in systems design it should be emphasized that analysis and design are not necessarily consecutive tasks in the sense that all the fact-finding is complete before the design stage begins. Continual reference back for further information may be necessary during the design of the new system.

Similarly, the steps involved in the design stage are not necessarily consecutive and may involve the systems analyst in going back over earlier steps to carry out more detailed design. Bearing this in mind, the stages of systems design can be carried out under the following headings:

The Nature of the System

This identifies the computer processing method(s) to be used in the system. The possible methods (which are described in Chapter 6) include batch, real-time and time-share processing, as well as systems controlled by database management systems. Of course, a system may use a combination of processing methods.

Output Specification

Logically, the systems analyst must decide what the system is required to output before deciding how to produce it.

It will already be known, in some detail, what output is required of the system, as this is identified at the investigation stage. In considering the design of screen or printed output, the systems analyst will have to consider the following factors:

Content.   One of a number of outputs from a stock control system, for example, could be a printed stock report of items whose quantities have fallen below preset minimum stock levels. The details of those data items which are to be included in the stock report will be decided at the design stage. The content and presentation of the report will depend on the requirements of those who are to make use of it. If, for instance, the report is to go to the Purchasing Department for the manual preparation of stock orders, then the report need not necessarily contain details of suppliers as this information will already be held by the purchasing department. If, on the other hand, orders are to be generated automatically and printed by the computer, the supplier's names and addresses will need to be accessible 'on-line' at the time the orders are produced.

Volume.   The volume of output obviously has significance in terms of selecting appropriate output devices.

Sequence.   The sequence in which output is required, for example whether it should be random or sequential will be one of the factors considered in choosing the file organization method and storage media.

Frequency.   How frequently the information will be required has to be considered in conjunction with the volume of demand. If, for example, a large volume of printed output has to be produced daily, this will occupy a printer for lengthy periods when it may be required for other output. The solution may involve the timing of the output, perhaps at the end of the day when the main tasks are finished. On the other hand the purchase of an additional fast laser printer may solve the problem.

If a job which produces printed output cannot proceed because a printer is temporarily unavailable, the technique of SPOOLing (Simultaneous Peripheral Operation On Line) can be used. This allows spooling or queuing of output to a storage device such as disk or tape until the printer is available, when it is despooled. Peripherals can operate autonomously after the initial data transfer command has been given by the processor and so computer processing can continue during the printing process.

File Design

File design is a process which must consider the contents of individual records, the sequence in which records are held on the storage medium and the order in which they may be accessed. In determining the most appropriate file organization and access methods for any particular application, a number of factors may be taken into account:

The 'Hit Rate'.   This defines the proportion of a master file's records which need to be accessed in one run and is expressed as a percentage.

Example

During an invoicing 'run', a customer master file containing, say 1000 records, may be processed with customer order transactions affecting 850 of the customer records. The *hit rate* for that run would be (850 ÷ 1000) × 100 or 85%.

Access Requirements.   Although the decision as to which file organization method to use can be complex, as a general, if rather simplistic rule, a 'high' hit rate of, say 80% would indicate the need for sequential access to a file, perhaps as part of a batch processing system. There may, of course, also be a need for random access to individual records in the same file and this would suggest that both sequential and random access should be provided. An example of such a situation is given below.

Example

In the above example of an invoicing application, the most efficient method of processing the file would be in sequence, so the master file would probably be sequenced according to the Customer Number key field and the transactions sorted into the same sequence. In addition, however, the users would wish to access customer records directly to check on customer balances, so random access is necessary.

Indexed sequentially organized files (Chapter 5) provide both these access facilities. Where the hit rate is 'low', say 15%, this would indicate that only random access is needed. Random organization (Chapter 5) fulfils this need, without the use of the large file indexes required with the indexed sequential method.

The file organization method clearly has consequences for the choice of storage media, either serial or direct. As is explained in Chapter 18 on Peripherals, magnetic tape only allows serial or sequential access, so where there is a need for any direct access, magnetic disk is the only real option. However, decisions still need to be made on the capacity and speed of access which is needed; there are wide variations in the performance characteristics of storage devices, even in a single category such as magnetic disk (Chapter 18 Peripherals).

Integrated Processing Requirements.   Sometimes, a single input may update more than one master file. For example, the value of a payment received by a retailing firm from a customer, in settlement of their account, may be input once and used by the applications program to update both the customer's account and the firm's cash or bank account.

Input Specification

The systems analyst must consider:

The content of input records.   The data requirements of a system will comprise information held on master files which, together with current transaction data, produces the required output.

Example

Data from customer orders for quantities of items specified by Item Code may be input to an Invoicing system to produce the necessary customer invoices. To obtain the output, the input data will need to be used to extract prices of items from the stock master file and calculate the value of goods ordered.

Source document design.   Source data is usually recorded on pre-printed documents in order to standardize the format of input data according to computer requirements. Properly designed source documents also assist accuracy and checking procedures. The design of the form should take account of the order in which data items are to be keyed in. It will often detail the maximum size (number of characters) and the mode of characters permitted, for example, alphabetic or numeric. Simple explanatory notes to help in its completion may appear on the form, but procedure manuals and staff training will generally be necessary for efficient and speedy form completion.

Dialogue design.   This concerns the structuring of the 'conversation' between the user and the computer. The dialogue makes use of the screen for the display of system prompts, user responses and system responses. User input is usually via a conventional keyboard, although other devices, such as the mouse or touch screen (Chapter 18 Peripherals), may also be used.

Volume and frequency of input.   This will have consequences for the choice of input device. Large volumes of input data will normally be encoded onto tape or disk for faster data input, such as that which occurs in large batch processing systems. Smaller volumes on the other hand, may be input via a VDU, validated and processed immediately.

Timing of input.   If the input needs to be carried out at the same time as other applications then a system priority has to be established or a larger number of input devices may have to be used.

The input must be scheduled so that the master files are kept as up-to-date as is necessary for users. In a real-time airline booking system, for example, the input needs to be immediate if customers are to be dealt with promptly and flight records kept up-to-date.

Processing Tasks

The clerical, machine-assisted and computerized procedures have to be finalized, based on the information gathered during the investigation stage. Specifications will be produced which fully detail the clerical tasks to carried out by staff at all stages of human involvement. For example, in a batch processing system, descriptions will be provided for the Data Control staff of the procedures for batching input documents and for calculating batch control totals. Program specifications are produced, which describe in detail the processing tasks to be carried out by computer. These specifications will be used, either by programmers to write the necessary applications software, or as a basis for deciding on which 'off-the-shelf' package(s) to buy.

System Implementation

User Involvement

Although a new system often aims to reduce the workload of users in the long run, during the implementation period it is usual to continue with the work of the existing system, in parallel, until the new system is fully tested. Additionally staff will be occupied with activities needed to introduce the system, such as converting files to computer storage media, reading user documentation and following training programmes.

There are several clearly identifiable areas of activity in the implementation of a new system:

     (i) Development and testing of programs.

    (ii) Conversion of files.

   (iii) Education and training of staff.

   (iv) Introduction of new clerical procedures.

    (v) The changeover plan - 'going live'.

Development and Testing of Programs

At the end of the design stage, the programming teams are presented with a *Program Specification* which sets out the system requirements in terms of what the computer is required to do, in other words the computer processing tasks. The programmers, using a programming language, code the programs according to the requirements in the program specification. The program specification also includes a testing plan which, through the use of properly selected input data, tests the working of the programs for the reliability and accuracy of the output.

Conversion of Files

Existing manual files need to be encoded onto the chosen storage media and this can be a formidable task. The encoding of large files will be a time-consuming process and coupled with the fact that 'live' transaction data will change the values in the master files, they may need to be phased into the computer system in stages. In a stock control system, for example, records for certain categories of stock item may be encoded and computer processed, leaving the remainder to be processed by existing methods and encoded at a later stage.

In favourable circumstances, a large scale encoding exercise may be undertaken to initially create the file and then, through an application program, transactions which have occurred since the encoding began can be used to update the file to reflect the correct values. Users will have to be made aware of which records have already been encoded into the system so that they can properly update them as transactions occur.

Where new files which did not previously exist are to be created, then the task is even more extensive in that the data has to be collected and organized before encoding. The validation of data before it is used in a computer system is vital so that users can rely on the accuracy of the output from the system. Validation is one of the system controls described in Chapter 8.

If a business has inadequate staffing to cope with the encoding exercise, a computer bureau (see Computer Services at the end of this chapter) may be used. Where possible, the bureau's staff should carry out the work on site, because the records will be needed for the continued operation of the business.

An additional problem is that records in their existing state may not conform with the file layouts designed for the new system and the data may have to be copied onto special-purpose input forms to assist with accurate encoding.

Education and Training of Staff

The education and training of the users of the system is vital if it is to be operated correctly and the full benefits are to be obtained.

Management need to be educated so that they can recognise how the system can provide the information they need. Generally, managerial staff will not carry out routine data entry, but some basic skill in using a VDU may be necessary to allow them for example to make immediate enquiries from a database. In a decentralized system, the need for such training will be greater than in a centralized system where only specialist computer staff are involved with computer processing. The role of different staff and the effects of computerization in terms of their training needs are discussed in Chapter 9.

The main categories of staff who will require education and/or training include:

Management;

Clerical Staff;

Data Control and Data Preparation Staff;

Computer Operations Staff.

By the time the system is ready to 'go live', all staff involved with the system should be competent to operate it efficiently. They should also have sufficient knowledge to assess its effectiveness. In other words, "does it do what it is supposed to do reliably and at the right time?".

Deciding when to carry out the training can be difficult. If too early, some staff will have forgotten what they have been taught by the time the system is introduced. If too late, staff may feel panicked because they have not been properly prepared. Training programmes should, as far as possible, be designed to suit the working conditions of staff and the time-scale for implementation. It may be that residential courses will be needed for supervisory staff, who will then carry out the 'on the job' training of subordinate staff. This latter task may involve staff working extra hours because the existing system may still have to be operated prior to the implementation and for sometime afterwards during a period of *parallel running.*

Introduction of New Clerical Procedures

The computer programs that have been developed or purchased form only part of the whole information processing system. To function correctly they have to be supported by the clerical procedures designed to interface with them. Testing of the system should also cover the operation of manual procedures such as the preparation and handling of source documents, the batching of input and preparation of control totals prior to input and dealing with error and other reports produced as output.

The Changeover Plan - 'Going Live'

'Going live', as the term suggests, involves using real data and using the system in the day-to-day operation of the organization. Prior to this the system should have been tested in simulated conditions and at that stage no reliance should have been placed on it. Even if careful preparations for its introduction have been made, a system will rarely function properly at first. For this reason, a system's initiation should not be on an 'all or nothing' basis and should be supported by the existing system until it can be relied upon. Comparisons with the output of the existing system will help spot any inaccuracies and inconsistencies in the new system's output. There is no set period for parallel running as this will depend on the particular system and the circumstances surrounding it. Pilot Running involves using a new system on only a limited area of the organization. An example could be the selection of a particular department to be involved in a new Personnel Recording system before the system's full implementation for all departments. This is a reasonably safe strategy, but Murphy's Law may dictate that the transactions which cause errors will be amongst those which do not pass through the pilot system.

Maintenance and Review

Maintenance

After its initial introduction, a system will not remain static. Dealing with necessary changes to a system is termed *System Maintenance.* Problems will probably become apparent as the system is operated but even if they do not the information needs of the users will no doubt change. Some changes will come from within the organization as new possibilities for the system are identified. Others may be enforced on the organization because of changes in the external environment. Such changes may be in customer demand, the introduction of new or stronger competition in the market, mergers with other organizations and so on.

The most important catalyst for change is probably the desire for better and more timely information by management to assist their decision-making and planning. At the design stage, the systems analyst should have allowed for the possibility of change. The analyst should have made it possible for changes to be made in the contents of files, output reports and processing routines without having to embark on complete program rewrites. The modification of software as needs change is part of every programmer's job and is called *Software Maintenance*. The hardware selected should be expandable perhaps in terms of memory, backing storage or in numbers and types of peripherals. Generally such expandibility can be assured by not purchasing a system at the top of a range.

Review

The systems analyst should regularly review each system with the relevant managers at least once a year. The system's performance needs to be evaluated in terms of the current user requirements. If differences are found then the cause has to be identified. It may be that the system has to be changed from its original specification, or it may be that the inadequacies are caused by improper implementation. There are a number of signs which can indicate inadequacies in a system, including:

(i) output which is continually behind schedule;

(ii) a regular backlog of input documents awaiting attention;

(iii) a significant increase in errors;

(iv) negative comments from staff operating the system regarding problems or positive suggestions for improvement;

(v) related information systems being kept waiting for data from the offending system;

(vi) customer complaints or loss of business as a result of poor service;

(vii) the necessity for regular, excessive overtime by staff to clear backlogs of work.

Thus a regular review of the operation of the system is necessary if the need for system maintenance is to be identified quickly and remedial action taken.

Computer Services

There are companies who offer a range of hardware and software services; some have spare capacity over and above that which is required for their normal business operations, which they offer on a rental basis, whilst others exist solely for the purpose of computer service provision. The services include the provision of:

- standard, off-the-shelf packaged software;

- tailor-made software;

- consultancy;

- complete hardware and software packages;

- hardware and software rental;

- aid in data preparation and transcription.

Such companies are known variously as computer bureaux, software consultancies, software houses and systems houses. The rental of computer services is expensive but may be appropriate for an organization which only has a temporary need for a computer, or where an increased facility is needed during an unusually busy period. Where access is given to a central mainframe computer operating under a time-sharing operating system, clients are charged for the time which they are *logged on* to the computer. Thus, with the use of a VDU and telephone link, a user can be linked to a powerful mainframe computer and have the impression of sole use. The computer is, in fact, sharing its processor time amongst many users. Such use assumes that the software required by the user is available on the central computer.

Assignment   *Revamping the System*

A Systems Analysis Project

Revamp Limited is an electrical contracting company based in Blackpool in Lancashire. There are two directors, one of whom is responsible for management of jobs on site and estimating for possible contracts, the other being occupied with pricing, cost control and general maintenance of the company's accounts. The company employs a workforce of fifty, although there are periods, usually in winter, when fewer are employed.

All systems are manual at present, but it is in the particular area of cost control where the manual system fails to provide management with information vital to the profitability of the company. In addition, pricing of jobs is a time-consuming process and savings could be made with the use of a microcomputer system. Micro Systems Limited is a computer bureau based in Blackpool and the directors of Revamp Limited have requested the bureau to carry out an investigation of the job and cost control systems, with a view to their computerization.

You are employed by the bureau as a trainee systems analyst and you have been given nominal control of this project. The following information is provided by the directors of Revamp Limited.

General description of the Job Costing and Cost Control System, currently operating at Revamp Limited.

The system provides an estimate of costs, including profit, relating to individually identifiable jobs or contracts. The estimate or price quoted to the main contractor or customer is generally maintained when the job is completed, so it is vital that the original estimate does not fall short of the actual costs incurred.

The job costing does not present any great problems to the firm (except that it is time consuming), but during the progress of a job there is insufficient time to maintain close monitoring of costs. This can result in situations whereby the original cost has been exceeded before the job is complete. Although the original price is usually agreed to be the final price, if the situation mentioned should occur, it may be possible to take some remedial action with the customer or contractor before the job has progressed too far.

Procedures

Pricing or Job Costing

1. Having received a request from a customer or contractor to give a quotation for a job, one of the directors visits the site and estimates the quantities of materials and labour needed to complete the job.

2. The estimated quantities are used to calculate a job cost, by reference to price catalogues.

3. The job is given a unique number and a record of the job is kept in the job file.

Cost Control

4. Once the job is accepted, invoices for materials purchased are charged to the relevant job. A supply is 'tied' to a job by recording the job number on the invoice.

5. In addition to charging materials to a job, labour (including overheads) is also charged, labour being treated as just another supplier.

6. When the job is complete, an invoice for the quoted price is sent to the customer and provided that the amount is greater than the actual cost, a profit is made.

Task

1. Identify any other information you may need to make a proper analysis of the system.

2. Having identified the kinds of information you need, build a more detailed picture of the system, by suggesting the kinds of values you may expect to find. For example, you may feel that the maximum number of jobs likely to be in progress at any one time is about thirty five.

3. Produce a Feasibility Report concerning the job costing and control systems and include the following sections:

(a) An outline description of the application. Identify the overall business and individual system objectives which are to be satisfied;

(b) A more detailed description of the system's existing operation, its good and bad points and the means by which a new system could improve upon it;

(c) A description of how a new system would operate and its expected costs and benefits;

(d) Possible alternatives and recommendations;

(e) Costs of development and timescale for development and implementation (if the recommended system is adopted).

The study should concentrate on the application and the scenario outlined in the assignment.

4. Produce a System Specification, including the following sections:

(a) Nature of the System;

(b) Output Specification;

(c) File Design;

(d) Input Specification;

(e) Processing Tasks.

5. Identify the information gathering methods available to you and suggest, with reasons, which are most appropriate to this situation.

Chapter 8

System Controls

The Need for Control

Computerized information systems present particular problems for the control of data entering the system, because for much of the time this data is not in human-readable form. Even when it is stored, the information remains in this state unless it is printed out or displayed on a VDU screen. If proper system controls are not used, inaccurate data may reach the master files or unauthorized changes to data may be made, resulting in decision-making which may be based on incorrect information.

System controls can be divided into two main types, according to the purposes they serve:

    (a)   Data Accuracy;

    (b)   Data Security.

Data Accuracy

It is extremely important to ensure that all relevant data is processed and that accuracy is maintained. Broadly there are two methods used to achieve these aims – *verification* and *validation*.

Data Control in a Batch Processing System

The controls which are used will depend on the type of processing method in operation, but batch processing provides the greatest opportunity for exerting control over the data, from the input stage through to the output stage.

The stages involved in a batch processing system cycle can be illustrated by the example of a systems flowchart for a payroll run shown on the following page. The following controls can be used at certain stages within the cycle:

Clerical Controls

These can be used at any stage in the cycle when the data is in a human readable form. The types of check include:

    (i) visual checking of source documents to detect missing, illegible or unlikely data values. An example of an unlikely data value could be a total of 100 in the weekly overtime hours entry for an individual worker;

    (ii) the verification of entries by checking them against another source. An example of such referencing could be checking in the price catalogue for the price of a stock item on an invoice;

    (iii) the re-working of calculations on a source document, for example, the checking of additions which make up the total quantity of an item on an order form.

Systems Flowchart - Batch Processing of Payroll

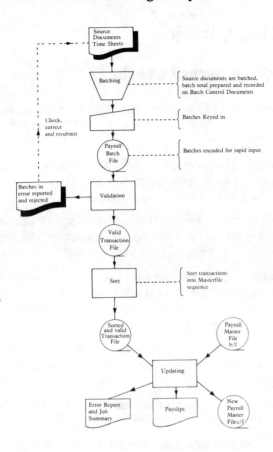

Verification

Before processing, data has to be transcribed from the source documents onto a computer input medium. This usually involves a keying operation to encode the data onto magnetic tape or magnetic disk. This stage can be prone to error, particularly if large volumes of data are involved. Verification is a process, which is usually machine-assisted, to ensure that the data is encoded accurately. Magnetic tape encoders (*key-to-tape* systems) for example, can operate in two modes, record and verify. The operation involves one person keying the data in the record mode, after which a second person re-keys the data with the machine in verify mode. In effect the machine 'reads' the data from the first keying operation and then checks it against the second keying as it occurs. The machine signals if characters do not agree, thus indicating a possible transcription error. Key-to-disk systems operate on a similar principle.

Validation

This process is carried out after the data has been encoded onto the input medium and involves a program called the *data vet* or *validation program*. Its purpose is to check that the data falls within certain parameters defined by the systems analyst. A judgement as to whether or not data is valid is made possible by the validation program. It cannot ensure absolute accuracy. That can only be achieved by the use of all the clerical and computer controls built into the system at the design stage. The difference between validity and accuracy can be illustrated by the following example.

A company has established a Personnel file. Each record in the file may contain a data item, the Job Grade. The permitted values of job grade are A, B, C or D. An entry in an individual's record may be valid and accepted by the system if it is recorded as A,B,C or D, but of course this may not be the correct grade for the individual worker concerned. Whether the grade is correct can only be determined by accuracy checks such as those discussed earlier.

Types of Validation Check

Character, Data Item and Record Checks

Size.   The number of characters in a data item value is checked. For example, an account number may require 6 characters and if there are more or less than this, then the item is rejected.

Mode.   It may be that particular data item values must contain particular types of character, for example alphabetic or numeric. If the system is programmed to accept only numbers then letters would be rejected.

Format.   This refers to the way characters within a value are organized. For example, an Item Code may consist of 2 alphabetic characters followed by 6 numeric characters. The system would reject any entry which did not correspond to this format.

Reasonableness.   Quantities can be checked for unusually high or low values. For example, a gas consumer with one small appliance may have a meter reading which would only be appropriate to a consumer with a large central heating system. If such a value was entered, the system would not accept it.

Presence.   If a data item must always have a value then it can be checked for existence. For example, the data item type 'Sex' in a Personnel record would always have to have an M or F entry.

Range.   Values are checked for certain upper and lower limits, for example, account numbers may have to be between 00001 and 10000.

Check Digits.   An extra digit calculated on an account number can be used as a self checking device. When the number is input to the computer the validation program carries out a calculation similar to that used to generate the check digit originally and thus checks its validity. This kind of check will highlight transposition errors caused by, for instance, keying in the digits in the wrong order.

All the above checks can be carried out prior to the master file updating stage. Further checks on data can be made through the use of a validation program at the update stage, by comparison with the master file. They are as follow:

New records.   When a new record is to be added to the master file, a check can be made to ensure that a record does not already use the entered record key .

Deleted records.   It may be that a transaction is entered for which there is no longer a matching master record.

Consistency.   A check is made that the transaction values are consistent with the values held on the master record which is to be updated. For instance a deduction for pension contributions by an employee who is not old enough to be in a pension scheme would obviously be inconsistent.

Validation using Batch Controls

These checks are only possible in a batch processing system.

Batch Totals

The purpose of batch totals is to allow a conciliation of manually produced totals for a batch with comparable computer produced totals. Differences are signalled and the batch is rejected for checking and re-submission.

Preparation of Batch Totals. Following the arrangement of source documents into batches of say 30 in each batch, totals are calculated on add-listing machines for each value it is required to control. On an order form, for example, quantities and prices may be separately totalled to provide two control totals. Totals may also be produced for each account number or item code simply for purposes of control although they are otherwise meaningless. For this reason such totals are called *hash* or *nonsense* totals. The totals are recorded on a batch control slip attached to the batch, together with a value for the number of documents in the batch and a batch number. The batch number is kept in a register held by the originating department so that missing or delayed batches can be traced.

A typical Batch Control Slip may be as follows:

Dept Ref: Sales	Date 30/01/86
Data Type: Orders	Batch No. 23
Number in Batch: 40	
Quantity Total: 30450	
Price Total: 13223.66	Prepared by: JE Checked by: PMC
Item-code Total: 576126	Entered by: DR

It should be noted that hash totals may produce a figure which has a large number of digits, so extra digits over and above the original length of the data item are truncated.

Reconciliation of Batch Totals. The details from each batch control slip are entered with each batch of transactions at the encoding stage. The serial transaction file which results will be arranged thus:

| BT1 | TR | TR | TR | TR | TR | BT2 | TR | TR | TR | TR | TR | BT3 | TR | TR | TR | TR . . . |

BT = Batch Total   TR = Transaction record

The serial transaction file is processed from beginning to end by the validation program. The sum of the transaction records relating to each batch should match the batch total. If any validation error is detected, either by differences in batch totals or through the character or data item checks described earlier, the offending batch is rejected to be checked and re-submitted. The rejected batches are reported on a computer printout.

Validation During Updating

Checks can be made in the manner described earlier on transactions for deleted or new records, or data which is inconsistent with the relevant record on the master file.

The above controls can be used in conjunction with proper clerical procedures to ensure that as far as possible, the information stored on the master files is accurate.

File Controls

In addition to controlling the accuracy of data entering the system it is essential to check both that the data is complete and that all relevant data is processed. This can be done through the use of file controls on the transaction file.

Following the validation of the batches of transactions, correct batches are written to another file to be sorted and used for updating the relevant master file. During validation, the validation program accumulates totals for all the correct batches. These can be used during the update run to ensure that the whole transaction file is processed.

Validation in On-Line Systems

On-line systems as described in Chapter 6 tend to be interactive and transactions are processed immediately with the master files at the data entry stage. The main controls which can be introduced to such systems include:

(i) the character, data item and record validation checks described earlier. Error messages are displayed on the screen at the time data is entered and require immediate correction at that time;

(ii) visual verification. At the end of each transaction entry, the operator is given the opportunity to scan the data on the screen and to re-enter any incorrect entries detected. This usually takes the form of a message at the bottom of the screen which is phrased in a way such as "Verify (yes or no)";

(iii) the use of well-trained data entry operators. They should have sufficient knowledge of the data being entered and the application it serves, to respond to error messages and make corrections to data accordingly.

Of course in a batch processing system, data entry is simply a keyboard skill, requiring little knowledge of the data and little use of initiative and this contrasts with the need for well trained data operators mentioned in (iii) above.

Data Security

The controls used have several main functions:

(i) to prevent loss of data files caused by software or procedural errors, or by physical hazards;

(ii) to protect data from accidental or deliberate disclosure to unauthorized individuals or groups;

(iii) to protect the data from accidental or deliberate corruption or modification. This is known as maintaining *data integrity*;

(iv) to protect the rights of individuals and organizations to restrict access to information which relates to them and is of a private nature, to those entitled or authorized to receive it. This is known as *data privacy*.

Security Against Data Loss

The loss of master files can be an extremely serious occurrence for any organization so properly organized security procedures need to be employed. Among commercial organizations that have lost the major part of their information store, a large percentage subsequently go out of business.

Master Files

The main causes of data loss are as follow:

Environmental hazards   - such as fire, flood and other natural accidents;

Mechanical problems   - for example the danger of disk or tape damage caused by a drive unit malfunction;

Software errors   - resulting from programming error;

Human error.   A wrong file may be loaded, the wrong program version used, a tape or disk mislaid, or physical damage caused to tape or disk;

Malicious damage.   It is not unknown for staff to intentionally damage storage media or misuse a program at a terminal.

The standard solution to such problems is to take regular copies of master files and to store the copies in a separate secure location. It is also necessary to maintain a record of transactions affecting a file since the last copy was taken, so that if necessary they can be used to reconstruct the latest version of the file. The method used to achieve this is referred to as the Grandfather, Father and Son (Generation) System.

Magnetic Tape Files

When a tape master file is updated by a tape transaction file the physical nature of the medium makes it necessary for a new tape file to be produced (This is discussed in Chapter 18). As the following systems flowchart illustrates, the updating procedure provides a built-in security system.

Tape File Security - Generation System

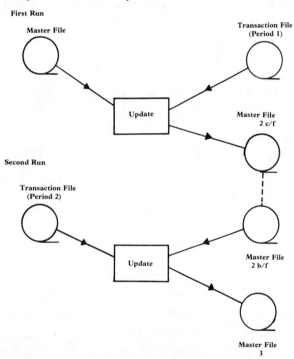

In the First Run, Master File 1 is updated by the transactions file to produce Master File 2 as its *son*. Master File 1 is the *father*. Should the *son* file be damaged and the data lost, it can be recreated from the *father* master file and the relevant transactions.

At the end of the Second Run, Master File 1 becomes the *grandfather*, Master File 2 becomes the *father* and Master File 3, the son.

Each *generation* provides security for subsequent files. The number of generations used will depend on the policy of the organization. Three generations is usually regarded as providing sufficient security and the oldest files are re-used by being overwritten as each cycle of generations is completed.

Magnetic Disk Files

Security Backups.   Disk files can be treated in the same way as tape files in that the updating procedure may produce a new master file leaving the original file intact. On the other hand, if the file is updated *in situ* (which in so doing overwrites the existing data), then it will be necessary to take regular backup copies as processing proceeds. The frequency with which copies are taken will depend on the volume of transactions affecting the master file. If the latest version of the master file is corrupted or lost, then it can be recreated using the previous backup and the transaction data received since the backup.

Transaction Logging.   In an on-line system, transactions may enter the system from a number of terminals in different locations, thus making it difficult to re-enter transactions to re-create a damaged master file. One solution is to *log* all the transactions onto a serial transaction file at the same time as the master file is updated. Thus the re-creation process can be carried out without the need for keying in the transactions again.

The following systems flowchart illustrates this procedure.

System Flowchart - Master File Backup and Transaction Log

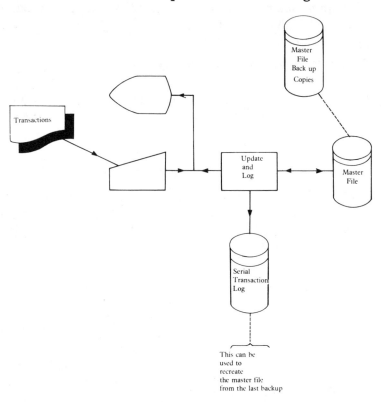

Data Security to Prevent Unauthorized Access

Unauthorized access to a system may:

- provide vital information to competitors;

- result in the deliberate corruption of the data. There is a documented case in the USA of young 'hackers' filling a database with graffiti resulting in a cost of thousands of dollars to reconstruct the data base;

- allow fraudulent changes to be made to data by employees or others;

- result in loss of privacy for individuals or organizations if the information is confidential.

To avoid such hazards an information system should be protected:

- physically;

- by administrative procedures;

- by software;

To detect any unauthorized access or changes to the information system:

- Users should require authorization (with different levels of authority depending on purpose of access);

- User actions should be logged and monitored;

- Users should be identifiable;

- The files should be capable of being audited;

- The actions of programmers should be carefully controlled to prevent fraud through changes to software.

Methods of Protection

Physical Methods.   It is necessary to protect the hardware in the main computer installation and terminals at remote sites.

Methods include, locks on doors, security staff and alarm systems (infra-red systems to detect body heat and movement are commonly used). Computer systems with terminals at remote sites present a weak link in any system and they must be properly protected. Software plays an important role in this. Disk and tape libraries also need to be protected, otherwise it would be possible for a thief to take file media to another centre with compatible hardware and software.

A variety of methods may be used to identify a system user. They include:

Identity Cards. Provided they are not copyable and have a photograph they can be effective and cheap. The addition of a magnetic strip which contains encoded personal details including a personal identification number (PIN), which the holder has to key in, allows the user to be checked by machine. This method is used to allow access to service tills outside banks.

Personal Physical Characteristics. Voice recognition or fingerprint comparison provide effective, if expensive, methods of identification.

Such methods are only effective if the supporting administrative procedures are properly adhered to.

Software Methods.   Access to files can be controlled at different levels by a series of passwords, which have to be keyed into the terminal in response to a series of questions displayed on the screen. An example of the use of different levels of security can be found in a Personnel Department. A typist may be able to use a program to retrieve information regarding an employee's career record but only the personnel manager is authorized to use a program to change the information held in the record.

'Hackers' are people who specialize (for fun or fraud) in breaking through the software protection to gain access to an information system's files. The passwords used therefore, should be carefully chosen, kept secure (memorized and not divulged) and changed frequently.

Using people's names for example, may allow entry by guessing or by trial and error.

Even if the terminals linked to a system are protected, an experienced hacker equipped with telephone, microcomputer and modem (a device to allow transmission of computer data over telephone lines) may gain access to a computer system's files while the system is in operation. The password controls may prevent access but if the data signals being transmitted along the telephone lines or via satellite are not properly protected, hackers can pick up the signals and display them on their own machines. To prevent such intrusion, *data encryption* methods are used to protect important and confidential information during transmission from one centre to another. As the power and speed of computers has increased, so the breaking of codes has been made easier.

Code designers have produced methods of encryption which are currently unbreakable in any reasonable time period, even by the largest and most powerful computers available. An example of such an elaborate coding system is illustrated by the operation of the Electronic Funds Transfer (EFT) system. This is used by banks and other financial institutions to transfer vast sums of money so these transmissions are protected by the latest data encryption techniques.

Security to Maintain Data Integrity

Data integrity refers to the accuracy and consistency of the information stored and is thus covered by the security methods outlined above.

Security to Maintain Privacy of Data

The rights of individuals and organizations concerning their confidential records are similarly protected by the methods outlined earlier. In addition, legislation by parliament (the Data Protection Act 1984) attempts to exert some control by requiring any persons or organizations holding personal information on computer files to register with the Data Protection Registrar. Some countries have 'Freedom of Information Acts' which allow the individual to see any personal information stored in their own files, except where national security is thought to be threatened. It is generally accepted that the Data Protection Act falls far short of complete freedom of information.

Assignment   *Entering the Exams*

Barneswell College of Further Education has a student population of approximately 1500 part-time students and 500 full-time students and offers a wide range of courses for single subject examinations offered by the GCSE Boards and other bodies, such as the City and Guilds Institute and the Royal Society of Arts. In addition, there are many vocational courses relating mainly to 'white collar' work in commerce, local and national government and industry. Although the college has an academic Computing section, staff from the section are not expected to be involved in any computerized administration systems.

The college is currently developing computerized systems to cover a variety of applications including, amongst others, examination entries, student records, and resource management, as part of an Educational Management Information System.

The college office already possesses two stand-alone, hard disk, PS/2 microcomputer systems, which the examinations officer, Dave Gubbins, has already used for the recording of examination entries for City and Guilds students. These will be linked into a college-wide, multi-user system, to be installed in the college in the near future.

The examination officer's experiences with computer systems so far, have not been entirely happy. Following the keying of exam entry details, 350 in all, the relevant disk file was corrupted and all data relating to the exam entries was lost. At this stage, no hard copy had been produced and the only solution was to re-enter all the examination details. Dave Gubbins was extremely upset because the keying exercise had to be carried out the evening before the submission date to the City and Guilds Institute. He is keen to ensure that such occurrences are not repeated in any new system.

Task

You are employed by the college to advise management on the administrative applications required of the new computerized system and your current concern is to produce a report on data security for the Project Development Group.

Produce a formal report, giving your reasoned recommendations for the following:

1. the prevention of loss of data from computer files;

2. the maintenance of security against unauthorized access to computer files.

Your recommendations should identify procedural and computer controls which may be of service.

Developmental Task

Examine the college's responsibilities under the 1984 Data Protection Act.

Chapter 9

Organizational Consequences of Computerization

The introduction of a computer to an organization cannot be effective if computerization simply means the transfer of manual files to computer storage and the automation of some of the existing clerical procedures. To achieve the full potential of computerization, an organization needs to implement certain changes which will affect its environment, its staff and its form of management.

Changes in the Organization's Environment

Computer hardware has to be kept in a suitable environment if it is to operate correctly. Although physical protection of hardware has improved considerably over recent years, large mainframe and mini computer systems need to be maintained in a relatively dust-free atmosphere within controlled moderate temperature ranges. Microcomputers tend to be more tolerant of their surroundings and can be accommodated in the relatively basic surroundings one would expect to find in any small office.

If computers have to operate in tough physical environments, for example, on warships or in battle tanks then the hardware can be designed accordingly. Fortunately, most organizations have less harsh surrounding in which to work. Nevertheless, there are generally some changes which need to be made in the *physical requirements* of the environment.

The Physical Requirements Necessary to Accommodate Computers

Controlled Moderate Temperature Range

Most office environments will be suitable in this respect but the precise requirements will depend on the hardware to be used and the manufacturer's specification. More often than not, problems are caused by the overheating of equipment. Thus hardware should not be sited next to a radiator or in direct sunlight.

Clean Surroundings

As previously indicated, the cleanliness required of the environment will depend on the type of hardware in use. In general however, dust will cause problems, particularly with storage media such as tapes and disks. For the larger organization this may mean the installation of air conditioning within a separate room for the mainframe or mini computer system.

Electrical Installation

Although computers operate from the standard electricity supply, it is essential that a separate power supply is installed to prevent problems of cut-out and possible loss of information if the circuits are overloaded. In some cases where reliability is vital, a backup power supply may be needed to cut in if the main supply fails. Magnetic storage media such as disk or tape should not be stored next to power supplies as the surrounding magnetic field may corrupt the data.

Lighting

Where natural light is at times inadequate then suitable artificial lighting will be necessary. In most office situations where manual clerical operations are already carried out, then normal electric lighting is probably sufficient. Lighting also has to be considered in terms of its possible effect on the reflective surfaces which may surround computer equipment. For this reason the casings on hardware are usually of a matt finish. Some computer screens may not have non-reflective qualities so the positioning of equipment in relation to both natural and artificial lighting will have to be taken into account to avoid reflective glare. Although most computer monitors have brightness and contrast control, direct sunlight can make the characters on a screen practically invisible. Artificial lighting which is too intense or badly positioned can also cause screen glare.

Noise Control

Sources of noise from computer equipment are in the main:

> (i) Impact printers;
>
> (ii) Cooling fans built into the computer itself.

Printer noise varies with the type of printer. Impact printers, such as the daisy wheel or dot matrix type, obviously make more noise than laser printers which do not use an impact mechanism. Noise can be controlled through the use of insulating containers. Where printers are part of a mini or mainframe system, noise will need to be controlled for the benefit of the computer operations staff but it is likely that a separate room will contain all the main computer resources so other parts of the organization will be unaffected. In smaller organizations the use of microcomputers and dot matrix printers can lead to a noisy environment but insulating containers, sound absorbent screens and carpeted floors can help.

Cooling fans within computer equipment tend to cause a background noise to which people soon become used. It is not as loud as printer noise but it can be at a level which may result in unnecessary stress for office staff. Again sound absorbent screens around the computer can help protect staff from such noise but properly serviced equipment helps avoid worn and noisy fans.

Effects on Staff

The effects on staff within an organization will be extremely varied and the degree of

effect will depend on the extent of involvement individual staff have with a computerized system.

Computerization within an organization tends not to be an instantaneous event
affecting all functional areas at the same time. It tends to be progressive, sometimes
planned and sometimes piecemeal.

Consider the following situation in a commercial trading organisation:

(i) Assume that Sales Order Processing (SOP) is computerized and that the
output includes Picking Lists (these are lists of products and quantities
of each that need to be retrieved from the warehouse to satisfy customer
orders).

(ii) Assume further that Stock Control in the warehouse is not computerized
but that the staff will receive computer printed picking lists.

(iii) Assume finally that the Accounting function is not computerized. Staff
in Accounting will receive sales details on computer printout from SOP
from which they will produce invoices to send to customers.

Effects on Clerical Staff

The staff in these three departments, SOP, Stock Control and Accounting are all
affected by computerization but to varying degrees.

Least effected are staff in Stock Control and Accounting who only receive computer
output. They have to become familiar with the reading and interpretation of computer
printouts. This is not a difficult task, but one which requires some adjustment on the
part of staff.

At a more complex level, the staff in SOP are more significantly effected. The effects
will require education and training for staff in the various parts of the computerized
process as follow:

Preparation of Input Data

Computerization imposes a discipline on clerical and management procedures. To deal
with data correctly it needs to be presented accurately and in a form suitable for input
to the computer. Usually, prior to data entry, all source data, (in this case customer
orders) have to be recorded on standard, specially designed Source Documents which
match the order of data requested by the computer software. For example, if the first
item of data required by the computer is an order number, then this should be the first
data item on the source document. The second data item required should be next and
so on.

Therefore, however the orders are received, by telephone, by word of mouth at the
sales desk or by post, the first job is to transcribe the details onto the Source Document.
Such tasks need to be documented in office procedure manuals and staff need to be
instructed in their proper execution.

Data Entry

Staff involved in this task will need to develop keyboard skills. Even if the data entry
operators are already skilled typists, some training or period of familiarization is
required to use a computer terminal correctly.

Training will be needed in the day-to-day operation of the software. These include
'signing on' with codes and passwords, familiarity with computer screen prompts and
the correct responses to make, dealing with simple error conditions when an incorrect
key is pressed and correcting or editing keying errors during data entry.

Where the volume of data entry is such that a member of staff can be fully occupied
with this task there are health and safety considerations to be examined. There are for
example recommended guidelines concerning time limits for personnel operating

VDU's. Headaches and eye strain can result from prolonged viewing of a computer screen.

Where the volume of data entry is limited, the specialist staff may not be justified and a number of clerical staff with a variety of duties may have to 'take their turn' at the keyboard. Thus more staff will need some basic training in the use of the system.

Effects on Managerial Staff

The day-to-day clerical routines will not usually directly involve managerial staff although this will depend on the size of the organization and the hierarchical staffing structure. However, their necessary involvement in the development, introduction and implementation of a computerized system and their responsibilities for the efficient running of their departments mean that the effects of computerization on the working lives of managers can be even more emphatic than the effects on clerical staff.

To continue the Sales Order Processing example, the manager of that department may:

  (i) be closely involved in a consultative role with systems analysts in the analysis of the old manual system and the design of the new computerized system;

  (ii) have to maintain communication with the staff in the SOP department to ensure that:

    – their views are taken into account;

    – envisaged changes are reported to them.

    This communication is vital if the staff are to feel 'involved'.

  (iii) require some computer education and training. A prerequisite of communication between staff is that the manager has developed some computer 'awareness' and computer 'literacy' sufficiently to understand the role of the computer and the changes in procedures within his department which are necessary.

This educational or training need has to be satisfied if the manager is to be effective in the role of ensuring that the operational procedures are being followed and that efficiency is being maintained. Without knowledge of the powers and limitations of a computerized system a manager cannot assess its effectiveness or suggest improvements.

At the managerial level of involvement, it may seem that the more mundane skills of operating a VDU are not needed. Often this is not so. A manager may wish to access files from a terminal in the office, so a minimal level of skill is required.

Other Computer Applications Involving Management

There are a number of computer applications which make use of 'content free' software. This refers to software which is not fixed to one application or type of data. Such software packages are available for Spreadsheet work, and Database or File Management.

There is an increasing awareness that microcomputers or terminals linked to a central computer can be used by managers and executive staff (although not exclusively) to aid their decision-making, with the provision of more and higher quality information.

An example may illustrate this point. Spreadsheet packages can be used for the preparation of cash budgets and sales forecasting with the added facility of generating 'what if' projections. So a cash budget based on current and anticipated figures of cash due in and out of the organization over the next few months, can be quickly modified to present the results of an alternative strategy of say, an injection of cash from a bank loan.

Database packages can be used by managers for their own local information store on which they can make enquiry. In addition, where a database is held centrally, a manager could access files through the use of a Query Language (This is discussed in Chapter 6). To use such a language requires training, similar to that required by a programmer albeit at a simpler level.

The efficient and effective use of such packages demands a high level of knowledge and skill which will probably require some sort of training programme, perhaps with the software supplier.

Effects on Managers not yet involved

The use of such facilities by one departmental manager or the issue of a general directive from top management within an organization will place pressure on other managers to follow suit. Of course the pressure may be in the other direction where departmental managers wish to get involved and pressurize top management for training and the introduction of new computerized systems

Changes in Job Descriptions

It can be seen from the previous section that where computerized systems are used within an organization and new staff are to be recruited, the job descriptions in advertisements should include a request for computer knowledge or skill, in the area which the job demands. Existing staff will have to have their job descriptions modified. In some circumstances this can mean an upgrading of the skill or professional level which may attract a higher salary. It can lead to delay in the introduction of computer systems. In local government, for example, some secretarial staff were prevented from using word processors because their union demanded an increase in their job grading. In some jobs it can lead to what is considered to be de-skilling. For example, in the newspaper industry the traditional skill of metal typesetting is now obsolete.

Effects on Functional Relationships

Earlier in this chapter, it is explained that computerization effects the ways in which different functions such as Sales and Accounts relate to each other, in terms of how information flows between them and the activities in which each is engaged.

Without computers, the Sales and Accounting departments would maintain their own files. Transaction data such as a customer order would be used to update each of the department's files separately. Each department would be responsible for maintaining its own files thus creating separate autonomous areas within an organization, each led by a Head of Department or similar executive staff member. Each department would tend to have its own working practices and provided information was presented to other departments in a form they could use, there would perhaps be little need for change.

Computerization imposes discipline and standardization. Information flows between departments may have to pass through a computer process and although the user requirements should take priority over what is convenient for the computer, some modifications will need to be made to the ways in which data is presented to the computer for processing. Earlier in this chapter, the example was used of customer order details being transcribed onto Source Documents designed to be compatible with the order of input to the computer.

A feature of manual systems is the separateness of related operations. For example a customer order will be used to update the customer file, the stock file and to produce a customer invoice in separate operations carried out in each separate functional area. A computerized system could allow these tasks to be carried out with a single input of the data.

Inter-departmental Conflict

Organizations are formed to allow a rational and coordinated approach to the achievement of certain aims which may be the provision of a service or product for which there is a profitable market. The problem is that organizations are made up of individuals who may not always be rational. Each individual has his or her own ambitions, fears and emotions. Management styles may well stem from such personal characteristics. This may lead to competition between department heads rather than cooperation in achieving the common aims of the organization as a whole.

Personal Fears

To many people, computerization is a venture into the unknown and many individuals feel threatened because they have insufficient knowledge or experience to give them adequate control over their own futures. Being made to look a fool, or worse, the possibility of being made redundant by computerization can be the main obstacle to the acceptance of change.

Resistance to Change

Sometimes because of inter-departmental rivalry or simply incompetence, a manager may keep secret certain facts which computerization may make available. This is another reason for resistance to the introduction of computerized systems.

Managers are forced to change their style of management because of the introduction of computers and may attempt to resist the threat to their power, by doing less than they might to make the innovation work and by constantly finding fault, without making constructive suggestions.

'The Enthusiast'

An alternative reaction, which is usually irrational, is the whole-hearted, eager acceptance of computerization as being the ideal solution to every problem. There are many circumstances where computerization is inappropriate or where the immediately available standard package is far from ideal.

Because organizations are made up of individuals, computer systems should be designed with the full cooperation of management and staff, enlisting their help wherever possible so as to take proper account of their individual or at least departmental information needs.

Effects on Management Style

Many managers work intuitively and have confidence in their own methods which have served them well. Such 'flying by the seat of the pants' often leads to a natural derision for any system designed by 'experts' and 'theorists'. Of course such confidence is usually based on previous success and the specialist in computer systems will often be young and, as far as the experienced manager is concerned, 'wet behind the ears'. Thus the computer specialist may have a difficult job in convincing existing management that a new computerized system will be an improvement on the old. The systems analyst will need to have the interpersonal skills to deal with such resistance.

One feature of computerized systems is the increase in the volume of information available to a manager and the speed with which it can be obtained. A resulting danger is that the manager may become too concerned with the low level decisions within his department, thus interfering with the responsibilities of lower levels of management or supervisory staff. The problem can be more serious if it extends upwards from departmental to corporate management. Information which should have been seen by the department manager may have been seen by the chief general manager first. Too much information and the wrong type of information can be worse than insufficient information.

Effects of Decentralization of Computing Power

Centralized and distributed systems are discussed in Chapter 6. Broadly, the development of systems using the combined technologies of computing and telecommunications have decentralized computer usage. A wide variety of systems is available to support decentralization, including Wide Area and Local Area Networks and stand-alone microcomputer systems. The main benefits for an organization may be as follow:

(i)   The delegation of control of some information processing to branch level management, hopefully resulting in systems which respond to local requirements. The control of information processing systems is thereby the responsibility of those who use them;

(ii)   More rapid, up-to-date information at the local level, because it is processed locally;

(iii)   The rapid distribution of centrally produced information via network systems;

(iv)   Provided that the local systems are linked to a central facility, then information which is locally produced can be transmitted and stored so as to be available at a corporate level. Overall control is not lost, but enhanced.

The above benefits are not automatic and may have certain implications for an organization. The main implications are:

(i)   New hardware and software needs to be purchased, which is compatible with any existing centralized facility;

(ii)   Local management and workers need to be trained in the operation of any new system introduced, if the maximum benefit is to be obtained. The use of microcomputers with, for example, database and spreadsheet packages requires extensive training of users. This can be expensive;

(iii)   A complete re-appraisal of specialist staffing may be needed as a result of decentralization. For example, systems analysts already familiar with the design and implementation of distributed systems may need to be recruited;

(iv)   Specialist personnel, including programmers and operators, may be needed at the local level;

(v)   Decentralized systems present new problems in terms of controlling the security of information (Chapter 8). The added risks must be considered and covered.

Assignment   *The Legal Network*

Barnes, Nesbit and Walker is a firm of solicitors based in Durham City, County Durham. Mr. Barnes is a senior partner and rather old-fashioned in his ideas on running the practice. He would rather dictate letters to his secretary than use a dictaphone. The two junior partners, Alun Nesbit and Rachel Walker, are keen to improve the efficiency of the practice. It is the intention to install a Local Area Network (LAN), using microcomputer systems as workstations and to computerize many of the office procedures. For example, legal documents will be prepared using a word processing package and high quality output obtained with a laser printer. The practice employs three personal secretaries, four copy typists and five general clerical staff. The management of clients' accounts will be made easier, in that each partner will have a workstation in their office to enter client charges as and when they occur.

Task

You are employed as a trainee office manager/ess by the practice. Mrs. Walker calls you into her office and asks you to prepare an informal report covering the following matters:

1. How the introduction of computers may affect the office and clerical staff;

2. The problems which may be encountered in trying to persuade Mr. Barnes to use the new system and suggestions as to how they may be overcome;

3. Training implications and possible strategies;

4. Physical preparations which need to be made for the installation of the computer network.

Developmental Task

Contact your local government offices and ask for a copy of their health and safety guidelines for VDU operators. Use the guidelines to draw up a staff notice for those using VDUs in the firm of Barnes, Nesbit and Walker.

Chapter 10

Software

Introduction

Software is the generic term which is used to describe the complete range of computer *programs* which will convert a general-purpose digital computer system into one capable of performing a multitude of specific functions. The term *software* implies its flexible, changeable nature, in contrast to the more permanent characteristics of the hardware or equipment which it controls.

The particular type, or types, of software controlling the computer system at any particular moment will determine the manner in which the system functions. For example, a certain type of software might cause the computer to behave like a wordprocessor; another might turn it into an accounting machine; another may allow it to perform a stock control function. In other words the behaviour of the computer is entirely determined by the item of software currently controlling it.

Computer programs

The terms *software* and *program* tend to be used synonymously, so what precisely is meant by the term 'computer program'?

At the level at which the computer operates, a program is simply a sequence of numeric codes. Each of these codes can be directly converted by the hardware into some simple operation. Built into the central processing unit (CPU - the heart of the computer) is a set of these 'simple operations', combinations of which are capable of directing the computer to perform complex tasks. Computer programs, in this fundamental form, are termed *machine code*, that is code which is directly 'understandable' by the machine.

The numeric codes of the program are in binary form, or at least the electrical equivalent of this numbering system, and are stored in the immediate access store (the *memory*) of the computer. Because this memory is volatile (its contents can be changed), it is possible to exchange the program currently held in the memory for another when the computer is required to perform a different function. For this reason the term *stored program* is often used to describe this fundamental characteristic of the modern digital computer.

Instruction sets

The collection of numeric codes which directs the computer to perform such simple operations as those mentioned above is called the *instruction set*. A typical computer would have some or all of the following types of instructions and, in addition, other more specialised instructions:

(a) **Data transfer.** This allows data to be moved within the CPU, between the CPU and the memory of the computer system or between the CPU and external devices such as printers, VDUs and keyboards;

(b) **Arithmetic operations.** Such instructions direct the computer to perform arithmetic functions such as addition, subtraction, multiplication, division, increment, decrement, comparison and logical operations such as AND, OR and NOT;

(c) **Shift operations.** These move data to the left or right within a *register* or memory location;

(d) **Transfer of control.** This directs the machine to skip one or more instructions or repeat previously encountered instructions.

The Fetch-Execute Cycle

A program, consisting of a combination of the instructions outlined above, is run or *executed* by retrieving or *fetching* each instruction in turn from the memory store of the computer, decoding the operation required and then performing this operation under the direction of the CPU. This sequence of events is termed the *fetch-execute* cycle.

On completion of each current instruction, the next instruction in the program's logical sequence of execution will be fetched from store automatically. This process ends or *terminates*, under normal circumstances, when a halt instruction in the program is recognised by the computer. The term *automatic sequence control* is often used to describe this characteristic of most current digital computers.

An Example of A Machine Code Program

The following example illustrates some of the concepts outlined above. Suppose that a computer has currently in its main store memory a simple machine code program to add two numbers together and store the result in memory. It could be shown as follows:

Address	Memory	Operation
Binary Code representing a location in the memory	Contents of each Location represented in Binary Code	
1000	1010010100010100	Load the number specified in the instruction into an internal register
1001	1110100010101110	Add the number specified here to the contents of the internal register
1002	1000100011101011	Transfer the result to the specified area of memory.
1003	1111111111111111	Halt

Each instruction in turn, starting with that resident in memory location 1000, would be fetched from memory, decoded and executed. This process would continue until the halt instruction in location 1003 was decoded.

The particular binary code or combination of binary digits (0s or 1s) in the instruction, causes the decoding circuitry of the CPU to transmit to other components of the hardware, the sequence of control signals which is necessary to perform the required operation.

Programming Languages

When it is considered that a typical program might contain tens of thousands of machine code instructions it might seem that programming is a formidable task, well beyond the capabilities of all but the most determined and meticulous of computer professionals. Indeed, if machine code were the only computer language in use, it is extremely unlikely that society would today be experiencing such a widespread presence of computers in almost every aspect of industrial, commercial, domestic and social life. Fortunately for the computer industry, programming techniques have evolved along with advances in hardware. There is now a proliferation of programming languages designed to allow the programmer to concentrate most of his attention on solving the problem, rather than on the tedious task of converting the solution to machine code form.

In the history of programming languages, one of the first significant innovations was the development of assembly languages. A program written in an assembly language is much more readable and understandable than its equivalent in machine code; the problem arises, however, that it is no longer directly executable by the computer. For example, a program, in some typical assembly language, equivalent to that given earlier in the chapter for the addition of two numbers, might take the following form:

LD	R,N1	LoaD register, R, with contents of location N1
ADD	R,N2	ADD contents of location N2 to contents of R
ST	R,N3	STore the result in location N3
HLT		HaLT

Notice that the operation codes LD, ADD, ST and HLT (representing LOAD, ADD, STORE and HALT respectively) are now easily recognisable and easy to remember; such *mnemonics*, or 'memory aids', are chosen for these reasons. The references, N1,N2 and N3, relate to memory locations and are called *symbolic addresses* and in many assembly languages it is possible to use meaningful names such as HRS or RATE to indicate the type of data stored there. The internal register, R, may be one of several available within the computer for use by the programmer.

The CPU is unable to decode instructions in this form; they must first be converted into the equivalent machine code. An *assembler* is a machine code program which performs this function. It accepts an assembly language program as data, converts mnemonic operation codes to their numeric equivalents, assigns symbolic addresses to memory locations and produces as output the required machine code program. (This is represented in the diagram below).

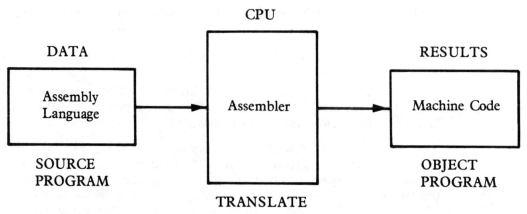

The assembly language program is termed the *source program* and the final machine code program is the *object program*.

Having an assembler means, of course, that it can be used to produce an improved version of itself! (This is illustrated in the following figure).

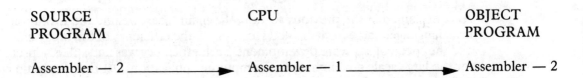

SOURCE PROGRAM	CPU	OBJECT PROGRAM
Assembler — 2 ⟶	Assembler — 1 ⟶	Assembler — 2

Thus there is no need to write any machine code programs at all and a considerable burden has been removed from the programming task; the computer itself now does much of the work required to produce the object program.

Though assembly languages aid the programmer considerably, they are still closely related to machine code; there is a 1:1 correspondence between a machine code instruction and one in assembly language. In other words each machine code instruction must have a matching assembly language instruction. This fundamental correspondence has led to the term *low-level* being applied to this type of programming language as they are not sufficiently sophisticated to allow one assembly language instruction to represent several instructions in machine code.

Computer scientists recognised, however, that most programs could be broken down into a collection of smaller identifiable tasks and that no matter what the program, such tasks were always present in some recognisable form, though probably occurring in different logical sequences.

For instance, the majority of programs require the evaluation of arithmetic expressions such as

$$X + Y \times Z - P / Q$$

in other words expressions involving combinations of the four arithmetic operators

$$+, -, \times \text{ and } /.$$

Most programs will produce some form of visible output, whether printed on paper or displayed on a screen; most programs require data to be input for processing.

All of these tasks require lengthy, complicated sequences of instructions, but significantly, they can all be stated in a generalised form, and can therefore be implemented using generalised machine code programs. *High-level* languages make extensive use of this characteristic. A high-level language is almost entirely constructed of these generalised sets of instructions or *statements*. A single statement, for instance, in a high-level language can specify the evaluation of a complex arithmetic expression requiring many machine code instructions. The translator required for such a source language is therefore much more complex than an assembler, since each source language statement will generally generate many machine code instructions.

Taking the simple addition program introduced earlier to its conclusion, the program in a high-level language might merely reduce to the single statement

$$N3 = N1 + N2$$

meaning that the symbolic address N3 is to store the sum of the contents of the memory's locations represented by the symbolic addresses N1 and N2. Notice that the programmer no longer needs to concern himself over the precise mechanics of the addition: the translator takes care of that automatically.

High-level languages are often termed *procedure orientated* or *programmer orientated* languages, because they are designed for the benefit of the programmer interested in a certain type of application or procedure. For instance, some languages are particularly suitable for business applications, others for scientific programming and others for educational use.

The Evolution of High Level Languages

As is explained in the previous section, the main thrust behind the evolution of high level languages came from the need to improve the efficiency of the programming task and the speed of software development. Such efficiency was and still is, a prerequisite for the large scale development of computing applications. At first, the main applications were scientific and mathematical and largely sponsored by the military for their own purposes, but massive developments in the fields of business and commerce soon followed. The languages designed for science and business, notably and respectively FORTRAN and COBOL, are not suitable for the development of other potential applications using, for example, artificial intelligence and knowledge-based systems (Chapter 11 Categories of Software - Expert Systems). For these and other less popular applications, new languages had to be developed. High level languages are often classified as being general-purpose or special-purpose. As the following case studies show, most languages are specialized in some degree and any single language can only be slotted into any particular category by comparison with other languages.

There are literally hundreds of high level languages, but included in the following paragraphs are those which have found, at one stage or another, widespread acceptance in their particular application areas.

FORTRAN (FORmula TRANslation)

FORTRAN was developed in the mid-1950s by IBM, for use on the then newly released IBM 704 computer. Its facility for using generally accepted arithmetic notation, such as, A = (B − C) × D, makes it suitable for use in scientific, mathematical and engineering applications. Before the arrival of FORTRAN, programming was carried out using assembly languages and the high cost of programmer time was the major factor which triggered FORTRAN's development. Following an idea by John Backus, an employee of IBM, a FORTRAN team was formed by the company to design and produce a programmer-orientated language, which provided mathematical facilities and which could be converted into efficient machine code. At the time, computer memory was extremely expensive and although assembly language programming is time-consuming, the assembled machine code is extremely efficient, both in terms of memory requirements and execution time. High level languages, on the other hand, produce relatively inefficient machine code. Despite scepticism from seasoned assembly language programmers, FORTRAN was an immediate success and during the 1960's a number of 'dialects' were developed for use on a wide range of machines. Since 1957, a number of FORTRAN language standards have been set, but most current implementations conform to the ANSI 77 (American National Standards Institute) standard. FORTRAN is available for most mainframe and mini computer systems.

ALGOL 60 (Algorithmic Language)

Like FORTRAN, ALGOL was designed for the solution of mathematical and scientific problems. The first draft of the language was developed in 1958 as a joint venture between specialists from the USA and Europe. ALGOL 58, as it became known, was revised in 1960 when it became apparent that improvements were needed and that IBM's backing of FORTRAN would make the latter language predominant in the USA. The developers of ALGOL 60 hoped to produce a general-purpose, clearly structured and machine independent language; FORTRAN did not, at the time, fulfil these criteria. The 1960 revision of ALGOL involved two notable people, John Backus, the initiator of FORTRAN and Peter Naur. They devised a standard notation to describe the syntactical structure of the language; this notation is known as Backus-Naur Form (BNF) and is now a commonly used method of describing the syntactical structure of any high level language. ALGOL's place in the evolution of high level languages is secure because of its contributions to the theory of language design, including the ideas of block structure, local and global variables (any variable can be assigned a 'scope' within a program, that is, for 'local' use in one subroutine or procedure only, or 'globally' throughout a program) and the *if ... then ... else* construction. Unfortunately, ALGOL 60 did not achieve its general-purpose status and like FORTRAN, became scientifically orientated. ALGOL 60 is appreciated for the elegance of its structure but is criticized for its clumsy and weak input facilities and has never achieved the popularity of FORTRAN. Revisions of ALGOL 60, notably ALGOL 68, have so extended the language, that they should be regarded as separate languages.

COBOL (COmmon Business Orientated Language)

Issued around 1958, COBOL is still the most widely used programming language for the development of business applications on mini and mainframe computers. The special demands of business applications could not be satisfied by the existing scientific language of FORTRAN and COBOL was designed specifically to meet those demands, which concern:

Files

Business systems tend to deal with large volumes of data, which are organized into files with clearly structured contents. For example, a customer file contains records of all a business's customers, but the types of information (the data item types) held for each customer tend to be identical. Thus, each customer record may comprise an account number, a name, an address, a credit limit and an outstanding balance;

Outputs

The outputs from business systems are often in summary form, so means for producing neatly formatted reports are essential. Numerical values must be printed in a form expected by business people - with currency signs, commas and decimal points in the expected positions and with credit and debit signs, as needed.

The initial impetus for a business language came from the U.S. Department of Defense, which wanted to computerize its everyday commercial systems. A steering committee called Codasyl (Conference on data systems languages) was set up in 1958 to oversee the development work being carried out by the several committees formed from representatives of computer manufacturers, major computer users and USA government departments. The resulting language was issued as COBOL 60 and it soon became available on several different makes of computer. Following several revisions of the language, a version was accepted by the American National Standards Institute (ANSI) in 1968. The involvement of different computer manufacturers should have ensured the achievement of the aim to make COBOL machine independent. However, as is the case with other high level languages, different dialects evolved, thus preventing complete program portability. COBOL is a verbose language and program statements can be written using English-type commands and data names. Although this verbosity makes COBOL coding easier to understand than that written in most other languages, it is a large and complex language, which often seems extremely difficult for beginners. The heavy investment of COBOL in existing software is likely to secure its future for some time to come.

BASIC (Beginner's All-purpose Symbolic Instruction Code)

The BASIC language was developed by Professors John Kemeny and Thomas Kurtz, in the mid-1960s, at Dartmouth College in the USA. Making use of the standard mathematical notation used by FORTRAN, BASIC was designed principally for use on time-sharing systems and as a simple, introductory programming language. It was aimed at those who were not necessarily planning to become professional programmers, but were using computing as a supporting subject for other disciplines studied at college.

BASIC has few grammatical rules. Programs are developed interactively by the user and can be written without knowledge of any complex programming techniques. Since its release in 1964, BASIC has become the world's most popular educational programming language and is offered as a standard language with most microcomputer systems. BASIC has evolved to become an extremely powerful business and scientific programming language and amongst the numerous dialects, Microsoft's version is one of the most popular, largely because of its association with IBM machines.

A major criticism of the BASIC language is that it gives very little support to structured programming techniques. For this reason, an increasing number of educational institutions are now teaching programming with Pascal (see later in this section) rather than BASIC.

PL 1 (Programming Language 1)

The PL1 language was introduced by IBM with their 360 series computers in 1966. At the time, programmers already had a choice of languages: FORTRAN or ALGOL for mathematical work; COBOL for business applications; assembly language for systems software development, and languages, such as LISP or SNOBOL, for specialized applications. Using such a range of languages posed problems for computer installations, not only in terms of programmer training, but also in the support and maintenance of all the relevant language translators (see next section). It was intended that PL1 should combine the features of these languages and thus be applicable to any type of problem.

Like ALGOL and Pascal, it has a block structure and a particular feature is its powerful string handling facilities, similar to those of BASIC. Features of COBOL are also included; record structures are defined in levels, although not in a separate data division and variables can be declared as particular data types.

The result of including all these features was an enormous language which was extremely difficult to learn in its totality. The intention was that a programmer would only learn a subset of the language, whichever was appropriate to the problem in hand. PL1 has never gained widespread popularity, partly because smaller, more elegant languages have been developed in addition to those which were already established and partly because its use is limited to the equipment of its developer, IBM.

RPG (Report Program Generator)

As the name of this programming language suggests, it is used for generating reports. The word 'reports' is used in its broadest sense, because RPG can be applied to applications requiring the production of, for example, invoices, cheque payments or payslips.

RPG is a specialized language, in that it can only be used for the generation of report material. Although COBOL may be described as a specialized language for business applications, it may be used for the production of many types of programs and is therefore, by comparison with RPG, a general-purpose language.

IBM developed RPG in response to their customers' demands for an efficient and cost-effective tool for producing reports. The language was released in 1961 for implementation on the IBM 1401 computer and rapidly gained widespread popularity. RPG is also available on various non-IBM systems and has been expanded to include extra facilities, for example, the ability to handle arrays.

Pascal

Named after the French mathematician and philosopher, Blaise Pascal, the Pascal programming language was originated by Niklaus Wirth and colleagues at the Institute of Informatics in Zurich. In designing the new language, Wirth's aim was to make it particularly suitable for teaching programming to university students and to this end, he looked to Algol 60 as a source of inspiration. Like Algol 60, Pascal uses a block structure and provides the facility to declare local and global variables (see explanation under the Algol section). The *if ...then* and *if ... then ... else* constructions of Algol 60 are also used in Pascal. Iteration is provided for with *repeat ... until ...* and *while ... do.* Pascal was published in 1971 and then issued in revised form in 1973. It has achieved popular success, particularly in scientific and educational spheres. Pascal's success in educational institutions stems mainly from its suitability for teaching structured programming techniques. Early criticisms of Pascal concentrated on its poor input/output facilities and subsequent revisions have provided for improved character string handling and random, as well as sequential, file organization and access.

C

The C language was created specifically to develop the UNIX operating system from an earlier version. This latter operating system was written in a low level assembly language and was thus heavily machine dependent and difficult to transfer to different machines. C spans the gap between high and low level languages. It is machine-independent, more so than most other high level languages, but is also low level in that it can be readily translated into the machine code of most computers.

For its high level features, C follows the good examples set by Algol 60 and Pascal as block structured languages. There is, however, no provision for the use of procedures. Instead, a program may call upon a number of functions to perform particular tasks. C provides all the modern control constructs, including *if ... then ... else* for conditional branching, the *case* construction for multi-way branching, and for iteration, *while* (tests the condition at the start of each iteration) and *do ... while* (tests the condition at the end of each iteration).

C is rapidly increasing its popularity as a concise, efficient programming language and is used for the development of a wide range of applications and systems software.

All the programming languages described so far are *procedural*. This means that they provide facilities for the programmer to detail explicitly how a program must 'navigate' through a file or database to obtain the necessary output. The programmer must, for example, code procedures such as 'read the first master record, process it, read the next, process it and so on until the end of the file is reached'. The following languages of LISP and PROLOG fall into different categories.

LISP (LISt Processing)

LISP is categorized as a language for *functional* programming. Although LISP is one of the oldest computer languages (nearly as old as FORTRAN), it is used extensively in one of the most innovative of today's research areas - artificial intelligence. LISP was developed around 1960 by J. McCarthy at the Massachusetts Institute of Technology. In its early years, LISP was restricted to only a few makes of machine on which it could be run efficiently. As its popularity increases, it is becoming available on more and more machines; most mainframes and an increasing number of microcomputers now support a version of LISP.

LISP was designed as a purely functional language. By this it is meant that statements in LISP look like functions. For example, the function which adds numbers in LISP is called PLUS and is written:

(PLUS 2 3)

The function PLUS operates on the 'arguments' 2 and 3. All statements are written in this way.

LISP is, however, primarily a language for manipulating symbols rather than performing complex numeric calculations. It treats all forms of data as being elements of lists and has facilities for conveniently manipulating these lists in various ways. Moreover, the language is extensible in that users can create their own functions to be used like any of those supplied.

Programs in LISP are developed interactively. Typing the name of a function, followed by its arguments, causes the function to be performed and the result displayed. In the example (PLUS 2 3), LISP would return the number 5 as soon as the function has been entered. This characteristic is one of the strengths of the language, in that programs are written in small, easily testable steps, the effects of which can be seen immediately.

PROLOG (PROgramming in LOGic)

PROLOG is described as a *declarative* language, as opposed to languages such as COBOL and Pascal, which are procedural. In PROLOG, the programmer defines (or 'declares') relationships and leaves the interpreter to extract relevant information from them. Its main function is to extract information from computer databases. PROLOG was developed in 1972 at Marseilles University, but further research and development of the language has continued in other parts of the world, notably in the UK and Japan.

The language has been adopted as the basis of software development for the Japanese fifth-generation project, because of its relevance to research in artificial intelligence. It has been used extensively in the development of expert systems because it includes facilities ideal for this type of application.

Its value as a database language can be attributed to three main characteristics:

(i) a database defined in PROLOG can be extended readily without any special provision for this growth needing to be made. This is in contrast to languages such as BASIC or COBOL where new information or requirements may require a complete software revision;

(ii) Databases can be merged or pooled with great ease; systems can be extended without the necessity of extensive forward planning.

(iii) The language has, built in, the facility for drawing logical conclusions from a user's inputs, and for extracting information embedded in complex sequences of rules.

Translators

It has already been noted that assemblers translate assembly language programs into machine code and that translators for high-level languages must perform a similar function. However, the precise mechanism by which this is accomplished for high-level languages varies considerably from language to language.

There are two main types of high-level language translators (or language processors as they are often known):

(a) compilers;

(b) interpreters.

It is important from a programming point of view to be quite clear about the difference between the two.

Compilers

The following figure illustrates the way in which a compiler is used to produce an executable program.

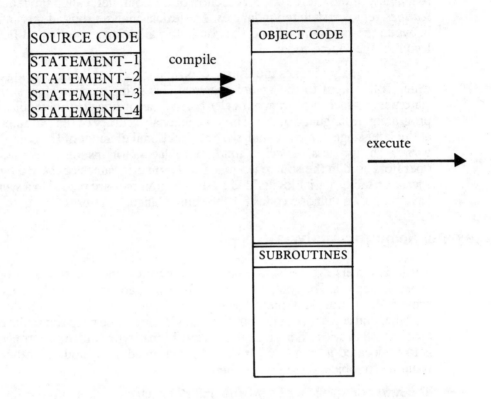

A compiler is essentially a sophisticated assembler, taking the source program and processing it to produce an independent object program in machine code. In addition, a compiler will often have access to a library of standard routines and special routines appropriate to the application area for which the language was designed; this collection of subroutines is called the *run-time library*. Included in this library of machine code subprograms will be routines for performing arithmetic operations, input/output operations, backing-storage data transfers and other commonly used functions. Whenever the source code refers to one of these routines specifically, or needs one to perform the operation specified, the compiler will ensure that the routine is added to the object program.

Note that the final object code is independent of both the source code and the compiler itself, that is neither of these two programs needs to be resident in main store when the object code is being executed. However, any alterations to the program necessitates modification and re-compilation of the source code prior to executing the program again.

Examples of compiled languages are FORTRAN, COBOL and PASCAL.

Compilation Stages

The compilation process can be broken down into a number of distinct stages:

- lexical analysis;

- syntax analysis and semantic analysis;

- code generation.

Lexical Analysis

Most programming languages allow a certain amount of *redundancy* in the preparation of the program. This means that, for example, spaces can often be inserted to aid readability of the source code. A section of the compiler, called the *lexical analyser* or *scanner*, removes such redundancies. The lexical analyser thus adopts an interface role between the programmer and the computer, allowing some limited flexibility in the layout of the source code.

The lexical analyser takes the source code and translates it into a string of characters, which is the input to the *syntax analyser*. This string of characters should comprise statements which are grammatically correct according to the requirements of the programming language in use. The grammatical accuracy of the statements is checked at the later stage of syntax analysis, by a functional element of the compiler called the *parser*. The process of *lexical analysis* replaces, for instance, reserved words and operators used in the source language with numeric values or *tokens*, by reference to a look-up table. Variables defined by the programmer are placed in a *symbol table* and have their own numeric codes for the source language in use.

Syntax and Semantic Analysis

These analysers do the actual hard work of breaking the source program into its constituent parts. The complete source program is analysed into blocks, which are then broken down into statements, which are further analysed into instruction words, variables and constants. Each variable used in the source program is placed in a *symbol table*, together with a declaration of its attributes - type (numeric, string etc.), where it is to be located in memory (its object program address) and any other information required for object code generation.

The *syntax* or grammar of a programming language consists of the rules which define a legal program statement, as opposed to a meaningless string of characters. The rules determine the correct arrangements of words. In English, for example, the sentence

> *the tree is biting the dog*

can be determined as *grammatically* correct by reference to the rules of English grammar. Conversely, the rules can be used to determine that

> *dog tree the biting*

is grammatically incorrect.

The grammar or syntax of the Pascal programming language can be used to determine that the program statement

> *net := gross − deductions;*

is correct, and that

> *gross − deductions := net;*

is not.

The process of *parsing* a program for syntactical accuracy is a function of the compiler.

Semantic analysis is concerned with checking, to an extent, the meaning or interpretation to be placed on words. Normally, correctness of meaning will be determined in conjunction with other words in the program. Thus, for example, every *if* in a Pascal program must be checked for an accompanying *endif* and every *begin* must have an *end.* In the COBOL language, a declaration such as the following,

> 77 End-file   PIC A VALUE IS ZERO.

in the WORKING-STORAGE SECTION is syntactically correct, but semantically incorrect because an attempt is made to initialize an alphabetic field with a numeric value. Similarly, suppose that a declaration

        01   Code   PIC 99.

                88   Code-range   VALUES ARE 01 THRU 50.

is made in the WORKING-STORAGE SECTION and then the statement

        MOVE 35 TO Code-range.

is used in the PROCEDURE DIVISION; the attempt to move a value to a condition-name is semantically wrong; the statement should probably have read:

        MOVE 35 TO Code.

To make proper use of the condition-name Code-range, the statement

        IF NOT Code-range THEN PERFORM Code-error.

would allow appropriate action to be taken if a 'code' value is found to be outside of the range 01 to 50.

Thus, although a program statement may be syntactically correct, an error in semantics will prevent the machine from understanding it.

Code Generation

By this stage, it can be assumed that the syntax analyser has found the source program to be *grammatically* correct, because the existence of any syntax errors would have terminated the translation process. The production of the object or machine code from the *tokenized* source program requires that the code is scanned, expressions are translated and machine addresses of instructions and variables (the latter by reference to the *symbol table*) are incorporated into the object code.

Linking

Frequently, the object code produced by the compiler comprises separate modules of machine code which are related to each other via call and return addresses; the separate modules may also share common data. The object code may also make reference to library routines, held externally from the main program block. The function of the linker program, or *linkage editor*, is to incorporate the absolute call and return addresses of any external routines (*closed subroutines*) which are to be used by the program, as well as those needed to link the various modules of machine code produced by the compiler. Sometimes, linking is carried out as part of the compilation process.

Interpreters

The procedure used by interpreters is entirely different from that of compilers. The figure on the next page illustrates this fundamental difference.

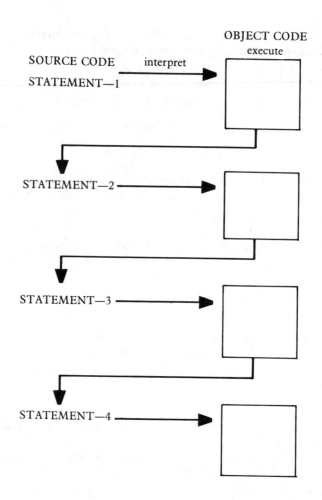

The source code statements are translated and executed separately, as they are encountered, while the source code is being processed by the interpreter. The object code that is actually executed is held within the interpreter; the latter merely identifies from the source statement which piece of machine code is relevant and causes it to be executed. On completion of a statement, control returns to the interpreter which then processes the next logical statement in the program sequence.

It might, therefore, seem that an interpreter is faster, more efficient and generally far superior to a compiler, but in fact the converse is almost invariably true. An interpreter must do a considerable amount of work before it can even begin to cause a source statement to be executed; on the other hand, a compiler has already done this work during compilation. Moreover, should a section of source code be repeated one or more times, an interpreter must re-interpret the section each time. Consequently interpreted programs tend to run significantly slower than equivalent compiled programs.

Because the translation and execution phases are interwoven, the interpreter must be resident in memory at the same time as the source code. If memory space is at a premium, this can be a severe limitation of an interpreted language.

On the credit side, interpreted languages generally allow program changes to be made more easily; it is merely necessary to make the modifications to the source code which is then immediately ready for execution.

Interpreted languages include BASIC and LISP.

Software Trends

In this section we briefly examine a number of types of software which are rapidly increasing in importance. Each category examined continues the trend of making things easier for the user: *WIMPs* are *Graphic User Interfaces* (or GUI's) which use screen graphics to help the user to control programs and operating systems; *Fourth Generation Languages* allow the user to concentrate on the problem solution strategy and leave the programming details to the computer; *Expert Systems* assist non-experts to make informed judgements in specialised areas.

WIMPs

The term "WIMP" refers to a computer software environment designed to be particularly easy to use. Characteristic of this type of system is the use of a combination of *Windows, Icons, Mice, Pointers and Pull-down menus*. The idea was pioneered by Apple Computers when they put their Lisa and Macintosh computers on the market in the early eighties. Though fairly slow to emulate this innovative approach, an increasing number of computer manufacturers are providing similar systems as standard features. Most systems use a device called a *mouse* to control the operation of the software. A mouse is a small, hand-held device connected to the computer by a flexible lead and incorporating one or more buttons. The mouse is moved over a flat surface near to the computer and, by means of an electronically monitored roller, it is linked to an image of a pointer which mirrors its movement on the monitor.

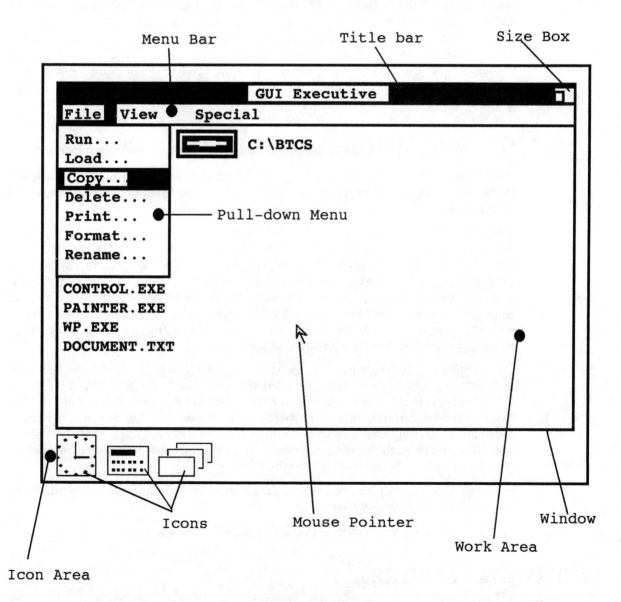

A typical WIMP environment is shown above. The system Window shown above has a number of common features:

- a mouse-controlled pointer. As the mouse is moved forward and backward and side to side, the pointer follows the movement on the screen; this allows the user to "point" at special areas of the screen and click a button on the mouse to indicate selection of an item;

- a title bar which declares the current application;

- a size box allowing the window to be contracted or expanded;

- a menu bar of menu titles indicating the presence of pull-down menus. These are selected using the mouse pointer.

- an icon area showing the existence of any utilities which can be "clicked";

- a list of items, in this case file names, which can be selected by pointing and clicking. These items may be data files, program files or command files depending on the nature of the current application.

Just as an operating system is a simplified interface to the complexities of the computer system, so the WIMP environment, when used in the manner described above, can be a convenient interface to the operating system. As such it can be used by the layman to perform file management functions such as creating, copying, renaming and deleting files, formatting and verifying disks or running applications. Moreover, there is a welcome trend towards designing application programs to run under the same style of environment, thus bringing a uniformity to the presentation and operation of applications.

Fourth Generation Languages

In order to provide a context that allows the concept of a fourth generation language to be appreciated, it is necessary to review briefly the main characteristics of the preceding three generations of languages.

First generation languages were Machine Code, the first true form of programming language, in which the computer was programmed directly using numeric codes. Evolving from this original form, assembly languages, the second generation, eased the programming task by making the computer take care of a number of functions that were not directly related to the processing problems being addressed. High-level languages represent the third generation of programming languages and are characterised by the concise way they allow a problem to be defined; consequently, these languages are relatively easy to learn and use.

Fourth generation languages represent the latest innovation in the evolution of programming languages, allowing a programmer to specify the problem to be solved in relatively general terms and leaving the computer to fill in the programming details. Such languages continue the tradition of reducing the work of the user and increasing the load on the computer. The terms "Fourth Generation Language", and its contraction, 4GL, are subject to a wide variety of interpretations and definitions, but they all have a number of characteristics in common:

- easier to use than existing high-level languages, particularly by non-specialists;

- more concise than existing high-level languages;

- the language is closer to natural language;

- user-friendly;

- non-procedural.

With the possible exception of the last one, these points are self-explanatory. The terms "non-procedural" and "declarative" refer to languages which allow the user to define a goal and leave the computer to determine (within bounds) how to achieve it. To illustrate the difference, compare the following two sets of instructions for making a cup of tea:

(1) – Boil the kettle;

   – Put two teaspoons of tea in the teapot;

   – Pour boiling water into the teapot until it is three-quarters full;

   – Wait at least five minutes for the tea to infuse;

   – Put a small amount of milk in a teacup;

   – Pour tea into the cup until it is almost full.

(2) – Make tea for one person;

   – Pour out one cup, with milk.

The first list defines the procedure, step by step, for making a cup of tea. The instructions imply that the procedure is not familiar to the tea maker; this is not the case in (2) where the implication is that the tea maker already has the required knowledge and merely needs to be told how much tea to make and whether milk is required. The person issuing the command in (2) is not interested in the precise way that the task is accomplished as long as the tea that arrives tastes good and does not take an unreasonable length of time. (1) represents procedural programming and (2) the declarative approach.

Two examples of current software systems which fit this loose definition of a 4GL are *Structured Query Languages (SQL's)* and *Program Generators*.

Structured Query Languages

Developed by IBM, SQL's operate on relational databases and are becoming the recognised standard for this type of application. Briefly, a relational database is one in which the database is considered to be a table(relation) of rows, which are equivalent to records, and columns, which are related to fields within records. New relations can be created in response to user queries. An SQL simplifies the task of specifying queries by allowing the user to use a series of key-words. The resulting query, while not being in natural language, is easily understandable to the non specialist and certainly more user friendly than many other query languages.

The general form of an SQL query is:

SELECT Name(ie field) FROM Table(ie file)

WHERE   ....

AND   ....

AND   ....

A query in this form can be used to extract rows(records) from tables subject to criteria which may depend on the contents of other tables. The conditions specified in the query allow the user to filter out only those rows of interest. In addition, standard functions are provided to simplify sorting procedures and report production. So a user could add statements such as

ORDER by Name

PRINT

For example, suppose a database, called 'CUSTBAL', consisting of customer accounts contained the following data in tabular form:

CUSTBAL

Name	ACno	Balance
Green	1537	67.98
Jones	1342	−22.42
Smith	1234	123.55
White	2316	−33.45
Yourdon	1466	−650.50

Suppose also that another table, called 'CUSTTYPE' contained the following columns:

CUSTTYPE

ACno	ACtype
1234	A
1342	B
1466	A
1537	C
2316	A

Then, a user, wishing to have a printout of all customers with account type A whose balance is in the red, might use the query:

SELECT Name FROM CUSTBAL WHERE

CUSTBAL.Balance < 0

AND CUSTBAL.ACno = CUSTTYPE.ACno

AND CUSTTYPE.ACtype= 'A'

ORDER BY Name

PRINT

This user query would produce the report

White

Yourdon

Other SQL's such as NATURAL allow the formation of very similar query structures.

Program Generators

One such system accepts a type of pseudocode as the source/specification language and uses it to generate the appropriate COBOL program. Pseudocode allows expression of processing requirements in very high-level, well structured terms which are not specific to a particular programming language. This is comparable to the way a compiler operates, accepting a high-level language as source code to generate a machine code program. In this case the output from the 4GL is the source code for a high-level language (ie COBOL). The specification language may be related to a system design technique such as Jackson Structured Design.

Fifth Generation Computers

At about the beginning of the 1980's, the Japanese announced their intention to produce the next or 'Fifth Generation' computers - machines exhibiting 'artificial intelligence' and operating enormously faster than current computers. These were to be based on new principles of operation, closer to the way that human beings are thought to perform processing tasks. Not only would new and faster hardware need to be designed to achieve these aims, but the software to drive it would need to be correspondingly much more sophisticated.

The Japanese identified a large number of goals to be achieved within a decade, one of which, the widespread use and support of knowledge-based systems, is of particular relevance in the present context.

Knowledge-based systems can be applied to a variety of applications including knowledge-based management, problem solving, inference and human interaction. An expert system is an example of a knowledge-based system for making logical inferences. "Intelligent Assistants" for management and "Intelligent Tutors" in education are further examples of such systems.

An expert system uses a knowledge-base of rules, that can be applied to data, as one component of its structure; such sets of rules serve to guide intelligently the directions that computations should take. This is particularly important when data is to be extracted from very large databases quickly. However, another important component of an expert system, and many other software applications, is the human/computer interface. The language used for this interaction between user and computer should be comfortable for the user and thus a great deal of research is being done on natural language interfaces. This research encompasses voice recognition and synthesis as well as written communication.

Whether the Japanese achieve their targets or not, in the near future we will see in the market place the fruits of the enormous research commitment undertaken by them and their competitors; the HAL computer in Arthur C. Clarke's "2001" may well be a reality by that very date, but by then it will probably be small enough to stand in a corner of your desk!

Assignment   *Turbo Cars*

Turbo Cars is a small car repair business operating from a back street garage in South Shields. The owner, Ray Pitts, has bought himself a second-hand Apple microcomputer, equipped with twin disk drives, a printer and a version of the C/PM operating system. He plans to keep computer records of his stocks of spares. A friend of his, Tom Finney, who runs a small motorist's discount shop, has an IBM system which supports the MS/DOS operating system; he uses the system for his business accounting applications. Tom is a computer enthusiast and has already written his own stock control program, using the COBOL programming language. He has given Ray Pitts a copy of the program listing which will require some modification for the Apple system.

Unfortunately, Tom Finney has moved out of the area and cannot be contacted. Ray Pitts knows that you have some knowledge of computing and asks you why the COBOL coding needs to be changed and why Tom Finney told him that he would need a COBOL compiler.

Task

You are going to visit Ray Pitts at his home to explain matters to him. Prepare some notes for him, explaining why the source code needs to be changed and the role that the compiler plays in providing an executable program.

In a role play exercise with other members of your group, give your explanations and tactfully offer some advice on alternative actions he may take.

Developmental Task

Research some different programming language dialects. BASIC will probably be the most familiar to you and it should be possible to identify a number of variations in the range and format of instructions available, for different versions of the language. Use any examples you find to illustrate your explanations to Ray Pitts.

Chapter 11

Categories of Software

The tree diagram in the figure below illustrates the different categories of software and, to some extent, their relationships to each other. This chapter begins by examining the distinction between systems and applications software.

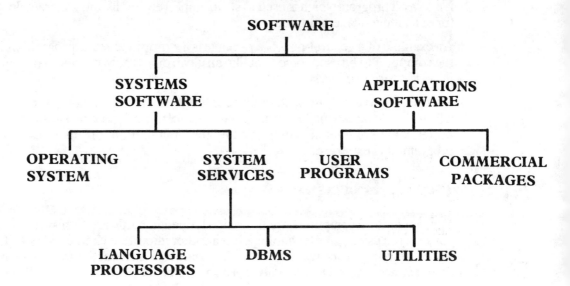

The term *systems software* covers the collection of programs usually supplied by the manufacturer of the computer. These programs protect the user from the enormous complexity of the computer system, and enable the computer to be used to maximum effect. Without systems software a modern digital computer would be virtually impossible to use; as computer hardware has evolved, so systems software has been forced to become more and more complex in order to make effective use of it. The relationship between a user program and the systems software invisibly allowing its operation, was once amusingly compared to an elephant riding on the back of a mouse, such is the size and complexity of systems software compared to the individual programs it supports.

Broadly speaking, systems software consists of two elements:

(i) those programs concerned with the control and co-ordination of all aspects of the computer system, namely the *Operating System*;

(ii) a number of other programs providing various services to users. These services include compilers and interpreters for any languages supported by the system, database management systems (DBMS) for the manipulation of large volumes of data, and utility programs such as program editors and other aids to programming.

Applications software refers to programs which have some direct value to the organization, and will normally include those programs for which the computer system was specifically purchased. For example, a mail order company might acquire a computer system initially for stock control and accounting purposes, when its volume of business begins to make these functions too difficult to cope with by manual means. Applications programs would be required to record and process customers' orders, update the stock file according to goods sent or received, make appropriate entries in the various accounts ledgers, etc.

Commercial packages come in two main categories:

> (i) special-purpose packages;

> (ii) general-purpose packages.

A package consists of one or more programs on some form of file medium (such as magnetic disc). It will be accompanied by documentation explaining in detail how the programs function and how they are used. An example of a special-purpose package is a payroll program which is used to store employee details and generate details of pay for each individual employee.

An example of a general-purpose package is a wordprocessor, a program which allows the computer to be used somewhat like an electronic typewriter and is therefore useful in a wide variety of ways.

User programs are those written by people within the organization for specific needs which cannot be satisfied by other sources of software. These program writers may be professional programmers employed by the organisation, or other casual users with programming expertise.

Systems Software

First generation computers are normally defined in hardware terms, in that they were constructed using valve technology, but another important characteristic of this generation of computers was the equally primitive software support provided for programmers and other users. Modern computers perform automatically many of the tasks that programmers in those days had to handle themselves; writing routines to control peripheral devices, allocating programs to main store, executing programs, checking peripheral devices for availability, as well as many other routine tasks.

In subsequent generations of computers, manufacturers started addressing themselves to the problem of improving the programming environment by providing standard programs for many routine tasks. Many of these routines became linked together under the control of a single program called the *executive, supervisor,* or *monitor,* whose function was to supervise the running of user programs and, in general, to control and co-ordinate the functioning of the whole computer system, both hardware and software. Early programs of this type have evolved into the sophisticated programs collectively known as *Operating Systems.*

Systems software has three important functions:

> (i) to facilitate the running of user programs;

> (ii) to optimise the performance of the computer system;

> (iii) to provide assistance with program development.

The operating system takes care of the former two requirements and language processors (such as assemblers and compilers), editors, diagnostic routines and other utility programs aid the third requirement.

Operating Systems

If a computer system is viewed as a set of resources, comprising elements of both hardware and software, then it is the job of the collection of programs known as the Operating System to manage these resources as efficiently as possible. In so doing, the operating system acts as a buffer between the user and the complexities of the computer itself. One way of regarding the Operating System is to think of it as a program which allows the user to deal with a simplified computer, but without losing any of the computational power of the machine. In this way the computer system becomes a virtual system, its enormous complexity hidden and controlled by the Operating System and through which the user communicates with the real system.

The Main Functions of Operating Systems

Earlier it was stated that the function of an operating system is to manage the resources of the computer system. These resources generally fall into the following categories:

Central Processing Unit (CPU).   Since only one program can be executed at any one time, if the computer system is such that several users are allowed access to the system simultaneously, in other words a *multi-user* system, then access to the CPU must be carefully controlled and monitored. In a *timesharing* multi-user system each user is given a small *time-slice* of processor time before passing on to the next user in a continuously repeating sequence. Another common scheme is to assign priorities to users so that the system is able to determine which user should have control of the CPU next.

Memory.   Programs (or parts of programs) must be loaded into the memory before they can be executed, and moved out of the memory when no longer required there. Storage space must be provided for data generated by programs, and provision must be made for the temporary storage of data, caused by data transfer operations involving devices such as printers and disk drives.

Input/Output (I/O) Devices.   Programs will request the use of these devices during the course of their execution and in a multi-user system conflicts are bound to arise, when a device being utilised by one program is requested by another. The Operating System will control allocation of I/O devices and attempt to resolve any conflicts which arise. It will also monitor the state of each I/O device and signal any faults detected.

Backing Store.   Programs and data files will usually be held on mass storage devices such as magnetic disk and tape drives. The Operating System will supervise data transfers to and from these devices and memory and deal with requests from programs for space on them.

Files.   These may be regarded as a limited resource in the sense that several users may wish to share the same data file at the same time in multi-user systems. The Operating System facilitates access to files and ensures restricted access to one program at any one time for those files which are to be written to.

Resource allocation is closely linked to one part of the Operating System called the *scheduler*. The term *scheduling* refers to the question of when, in a multi-user system, should a new process be introduced into the system and in which order the processes should be run.

The above is by no means an exhaustive list of the functions of an Operating System. Other functions include:

- interpretation of the command language by which operators can communicate with it;

- error handling. For example, detecting and reporting inoperative or malfunctioning peripherals;

- protection of data files and programs from corruption by other users;

- protection of data files and programs from unauthorised use;

- accounting and logging of the use of the computer resources.

System Services

Often a manufacturer will provide a number of programs designed specifically for program or application development. Three such aids are:

(i)   Language Processors;

(ii)   Database Management Systems;

(iii)   Utility Programs.

Language Processors

Translators such as assemblers, compilers and interpreters fall into this category. The characteristics of these types of programs have been explored earlier in this chapter, though it is worth noting here, that in terms of program development they generally offer a valuable service in addition to those previously described. During the program development process it is very easy for programmers to write program instructions in violation of the rules for their formation. These are called *syntax errors* and will normally be detected by a compiler. This may occur, for instance, as it scans the instruction and attempts to parse it (that is split it into recognisable chunks prior to converting it into machine code). The compiler will report all such errors that it is capable of detecting, by terminating the attempted compilation, specifying the nature of the errors, and indicating at which source statements they occurred. This report, usually called an *error listing*, is an invaluable aid to producing an executable (though not necessarily correct) program.

Database Management System (DBMS)

The term 'database' is used to describe a form of mass storage file organisation where the user is not directly concerned with layout, structure, or location of files; he or she only defines the information that is to be stored, and the form in which any reports derived from the data are to be presented. For this method of processing to be possible, a great deal of generalised software must be provided and, since such software must be closely related to many of the routines within the Operating System, manufacturers will often provide such a DBMS either with the rest of the computer system when purchased, or offer it as an additional piece of software to be purchased as and when required.

Utility Programs

As part of the systems software provided with a computer system there are a number of utility programs specifically designed to aid program development and testing. These include:

Editors.   These permit the creation and modification of source programs and data files. The facilities offered by these programs usually include such things as character, word and line insertion and deletion, automatic line numbering, line tabulation for languages which require program instructions to be spaced in a specific manner, the storage and retrieval of files from backing storage, and the printing of programs or other files.

Diagnostic and Trace Routines.   Programs in which the appropriate translator can find no fault will often contain errors in logic, known as *bugs*, which only become apparent when the program is run and produces results which are contrary to expectations. These *run-time* errors are often very difficult to detect and may lead to long delays in the implementation of the program. Certain types of run-time errors will produce diagnostic messages to be produced by the operating system, but errors in the logic of a program must be isolated by the programmer himself.

A Trace routine will allow the user to follow the path taken through the program so that it may be compared with the expected route; thus the point at which any deviation occurred can be detected. Breakpoints may be inserted at strategic points in the program, such that when they are encountered, program execution is halted temporarily to allow the current state of the program variables to be examined and displayed in order to check their validity. Other similar facilities can be called on from these packages to speed the *debugging* process.

File Managers. These simplify and facilitate a number of operations connected with program development and maintenance such as:

(i) keeping backup copies of important files;

(ii) deleting files and creating space for new ones;

(iii) merging files;

(iv) listing details of current files held on backing storage;

(v) sorting file names into specified orders.

Without the help of such dedicated programs, operations such as these could be extremely time-consuming and consequently expensive.

Applications Software

An analysis of the uses to which companies and individuals put computers would reveal that the same types of tasks appear time and time again. Many organizations use computers to facilitate payroll calculations, others to perform stock control functions, accounting procedures, management information tasks and numerous other common functions.

These types of programs are classed as *applications software*, software which is applied to practical tasks in order to make them more efficient or useful in other ways. Systems software is merely there to support the running, development and maintenance of applications software.

An organisation wishing to implement one of these tasks (or any other vital to its efficient operation) on a computer has several alternatives:

(i) Ask a software house to take on the task of writing a specific program for the organisation's needs;

(ii) Use its own programming staff and produce the software 'in house';

(iii) Buy a commercially available program 'off the shelf' and hope that it already fulfils, or can be modified to fulfil, the organisation's requirements;

(iv) Buy a general purpose program, such as a database or spreadsheet package, that has the potential to perform the required functions.

The final choice will depend on such factors as the urgency of the requirements, financial constraints, size of the company and the equipment available.

It is beyond the scope of this book to enter into a discussion regarding either the strategy for making such a decision or to investigate specific items of software available for specific applications; but, with the immense and growing, popularity of general purpose packages, particularly for personal-business microcomputers, it is worth looking in more detail at this category of software.

General Purpose Packages for Microcomputers

Discussion of this class of software will be restricted here to the following headings , though they are not intended to represent an exhaustive list of all the categories of general purpose packages which are available:

(a) Wordprocessors

(b) Ideas or Thought Processors

(c) Spreadsheets

(d) Databases

(e) Graphics packages

(f) Expert System Shells

(g) Integrated packages

What characterises these software types as belonging to the category of general-purpose packages is that they have been designed to be very flexible and applicable to a wide range of different applications. For instance, a spreadsheet can be used as easily for simple accountancy procedures as for stock control; a database can be used with equal facility to store information on technical papers from journals, stock item details and personnel details for payroll purposes.

The suitability of a particular general-purpose package for a specific application will be largely dependent on the characteristics of the package. Though the general facilities afforded by different database packages may be roughly equivalent (for instance every package performs basically the same functions), each manufacturer will adopt its own style of presentation and will provide certain services not offered by its competitors. A prospective buyer should have a clear idea of the main uses for which the package is to be purchased right at the outset, because some packages may be much more suitable than others.

Advantages of general-purpose software compared to other forms of applications software are as follow:

(i) Because large numbers of the package are sold prices are relatively low;

(ii) They are appropriate to a wide variety of applications;

(iii) As they are already perfected they allow a great reduction in the time and costs necessary for development and testing;

(iv) They prove suitable for people with little or no computing experience;

(v) They are very easy to use;

(vi) They have been thoroughly tried and tested;

(vii) Most such packages are provided with extensive documentation.

Some of the disadvantages are as follow:

(i) Sometimes the package will allow only a clumsy solution to the application;

(ii) The user must still develop the application. This requires a thorough knowledge of the capabilities of the package, and how to make the best use of them;

(iii) The user will need to provide his own documentation for the particular application for which the package has been tailored;

(iv) Unless the software is used regularly, it is easy to forget the correct command sequences to operate the package, particularly for people inexperienced in the use of computer software of this type;

(v) The user must take responsibility for his own security measures to ensure that vital data is not lost, or to prevent unauthorised personnel gaining access to the data.

Wordprocessors

The wordprocessor performs much the same function as a typewriter, but it offers a large number of very useful additional features. Basically a wordprocessor is a computer with a keyboard for entering text, a monitor for display purposes, and a printer to provide the permanent output on paper. A wordprocessor is really nothing more than a computer system with a special piece of software to make it perform the required functions; some such systems have hardware configurations specifically for the purpose (such as special keyboards and letter-quality printers) but the majority are merely the result of obtaining an appropriate wordprocessor application package.

Wordprocessors are used for such purposes as producing

- letters
- legal documents
- books
- articles
- mailing lists

and in fact any type of textual material.

Some of the advantages they have over ordinary typewriters are as follow:

- typing errors can be corrected before printing the final version;
- the availability of such automatic features as page numbering, the placing of page headers and footers and word-line counting;
- whole document editing such as replacing every incidence of a certain combination of characters with another set of characters. For instance, replacing each occurrence of the name 'Mr. Smith' by 'Mrs. Jones';
- printing multiple copies all to the same high quality;
- documents can be saved and printed out at some later date without any additional effort.

However, wordprocessors do have some drawbacks. For instance, prolonged viewing of display monitors can produce eyestrain. They are generally considerably more expensive than good typewriters, and to be used properly, a certain amount of special training is required.

On the whole, wordprocessors are now firmly established in the so-called 'electronic office' and there is no reason to suppose that their use will not continue to expand.

Ideas Processors

As the name suggests, software of this type enables users to process ideas or thoughts. Ideas, opinions and thoughts are generally unstructured and cannot, therefore, be processed in any useful way by a word processor or organized into files in a database. Ideas processors allow the user to organize and analyse unstructured information of a variety of different types, such as, for example, notes, memos, concepts, which are stored in a variety of different forms, for example, diaries, reference books, reports, files etc. A well known package is Agenda from Lotus. The package allows the user to enter random, spontaneous information in the same way as it would be jotted down on a notepad; such 'jottings' are known as *items*. These items can then be placed in Categories; in other words the items can be indexed with any key required by the user, for example, name, date, place, product, area and town. Items can then be re-categorized at will and the user can then view them by category.

Spreadsheets

Just as wordprocessors are designed to manipulate text, spreadsheets are designed to do the equivalent with numerical information. A spreadsheet program presents the user with a blank grid of *cells* each of which is capable of containing one of three types of information:

> - a label consisting of alphanumeric characters;
>
> - a number;
>
> - a formula, which may make reference to other cells.

These are sufficient to allow a wide range of applications to be implemented in a very convenient and easily understandable way. For example, suppose that a small business dealing in the sale of personal computer systems wishes to use such a program to record on a monthly basis, the sales values attributable to each of its four salespersons. The spreadsheet might be set up as shown on the following page.

Column A contains labels describing the systems purchased. Column B the sales value of the item, and the remaining four columns contain the calculated commissions for the salespersons. The actual sales data in columns A and B, and the commissions, are typed in at the appropriate places according to who made the sales. The totals, however are calculated by the program through formulae installed in the cells B50 to F50. Such a formula might be written as

> @SUM(B4..B49)

and it would automatically calculate the sum of the contents of cells B4 to B49. Installed in cell B50, it would produce the figure '88860.00'; any empty cells, or those containing labels, would be treated as having a value of zero. Any change in the data on the spreadsheet would cause all the calculations to be repeated.

This automatic calculation facility gave rise to the expression *what if* which is often used to describe an important capability of spreadsheets. It is possible to set up complex combinations of inter- dependent factors and see *what* happens to the final result *if* one or more of the factors is changed. The spreadsheet, once set up, takes care of all the recalculations necessary for this type of exercise.

	A	B	C	D	E	F	G
1	ITEM	SALE		COMMISSION			
2		VALUE					
3			John	Jim	Joan	Janet	
4	IBM PC	2000		100			
5	Amstrad 1512	670			33.50		
6	IBM XT	3200				160	
7	Compaq	1800		90			
8	Olivetti	1900	95				
		etc					
50	TOTAL SALES	88860.00	265.50	468.30	922.80	565.90	
51							
52	TOTAL COMMISSION	2221.50					

The earliest program of this form was called 'Visicalc' and it ran on an Apple Micro-computer. Many such programs now exist, having capabilities far exceeding those of Visicalc, but they still closely resemble the original concept in appearance and operation.

Spreadsheets have a number of attractive features compared to traditional programming solutions to processing needs:

- designed for laymen;
- easy to learn and use;
- wide range of uses;
- relatively cheap;
- easily modified;
- well tried and tested;
- provide quick development time.

On the debit side, they tend to be:

- too general purpose and therefore provide satisfactory rather than ideal solutions;
- the problem must still be analysed and a solution method identified.

Database

At one time database programs, or Database Management Systems (DBMS) as they are often called, were restricted to mainframe computers because of the large memory requirements demanded of such applications. Currently, however, even personal business microcomputers have sufficient internal memory (1 megabyte - roughly 1 million characters of storage - is quite common) to make such applications not only feasible but also extremely powerful.

These programs allow files, comprising collections of records, to be created, modified, searched and printed. A good database program will offer, as a minimum, the following facilities:

- user-definable record format allowing the user to specify the fields within the record;

- user-definable input format to allow the user to define the way the data is to be entered into the computer;

- file searching capabilities for extracting records satisfying certain criteria from a file;

- file sorting capabilities so that records can be ordered according to the contents of a certain field;

- calculations on fields within records for inclusion in reports;

- user-definable report formats, so that different types of reports containing different combinations of record fields may be produced.

Recently, an innovative feature has begun to appear with database programs. Some software houses are adding *natural language* interfaces to their programs to allow users to state their requirements in (almost) ordinary English. This is a very attractive feature to inexperienced users of computers. For instance, if the system has been set up for a personnel file of employees of a business, the enquirer might want to know how many of the employees are earning less than a certain salary. The question to the program could be phrased:

"Print the names and departments of employees whose salaries are less than '£6000'"

and the program would search the file and print the required details for all those records satisfying the stated criterion.

The main value of such a facility is the brevity with which quite complicated requirements may be stated; English is a very expressive and concise language compared to formal query languages or menu-driven strategies for information retrieval programs. However, natural language processing is still in its infancy and programs offering this facility generally are able only to cope with a very limited form of English. The user, to get the most benefit from the free-form style of input, must be very much aware of the nature of these restrictions, otherwise a great deal of time will be wasted in phrasing questions in a form that the system is unable to 'understand'.

Graphics Packages

These generally fall into three categories according to their main area of use:

- Business graphics;

- Graphic design;

- Desktop publishing.

Business graphics packages allow the production of such things as Bar Charts, Line Graphs and Pie Diagrams; diagrams of a statistical nature likely to be included in business reports.

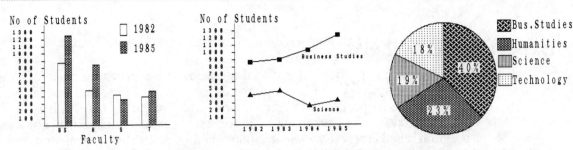

Packages for graphic design consist of a collection of special functions aimed at aiding the graphic designer. The artist uses the screen as his canvas and a light-pen (or equivalent device) as his brush. They generally allow work of professional quality to be produced in a relatively short amount of time, and include such facilities as

- large colour palette

- geometric figure drawing, e.g. lines, rectangles, circles

- filling areas with colour or patterns

- undoing mistakes

- moving/copying/deleting/saving areas of the screen display

- choice of a variety of character fonts

- printing the finished design.

A familiar example
of a computer graphic

Desktop publishing programs are designed to facilitate the production of documents such as posters, illustrated articles and production of documents such as posters, illustrated articles and other documents which combine large amounts of text with illustrations, the type of thing we frequently see in newspapers. As such they tend to contain a number of facilities in common with graphic design packages, but emphasise the printing aspect much more and generally just work in black and white. These packages place a lot of emphasis on being able to experiment with arranging sections of the document and seeing its overall appearance. Text is also given more importance; a rudimentary wordprocessor may be provided, or text may be *imported* from a prepared file, and the user is generally able to experiment with different type fonts on text already displayed on the screen.

An example of
desktop publishing

Expert System Shells

Pure research in the field of artificial intelligence has had a number of practical spin-offs. One such spin-off has been the development of programs known as *Expert Systems*. These are programs designed to be able to give the same sort of help or advice, or make decisions, as a human expert in some narrow field of expertise. For instance, a program called *Prospector* is capable of predicting the existence of mineral ores given various pieces of information gathered from physical locations. In the same way that, given certain evidence, an expert might say that a particular site looked favourable for containing ore, *Prospector* indicates the probability of the existence of the ore. *Prospector* is in fact attributed with the discovery of an extremely valuable quantity of molybdenum which had previously been overlooked by human experts.

Expert systems have been developed in all kinds of areas which have traditionally been the responsibility of human experts, including medical diagnosis; decisions in areas such as this are so important, however, that it would be foolish to blindly accept the pronouncement of a computer. For this reason, expert systems have built-in the ability to 'explain' the reasoning behind any conclusion so that this chain of reasoning can be checked and verified (or rejected) by a human.

A typical expert system has three main components:

(i)   a *knowledge base* consisting of facts and rules by which facts can lead to conclusions. For example, the rule

   IF (1) STEM is woody

AND (2) POSITION is upright

AND (3) ONE MAIN TRUNK is NO

   THEN TYPE is SHRUB

could be one of many in an expert system knowledge base for botanical classification;

(ii)   an *inference engine* which processes the knowledge base;

(iii)   a *user interface* to facilitate communication with the user.

The term *Shell* is given to expert systems which have been given no specific knowledge base, only the inference engine and user interface; the knowledge base has to be provided by the user. An expert system shell can thus be used to provide advice or help in a number of areas of expertise, providing it is given the appropriate knowledge base for each area.

For example, an expert system shell could be used to give advice on the legal procedures and sequence of steps necessary for selling a house (what solicitors call 'conveyancing'), or to give advice about possible causes and cures of diseases in houseplants, or diagnosing faults in cars. Not only could these applications be of practical use, but they could also be instructive, because the user could ask for and obtain the reasons behind any conclusions.

One of the problems of using such shells, is the determination of the rules which represent the wisdom of a human expert; many experts are not consciously aware of the precise reasoning processes they themselves use in order to come to some conclusion, yet in order to produce an expert program, these processes must be defined in a form that is usable. The process of determining the knowledge base rules is known as *knowledge elicitation* or *knowledge acquisition* and is performed by *knowledge engineers*.

Integrated Packages

Once it became evident that packages such as those described above were going to become more and more in demand, software houses started producing packages which offered integrated combinations of wordprocessors, databases, spreadsheets, graphics and more recently, expert system shells. In fact one integrated package called Lotus 123, offering spreadsheet, database and business-type graphics, became the most successful ever general purpose applications package for microcomputers. Its huge success can be attributed to several important factors typifying the many variations of the program which have since appeared on the market:

(i)   The extremely *user-friendly* presentation - facilities are selected by choosing options from menus, which call up further menus until the actual operation required is displayed and performed. There are on-line help facilities which the user can have displayed at any time;

(ii)   The same data can be used for each of the three main applications: for calculations, information retrieval or to provide data for the production of diagrams such as bar charts or pie diagrams;

(iii)   The large number of special functions by which almost every need can be met;

(iv)   The same command sequence and menu structures are used for each of the three functions, making the package very easy to learn;

(v)   Relatively cheap considering the number of functions supplied in the one package.

Integrated packages offering even more functions are now on the market. Many now offer wordprocessing in addition to the three original functions. A recent development combines these four with an expert system shell and a natural language interface to the database. One reviewer of this package noted that, although the program could do just about everything, it was so complicated that it was difficult to get it to do anything! Fortunately this is not generally true of integrated packages which are what can be considered (at least for the moment) the ultimate in general purpose applications programs.

Assignment   *Williamson's Operating System*

R. & G.H. Williamson Limited is a small building company based in Kendal. The high quality of their work has led to the rapid expansion of the business, which now employs over thirty full-time workers who are skilled in various aspects of building work. The company is owned by Gareth and Robert Williamson who carry out initial job estimates on site. The two directors plan to buy a computer system, primarily to carry out their general accounting procedures. They have already approached Sys-Time Ltd, a software house, but were disappointed with the advice which they received, partly because they themselves were a little vague about their requirements and partly because Sys-Time 'blinded them with science'.

You are employed as a trainee office manager and Gareth Williamson, being aware of your knowledge of computing, has asked you to explain to him the significance of a few of the terms that the Sys-Time consultant threw at him. He wants you to brief him so that he is better prepared when he meets the representative of another software house.

Task

Gareth Williamson wants to understand the meaning and significance to him of the terms:

(a)   operating systems;

(b)   integrated package;

(c)   spreadsheet;

(d)   wordprocessor;

(e)   database;

(f)   WIMPs.

Prepare notes explaining all these terms and suggesting the relevance and potential usefulness of each to his company.

Developmental Task

Identify particular commercial packages/versions belonging to each of the software categories listed above.

Chapter 12

Program Design

Introduction

One of the major problems which confronts the beginner faced with the task of writing a computer program, is where to start. How is it possible to organise program instructions to perform the required task, and how can the programmer be sure that the finished program will always perform as desired? The aim of this chapter is to answer these questions by introducing a program design technique which replaces inspiration with a simple logical sequence of steps which are easy to learn, understand and apply.

The technique is called *Jackson Structured Programming*, or *JSP*, and is fully described by Michael A. Jackson in his book 'Principles of Program Design'. The method has the following characteristics:

    (i) it depends on the application of a small number of simple, clearly defined steps;

    (ii) it can be taught because of (i);

    (iii) it is practical, resulting in programs which are easy to write, understand, test and maintain.

JSP is a *top-down* programming technique in which the programmer, starting from the premise that the complete program will be too difficult to comprehend in its entirety, breaks the problem down into a sequence of manageable components. Each such component is then broken down into smaller parts, and so on until a level is reached which cannot easily be further simplified. Without this technique, a programming problem can be too large and complex in its complete form. This process produces a program structure resembling a tree diagram as shown below:

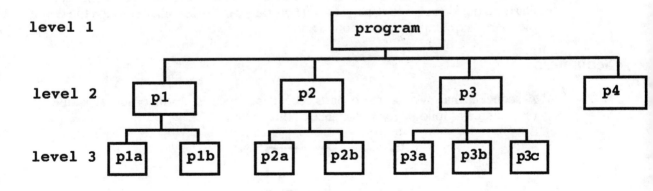

Each level lists the procedures (p1, p2 etc.) which provide a complete description of the program. The amount of detail increases with the level number. Thus the program can be considered equally to consist of the sequence p1..p2..p3..p4 or

p1a..p1b..p2a..p2b..p3a..p3b..p3c..p4.

p1a and p1b, for example, provide a more detailed picture of p1.

Basic Components of JSP Design

There are only four basic components:

(i) *Elementary Components* which are not further subdivided into constituent parts;

(ii) a *Sequence* of two or more parts occurring in order;

(iii) a *Selection* of one part from a number of alternatives;

(iv) an *Iteration* in which a single part is repeated zero or more times.

Each separate part of a sequence, selection or iteration may be a sequence, a selection or an iteration, so there is no limit to the complexity of structure which can be formed. For example, a sequence of three parts may be:

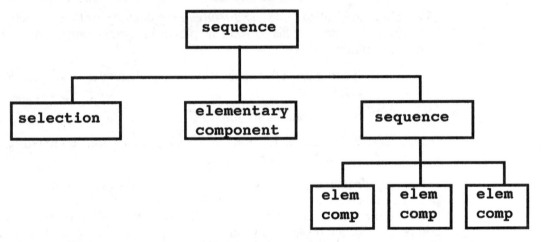

The structures developed using combinations of these four component types are equally useful for describing data structures as they are for describing program structures. This property forms the basis of JSP design, which uses descriptions of data structures to define the fundamental structure of the program. The next sections illustrate the idea of data structures and how they can be described through the use of the four basic components identified above.

Sequences

A sequence has two or more parts, occurring once each, in order. It would be represented as follows, for a sequence of three parts:

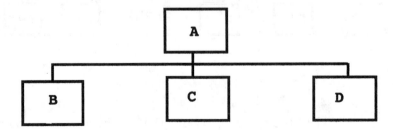

If we wish to describe a pack of cards which has been sorted into suits, we might consider it as being a sequence of four suits:

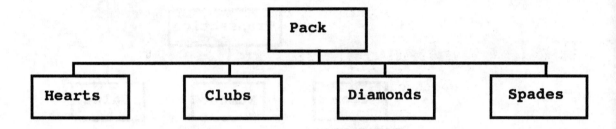

A meal might be considered to be a sequence of starter, main course and dessert:

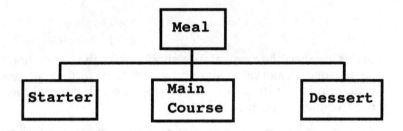

A file consisting of a header record (describing certain characteristics of the file, for instance) followed by a set of data records can be regarded as a sequence of two parts:

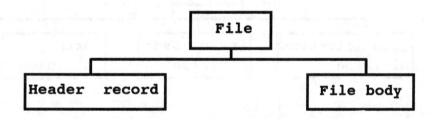

A computer-generated report of a sales file might consist of a list of transaction details giving item description, number sold and total selling price, followed by a grand total of the sales value:

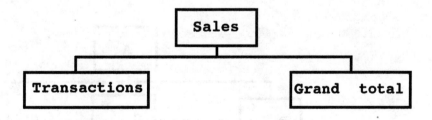

Each transaction could itself be regarded as a sequence of three parts: item description, number sold, and sales value. In fact the item description might also be recognised as a sequence of code number and name.

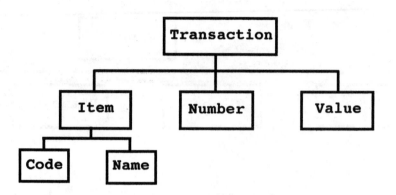

In this instance, the elementary components of the transaction would be code number, name, number, and value, since none of these is further defined. This hierarchical type of description illustrates the way in which a simple concept such as a sequence can give rise to quite complicated structures.

As a final example of a sequence, a COBOL program which consists of four divisions could be represented as the sequence

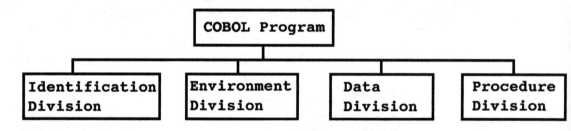

The examples illustrate that it is just as easy to describe a data structure as it is to describe a sequence of processes.

Selections

The selection component indicates what choices are available when a choice is to be made of one single part from several alternatives:

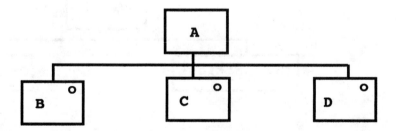

The small circles in the three boxes show that A is a selection and that only one of the three items is to be selected.

Suppose it is wished to represent the possible results when two people cut a pack of cards in order to see who has the higher card. The process could be represented as a sequence of two actions, the second of which can have one of two possible outcomes:

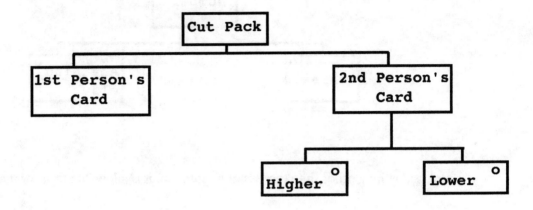

We could use this notation to describe a menu having a number of alternatives for each course:

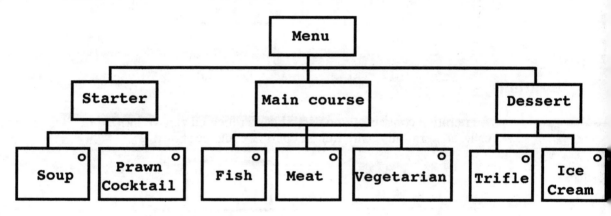

Similarly, in the sales file report described earlier, we might wish to differentiate between cash sales and credit sales for each transaction:

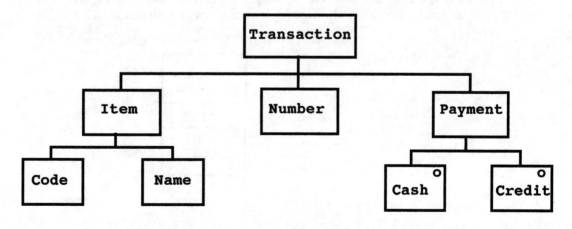

Sometimes a selection will consist of only one part which will be of interest while any other possibility is of no interest. For example, if we wished to count the number of times that three shows when a dice is thrown, it could be represented as follows:

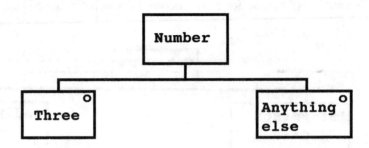

But as anything other than three is of no interest, it is allowable to show it as:

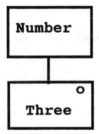

Iterations

An iteration consists of one part which is repeated zero or more times. Diagrammatically, an iteration A with iterated part B, could be shown as:

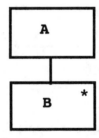

The asterisk indicates that B is repeated zero or more times, and A represents the complete process. A shuffled pack of cards can be represented as:

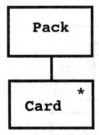

and the pack organised into suits would be:

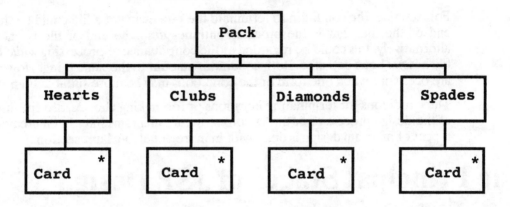

A file consisting of a header record followed by a set of data records becomes:

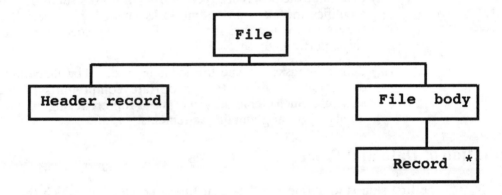

and our sales report can now show that the report consists of a number of lines, each showing the details of one transaction:

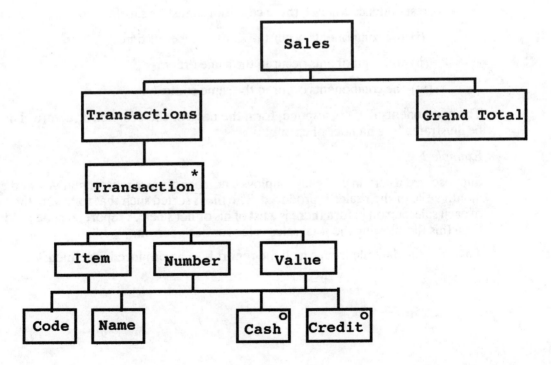

The iterated part of a process continues until some terminating condition is encountered, or only while some condition holds true.

For example, the condition to terminate the processing of a file could be the physical end of the file, that is the process continues *until* the end of file is encountered; alternatively, this could be regarded as the continuance of processing *while* the end of file has *not* been detected. Both conditions amount to the same thing. However, there are occasions when one form of the conditions may be more suitable than the other.

The conditions for terminating iterations or for making choices, are specified as part of the design process after the various structure diagrams have been created and this aspect of program design is dealt with in more detail in a later section.

The Principal Stages of JSP Design

The basic design technique is a three-step procedure:

(i) define the structure of the data to be processed;

(ii) determine the program structure from the data structures. This, in effect, identifies the main processing tasks needed to process the data. The program structure thus formed will generally need filling out when step (iii) is performed;

(iii) define the tasks to be performed in more detail by allocating elementary operations available to appropriate components of the program structure. Such elementary operations represent single (or at least small numbers) of programming statements.

Definition of Data and Program Structures

The first step is to define the data structures. The form in which the data is to be supplied to the program must be clearly stated, and the form of the data to be output from the program must also be defined. In addition, it is necessary to identify *correspondences* between all the data structures in order to combine them to form the program structure.

For a correspondence to exist, three conditions must be satisfied:

(i) the components occur the same number of times;

(ii) the components occur in the same order;

(iii) the components occur in the same context.

The components that correspond, form the basis of the program structure. This can be illustrated by a number of examples.

Example 1

Suppose that a certain company employs a number of sales representatives, and every month a file of their sales is produced. The file is sorted such that following the name of each salesperson in turn there is a list of his or her sales. A report must be produced from this file showing the total sales value for each person.

To begin, the data file from which the report is to be produced is defined:

This indicates that the sales file is an iteration of salesperson (there are a number of salespersons records), and salesperson is an iteration of sale (each salesperson has a number of sales figures).

The summary report that is required looks like this:

```
MicroPhile Computers

Sales Summary   Dec 1987

Salesperson          Total Sales (£)      Commission (£)
_____

J. Smith                 3275.62              263.56
H. Morgan                4456.40              345.22
P. Sheridan              3986.80              286.45
.....................    ....................  ....................
.....................    ....................  ....................
A. Morrow                2269.50              200.34
                         _____           _____

TOTALS                   52986.28             5032.66
                         _____           _____
```

The data structure would have the following representation:

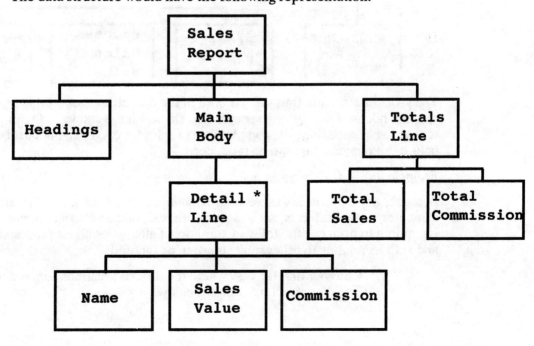

The Sales Report is a sequence of Headings, Main Body and Totals Line. The Main Body is an iteration of Detail Line which is to contain three items of information: Name, Sales Value and Commission. The Totals Line is a sequence of Total Sales and Total Commission.

The correspondences are

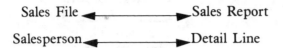

Sales File ⟷ Sales Report

Salesperson ⟷ Detail Line

The first correspondence is quite obvious since it is the sales file which is used to produce the sales report.

The second correspondence results from the fact that for each salesperson a single line is required which is the sales summary for that person.

It is usual to draw the data structures side-by-side with arrowed lines indicating the correspondence.(This is shown in the previous figure).

The two structures are now combined into a program structure in which the components represent processing operations:

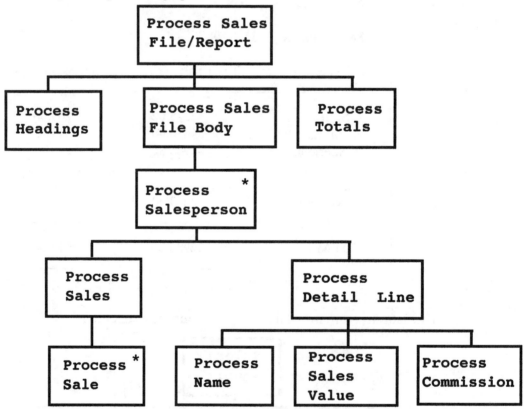

The program structure thus reflects both of the data structures used in its design. The correspondence between Salesperson and Detail Line is shown in the program structure as a sequence since the complete set of sales for each person must be processed before the summary line can be produced.

Example 2

A sequential file consists of records containing details of magazine articles about computer-related subjects, such as hardware, software and programming. A program is required to print out the titles and authors of all articles about programming. Titles and authors relating to other subjects are to be ignored.

(i) Consider first the case where the articles are in random order of subject. The data structure is shown below.

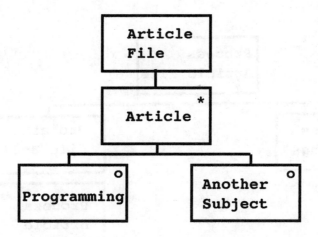

The output structure is of the form:

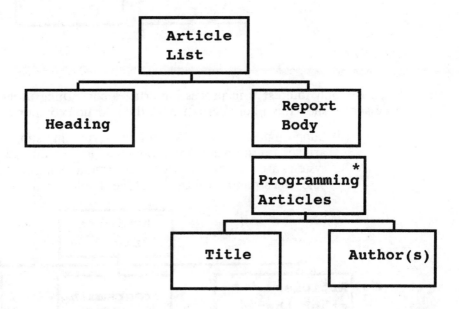

The correspondences in this case are:

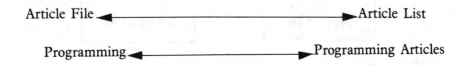

The second correspondence is between the Programming component of Articles in the Article File and the Programming Articles component of the selection in the Article List report. Because the file is not sequenced according to subject, it is necessary for the whole Article File to be processed to allow the extraction of Programming articles as and when they are reached.

The program structure is then

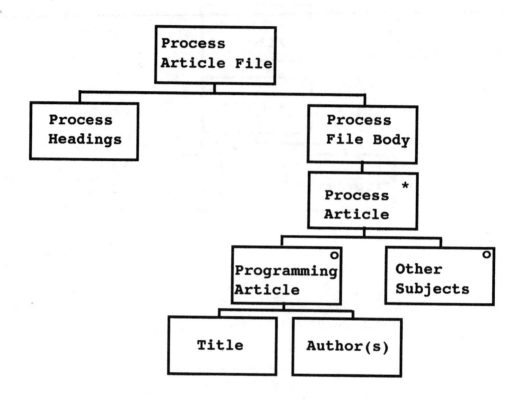

Since the only interest is in processing articles concerning programming, it is not necessary to show the other alternative for the selection component.

(ii) Suppose now that the file has been sorted into subject order, so that all articles on software are grouped together, all articles on operating systems are together, all articles on programming are together and so on. The data structure for the input file is now as follows:

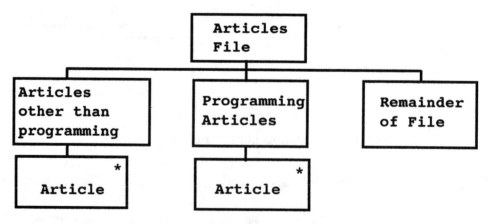

where the file now may be considered to consist of three parts:

(i) a number of articles not relating to programming;

(ii) a number of articles on programming;

(iii) the rest of the file, which is of no interest.

Notice that in this instance the selection component is missing, and it is replaced by two iterations, one of unwanted records and the other of records of interest. The report structure is still the same, but the correspondence is now between Programming Articles in the Articles File and Report Body in the report file. The sorting of the file into subject order means that the records on programming are grouped together and therefore correspond directly to the data required in the report.

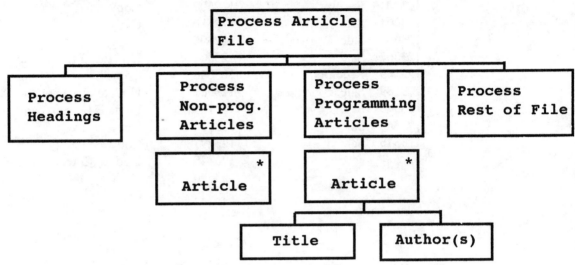

Notice that the final procedure, Process Rest of File, does not involve an iteration; once the subject changes from programming to something else, the processing is finished and the program in effect stops.

Example 3

The examples above deal with the process of combining a single input file with a single output file to produce a program structure. However there are an important class of processing problems which involve two input files whose records need to be *matched* or *collated*.

The process might, for example, require the matching of a Master File of items of stock and a Transaction File containing details of items received from suppliers or sold to customers. If both of these files are in some particular order (for instance in ascending order of stock reference number) then updating the Master File involves reading a transaction record and then attempting to find a stock record in the Master File with the same key value (in this case, the stock reference number). If it is assumed that there should be a stock record for every transaction then, in the process of comparing a transaction record key value with a stock record key value, a number of situations can arise:

(i)   The transaction record key has a value which is greater than the stock record key. In this instance the stock record does not have a matching transaction and does not require updating. The stock record merely needs to be copied to the file holding the updated stock records. We will call this new file the Updated Master File;

(ii)   The transaction record key is the same value as the stock record key. Here it is necessary to determine the nature of the transaction, whether it is a sale or receipt, before processing the stock record. The updated record will then be written to the Updated Master File;

(iii)   The transaction record key has a value which is less than the stock record key. This situation should not arise in this example and therefore indicates that an error has occurred, possibly as a result of the transaction file being out of sequence. To help clarify the nature of the

processing tasks, consider the following table showing a
list of transaction record keys, type of transaction and
keys of records in the Master File to be updated:

Trans	Type	Master File	Action
123001	Receipt	122500	Copy
123001	Sale	122570	Copy
123001	Sale	122595	Copy
123067	Sale	123001	Update (3 trans) and Write
123189	Receipt	123048	Copy
123189	Sale	123067	Update (1 trans) and Write
123345	Sale	123189	Update (2 trans) and Write
123345	Sale	123224	Copy
123345	Sale	123297	Copy
		123345	Update (3 trans) and Write
		123890	Copy
		....	Copy
	etc		....
		....	Copy
		134347	Copy

Notice that it is possible to have several transactions for the same stock record in the
Master File. The first three records of the Master File do not have any matching
transaction records and therefore are copied to the Updated Master File without
modification. All stock records occurring after the end of the Transaction File are also
written to the new Updated Master File.

The data structures and correspondences for this example are therefore

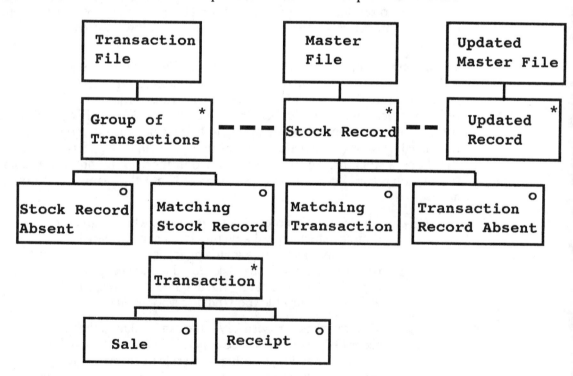

The Transaction File is considered to contain a number of groups of transactions, each
group containing records with the same key value (stock reference number); each
record in the group is used to update a single stock record from the Master File. In the
table described earlier, the stock item with key value 123001 has a group of three
transactions comprising a receipt and two sales transactions, whereas stock item 122570
has no transactions associated with it (that is, the transaction record is absent).

The outline program structure is

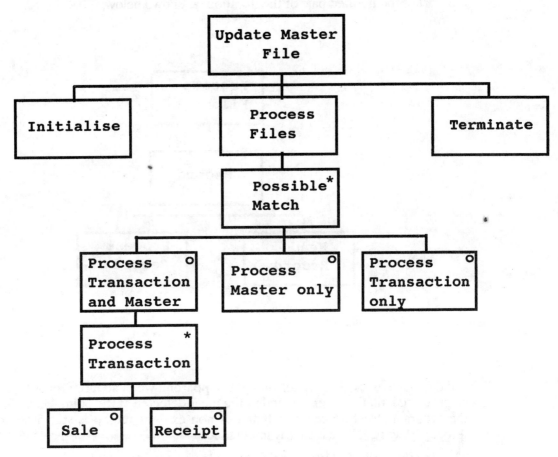

Before describing the final stage of the design process, it is important to note that in this example it is assumed that before the iteration "Process Master File" is commenced, there is a pair of records ready for testing for a "Possible Match"; this means that a record from each of the files has been read in preparation for processing. The very nature of the iteration must be tested at the commencement of the iteration, and in this instance the end of the Master File and the Transaction File is the required condition for termination of the iteration. Reading a sequential file and performing some processing until there are no more records left to process (that is, when the end of the file is detected) would thus require the following program structure:

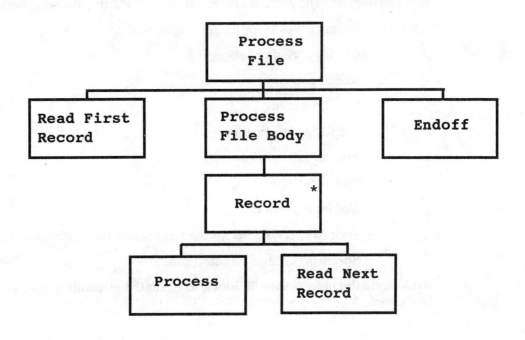

Compare this scheme with the perhaps more obvious approach of reading a record at the start of the iterated part of the iteration, as shown below,

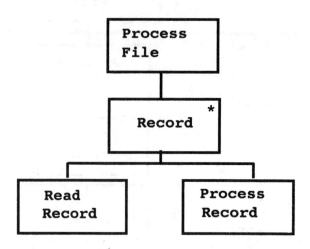

and the inadequacy of the latter should be apparent: when no more records remain to be processed, that is, when the end of the file is detected at the point "Read Record", the program structure requires that this non-existent record is still processed (by 'Process Record')! This is clearly impossible.

The technique, illustrated in the first example above, of reading the first record as soon as possible and subsequently reading at the completion of the processing of a record, is called *reading ahead*. It is important to note that the processing of each record *concludes* with reading another record, so that there is always a record ready for processing, and the end of the file can be detected at the end of each iteration.

Allocation of Elementary Operations

The final stage in the design technique is to allocate elementary operations to the program structure. The elementary operations include the following types :

> Opening files ready for reading or writing;
>
> Closing files after processing;
>
> Reading records;
>
> Writing records;
>
> Displaying information;
>
> Printing information;
>
> Incrementing counts;
>
> Making calculations;
>
> Specifying conditions for the termination (or continuance) of iterations;
>
> Specifying criteria for selections.

To illustrate the process we will list and allocate the elementary operations required for Example 3.

Initialisation operations:

    1. Open Master File for Input

    2. Open Updated Stock File for Output

    3. Open Transaction File for Input

Program Termination operations:

    4. Close Master File

    5. Close Updated Stock File

    6. Close Transaction File

    7. Stop

Input/Output operations:

    8. Read Master File

    9. Read Transaction File

    10. Write Updated Stock Record

Processing operations:

    11. Subtract number of sales from stock level

    12. Add receipts to stock level

    13. Display error message: "No stock record for this transaction"

    14. Store transaction record key

Iteration conditions:

    C1. Until End of Master File and Transaction File

    C2. Until change of transaction record key

Selection conditions:

    C3. Transaction record key matches stock record key

    C4. Transaction record key > stock record key

    C5. Transaction record key < stock record key

    C6. Transaction type = Sale

    C7. Transaction type = Receipt.

It is now possible to add some detail to the program structure diagram:

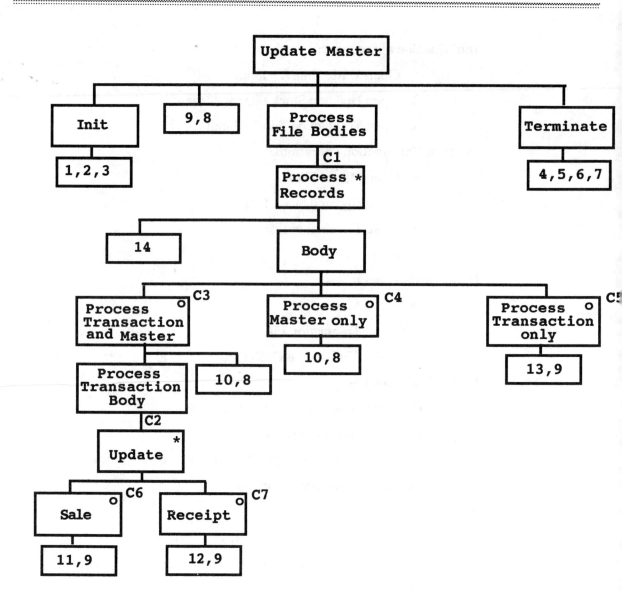

Examination of the program structure above might suggest the possibility of 'improving' its efficiency by combining such operations as "9. Read Transaction File" or "8. Read Master File", both of which appear to be repeated unnecessarily. For example, operation 9 could be extracted from the Sale and Receipt operations and it could become a separate operation following the selection:

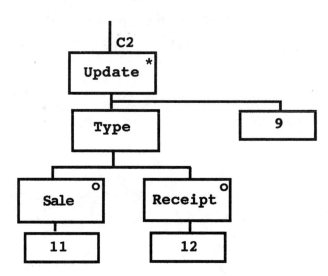

Though this simplified program structure would still be correct, the danger is that should it be necessary to modify the program at some later date, unnecessary complications might result. In his book "Principles of Program Design", M.A. Jackson, talking about this process of program optimisation, provides two rules:

> Rule 1: Don't do it

> Rule 2: Don't do it yet

meaning that it is best, in the interests of program clarity, not to optimise the structure at all, but if you must do it, first begin within an unoptimised structure and then optimise it later.

To summarise, the steps by which the final program structure is defined are as follow:

1.   Define the structure of the data to be processed. In many data processing applications these will be files.

2.   Define the structure of the desired result of the processing. This output could be in the form of files or printed reports for instance.

3.   Identify the correspondences between the data structures in order to help to clarify the program structure.

4.   Define the outline program structure by combining the data structures and utilising the correspondences identified.

5.   List the elementary operations, grouped under the headings:

      Initialisation

      Program termination

      Input/Output

      Processing

      Iteration conditions

      Selection conditions.

6.   Assign these elementary operations to each part of the outline program structure. These elementary operations should be capable of being easily converted into one or more instructions in the target language. If the program structure has been defined well, the elementary operations should be easy to identify.

7.   Under some circumstances it may be necessary to fill out the program structure with additional operations. A typical example of this is when the reading ahead approach to file processing is incorporated. The outline program structure might look like this:

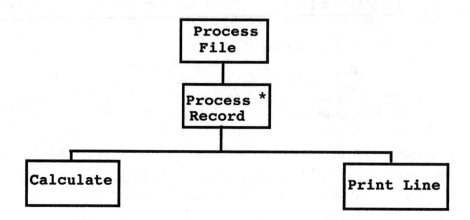

When more detail is added, it might then become

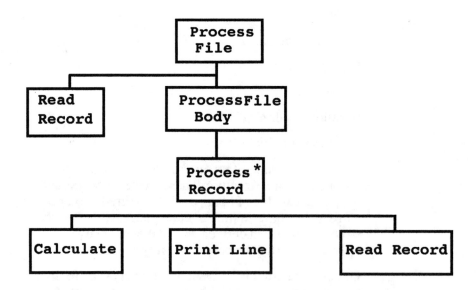

Assignment   *The Squash Club*

The Arnside Squash Club in Guildford, Surrey, has a large and thriving membership, running about sixteen leagues held over six-week periods. Each league has five players and each member of a league must play at least three games during the six weeks, to stay in the league. At the end of six weeks, the points for each player are totalled and new leagues are drawn up according to the points placings. The club is run by a committee of six members, plus a chairperson and secretary.

The club has bought an Archimedes microcomputer system with twin disk drives, a monitor and a printer, which they intend to use for the membership records and league placings. A database package is to be used for the membership records, but the club's secretary, Bill Norris, has volunteered to write programs to set up and record the progress of the squash leagues. Although Bill has a good working knowledge of the BASIC language, he is unfamiliar with the techniques used by professional programmers to plan and develop their programs. You are a member of the club committee and as a trainee programmer with a local firm, you have gained some experience of program development techniques.

Task

1. **Explain the need for programming standards;**

2. **Write a set of formal guidelines for Bill Norris, explaining the stages he should follow, from the initial consideration of the problem to the production of a fully operational program;**

3. **Suggest the techniques and programming aids he may use during each stage.**

Chapter 13

Pseudocode

Pseudocode, or *schematic logic* as it is sometimes termed, offers a transition stage between the two-dimensional form of the program structure diagram and the final *top-to-bottom* program coded in the target language. Programmers generally find pseudocode easier to use when actually coding programs. In fact, some recent high-level languages accept pseudocode as the source language and convert it to a language such as COBOL automatically.

Another use of pseudocode is in the presentation of algorithms, that is, as a formal way of describing a processing technique, without any attempt to produce a program from it. (Numerous examples of this occur in the chapters on data structures and sorting techniques).

The pseudocode presented here is similar in form to Pascal, a language well known for its structured format.

Each of the structures discussed in the previous chapter has its equivalent form in pseudocode. For example, a sequence of the elementary operations P1, P2 and P3 in pseudocode would be:

```
begin
   P1
   P2
   P3
end
```

For example, a pseudocode sequence might be:

```
begin
     Add 1 to count
     Accumulate month total
     Accumulate year total
end
```

This sequence consists of three elementary operations which are to be executed in the order shown.

Selections can be expressed in a number of ways in pseudocode depending on the number of alternatives. The simplest form is where a single operation is to be performed if a certain condition is true:

```
if C1 then P1
```

Example:

```
if new page then print heading
```

Where several operations are to be performed it would be written

```
if C1 then
       P1
       P2
       P3
endif
```

Example:

```
if new page then
        print page heading
        print page number
        print column headings
endif
```

For a selection of one operation from two we would write

```
if C1 then
        P1
else
        P2
endif
```

where C1 is a condition which when true causes operation P1 to be executed, and when false causes P2 to be executed.

Example:

```
if batch record then
        check batch totals
        print batch status report
else
        process data record
        read next record
endif
```

Where there is to be a selection of one operation from a number of alternatives, the pseudocode takes the form

```
if        C1 then P1
else if C2 then P2
else if C3 then P3
else if C4 then P4
    etc.
endif
```

Example:

```
if        record type = "A" then Add record to file
else if record type = "D" then Delete record from file
else if record type = "T" then Update record
endif
```

Iterations may also be expressed in a number of ways. Where it is known at the beginning of the loop the number of repetitions to be performed, we can write

```
for var := a to b
        P1
        P2
        P3
        etc.
endfor
```

where *var* is a control variable which starts at the value of *a* and increases in unit increments each time the operations P1, P2 ... have all been executed. The loop terminates when *var* exceeds the value of *b*.

Example:

```
for i := 1 to 10
        read X
        s := s + X
endfor
```

This would read ten numbers and accumulate them in *s*.

If the number of repetitions is not known in advance, then the *while* form can be used:

```
while C1
      P1
      P2
      P3
      etc.
endwhile
```

Example:

```
while not end of file
      process record
      increment record count
      read next record
endwhile
```

A third way to represent iteration is shown below:

```
repeat
      P1
      P2
      P3
      etc.
until C1
```

Here, C1, the condition for terminating the iteration, is at the end of the sequence of operations to be repeated. This means that these operations will be executed at least once; with the *while* construct the operations to be repeated need not be executed at all if the termination condition is true initially.

Example:

```
repeat
      read keyboard
until key pressed
```

With reference to our stock file example (example 3) at the end of the previous chapter, the program structure, when converted to pseudocode, starts to take on the appearance of a computer program, as shown below. Note that comments are enclosed in braces: {...}

```
begin
 {open files}
 open transaction file for input
 open master file for input
 open updated stock file for output
 {read first record in each file ready for processing}
 read transaction file
 read master file
 {start of main processing loop}
 while more transactions
    store transaction record key in temp-key
       if  transaction record key = stock record key then
       {update master record with each matching transaction}
       while transaction rec key = temp-key
        if type = sale then
           subtract no. of sales from stock level
           read transaction file
        else if type = receipt then
           add receipts to stock level
           read transaction file
        endif
       endwhile
       write updated stock record
       read master file
    else if  transaction record key > stock record key then
       {just copy master record to updated stock file}
```

```
            write updated stock record
            read master file
        else if transaction record key < stock record key then
            {transactions probably out of sequence}
            display error message
            read transaction file
        endif
    endwhile
    close transaction file
    {transfer any remaining master file records}
    while more master file records
        copy master record to stock record
        write updated stock record
        read master file
    endwhile
    close master file
    close updated stock file
end
```

Notice that the indentation of components helps to clarify the program structure and make the logic easy to follow. However, more complex program structures, with greater depths of embedded components, may become rather cumbersome if written in this manner. Under such circumstances it is preferable to make reference to "chunks" of components, or *procedures,* so that the logic of the program does not become obscured by too much detail. The pseudocode above, for example, could have been written in a modular form using procedures as illustrated below:

```
begin
 procedure initialise {open files}
 {read first record in each file ready for processing}
 read transaction file
 read master file
 {start of main processing loop}
 while more transactions
    procedure process_transactions
 endwhile
 close transaction file
 {transfer any remaining master file records}
 procedure transfer_remaining_records
 procedure terminate
end
{Procedure definitions:}

define procedure initialise
begin
 {open files}
 open transaction file for input
 open master file for input
 open updated stock file for output
end

define procedure process_transactions
begin
    store transaction record key in temp-key
      if   transaction record key = stock record key then
         procedure update
         write updated stock record
         read master file
      else if  transaction record key > stock record key then
         {just copy master record to updated stock file}
         write updated stock record
```

```
            read master file
        else if transaction record key <stock record key then
            {transactions probably out of sequence}
            display error message
            read transaction file
        endif
end

define procedure update
begin
  {update master record with each matching transaction}
  while transaction rec key = temp-key
    if type = sale then
        subtract no. of sales from stock level
        read transaction file
    else if type = receipt then
        add receipts to stock level
        read transaction file
    endif
  endwhile
end

define procedure transfer_remaining_records
begin
  while more master file records
    copy master record to stock record
    write updated stock record
    read master file
  endwhile
end

define procedure terminate
begin
 close master file
 close updated stock file
end
```

This arrangement for pseudocode has the added advantage of resembling the way that languages such as Pascal allow programs to be written, and it also facilitates the adoption of a top-down approach to program development.

Chapter 14

Coding the Program

Coding the Program

Introduction

The program design stages discussed in the previous two chapters serve to define the structure of a program and the operations that it must perform. In order to implement the program, these operations must subsequently be realised in the syntax of the target language, and this is the task to be discussed here.

We have adopted the approach of implementing the same simple task involving text processing in three widely used languages, namely BASIC, Pascal and C, in order to compare the syntax of the three languages. As far as possible, within the constraints of the three languages, the programs have been written so that they may be compared easily. The problem is first described with the aid of pseudocode, which is then translated into each of the target languages in turn. The programs are described only briefly, with particular attention being paid to structured programming; it has been assumed that the reader has had some programming experience with at least one of these languages, so that explanations of common programming principles may be kept to a minimum.

The following language implementations have been used to produce the three programs presented here:

BASIC	Microsoft BASIC
Pascal	Borland Turbo Pascal
C	Borland Turbo C

Note that a brief general description of each of these languages is provided in Chapter 10, and a complete chapter has been devoted to programming in COBOL.

A Text Processing Problem

The task that is to be implemented is related to natural language processing which deals with the problem of being able to handle instructions written in ordinary English. One of the first requirements of a program designed to analyse natural language might be to isolate the separate words in a sentence and perhaps convert all lower case letters to upper case to facilitate further processing; this is the task to be addressed here.

The program is required to perform the following operations:

(i) Read and store a complete sentence entered at a keyboard.

(ii) Identify the start and end of each individual word in the sentence by storing a pair of pointers in a two-dimensional array.

(iii) Convert any lower case characters in the sentence to upper case.

(iv) Print the individual words in the sentence on separate lines.

For example, suppose that the following sentence is to be processed:

```
0         1            2            3            4
1234567890123456789012345678901234567890
     Print  all  account    names
```

The program needs to set up an array with start and end pointers as shown below:

	Word	Start	End
1	Print	6	10
2	all	13	15
3	account	18	24
4	names	28	32

The pseudocode and the programs all use a two dimensional array, *wordptr*(20,2) to store these pointers. The first subscript is the word number, allowing a maximum of 20 words, and the second subscript is for the two pointer, so that for the third word "account",

$$wordptr(3,1) = 18 \quad and \quad wordptr(3,2) = 24$$

As each character in a word is scanned, it is tested for being an ASCII character in the range 97 to 122, that is a lower case character; if it is in that range then it is converted to a capital letter by subtracting 32 from its ASCII value (because upper case letters are in the range 65 to 90).

The variable *wordcount* is incremented each time a new word is detected; the variable *ptr* specifies the position within the sentence of the current character being scanned; *len* stores the length of the sentence stored in the string variable *sentence*; the notation *sentence(ptr)* is used to indicate the character at the position given by *ptr* (thus when *ptr* has the value 9, *sentence(ptr)* is the letter "n").

All of the words are printed out in order after the complete sentence has been scanned:

```
PRINT
ALL
ACCOUNT
NAMES
```

The pseudocode for the procedures outlined above is as follows:

Pseudo-code for Example Programs

```
begin
   ptr := 1
   wordcount := 0
   read sentence
   len := length of sentence
   {Process each character in the sentence}
   while ptr less than or equal to len
         add 1 to wordcount
         {Find first non-blank character}
         while (sentence(ptr) equals blank) and (ptr < len )
           ptr := ptr + 1
         endwhile
         {Store pointer to start of word}
         wordptr(wordcount,1) := ptr
         {Find end of word}
         while (sentence(ptr) <> blank) and (ptr < len)
            {Convert any lower case characters to upper case}
            if sentence(ptr) is a lower case letter then
                sentence(ptr) := equivalent upper case letter
            endif
           ptr := ptr + 1
         endwhile
         {Store pointer to end of word}
         wordptr(wordcount,2) := ptr - 1
   endwhile
```

```
        {Print all of the words}
        for i := 1 to wordcount
            print characters between wordptr(i,1) and wordptr(i,2)
        endfor
end
```

The BASIC Implementation

Program Listing

```
10    DIM WORDPTR(20,2)
20    PTR = 1
40    WORDCOUNT = 0
45    BLANK$ = " "
47    PRINT "Type sentence followed by <Enter>:"
50    INPUT SENTENCE$
60    L=LEN(SENTENCE$)
65    REM Process each character in the sentence
70    WHILE PTR <= L
80      WORDCOUNT = WORDCOUNT + 1
85      REM Find first non-blank character
90      WHILE (MID$(SENTENCE$,PTR,1) = BLANK$) AND (PTR < L)
100       PTR = PTR + 1
110     WEND
120     REM Store pointer to start of word
125     WORDPTR(WORDCOUNT,1) = PTR
127     REM Find end of word
130     WHILE (MID$(SENTENCE$,PTR,1) <> BLANK$) AND (PTR < L)
131     REM Convert any lower case characters to upper case
132       ASKEY=ASC(MID$(SENTENCE$,PTR,1))
134       IF ASKEY> = 97 AND ASKEY <= 122 THEN
              MID$(SENTENCE$,PTR,1) = CHR$(ASKEY-32)
140       PTR = PTR + 1
150     WEND
160     REM Store pointer to end of word
170     WORDPTR(WORDCOUNT,2) = PTR - 1
185 WEND
187 PRINT "Here are the words of the sentence in upper case: "
188 REM Print all of the words
190 FOR I = 1 TO WORDCOUNT
200   PTR = WORDPTR(I,1)
210   WORDLEN = WORDPTR(I,2) - WORDPTR(I,1) + 1
220   PRINT MID$(SENTENCE$,PTR,WORDLEN)
230 NEXT I
240 END
```

Program Notes

1.   In BASIC, arrays must be declared in a DIM (DIMension) statement prior to using an array variable, hence the first statement

```
        10    DIM WORDPTR(20,2)
```

Unlike Pascal and C, each line in a BASIC program must have a line number indicating the sequential order of executing instructions.

Other variable types do not need to be declared prior to use. String variables, such as BLANK$ and SENTENCE$, are denoted by the presence of a $ sign at the end of the variable name.

2.   The PRINT statement produces output on the computer's VDU. Text literals are enclosed in speech marks and, unless it is terminated with a comma or semi-colon, a

PRINT statement will automatically generate a line feed. Thus the statement

```
47   PRINT "Type sentence followed by <Enter> "
```

produces the message

```
Type sentence followed by <Enter>
```

on the screen.

3. INPUT accepts input from the keyboard and stores the data in the specified variable. The input must be terminated by pressing the <Enter> key (sometimes labelled <Return>).

4. The LEN function returns the length of the string argument.

5. REM is used for comments. The BASIC interpreter ignores REM statements.

6. WHILE repeatedly executes all statements up to the next WEND encountered as long as the specified condition is true. Thus the statements between lines 70 to 185 are repeatedly executed while the value of PTR is less than or equal to LEN (the length, in characters, of the sentence). When PTR exceeds LEN, the loop is terminated and line 187 is executed.

7. The function MID$(SENTENCE$,PTR,1) returns a string consisting of the single character at position PTR within SENTENCE$. The third argument of the function, in this instance "1", specifies how many characters are to be extracted starting at the position specified by the second argument. Thus, the conditional expression

```
MID$(SENTENCE$,PTR,1) = BLANK$
```

compares the character at position PTR with a space, and will either be true or false.

The IF statement requires a conditional expression which evaluates to true or false; if the condition is true, the statement(s) following the word THEN are executed, otherwise these statements are ignored. BASIC also supports the use of the word ELSE which is followed by an alternative set of statements to be executed if the condition is false.

8. The function ASC() returns the ASCII value of the single character string argument. Thus ASC(MID$(SENTENCE$,PTR,1)) returns the ASCII value of the character at position PTR. CHR$() does the reverse of this by returning the character represented by the ASCII code supplied as its single argument. Thus , if the variable ASKEY contained the value 98 (the ASCII code for the letter "b"), CHR$(ASKEY-32) would return the character "B" which has ASCII code 66 (that is, 98 - 32).

9. Line 134 tests the current character for lower case and, if true, replaces it with the equivalent upper case character.

10. BASIC also supports the use of a FOR..NEXT loop which repeats the statements between FOR and NEXT a predefined number of times. A control variable is set to a starting value and is automatically incremented every time the loop is completed until it exceeds a specified value. Thus

```
FOR I = 1 TO WORDCOUNT
. . . .
. . . .
NEXT I
```

sets the control variable I to 1 and repeats the appropriate statements until I exceeds the value stored in WORDCOUNT.

In this instance, the FOR..NEXT loop spanning lines 190 to 230 is used to print each individual word in the sentence.

The Pascal Implementation

Program Listing

```
program sepsen(input,output);
const blank=' ';
var     ptr, wordcount, i,
          askey, len, wordlen :integer;
                    wordptr    :array[1..20,1..2] of integer;
                    sentence   :string[255];
begin
  ptr:=1;
  wordcount:=0;
  writeln('Type sentence followed by <Enter>:');
  readln(sentence);
  len:=length(sentence);
  {Process each character in the sentence}
  while (ptr <= len) do
    begin
      wordcount:=wordcount + 1;
      {Find first non-blank character}
      while (sentence[ptr] = blank) and (ptr < len) do
        begin
         ptr:=ptr + 1;
        end;
      {Store pointer to start of word}
      wordptr[wordcount,1]:=ptr;
      {Find end of word}
      while (sentence[ptr] <> blank) and (ptr < len) do
        begin
        {Convert any lower case characters to upper case}
         askey:=ord(sentence[ptr]);
         if (askey >= 97) and (askey <= 122) then
                 sentence[ptr]:=chr(askey-32);
         ptr:=ptr + 1;
        end;
      {Store pointer to end of word}
      wordptr[wordcount,2]:=ptr - 1;
    end;
  writeln('Here are the words of the sentence in upper case: ');
  {Print all of the words}
  for i:= 1 to wordcount do
    begin
     ptr:=wordptr[i,1];
     wordlen:=wordptr[i,2] - wordptr[i,1] + 1;
     writeln(copy(sentence,ptr,wordlen));
    end;
end.
```

Program Notes

1. A Pascal program must be assigned a name at the beginning of the program. The parameters inside the brackets in the statement

```
        program sepsen(input, output);
```

indicate that the keyboard and the VDU are to be used for input and output purposes respectively.

2. All variables and constants must be declared at the beginning of the program. The type of each variable must be specified.

3.   The keyword *begin* indicates the start of the executable code, and the end of the code is denoted by *end* followed by a period.

4.   The end of a statement is usually indicated by a semi-colon, though there are certain occasions where this is not necessary.

5.   *writeln()* is used in this instance to display a string literal on the VDU, though it may also be used to write data to disk files. It automatically produces a line feed after displaying the item(s) enclosed in brackets. It is comparable to the *PRINT* statement in BASIC.

readln() is the equivalent of INPUT in BASIC for accepting data typed in at a keyboard.

6.   Comments are enclosed in braces {....} or (*.....*) and are ignored by the compiler.

7.   Blocks of statements, that is, a sequence of one or more statements, are enclosed between *begin* and *end* keywords.

8.   Unlike the equivalent instruction in BASIC, the *while .... do* statement in Pascal does not have a special end keyword; if more than a single statement is to be repeated, the statements are blocked as described in note 7 above.

As usual, the *while* loop terminates when the specified condition becomes false.

9.   Array elements are enclosed in square brackets. The array element *sentence[ptr]* refers to the single character at the position specified by the contents of the integer variable *ptr*.

10.   The *ord()* function returns the ASCII value of the character supplied as its argument; this is similar to the *ASC()* function in BASIC. Similarly, the *chr()* function returns the character equivalent to the ASCII code supplied as the argument to the function, as does the *CHR$()* function in BASIC.

11.   The *for...do* loop in Pascal again uses the block structure approach when repeating more than a single statement. The control variable is used in the same manner as for BASIC.

12.   *copy()* is a function which returns a substring of its first argument in an identical manner to *MID$()* in BASIC.

The C Implementation

Program Listing

```
#include <stdio.h>
main()
{
    int ptr, wordcount, i, len, askey, wordlen,
        wordptr[20][2];
    char *blank, sentence[256];
    blank = " ";
    ptr = 0;
    wordcount = 0;
    puts("Type sentence followed  by <Enter>:\n ");
    gets(sentence);
    len = strlen(sentence) - 1;
    \*Process each character in the sentence*\
    while (ptr <= len)
       {
         wordcount = wordcount + 1;
         \* Find first non-blank character *\
         while ( *(sentence + ptr)  == *blank && ptr <= len )
           {
             ptr = ptr + 1;
```

```
        }
        \* Store pointer to start of word *\
        wordptr [wordcount] [1] = ptr;
        \* Find end of word *\
        while ( *(sentence + ptr) != *blank && ptr <= len )
          {
            \* Convert any lower case characters to upper case *\
            askey = *(sentence + ptr);
            if (askey >= 97 && askey <= 122)
                *(sentence + ptr) = askey - 32;
            ptr = ptr + 1;
          }
        \* Store pointer to end of word *\
          wordptr [wordcount] [2] = ptr - 1;
        }
    puts("Here are the words of the sentence in upper case:\n");
    \* Print all of the words *\
    for (i =1; i  wordcount; i++)
      {
        ptr = wordptr [i] [1];
        wordlen = wordptr [i] [2] - wordptr [i] [1] + 1;
        *(sentence + ptr + wordlen) = 0;
        puts (sentence + ptr);
      }
    },
```

Program Notes

1.   The first line of the program is a directive to the compiler specifying a library of functions concerned with standard input-output operations.

2.   *main*() declares that the mainline program code follows.

3.   Braces, that is { and }, are used to specify blocks of code in the same way that *begin* and *end* are used in Pascal.

4.   Variables must be declared at the beginning of the program. Again this is similar to Pascal. Arrays of more than one dimension must be declared with the size of each subscript enclosed in square brackets: *wordptr[20][2]*.

Strings are handled by means of pointers. Thus, the intepretation of *sentence[256]* is that 256 bytes are to be reserved starting at the memory address stored in the pointer *sentence*. The asterisk(*) is an indirection operator and indicates that, for example, *blank* is to be regarded as a pointer to a string which is yet to be defined. The assignment

```
        blank = " "
```

assigns the starting address of the string (a single space in this instance) to the pointer variable *blank*.

5.   The *puts* verb is used to display the contents of strings on the VDU according to the format specified by the literal between the quotation marks. The statement

```
        puts("Type sentence followed  by <Enter>:\n ");
```

causes the message

```
        Type sentence followed by <Enter>:
```

to be displayed, followed by a line feed (because of the presence of the \n).

6.   The *gets* verb stores alphanumeric data entered at the keyboard at the memory location specified. Thus

```
        gets (sentence);
```

stores the characters typed in at the keyboard starting at the location contained in the string pointer *sentence.* Strings are stored in ASCII code terminated with ASCII 0.

7.   Relational expressions use identical relational operators to those in Pascal except for the equality and inequality operators: in Pascal they are = and <> respectively; in C they are ==, for equality, to differentiate it from assignment, and != for inequality. Logical operators have their own symbols: && means and, || means or, ! means not. Thus the compound relational expression

```
( *(sentence + ptr) == *blank && ptr <= len )
```

means: "the character at memory location *(sentence + ptr)* is the same as the character at the memory location given in *blank,* and *ptr* is less or equal to *len*".

This expression will have a value of true or false.

8.   The *for* loop, again, should be fairly recognisable: the keyword *for* is followed by three expressions separated by semi-colons. The first expression defines the initial value of the control variable; the second expression is the condition for continuation of the iteration; the third expression usually specifies how the control variable is to be modified (*i++* means increment *i*).

9.   The manner in which the words are printed out at the end of the program diverges slightly from the other two versions of the program because of the way that strings are handled in C. The statement

```
*(sentence + ptr + wordlen) = 0;
```

inserts a string terminator at the end of the word to be printed by merely replacing a blank with the value 0. Remember that the * means "the location pointed to by", so *(sentence + ptr + wordlen)* is the address of the first space after the current word. The word is then printed using

```
puts(sentence + ptr);
```

Assignment   *Bugbusters Ltd.*

As a junior programmer for Bugbusters Ltd., a software house noted for its wide experience and varied programming services, you have been asked by a customer to tailor a standard file updating program to the particular dialect of the programming language that his computer supports. The source code that is to be used is that of the program listed on page 188.

Task

Identify various forms of control structures implemented in the target dialect of the required language (that is, the high level language you are currently using, or are familiar with) and convert the program given on page 188 to that dialect.

Developmental Task

In order to test the program it will be necessary to create two files: a Master Stock File and a Transaction File (see the chapter on documentation for the details of these files). You may need to write simple programs to create the files or use a text editor if such is available.

Chapter 15

Program Debugging and Testing

Introduction

This part of the chapter examines the processes used to debug and test a program. Once the program has been written, it must go through two stages in order to remove errors which almost inevitably will be present. No matter how much care has been taken in the design and coding of a program,it is very likely to contain errors in syntax, that is incorrectly formed statements, and almost as likely to also contain errors in logic. *Debugging* is the term given to the process of detecting and correcting these errors or *bugs*.

The first stage in the removal of errors is the correction of syntax errors and obvious errors in logic. Fortunately for the programmer, modern interpreters and compilers provide considerable assistance in the detection of syntax errors in the source code. Malformed statements will be reported by a compiler after it has attempted to compile the source code; an interpreter will report illegal statements as it attempts to execute them. Logic errors, however, are largely undetectable by the translating program. These are errors which cause the program to behave in a manner contrary to expectations. The individual statements in the program are correctly formed and it runs, but the program as a whole does not work as it should; it may give incorrect answers, or terminate prematurely, or not terminate at all.

Hopefully, even the most puzzling logic errors, once detected, can eventually be removed. But how can the programmer be confident that the program will continue to behave properly when it is in use? The answer is that the programmer can never be absolutely certain that the program will not fail, but by the careful choice of test data in the second stage of the debugging process, the programmer can test the program under the sort of conditions that are most likely to occur in practice. Test data is designed to determine the robustness of the program, in other words, how well it can cope with unexpected or spurious inputs as well as those for which it has been designed specifically to process.

Syntax and Logic Errors

Because translation programs such as compilers must contain detailed rules concerning the allowable structures of statements in the language, they are generally able to provide the programmer with quite detailed information on the cause and location of syntax infringements. A COBOL compiler for example, having attempted to compile a source program, might produce an error report of the following form:

```
64 E - Syntax error (resumption at next PARAGRAPH/VERB): DIASPLAY
65 E - Syntax error (resumption at next PARAGRAPH/VERB): LOOP3
70 E - Bad nesting of DO/END-DO.
84 E - Procedure-name is unresolvable: AMEND-ALLOW

--- End of compilation ----------
Number of errors found:         4
Number of warnings given:       0
Number of source lines:       354
-----------------------------------
```

Each line of the report gives the following information:

(a)　　the line in the source code at which the error was located;

(b)　　the degree of severity of the error, that is to what extent it has prevented the production of the object code;

(c)　　a description of the error;

(d)　　the offending part of the statement if this can be isolated.

After correcting the source code, the program must be recompiled. Further errors may then be revealed and the process repeated. Only after the program has been compiled successfully, with no errors reported, should the object code be run. At this stage the operating system may report difficulties in attempting to execute the object code. For instance, if the program attempts to read a file which has not been opened prior to the read instruction, the operating system might halt execution of the program and report the detection of this *run-time* error. This constitutes an error in logic which the compiler is unable to detect; the error only becomes apparent when the program is run. Generally, the nature of the run-time error and perhaps its location in the source code will be reported, again with an error code through which further information might be obtained.

With a compiled programming language the programmer can be confident that all syntax errors have been removed from the program; the compiler itself will report this fact. However, since an interpreter only processes instructions as they are encountered, a syntax error in a statement will only be detected if that statement is executed. As a result, a complex program written in BASIC for instance, might hide a number of syntax errors which may only reveal themselves after the program has been run several times. For example, the following program statement contains a syntax error which might not reveal itself immediately:

> . . . .
>
> . . . .
>
> 100 IF code　 = 89 THEN GOTO SUB 2000
>
> . . . .

The fact that the instruction should have read

> 100 IF code = 89 THEN GOSUB 2000

would only become apparent when the variable 'code' actually had the value 89. Any other value would cause the coding following the condition in the statement to be ignored and allow the syntax error to remain hidden.

This same instruction could also hide a logic error. If line 2000 did not exist then it would be impossible to execute the subroutine starting at this point. Again the error might not become apparent immediately.

These examples illustrate the importance of testing a program thoroughly using data which will exercise every part of the program.

Detecting Logic Errors

Frequently logic errors do not prevent the program from executing, rather they cause some sort of processing error. The symptoms of the error may be obvious, but the cause might not be so apparent. Every programmer comes up against the logic error which 'cannot' exist; the coding appears to be perfectly correct and yet the program behaves incorrectly. No matter how many times the coding is scrutinised, there seems to be no reason for the problem. The mistake that many beginners at programming make is to spend an inordinate amount of time looking at program listings in order to find the error; though intuitively this seems to be the obvious approach, in practice it is a sort of 'gumption trap' which can waste a great deal of time and result in a great deal of frustration. It seems easier to stare at a listing in the belief that the error must eventually reveal itself rather than having the gumption to adopt some positive and systematic approach which might appear to involve more unnecessary work.

If, after examining a program listing for a reasonable amount of time, the cause of the error remains elusive, there are a number of courses of action which will probably be much more productive than continuing to pore over the listing:

(i) Ask a fellow programmer to listen critically while you explain the operation of the program and the way it is behaving. Quite often you will see the cause of the error as you are making the explanation. Alternatively, your helper might recognise the type of error and its probable cause from his/her own experience, or might ask a question which makes you reconsider some aspect of the program which you have assumed to be correct or had no direct bearing on the problem. It is surprising how often this technique works.

(ii) Examine the values of key variables while the program is running. Install temporary lines of coding throughout the program to display the value of variables and to pause until you press a key. For example, in COBOL you might insert the statements

DISPLAY "AT PARAGRAPH/PROC-REC/ ", inrec.

ACCEPT dummy.

The DISPLAY statement indicates the current position in the program, and the contents of the variable "inrec". The ACCEPT statement causes the program to wait until "dummy" (defined in the WORKING-STORAGE SECTION as PIC X) is given a value (pressing the RETURN /ENTER key is sufficient). In BASIC, PRINT and INPUT instructions can be used to perform the equivalent operations.

Comparison of the values actually displayed with expected values will normally indicate the likely source of the error.

(iii) Use debugging utilities provided in the language itself or separately in the system software. Several versions of BASIC have a trace facility which, when turned on, displays the line number of statements prior to their execution. Sometimes a particular implementation of a language will provide more sophisticated debugging facilities which will display the values of particular variables as they are encountered during program execution. Minicomputer systems and mainframes will usually have special debugging software which can be used with any of the languages supported by the system. It is up to the programmer to investigate the debugging aids available and make good use of them.

Test Data

When the programmer feels that the most obvious program errors have been detected and removed, the next stage is to test the program using carefully selected data. The nature of the test data should be such that:

(i) every statement in the program is executed at least once;

(ii) the effectiveness of every section of coding devoted to detecting erroneous input is verified;

(iii) every route through the program is tried;

(iv) the accuracy of the processing is verified;

(v) the program operates according to its original design specification.

In order to achieve these aims, the programmer must be inventive in the design of the test data. Each test case must check something not tested by previous runs; there is no point in proving that a program which can add successfully a certain set of numbers can also add another similar set of numbers. The goal is to strain the program to its limit, and this is particularly important when the program is to be used frequently by a number of different people.

There are three general categories of test data:

Normal data. This includes the most general data which the program was designed to handle.

Extreme values. These test the behaviour of the program when valid data at the upper and lower limits of acceptability are used. The process of using extreme values is called *boundary testing* and is often a fruitful place to look for errors. For numeric data this could be the use of very large or very small values. Text could be the shortest or longest sequence of characters permitted. A program for file processing could be tested with a file containing no records, or just a single record. The cases where zero or null values are used are very important test cases, frequently highlighting programming oversights.

Exceptional data. Programs are usually designed to accept a certain range or class of inputs. If *illegal* data are used, (that is data which the program is not designed to handle), the program should be capable of rejecting it rather than attempting to process it. This is particularly important when the program is to be used by people other than the programmer, since they may be unaware of what constitutes illegal data. From the outset a programmer should assume that incorrect data will be used with the program; this may save a great deal of time looking for program errors which may actually be data errors.

Top-down Testing

Top-down program design techniques, such as those discussed earlier in this chapter lend themselves to methodical testing. In top-down design, the program is designed by defining the main sections of the program first. These sections are then defined in terms of sub-sections of procedures which themselves may be further defined. Top-down testing proceeds in a similar manner. As a level of the program is coded, it can be tested by using program *stubs* for uncoded lower levels. Stubs are 'empty' sections of the program which do nothing when executed. For example, in COBOL a program stub could be a paragraph merely containing the word EXIT which does nothing when executed:

. . . .

. . . .

PROC5.

EXIT.

PROC6.

etc.

. . . .

. . . .

However, the paragraph PROC5 can still be *performed* from a higher level section of the program and thus allow the accuracy of the logic of this higher level to be investigated.

In this way the complete program need not exist in order for parts of it to be tested thoroughly. As the skeleton is fleshed out, more test data can be used. Thus the test data grows in parallel with the production of the program coding. Furthermore, the overall logic of the program can be tested right at the outset, and continues to be tested as more coding is added.

Validation

At some point the programmer must decide that the program has had sufficient testing. He or she will be confident that the program will operate according to specification and without 'crashing' or 'hanging up' under extreme or unexpected circumstances; the reputation of a professional programmer relies on this. Prior to release, the final testing is then performed by the user for whom the program was developed. The programmer may have overlooked areas of difficulty because it is often difficult to view a program objectively or entirely from the point of view of the user. If this is the case then the program will be modified and re-tested until all user requirements are met.

Chapter 16

Program Documentation

Introduction

The purpose of documentation is to provide the user with all the information necessary to fully understand the purpose of the program and how that purpose has been achieved. The precise form that the documentation takes will be determined by a number of factors:

    (i) The type of program;

    (ii) Who is likely to use the program;

    (iii) Whether it will be necessary to modify the program coding after it has been finally tested and accepted.

This section will explore these factors and provide general guidelines for the contents of the documentation, but because of the wide variety of opinion regarding its format, no particular documentation standard will be advocated. The section concludes with an example of how a program might be documented.

Documentation Requirements

A program which validates a temporary file prior to creating it permanently will probably require a minimum of user interaction and only a small number of instructions for the benefit of the person who will run the program. However, at some later date, it might be necessary for the author of the program, or a different programmer, to modify it. This possibility means that the structure of the program will have to be explained in great detail, and test procedures to ensure its correct operation will have to be provided.

A general purpose program such as a spreadsheet, designed for naive users, will entail the provision of extremely detailed instructions regarding its function and use. Such programs are generally accompanied by extremely detailed user manuals and tutorials. On the other hand, users would not be expected (and definitely not encouraged) to modify the program coding; thus no details would be provided regarding the way the program has been written. This latter type of documentation would only be required by the people responsible for producing the program.

In addition to the documentation requirements of users and programmers, there is a third category of person to be catered for. These are people such as managers who are neither likely to use programs extensively nor want to attempt to modify them. They merely need to have an overview of the program - its function, capabilities, hardware requirements etc.

Thus there are many factors governing the coverage of documentation, and for this reason, in the next section, it is only possible to provide a checklist of items which might reasonably be included.

Documentation Checklist

The documentation for a simple program generally falls into four sections:

    (i) Identification

    (ii) General specification

    (iii) User information

    (iv) Program specification.

Most users will need access to the first three sections; in general the fourth section will only be needed if the program is to be modified. The amount of detail in each section will depend entirely on the particular application and, to some extent, the implementation language. COBOL, for example, is largely self-documenting: it contains an Identification Division containing all the information listed in the first section below. The Data Division of a COBOL program contains precise details regarding all of the files used by the program and which devices are required. The Procedure Division is written in 'English-like' sentences which are generally easy to understand, even by a non-programmer. Consequently, a program written in COBOL will generally require less documentation than one written in BASIC.

The following checklist is a guide to what might reasonably be included in the documentation for a program:

Identification

- title of program;

- short statement of its function;

- author;

- date written;

- language used and version if relevant;

- hardware requirements.

General specification

- description of the main action(s) of the program under normal circumstances;

- systems flowcharts;

- description of data structures, including data structure diagrams and file specifications;

- restrictions and/or limitations of the program;

- equations used or references to texts explaining any complex procedures/techniques involved;

User information

- format of input required, e.g. source document or screen mask;

- output produced, e.g. typical printout or screen display;

- detailed instructions for initially running the program;

- medium on which program located, e.g. floppy disc(s);

Program specification

- structure charts;
- pseudo-code;
- annotated listing;
- testing procedure including test data and expected output.

Example of Documentation

A simple stock file updating problem illustrating various aspects of program development is used to illustrate how a program might be documented. The implementation language is assumed to be BASIC since good documentation is particularly important for programs written in languages which, unlike COBOL, do not contain self-documentation characteristics.

Documentation Example

Identification

Program ID : STOCK-FILE UPDATE.

Author : Nick Waites.

Purpose : To update a master stock file with a transaction file containing details of sales and receipts of stock items.

Date written : March 1987.

Language: BBC BASIC II.

Hardware: BBC Model B, Single 40 track floppy disc drive.

General Specification

Operation of Program

The purpose of the program is to read a sequential transaction file held on floppy disc and use it to update a sequential file containing records of stock items. The transaction file comprises a set of records containing details of stock items received from suppliers, and records containing details of stock items sold. Each record in the transaction file will be used to modify a corresponding record on the master file. There may be several transaction records for each record on the master file. Where the transaction is a sale, the number sold will be subtracted from the current stock level; receipts will be added to the current stock level. The transaction file is assumed to have been pre-sorted such that all orders relating to a particular record are grouped together. Once all transactions for a record have been processed, the updated record is written to a new stock file, again sequentially organized.

Systems Flowchart

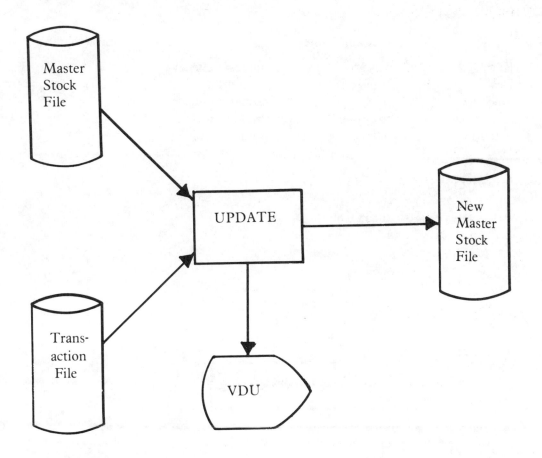

Data Structures

    (i)   Master stock file.

        (a) Structure diagram:

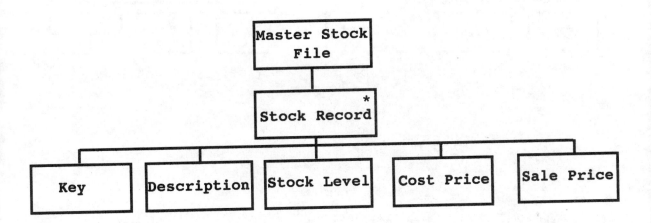

(b) File Definition:

File Name: Masterfile

Field	Program name	Type	Size(char)
Key	mastkey	numeric integer	
Description	descript$	alphabetic	30
Stock level	stock	numeric integer	
Cost Price	costprice	numeric real	
Sale Price	sellprice	numeric real	

(ii)   Transaction File.

(a) Structure Diagram:

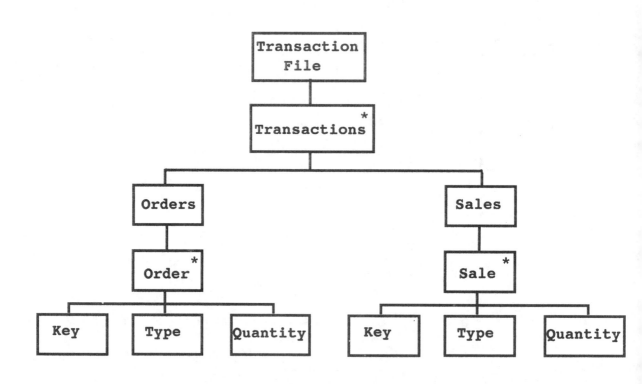

(b) File Definition:

File Name: Transfile.

Field	Program name	Type	Size(char)
Key	transkey	numeric integer	
Type	type$	"SALE" or "ORDR"	4
Quantity	quantity	numeric integer	

(iii) New stock file.

(a) Structure diagram:

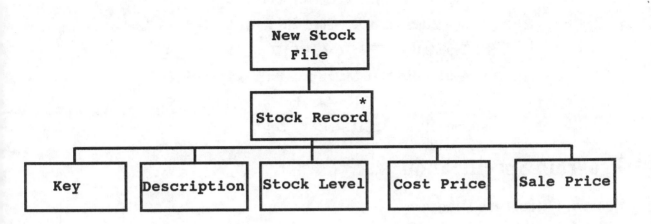

(b) File Definition:

File Name: Newfile

Field	Program name	Type	Size(char)
Key	mastkey	numeric integer	
Description	descrip$	alphabetic	30
Stock Level	stock	numeric integer	
Cost Price	costprice	numeric real	
Sale Price	sellprice	numeric real	

Restriction/limitations

The program operates under two important assumptions:

(i) The transaction file has been thoroughly validated.

(ii) The transaction file has been sorted into the same sequential order as the records in the master stock file, namely, ascending order of key field.

In addition, since the program creates a new master stock file (Newfile) whenever it processes the transaction file against the current master stock file (Masterfile), the new file must be renamed. This procedure is defined in the following section.

User Information

This program constitutes one element of a suite of programs forming a simple stock control system. The other processing tasks on which this program relies are defined and explained in companion documents. The complete system documentation, of which this is a part, defines the interrelationships between the program and files in the system.

The following steps are required in order to update the current master stock file using a previously created, sorted and validated transaction file:

(i) Insert the program disc labelled "SCSPROG1" into the disc drive.

(ii) Type LOAD "UPDATE" <RETURN>

(iii) Insert the data disc labelled "SCSDATA1" into the disc drive.

(iv) Type *DELETE MFcopy <RETURN>

(v) Type *RENAME Materfile MFcopy <RETURN>

(vi) Type *RENAME Newfile Masterfile <RETURN>

(vii) Type RUN <RETURN>

Program Specification

Program Structure Diagram

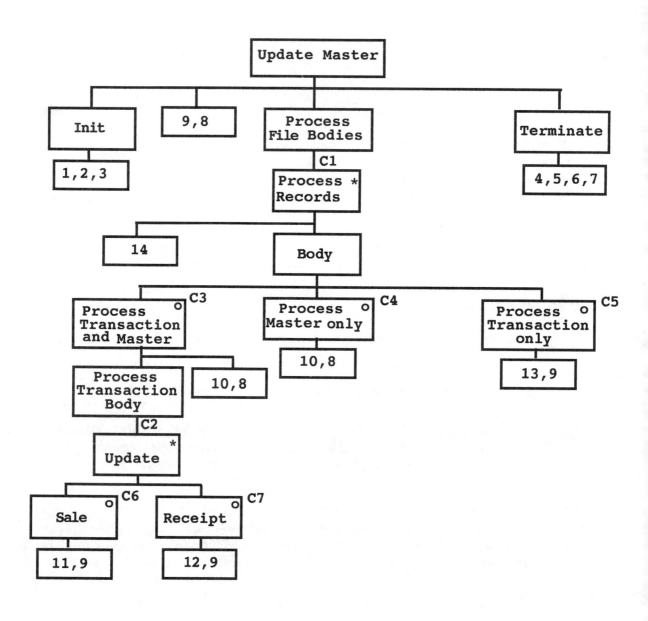

Operations

Initialisation operations:

1. Open Master File for Input

2. Open Updated Stock File for Output

3. Open Transaction File for input

Program Termination operations:

4. Close Master File

5. Close Updated Stock File

6. Close Transaction File

7. Stop

Input/Output operations:

8. Read Master File

9. Read Transaction File

10. Write Updated Stock Record

Processing operations:

11. Subtract number of sales from stock level

12. Add receipts to stock level

13. Display error message: "No stock record for this transaction"

14. Store transaction record key

Iteration conditions:

C1. Until End of Master File and Transaction File

C2. Until change of transaction record key

Selection conditions:

C3. Transaction record key matches stock record key

C4. Transaction record key > stock record key

C5. Transaction record key < stock record key

C6. Transaction type = Sale

C7. Transaction type = Receipt

Pseudocode

UPDATE
MASTER seq

    INIT seq

        Open Transaction File for Input;

        Open Master File for Input;

        Open Updated Stock File for Output;

    INIT endseq

        Read Transaction File;

        Read Master File;

PROCESS
FILE
BODIES iter until end of Transaction File and Master File

    PROCESS RECORDS seq

        Store transaction record key in Temp-key;

        BODY select transaction record key = Stock record key

            PROCESS
            TRANS
            BODY iter while transaction rec key = Temp-key

                UPDATE   select type = Sale

                        Subtract no. of sales from stock level;

                        Read Transaction File;

                UPDATE   or type = Receipt

                        Add receipts to stock level;

                        Read Transaction File;

                UPDATE   endselect

            PROCESS
            TRANS
            BODY   enditer

            Write Updated Stock record;

            Read Master File;

        BODY or transaction record key > stock record key

            Write Updated Stock record;
            Read Master File;

        BODY or transaction record key < stock record key

            Display error message;

            Read Transaction File;

        BODY endselect

    PROCESS RECORDS endseq

PROCESS
FILE
BODIES enditer

    TERMINATE   seq

        Close Transaction File;

        Close Master File;

        Close Updated Stock File;

    TERMINATE   endseq

UPDATE
MASTER   endseq

Program Listing

```
10   REM * UPDATE MASTER STOCK FILE sequence *

20   REM * INIT seq *
30        Transfile = OPENIN("transdata")
40        Masterfile = OPENIN("mastdata")
50        Newfile = OPENOUT("newdata")
60   REM  * INIT endseq *

80   INPUT # Transfile, transkey, type$, quantity
90   INPUT # Masterfile,mastkey,descrip$,stock,costprice,sellprice

100  REM * PROCESS FILE BODIES iterate UNTIL end of Trans AND Mast *
110  IF EOF(Transfile) AND EOF(Masterfile) GOTO 530

115       REM * PROCESS RECORDS sequence *
120       LET tempkey = transkey
130       REM * BODY select transaction key = stock key *
135       IF transkey<> mastkey GOTO 340
140          REM * PROCESS TRANS BODY iterate WHILE transkey = tempkey
145          IF transkey <> tempkey GOTO 310

150          REM * UPDATE RECORDS type = Sale *

160            IF type$ <> "SALE" GOTO 200
170            LET stock = stock -  quantity
180            INPUT # Transfile, transkey, type$, quantity
190            GOTO 300

200          REM * UPDATE RECORDS type = Receipt *
220            LET stock = stock + quantity
230            INPUT # Transfile, transkey, type$, quantity

300          REM * UPDATE RECORDS endselect *
305          GOTO 140
310          REM * PROCESS TRANS BODY end iteration *

320          PRINT # Newfile,mastkey,descrip$,stock,costprice,sellprice
330          INPUT # Masterfile,mastkey,descrip$,stock,costprice,sellprice
335          GOTO 500

340       REM * BODY or transkey > mastkey *
345       IF Transkey <  mastkey GOTO 380
350          PRINT # Newfile,mastkey,descrip$,stock,costprice,sellprice
360          INPUT # Masterfile,mastkey,descrip$,stock,costprice,sellprice
370          GOTO 500

380       REM * BODY or transkey <  mastkey *
390          PRINT " Transactions out of order "; transkey, mastkey
400          INPUT # Transfile, transkey, type$, quantity

500       REM * BODY end selection *

510       REM * PROCESS RECORDS end sequence *

520       GOTO 100
530  REM * PROCESS FILE BODIES end iteration *

535  REM * TERMINATE sequence *
540       CLOSE # Masterfile
550       CLOSE # Transfile
560       CLOSE # Newfile

570  REM * UPDATE MASTER STOCK FILE end sequence *
575  REM * TERMINATE end sequence *
580  END
```

Testing Procedure

In order to facilitate the process of testing the program's operation, two special files have been prepared. The first file called 'MFtest' contains a small number (5) of stock records (see Table 1). The other file 'TRtest' contains a number of transactions (see Table 2). When the program has been run using these special files, an updated master file called 'newfile' is created. The expected contents of this file are shown in Table 3.

The procedure required for testing the program is as follows:

(i) Insert the disc labelled "SCSPROG1" into the disc drive.

(ii) Type LOAD "UPDATE" <RETURN>

(iii) Insert the disc labelled "SCSTEST1" into the disc drive.

(iv) Type RUN <RETURN>

(v) Type CHAIN "REPORT1" <RETURN>

The contents of the newly created file will be displayed on the screen. (The contents of the file may be printed out by using the program REPORT2 instead of REPORT1).

The file displayed (or printed) should match that in Table 3.

Key Field	Description	Level	Cost	Sale
100011	Apple Juice	36	1.30	1.60
100027	Honey comb	20	0.35	0.50
100039	Long Grain Brown Rice (Organic)	44	0.32	0.41
100122	Sultanas (Australian)	22	0.55	0.69
100343	Shoyu (Japanese)	10	1.23	1.57

Table 1: Initial Contents of Master File

Key Field	Type	Quantity
100011	ORDR	12
100011	SALE	3
100011	SALE	5
100039	SALE	6
100039	SALE	2
100122	SALE	11
100122	ORDR	30
100122	SALE	5

Table 2: Transaction File

Key field	Description	Level	Cost	Sale
100011	Apple Juice	40	1.30	1.60
100027	Honey comb	20	0.35	0.50
100039	Long Grain Brown Rice (Organic)	36	0.32	0.41
100122	Sultanas (Australian)	41	0.55	0.69
100343	Shoyu (Japanese)	10	1.23	1.57

Table 3: Final Contents of Master File

Assignment *Documentation Standards*

Though BTEC do not specify any particular documentation standards for programs, they do recommend that a suitable set of standards is adopted and used for all programming exercises.

Task

Identify a suitable system of documentation standards and use them when documenting programs that you write. (BTEC provide guidance for documentation and also suggest that the standards provided by NCC are equally suitable).

Chapter 17

Computer Systems

The Computer

The Computer as a System

Any *system* consists of a number of separate elements working together to achieve a common aim. A car, for example, is a form of transport system comprising such elements as an engine, wheels and a gear box. Its aim is to transport people from one place to another. The system will only operate successfully if all these major components work. An essential additional element is the driver, without whom the car is simply a motionless piece of metal.

In the same way a *computer system* consists of a number of individual elements working together with the common aim of processing *data* to produce *information*.

Data   ⇨   Process   ⇨   Information

As computer processing is carried out electronically, a computer system may also be called an Electronic Data Processing System.

Data and Information

The difference between data and information can be illustrated by a simple example. If a company wishes to provide the information necessary to produce a customer invoice (which notifies a customer of the amount owed in respect of an order), several separate items of data need to be processed, including the prices and quantities of items ordered by the customer. To be described as information, the computer's output must be relevant and useful to the user receiving it.

The Elements of a Computer System

The elements which make up a computer system are called *hardware* and *software*. The system requires both, as neither can perform any useful function without the other.

Hardware

The term *hardware* is used to describe all the physical electronic and mechanical elements forming part of a computer system.

Software

The term *software* describes the instructions or programs which the hardware needs in order to function.

Another term, *firmware*, is used to describe programs which are 'hardwired' into the computer using integrated circuit 'chips'. Such storage is termed Read Only Memory (ROM). ROM is *non-volatile*, in other words the programs are not lost when the machine is switched off. Also, the contents cannot be overwritten by other programs or data.

Hardware

The Elements of Hardware

The hardware of a computer system comprises the following elements:

Input

To allow the computer to process data it must be in a form which the machine can handle. Before processing, data is normally in a *human readable form*, for example, as it appears on an employee's time sheet or a customer's order form. Such alphabetic and numeric (decimal) data cannot be handled directly by the internal circuitry of the computer. Firstly, it has to be translated into the binary format which makes the data *machine-sensible*. There are a wide variety of input devices which carry out this function but the most common are keyboard devices.

The function of an input device, therefore, is to translate human readable data into a machine-sensible form which the computer can then handle.

Data is transferred from the input device to Main Memory.

Main Memory

The main memory has two main functions:

 (a) to temporarily store programs currently in use for processing data;

 (b) to temporarily store data:

  (i) entered via an input device and awaiting processing;

  (ii) currently being processed;

  (iii) which results from processing and is waiting to be output.

Central Processing Unit (CPU) or 'Processor'

The CPU carries out instructions and consists of two elements:

The Arithmetic/Logic Unit(ALU). The ALU carries out arithmetic operations such as addition, multiplication, subtraction and division. It can also make *logical* comparisons between items of data, for example, it can determine whether one value is greater than another. Such logical operations can also be performed on non-numeric data.

The Control Unit. The control unit controls the operation of all hardware, including input and output devices and the CPU.

It does this by fetching, interpreting and executing each instruction in turn. The *Fetch-Execute* cycle is described in detail in Chapter 22.

When an instruction (such as an input instruction to accept data via a keyboard) is to be executed, the control unit sends the appropriate signals to the keyboard device. Similarly, an instruction involving an arithmetic computation will be signalled to the ALU which carries out such functions.

Output

Output devices perform the opposite function of input devices by translating machine-sensible data into a human-readable form, for example, onto a printer or the screen of a visual display unit (VDU). Sometimes, the results of computer processing may be needed for further processing, in which case, they are output to a storage medium which retains it in machine-sensible form for subsequent input. Usually, the storage medium will be magnetic disk or tape.

Backing Store

Backing store performs a filing function within the computer system. In this context it is important to consider a couple of important concepts.

Memory Volatility.   It is not practical to store data files and programs in main memory because of its *volatility*. This means that the contents of the main memory can be destroyed, either by being overwritten as new data is entered for processing and new programs used, or when the machine is switched off. Such volatile memory is termed Random Access Memory (RAM).

Retrievable Data.   Backing storage media provide a more permanent store for programs (which may be used many times on different occasions) and data files (which are used for future reference or processing).

When the results of processing are output to a printer or VDU screen, the user is provided with visual information which is not normally retrievable by the computer unless it is also recorded on a backing storage medium such as magnetic tape or disk. The following example illustrates some aspects of file storage.

Example

In a payroll operation, data on hours worked by employees, together with other relevant data for the current pay period, needs to be processed against the payroll details held on the payroll master file in order to produce the necessary payslips. The payroll master file is stored on backing store and is placed *on-line* when needed for processing. Any such files can be stored indefinitely on backing storage media. Magnetic disk and magnetic tape are re-useable. When a file is no longer required, it can be overwritten by new data.

Peripherals

Those hardware devices which are external to the CPU and main memory, namely those devices used for input, output and backing storage are called *peripherals*.

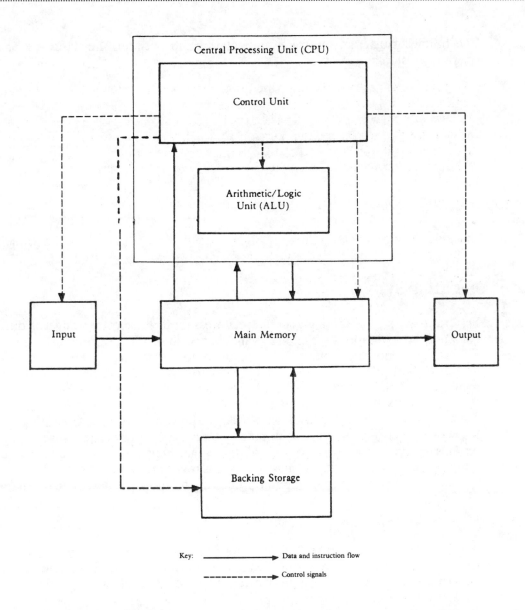

Key: ——————▶ Data and instruction flow

- - - - - - -▶ Control signals

The above diagram illustrates the relationships between the various hardware elements. It illustrates the data flow through the system and the flow of control signals from the control unit. The diagram illustrates what is usually called the *logical structure* of the computer.

Software

Software is examined in great detail in Chapter 11. Introduced here, are some basic concepts which allow a simple understanding of computer systems. The role of software is to run the hardware. Software can be broadly divided into two types:

(a)   Systems Software;

(b)   Applications Software.

Systems Software

Systems software is *dedicated* to the general organization and running of the computer system, in other words such software is written specifically for that purpose. Standard tasks, such as handling files on disk and tape systems, are common to most computer applications and are controlled by a particular group of systems programs called the *Operating System*.

The following diagram illustrates the relationship between the hardware and the operating system:

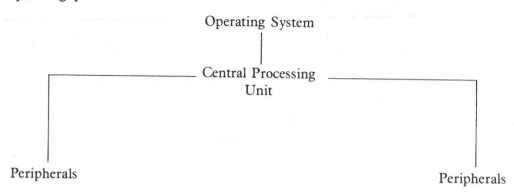

Types of Operating System

Different types of operating system are necessary to handle the range of different computer configurations which are available and the variety of processing modes in which they can operate. For example, a microcomputer system with keyboard, monitor, disk drive and printer, requires a much less sophisticated operating system than a mainframe computer system with a large number and variety of input, output and storage devices. Computer systems which allow multi-user operation, that is, the serving of more than one user at a time, require a multi-user operating system. Conversely, single-user microcomputer systems require only single-user operating systems. There are a variety of operating systems which serve the requirements of different computer processing methods such as real-time processing, batch processing and time-share processing. Computer processing methods are described in Chapter 6.

Applications Software

Applications programs make the computer function in a specific way for a particular user requirement, for example, for use in stock control or invoicing. Increasingly, many applications are catered for by pre-written Applications Packages.

A Classification of Computer Systems

Computer systems can be classified according to the following characteristics:

(a)   Purpose;

(b)   Size and Complexity;

(c)   Generation (Place in Historical Development).

Purpose

There are two categories under this heading:

General Purpose Computers

As the term suggests, general purpose machines can carry out processing tasks for a wide variety of applications and most organizations will make use of this type of machine.

Dedicated or Special Purpose Computers

In their logical structure, these machines are fundamentally the same as the general purpose machine except that they have been programmed for a specific application. Dedicated word processors provide one example. The advent of cheap, microprocessor-based systems has led to an expansion of their use in controlling machines and many household products such as washing machines and microwave ovens are controlled by such systems.

Size and Complexity of Computer Systems

It should be emphasized that the following categories are only broad guidelines and changes in technology are continually blurring the differences between them. However, the generally accepted categories of computer system are as follow:

Mainframe Computers

Mainframe computer systems are the largest and most powerful type of computer and are used by large organizations such as banks, airlines and government departments.

They usually support a large number and variety of peripherals and can process a number of applications concurrently. This is called *multiprogramming*. The mainframe's power stems from the phenomenal speeds of the processor and the large size of the main memory.

Mainframes may also be used for Wide Area Networks (these are examined in detail in Chapter 23). For example, in the case of an international airline with offices throughout the world, incoming and outgoing communications traffic will probably be controlled by minicomputers (this is referred to as *front end processing* or simply FEP), leaving the mainframe free to carry out the main processing tasks. It may be necessary to employ two mainframes working 'back to back', either to share the processing load or to provide a backup in the event of the breakdown of one processor. In this case also, a minicomputer will be employed to control the flow of data between the processors. The use of two processors working in tandem is known as *multiprocessing*.

Mainframe computers are generally accommodated in special-purpose, air-conditioned rooms to ensure trouble free operation.

Minicomputers

Minicomputers are scaled-down versions of mainframe computers. The division between the two types becomes rather blurred when referring to small mainframes and large 'minis'. Costing less and being robust enough to operate without a special environment, they can be used in *real-time* applications such as controlling manufacturing processes in an engineering factory. They are also used by medium sized organizations for all their processing needs or by larger organizations as part of a network system.

Minicomputers can support a number of applications concurrently and are often used with *time-share* operating systems (this is discussed in some detail in Chapter 6) and intelligent terminals to provide organizations with decentralized processing facilities. Used in this way, many applications such as word processing, invoicing and customer enquiry can be carried out by users in their own departments. Generally, the volumes of input will be relatively small. This contrasts with the multiprogramming mode of operation often used in mainframe systems where large volume, batch processing jobs are processed centrally and users are not directly involved.

Microcomputers

Microcomputers were originally unique in their use of single 'chip' processors. The Central Processing Unit (the control unit and arithmetic/logic unit) are stored on a single 'chip' to form a microprocessor. A whole series of such processor chips are currently in use, including, for example, those manufactured by Motorola and Intel.

Originally, microcomputers were only capable of supporting a single user and a single application at any one time. The increase in processor speed and memory capacity and the facility for networking (for multi-user operation) now permits their use for *multi-tasking* (the running of several tasks concurrently by one user). It is now extremely popular to link microcomputers into a Local Area Network, to allow sharing of disk and printer facilities, as well as electronic communications between users (Electronic Mail). They can now support applications packages previously restricted to mini and mainframe systems, including, for example, those used for database and computer aided design (CAD) work.

The low cost of microcomputers and the increase in the range of software available, makes their use possible in almost any size and type of organization. In the small firm, a microcomputer may be used for word processing, stock control, costing, and general accounting. In the larger organization they may be used as *intelligent* terminals in a distributed processing system (Chapter 6). Such systems provide the user with the processing facilities of a central mini or mainframe computer and at the same time, a degree of independent processing power through the use of the microcomputer's own processor and memory store.

Generations of Computers

Since the first electronic computers were built in the 1940s, a number of developments in electronics have led to computer hardware being categorized by 'generation', that is, its place in the history of the computer. These generations can be simply defined as follows:

First Generation

During the 1940s, this first generation of computers used electronic components including vacuum tubes. The first computer to allow a program to be stored in memory (a stored-program computer) was EDSAC, developed at the University of Manchester. The vacuum tubes were fragile, subject to overheating and caused frequent break-downs.

Second Generation

The introduction of low-cost and reliable transistors allowed the computer industry to develop at a tremendous rate during the late 1950s. The cost and size of the machines was radically reduced so it became possible for large commercial organizations to make use of computers. Examples of such machines include LEO III, UNIVAC and ATLAS.

Third Generation

The development of integrated circuit (IC) technology in the mid-1960s heralded the development of more powerful, reliable and compact computers, such as those of the IBM 360 series.

Fourth Generation

This generation is typified by large scale integration (LSI) of circuits which allowed the development of the microprocessor, which in turn allowed the production of the microcomputer. All computers used today make use of such silicon 'chip' technology.

Fifth Generation

At present, most computers are still of the fourth generation variety. Developments are continuing towards expanding memory size, using very large scale integration (VLSI) techniques and increasing the speed of processors. This increasing power is allowing the pursuit of new lines of development in computer systems:

(i)   More human orientated input/output devices using voice recognition and speech synthesis should allow communication between computers and humans to be more flexible and 'natural'. In the future, the aim is to allow computers to be addressed in languages natural to the users. Current techniques on some microcomputers allow acceptance of some spoken commands. Others allow the selection of user options displayed as graphics on the screen via a hand-held 'mouse'.

(ii)   Parallel processing techniques. Mainframe computers with several internal processors are moving computer processing away from the sequential (one instruction after another) operation of earlier generations. The transputer, which was developed by INMOS as a computer on a 'chip', can be used as the basic building block for a number of new computer architectures including parallel processor computers. Parallel processing radically increases the power of the computer to handle the complex programming needed for 'expert' systems and artificial intelligence (AI). Expert systems already exist for medical diagnosis, and legal advice. The main applications to benefit from parallel processing are likely to be those which make extensive use of graphics, for example, computer-aided design (CAD).

Existing sequential programming languages (such as BASIC, COBOL, Fortran and Pascal) will be inappropriate to make proper use of parallel processing machines. A new group of languages based on Prolog (PROgramming in LOGic) should allow logic programming techniques to maximize use of parallel processing computers.

Assignment   *Taking Stock*

Perkins Ltd. is a private limited company which runs a discount warehouse in Leeds. The warehouse sells a wide range of DIY, gardening and car maintenance goods. The profitability of the company depends on a rapid stock turnover and minimum levels of stock. At the same time, customers expect to be able to buy any of the items advertised in the company catalogue on demand.

To help achieve these objectives, the company uses a minicomputer system for stock control and most of its other applications. At present, the stock control system is run on a batch processing basis, transactions for stock issues and receipts being posted to the master file, at the end of each day. This delay means that the stock master file does not always reflect the up-to-date position and it has been decided that a new system is to be introduced to enable transactions to be posted to the master file as soon as stock is sold or received. The new system uses VDU terminals which are linked to the minicomputer and data entry is to be carried out interactively. This means that data is entered in response to message prompts on the screen. Errors are indicated on the screen as they occur and the data entry operator has to correct them immediately.

The new system will require more highly trained operators than are necessary for a batch data entry system and a staff training programme is to be introduced.

Task

You have previous experience of an interactive stock control system and, in your present role as data entry supervisor, are to be involved in the staff training programme. The Management Information Services Manager believes some basic understanding of the role of the computer helps staff in their work and has asked you to give an introductory talk or other form of presentation to the data entry staff, concerning the new system and the role of the computer in it. Your talk should cover the following points:

1.   a description of the information flows from data collection to the updating of the master files and the production of stock reports.

2.   a diagram, appropriately simplified, which illustrates the logical structure of a computer system and the functions of each component in the structure.

3.   a description of the relationships between each stage of processing in the stock control system and the functional components described in 2.

You may use any form of presentation you wish and it may include, for example, the use of flip charts, OHP slides, wall displays, video, handouts, etc. It may also be appropriate to develop the presentation as part of a group project.

Developmental Task

Use a stock control package and for one processing routine, for example, the entry of transactions for goods issued, produce a simple user manual describing the prompts which appear on the screen and the necessary responses.

Assignment   *A New System for Milford*

Milford Communications Limited is a small company based in Cirencester specializing in the manufacture of telephone equipment for the United Kingdom market. Its business has grown dramatically in the last few years, since the removal of British Telecom's monopoly on the supply of telephone equipment. The business has taken advantage of the popular demand for sophisticated telephone handsets which 'remember' a range of regularly used telephone numbers specified by the user.

There are twenty five staff at the Cirencester Head Office and all the office administration systems are computerized, using a number of 'stand-alone' microcomputer systems and software packages. The financial director, Arthur Danish, is confident that the business can be further expanded by improving the efficiency of the information processing systems. At present, the separate microcomputer systems do not facilitate management in obtaining a 'global' view of the organisation's operation. You are employed as a systems development assistant, responsible to Mr. Danish and he has asked you to produce a report on the alternative computer systems which may be of use in this situation.

Task

1. **Prepare an informal report for Mr. Danish, in which you consider the various alternative types of computer system which may be used in the organization. Also present any arguments for and against each alternative.**

2. **As an appendix to your report, explain the significance of systems software and the purchases which may be needed, in addition to the computer hardware.**

Developmental Task

Research from computing magazines, or journals, a range of computer systems which could be used in this situation and produce a table detailing the approximate costs, general features and limitations of each system. Make argued recommendations as to the type of system which is likely to be most appropriate.

Chapter 18

Peripherals

Overview of Peripherals

As the name suggests, peripheral devices are the external elements of the computer system described in Chapter 17. They provide a means of communication between the central processor and its human operators. Peripheral devices can be categorized according to their general function. These functions are identified at the beginning of Chapter 17 as part of the logical computer configuration. The functions are:

> (i) Backing Storage;
>
> (ii) Input and Output.

There are two sections in this chapter. The first deals with Backing Storage devices and media and the second with Input and Output peripheral devices.

Backing Storage

All backing storage systems consist of two main elements, a *device* and a *medium*. For example, a disk drive is a device and a magnetic disk is a storage medium. Under program control, data files are generally read from and written to via the storage device which is connected on-line to the CPU. The most important kinds of backing storage devices in use today are those using magnetic tape and magnetic disk.

Magnetic Tape

Despite the continued evolution of disk storage, magnetic tape continues to be used in most large scale computer installations as a cheap and secure method of storing large volumes of data which are normally processed in a serial fashion. It is also useful for the storage of historic files where rapid access to individual records is not essential. An example of the former use is in the processing of an organisation's payroll. An example of storing historic data on tape is provided by the Police National Computer system in Hendon. Here, millions of records of current criminal activity are kept *on-line* and are directly accessible from magnetic disk. Records which are not currently 'active' are held *off-line* on magnetic tape. When a record needs to be retrieved, the relevant tape has to be placed on-line and searched until the required record is found. It would be inefficient and expensive to keep all records, no matter how old, on-line all the time.

General Features of Magnetic Tape

The tapes used on mainframe and minicomputer systems are stored on detachable reels up to 26.7cm in diameter. A tape is usually between 0.38cm and 2.54cm wide. It is made of plastic and is covered with a coating which can be magnetized. The most commonly used tapes are 1.27cm wide. In larger systems, tapes may be 730m in length and able to record 15000 bytes of information per cm.

A particular type of cartridge tape, which looks like a cassette tape but is slightly larger, is often used as a backup for 'hard' disk on microcomputer systems. These tapes have huge capacity (up to 60mb - million bytes) and can copy the contents of a hard disk in a few minutes. This type of tape is called a *streamer* tape.

The rest of this section concentrates on the large reel-to-reel systems.

Processing Tapes

A tape must be mounted on an on-line *tape unit* when it is to be used by a computer system. The figure below illustrates the main features of a large tape unit for reel-to-reel tapes.

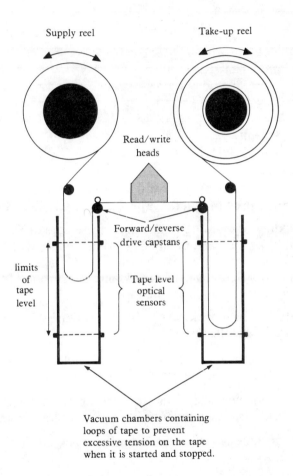

Large Magnetic Tape Unit

It can be seen from the figure that there are two reels. The supply reel contains the tape that is to be read from or written to by the computer system. The takeup reel collects the tape as it is unwound from the supply reel. During processing, the tape is propelled past separate *read* and *write* heads at high speed. As is explained in Chapter 5, data is transferred between tape and main memory in physical blocks. A small gap called the *inter block gap* is left between each block of data, to allow the tape to decelerate and stop and accelerate again to the correct speed for data transfer. To keep the tape at the proper tension, even during acceleration and deceleration, vacuum chambers are used to allow some slack in the tape beneath each reel. The optical level sensors in each vacuum chamber detect the level of 'droop' and when necessary, signal the supply reel to release more tape or the takeup reel to takeup more tape.

When processing is finished, the tape is rewound onto the supply reel, which is then

Data Storage on Magnetic Tape

The figure below shows how data is stored on magnetic tape. The coding system used is either ASCII or EBCDIC (which is used for IBM equipment),

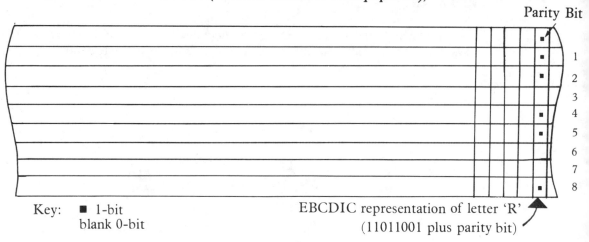

Parity Bit

Key: ■ 1-bit
       blank 0-bit

EBCDIC representation of letter 'R'
(11011001 plus parity bit)

Data Storage on Magnetic Tape (Nine-Track, Even Parity)

The coding systems are binary and in the case of EBCDIC, each character is represented by a group of 8 binary digits (bits), either 0 or 1, plus a parity bit (for checking transmission errors), across the width of the tape. As the figure shows, each 0 or 1 bit is accommodated in a single track and each group of bits representing one character occupies one frame across the tape.

The method of representing a 0 or 1 bit depends on the recording system in use but simplified examples are as follows:

> (a) the presence of a magnetic field to represent 1 and the lack of a magnetic field to represent 0;

> (b) the 0 and 1 bits are represented by magnetic fields of opposite polarity, say north for 1 and south for 0.

The tape unit reads across the nine tracks in a frame to identify the character represented.

Blocking Data on Magnetic Tape

The organization of files on magnetic tape is described in Chapter 5, so this section deals with the operational characteristics of storing data on tape.

In order to transfer data to or from tape, the tape has to pass the read-write heads at a particular speed. Data transfer takes place in *blocks* because, for example, it is not generally possible to read a complete logical file into memory at one time. Instead, suitably sized blocks are transferred to be processed in turn, requiring the tape to stop and start repeatedly. The inter-block gap allows for such stops and starts.

As is explained in Chapter 5, a file is made up of a number of *logical* records. For example, a stock file contains a logical record for each commodity in stock. Generally, a logical record will not be large enough to constitute a physical record or block, so a number of logical records are grouped for transfer at one read or write instruction. The number of logical records in each physical record indicates the *blocking factor*. Large blocks save space (fewer inter-block gaps) and speed processing. Memory size is a limiting factor on the size of blocks.

To speed processing, many computer systems contain special high-speed memory areas called *buffers*. A buffer acts as a waiting area for a transferred block from where it can be quickly accessed and processed by the CPU. *Double* buffering makes use of two buffers which work 'in tandem' to speed processing. The following diagram illustrates the buffering process.

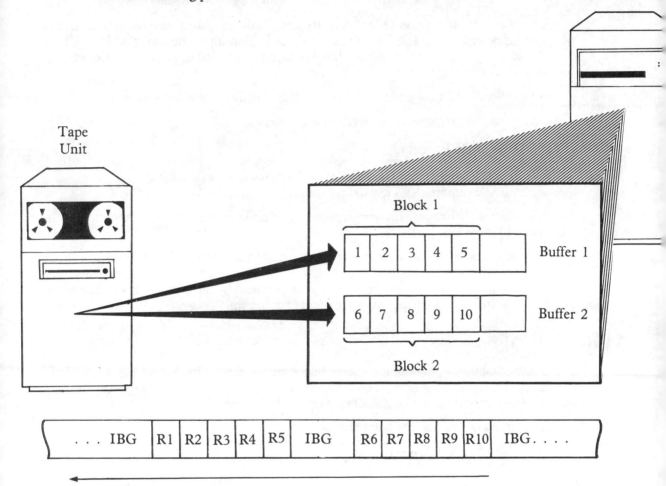

Direction of read

1BG	= Inter-block Gap
Rn	= Logical record number

Buffering of Blocks of Data in Main Memory

If the records are blocked as shown above, the systems software initially places the first block into buffer 1 and the second into buffer 2. *Read* instructions from the applications program retrieve the data from these buffers. The CPU can retrieve logical records faster from the buffer than from tape. As soon as all logical records from buffer 1 have been processed, the reading process transfers to the logical records in buffer 2. Meanwhile, the next block on tape can be transferred into buffer 1 and so on.

Security of Files on Magnetic Tape

There are two major areas of concern:

(i) It is important that the correct file is used in a file processing operation to ensure correct results. Thus, the subject of the file and the version must be identifiable. For example, it is no good

producing monthly payslips using information from a payroll
master file three months out of date.

(ii)   A tape file must be protected against accidental erasure. This
may occur because tapes are reusable and when a file is no
longer required it can be overwritten by new information.

To ensure that the correct file is used for any particular job, a tape file usually has an
internal header label. The label appears at the beginning of the tape and identifies it.
The identifying information in the label is usually recorded under program control or
by a data encoding device.

A tape header label usually contains the following items of information:

(a)   File name e.g. *Payroll, Stock, Sales;*

(b)   Date created;

(c)   Purge date - the date from which the tape is no longer
required and may be re-used.

The label is checked by the program, before the file is processed, to ensure that the
correct tape is being used.

A device called a *file protection ring* can be used to prevent accidental erasure. When
tapes are stored off-line, the rings are not fitted. To write to a tape, the ring must first
be fitted to the centre of the reel. A tape can be read by the computer whether or not
a ring is fitted. The simple rule to remember is 'no ring, no write'.

Magnetic Disks

Many computer applications require fast, direct access to individual records within a
file and this facility is provided by magnetic disk. For this reason, magnetic disks are
the most important backing storage media in use today.

Two popular types of magnetic disk are:

(i) Hard disks;

(ii) 'floppy' or flexible disks.

Hard Disks

General Features

The disk is usually made of aluminium with a coating of a magnetizable material on
which data can be recorded. Records are stored in concentric rings or *tracks*. The
method of encoding is fundamentally the same as that for tape, except that the
magnetic states representing binary patterns are stored in single-file around the tracks.
The diagram on the following page illustrates these features.

Each track is divided into a number of *sectors* and each sector has a given storage
capacity. Each track and sector has a physical *address* which can be used by software
to locate a particular record or group of records. The central area of the disk is not
used, because to do so would necessitate a higher packing density than can be read or
recorded by the read-write head. The number of tracks and sectors is known as the
disk's *format*. The sector size can either be fixed permanently or can be altered by
software. The former is known as *hard* sectoring and the latter as *soft* sectoring.

Hard Sectoring

The position of each sector can be indicated by a slot or reflective marker which can be detected by sensors in the drive unit. As the smallest unit of data transfer between disk and CPU is a sector (*block*), this means that any application is restricted to the disk's block size. Consider, for example, an application which uses logical records of 64 bytes, stored on a disk with 512 byte *hard* sectors. A minimum of 8 logical records needs to be transferred to memory even if only one is required out of the sector.

Soft Sectoring

This method allows the sectors to be set by software. All microcomputer systems use soft sectoring.

The Addressing Structure of a Magnetic Disk

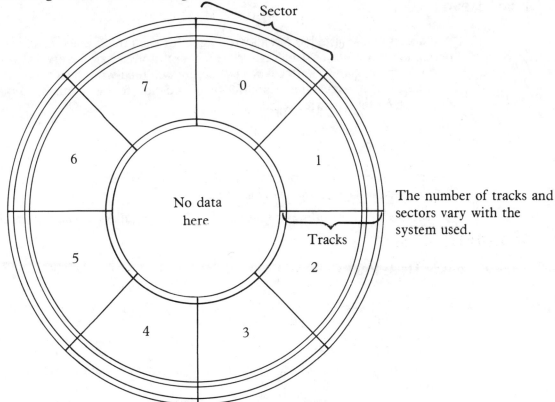

The number of tracks and sectors vary with the system used.

Operational Characteristics

During computer operation, the disk revolves continuously. The read-write head does not actually touch the disk surface as this would result in rapid wear of the disk surface and the head. Instead, the head 'floats' very close to the surface of the disk, so that information can be recorded on or read from the concentric tracks. The head is shaped so that as the disk revolves at high speed, a flow of air forces the head a minute distance above the surface. When the disk is not revolving, the air pressure beneath the head is reduced. This may result in a 'head crash' which causes damage to both the disk surface and the read-write head. Two main methods are available to prevent such an occurrence.

Firstly, the head can be automatically retracted away from the surface before the disk stops revolving. An alternative method, used on *Winchester* drives, is to make the head 'take-off' and 'land' as necessary on the disk surface. To prevent disk damage, the surface is lubricated and the whole unit is hermetically sealed to prevent dust from entering. This second method allows the head to fly closer to the surface than on conventional drives, thus increasing the reading accuracy and enabling greater packing density.

The use of flying heads requires the disk drive environment to be completely free from dust and other impurities which may cause a 'head crash'. A human hair or even a smoke particle can be large enough to cause damage. The IBM 3360 disk heads, for example, glide 17 millionths of an inch above the recording surface. A human hair is approximately 2500 millionths of an inch.

There are two main approaches to the design of the access mechanization of the read-write head:

   (i) *Fixed* head;

   (ii) *Moveable* head.

Fixed Head Disks

The access mechanism has a read-write head for each track. Each head is positioned permanently over its particular track so no lateral motion is necessary. However, a disk with 400 tracks on two surfaces would require 800 read-write heads mounted onto a fixed access arm. Access time is shorter than is possible for moveable head systems, but their high cost has restricted their use.

Moveable Head Disks

This mechanism only uses one read-write head per disk surface. The head is moved to the required track by a moveable arm.

In order to increase on-line storage capacity, a stack of disks can be formed into a *disk pack.*

Exchangeable Disk Packs

Disks are often assembled into groups of six, eight, ten or twelve and mounted on a central spindle which rotates all the disks at the same speed. There is sufficient gap between each surface to allow read-write heads to move in and out between the disks. Only one head may be actively reading or writing at any one time. The disk pack is enclosed in a plastic shell, to protect the disk surfaces from dust or other foreign objects.

The diagram below illustrates the disk pack and the access mechanism.

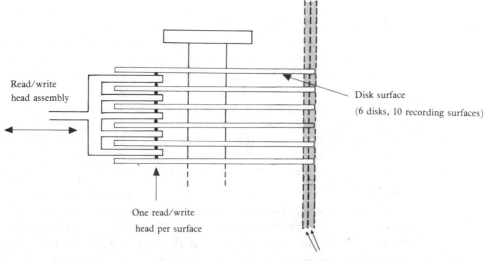

The disk pack is generally loaded from the top of the disk unit. Because the disk pack can be removed and exchanged, the heads remain in their retracted position when the pack is not in place and when the disks are not revolving at their full operating speed.

Disk Cylinders

The concept of the *cylinder* is explained in Chapter 5. Briefly, if there are ten possible recording surfaces with 200 tracks per surface, there are 200 imaginary, concentric *cylinders*, each consisting of ten tracks. Each vertical plane of tracks is a cylinder and as such is equivalent to a track position to which the heads on the access mechanism can move. With a moveable head system, all the read-write heads are fixed to a 'comb' so that each is in the same cylinder at any one time. Sequential files are applied to a disk pack on a cylinder-by-cylinder basis so that all records in a cylinder can be processed with the heads in one position.

Single Exchangeable Disks

Single exchangeable disks are also known as *cartridge* disks and can be inserted into the front of the disk unit, in which case, part of the disk cover automatically slides to one side to allow the read-write heads to move in, or it can be 'top loaded' and the plastic cover removed by the operator once the disk is in place. As is the case with the exchangeable disk pack, the moveable heads remain in the retracted position except when the disk is revolving at full speed.

Winchester Disks

When first introduced, Winchester disks were designed for large computer systems and are still popular on such systems. They are now used as an alternative to floppy disks on microcomputer systems. Winchester disks provide a much greater volume of on-line storage and faster access to programs and data than is possible with floppy disks.

Winchester disk systems consist of packs of hard disks, stacked in the same way as the exchangeable disk pack systems described earlier. The disks are not removable and are hermetically sealed in the storage units together with the read-write mechanism. The contamination-free environment in which the disks are stored allows very high speeds of rotation, typically, 3600 revolutions per minute. Storage capacities are increasing as technology advances, but commonly available systems for microcomputers provide up to 300 megabytes of storage.

Winchester disk units can be stored internally within the computer unit. For example, in the IBM PS/2 it is placed in the position normally occupied by one of the two floppy disk drives. Large volume storage presents problems in terms of security backup. A large number of floppy disks would need to be used to back up one Winchester disk, so many systems are stored externally and provide a built-in slot for a tape cartridge. The tape backup system is known as a *tape streamer* and can be used with both internally and externally housed hard disk systems.

Disk Access Time

'Access time' is the time interval between the moment the command is given to transfer data from disk to main memory and the moment the transfer is completed. In a moving head system the retrieval of data involves three identifiable tasks.

Seek Time

Suppose, for example, the read-write head unit is in cylinder 5 and that data is required from cylinder 24. To retrieve the data, the mechanism must move inwards to cylinder 24. The time taken to accomplish this movement is known as the *seek time*.

Rotational Delay

When a read or write instruction is issued, the head is not usually positioned over the sector where the required data are stored, so there is some *rotational delay* while the disk rotates into the proper position. On average, the time taken is half a revolution of the disk pack. This average time is known as the *latency of the disk.*

Data Transfer Time

This is the time taken to read the block of data into main memory.

Two strategies can be used to reduce disk access time. The first solution is to store related records in the same cylinder so that head movement is minimized. This strategy is usually adopted for sequential files when the records are to be accessed sequentially. Even with random files it is sometimes possible to group related records in the same cylinder. The second solution is to use the fixed head disks described earlier. As each track has its own read-write head, no seek time is involved. It has to be said, however, that this second option is no longer used in disk drive systems.

Floppy Disks or Diskettes

Floppy disks are physically and operationally different from hard disks. They are flexible and encased in a square plastic protective jacket. The diskette revolves inside the jacket at approximately 360 revolutions per minute, more slowly than a conventional disk. The jacket is lined with a soft material which helps to clean the diskette as it revolves. The read-write head makes contact with the diskette surface when data transfer is in progress and withdraws at other times to reduce wear. The diskette does not rotate continuously. A diskette will eventually wear out after about 500 to 600 hours of contact. Some systems offer a non-contact flying-head system which allows the diskette to revolve at 3000 rpm. This removes the problem of wear and speeds access time.

The following diagram shows the component parts of one type of floppy disk, the 5.25 inch, which is still extremely popular, despite increasing competition from its more robust 3.5 inch rival (described later).

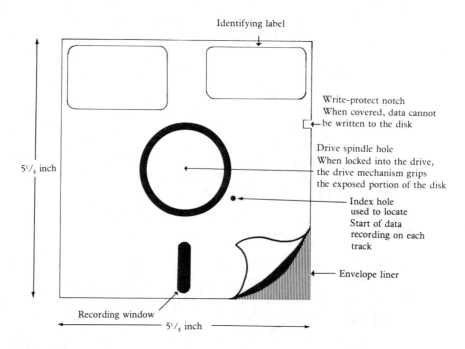

There is a slot in the jacket to allow the read-write head to access the diskette and a central hole for the drive shaft. The diskette has to be inserted into the disk drive and then locked into place by closing the drive door. The locking-in step locks the drive shaft into the central hole in the disk.

Types of Floppy Disk

Floppy disks are available in two sizes according to diameter - 5.25 inches and 3.5 inches. Diskettes can be either 40-track or 80 track and the number of sectors can be varied (soft-sectoring is used). Suppose, for example, that a diskette has 80 tracks and that a particular computer system formats the diskettes into 9 sectors. Formatting causes it to be divided up into nine sectors 0 to 8 as shown below. Thus with 80 tracks and 9 sectors, the diskette has 720 addressable locations. Soft sectoring is used because the operating systems of different computers use different addressing formats. Thus, in principle, standard diskettes can be sold which only require formatting to be used on a particular machine. The formatting procedure also sets up a *directory* which is automatically maintained by the computer system to keep track of the contents of each location.

Formatted Floppy Disk

The floppy disk is addressed according to Track number and Sector number. In this illustration, the formatting allocates 9 (sectors) x 80 (tracks) = 720 addressable locations. Each location can accommodate, say 256 bytes.

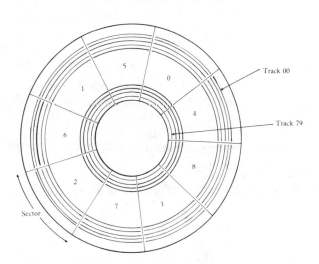

Diskettes are recorded in one of several bit-densities. Single-density diskettes can store 3200 bits per inch in terms of the innermost track of the diskette (this is obviously shorter than the outer tracks). Most diskettes are now double-density, recording 6400 bits per inch or quad-density with 12800 bits per inch. To further increase capacity, double-sided diskettes are also available, although to take advantage of these greater capacities, the disk drive unit must be able to write-read at the required density and access both sides of the diskette.

3.5 inch Disks

The 3.5 inch disk is stored in a rigid plastic casing which makes it more robust than its 5.25 inch counterpart. A metal sliding shutter which covers the recording surface access slot slides open when the disk is placed in the drive unit. The greater protection provided by this casing allows data to be recorded more densely on a 3.5 inch disk than is generally practicable on a floppy disk. A storage capacity of 1.44mb is typical.

A small hole with a sliding shutter located in one corner of the casing acts as the *write protect* slot. The drive unit uses an infra-red light source to determine whether or not the slot is open. An open slot indicates that the disk is *read only*. This is opposite to the condition used with a 5.25 inch floppy disk drive when a covered slot indicates 'read only'.

Alternative Backing Storage Devices and Media

Magnetic tape and disk systems account for a very large proportion of all storage systems in use, but there are a number of alternative systems. These include:

(i) optical disks;

(ii) magnetic bubble memory.

Optical Disks

The optical disk uses laser beam technology to allow data to be recorded and read using bit-densities several times greater than a typical magnetic disk. Data is recorded as bit-patterns using high-intensity laser beams to burn tiny holes into the surface of the disk. The data can then be read from the disk using a laser beam of reduced intensity. A similar technology is used for Compact Disk (CD) digitized recordings of music and film. Its application in computing is still in the early stages of development but it is likely to have a profound impact on backing storage usage.

There are two main types of optical disk system presently available.

CD-ROM (Compact Disk-Read Only Memory) Systems

As the title suggests this type of disk only allows the computer to read data from the disk. The disk is pre-recorded by the manufacturer. It is of no use for the storage of data which requires updating. Its main application is for Interactive Video Disk systems. A video disk can store text, images and audio signals and is of use in advertising, training and education. Sequences of film and sound can be retrieved under computer control.

WORM (Write Once, Read Many)

The large storage capacity of optical disks means that the writing facility can be used for a considerable period before all space is used up. Storage capacities are measured in gigabytes (thousands of millions of characters), way beyond the capacity of any magnetic disk systems. Optical disk systems which provide an erase facility are available but are still too expensive for most users.

Apart from its vast storage capacity, the optical disk is less prone to environmental hazards such as dust. The main reason for this is that the read signal is more intense and the laser head can be fixed 2mm from the disk surface, allowing dust and other particles to pass underneath.

The large investment in conventional hard disk systems, both in terms of hardware and software, is likely to slow the widespread introduction of optical disk for backing storage.

Magnetic Bubble Memory

Unlike disks and tapes, which are electro-mechanical devices, magnetic bubble memory has no moving parts at all.

Bubbles are formed in thin plates of magnetic material as tiny cylindrical *domains*. The presence of a bubble in a location represents a 1-bit and the absence of a bubble, a 0-bit. The bubbles can be moved within the magnetic layer by tiny electrical forces, thus altering the bit patterns. Bubbles can be created and destroyed by similar forces.

Because there are no moving parts, bubble memory is potentially more reliable than its electro-mechanical counterparts but as yet it has not been brought into general use for a variety of reasons. Firstly, storage capacities and access times for magnetic disks are continually being improved. Secondly, except for very small systems, magnetic bubble memory is more expensive per bit of storage, than magnetic disk. This is likely to remain so until increased volume of production brings down production costs. Its non-volatility makes it a possible alternative to the small disk memories used on some microcomputer systems. Currently, magnetic disk provides better access times than bubble memory.

The main applications of magnetic bubble memory are for memory units in terminals, microcomputers, robots and telecommunications equipment where the memory capacity required is not large. It appears that magnetic bubble memory has failed to make any real impact on storage systems.

Input and Output Devices

Overview of Input and Output Equipment

This section is concerned with equipment designed for input, output or both.

The most common methods of input involve the use of *display* devices such as the Visual Display Unit (VDU) and the first part of this section deals with such equipment. Printers are the next devices to be considered in that they provide 'hard copy' output of the results of computer processing, sometimes at incredible speeds.

The next part examines equipment which automates input and removes the need for keyboard data entry. Equipment in this category includes, for example, OCR (Optical Character Recognition) devices and Bar Code Readers.

Finally, an examination is made of some special-purpose output devices involving output onto microfilm and speech synthesis.

Display Devices

Visual Display Unit

The most commonly used device for communicating with a computer is the Visual Display Unit (VDU). Input of text is via a full alphanumeric keyboard and output is displayed on a viewing screen similar to a television. The term VDU terminal is normally used to describe the screen and keyboard as a combined facility for input and output. On its own, the screen is called a *monitor*. In order that an operator can see what is being typed in via the keyboard, input is also displayed on the screen. A square of light called a *cursor* indicates where the next character to be typed by the operator will be placed.

Display Screen Characteristics

Text and Graphics

Most display screens provide both a *text* and *graphics* facility. Text consists of letters (upper and lower case), numbers and special characters such as punctuation marks. Most applications require textual input and output. Graphics output includes picture images, such as maps, charts and drawings. In business applications, for example, a company's sales figures can be graphed on the screen if the screen provides graphical output. Most computer games rely on graphics.

Screen Resolution

A screen's resolution dictates the clarity or sharpness of the displayed text or graphics characters. The achievement of high quality graphics generally requires a higher resolution or sharper image than is required for textual display. Images are formed on the screen through the use of *pixels*. A pixel is a tiny dot of light on the screen and the resolution is determined by the number of pixels on the screen. The greater the density of pixels, the greater the resolution.

Resolution is measured by the number of columns and rows of pixels, for example, a resolution of 720 × 350 indicates 720 columns × 350 rows = 252,000 pixels.

Dot Matrix Characters

Textual characters are usually formed using a matrix of pixels as is shown in the following example. As with screen resolution, the clarity of individual characters is determined by the number of pixels used. Selected dots within the matrix are illuminated to display particular characters. A 10 × 14 matrix obviously gives greater clarity and definition than a 5 × 7 matrix and many display screens use even greater resolutions. Although both upper case and lower case can be accommodated in a particular size matrix, it is usual to add extra rows for the 'tails' of lower case letters such as g,p,y,j. Different character sets can be displayed using dot matrix representation.

A 5 × 7 Pixel Dot Matrix Forming The Letter 'F'

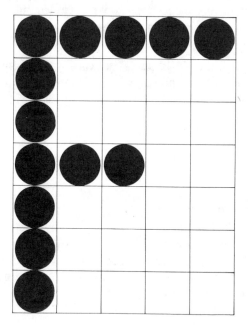

Graphics Display with Bit Mapping

To provide maximum control over the screen display, each pixel can be individually controlled by the programmer. This allows maximum flexibility in the design of individual images. Where image movement is required, in for example computer games, this is achieved in a similar manner to filmed cartoons. Smooth movement is simulated by making minute changes to the shape and location of the image. This requires the high degree of precision available at the individual pixel level. Apart from movement simulation, bit mapping allows the drawing of extremely complex and life-like pictures and is therefore used in the development of, for example,application packages for Computer Aided Design (CAD).

Monochrome and Colour

A monochrome screen uses one colour for the foreground and another for the background. White on black is not generally favoured because of indications from various research studies that users suffer greater eye fatigue than is the case with some other combinations. Green on black or amber on black are the most favoured combinations. Most screens offer a *reverse-video* feature which enable characters to be highlighted by selective switching of the foreground and background colours.

Colour is generally achieved through combinations of red, green and blue (RGB). A greater variety is obtained by mixing alternate pixels of different colours. In close proximity to one another, they appear to merge and produce a different colour. If a wider range of colours is directly available, then many more variations can be created by such illusion. Colour displays require a great deal of memory, but the fall in memory costs is facilitating an increased sophistication in applications which use colour, even those based on microcomputer systems.

Dumb and Intelligent Terminals

A *dumb* terminal is one which has no processing power of its own, possibly no storage, and is entirely dependent on a controlling computer. Where a terminal is connected via a telecommunications link, each character is transmitted to the central computer as soon as it is entered via the operator. This makes editing extremely difficult and slow and for this reason, they are not generally used for remote data entry.

An *intelligent* terminal has some memory and processing power and as such, allows the operator to store, edit and manipulate data without the support of the computer to which it is connected. The processing facility is provided by an internal processor, usually a microprocessor. Storage is normally in the form of *buffer* memory in which several lines of text can be held and manipulated before transmission. The facility may also include local backing storage on floppy disk and a printer.

A number of tasks required for text editing involve the use of control codes and these can be built into ROM (Read Only Memory) or magnetic bubble memory, both of which are non-volatile. Typical control codes are those which, via single key-presses, execute functions such as clearing the screen, moving the cursor up or down, and homing the cursor to the top-left of the screen. Function keys for these and other functions are generally specifically marked.

It is also likely that the terminal is programmable, probably in BASIC, thus allowing specific routines to be developed for validation of data.

Microcomputer systems are often used as intelligent terminals.

Keyboards

Computer keyboards are generally organised with a full QWERTY layout, a separate numeric keypad (useful when data includes a high proportion of numeric characters) and several function keys. The number of function keys varies from one keyboard to another. Keyboards designed specifically for use in word processing have many function keys dedicated to the task of text manipulation. Other general-purpose function keys may be given specific functions by whatever software package is being used. The desirable qualities of a keyboard are reliability, quietness and light operating pressure and in these terms keyboards vary dramatically.

Many keyboards are detachable, enabling the operator to position it to suit personal comfort. Usually the keyboard remains physically connected via a stretch-coil but a few systems use infra-red in a similar fashion to the remote control unit of a television set or video recorder.

Concept Keyboards

In specialist applications, the standard keyboard is not always the most convenient method of input. In a factory, for example, a limited number of functions may be necessary for the operation of a computerized lathe. These functions can be set out on a touch sensitive pad and clearly marked. This is possible because all inputs are anticipated and the range is small. The operator is saved the trouble of typing in the individual characters which form instructions.

Concept keyboards also have application in education, particularly for the mentally and physically handicapped. Instead of specific functions, interchangeable overlays, which indicate the functions of each area of the keyboard allow the user to design the keyboard to particular specifications. For example, if the responses required by a user are limited to 'yes' and 'no', the overlay is simply divided into two parts, one for each response. The keyboard is housed in a flat, wipe clean, touch sensitive aluminium box. The membrane on which overlays are placed is divided into a matrix of cells, for instance 128 on a 16 × 8 format. The cells have to be programmed to conform to the desired overlay.

Alternatives to Keyboards

Two methods of input make use of the screen display itself.

Touch Screen

Touch screen devices allow a screen to be activated by the user touching the screen with a finger. This is particularly useful where a menu of processing options is available on the screen for selection.

Light Pen

A light pen is shaped like a pen and contains a photo-electric or light-sensitive cell in its tip. When the pen is pointed at the screen the light from the screen is detected by the cell and the computer can identify the position of the pen. By *mapping* the screen to allocate particular functions to particular locations on the screen, the position of the pen indicates a particular function. The light pen enables specific parts of a picture on display to be selected or altered in some way, making it particularly useful for applications such as computer aided design (CAD).

Devices to control cursor movement include the *joystick*, the *mouse* and the *crosshair cursor*.

Joystick

The joystick is similar to a car's gear lever, except that fine variations in the angle of movement can be achieved. The cursor movement is a reflection of the movement of the joystick in terms of both direction and speed. It is commonly used for computer games and for CAD.

Mouse

The mouse has a roller which dictates cursor movement. The user can move the cursor by moving the mouse across a flat surface. It is very popular with 'user friendly' software which requires the user to select from displayed screen options. A select button is fitted on the mouse to enable the user to choose a particular screen position or function.

Crosshair Cursor

The crosshair cursor has a perspex 'window' with 'cross hairs' rather like a telescopic rifle's sighting mechanism. It can be moved over hard-copy images of maps, or survey photographs and allows precise selection of positions through the crosshair 'window'. The images are digitized into the computer's memory and can then be displayed on the screen for modification. The keyboard or a keypad built into the device can be used to enter additional information, for example to identify rivers or roads on a digitized map.

Printers

Printers can be categorized according to *speed* of operation and the *quality* of print. Printers are also identifiable as either *impact* or *non-impact* devices.

Impact Printers

Impact printing uses a print head to strike an inked ribbon which is located between the print head and the paper. Individual characters can be printed by either a dot-matrix mechanism or by print heads which contain each character as a separate font (solid font type).

Dot Matrix Printers

Characters can be formed from a matrix of dots, typically a 7×7 or 9×7 matrix. The density of the matrix largely determines the quality of the print. The impact is carried out by a number of 'needles' which can be projected or withdrawn according to the pattern that is required. A ROM (Read Only Memory) 'chip' within the printer provides it with a character set. Certain built in functions such as automatic line feed and alternative character sets can be altered by switching small *dip* switches inside the printer. The intensity of print can be improved by passing the print head over a line twice (double-strike). In summary, a dot matrix printer can be programmed to effect a wide variation of printing results

Graphical Output

Printers which support bit-mapping (software control over individual pins in the matrix head) can produce graphical output. Without colour, pictorial effects can be achieved by double-striking to emphasize some areas of print and by moving the paper in very small increments rather than a line at a time.

Solid Font Printing

A solid font head uses a separate font for each character and character sets have to be altered by changing the head.

Because they form a solid image, they have until recently, provided a better quality of print than the dot-matrix type. There are a number of types, three of which are described below.

Daisy-wheel Head

As the name suggests, character fonts are attached to 'petals' on a central wheel which has to revolve to place a particular character in the print position. Inevitably, the considerable movement required between each character print means that daisy-wheel printers operate relatively slowly, about 30 to 60 characters per second. The quality of print is very high which makes it a popular device for the production of, for example, legal documents and other output where image is vital. Laser and ink jet printers, as well as new dot matrix printers are providing increasing competition and the daisy wheel is likely to become less popular.

Cylinder Print Head

This type is only used on teletypewriter or teleprinter terminals and is consequently becoming uncommon. A teletypewriter has a keyboard and printer only and although largely replaced by the VDU, is still used for telex communications. The cylinder print head has 64 symbols embossed on a cylinder. Lower-case characters are not provided. An individual character is selected through a clockwise or anti-clockwise turn and an appropriate vertical movement of the head. Impact with the ribbon is achieved by a hammer which strikes the back of the print head whenever a character is to be printed.

Golf-ball Head

The golf-ball head also has characters embossed on its surface but it differs from the cylinder print head in three main ways. Firstly, the spherical shape accommodates a wider range of characters than the cylinder shape. Secondly, different character sets can be obtained by changing the print head. Thirdly, the head is made to strike the ribbon by a cam mechanism. No hammer strikes the head. Individual characters are obtained by the rotation and tilting of the head.

Dot-matrix printers are much faster than solid-font printers. Speeds of 100 to 300 characters per second are common for low-speed, impact dot matrix printers.

All the printers described above are *character* printers in that they print a single character at a time. Faster printing can be achieved by *line* and *page* printers

Line Printers

A line printer prints a complete line of characters, rather than in the serial fashion used by character printers.

Two types of line printer are described here, the *barrel* or *drum* printer and the *chain* printer.

Barrel Printer

The barrel printer has a band with a complete set of characters at each print position. Each print position has a hammer to impact the print ribbon against the paper. There are usually 132 print positions on the barrel. The mechanism is illustrated below.

132 bands

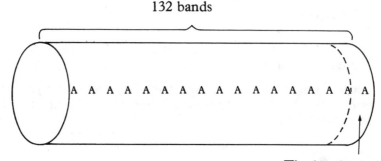

The band at each printing position consists of all characters available

One complete revolution of the barrel exposes all the characters to each print position. Therefore a complete line can be printed in one revolution. The characters on the barrel are arranged so that all characters of the same type are in the same horizontal position. Thus, in a line of print, any required As can be printed, then Bs and so on, until the complete line is printed. The barrel revolves continuously during printing, the paper being fed through and the process repeated for each line of print. Typical printing speeds are 100 to 400 lines per minute.

Chain Printer

The chain printer mechanism is illustrated below.

Several complete sets of characters are held on a continuous chain which moves horizontally across the paper. The ribbon is situated between the chain and the paper and an individual hammer is located at each of the 132 print positions. A complete line can be printed as one complete set of characters passes across the paper. Thus, in one pass as many lines can be printed as there are sets of characters in the chain. Printing speeds are higher than is possible for barrel printers.

Chain Printer

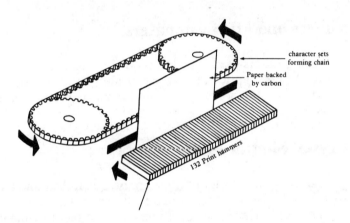

Line printers are expensive compared with character printers but may well be necessary where large volume output is required. Printing speeds of up to 3000 lines per minute are achieved with impact line printers. Even higher speeds are possible with non-impact printers.

Non-Impact Printers

Most non-impact printers use dot-matrix heads. They do not require mechanical hammers and print heads do not strike the paper. A variety of printers are available using a wide range of technologies. The most popular are as follow.

Thermal Printers

Characters are burned onto heat-sensitive thermographic paper. The paper is white and develops colour when heated above a particular temperature. The heat is generated by rods in the dot-matrix print head. By selective heating of rods, individual characters can be formed from the matrix. Printing can be carried out serially, one character at a time or, through the use of several heads, on a line-by-line basis. Serial thermal printing is slow but speeds in excess of 1000 lines per minute are possible with line thermal printing.

Electrosensitive Printers

This type produce characters in a similar fashion to the thermal printer except that the paper used has a thin coating of aluminium which covers a layer of black, blue or red dye. Low voltage electrical discharges in the matrix rods produce sparks which selectively remove the aluminium coating to reveal the layer of dye underneath. Operated as line printers with heads at each print position, printing speeds in excess of 3000 lines per minute are achieved.

Laser Printers

Laser printers use a combination of two technologies, electro-photographic printing used in photo-copying and high intensity lasers. A photoconductive drum is initially charged and then a high intensity laser beam selectively discharges areas on the drum. As with photocopiers, toner material is spread over the surface to form an ink image. This is then transferred to the paper and made permanent through heating. Achieving print speeds of 21,000 lines per minute, the laser printer is used in very large systems requiring exceptionally high speed output.

Effectively, complete pages are printed at one time so they come under the heading of *page* printers.

Laser Printers and Microcomputers

Laser printers used to be too costly for use in a microcomputer environment, but with rapidly falling prices, they are providing some competition for the dot matrix printers. Although still more costly than dot matrix printers, laser printers offer greater speed and quality.

Liquid Crystal Shutter Printer

Liquid crystal shutter printers are based on the same technology as the generally more expensive laser printers, but do not rely on a laser for the light source. In laser printers, the laser is fixed in one position, so to complete an image the width of a page, the beam is reflected from a rotating mirror which moves the laser beam horizontally across the drum. This scanning action involves some complicated mechanical machinery which, together with the laser, forms a major part of the component costs. Liquid crystal shutter printers, on the other hand, use a powerful halogen light bulb as their light source and an array of liquid crystal shutters (the same technology used for liquid crystal displays (LCD) on watches and portable computer display screens) to control which positions on the photo-sensitive drum are exposed at any one time. In the Crystal Print 2, the array contains 2400 shutters, sufficient to produce a full page-width image at one go. In a liquid crystal shutter printer, moving parts are limited to the revolving drum and the paper and this makes the machine simpler and cheaper to service than its laser counterpart.

Ink Jet Printers

Ink jet printers spray high-speed streams of electrically charged ink droplets from individual nozzles in the matrix head onto the paper to form characters. Many will hold colour cartridges to produce excellent colour output.

Ink jet printers provide a possible alternative to the laser printer.

Summary of Printers

Generally speaking, the smaller, low speed, character printers are of use with microcomputer systems, but the increasing popularity of such systems has demanded increased sophistication in small printers. Features which have improved printing speeds include *bi-directional* printing (printing in two directions) and *logic-seeking* which allows the printer to cut short a traverse across the paper if only a few characters are required on a line.

The most popular printers for microcomputers are, impact dot-matrix, daisy-wheel, electro-sensitive, ink jet and laser.

Data Capture Devices

Source data is normally collected in human-readable form. For example, customer orders are recorded on order forms and weekly pay details may be recorded on time sheets. Prior to processing, such data has to be translated into machine-sensible form and this usually involves a keying operation. There are a number of *data capture* devices available which allow data to be collected in a printed or hand-written form directly readable by a computer input device.

Optical Character Readers (OCR)

OCRs are designed to read stylized characters which are also readable by humans. There are a number of designs for such characters but any individual design is known as the character *font*. There are a number of industry standard fonts and an example selection from an optical character set is shown below.

The OCR reflects light off the characters and converts them into digital patterns for comparison with the stored character set. Originally, a highly stylized appearance was preferred to aid machine recognition but some OCRs can read the character sets of popular makes of office typewriter. Ideally, OCRs should be able to read any characters but the wider the range of styles that need to be read, the more difficult becomes the recognition process. In some applications, a restricted character set of, perhaps numerals and certain alphabetic characters may suffice and the reading process becomes quicker and more accurate. Nevertheless, large OCRs are capable of reading several character sets comprising more than 300 characters.

```
ABCDEFGHIJKLMN
OPQRSTUVWXYZ
1234567890.
```

The reading of hand-printed characters presents particular problems because of the almost infinite variation of printing styles. Recognition is possible provided that the person preparing the data has a visual guide of the preferred style. The character set will usually be limited to numerals and a few alphabetic characters.

Artificial intelligence techniques are being applied to OCRs to allow the 'learning' of new character sets.

Applications of OCR

OCR is often used to capture sales data at the point-of-sale (POS). A POS terminal is essentially an electronic cash register linked to a computer or with storage of its own. Data captured at the terminal can, for example, be sent to update computer files. Sometimes POS registers have direct-access memory to hold product prices and descriptions, so that the details can be printed on the customer receipt. An OCR-character-coded price label, attached to each product, can be scanned with a wand (light pen) or laser 'gun'.

Optical Mark Readers (OMR)

An OMR is designed to read marks placed in preset positions on a document. The document is preprinted and the values which can be entered are limited as each value is represented by, for example, a box in a certain position. Thus, a suitable application for OMR is a multi-choice exam paper, where the answer to each question has to be indicated by a pencil mark in one of several boxes after the question. The figure on the next page illustrates such a form:

The OMR scans the document for boxes containing pencil marks and thus identifies the values selected.

Optical mark readers can read up to 10,000 A4 documents per hour.

Bar Code Readers

The bar code is also an optical code which is normally read by a light pen. The code makes use of a series of black bars of varying thickness. The gaps between each bar also vary. These bars and gaps are used to represent numeric data. The values represented are often printed underneath in decimal form.

A BAR CODE

Bar codes are commonly used to store a variety of data such as price and stock code concerning products in shops and supermarkets. A sticker with the relevant bar code (itself produced by computer) is attached to each product. Sometimes, the check-out will have a built-in scanner station over which the goods pass. This is convenient if packages are of regular shape but soft packages with creases may cause problems for the scanner. In such cases, the light pen or wand provides a more practical solution. By using the data from the code, the cash register can identify the item, look up its latest price and print the information on the customer's receipt.

Another useful application is for the recording of library issues. A bar code sticker is placed inside the book cover and at the time of issue or return it can be scanned and the library stock record updated. By providing each library user with a bar coded library card, the information regarding an individual who is borrowing a book can be linked with the book's details at the time of borrowing.

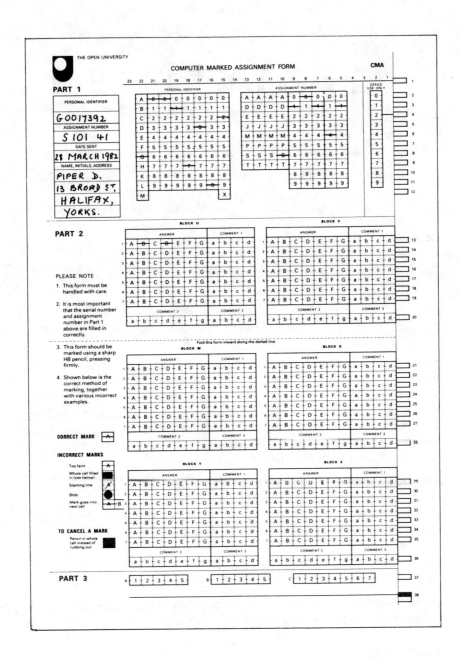

Magnetic Ink Character Reader (MICR)

This particular device is employed almost exclusively by the banking industry, where it is used for sorting and processing cheques in large volumes. The millions of cheques which pass through the London Clearing System could not possibly be sorted and processed without the use of MICRs.

Highly stylized characters, usually of the E13B font illustrated on the next page, are printed along the bottom of the cheques by a special printer, using ink containing iron oxide. The MICR first magnetizes the characters as the cheque passes through and then decodes them by induced voltage signals. A high degree of reliability and accuracy is possible, partly because of the stylized font, but more importantly, because the characters are not affected by dirty marks. This is obviously important when cheques may pass through several hands before reaching their destination. Such marks may cause problems for an optical character reader.

0123456789

Amount symbol   Dash symbol   "On-us" symbol   Sorting Code Symbol

Digitizers

Examples of digitizers in use are provided by the light pen, the mouse and the joystick, described earlier.

Another name for a digitizer is an Analogue to Digital converter (ADC). Data is often not in digital format but is instead a measurement, for example, of temperature changes or changes in light intensity. Such data is in analogue form. Temperature is normally measured by the movement of mercury in a thermometer and light intensity by movement of a pointer on the dial of a light meter. By reflecting these measurement changes with voltage changes, they can then be converted to the digital signals useable by the computer with an ADC or digitizer.

A particularly useful device for collecting pictorial data is the *graphics tablet*. A pen-like stylus enables the user to 'draw' on the tablet and reflect the results on the computer screen or store the results for future manipulation. The tablet is addressable by the computer through a matrix of thousands of tiny 'dots', each of which reflect a binary 1 or 0. When a line is drawn on the tablet, the stylus passes over these dot locations, causing the binary values in memory to change. Thus a particular drawing has a particular binary format which can be stored, manipulated or displayed.

Digitizers are used in other applications, for example, in the capturing of photographic images, via a 'digitizing' camera and the subsequent production of a digitized image.

Voice Recognition Devices

Human speech varies in accent, personal style of speech and pitch and the interpretation of the spoken word makes the development of voice recognition devices a difficult process. In normal conversation, humans make assumptions about the listener, often cutting sentences short or emphasizing a point with a facial expression. Voice recognition devices to deal with complete human language are unlikely to be developed for some time to come.

There are however, devices which can be 'trained' to recognize a limited number of words spoken by the individual doing the training. Devices can be used to give commands for machinery control, for example, 'up', 'down', 'left', 'right', 'fast', 'slow' etc. Paralysed persons can control a wheelchair or lighting and heating through a voice recognition device controlled by a microprocessor.

Special-Purpose Output Devices

Computer Output Microform (COM) Recorders

COM recorders record information from computer storage onto microfilm or microfiche. Microfilm is a continuous reel, whereas, microfiche is a sheet of film with a matrix of squares or pages. Either form can be viewed with a magnifying viewer. COM can result in large savings in paper costs, storage space and handling. For example, a 4 inch × 6 inch microfiche sheet can store the equivalent of 270 printed pages.

COM is particularly useful for the storage of large amounts of information which do not need to be updated frequently.

Graph Plotters

A plotter is a device designed to produce charts, drawings, maps and other forms of graphical information on paper. There are a variety of methods for producing the image.

Pen Plotters

Pen plotters use an ink pen or pens to create images on paper. There are two types:

(i) Flatbed plotters;

(ii) Drum Plotters.

A *flatbed* plotter is illustrated below.

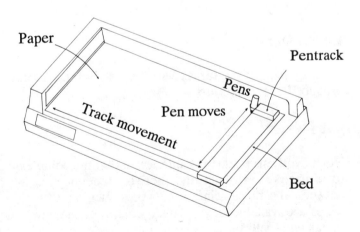

It looks like a drafting board with pens mounted on a carriage which moves along guide tracks. The paper is placed on the 'bed'. The pens can be raised or lowered as the image being created requires and different coloured pens can be brought into use at various stages of the process. Drawing movements are executed by movement of the carriage along the tracks and by the pens along the carriage. The size of paper which can be accommodated is limited by the size of the plotter 'bed', but this can be extremely large.

A *drum* plotter has a different drawing mechanism. Instead of the paper remaining still, it moves to produce one of the lateral movements whilst the pens move to execute the other movements. In order to control the paper, the drum plotter uses sprocket wheels to interlock with the paper. The main advantage of the drum plotter is its ability to handle large sheets of paper. The operation of a drum plotter is illustrated below.

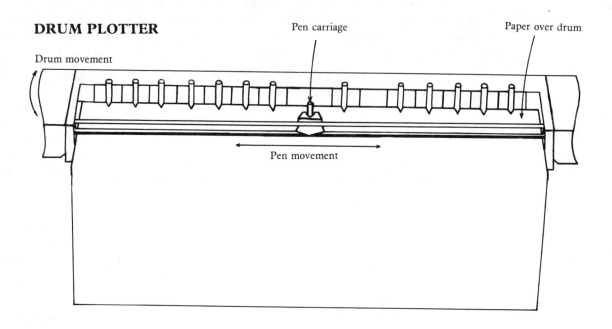

DRUM PLOTTER

Pen carriage

Paper over drum

Drum movement

Pen movement

Electrostatic Plotters

The electrostatic plotter is relatively fast, but the output is of poorer quality than that produced by pen plotters.

Voice Output Devices

Voice synthesis is still in its infancy, in that the complexities of human speech have yet to be mastered satisfactorily. There is a tendency for such devices to become confused between the pronunciation of words such as 'though' and 'plough'. Speech ROM 'chips' are available for many microcomputer systems. Educational applications include 'speak and spell' and arithmetic. Large scale application is possible where the range of output can be anticipated, for example, stocks and share prices, railway timetables, speaking clock etc. Such services may be provided via an answerphone service.

Assignment *Gotta Lot of Bottle*

Fine Wines Limited is a medium sized company with a chain of off-licence shops in the Somerset area. Its Registered Office and central warehouse are in Bath. A minicomputer is used for most of the company's accounting and administrative applications. A telecommunications link between warehouse and main office allows the updating of stock files via VDU terminals at the warehouse. In addition, a printer at the warehouse is used to print details of orders from the various shops in the off-licence chain. Each week, the company's delivery lorries deliver the goods ordered by each shop manager a week previously. At the same time, the driver collects the completed order forms for the following week's delivery. The drivers return the order forms to the Bath office where they are keyed in and processed.

You are employed by Compudata, a software house based in Bristol, as a trainee systems analyst. Fine Wines Ltd. have approached Compudata regarding the improvement of the order collection procedures. It is apparent that the data collection procedure could be automated because the Fine Wines order forms are designed with pre-printed item lists and choices of quantities which can be ordered. In other words, all the shop manager has to do is tick chosen quantity boxes next to selected items in the list. Your team leader, Ken Barlow, has given you the task of preparing a preliminary report for presentation to Fine Wines Limited, outlining the use of Optical Mark Reading (OMR) techniques to automate order collection.

Tasks

1. Prepare a preliminary report for Fine Wines Ltd., outlining the OMR proposals and briefly explaining the principles of the technique. In addition explain how the present design of forms may be utilized and how they must be completed by the shop managers. Identify any extra equipment which needs to be purchased.

2. In order to give Fine Wines Limited some element of choice, briefly outline any possible alternatives they may adopt for their order collection procedures.

Chapter 19

Number Systems

Introduction

Although the denary number system has proved to be the simplest for humans to use, it is more convenient for computers to use the binary number system. As is explained in more detail in Chapter 20, the electronic components used in computers can be in one of two physical states, which can be used to represent 0 and 1, the two digits of the binary number system. This chapter explains the basis of this and other number systems relevant to the subject of computing.

General Principles of Number Systems

The Radix or Base of a Number System

First consider the denary system. There are ten symbols, 0 to 9 and the base or radix of a number system is simply the number of different symbols it uses. Thus, the denary number system has a radix or base of 10.

Place Value

Each symbol can be given a weight or *place value*, according to its position within a number. In the denary system, each place value is a power of ten. Thus, for denary integers the place values (starting from the least significant digit on the right) are units, tens, hundreds, thousands etc. The concept of place value can be illustrated with the following example of an integer number, 1263:

Power of ten	10^3	10^2	10^1	10^0
	1000's	100's	10's	units
	1	2	6	3

The normal representation of 1263 can be seen as:

$$1 \times 1000 + 2 \times 100 + 6 \times 10 + 3 \times 1$$

It should be noted that any number raised to the power of zero is 1.

The value of a fractional digit is also determined by its position within a number, except that the power is negative.

Power of ten	10^{-1}	10^{-2}

The normal representation of 0.75 or ¾ can be seen as:

$$7 \times \tfrac{1}{10} + 5 \times \tfrac{1}{100} = \tfrac{75}{100} = \tfrac{3}{4}$$

The Binary System

The binary system uses two symbols 0 and 1. Thus, it has a base or radix of 2. The denary system uses powers of ten and the binary system uses powers of two. Each binary digit (bit) is weighted with a power of two according to its position within a number. Some of the place values are shown below:

Integers					Fractions		
16	8	4	2	1	½	¼	⅛
2^4	2^3	2^2	2^1	2^0	2^{-1}	2^{-2}	2^{-3}

Thus the binary number 11001.11 is equivalent to:

$$1 \times 2^4 + 1 \times 2^3 + 0 \times 2^2 + 0 \times 2^1 + 1 \times 2^0 + 1 \times 2^{-1} + 1 \times 2^{-2}$$

$$= 16 + 8 + 0 + 0 + 1 + ½ + ¼$$

which equals denary 25¾

The following table shows the binary equivalents of 1 to 10 in the denary system:

Denary	Binary
1	00001
2	00010
3	00011
4	00100
5	00101
6	00110
7	00111
8	01000
9	01001
10	01010

Using the place values for the binary system shown earlier, it is easy to see how each of the denary numbers in the table equates with its binary representation.

Binary - Rules of Arithmetic

Addition Rules

$$0 + 0 = 0$$
$$0 + 1 = 1$$
$$1 + 0 = 1$$
$$1 + 1 = 0 \quad \text{plus 1 carried forward}$$

Example

```
 011010
 110100 +
1001110
```

Note that the 1 on the left hand end of the number has been carried forward.

Example

```
101100
000010 +
101110
```

The rules for binary addition are needed when studying computer arithmetic in Chapter 22.

Octal and Hexadecimal Numbers

These number systems are often used as a shorthand method for representing binary numbers. As can be seen from the binary numbers listed above, they are very confusing to the eye and it is difficult, even with small groupings, to distinguish one pattern from another. Where it is necessary for the computer's binary codes to be written or read by programmers, for example, then it is invariably more convenient to use alternative coding methods. Octal and hexadecimal (hex) notations are used because they are more readily converted to or from binary than denary notation.

It must be emphasized that computers can only handle binary forms of coding. Therefore octal and hexadecimal codes must be converted to binary before they can be handled by the computer.

Octal Coding

The octal number system has a base of 8, using 0 to 7 as its symbols. Some of the place values are shown below:

Integers				Fractions		
512	64	8	1	$\frac{1}{8}$	$\frac{1}{64}$	$\frac{1}{512}$
8^3	8^2	8^1	8^0	8^{-1}	8^{-2}	8^{-3}

The coding of binary numbers in octal is straightforward. Three binary digits will allow $8\,(2^3)$ different patterns of bits, sufficient to represent each of the octal symbols. These are as follow:

Binary Number	Octal Coding
000	0
001	1
010	2
011	3
100	4
101	5
110	6
111	7

A binary number can be split into groups of 3 bits, starting from the right-hand side, as the following example shows:

Binary number (16 bits)	0	111	001	101	100	110
Octal coding	0	7	1	5	4	6

Because the 16 bits will not divide exactly into groups of 3, the left-most or Most Significant Bit (MSB) can only take the values 0 or 1.

A more commonly used system is the hexadecimal coding system.

Hexadecimal Coding

The hexadecimal number system has a base of 16, and uses the following symbols:

0 to 9 and A to F (used for the numbers 10 to 15 in the denary system)

The letters A, B, C, D, E and F are used to bring the number of unique symbols up to sixteen. The place values can be illustrated as follows:

Integers				Fractions		
4096	256	16	1	$\frac{1}{16}$	$\frac{1}{256}$	$\frac{1}{4096}$
16^3	16^2	16^1	16^0	16^{-1}	16^{-2}	16^{-3}

A group of 4 bits will provide 16 possible unique patterns, the number required to represent all the symbols of the hexadecimal number system. These are as follow:

Binary Number	Hexadecimal Coding
0000	0
0001	1
0010	2
0011	3
0100	4
0101	5
0110	6
0111	7
1000	8
1001	9
1010	A
1011	B
1100	C
1101	D
1110	E
1111	F

Therefore, a binary number can be coded by grouping the bits into groups of four, starting from the right-hand side and using the appropriate hexadecimal symbol for each group, as the following example shows:

Binary number (16 bits)	1100	0011	1111	0110
Hexadecimal Coding	C	3	F	6

Hexadecimal coding is more commonly used because most computers now organize their internal memory in 8-bit groupings (*bytes*) or multiples of bytes. These groupings conveniently divide into 4-bit *nibbles* which can be coded in the 'shorthand' of hexadecimal.

A knowledge of hexadecimal is essential for the interpretation of computer manufacturers' manuals, which use the coding system extensively to specify memory and backing storage features. Programmers using low level languages, such as assembly code, also need to be familiar with this number system.

Assignment   *Position Counts*

You are a member of a race of one-armed people and have developed a number system based on your five available fingers. The chief of your tribe is interested because the present two-digit number system based on the number of ears each person has is inadequate for the extensive trading carried out with neighbouring tribes.

Tasks

1.   Produce some explanatory notes to help you present your talk to the rest of the tribe. The notes should include references to place value, the radix or base of the number system, and a table showing several integer and fractional values either side of the radix point. Also provide a two-column table showing several quinary numbers and their binary equivalent. Explain any benefit the quinary system may provide compared with the existing binary system.

2.   Present the talk to the rest of the 'tribe'.

Developmental Task

Try designing a duo-decimal (base 12) number system.

Chapter 20

Data Representation

The Need for Data Representation

The distinction made between data and information at the beginning of Chapter 17 is not relevant here. Data in this context is a general term which covers any data or information which is capable of being handled by the computer's internal circuitry, or of being stored on backing storage media such as magnetic tape or disk.

To be processed by computer, data must be in a form which the computer can handle; it must be *machine-sensible*.

Data Coded in Binary

To be 'machine-sensible', data has to be in binary format. In Chapter 19, it is explained that the binary number system uses only two digits, 0 and 1. Both the main memory and external storage media, such as magnetic disk and tape, use patterns of the electrical/magnetic representations of the digits 0 and 1 to record data and instructions.

Why Binary? - Bi-stable Devices

Computer storage uses two-state or *bi-stable* devices to indicate the presence of a 0 or a 1. The circuits inside a computer represent these two states by being either conducting or non-conducting, that is, current is either flowing or is not flowing through the circuit. A simple example of a bi-stable device is an electric light bulb. At any one time it must be in one or other of two states, on or off. Magnetic storage media use magnetic fields of two possible polarities (north and south) as bi-stable devices to represent 0 and 1.

To understand the benefits of using binary representation, consider the electronic requirements which would be necessary if the decimal (denary) system were used. To record the digits 0 - 9, a computer's circuitry would have to use and accommodate ten clearly defined physical electronic states. This would require extremely reliable components to avoid the machine confusing one physical state with another. With bi-stable devices, slight changes in performance do not prevent differentiation between the two physical states which represent 0 and 1.

Coding of Data

Much of the data processed by computer and stored on backing storage is represented by *character* codes. The codes used inside the computer are referred to as *internal* codes, whereas those used by various peripherals are termed *external* codes. Data transferred between peripheral devices and the processor may utilize a variety of binary character codes, but when processing data the processor will tend to use a particular internal code, which will vary with machines of different manufacture. Sometimes, an external character code may continue to be used for storage of data in main memory; alphabetic data remains in character code form during computer processing. On the other hand, numeric data presented by a peripheral in character code form is converted to one of a number of numeric codes for processing purposes. Code conversion may be executed within a peripheral, within the interface device between a peripheral and the processor, or within the processor itself.

Characters may be grouped according to the following categories:

- alphabetic (upper and lower case);
- numeric (0 to 9);
- special characters (apostrophe, comma, etc);
- control characters and codes.

Control characters are used in data transmission, perhaps to indicate the start or end of a block of data; control codes can be used to affect the display of data on a VDU screen and include those which cause, for example, carriage return, delete, highlight or blinking. Control characters and codes do not form part of the data which is to be usefully processed, but are necessary for its control.

The range of characters which can be represented by a computer system is known as its Character Set. The ASCII (American Standard Code for Information Interchange) code, illustrated in the following table, uses seven *binary digits* (*bits*) to represent a full range of characters:

ASCII Character Set (Extract)

Data passing between a peripheral and the computer is usually in character code, typically ASCII or EBCDIC (shown in the following table).

Character	ASCII 7-Bit Representation	Character	ASCII 7-Bit Representation
0	0110000	I	1001001
1	0110001	J	1001010
2	0110010	K	1001011
3	0110011	L	1001100
4	0110100	M	1001101
5	0110101	N	1001110
6	0110110	O	1001111
7	0110111	P	1010000
8	0111000	Q	1010001
9	0111001	R	1010010
A	1000001	S	1010011
B	1000010	T	1010100
C	1000011	U	1010101
D	1000100	V	1010110
E	1000101	W	1010111
F	1000110	X	1011000
G	1000111	Y	1011001
H	1001000	Z	1011010

Extended Binary Coded Decimal Interchange Code (EBCDIC) (Extract)

Character	EBCDIC 8-Bit Representation	Character	EBCDIC 8-Bit Representation
0	11110000	I	11001001
1	11110001	J	11010001
2	11110010	K	11010010
3	11110011	L	11010011
4	11110100	M	11010100
5	11110101	N	11010101
6	11110110	O	11010110
7	11110111	P	11010111
8	11111000	Q	11011000
9	11111001	R	11011001
A	11000001	S	11100010
B	11000010	T	11100011
C	11000011	U	11100100
D	11000100	V	11100101
E	11000101	W	11100110
F	11000110	X	11100111
G	11000111	Y	11101000
H	11001000	Z	11101001

This popular 8-bit character code has a 256 character set and is generally used with IBM and IBM-compatible equipment.

Parity Checking of Codes

The ASCII code shown earlier is a 7-bit code. An additional bit in the left-most (most significant bit) position is used for detecting single bit errors which may occur during data transfer. Such errors may result from a peripheral fault or from corruption of data on storage media.

The scheme used for detecting errors is simple. There are two types of parity, namely *odd* and *even*, though it is of little significance which is used. To record odd parity, the parity bit is set to 1 or 0 in order that there are an odd number of bit 1s in the group. Conversely, even parity requires that the parity bit is set so that there are an even number of bit 1s in the group.

Examples of these two methods are shown below:

Data	Odd Parity	EvenParity
1001010	01001010	11001010
0101101	10101101	00101101
	↑	↑
	parity bit	parity bit

If even parity is being used and the main store receives the grouping 10010100 then the presence of an odd number of bits indicates an error in transmission. Provided an odd number of bits are corrupted all transmission errors will be detected. However, an even number of bits in error will not affect the parity condition and additional controls can be implemented which make use of parity checks on blocks of characters (*block check characters* - BCC).

Data Storage in Main Memory

Character codes, such as the ASCII code described earlier, are primarily of use during data transfer between a peripheral and the main memory. They are also generally used to represent non-numeric data inside the computer. Numeric data is usually converted to one of a number of numeric codes.

Binary Coded Decimal (BCD)

As the name suggests, BCD uses a binary code to represent the decimal digits. It is a 4-bit code and is only used for the representation of numeric values. Each of the ten digits used in the decimal system is coded with its binary equivalent as follows:

Decimal Digit	0	1	2	3	4	5	6	7	8	9
BCD Code	0000	0001	0010	0011	0100	0101	0110	0111	1000	1001

In this way, any number can be represented by coding each digit separately.

A decimal value of 624 would be coded as follows:

Decimal	6	2	4
BCD	0110	0010	0100

A number of points need to be made regarding this coding method:

- only ten of the sixteen (2^4) possible unique combinations available with each 4-bit group is used;
- a decimal number in BCD generally uses more bits of storage than a pure binary representation of the number;

Example

Decimal	BCD	Pure Binary
1265	0001 0010 0110 0101	10100001001
	16 bits	11 bits

- more complex electronics are required to carry out arithmetic on data in BCD form than are necessary for pure binary numbers.
- although 4 bits are sufficient for BCD representation, the sixteen possible binary patterns are clearly not enough to represent all alphabetic and special characters as well. To allow the coding of alphabetic and other characters, more bits are often used; the standard 6-bit BCD code allows the representation of a 64 character set and the EBCDIC code described earlier provides for a 256 character set.

BCD is, nevertheless, a very popular method of representing numbers within a computer.

Internal Parity Checks

Most mini and mainframe computers use parity bits to detect and sometimes correct, data transfer errors within the computer, so the actual length of codes is extended accordingly.

The Structure of Main Memory

Main memory is divided into a number of cells or *locations,* each of which has a unique name or *address* and is capable of holding a unit or grouping of bits which may represent data or an instruction. More is said about instructions in Chapter 22. Memory locations are normally addressed using whole numbers from zero upwards.

Size of Locations

The size of memory location used varies from one make of computer to another and is related to the coding methods used and the number of bits it is designed to handle as a unit.

Memory Words

A memory word is a given number of bits in memory, addressable as a unit. The addresses of memory locations run consecutively, starting with address 0 and running up to the largest address. Each location contains a word which can be retrieved by specification of its address. Similarly, an instruction to write to a location results in the storage of a word into the quoted address. For example, the word 01100110 may be stored in location address 15 and the word 11000110 in location address 16. A memory word may represent data or an instruction. The topic of memory addressing is dealt with in Chapter 22. The number of bits which is stored in a location is known as the memory's *word length.* Thus, memory which handles memory words of 16 bits is known as 16-bit memory, whilst that which makes use of 32-bit words is known as 32-bit memory. In practice, a machine may use memory words of different lengths for different operations. Word length is one of the most important design characteristics of computers, in that it can be fundamental to the efficiency and speed of the computer. Generally, the larger and more powerful the computer, the greater the word length. Until recently, 32-bit and 64-bit words were largely used by mainframe and minicomputer systems exclusively. When first introduced, microcomputers were 4-bit or 8-bit machines, but advances in technology have made 16-bit and 32-bit microcomputers commonplace.

Bytes

Words can usually be broken down into smaller units called *bytes.* An 8-bit unit is called a byte. In an 8-bit computer, the terms 'byte' and 'word' are interchangeable. A 16-bit computer, for example, may be able to access a 16-bit memory word in two 8-bit bytes.

Nibbles

In 4-bit microprocessors, the 4-bit word is known as a *nibble.* Two nibbles form a byte.

The need to refer to bytes arises from the fact that a location may contain more than one separate grouping of bits, each of which has a separate purpose. As explained above, the coding systems used for numeric and non-numeric data are different and thus need different storage requirements. This has led to a number of different memory structures, based on different word lengths, which have sufficient flexibility to accommodate the requirements of both numeric and non-numeric data.

Alternative Memory Structures

Byte Machines

In such machines the memory is structured with locations having a fixed length of 8 bits. This makes possible 256 different bit patterns ($2^8 = 256$). Thus, the full ASCII character set (described earlier) can be represented. In addition, two 4-bit BCD numeric characters will fit into each 8-bit location.

Data Storage in a Byte Machine

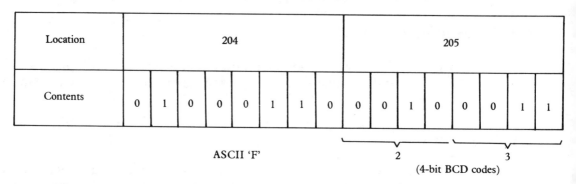

Location	204	205
Contents	0 1 0 0 0 1 1 0	0 0 1 0 0 0 1 1

ASCII 'F'   2   3
                              (4-bit BCD codes)

Word Machines (Fixed Word Length Computer)

In this design, data is handled a word at a time; one word = one location. The unit of transfer between the processor and the main memory is always the same size. Word lengths include 16, 24, 32 and 64 bits. Several characters may be packed into one word, for example, four 4-bit BCD digits or two 8-bit EBCDIC characters in a 16-bit word. Frequently, storage is wasted if only part of a word is occupied, for example, when one 8-bit EBCDIC character is held in a 16-bit word.

Variable Word Length Computers

This type of computer allows a word to be of variable length by using one or more locations at the time of data transfer. If, for example, the characters 'CAT' were to be stored, the word length could be set to one and each character referred to separately. Alternatively, the word length could be set to three to allow 'CAT' to be referred to all at once. The byte machine provides an example of a variable word length computer.

Number Representation inside the Computer

To be of practical use, a computer must be able to store, manipulate and differentiate between positive and negative numbers.

There are a number of different ways this can be done. The most common are:

(i) sign and magnitude;
(ii) complementation.

Before describing these methods convention states that, in common with other number systems, the right-most digit in a binary number is the Least Significant Bit (LSB) and the bits increase in significance until the Most Significant Bit (MSB) in the left-most position.

Sign and Magnitude

With this method, the MSB position is occupied by a bit 0 or a bit 1 to indicate, respectively, either a positive or negative sign. The remainder of the binary word holds the *absolute* (independent of the sign) magnitude of the number. The following examples illustrate this method in a 16-bit word:

sign bit (0 for +)
+33   0000000000100001
sign bit (1 for −)
−28   1000000000011100

Complementation

Complementation enables a computer to carry out subtraction by addition.

Tens Complement

The tens complement of a single decimal digit is found by subtracting the digit from ten. Thus the tens complement of 4 is $(10 - 4)$ which is +6. In the decimal system, subtracting a decimal number is equivalent to adding the tens complement of that number. Consider the following subtraction:

$$8 - 3 = 5$$

By switching the number 3 to its tens complement $(10 - 3 = 7)$ the calculation becomes:

```
 8
 7+
 ──
 15
  ↑
```

ignore the final carried digit

A more detailed explanation of the process of number complementation is given in Chapter 24 on Arithmetic Operations. There is no benefit in using tens complement for subtraction because the process of complementation itself involves subtraction. However, this is not the case with binary complementation.

Binary Complements (Ones and Twos Complement)

The twos complement of a binary number is generated by the following stages:

(i) The number is converted to its *ones* complement by switching the values of all the bits in the number. In other words all ones are 'flipped' to zeroes and all zeroes are 'flipped' to ones. The following examples illustrate the ones complements of some binary numbers:

Binary number	Ones complement
001101	110010
100100	011011
001001100	110110011

(ii) The ones complement of the binary number is then converted to *twos* complement by adding 1. For example:

Binary number	0001001
Ones complement	1110110
	1 +
	───────
	1110111

To follow the computer arithmetic examples in this chapter, the rules for binary addition need to be understood and these are listed in Chapter19 on Number Systems.

Binary Subtraction

Subtraction can be carried out by negating the second number (known as the *subtrahend*), in this case by conversion to twos complement form and adding it to the first number (called the *minuend*). The ease with which binary numbers can be switched from positive to negative and vice-versa by complementation, makes subtraction by addition suitable for computers. Consider the following examples, assuming a 6-bit word length.

Example

$$29 - 7 = 22$$

Minuend	0 1 1 1 0 1	29
Subtrahend	0 0 0 1 1 1	7−

Using twos complement:

Convert subtrahend to twos complement:

	0 0 0 1 1 1
Ones complement	1 1 1 0 0 0
	1 +
Twos complement	$\overline{1\ 1\ 1\ 0\ 0\ 1}$

Minuend		0 1 1 1 0 1
Subtrahend (twos complement)		1 1 1 0 0 1+
	Result	$\overline{1\ 0\ 1\ 0\ 1\ 1\ 0}$

↑
ignore the carried bit

The answer 010110 converts to decimal as $0 + 16 + 0 + 4 + 2 + 0$, which equals 22.

Example

Consider the following example where the minuend is smaller than the subtrahend, resulting in a negative answer:

$$7 - 9 = -2$$

Minuend	0 0 0 1 1 1	7
Subtrahend	0 0 1 0 0 1	9−

Using twos complement:

Convert subtrahend to ones complement:

	0 0 1 0 0 1
Ones complement	1 1 0 1 1 0
	1 +
Twos complement	$\overline{1\ 1\ 0\ 1\ 1\ 1}$

Minuend		0 0 0 1 1 1
Subtrahend (twos complement)		1 1 0 1 1 1+
	Result	$\overline{1\ 1\ 1\ 1\ 1\ 0}$

The answer converts to decimal as $-32 + 16 + 8 + 4 + 2 + 0$, which equals −2.

The MSB is the sign bit which, in twos complement, is part of the number. No provision is needed for separate explicit sign representation. The sign is implicit, unlike sign and magnitude representation which uses the sign bit explicitly to indicate a positive or negative value.

negative value.

As the above examples show, a positive value is indicated by a 0 and a negative value by a 1 in the MSB position. Thus, a 1 in the MSB position means its place value is negative (in the example above, it is -32). The addition of those lower significance place values which contain a bit 1 results in a negative value (in the above example, $-32 + 16 + 8 + 4 + 2 + 0 = -2$).

Number Range and Arithmetic Overflow

The number range of a word in a computer is limited by the number of bits in the word and the fact that the MSB is needed to indicate the sign (unless of course the number is an unsigned integer). This applies whatever method is used to indicate the sign of numbers. Thus in an 8-bit computer using two's complement, the maximum number which can be represented is either $+127$ or -128, as the following figure shows:

```
Bit  7 6 5 4 3 2 1 0
     0 1 1 1 1 1 1 1 (64 + 32 + 16 + 8 + 4 + 2 + 1 = +127)
     ↑
MSB
(sign bit)
```

```
Bit  7 6 5 4 3 2 1 0
     1 0 0 0 0 0 0 0 (−128)
     ↑
MSB
(sign bit)
```

With sign and magnitude, the maximum negative value is -127.

```
Bit  7 6 5 4 3 2 1 0
     1 1 1 1 1 1 1 1 − (64 + 32 + 16 + 8 + 4 + 2 + 1) = −127
     ↑
MSB
(sign bit and not part of the number)
```

Detection of Overflow

If the result of an operation involving two numbers exceeds the maximum permitted by the word, then overflow occurs. For example, in an 8-bit word machine using integer arithmetic any result outside the range -128 to +127 would overflow.

This needs to be detected by the computer so that an incorrect result is not overlooked. The hardware in the ALU detects an overflow condition by comparing the states of the carry in to, and the carry out from, the sign bit. If they are not equal, overflow has occurred and the answer is incorrect.

Consider the following twos complement examples, assuming an 8-bit word:

Example a

$64 + 4 = 68$

```
sign bit
Bit  7 6 5 4 3 2 1 0
     0 1 0 0 0 0 0 0      +64
     0 0 0 0 0 1 0 0      + 4
     ‾‾‾‾‾‾‾‾‾‾‾‾‾‾‾
     0 1 0 0 0 1 0 0      =68
   0   0
   ↑   ↑
carry out   carry in
```

The carry in and the carry out are equal so the answer is within the word length's range.

Example b

$$-12 + 68 = 56$$

```
sign bit
Bit   7 6 5 4 3 2 1 0
      1 1 1 1 0 1 0 0   - 12
      0 1 0 0 0 1 0 0   + 68
      0 0 1 1 1 0 0 0   = 56
    1   1
    ↑   ↑
carry out  carry in
```

The carry in and the carry out are equal so there is no indication of overflow.

Example c

$$96 + 64 = 160$$

```
sign bit
Bit   7 6 5 4 3 2 1 0
      0 1 1 0 0 0 0 0   + 96
      0 1 0 0 0 0 0 0   + 64
      1 0 1 0 0 0 0 0   = -96 incorrect
    0   1
    ↑   ↑
carry out  carry in
```

The answer appears to be negative because the sign bit is set to 1. The answer will be detected as incorrect in this example because the carry in to and the carry out from the sign bit are *not* equal.

Overflow will also occur when two negative numbers are added to produce a sum beyond the range of the word.

An overflow 'flag' (a single bit) in the condition codes or status register is set as soon as an overflow occurs. Thus, following the execution of an arithmetic process, a programmer can include a single test on the overflow flag to determine whether or not incorrect results are due to arithmetic overflow. Other machines may use the flag to implement an 'interrupt' (which interrupts the CPU operation) to suspend processing and display an error message.

The problem of limited number range and the need for accuracy can be overcome by the use of two or more words of memory to store a single number.

Integer and Real Numbers

Integer Numbers

Earlier in this chapter, it is pointed out that the word length of a particular machine places limits on the range of numbers which can be stored. The example of an 8-bit machine was used to illustrate a number range restricted from −128 to +127. Similarly, a machine which uses a 16-bit word length can only store numbers ranging from +32767 to −32768. These number ranges also assume that machine use is limited to whole or *integer* numbers (which have no fractional element). Although a programmer could choose to restrict numbers to integer format, machines without the facility to handle fractions are uncommon.

Real Numbers

Real numbers include all the integers and fractions of a number system, that is, all numbers above and below zero and including zero.

Many computer applications require the use of numbers with a fractional element, that is, real numbers. Such numbers are represented in binary with a binary *point* to separate the integer and fractional parts of the number, for example, 1101·11. Clearly, mixed numbers provide a greater level of accuracy than integer numbers but at the cost of increased storage requirements. There are two basic methods of storing real numbers:

      (i) Fixed-point Representation
     (ii) Floating-point Representation

Fixed-point Numbers

Fixed-point numbers are stored with the binary point imagined to be immediately to the right of the units column. The position of the binary point is fixed by the programmer and can be moved. The binary point is said to have an 'assumed' position which gives meaning to a number.

Example

Using an 8-bit word, the programmer assumes the binary point to be fixed as follows:

Binary point
↓

	bit	7 6 5 4 3 2 1 0	decimal
binary number		0 0 0 0 1 0 1 1	2·75
binary number		0 1 1 1 0 0 0 1	28·25

If the binary point is assumed to be as follows then the same binary groupings take on different values (shifting the point one place to the left halves the number, whilst a single shift to the right doubles it - for clarification of this, refer to Chapter 22 on Computer Instructions):

Binary point
↓

	bit	7 6 5 4 3 2 1 0	decimal
binary number		0 0 0 0 1 0 1 1	1·375
binary number		0 1 1 1 0 0 0 1	14·125

Therefore, a programmer must keep track of the point position in order to know the value of stored numbers. This problem is of concern to the programmer using low level languages.

To avoid confusion, the programmer can, either:

    (i) avoid moving the assumed point for a particular type of value throughout the program, or
   (ii) define particular types of values as being wholly *integer* (the point is always after the right-most digit) or wholly *fractional* (the point is always before the left-most digit).

To maintain accuracy, a storage location must be large enough to accommodate *all* the digits of the number. This can present problems when the number is very large or very small. Floating-point number representation helps overcome this problem at the cost of slower computation and decreased accuracy; this latter point is discussed later.

Floating-point Numbers

A *mantissa* and *exponent* can be used to represent a number. The number 6,800,000, for example, can be written as:

$$0\cdot 68 \qquad \times \qquad 10^7$$
$$\text{mantissa} \qquad\qquad \text{exponent}$$

Similarly the number, $0\cdot 0000564$ can be written as:

$$0\cdot 564 \qquad \times \qquad 10^{-4}$$

The above decimal examples make use of what is referred to as Standard Index Form, which is dealt with in detail in Chapter 24 on Arithmetic Operations.

Binary numbers are similarly represented:

		mantissa		exponent
$101\cdot 0101$	as	$0\cdot 1010101$	$\times$	2^3
$0\cdot 0011001$	as	$0\cdot 11001$	$\times$	2^{-2}

In floating-point notation, the point is not fixed by the programmer. Instead it remains in a position at the left of the mantissa, as shown in the above examples. Floating-point notation is based on the expression:

$$m \times r^e \text{ where } m \text{ is } + \text{ or } - \text{ and } e \text{ is } + \text{ or } -$$

'm' is the mantissa, 'r' is the radix (base) and 'e' is the exponent (power). In binary the radix (r) is 2.

Fixed-point numbers can be converted to floating-point numbers by a process called *normalization*. As the above examples show, if the number is greater than 1 then the point 'floats' to a position immediately before the most significant bit. This part becomes the mantissa (m). The point in the following example has moved 4 places and the exponent (e) is therefore, 4

Fixed-point		Floating-point		
		Mantissa		Exponent
$1110\cdot 001$	becomes	$0\cdot 1110001$	$\times$	2^4

If the number is a fraction and a bit 1 does not immediately follow the point, then the point 'floats' to the right of any leading zeros, until the first non-zero bit is reached, as in the following example:

Fixed-point		Floating-point		
		Mantissa		Exponent
$0\cdot 0011101$	becomes	$0\cdot 11101$	$\times$	2^{-2}

With normalized positive numbers the binary point must not be followed immediately by a zero. Conversely, normalized negative numbers require that the binary point is not followed immediately by a one. Any normalized binary mantissa must be a fraction falling within the range $+0\cdot 5$ (decimal) to less than $+1$ for positive values and -1 to greater than $-0\cdot 5$ for negative values. The range of possible normalized mantissas, given a 4-bit allocation, is given below.

Positive Mantissas	Denary/ Fractional Equivalent	Negative Mantissas	Denary/ Fractional Equivalent
$0\cdot 100$	$+\frac{1}{2}$	$1\cdot 000$	-1
$0\cdot 101$	$+\frac{5}{8}$	$1\cdot 001$	$-\frac{7}{8}$
$0\cdot 110$	$+\frac{5}{8}$	$1\cdot 010$	$-\frac{3}{4}$
$0\cdot 111$	$+\frac{5}{8}$	$1\cdot 011$	$-\frac{5}{8}$

The decimal values shown assume a zero exponent.

Storage of Floating-point Numbers

Floating-point numbers are always stored in two parts:

(i) The *mantissa*, the length of which is determined by the precision to which numbers are represented. Clearly, if fewer bits are allocated to the mantissa (which is always a left-justified fraction) then less precision is possible.

(ii) The *exponent*, which is usually allocated one-third to one-half of the number of bits used for the mantissa.

The following example is based on an 8-bit machine, where two words are used to store each floating-point number in twos complement form.

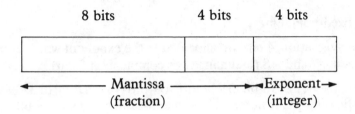

Of the 16 bits available, 12 bits are used for the mantissa and 4 bits for the exponent.

The binary point in the mantissa fraction is immediately to the right of the sign bit, which is 0 for a positive and 1 for a negative floating-point number. The following examples illustrate these features.

Positive Floating Point Number

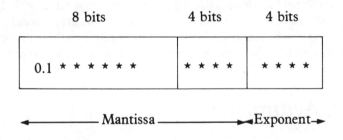

Negative Floating Point Number

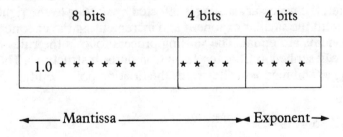

In twos complement form, the most significant digit to the right of the binary point is 1 for a positive and 0 for a negative floating-point number. It should be noticed that the sign bit and the most significant non-sign bit differ in both cases. As is explained earlier, any representation where they are the same indicates that the mantissa needs to be normalized. This may be necessary after any floating-point arithmetic operation.

Floating-point Conversion

To obtain the denary equivalent of a floating-point representation requires the mantissa to be multiplied by 2, raised to the power of 'e', which has the value stored in the exponent part of the number. Thus, if 'e' has the value 5:

$$\begin{array}{cc} \text{mantissa} & \text{exponent} \\ 0 \cdot 1 1 0 1 0 0 1 \times & 2^5 \end{array}$$

Converted to denary, this becomes:

$$(\tfrac{1}{2} + \tfrac{1}{4} + 0 + \tfrac{1}{16} + 0 + 0 + \tfrac{1}{128}) \times 2^5$$

$$= {}^{105}\!/_{128} \times 32 = 26\tfrac{1}{4}$$

or in fixed-point binary, $1\,1\,0\,1\,0 \cdot 0\,1$

In the illustration, 4 bits are allocated to the exponent which allows 'e' to have a value between +7 and −8 (assuming twos complement form).

Alternatively, in a 16-bit machine, two words with a total of 32 bits may be used to store each floating-point number. The mantissa may occupy 24 bits, leaving 8 bits for the exponent. In such a representation, the exponent 'e' could have a value between +127 and −128 (assuming twos complement).

Alternative Floating-point Forms

Different machines use different methods for coding floating-point numbers. The mantissa may be coded in twos complement, as described above, or it may be stored as sign and magnitude. The advantage for machine arithmetic of storing numbers in twos complement form has already been identified, but machines with the circuitry to handle floating-point numbers may also have the facility to carry out subtraction without twos complement representation. The above illustrations of floating-point numbers assume that the exponent is also stored in twos complement form. In practice, the exponent is often stored in sign and magnitude.

Floating-point Arithmetic

Addition

To add two floating-point numbers, they must both have the same value exponent.If they differ, the necessary scaling is effected by *shifting* to the right the mantissa of the number with the smaller exponent and incrementing the exponent at every shift until the exponents are equal. The shifting process follows the rules for arithmetic shifts, which are described in Chapter 22 on Computer Instructions. The following example, assuming a 6-bit mantissa, illustrates the floating-point addition procedure:

Example

$6 \cdot 75 + 12 \cdot 5 = 19 \cdot 25$

	Mantissa		Exponent
Bit	5 4 3 2 1 0		
6·75	0·1 1 0 1 1	×	2^3
12·5	0·1 1 0 0 1	×	2^4

Step 1

The mantissa with the smaller exponent is right-shifted and the exponent incremented thus:

$$0 \cdot 11011 \quad x \quad 2^3$$

becomes

$$0 \cdot 01101 \quad x \quad 2^4$$

As a result a bit 1 is lost from the least significant bit position.

Step 2

The mantissas are added:

Mantissa	Exponent
0·01101	
0·11001 +	
1·00110	x 2^4

This is clearly incorrect as the sign bit is now 1, indicating a negative value, when the result should be positive. The method by which the computer detects this type of error is explained earlier in this chapter. The mantissa is beyond the permitted range (see previous section) for a positive number and normalization is required; the mantissa is shifted one place to the right and the exponent is incremented accordingly:

$$0 \cdot 10011 \quad x \quad 2^5$$

This floating-point value represents:

$$0 \cdot 10011 \quad x \quad 32$$
$$= \quad (½ + 0 + 0 + 1/16 + 1/32) \times 32$$
$$= \quad 19$$

Some loss of accuracy has resulted (19 instead of 19·25). The loss of accuracy results from the right-shift operation required to equalize the exponents; a significant bit is lost when the binary value for 6·75, 0·11011 became 0·01101. The decimal value of this discarded bit is its fractional value of 1/32 multiplied by the exponent (before scaling) of 2^3 (8), giving a result of 0·25. Although a further right-shift is needed to normalize the result, the discarded bit is a 0 and does not produce any additional inaccuracy.

Subtraction

The procedures for subtraction are the same as for addition except that the mantissas are subtracted. This can be achieved by negating the subtrahend and then adding it to the minuend. Consider the following example, assuming a 6-bit word and a twos complement mantissa and exponent.

Example

$$12 \cdot 5 - 6 \cdot 75 = 5 \cdot 75$$

This can be expressed as $12 \cdot 5 + (-6 \cdot 75) = 5 \cdot 75$

	Mantissa	Exponent
Bit	5 4 3 2 1 0	
12·5	0·11001 x	2^4
6·75	0·11011 x	2^3

Step 1

Right-shift the mantissa with the smaller exponent and increment the exponent, repeatedly if necessary, until the exponents of the two numbers are equalized. In this case, only one right-shift is needed.

$$0\cdot11011 \qquad \times \qquad 2^3$$
becomes $\qquad 0\cdot01101 \qquad \times \qquad 2^4$

Note that the right-shift of one place has resulted in the loss of a bit 1 from the LSB position and thus some loss of accuracy.

Step 2

Negate the subtrahend by finding the twos complement of its mantissa:

$$6\cdot75 \quad 0\cdot01101$$
$$\text{Ones complement} \quad 1\cdot10010$$
$$1 +$$
$$\text{Twos complement} \quad \overline{1\cdot10011}$$

Step 3

Add the mantissas $\quad 0\cdot11001$
$$1\cdot10011$$
$$\overline{10\cdot01100} \quad \times \quad 2^4$$
$$\uparrow$$
ignore carry

Step 4

If necessary, normalize the result. In this case, the answer is not in normal form because the sign bit and the most significant bit to the right of the binary point are the same (this is explained earlier in the chapter).The result can be normalized by carrying out a left-shift of one on the mantissa and decrementing the exponent accordingly, to produce:

$$0\cdot11000 \quad \times \quad 2^3$$
$$= \qquad (\tfrac{1}{2} + \tfrac{1}{4}) \times 8$$
$$= \qquad 6$$

Note that a zero is inserted into the least significant bit position. The floating point process has resulted in some significant loss of accuracy (6 as opposed to $5\cdot75$).

Maintenance of Arithmetic Precision

Floating-point arithmetic precision can be improved by:

(i) increasing the number of bits allocated to the mantissa;
(ii) rounding.

Mantissa Length

Increasing the number of bits allocated to the mantissa will improve precision but inaccuracies can never be completely eliminated. In practice, memory words are much longer than those used for illustration here and where memory words are of insufficient length to ensure acceptable accuracy, two adjacent locations may be used. Machines which make use of this method are providing what is referred to as double-precision floating-point facilities.

Rounding

The subtraction example above demonstrates a loss of accuracy through truncation; a significant bit is lost when the mantissa is shifted one place to the right in order to equalize the exponents of the minuend and the subtrahend. If a computer process requires a series of calculations, each using the results of previous ones, repeated truncation may accrue considerable inaccuracy and this will be reflected in the final result. As can be seen from the earlier example of floating-point addition, the process of normalizing the result also requires the shifting or justification of the mantissa. Consider the following example, which only shows the mantissas to illustrate the normalization process:

Mantissa	$0 \cdot 1\,0\,0\,1$
Mantissa	$0 \cdot 1\,1\,0\,0\,+$
Result	$\overline{1 \cdot 0\,1\,0\,1}$ Note that the sign bit has changed to 1
	$\overline{0 \cdot 1\,0\,1\,0\,1}$ Correct result after right-justifying
	$\uparrow$
	discarded bit

Normalization has resulted in the loss of a bit 1 from the least significant bit (LSB) position and consequent loss of accuracy. Rounding dictates that if the last bit to be discarded (the most significant of those which are lost) during an arithmetic shift is a 1, then 1 is added to the least significant retained bit. Consider an 8-bit mantissa rounded as follows:

$1\,0\,1\,0\,1\,1\,0\,1$	rounded to 7 bits becomes	$1\,0\,1\,0\,1\,1\,1$
	rounded to 6 bits becomes	$1\,0\,1\,0\,1\,1$
	rounded to 5 bits becomes	$1\,0\,1\,1\,0$
	rounded to 4 bits becomes	$1\,0\,1\,1$

The accumulated errors caused by repeated truncation of values during a lengthy arithmetic process can partially, though not entirely, be avoided by rounding. In practice, rounding can sometimes result in greater inaccuracies than would result without rounding. Many rounding algorithms exist to try to overcome this problem and the type of inaccuracy which occasionally occurs will depend on the rounding algorithm used.

Floating-point Multiplication and Division

To multiply two floating-point numbers, the mantissas are multiplied and their exponents are added. Floating-point division is carried out by dividing the mantissas and subtracting their exponents. The details of these processes are beyond the scope of this chapter, but the principles of integer division and multiplication used by computers are described in Chapter 24 on Arithmetic Operations.

Hardware and Software Control of Computer Arithmetic

The execution of computer arithmetic operations often involves a mixture of hardware and software control. Increasingly, to improve processing efficiency, many computers are equipped with additional circuitry to handle floating-point numbers directly.

Assignment   *Floating Point*

Task

1.   If a computer using floating point arithmetic provides 18 bits for the mantissa and 6 bits for the exponent, calculate the approximate range of numbers which can be represented.

2.   Normalize the following decimal numbers into standard form.

   (i) 42
   (ii) 259
   (iii) −127
   (iv) −72654
   (v) 245·75
   (vi) $26·5 \times 10^2$
   (vii) $8·125 \times 10^{-3}$

3.   Show how each of the decimal numbers in Task 2 would be represented in a binary register using the floating point format detailed in Task 1. Assume twos complement for both mantissa and exponent.

4.   Carry out the following subtractions in binary using twos complement arithmetic. Assume an 8-bit word.

   (i) 105 − 42
   (ii) 72 − 94

5.   Use the following addition sum to illustrate arithmetic overflow and explain how the computer's circuitry would detect it.

   75 + 96

Assume an 8-bit word and twos complement representation.

Chapter 21

Computer Logic

Introduction

In Chapter 20 it was explained that data and instructions in a digital computer are represented by the binary numbering system. Internal registers and locations within the memory of the computer must be able to 'remember' data and instructions as sequences of binary digits. The ALU must be able to perform arithmetic on numbers held in this form, and the decoding circuitry of the Control Unit must be able to recognise and interpret program instructions represented by binary numbers. All of these functions, and many more, are performed by logic circuits.

Computer logic is based on a branch of mathematical logic called Boolean Algebra (named after the English mathematician George Boole) which allows the symbolic manipulation of logical variables in a manner very similar to the manipulation of 'unknowns' in an ordinary algebraic expression of the form

$$x.(y+z) \text{ or } x.y + x.z$$

Just as laws are needed for ordinary algebraic expressions, fundamental laws exist for the manipulation of Boolean expressions. By means of these laws, complex logical expressions, representing logic circuits, can be analysed or designed.

This chapter introduces the foundations of Boolean Algebra, its relevance to computer circuitry, and the processes by which such circuitry may be designed and analysed.

Boolean Variables

A Boolean variable has one of two values, normally represented by 1 and 0. In terms of computer circuitry, a Boolean variable represents a voltage on a line which may be an input to a logic circuit or an output from a logic circuit. For instance, a value of 1 might represent five volts and a value of 0, zero volts. Boolean variables are denoted by letters of the alphabet. Thus the variables X, Y, Z, P, Q, R are each able to represent a value of 1 or 0.

Gates

The term 'gate' is used to describe the members of a set of basic electronic components which, when combined with each other, are able to perform complex logical and arithmetic operations. These are the types of operations associated with the ALU (Arithmetic and Logic Unit) of the CPU. For present purposes, the physical construction of the gates is of no direct concern, and the discussion will be restricted to their functions only.

The 'Or' Gate

Gates have one or more inputs but only a single output. The nature of the gate determines what the output should be given the current inputs. For example, the OR gate could be defined as follows:

Truth Table for 'OR' Gate

INPUTS		OUTPUT
X	Y	X OR Y
0	0	0
0	1	1
1	0	1
1	1	1

The output is 1 if the
X input OR the Y input is 1

X and Y are Boolean variables capable at any time of having the value 1 or 0. Thus at any instant X could have a value of 0 and Y a value of 1, or X could have a value of 1 and Y could have a value of 1; there are four such combinations of the values of X and Y as shown in the table above. With an OR gate, when there is at least one 1 in the input variables, the output is 1. The third column of the table shows the output produced by each combination of the two inputs. The complete table is known as a *truth table* and completely defines the operation of the OR gate for every combination of inputs. As will be shown throughout this chapter, truth tables are extremely useful for describing logic circuits.

Symbolically, the combination of X and Y using an OR gate is written

X OR Y   or   X + Y   (read as "X or Y")

Both forms mean that X and Y are inputs to an OR gate. The second form is that required for Boolean Algebra and the " + " is known as the OR operator.

The symbol used when drawing an OR gate in a logic circuit is

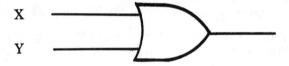

Gates are the physical realisations of simple Boolean expressions. The design of logic circuits is performed symbolically using Boolean Algebra. A Boolean algebraic expression can then be converted very easily into a logic circuit consisting of combinations of gates.

The OR gate is only one of several which are used to produce logic circuits. The other gates of interest are AND, NOT, EOR, NAND and NOR. The first two, in conjunction with the OR gate, are of the greatest importance since these three are directly related to the Boolean operators used in Boolean Algebra.

The 'And' Gate

The AND gate is defined by the following truth table:

Truth Table for 'AND' Gate

X	Y	X AND Y
0	0	0
0	1	0
1	0	0
1	1	1

The output is 1 when the
X input AND the Y input are 1s

This time, the gate only produces an output of 1 when both inputs are 1s. The Boolean operator equivalent to the AND gate is the AND operator ".", and is written

X.Y (read as "X and Y")

The symbol for the AND gate is

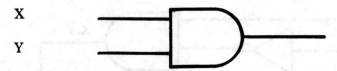

X

Y

The 'Not' Gate

The third important gate is the NOT gate which has the truth table

Truth Table for 'NOT' Gate

X	NOT X
0	1
1	0

This gate only has a single input which is inverted at the output. A NOT gate is often called an "inverter" for this reason.

The symbol for a NOT gate is

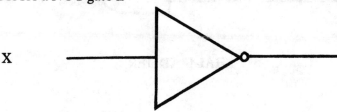

X

and it is written $\overline{X}$ or $\sim X$ in Boolean expressions.

Example of a Useful Logic Circuit

At this point it is worth considering an example of a widely used logic circuit to illustrate the relevance of this chapter. The circuit, which is called a *half adder*, performs the addition of two binary digits to give a sum term, S and a carry term, C, both being Boolean variables. The inputs to the circuit are X and Y representing the two binary digits to be added. The rules for binary addition are

$$0 + 0 = 0 \text{ carry } 0 \quad (00)$$
$$0 + 1 = 1 \text{ carry } 0 \quad (01)$$
$$1 + 0 = 1 \text{ carry } 0 \quad (01)$$
$$1 + 1 = 0 \text{ carry } 1 \quad (10)$$

The equivalent truth table is

X	Y	S	C
0	0	0	0
0	1	1	0
1	0	1	0
1	1	0	1

The requirement is for a combination of AND/OR/NOT gates to give two separate outputs for (S)um and (C)arry given any two binary digits represented by X and Y. The circuit is as follows:

Notice that the various gates have the same X and Y inputs.

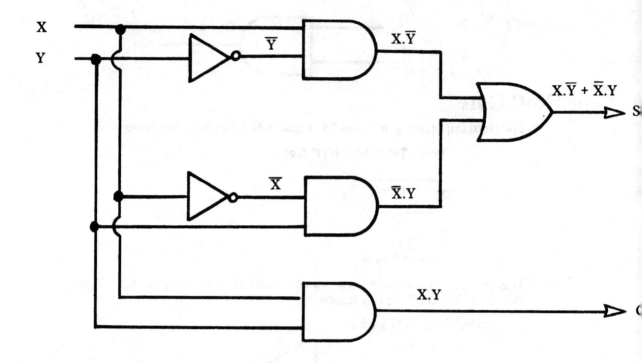

HALF ADDER

and the equivalent Boolean expressions for S and C are

$$S = X.\overline{Y} + \overline{X}.Y$$

$$C = X.Y$$

To prove that the circuit actually works a truth table is constructed showing the output from every component in the circuit from stage to stage, given the inputs to that stage:

X	Y	$\overline{X}$	$\overline{Y}$	$X.\overline{Y}$	$\overline{X}.Y$	$X.\overline{Y}+\overline{X}.Y$ (S)	X.Y (C)
0	0	1	1	0	0	0	0
0	1	1	0	0	1	1	0
1	0	0	1	1	0	1	0
1	1	0	0	0	0	0	1

Thus if X=0 and Y=0, $\overline{Y}$=1 and using the truth table for the AND gate, $X.\overline{Y} = 0.1 = 0$ and $\overline{X}.Y = 1.0 = 0$. The rightmost OR gate in the diagram has inputs $X.\overline{Y}$ and $\overline{X}.Y$, that is, 0 and 0, and using the truth table for the OR gate, it can be seen that this results in an output of 0 for S. Similarly, if X=0 and Y=0, the truth table for the AND gate shows that X.Y=0, that is C=0 for this combination of inputs.

Following this type of argument for the remaining rows in the truth table, it can be seen that the circuit produces exactly the right output for each combination of inputs to perform binary addition on the input bits. Thus a combination of a few elementary components has produced a most important circuit. A truth table allowed the operation of the circuit to be confirmed. Later it will be shown how the Boolean expressions representing the circuit can be derived directly from the first truth table defining the required operation of the circuit.

The Derivation of Boolean Expressions from Truth Tables

Suppose that it is required to produce a suitable logic circuit from the following circuit specification:

A circuit has two binary inputs, X and Y. The output from the circuit is 1 when the two inputs are the same; otherwise the output is 0.

The first step is to produce a truth table to define the circuit fully:

X	Y	OUTPUT
0	0	1
0	1	0
1	0	0
1	1	1

Each possible combination of X and Y has been listed. Where X and Y are the same, OUTPUT has been assigned a value of 1; where X and Y are different, OUTPUT has been assigned a value of 0.

The next step is to define, for each entry in the OUTPUT column having a value of 1, a Boolean expression involving X and Y which uniquely defines that value. So for the first row in the table, where X=0 and Y=0, the expression $\overline{X}.\overline{Y}$ has a value of 1; for any other combination of X and Y it has a value of 0. The expression therefore satisfies the requirement of uniquely defining this combination of values. The expression X.Y has a value of 1 only when X=1 and Y=1, otherwise it has a value of 0, and so it uniquely defines the last row in the truth table. Together the expressions $\overline{X}.\overline{Y}$ and X.Y will produce an output of 1 when X=0 and Y=0 or when X=1 and Y=1. Hence

$$\text{OUTPUT} = \overline{X}.\overline{Y} + X.Y$$

The following truth table confirms this result:

X	Y	$\overline{X}$	$\overline{Y}$	$\overline{X}.\overline{Y}$	X.Y	$\overline{X}.\overline{Y} + X.Y$
0	0	1	1	1	0	1
0	1	1	0	0	0	0
1	0	0	1	0	0	0
1	1	0	0	0	1	1

=OUTPUT

The circuit can now be drawn:

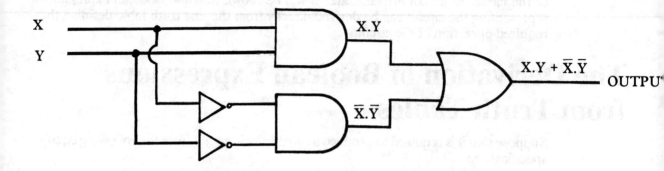

The process of converting a truth table to a Boolean expression is summarised as follows:

(a) Consider only the rows of the truth table for which the output is to be 1.

(b) Take each of these rows in turn and write alongside the row an expression containing the input variables connected by the AND operator. If the value of an input variable is 0 then it will appear inverted in the expression.

(c) Combine these expressions using the OR operator.

To provide another illustration of the process suppose that three binary signals, A, B and C, are required to represent a number in the range 0 to 4. The variable A represents the most significant digit of the binary number ABC, B is the next significant digit, and C is the least significant digit. A circuit is required to detect an illegal combination (that is the numbers 5 to 7) by producing an output of 1. The truth table is

A	B	C		OUTPUT	
0	0	0	(0)	0	
0	0	1	(1)	0	
0	1	0	(2)	0	
0	1	1	(3)	0	
1	0	0	(4)	0	
1	0	1	(5)	1	$A.\bar{B}.C$
1	1	0	(6)	1	$A.B.\bar{C}$
1	1	1	(7)	1	$A.B.C$

Therefore

$$\text{OUTPUT} = A.\bar{B}.C + A.B.\bar{C} + A.B.C$$

and the required circuit is

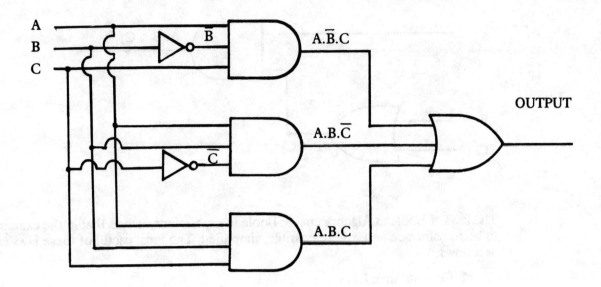

As an exercise, use a truth table to prove that the Boolean expression above does indeed produce the required outputs.

The Laws of Boolean Algebra

Though the circuit above does perform as specified, it is very inefficient; it uses more gates than are absolutely necessary to produce the required outputs. In fact rather than six gates, only two are necessary because, as the truth tables below show,

$$A.\bar{B}.C + A.B.\bar{C} + A.B.C = A.(B + C)$$

A	B	C	$\bar{B}$	$\bar{C}$	$A.\bar{B}.C$	$A.B.\bar{C}$	$A.B.C$	$(A.\bar{B}.C + A.B.\bar{C} + A.B.C)$
0	0	0	1	1	0	0	0	0
0	0	1	1	0	0	0	0	0
0	1	0	0	1	0	0	0	0
0	1	1	0	0	0	0	0	0
1	0	0	1	1	0	0	0	0
1	0	1	1	0	1	0	0	1
1	1	0	0	1	0	1	0	1
1	1	1	0	0	0	0	1	1

=OUTPUT

A	B	C	B + C	A.(B + C)
0	0	0	0	0
0	0	1	1	0
0	1	0	1	0
0	1	1	1	0
1	0	0	0	0
1	0	1	1	1
1	1	0	1	1
1	1	1	1	1

=OUTPUT

The circuit for the simplified expression is

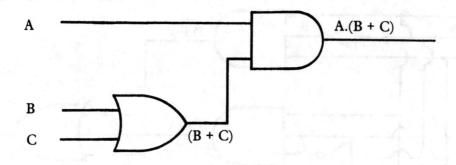

The laws of Boolean Algebra enable Boolean expressions such as that in the example to be transformed and, where possible, simplified. The most useful of these laws are as follows:

1. Commutative Laws.

(a) $X+Y=Y+X$;   (b) $X.Y=Y.X$

2. Associative Laws.

(a) $X+(Y+Z) = (X+Y)+Z$;   (b) $X.(Y.Z) = (X.Y).Z$

3. Distributive Laws.

(a) $X.(Y+Z) = X.Y + X.Z$;   (b) $X + Y.Z = (X+Y).(X+Z)$

4. De Morgan's Laws.

(a) $\overline{(X + Y)} = \overline{X}.\overline{Y}$;   (b) $\overline{(X.Y)} = \overline{X} + \overline{Y}$

5. Laws of Absorption.

(a) $X + X.Y = X$;   (b) $X.(X + Y) = X$

6. Laws of Tautology.

(a) $X + X = X$;   (b) $X.X = X$

7. Law of Complementation.

$$\overline{\overline{X}} = X$$

8. Other useful identities.

(a) $X + \overline{X} = 1$;   (b) $X.\overline{X} = 0$

(c) $X + 1 = 1$;   (d) $X.1 = X$

(e) $X + 0 = X$;   (f) $X.0 = 0$

Notice that with each of the first six laws, there is a connection between (a) and (b). Given one of these rules, the other may be derived by replacing the '+' operator with the '.' operator or vice-versa. Thus if it is known that $X + X.Y = X$, then the 'dual' of the rule, that $X.(X+Y)$, is also true. All identities in Boolean Algebra have this useful property.

To illustrate the use of these laws in the simplification of Boolean expressions, consider the expression derived earlier:

$$A.\overline{B}.C + A.B.\overline{C} + A.B.C$$

Simplification of this expression could proceed as follows:

(i) $A.\overline{B}.C + A.B.\overline{C} + A.B.C = A.\overline{B}.C + (A.B.\overline{C} + A.B.C)$

Rule 1 allows us to deal with terms in any order.

(ii) Considering the bracketed pair of terms,

$A.B.\overline{C} + A.B.C = A.B.(\overline{C} + C)$ by rule 3(a)

Here A.B is treated as if it were a single variable, and the expression is therefore of the form

$X.\overline{C} + X.C = X.(\overline{C} + C)$ where X represents A.B

(iii) Rule 8(a) shows that $\overline{C} + C = 1$, so that

$A.B.(\overline{C} + C) = A.B.1$

and by rule 8(d),

$A.B.1 = A.B$

(iv) Hence,

$A.\overline{B}.C + (A.B.\overline{C} + A.B.C) = A.\overline{B}.C + A.B$

(v) Again using rule 3(a),

$A.\overline{B}.C + A.B = A.(\overline{B}.C + B)$

This is of the form

$X.Y + X.Z = X.(Y + Z)$

(vi) Now consider the term $\overline{B}.C + B$.

Using rule 1(a), this can be rewritten $B + \overline{B}.C$, and now using rule 3(b),

$B + \overline{B}.C = (B + \overline{B}).(B + C)$

As in step (iii), $(B + \overline{B}) = 1$ and $1.(B+C) = (B+C)$.

Hence $B + \overline{B}.C = (B + C)$ and therefore

$A.(B + \overline{B}.C) = A.(B+C)$

Thus the original expression has been considerably simplified and confirms the identity stated earlier.

Fortunately, the process of simplifying expressions involving AND terms separated by OR operators can be performed in a much simpler way using the Karnaugh Map method. This method, as well as being quicker and less prone to error, is also more likely to result in the best simplification possible, particularly where four variables are involved. In certain cases, however, a knowledge of the laws of Boolean Algebra are required. Examples of such instances will be provided later.

Karnaugh Maps

A Karnaugh map consists of a two-dimensional grid which is used to represent a Boolean expression in such a way that it can be simplified with great ease. For example, consider the expression

$\overline{X}.Y + X.\overline{Y} + X.Y$

This expression involves two Boolean variables, X and Y. The number of different terms possible with two variable is four, and therefore the Karnaugh map for expressions involving two variables is a 2 × 2 grid:

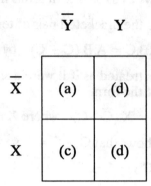

Each cell in the grid may be regarded as having a co-ordinate formed from a combination of X and Y. Thus the cell labelled (a) has the co-ordinate $\overline{X}.\overline{Y}$, (b) has the co-ordinate $\overline{X}.Y$, (c) has the co-ordinate $X.\overline{Y}$, and (d) has the co-ordinate $X.Y$. When entered onto the map, the expression quoted above translates as follows:

$$
\begin{array}{c|c|c|}
 & \overline{Y} & Y \\
\hline
\overline{X} & 0 & 1 \\
\hline
X & 1 & 1 \\
\hline
\end{array}
$$

Each '1' on the map indicates the presence of the term corresponding to its cell co-ordinate in the expression, and each '0' indicates its absence.

Using a further example, the expression $\overline{X}.Y + \overline{X}.\overline{Y}$ translates to

$$
\begin{array}{c|c|c|}
 & \overline{Y} & Y \\
\hline
\overline{X} & 1 & 1 \\
\hline
X & 0 & 0 \\
\hline
\end{array}
$$

Having drawn the appropriate Karnaugh map, the next stage is to attempt to identify a simplified expression. The procedure is as follows:

(i) Identify all pairs of adjacent '1's on the map. (Horizontally and vertically).

(ii) Draw loops around each pair.

(iii) Attempt to include every '1' on the map in at least one loop; it is allowable to have the same '1' in two different loops.

(iv) The aim is to include each '1' in at least one loop, but using as few loops as possible.

Thus the expression $\overline{X}.Y + X.\overline{Y} + X.Y$ becomes

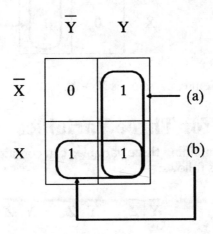

(v) Take each loop in turn and write down the term represented: the loop labelled (a) above spans both X and $\overline{X}$, but Y remains constant. The loop is therefore given the value Y. In the loop labelled (b), both Y co-ordinates are covered but X remains constant. This loop has the value X.

(vi) The loop values are ORed together. In the example, the expression is therefore equivalent to X + Y.

Karnaugh maps take advantage of a small number of the laws of Boolean Algebra. The Distributive Law allows terms with common variables to be grouped together:

$$X.\overline{Y} + X.Y = X.(\overline{Y} + Y) \quad (\text{ see rule 3(a) })$$

Another law (8(a)) gives the identity $\overline{Y} + Y = 1$.

And finally, law 8(d) says that $X.1 = X$.

The Karnaugh map allows this sequence of applications of laws to be performed in a single step:

the loop (b) representing $\quad X.\overline{Y} + X.Y$ becomes X.

'1's may be included in more than one loop because of the Law of Tautology (Tautology is saying the same thing twice). Thus X + X = X, and conversely, X = X + X. In other words, any term in an expression may be duplicated as many times as desired without affecting the value of the expression. So, given the expression

$$\overline{X}.Y + X.\overline{Y} + X.Y,$$

the term X.Y may be duplicated to give the equivalent expression

$$\overline{X}.Y + X.Y + X.\overline{Y} + X.Y,$$

where loop (a) is $\overline{X}.Y + X.Y$, and loop (b) is $X.\overline{Y} + X.Y$.

As a further example, the expression

$$X.\overline{Y} + \overline{X}.Y + X.Y$$

gives the map

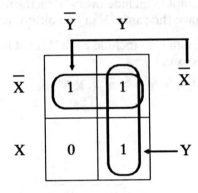

and the equivalent expression is $\overline{X} + Y$.

Karnaugh Maps for Three Variables

Expressions containing three variables can contain up to eight terms. The 3-variable map is drawn as follows:

	$\overline{Y}.\overline{Z}$	$\overline{Y}.Z$	$Y.Z$	$Y.\overline{Z}$
$\overline{X}$		(a)		
X			(b)	

This time a co-ordinate pair comprises an X variable and a YZ term.

For example, the cell (a) represents the term $\overline{X}.\overline{Y}.Z$, and (b) represents X.Y.Z.

The following map represents the expression $X.\overline{Y}.Z + X.Y.\overline{Z} + X.Y.Z$:

	$\overline{Y}.\overline{Z}$	$\overline{Y}.Z$	$Y.Z$	$Y.\overline{Z}$
$\overline{X}$	0	0	0	0
X	0	1	1	1

(a)   (b)

In loop (a), X and Z are common factors, but Y changes ($\overline{Y}.Z$ + Y.Z). The loop has the value X.Z. In loop (b), X and Y are constant but Z changes (Y.Z + Y.$\overline{Z}$). Thus (b) has value X.Y. The expression therefore simplifies to

X.Y + X.Z

and a further application of law 3(a) gives the final solution

$$X.\overline{Y}.Z + X.Y.\overline{Z} + X.Y.Z = X.(Y + Z)$$

With a 3-variable map, as well as looping pairs of '1's, it is necessary to look for groups of four '1's. For example, the map below could represent the expression

$$X.Y.Z + \overline{X}.\overline{Y}.Z + \overline{X}.Y.Z + X.\overline{Y}.Z$$

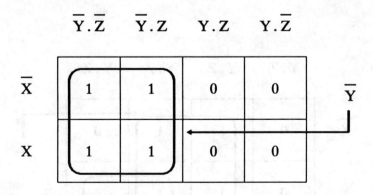

The single loop spans the X co-ordinate completely, and so X can be removed from the simplified expression. In the YZ terms spanned, Y changes and Z is constant. The simplified expression is merely Z.

Here are some further examples:

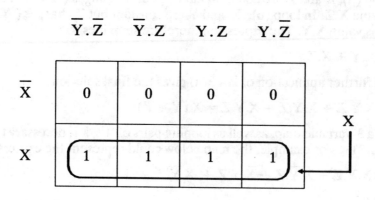

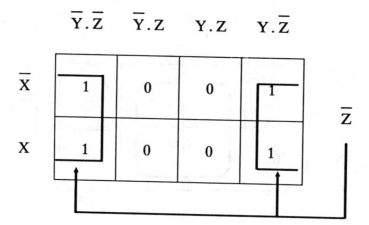

In this example the group of four is formed from opposite sides of the grid.

Below are some further examples with combinations of differnt types of loops illustrated.

Note that the largest groups are identified first, and then sufficient smaller groups so that every '1' is in at least one loop.

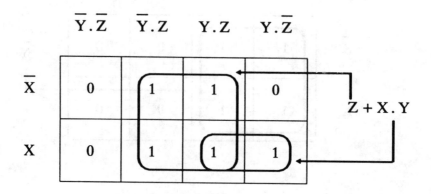

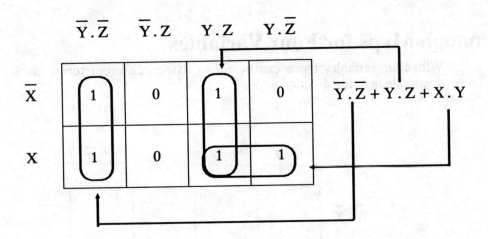

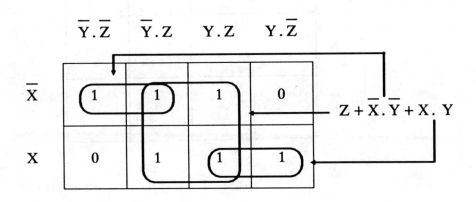

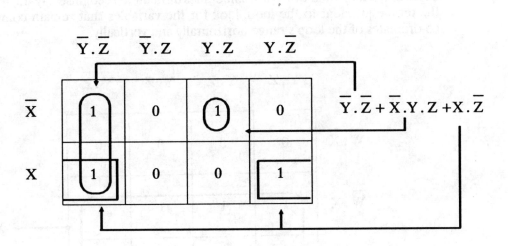

Karnaugh Maps for Four Variables

With four variables there can be up to sixteen different terms involved, and the 4-variable map is a 4 × 4 grid:

	$\overline{Y}.\overline{Z}$	$\overline{Y}.Z$	$Y.Z$	$Y.\overline{Z}$
$\overline{W}.\overline{X}$				
$\overline{W}.X$				
$W.X$				
$W.\overline{X}$				

It is necessary to look for groupings of 8, 4 and 2 with the 4-variable map. The following examples illustrate a number of possible groupings, including some that occur on the edges of the maps and which are sometimes difficult to recognise. Again, to determine the term equivalent to the loop, look for the variables that remain common to the co-ordinates of the loop's range horizontally and vertically.

	$\overline{Y}.\overline{Z}$	$\overline{Y}.Z$	$Y.Z$	$Y.\overline{Z}$
$\overline{W}.\overline{X}$	0	0	0	0
$\overline{W}.X$	1	1	1	1
$W.X$	1	1	1	1
$W.\overline{X}$	0	0	0	0

X

	$\overline{Y}.\overline{Z}$	$\overline{Y}.Z$	$Y.Z$	$Y.\overline{Z}$	
$\overline{W}.\overline{X}$	1	0	0	1	
$\overline{W}.X$	1	0	0	1	$\overline{Z}$
$W.X$	1	0	0	1	
$W.\overline{X}$	1	0	0	1	

	$\overline{Y}.\overline{Z}$	$\overline{Y}.Z$	$Y.Z$	$Y.\overline{Z}$
$\overline{W}.\overline{X}$	0	1	1	0
$\overline{W}.X$	0	1	1	0
$W.X$	0	1	1	0
$W.\overline{X}$	0	0	1	0

$$Y.Z + \overline{W}.Z + X.Z$$
$$= Y.Z + Z.(\overline{W} + X)$$

	$\overline{Y}.\overline{Z}$	$\overline{Y}.Z$	$Y.Z$	$Y.\overline{Z}$
$\overline{W}.\overline{X}$	1	1	0	1
$\overline{W}.X$	0	0	1	0
$W.X$	0	0	0	0
$W.\overline{X}$	1	1	0	1

$$\overline{X}.\overline{Z} + \overline{X}.\overline{Y} + \overline{W}.X.Y.Z$$
$$= \overline{X}.(\overline{Z} + \overline{Y}) + \overline{W}.X.Y.$$
$$= \overline{X}.(\overline{Z.Y}) + \overline{W}.X.Y.$$

The Design of Logic Circuits

The complete process of designing a logic circuit may be summarised as follows:

(i) Identify Boolean variables equivalent to the inputs to the circuit required.

(ii) Identify the outputs from the circuit.

(iii) Draw a truth table to define the output required for each possible combination of the input variables.

(iv) Derive an expression from the truth table for the output in terms of the input variables.

(v) Simplify this expression using a Karnaugh map.

(vi) Examine the simplified expression for possible further simplifications using direct applications of the laws of Boolean Algebra.

(vii) Draw the circuit using the appropriate gate symbols.

The following problem illustrates the process.

Four binary signals A, B, C, D represent a single Binary Coded Decimal (BCD) digit. A logic circuit is required to output logic 1 on the occurrence of an invalid combination of the signals, that is, when they represent a number in the range 10 to 15.

(i) The inputs to the circuit are clearly defined and it is assumed that A is the most significant digit and D the least significant digit.

(ii) The single output is to be 1 when the binary number represented by ABCD is in the range 10 to 15, that is, 1010 to 1111 in binary.

(iii) The truth table has 16 entries, representing the numbers 0 to 15.

A	B	C	D		OUTPUT	
0	0	0	0	(0)	0	
0	0	0	1	(1)	0	
0	0	1	0	(2)	0	
0	0	1	1	(3)	0	
0	1	0	0	(4)	0	
0	1	0	1	(5)	0	
0	1	1	0	(6)	0	
0	1	1	1	(7)	0	
1	0	0	0	(8)	0	
1	0	0	1	(9)	0	
1	0	1	0	(10)	1	$A.\overline{B}.C.\overline{D}$
1	0	1	1	(11)	1	$A.\overline{B}.C.D$
1	1	0	0	(12)	1	$A.B.\overline{C}.\overline{D}$
1	1	0	1	(13)	1	$A.B.\overline{C}.D$
1	1	1	0	(14)	1	$A.B.C.\overline{D}$
1	1	1	1	(15)	1	$A.B.C.D$

(iv) The expression for the output is given by

$$\text{OUTPUT} = A.\overline{B}.C.\overline{D} + A.\overline{B}.C.D + A.B.\overline{C}.\overline{D} + A.B.\overline{C}.D + A.B.C.\overline{D} + A.B.C.D$$

(v) The Karnaugh map is

	$\bar{C}.\bar{D}$	$\bar{C}.D$	$C.D$	$C.\bar{D}$
$\bar{A}.\bar{B}$	0	0	0	0
$\bar{A}.B$	0	0	0	0
$A.B$	1	1	1	1
$A.\bar{B}$	1	1	1	1

$A.B + A.C$

(vi) Using the Distributive law, 3(a), the expression $A.B + A.C$ may be written $A.(B + C)$.

(vii) This expression translates to the following logic diagram:

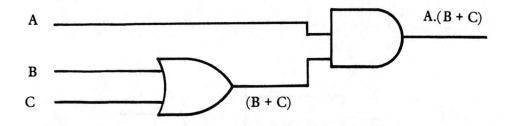

More Logic Gates

The gates that have yet to be defined are the NOR(Not OR), NAND(Not AND) and XOR (eXclusive OR) gates.

The truth table for the NOR gate shows that its outputs are the inverse of those for the OR gate:

X	Y	X NOR Y
0	0	1
0	1	0
1	0	0
1	1	0

Algebraically, the NOR gate is written $\overline{(X+Y)}$. Thus the gate appears to be formed from one OR gate and one NOT gate inverting the output from the OR gate. In practice, however, the OR gate outputs are generated from a single simple circuit and not by the combination of an OR gate followed by a NOT gate.

The symbol for the NOR gate is

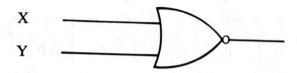

The truth table for the NAND gate shows that its outputs are the inverse of those for the AND gate:

X	Y	X NAND Y
0	0	1
0	1	1
1	0	1
1	1	0

In Boolean Algebra, the gate is written $\overline{(X.Y)}$. The comments above regarding the construction of the NOR gate similarly apply here: the NAND gate is not constructed from an AND gate followed by a NOT gate, but consists of a single circuit no more complex than the other gates.

The symbol for the NAND gate is

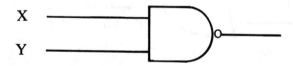

The Importance of the NAND gate and NOR gate

The importance of these gates may be attributed to two factors:

(i)   each may be manufactured cheaply and easily;

(ii) each can be used in the production of any circuit using AND/OR/NOT logical components. In other words, NOR gates and NAND gates can be used in the place of AND, OR or NOT gates.

These two properties mean that a logic circuit using, for instance, NOR gates only, can be produced easier and cheaper than the same circuit using combinations of three different types of components (AND, OR and NOT gates). A unit using a number of the same component is much easier to manufacture than one using several different components.

The following logic diagrams show how NOR gates and NAND gates may be used to represent the behaviour of AND, OR and NOT gates:

(i) NOT gate using NOR gate.

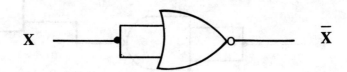

(ii) OR gate using NOR gates.

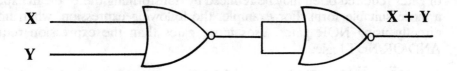

(iii) AND gate using NOR gates.

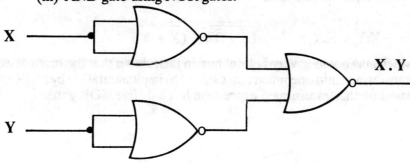

(iv) NOT gate using NAND gate.

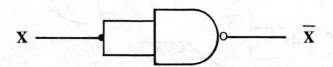

(v) AND gate using NAND gates.

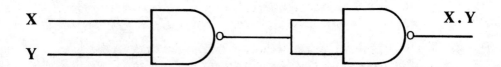

(vi) OR gate using NAND gates.

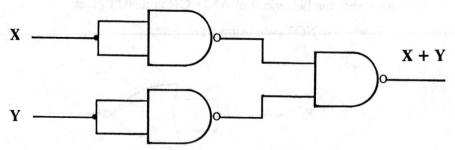

(As an exercise, write down Boolean expressions equivalent to the circuits shown above and prove their validity using truth tables).

It may appear from the diagrams shown above that circuits using NAND or NOR gates will generally require more gates than when using AND/OR NOT components. This may be true on occasions, but at other times fewer gates may be required. The number of gates required often may be reduced by transforming the Boolean expression into a more suitable form. For example, the following expression, when implemented directly using NOR gates, uses more gates than the expression requires using AND/OR/NOT logic:

$$X.\overline{Y} + \overline{X}.Y \quad (\text{2 AND gates, 2 NOT gates, 1 OR gate} = \text{5 gates})$$

However, it can be shown that the following identity is true:

$$X.\overline{Y} + \overline{X}.Y = \overline{\overline{(\overline{X} + \overline{Y})} + \overline{(X + Y)}}$$

which may not look very helpful but, in fact, shows that the original expression can be transformed into one much more suited to implementation by NOR gates . The circuit based on this transformed expression has only five NOR gates:

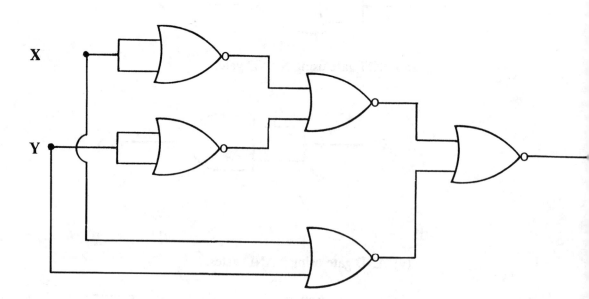

The Exclusive OR gate

This is usually abbreviated to XOR or EOR. The XOR gate has the following truth table:

X	Y	X XOR Y
0	0	0
0	1	1
1	0	1
1	1	0

The exclusive OR gate is so named because, of its output values, the case where both inputs are logic 1 is excluded; in the OR gate these inputs produce an output of 1. In effect, the XOR gate has an output of logic 1 when the inputs are different; when the inputs are the same, the output is logic 0.

Algebraically, the XOR gate is $X.\overline{Y} + \overline{X}.Y$ and the symbol that is frequently used is

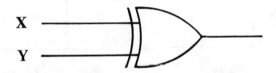

As an example of its use, suppose that it is required to generate an even parity bit (see Chapter 20) for a four bit word ABCD. The truth table for this problem is as follows:

A	B	C	D	Parity Bit	
0	0	0	0	0	
0	0	0	1	1	$\overline{A}.\overline{B}.\overline{C}.D$
0	0	1	0	1	$\overline{A}.\overline{B}.C.\overline{D}$
0	0	1	1	0	
0	1	0	0	1	$\overline{A}.B.\overline{C}.\overline{D}$
0	1	0	1	0	
0	1	1	0	0	
0	1	1	1	1	$\overline{A}.B.C.D$
1	0	0	0	1	$A.\overline{B}.\overline{C}.\overline{D}$
1	0	0	1	0	
1	0	1	0	0	
1	0	1	1	1	$A.\overline{B}.C.D$
1	1	0	0	0	
1	1	0	1	1	$A.B.\overline{C}.D$
1	1	1	0	1	$A.B.C.\overline{D}$
1	1	1	1	0	

The expression for even parity is thus

$$\text{Parity bit} = \overline{A}.\overline{B}.\overline{C}.D + \overline{A}.\overline{B}.C.\overline{D} + \overline{A}.B.\overline{C}.\overline{D} + \overline{A}.B.C.D + A.\overline{B}.\overline{C}.\overline{D} +$$
$$A.\overline{B}.C.D + A.B.\overline{C}.D + A.B.C.\overline{D}$$

and the Karnaugh map representation is

	$\overline{C}.\overline{D}$	$\overline{C}.D$	$C.D$	$C.\overline{D}$
$\overline{A}.\overline{B}$	0	1	0	1
$\overline{A}.B$	1	0	1	0
$A.B$	0	1	0	1
$A.\overline{B}$	1	0	1	0

As the map shows, there is no way of simplifying the expression. However, if the terms are grouped together as follows, a pattern begins to emerge:

Parity bit $= \overline{A}.\overline{B}.(\overline{C}.D + C.\overline{D}) + \overline{A}.B.(C.D + \overline{C}.\overline{D}) +$
$\overline{A}.B.(\overline{C}.\overline{D} + C.D) + A.B.(\overline{C}.D + C.\overline{D})$

Rearranging the terms,

Parity bit $= \overline{A}.\overline{B}.(\overline{C}.D + C.\overline{D}) + A.B.(\overline{C}.D + C.\overline{D}) +$
$\overline{A}.B.(C.D + \overline{C}.\overline{D}) + A.\overline{B}.(C.D + \overline{C}.\overline{D})$

Again, using the Distributive law, the first two and the last two terms can be grouped together to give

Parity bit $= (\overline{A}.\overline{B} + A.B).(\overline{C}.D + C.\overline{D}) + (\overline{A}.B + A.\overline{B}).(\overline{C}.\overline{D} + C.D)$

Notice that two of the terms in brackets are immediately recognisable as XOR functions. In addition it can be shown that

$$\overline{X}.Y + X.\overline{Y} = \overline{(\overline{X}.\overline{Y} + X.Y)}$$

Using this identity, the expression for parity becomes

Parity bit $= \overline{(\overline{A}.B + A.\overline{B})}.(\overline{C}.D + C.\overline{D}) + (\overline{A}.B + A.\overline{B}).\overline{(\overline{C}.D + C.\overline{D})}$

Now each bracketed term looks like an XOR gate and, treating each bracketed term as a unit, the complete expression has the form

$\overline{X}.Y + X.\overline{Y}$, where $X = (\overline{A}.B + A.\overline{B})$ and $Y = (\overline{C}.D + C.\overline{D})$

Thus the whole expression, and every term within it, represent XOR gates.

The equivalent circuit is

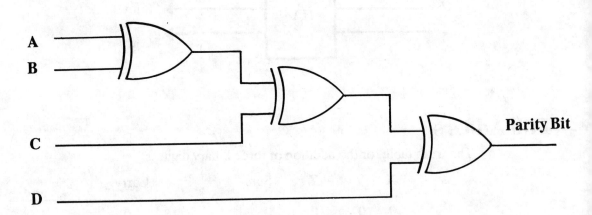

Logic Circuits for Binary Addition

The logic ccircuits which perform the function of addition in the Arithmetic and Logic Unit of the Central Processing Unit are called *adders*. A unit which adds two binary digits is called a *half adder* and one which adds together three binary digits is called a *full adder*. In this section each of these units will be examined in detail, and it will be shown how such units are combined to add binary numbers.

Half Adders

Earlier in this chapter, the function of a half adder was explained in order to illustrate the relevance of computer logic. Remember that the function of a half adder is to add two binary digits and produce as output the Sum term and Carry term. The operation of the half adder is defined by the following truth table:

X	Y	Sum		Carry	
0	0	0		0	
0	1	1	$\overline{X}.Y$	0	
1	0	1	$X.\overline{Y}$	0	
1	1	0		1	$X.Y$

Thus, the expressions for the Sum and Carry terms are given by:

Sum = $\overline{X}.Y + X.\overline{Y}$

Carry = $X.Y$

The circuit equivalent to these expressions was presented earlier.

The following symbol will henceforth be used for a half adder

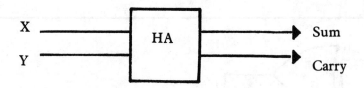

Full Adders

The truth table for the addition of three binary digits is

X	Y	Z	Sum		Carry	
0	0	0	0		0	
0	0	1	1	$\overline{X}.\overline{Y}.Z$	0	
0	1	0	1	$\overline{X}.Y.\overline{Z}$	0	
0	1	1	0		1	$\overline{X}.Y.Z$
1	0	0	1	$X.\overline{Y}.\overline{Z}$	0	
1	0	1	0		1	$X.\overline{Y}.Z$
1	1	0	0		1	$X.Y.\overline{Z}$
1	1	1	1	$X.Y.Z$	1	$X.Y.Z$

Considering the Sum term first, the expression derived from the truth table is

$$Sum = \overline{X}.\overline{Y}.Z + \overline{X}.Y.\overline{Z} + X.\overline{Y}.\overline{Z} + X.Y.Z$$

Grouping together the first and third terms, and the middle two terms gives

$$Sum = \overline{Z}.(\overline{X}.Y + X.\overline{Y}) + Z.(\overline{X}.\overline{Y} + X.Y)$$

Using the identity

$$\overline{\overline{X}.Y + X.\overline{Y}} = (\overline{X}.\overline{Y} + X.Y) \qquad \text{(the proof for this has been given earlier)}$$

the Sum term can be written

$$Sum = \overline{Z}.(\overline{X}.Y + X.\overline{Y}) + Z.\overline{(\overline{X}.Y + X.\overline{Y})}$$

which is of the form

$$\overline{Z}.S + Z.\overline{S} \text{ where } S = \overline{X}.Y + X.\overline{Y}$$

In other words, S is the sum term from a half adder with inputs X and Y, and Sum is one of the outputs from a half adder with inputs Z and S.

The Sum term can now be produced using two half adders:

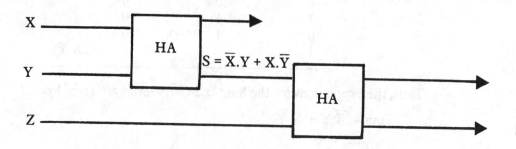

Returning to the Carry term, the expression derived from the truth table is

$$Carry = \overline{X}.Y.Z + X.\overline{Y}.Z + X.Y.\overline{Z} + X.Y.Z$$

Again gathering terms,

$$Carry = Z.(\overline{X}.Y + X.\overline{Y}) + X.Y.(\overline{Z} + Z)$$
$$= Z.(\overline{X}.Y + X.\overline{Y}) + X.Y \quad \text{since } \overline{Z} + Z = 1 \text{ and } X.Y.1 = X.Y$$

Substituting S for $\overline{X}.Y + X.\overline{Y}$ as before, the expression becomes

$$Carry = Z.S + X.Y$$

Both of these terms look like the carry term from a half adder: Z.S is the carry term from a half adder with inputs Z and S (the carry term from the second half adder in the diagram above); X.Y is the carry output from the first half adder in the diagram. The two carry outputs merely need to be ORed together:

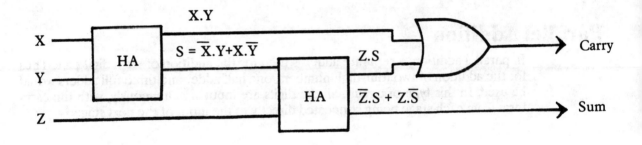

Adding Binary Numbers

So far, the circuits for addition have only been capable of adding two or three binary digits; more complex schemes are necessary in order to add two binary numbers each comprising several digits. Two approaches will be considered. The first adds numbers bit by bit, one pair of bits after another and is termed *serial addition*; the other accepts as inputs all pairs of bits in the two numbers simultaneously and is called *parallel addition*.

Serial Addition

Suppose that the numbers to be added have a four-bit wordlength, and the two numbers A and B have digits $a_3\ a_2\ a_1\ a_0$ and $b_3\ b_2\ b_1\ b_0$ respectively. The circuit for a four-bit serial adder is shown below:

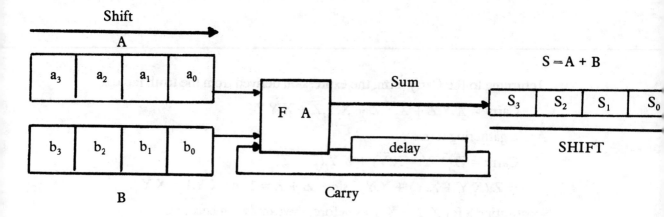

In this particular design, a single full adder is presented with pairs of bits from the two numbers in the sequence $a_0 b_0$, $a_1 b_1$, $a_2 b_2$, $a_3 b_3$. As each pair of bits is added, the sum term is transmitted to a shift register to hold the result, and the carry term is delayed so that it is added in to the next addition operation.

Though this method is cheap in terms of hardware requirements, it is not often (if at all) used in modern digital computers because of its slow operation. The degree to which hardware prices have dropped in recent years has resulted in the almost universal adoption of parallel addition.

Parallel Addition

In parallel addition, a separate adder is used for the addition of each digit pair. Thus for the addition of two four-digit numbers, one half adder and three full adders would be used. In this type of circuit, all the digits are input simultaneously, with the carry term from each stage being connected directly to the input of the next stage:

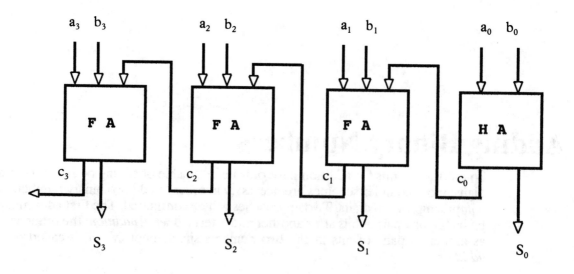

Though faster than serial addition, one fault of the type of parallel adder shown above is the successive carry out to carry in connections which cause relatively long delays;

more elaborate schemes are capable of overcoming this problem (at the expense of added circuitry).

The efficiency of the addition circuits is of particular importance in microprocessors where the functions of multiplication and division, as well as subtraction, often use these circuits. Larger computers (and many of the more recent 16 and 32 bit microprocessors) have special purpose circuitry for multiplication and division.

Exercises

1. *For each of the expressions below, simplify the expression using a Karnaugh map and draw a circuit of the simplified expression:*

    (i) $X.Y.Z + X.Y.Z + X.Y.Z$

    (ii) $A.B.C + A.B.C + A.B.C + A.B.C + A.B.C$

    (iii) $A.B.C.D + A.B.C.D + A.B.C.D + A.B.C.D + A.B.C.D + A.B.C.D$

    (iv) $W.X + X.Y + X.Y.Z + W.Y.Z + W.X.Y.Z$

2.   *Use truth table to prove the laws of Boolean Algebra.*

3.   *Given two binary signals X and Y, produce a truth table to define the difference of the two digits for every combination. There will be two outputs representing the difference and a "borrow". Hence draw the circuit for a "half-subtractor".*

4.   *Produce a truth table which defines the 4-bit product when two 2-bit numbers are multiplied together. (The largest number produced will be $3 \times 3 = 9$ which requires 4 bits). Simplify each of the four outputs using Karnaugh maps and produce a circuit for hardware multiplication of 2-bit numbers.*

Assignment   *Seven Segment Display*

The diagram below shows the layout of a seven segment display digit commonly used in calculators. Each segment of the display can be emphasised by applying a logic 1 to the input to that segment. By simultaneously emphasising the appropriate segments, the device can be used to display the digits 0 to 9.

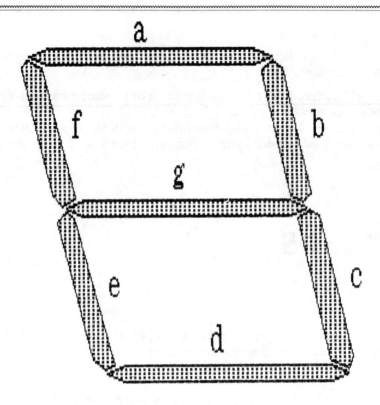

Layout of a seven-segment display digit.

Task

Design seven logic circuits, one for each segment, such that when four signals representing a binary-coded decimal(BCD) digit are applied to each circuit, the appropriate digit is displayed.

The truth table will have the following form:

INPUTS(BCD) A B C D	DIGIT	a	b	c	d	e	f	g
0 0 0 0	0	1	1	1	1	1	1	0
0 0 0 1	1	0	1	1	0	0	0	0
.... etc	....							
.... 1 0 0 1	 9	1	1	1	1	0	1	1

Chapter 22

Computer Instructions

Introduction

This chapter deals with activity of the Central Processing Unit (CPU) and the ways in which computer program instructions are stored, interpreted and executed in order that the computer can perform its tasks. Case studies of computer systems are provided at the end of this chapter to illustrate the application of some of the theories which follow.

In Chapter 20 it is stated that data can take various forms when stored in a memory word, namely:

- pure binary;
- coded binary, for example BCD;
- character codes, for example ASCII.

All the above are considered to be *data* and can be interpreted as such by the CPU. In order to perform any tasks, the CPU has to have access to computer *instructions*. During processing, data currently being processed and the instructions needed to process the data are stored in main memory.

Thus a memory word can also contain an instruction. A memory word containing an instruction is referred to as an *instruction word* and one containing data as a *data word*.

The Central Processing Unit (CPU)

The CPU has a number of *registers* which it can use to temporarily store a number of words read from memory. These registers are used to apply meaning to the contents of memory words. It should be noted that the contents of memory words cannot be determined as data or instructions simply by examining their contents in memory.

The CPU differentiates between data and instructions by placing:

- instructions in an *instruction register;*
- data in *data registers*.

A computer program stored in main memory comprises a sequence of instructions. Each instruction is transferred, in turn, into the CPU's instruction register, thus identifying the next operation which the CPU is to perform. The instructions are retrieved from consecutive memory locations, unless the last instruction executed requires the next instruction to be fetched from a different location. Instructions dealing with the latter circumstance are called *branch* or *jump* instructions. The various types of instruction are described later. The process of fetching, interpreting and executing instructions is called the *fetch-execute cycle*; the process may also be referred to as the *instruction cycle* or *automatic sequence control*.

As is indicated in Chapter 17, the *control unit* has the function of controlling all hardware operation, including the CPU itself. To understand the fetch-execute cycle it is necessary to be aware of the names and functions of the various registers used.

The Program Counter (PC)

The PC keeps track of the locations where instructions are stored. At any one time during a program's execution the PC holds the memory address of the next instruction to be executed. Its operation is possible because, in all computer systems, the instructions forming a program are stored in adjacent memory locations, so that the next instruction will normally be stored in an address a single increment more than the address of the last instruction to be fetched. By incrementing the address in the PC each time an instruction is received, the PC always has the address of the next instruction to be retrieved. The program counter is also known by a variety of other names, including the Sequence Control Register (SCR) and the Instruction Address Register (IAR).

Memory Buffer Register (MBR)

Whenever the contents of a memory word are to be transferred into or out of main memory, they pass through the MBR. This applies to both data and instructions.

Memory Address Register (MAR)

The MAR provides the location address of the specific memory word to be read from or written to via the MBR.

Current Instruction Register (CIR)

As the name suggests, the function of the CIR is to store the current instruction for decoding and execution.

Accumulators

These registers are situated within the arithmetic/logic unit (ALU) and provide a 'working area' for data fetched from memory. Numbers about to be added or subtracted can be copied, via the MBR, into the accumulators. The arithmetic result can be placed in one accumulator and from there, copied to a main memory location. All communications between the CPU and the memory take place via the MAR and the MBR, as the following diagram illustrates.

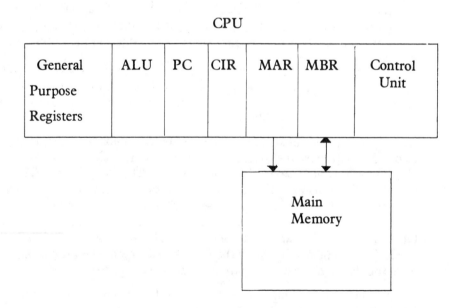

In order to fetch an instruction from memory the CPU places the address of the instruction in the MAR and then carries out a memory read; the instruction is then copied into the MBR and from there, into the CIR.

Similarly, an instruction which itself requires the reading of a particular data word causes the address of the data word to be placed into the MAR. The execution of the memory read then results in the copying of the addressed data word into the MBR, from where it can be accessed by the processor. The MBR acts as the point of transfer for both data and instructions passing, in either direction, between the main memory and the CPU.

Fetch-execute Cycle

The instruction fetch-execute cycle can be described as follows:

Fetch phase

– common to all instructions.

(i) the contents of the PC are copied into the MAR. The MAR now contains the location address of the next instruction and a memory read is initiated to copy the instruction word from memory into the MBR.

(ii) the PC is incremented and now contains the address of the next instruction.

(iii) the instruction word is then copied from the MBR into the CIR.

Execute phase

– the action taken is unique to the instruction.

(i) the instruction in the CIR is decoded

(ii) the instruction in the CIR is executed.

(iii) unless the instruction is a STOP instruction, then the cycle is repeated.

The fetch-execute cycle is carried out automatically by the hardware and the programmer cannot control its sequence of operation. Of course, the programmer does have control over which instructions are stored in memory and the order in which they are executed.

The cycle can be illustrated more simply with a flowchart, without detailed reference to all the registers.

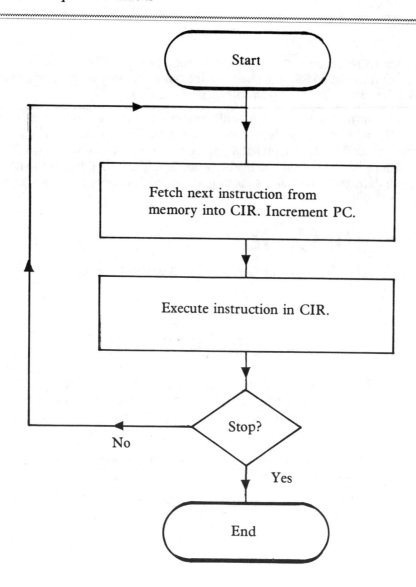

Types of Instruction

All the instructions available on a particular machine are known collectively as the *instruction set* of that machine. There are certain types of instruction commonly available in most computer systems. They can be classified according to their function as follow:

- arithmetic and logical operations on data;

- input and output of data;

- changing the sequence of program execution (branch instructions);

- transfer of data between memory and the CPU registers;

- transfer of data between registers within the CPU.

Instruction Format

An instruction usually consists of two main components, the *function* or *operation code* (*opcode*) and the *operand*. The opcode part of the instruction defines the operation to be performed, for example to add or to move data. The operand defines the location address in memory of the data to be operated upon. The storage of an instruction can be illustrated as follows using a 16-bit memory word:

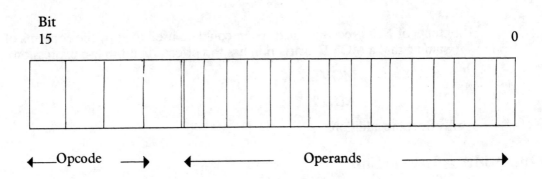

Thus, the most significant 4 bits determine the type of instruction and the remaining 12 bits specify the operand or operands to be used.

Three-address Instruction

If an expression requiring the use of three memory variables is to be accommodated by one instruction, then the instruction word will need to contain the address of each variable, that is three operands. An addition instruction can be expressed symbolically as,

ADD Z,X,Y

that is, add the contents of X to the contents of Y and store the result in Z.

The instruction word needs to be large enough to accommodate the three addresses and can be illustrated as follows:

OPCODE	ADDRESS	ADDRESS	ADDRESS

Because of the large number of bits required this format is not often used.

Two-address instruction

With this format only two addresses are available in the instruction, so that there is an implicit assumption that the result is to be stored in one of the operands (X or Y). This means that one of the original numbers is overwritten by the result (remember memory volatility).

If only one instruction is used, then adding the contents of X and Y and placing the result in X is expressed symbolically as,

ADD X,Y

and the instruction word format can be illustrated as follows:

OPCODE	ADDRESS	ADDRESS

In order to place the result in Z (as in the first expression) and to preserve the original contents of X, a preceding instruction could be used to copy the contents of X to Z. Assuming that a MOVE instruction has this effect, then the two expressions

> MOVE Z,X
>
> ADD Z,Y

will effect the addition.

One-Address Instruction

It should be obvious that this format only allows an opcode to refer to one operand and that two assumptions regarding storage are implicit. Firstly, as with the two-address format, it must be assumed that the result is to be stored in Z. Secondly, if only one operand can be referred to, the addition process must use another storage area for the second operand. Generally, a CPU general-purpose register, called the accumulator, is used. The single-address instruction is used where there is only a single accumulator, so the instruction does not need to refer to the accumulator. The instruction word format can be illustrated as follows:

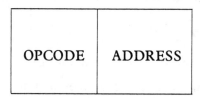

The processes needed to achieve the required result may be:

1. Copy the contents of one operand, X, into the accumulator. This operation uses a LOAD (accumulator) instruction.

2. ADD the contents of operand Y, placing the result in the accumulator. At the time of the addition, the contents of operand Y are in the MBR, having been read from memory as part of the instruction. An ADD instruction usually has this effect.

3. Copy the result from the accumulator into address Z using a STORE command.

The assembly language coding (Chapter10 Software) for the above process may be as follows:

Instruction	Effect
LDA X	copies the contents of X, via the MBR, into the accumulator;
ADD Y	reads the contents of Y into the MBR, adds them to the accumulator and places the result in the accumulator;
STO Z	copies the result from the accumulator into memory address Z, via the MBR.

One-and-a-half-Address Instruction

Where there is more than one accumulator, an instruction using the accumulator must indicate which one is to be used. Since the number of accumulators is generally small, the number of bits needed to refer to a single accumulator is usually less than the number needed for a memory location address. The processes for carrying out the example sum are the same as for the one-address format, except that a specified accumulator is used. The instruction word format can be illustrated as follows:

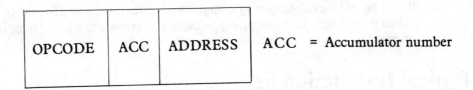

Zero-Address Instruction

This type of instruction is particularly popular with small machines because of its economy in size. Many microcomputer systems operate with a combination of one-address and zero-address instructions. A zero-address instruction does not specify any operands within it and relies on the use of a memory-based data structure called a *stack*, to provide the operands.

A stack consists of a group of adjacent memory locations, the contents of which are addressed by a stack pointer. The stack pointer is a register that contains the address of the current top of stack. Values can only be added (*pushed*) to, or removed (*popped*) from, the top of the stack, which is indicated by the current position of the stack pointer. The value of the stack pointer is incremented or decremented when an item is pushed or popped. A value located below the top item on the stack (as indicated by the stack pointer) cannot be removed until any values above it have been removed.

Consider, for example, an ADD instruction which requires the addition of two operands, X and Y. The operands X and then Y are pushed onto the stack; Y is thus at the top of the stack and is the first one which can be removed. The ADD instruction causes the popping of Y and X from the stack; they are added and the sum is pushed onto the top of the stack.

Although this instruction format is extremely short, additional instructions are needed in order to transfer operands from memory to the stack and from the stack to memory; obviously these instructions need to be longer in order to allow specification of memory addresses. They are similar to single instruction words, except that operands are copied to and from the stack rather than to and from the accumulator.

Instruction Format and Memory Size

Given a particular word length (the number of bit positions in a memory word), single-address instructions can directly (specify the actual memory address) address a larger number of memory locations than one-and-a-half or multiple-address formats because all the address bits can be used for one address. Many computers allow a variable length instruction word so that the number of bits available for the address portion of the instruction can be increased to allow a larger number of memory locations to be directly addressed. If, for example, there are 16 bits for the address, then the highest location which can be addressed is:

$$2^{16} - 1 = 65,535$$

Therefore, 65,536 locations can be addressed, numbered 0 to 65,535 (computer memory sizes are quoted in nK, K being 1024 and 'n' being a variable) and this example illustrates a 64K memory, that is, 64 x 1024 which equals 65,536.

By increasing the number of bits available for the address to, say 20, the number of locations which can be addressed is over a million. In practice, not all memory words need to be addressed directly. For example, to enable the direct addressing of all locations in a 256K ($256 \times 1024 = 262,144$) memory requires the use of 18 bits ($2^{18} = 262,144$). There are addressing techniques to reduce the number of bits needed for a memory address and some of these are described later in the chapter. An increase in word size also allows an increase in the number of bits available for the opcode and the possibility of an increase in the size of the instruction set. It has to be said, however, that a recent development in computer architecture, namely that of the RISC (Reduced Instruction Set Computer) processor, is making this latter benefit somewhat less relevant.

A Typical Instruction Set

The range of instructions available for any particular machine depends on the machine's architecture, in terms of word length and the number and types of registers used. For this reason it is only possible to list some typical types of instruction (the names LOAD etc are not actual mnemonic opcodes) some of which were used in the earlier example:

Load	copies the contents of a specified location into a register.
Add	adds the contents of a specified memory location to the contents of a register.
Subtract	subtracts the contents of a specified memory location from the contents of a register.
Store	copies the contents of a register into a specified memory location.
Branch	switches control to another instruction address other than the next in sequence.
Register-register	moves contents from one register to another.
Shift	moves bits in a memory location to the left or to the right for arithmetic purposes or for pattern manipulation.
Input/output	effects data transfers between peripherals and memory.
Logical operations (AND, OR, NOT)	which combine the contents of a register and a specified memory location or register.

These latter operations are described in Chapter 21 on Computer Logic. The first four instruction types in this list have already been explained in the earlier addition example, so the following sections deal with those remaining.

Branch Instructions

These instructions cause the program to divert from the sequence which is dictated by that of contiguous memory locations containing program instructions. A branch instruction causes the value of the Program Counter (PC) to be altered to direct the next instruction to be fetched from a location which is not physically adjacent to the current instruction. A branch may be *conditional* (dependent on some condition) or *unconditional*. In the latter case, the branch is always made, whereas in the former, the branch only occurs if a specified condition occurs. The conditions tested usually include tests on CPU register contents for zero, non-zero, negative and positive number values. The branch or jump may be to a specified address or simply to 'skip' the next instruction (or several instructions). In either case the program counter must be incremented accordingly to change its contents to the address specified by the branch instruction. Branching can be used to repeat a sequence of instructions in a *loop*. Usually this is conditional to avoid an unending program iteration.

Subroutines

A branch instruction to jump or skip to a specified instruction address does not necessarily involve a return to the original sequence once the branch has been made. To provide for such a return requires a special form of branching. There are circumstances when a group of instructions referred to as a subroutine needs to be executed more than once during a program's execution. It may be necessary, for example, to carry out a particular sequence of calculations at different points in a program. Instead of coding the instructions at each point where they are required, the coding can be written as a subroutine.

Whenever a subroutine is used or *called*, there must be a mechanism for returning control to the original program sequence. One method is to save the current contents of the PC in the first location of the subroutine before the branch to the subroutine is made. Upon completion of the subroutine the contents of the first location can be loaded into the PC and control returned to the calling program. The process of branching to a subroutine and then returning to continue the instruction sequence can be illustrated by the following diagram:

Main program

Instruction

Sequence

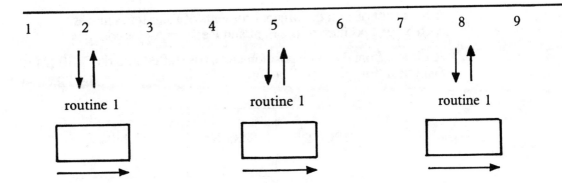

Alternatively, the return address may be placed on a *stack* (a memory facility described earlier in this chapter) and copied back into the PC to allow a resumption of the normal program sequence. The stack is particularly useful where subroutines are 'nested'; this means that a subroutine may be called from within another subroutine. The return addresses are placed onto the stack and removed in reverse order so that the last return address is the first to be removed. The technique is described in detail in Chapter 34 (Data Structures).

Register-Register Instructions

As the name suggests, instructions of this type are used to transfer the contents of one register to another. Its format is similar to that of the two-address instruction described in the previous section. It can be illustrated as follows:

OPCODE	REG1	REG2

Although operands to address memory are not used, the instruction allows two operands to address the registers involved. The number of registers available will tend to be small, perhaps two or three, so that a single byte may be sufficient to contain the two operands. In an 8-bit machine, such instructions may be two bytes long, one for the opcode and one for the two register addresses. Data transfers between registers within the CPU are carried out via a communications system which is a subdivision of the computer system's *architecture*.

Shift Instructions

A shift operation moves the bits in a register to new positions in the register. A shift can be either to the left or to the right and may be *logical* or *arithmetic*. Consider the following example which illustrates the concept of logical shifting.

Example

	Bit Position	5 4 3 2 1 0
At the start Register A contains		0 0 1 1 0 1

A *left* shift of 1 moves each bit one position to the left and

Register A now contains   0 1 1 0 1 0

Bit 5 (a 0) is lost and a 0 is shifted into the
(LSB) Least Significant Bit position.

A right shift of 1 on the original contents of Register A moves
each bit one position to the right and Register A now contains   0 0 0 1 1 0

A 1 is lost from the Bit 0 position and a 0 is shifted into the MSB (Most Significant Bit) position. The format of a shift instruction may be as follows:

OPCODE	REG No	No of shifts

The opcode indicates the type of shift, which may be one of the following:

Logical Shifts

Logical shifts are used for pattern manipulation of data and are not concerned with arithmetic operations. Thus the above examples illustrate logical shifts. Another type of logical shift involves rotation of bits in a register or location. Such shifts are called *rotational* or *cyclic shifts*.

Rotational Shifts

A rotational shift can be either to the left or to the right, as the following examples illustrate:

Example 1

A *right* rotational shift of one.

Before shift   After shift

1 1 0 1   1 1 1 0

The 1 in the LSB position is moved to the MSB position as each bit moves one place to the right.

Example 2

A *left* rotational shift of one.

Before shift   After shift

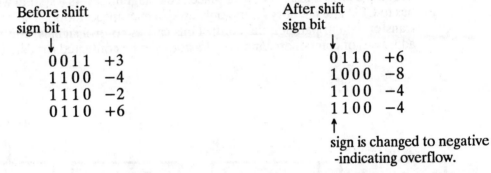

1011   0111

The 1 in the MSB position is moved to the LSB position as each bit moves one place to the left.

Arithmetic Shifts

Left and right shift operations are used for multiply and divide operations but arithmetic meaning must be maintained. A left shift of one doubles the number and a right shift of one halves the number. Computer multiplication can be carried out through a sequence of additions and shifts, and division by a sequence of subtractions and shifts. Some examples of arithmetic shifts using twos complement notation are as follow:

Example 1

A *left* shift of 1 (zeros are inserted into the LSB position)

Before shift
sign bit
↓

0 0 1 1	+3
1 1 0 0	−4
1 1 1 0	−2
0 1 1 0	+6

After shift
sign bit
↓

0 1 1 0	+6
1 0 0 0	−8
1 1 0 0	−4
1 1 0 0	−4

↑
sign is changed to negative
-indicating overflow.

Note that in the last example above the sign has been changed from positive to negative by the left shift operation. In these circumstances an overflow signal would be set.

Example 2

A *right* shift of 1 (where necessary, a 1 is shifted into the sign bit to preserve the sign)

Before shift
sign bit
↓

| 0 1 1 0 | +6 |
| 1 1 0 0 | − 4 |

After shift
sign bit
↓

| 0 0 1 1 | +3 |
| 1 1 1 0 | −2 |

↑
sign preserved by shifting
1 into the MSB position

Example 3

A right shift of 2 (again, the sign is preserved)

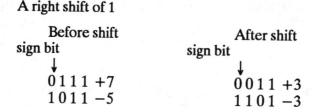

Before shift
sign bit
↓

1 0 0 0	−8
0 1 0 0	+4
1 1 0 0	−4

After shift
sign bit
↓

1 1 1 0	−2
0 0 0 1	+1
1 1 1 1	−1

Although the solution is not of concern in this text, it should be noted that right shifts truncate the number, so there are no halves. The examples below illustrate this point:

A right shift of 1

Before shift
sign bit
↓

0 1 1 1	+7
1 0 1 1	−5

After shift
sign bit
↓

0 0 1 1	+3
1 1 0 1	−3

Input/Output Instructions

Input/output (I/O) instructions are concerned with the transfer of data between peripherals and memory or between peripherals and registers in the CPU or processor.

The following diagram illustrates the architecture of the communication system which allows the data transfers to take place. The diagram shows a system with common I/O bus to CPU and memory (commonly used in microprocessors). The data bus is used to transfer data in parallel; the control bus carries control signals, and the address bus, addresses of components/memory locations to be contacted for data transfer.

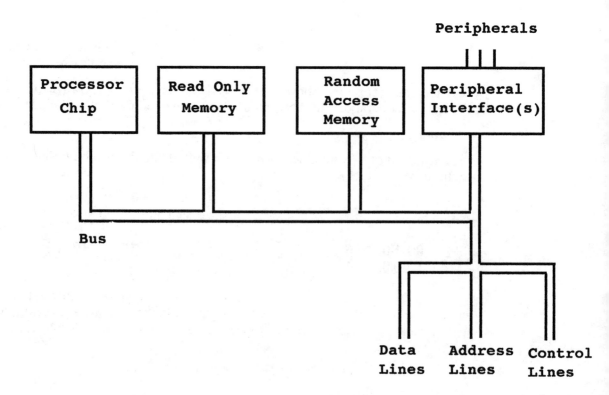

An interface unit has a special function. It converts control and data signals from the CPU into the forms necessary for the various peripherals. Conversely, it converts the input from various peripherals into the standard form useable by the CPU.

Direct Memory Access (DMA)

Not all data transfers between peripheral devices and the CPU are carried out under continual program control. Other schemes such as DMA allow data transfer to or from high speed storage devices such as tape or disk to be effected without continual CPU control. Data is transferred in blocks, as opposed to character by character. DMA is possible because of the ability of some peripheral devices to operate *autonomously*, that is, after the initial input or output instruction has been given by the CPU, the peripheral is able to complete the data transfer independently. To allow the memory to be accessed directly by a peripheral, instead of via the CPU, hardware known as a DMA controller is needed. For transfers from main memory to peripheral, the CPU supplies the DMA controller with the start address in memory of the data block to be transferred and its length. A transfer from, for example, a disk pack to memory would require the CPU to tell the DMA controller the relevant disk address and into which memory locations the data is to be copied. The DMA controller 'steals' memory cycles from the CPU while the data transfer is taking place. Meanwhile, the CPU can continue execution of its current program, although its operation is slowed slightly by the *cycle stealing*. DMA is an essential component to any computer system working in multi-programming mode.

Programmed Input/Output

Input and output which is under program control is termed *programmed* I/O. The CPU instruction set contains four types of I/O instructions:

(i) Input - to transfer data from peripheral to CPU;

(ii) Output - to transfer data from CPU to peripheral;

(iii) to set individual control flags in the I/O interface unit;

(iv) to test individual flags in the I/O interface unit.

A peripheral device is attached to an interface unit by a cable. The interface unit (usually inside the computer) is connected to one of a number of I/O slots. Each I/O slot has a fixed address by which a peripheral can be identified for input or output. There are 3 basic elements in an interface unit:

(i) A control bit or 'busy' register - used to signal a device to start input or output. This cannot be set by the device as it is under I/O control;

(ii) A flag bit or 'done' register - this is set by the device when the data transfer is complete. This flag can be tested or cleared by program instructions;

(iii) A buffer register for the storage of data transferred into (read by) or to be transferred from (written by) the device.

When a 'start read' instruction is given, *one* character is transferred between the interface buffer register and the device. One character is transferred in the opposite direction if a 'start write' instruction is given. Thus programmed I/O is on a character by character basis.

Data transfers can be under program control in two main ways:

– interrupts;

– polling.

Interrupts

This method allows the device to *interrupt* the CPU when a transfer is complete. The CPU does not have to continually test the flag bit and is free to carry out other tasks while a character is being transferred.

Polling

A simpler alternative is to use a CPU instruction to command the device to operate by setting the control bit and then repeatedly testing the flag bit (*polling*) to discover when the transfer is complete. Although simple to program, it is extremely inefficient in terms of CPU operation because the CPU operates at many times the speed of any peripheral device and is thus wasting much of its power 'waiting' for each character to be transmitted. The technique is appropriate for a microcomputer system where only a few external devices are interfaced and the processor has sufficient time to continually test the devices to see if they are ready.

For the polling alternative, the instruction sequence would be as follows:

For *input* from a specific device:

      (i) instruction to interface to set control bit for 'start transmit';

      (ii) send instruction to test flag bit. If flag bit indicates transfer complete, skip next instruction;

      (iii) branch to previous instruction;

      (iv) issue instruction to transfer character from buffer register into CPU accumulator;

      (v) issue store instruction to transfer character from accumulator to main memory.

For *output* to a specific device:

      (i) issue instruction to transfer character from CPU accumulator into buffer register of interface device;

      (ii) issue instruction to set control bit to start transfer;

      (iii) issue instruction to test flag bit and if set, skip the next instruction;

      (iv) branch to previous instruction.

The repetitive flag-test loop is necessary to ensure that a character transfer is completed before the next one is transmitted.

Memory Addressing Methods

The physical memory addresses ultimately used by the hardware are the *absolute addresses*. As explained earlier, addressing memory locations directly restricts the size of useable memory and for this reason a computer's instruction set will normally include facilities for addressing locations beyond those directly addressable with a given address length. Thus, absolute addresses may be referenced in a variety of ways and the addressing mode used is indicated in the operand of an instruction word. The format of an instruction word may be as shown on the following page.

	ADDRESSING	
OPCODE	MODE	ADDRESS

The following addressing modes are common to most machines:

Immediate Addressing

With this method, the operand to be accessed by the instruction is stored in the instruction word or in the word immediately following it in memory. In the former case, the operand would be fetched with the instruction and no separate memory read would then be necessary. In the latter case, an ADD instruction which employed this method of addressing would indicate that the operand is to be found immediately after the opcode in memory. In a byte organized machine, the first byte would contain the opcode, the execution of which would involve the fetching of the next byte in memory which contained the required operand. Computers based on the Intel 8080 or Motorola 6800 processor use this latter method for immediate addressing. The Intel 8080 provides the opcode ADI (add immediate) as part of its instruction set. Immediate addressing is useful when small constants or literals are required in a program, for example, a set value of 3 to be subtracted from the contents of a register at some stage in the program. It is inappropriate to use this method if there is any need for the value to be changed as this would require changing the program coding.

Direct Addressing

As the name suggests, this addressing mode specifies the actual or effective memory address containing the required operand, in the address field of the instruction word. The addressed memory location specified must be accessed to obtain the operand.

Indirect Addressing

With this method, the location address in the instruction word does not contain the operand. Instead, it contains the address containing the data item. Thus, an indirect address is, in effect, a pointer to the address containing the operand. For example, IAD 156 (indirect add) indicates that the address 156 contains the address of the required operand. If specific indirect addressing instructions are not provided, an instruction word may contain a 'flag' bit to indicate whether or not an operand is an indirect or direct address; the flag bit may be set to 1 if the address is indirect and to 0 if it is direct. In this way, an LDA (load accumulator) instruction is able to refer to a direct or indirect address by the appropriate setting of the flag bit. The following diagram illustrates the principle of indirect addressing.

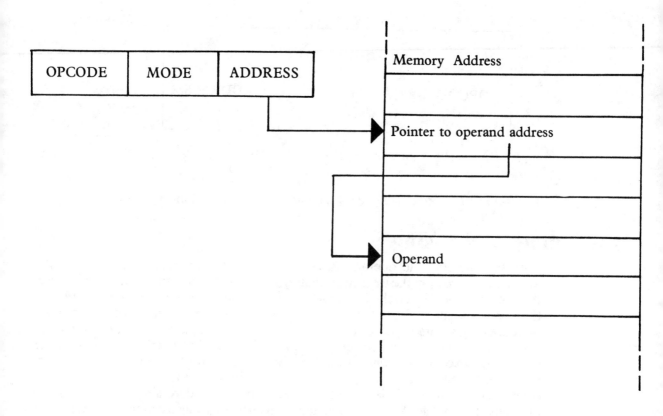

Indirect addressing is generally slower in execution than direct addressing as an extra *memory cycle* is needed each time the actual address is deferred. Indirect addressing is also known as *deferred* addressing and if the address is deferred more than once it is known as a *multi-level* address.

Relative Addressing

With relative addressing, the instruction word contains an *offset* address which indicates the location of the operand relative to the position of the instruction in memory. Thus, if an instruction is stored in address N and the offset is 5, then the operand is in address N + 5. It is a useful technique for branching a program, in which case the offset address will indicate the relative address of the next instruction to be fetched, rather than a data item. The program counter (PC) is used to calculate the effective address in that it contains the address of the current instruction. By adding the offset to the PC, the address is determined. The instruction set usually contains instructions which allow such program jumps to be made. Relative addressing is also used to move a block of *relocatable* code from one part of memory to another. The addresses in the instruction words can remain the same wherever the code is located in memory because the effective addresses are always relative to the position of the instructions.

Indexed Addressing

With this method, the effective address is calculated by the addition of an index value to the address given in the instruction. The index value is usually stored in either a general-purpose CPU register or a special *index* register.

The method can be employed by a programmer when an ordered block of data is to be accessed and each data item is to be processed in the same way. If the value of the index is N and the address in the instruction is X, then the effective address for an operand is N + X. The register is set to an initial value and incremented as the instructions step through the memory locations. A branch instruction is used to create a program loop to repeat the same set of instructions needed for each item of data in the block.

Case Study Examples

Instruction Formats

The DEC PDP-10

The PDP-10 uses a *one-and-a-half* instruction format in that each instruction allows a single main memory address and a register address (one of 16 available). The format is as follows:

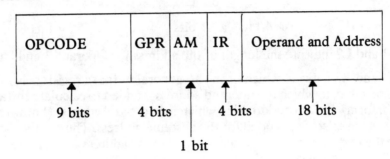

| OPCODE | GPR | AM | IR | Operand and Address |

9 bits   4 bits   4 bits   18 bits

1 bit

OPCODE	–	the instruction
GPR	–	the address of one of 16 general purpose registers
AM	–	the addressing mode - direct or indirect
IR	–	Index Register address - one of the same 16 general purpose registers which can be used specifically as an index register (e.g. for indexed addressing).
OPERAND ADDRESS	–	the main memory address containing the required operand.

As is explained in the text, the use of a number of general purpose registers requires the use of an address to specify the particular register in use. A system with only one general purpose register (accumulator) would not require an address as it would be implicit in any instruction which used it.

The IBM 360 System

The IBM 360 uses a variety of instruction formats based on the *two address* format. The following illustrate two of the instruction formats:

Register-Register Instructions

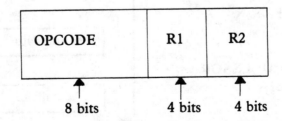

| OPCODE | R1 | R2 |

8 bits   4 bits   4 bits

R1 - the Register 1 operand address

R2 - the Register 2 operand address

Memory to Memory Instructions

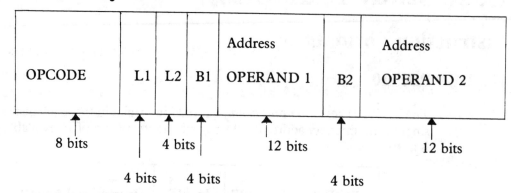

L1 and L2 indicate the length of the address for Operand 1 and 2 respectively.

B1 and B2 indicate which of the 16 general purpose registers is to be used to store a base value, to which the operand address is added to calculate the actual address. This is a form of *relative* addressing which uses a 'base' address (known as *base* addressing) to which offsets are added for the absolute address. The relative addressing described in the text uses an offset which is added to the address of the current instruction (value of the program counter).

CPU Architecture

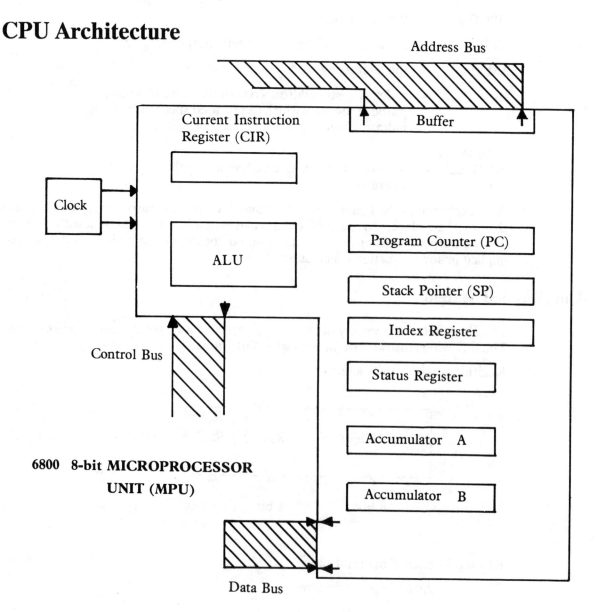

The following can be identified:

Bus

The diagram shows three buses, the data bus, the address bus and the control bus.

Data Bus

This bus carries data between the CPU and the main memory.

Address Bus

This carries the address of the memory word to be read from or written to main memory.

Control Bus

This bus carries control function signals, for example, to reset CPU registers and to prepare the processor for the beginning of a program.

Accumulators

There are two in the 6800 processor, A and B, which are used for holding data during arithmetic operations by the arithmetic/logic unit (ALU) and as work areas for some non-arithmetic operations.

Status Register

Each bit in the status register is assigned a particular meaning by the manufacturer and can be set as a 'flag' to indicate the occurrence of certain conditions, for example, an arithmetic overflow.

Index Register

This register is used in certain types of memory addressing instructions (see indexed addressing).

Stack Pointer

A stack is a collection or 'stack' of items used, for example, for storing return addresses for subroutines. The stack pointer indicates the item currently at the top of the stack or the first free space above it.

Clock

The clock produces a timing pulse to synchronize and co-ordinate events occurring within the processor.

Assignment

Addressing the Problem

Task

1.   **What is meant by the term 'absolute address'? A computer system uses:**

   Indirect addressing

   Relative addressing

   Indexed addressing

Explain carefully how the absolute address is obtained in each case.

2.   Explain which of the above addressing methods would be appropriate for the addition of an array of contiguous memory variables. Draw a program flowchart to illustrate the procedure for totalling a series of 30 numbers beginning in location 0040.

3.   Assuming a one-and-a-half address instruction format, explain the role of the various components of the 6800 processor (illustrated earlier) in the running of the program in Task 2.

Chapter 23

Computer Networks and Distributed Systems

This chapter looks at how computer networks have developed, some technical aspects of their construction and how they can be used to decentralize or distribute the data processing function.

Factors Favouring the Decentralization of Computing Power

Three main factors have encouraged many organizations to adopt a decentralized policy:

(i) Many organizations already have a number of computers installed at geographically separated sites. At first these systems tended to be used in isolation, but the need to extract and analyse information from the company as a whole, led to their connection via the telecommunication network;

(ii) The cost of computers has fallen dramatically, making it cost-effective for organizations to process and analyse data at the various points of collection;

(iii) The development of Local Area Networks of low-cost microcomputers with electronic office facilities (Chapter 6), has encouraged demand for local computer power and these networks can be readily connected to any central facility via telecommunications networks;

Data Communications and Computers

The combination of computer and telecommunications technologies has had a profound effect on the way computer systems are organized. The idea of a computer centre handling all computer processing, without any user involvement, is rapidly becoming obsolete. A computer network aims to distribute the processing work amongst a number of connected computers and to allow users direct control over processing.

A system which uses a central computer to control all processing, with a number of 'slave' terminals is not necessarily a computer network. The following section describes two pre-network systems which make use of the telecommunications and computer technologies. They are:

(a) Non-Interactive Systems;

(b) Interactive 'Dumb' Terminal Systems.

Non-Interactive Systems

Systems for the transmission of data from remote terminals to a central computer, have been in widespread use since the mid-1960s. Used for transfer of large volumes of data, they were known as Remote Job Entry (RJE) systems. At first, they tended to use terminals which only allowed one-way transmission. The way in which many banks used the system is described below as an example.

Example: The Transmission of Bank Transactions

Details of the customer transactions were transmitted by a *dial-up* telephone connection to the computer centre, at the end of the day. During the day, the transactions were keyed into *off-line* accounting machines which automatically punched the details onto paper tape. The paper tape was then loaded onto a paper tape reader, the computer link made and the data transmitted to the computer centre.

The system was extremely limited. It only provided a facility for transmitting data *to* the computer. The system did not allow the link to be used to retrieve information from the computer and no separate processing power was available at the transmitting branch. The system can be illustrated diagrammatically as follows:

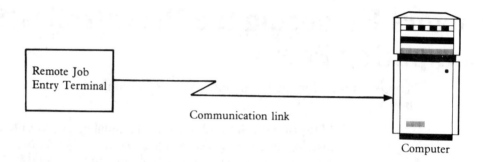

Similar systems developed using key-to-tape or key-to-disk systems for the data encoding process, but processing control was still completely centralized.

Interactive 'Dumb' Terminal Systems

Through the use of a teletypewriter (TTY) terminal or more recently, a VDU terminal, it became possible for the communication link to be two-way.

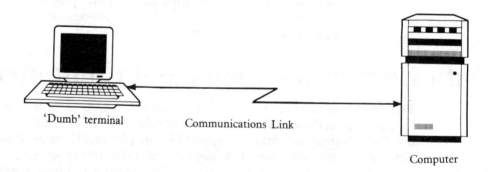

Both the TTY and VDU terminals acted as input and output devices and supported two-way communications. However, these devices had no processing power or storage facility of their own (*dumb*) and were entirely dependent on the central computer. Whenever the central computer was *down,* all users were deprived of any processing facility.

Neither of the above systems can be described as a network because all processing control is with a central computer system.

Computer Networks

Some computer networks use *intelligent* VDU or microcomputer terminals to permit some independent processing power at sites remote from the central computer. Other networks distribute even more processing power by linking together microcomputer or minicomputer systems. In this case, the terminals are computer systems in themselves. Because such networks distribute some processing power to a number of different sites, they are also known as *distributed* processing systems.

Applications of Computer Networks

Networks can be configured to suit almost any application, from the provision of a world-wide airline booking service to home banking. Terminals may be only a few hundred feet apart and limited to a single building, or they may be several thousand miles apart. Some major areas of use, or potential use, are as follow:

(i) Computer-aided education can be supported by a network which provides Computer-Assisted Learning (CAL) packages to suit a wide range of subject and course areas;

(ii) Public data bases can allow people to make, for example, airline, restaurant, theatre or hotel reservations from anywhere in the world, with instant confirmation. Home banking services, such as that provided by the Bank of Scotland can be accessed by Prestel subscribers. A potential area of use could be the newspaper industry. Subscribers could arrange for personalized newspapers which contained only those subjects of interest to them. Information could, of course, be completely up-to-date;

(iii) Electronic mail has the potential to make hand-delivered communications virtually obsolete and this is discussed in Chapter 6;

(iv) Teleconferencing allows discussion amongst individuals without their physical presence in one room. A meeting can be conducted by the typing of messages at terminals. All contributions to a discussion are automatically recorded for later reference .

Local Area and Wide Area Networks

Computer networks can be classified according to their geographical spread. A network confined to, say, one building with work-stations which are usually microcomputers distributed in different rooms, is known as a *Local Area Network (LAN)*. One particular type, known as a *Ring Network* can extend over a diameter of two or three miles. A computer network distributed nationally or even internationally makes use of telephone and sometimes, satellite links, and is referred to as a *Wide Area Network* (WAN). In large organizations with several branches, it is becoming popular to maintain a LAN at each branch for localized processing and to link each LAN into a WAN covering the whole organization. In this way, branches of an organization can have control over their own processing and yet have access to the organization's main database at headquarters. In addition, inter-branch communication is possible.

Network Topologies

Computer networks can be categorized according to their 'shape' or *topology*. Each terminal in a network is known as a *node*. If a central computer controls the network it is known as the *host* computer. The topology of a network is the arrangement of the nodes and the ways they are interconnected. The communication system within a network is known as the *subnet*. Data can be transmitted around the subnet either on a point-to-point basis or via a broadcast channel.

–   If *point-to-point* transmission is used, the data passes through each device in the network. Thus, if two devices wish to communicate, they must do it indirectly, via any intervening devices. Each device must have the facility to store the entire message and forward it when the output channel is free.

–   If a *broadcast* channel is used, a common communication channel is shared by all devices in the network. This means that any message sent by a device is received by all devices. The message contains the address of the device intended to receive it, so that the other devices can ignore it.

There are a number of recognized network topologies and some of the most common are described below.

Star Network

A star network generally has a central host computer at the hub, with the terminals or nodes connected directly to it. The following figure illustrates one particular type of star topology.

Switched Hub Star Network

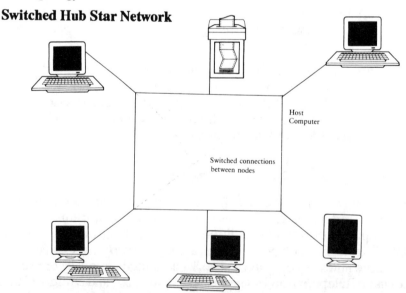

Host
Computer

Switched connections
between nodes

In this structure, all messages pass through the host computer, which interconnects the different users on the network. Thus, in this topology the host computer at the hub has a message switching function. Messages are transmitted point-to-point. The topology is particularly useful for intercommunications between pairs of users on the network (via the host). The network may consist of several computer systems (the nodes), connected to a larger host computer which switches data and programs between them. The star topology is less suitable where several nodes require access to another node.

Star Computer Network

The following star topology illustrates a popular form of network where the hub performs processing on information fed to it via the telephone system. In this case, the host computer has a processing rather than a message switching function.

Star Network

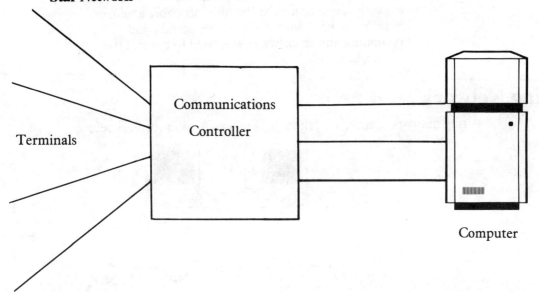

The star computer network is by far the most popular for WANS, because most large organizations start with a central computer at the head office, from which branch computer facilities are provided via the telephone network. The main aim is to provide computer communication between the branches and head office. Most other network topologies aim to provide communication between all devices on a network. The advantages of a star network topology are as follow:

(i) It is suitable for WANs where organizations rely on a central computer for the bulk of processing tasks, perhaps limiting the nodes to their local processing needs and the validation of data, prior to transmission to the central computer;

(ii) Centralized control of message switching allows a high degree of security control;

(iii) Each spoke in the star is independent of the rest and a fault in a link or device in one spoke, can be identified by the computer at the hub;

(iv) The data transmission speeds used can vary from one spoke to another. This is important if some spokes transmit using high speed devices, such as disk, whilst others transmit from low speed keyboard devices. The method of transmission may also vary. For example, one node may only require access to the network at the end of each day, in which case a *dial-up* connection may be sufficient. A dial-up connection uses the public telephone network and the user only pays for the time taken for transmission. Alternatively, other nodes may require the link for most of the working day, in which case a permanent leased line is appropriate. Leased lines provide a more reliable transmission medium and also allow higher speeds of data transmission.

The main disadvantages inherent in star networks are as follow:

(i) The network is vulnerable to hub failures which affect all
users. As a distributed processing system, some processing
is still possible at the nodes but inter-node communication
is lost when the host computer fails;

(ii) The control of communications in the network requires
expensive technology at the hub, probably a mini or
mainframe computer. Complex operating and
communications software is needed to control the
network.

Ring Network

A ring network connects all the nodes in a ring, as illustrated below.

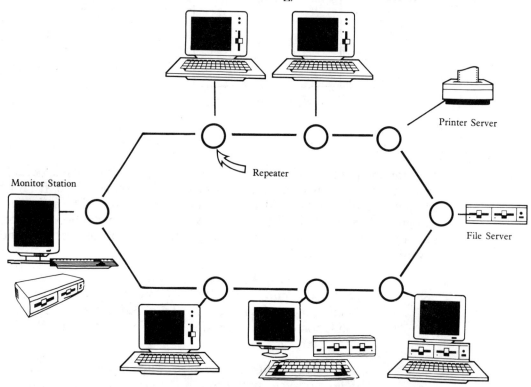

There is no host computer and none of the nodes need have overall control of access
to the network. In practice, a monitoring station is used for the control of data
transmission in the network. The topology is designed for LANs and the Cambridge
Ring is a popular configuration.

The ring consists of a series of *repeaters* which are joined by the physical transmission
medium. Repeaters regenerate messages as they pass around the network. The user
devices are connected to the repeaters. Thus, a message from one node, addressed to
another, is passed continually around the ring until the receiving node flags that it is
ready to accept it. Data is transmitted in mini-packets of about 40 bits and contains the
address of the sending node, the address of the receiving node and some control bits.
The ring network presents particular advantages:

(i) There is no dependence on a central host computer as
data transmission around the network is supported by all
the devices in the ring. Each node device has sufficient
intelligence to control the transmission of data from and to
its own node;

(ii) Very high transmission rates are possible;

(iii) Routing between devices is relatively simple because messages normally travel in one direction only around the ring;

(iv) The transmission facility is shared equally amongst the users.

The main disadvantages are as follows:

(i) The system depends on the reliability of the whole ring and the repeaters;

(ii) It may be difficult to extend the length of the ring because the physical installation of any new cable must ensure that the ring topology is preserved.

Loop Network

A loop network is similar in shape to a ring network, but priority of access to the network is controlled by a loop controller. Thus access to the network may not be equally shared amongst the nodes. Transmission rates also tend to be lower than for the ring. This is because communications are generally via the controller rather than direct from device to device. Communication is point-to-point. The topology is commonly used for the local handling of terminals by a large computer system.

Bus Network

The bus or highway network can be likened to a bus route, along which traffic moves from one end to the other. To continue the analogy, the stations are like 'bus stops' and the data like 'passengers'. Data can be placed on to the route or 'picked up' as it passes. The term *station* is used rather than *node* for this type of network. The communications subnet uses a broadcast channel, so all attached nodes can 'hear' every transmission. The topology is illustrated below and is typical of many LAN configurations. As is the case in the ring network, there is no host computer and all stations have equal priority in using the network to transmit.

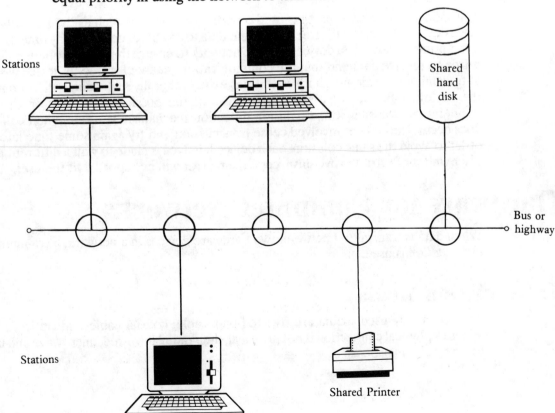

Local Area Network Access Methods

The three main methods of controlling access to a LAN are as follow:

Empty Slot Technique

This system is appropriate for networks in the shape of rings or loops, where messages are passed point-to-point in one direction. One or more empty slots or packets circulate continuously around the ring. When a device has information to transmit, it loads it into the slot, which carries it to its destination. At the time of loading, the destination address is placed in the slot and a 'full-empty' flag is set to 'full'. As the slot is passed from one repeater to another, no attempt will be made to load the slot as long as the flag is set to 'full'. When the slot reaches the destination device, the device's repeater reads the information without clearing the slot. Before passing it on, the repeater sets a 'received message' flag in the slot. When the slot again reaches the sending device, the flag is set to 'empty'. The destination device can check that the message was received by checking the 'received' flag. If the message was not successfully received, perhaps because the destination device was not 'listening', the sender device can check the acknowledgement flag and re-transmit in the next slot.

Token Passing Technique

This technique is also used for ring networks. An imaginary 'token' is passed continuously around the ring. The token is recognized as such by the devices, as a unique character sequence. If a device is waiting to transmit, it catches the token and with it, the authority to send data. As long as one device has the token, no other device can send data. A receiving device acknowledges the receipt of a message by inverting a 1-bit field.

Carrier Sense Multiple Access with Collision Detector (CSMA-CD)

This method of access control is used on broadcast systems such as the bus network. Each device is theoretically free to transmit data to any other device at any time. Before attempting to transmit, a device *polls* the network to ensure that the destination device is free to receive data and that the communications channel is free. A device wishing to transmit must wait until both conditions exist. Generally such delay will be no more than a few millionths of a second. Because of the possibility of collision through simultaneous transmission, a collision detection mechanism is used. When collision does occur, the devices involved cease transmission and try again some time later. In order to avoid the same collision, each device involved is made to wait a different time. If a number of retries prove unsuccessful, an error will be reported to the user.

Hardware for Computer Networks

When data is transmitted between two hardware devices in a network, a communication *medium* is used.

Transmission Media

The commonly used media are, twisted-pair cable, coaxial cable and optical fibre. Where a physical connection is not practical, then radio, infra-red, microwave and laser technologies may be used.

Twisted-pair Cable

Twisted-pair cable is formed from strands of wire twisted in pairs. It predates any other method and is still extensively used for standard telephone or telex terminals. Each twisted pair can carry a single telephone call between two people or two machines. Although twisted-pair cable is generally used for analogue signal transmission, it can be used successfully for digital transmission. Variation in the lengths of wire within pairs can result in signals being received out of phase, but this can be overcome by the frequent use of repeaters. The repeaters 'refresh' the signal as it passes to maintain its consistency. Although transmission rates permitted by such cable are lower than for some other media, they are acceptable for many computer applications.

Coaxial Cable

Coaxial cable is resistant to the transmission interference which can corrupt data transmitted via twisted-pairs cable. It thus provides a fast, relatively interference-free transmission medium. Its construction consists of a central conductor core which is surrounded by a layer of insulating material. The insulating layer is covered by a conducting shield, which is itself protected by another insulating layer. During network installation, the cable can be cut and connections made, without affecting its transmission quality. The quality of cable can vary and some low quality cable is unsuitable for data transmission over long distances. On the other hand, high quality cable can be quite rigid and difficult to install in local networks, where space is limited. Despite this difficulty, it is an extremely popular choice for LANs.

Optical Fibre Cable

Optical fibre cable consists of thousands of clear glass fibre strands which transmit light or infra-red rays instead of electrical signals. The data is transmitted by a light-emitting diode (two-state signals) or injection-laser diode. Transmission speeds of billions of bits per second are achieved. Repeaters are only required after several miles. The other end of the cable has a detector which converts the light pulses into electrical pulses suitable for the attached device.

Optical fibre cable is more expensive than electrical cable but is finding increasing use in LANs. However, its main application is for long-distance communications.

Radio Transmission

Infra-red Radiation

Infra-red radiation can be used within a single room with the use of an infra-red transmitter-receiver. Each device within range would also contain an infra-red transmitter-receiver. Infra-red communication provides a useful alternative to conventional cable in situations where cable would be a nuisance or hazard. As long as devices are in 'sight' of one another, infra-red provides a possible medium of communication.

Microwaves

Microwaves are high-frequency radio signals and can be used where transmitter and receiver are not 'in sight' of one another. The communication path must be relatively obstruction-free. Microwaves can be transmitted via earth transmitters or via communications satellites. Earth stations must be no more than 25-30 miles apart, because humidity in the atmosphere interferes with microwave signals. Each station in a communication path acts as a repeater station. Obviously, it is impractical to build sufficient repeater stations to deal with all transmissions, so communications satellites are used. Satellite communications are now fairly common and provide a cheaper and better trans-ocean transmission medium than undersea cable.

Data Transmission Techniques

Transmission Modes

Communications media can be classified according to whether or not two-way transmission is supported.

Simplex mode allows communication in one direction only and as such, is inappropriate for use in WANs.

SIMPLEX TRANSMISSION

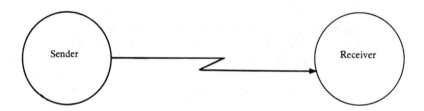

Half-duplex mode supports communications in both directions, but not at the same time.

HALF-DUPLEX TRANSMISSION

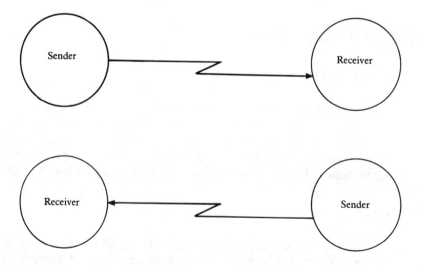

Duplex mode allows communication in both directions at the same time. In interactive systems, when on-demand enquiries are needed this mode is appropriate.

DUPLEX TRANSMISSION

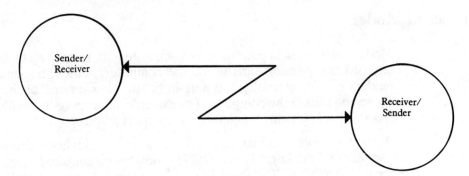

Types of Signal

There are two forms of signal which can be transmitted along a medium, *analogue* and *digital*. The telephone network is designed to carry the human voice and carries signals in continuous sine wave form. Computers handle data in digital form. The two wave forms are illustrated below.

Analogue and Digital Transmission

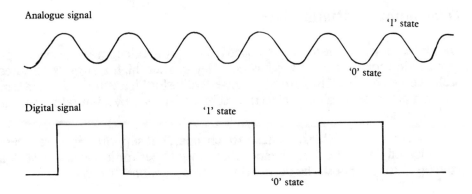

Any telephone link between computer devices requires a device to modify the signals transmitted. Developments are taking place to digitize all telephone transmissions and this will allow the telephone network to support computer transmissions directly. In the meantime a device called a *modem* is needed to *mo*dulate and *dem*odulate the signal. The modem for the transmitter device has to modulate the digital signal into analogue form for transmission along the telephone line. The modem at the receiver device has to carry out the reverse operation.

Modem in Telecommunications Link

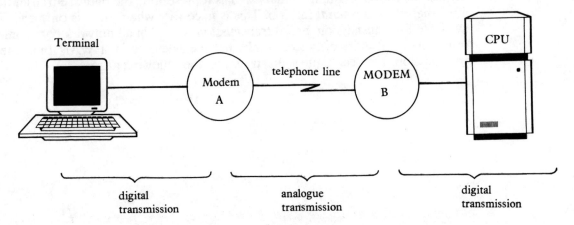

Modems are capable of both functions, so that two way communications are supported.

Types of Modem

Modems can be held externally in a separate unit, or on a system board plugged into one of the expansion slots inside the computer. Although space is saved when the modem is held internally, the plug-in board takes up one of the limited number of expansion slots in the computer. For example, other plug-in boards may be needed for an extra programming language or to support graphics.

Acoustic-coupler modems are connected to the telephone handset and convert the computer's digital signal into audible tones, for transmission as analogue signals down the telephone line. The receiving device converts the signal back to a digital form for processing. The user has to dial the number of the computer system, wait for a high pitched signal, and then connect the handset to the modem. The data transmission rate is lower than for other types of modem, but acoustic-coupler modems provide a simple computer connection for anyone with a terminal and a telephone.

Different modems provide different data transmission rates, measured in bits per second (bps or *baud*). Acoustic-coupler modems only allow a baud rate of about 300 bps. The transmission rate is also dependent on the type of line used.

Types of Telecommunications Lines

Dedicated lines.   These can be leased from British Telecom and provide a permanent connection for devices in a network. They provide high transmission rates and are relatively error free. They are only cost-effective for high volume data transmission, or when a permanent link is vital to the users. Charging is by a flat rate rather than when calls are made.

Dial-up or switched lines.   These are cheaper, but support lower transmission rates than leased lines. They are cheaper than leased lines for low-volume work and allow the operator to choose the destination of transmissions.

Communication Standards

Parallel and Serial Transmission

Devices differ in the ways they communicate or 'talk' with each other. One such difference is in the number of channels they use to transmit data.

Serial Transmission

With serial transmission, the binary signals representing the data are transmitted one after the other in a *serial* fashion. This is necessary when there is only one channel available for transmission. Serial transmission is used in all network communications other than for short distances. Links between devices in a WAN thus use serial transmission. The technique is illustrated on the following page.

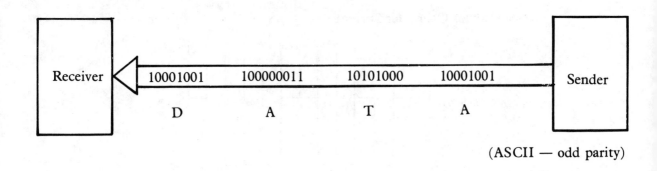

(ASCII — odd parity)

A standard device for serial communication between devices is the RS-232C interface.

Parallel Transmission

As the term suggests, data bits are transmitted as groups in *parallel*, as is illustrated below.

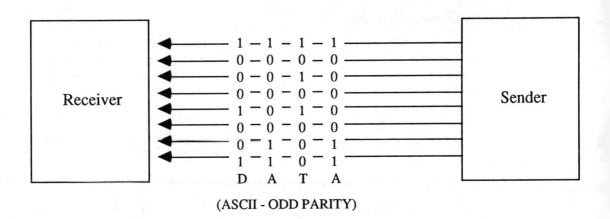

(ASCII - ODD PARITY)

This is obviously faster than sending them serially, but it is only practical over short distances. Communication between a computer and its nearby peripherals can be carried out using parallel transmission. This is particularly important where high-speed devices, such as disk or tape units, are concerned. Microcomputer systems often use parallel transmission to communicate with a nearby printer. An example of a popular standard device is the Centronics parallel interface.

Asynchronous and Synchronous Serial Transmission

Asynchronous Transmission

When a sending device transmits characters at irregular intervals, as does for example, a keyboard device, it is said to be transmitting *asynchronously*. Although the characters are not sent at regular intervals, the bits within each character must be sent in regular timing intervals. An asynchronous character generally has a format similar to that illustrated on the following page.

It can be seen from the diagram that the line has two electrical states, representing 1 and 0. Between characters, the line is in the 'idle' state, a 1 or *mark* condition. To indicate the start of a character, the first or *start* bit is set to 0. A *stop* bit follows each character. The machine at the receiver end 'listens' to the line for a start bit. When it senses this it counts off the regularly timed bits which form the character. When a stop bit is reached, the receiver switches to its 'listening' state. Because start and stop bits mark the beginning and end of each character, the time interval between characters can be irregular, or asynchronous.

Asynchronous Character Format

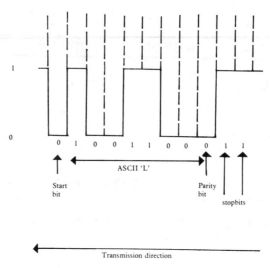

Synchronous Transmission

The start and stop bits used in asynchronous transmission are wasteful, in that they do not contain information. Where higher speed devices are involved, or where data can be buffered and transmitted in larger blocks, it is more efficient to send the data in timed or *synchronous* blocks. The following diagram illustrates the technique.

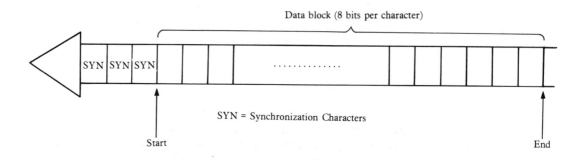

A variety of formats may be used, each having their own operating rules or *protocol*. Communications protocol is dealt with later in this chapter.

In synchronous transmission a data stream may be very long, so it is vital that the timing between transmitter and receiver is synchronized and that the individual characters are separated out. This is done by using a clock lead from the transmitter. Synchronization (SYN) characters are placed at the beginning of each data block and, in case timing is lost by line disturbance, several SYN characters may be situated at intervals within the data block. Thus if timing is lost, the receiver can re-time its bit groupings from the last SYN character. Like the start and stop bits used in asynchronous transmission, SYN characters are not part of the data and as such, have to be 'stripped' out by the receiver. Synchronous transmission is generally used for data speeds of 2400 bps and more.

Some VDU terminals are designed for high speed data transmission and use synchronous transmission. Many others use asynchronous transmission.

Communication Protocols

Many computer devices are now designed for use in networked systems. Manufacturers are now tending to conform to standard protocols which make their equipment useable in a variety of user networks. *Closed* networks which are restricted to one manufacturer's equipment and standards are not attractive to the user, because it restricts the choice of equipment which can be used. The aim of standardization is to achieve more *open* systems which allow users to select from a wider range of manufacturer's products. A Reference Model for Open Systems Interconnection (OSI) has been under development by the International Standards Organization (ISO) since 1977. Other standards, including SNA (IBM's System Network Architecture) and Ethernet are largely incompatible with one another. Certain standards in the OSI model have been set by manufacturers as their commercial products have gained in popularity. The move towards more open systems has gained momentum in recent years and, for example, non-IBM stations can now be attached to IBM's Token Ring Network.

The OSI reference model for communications protocol identifies a hierarchy of seven layers. The layers and their functions are briefly described below.

Application Layer

This is the highest layer in that it is closest to the user. It supports the transfer of information between end-users, applications programs and devices. Several types of protocol exist in this layer, including those for specific applications and those for more generalized applications, such as accounting, entry control and user identification. The applications layer 'hides' the physical network from the user, presenting a user-orientated view instead. For example, the user need not know that several physical computers are involved when accessing a database.

Presentation Layer

This layer covers standards on how data is presented to the end-user devices. The aim is to ensure that different devices, which may be using data in different formats, can communicate with one another. The presentation layer can, for example, handle conversions between ASCII and EBCDIC character codes. It may also carry out encryption to ensure data security during transmission over vulnerable telecommunication links. The presentation layer also attempts to deal with conversions between terminals which use different line and screen lengths and different character sets.

Session Layer

The session layer is concerned with the exchange of information between different applications and users; it is the user's interface into the network. When a user requests a particular service from the network, the session layer handles the dialogue.

Transport Layer

The data transmission system on any network will have its own peculiarities and the function of the transport layer is to 'mask' out any undesirable features which may prevent a high quality transmission for the network.

Network Layer

The function of the network layer is to perform the routing of information around the network and also to connect one network to another. The software can also carry out accounting functions to enable the network owner to charge users.

Data Link Layer

The physical data transmission media used in a network are subject to interference which can corrupt data and other signals. The data link layer handles data transmission errors and thus improves the quality of the network. The techniques used, for example, for the receipt and acknowledgement of data by a receiver device, are determined by the data link layer.

Physical Layer

The physical layer provides the means to connect the physical medium and is concerned with the transmission of binary data within the communication channel. Standards are set regarding the mechanical, electrical and procedural aspects of interface devices. For example, standards are set for the number of pins a network connector should have and the function and position of each pin.

Special Communications Equipment

A number of different machines and devices exist to improve the efficiency of telecommunications networks. The most notable are, multiplexers (MUX), concentrators and front-end-processors (FEP).

Multiplexers

Low speed terminals, such as those with keyboards, transmit at about 300 bps, whereas voice-grade telephone lines can support transmission speeds of up to 9600 bps. A *multiplexer* allows a number of low-speed devices to share a high-speed line. The messages from several low-speed lines are combined into one high-speed channel and then separated out at the other end by a demultiplexor. In two-way transmissions, both these functions are carried out in one unit at each end of the higher speed channel. The operation of a multiplexer linking several remote terminals to a host computer is illustrated on the following page.

Multiplexers use different methods to combine signals and separate them out.

Frequency Division Multiplexing (FDM) differentiates between the signals from different devices by using a different frequency range for each. Allowing for spacing between the different ranges, a 2400 bps circuit can handle twelve 110 bps terminals.

Time Division Multiplexing (TDM) provides a time slice on the higher-speed line for each terminal. The multiplexer has a number of registers, one per low-speed channel. Each register can store one character. The multiplexer scans each register in sequence, emptying the contents into a continuous stream of data to be transmitted. A multiplexer will send a null character whenever it finds an empty slot. Concentrators aim to overcome this wastage.

Multiplexers to Connect Low-speed Devices to a Host Computer

Concentrators

A concentrator greatly increases data throughput by increasing the number of low-speed channels and instead of transmitting a null character, empties the contents of the next full register. The data from each low-speed device is identified by extra identification bits and this constitutes an overhead.

Front-End-Processors (FEP)

A *front-end-processor* is the most sophisticated type of device for communications control and is usually a minicomputer held at the site of a mainframe host computer. Its main task is to handle all the communications traffic, leaving the mainframe free to concentrate on processing tasks. Its main tasks include:

- parity checking;
- 'stripping' of overhead characters from serial transmission, start-stop bits and SYN characters;
- conversion from serial to parallel transmission and vice versa;
- network control;
- network accounting;
- character conversion.

Assignment *Booking for Sunshine*

Sunshine Holidays Limited is a medium-sized company which operates a chain of travel agencies throughout the North of England. The company's Head Office is in the centre of Nottingham. A minicomputer system at Head Office is used for all the company's main information processing activities. At present there are no computer facilities at the individual travel agencies, although each agency does have a Prestel unit for checking on travel and holiday vacancies. A travel industry database called Travicom would be a useful service for the company in that the database specializes in travel and holiday information. Although Prestel provides relevant information, it also deals with many other subjects as well. The company's Managing Director, Bill Sissons is convinced that their future survival in the industry depends on the quality of the service they provide to their customers and that the latter can only be improved if communications between the agencies are enhanced. The most effective mechanism for this communication would seem to be through the establishment of computer links between the various agencies and Head Office. A link into Travicom is also seen as being an important contributor to improvement of services and this may be effected with the use of a Gateway from the existing Prestel connection. The company's competitors already make extensive use of the Travicom facility.

Sunshine Holidays Limited have approached Inter-net Limited, a company specializing in computer networks. You are employed by Inter-net Limited as a Sales Representative and the Sales Manager, Michael Turnpenny, has asked you to visit the offices of Sunshine Holidays to give a presentation on the systems available for Local and Wide Area Networks, which may fill their requirements. The company is interested in the idea of a Local Area Network at their Head Office, linked into a Wide Area Network to connect the agencies to the Head Office computer and to Travicom. It is likely that microcomputer systems with local storage and printing facilities would be used as terminals linking into the Wide Area Network.

Task

As a sales representative for Inter-net Limited, prepare a talk for presentation to the management of Sunshine Holidays Limited. Make use of diagrams to illustrate your talk. Your talk should introduce the concepts of Local and Wide Area Networks and describe in a non-technical way, the various configurations which may be used. Identify any hardware requirements. Suggest how the networks may be used to improve the communication and information processing systems within the company.

Assignment *A Database for Power*

Power Tools Limited is a small company with three DIY shops in Bradford and Leeds. The business was established by ex-joiner Harry Turner in 1968 with a single shop in Leeds. He joined forces with Geoff Baker, an accountant, to form the present company in 1982 and the two additional shops were opened in 1985. A new shop may be opened in Halifax in the near future. At present, you are employed as manager of one of the shops in Leeds. The directors are considering the use of microcomputer systems for the accounting tasks in the business. This follows their recent attendance at a one-day seminar entitled 'Small Business Systems'. Mr. Baker has asked you to investigate the benefits which may be gained from using a database system with all the shops connected to it via a computer network.

Task

Prepare an informal report for the directors, in which you explain the concept of a database system and the benefits it may provide in combination with a computer network. Give examples of the kind of information such a system may provide, which would not be readily available if the shops maintained separate systems.

Developmental Task

Use a database package to set up some simple files and use the query language to extract information according to various criteria.

Chapter 24

Arithmetic Operations

Introduction

The four fundamental processes of arithmetic are addition (+), subtraction (−), multiplication (×) and division (÷), and these are termed *arithmetic operations.* Arithmetic operations are performed on numbers which may be presented and described in different forms:

(a) *Integers* are whole numbers, such as 1, 2, 3, 6, 25;

(b) *Common fractions* (or *vulgar fractions*) are numbers like ½, ⅝, ⅗, ⁹⁄₁₀, each representing a part of a whole number;

(c) *Decimal fractions*, where the fractional part of the number is separated from the whole part by a dot called a *Decimal Point* as in $1\cdot237$, $2\cdot2$, $13\cdot986$;

(d) *Directed* (or *Signed*) *numbers* are preceded by a (+) or a (−) to indicate a positive quantity or a negative quantity respectively: $+13$, -21, $+13$, $-\frac{1}{3}$, $-235\cdot68$. The + sign is usually omitted for positive numbers;

(e) *Indexed numbers* are shown as a number raised to a power. For example, the indexed number 3^3 represents $3 \times 3 \times 3$, and 10^2 represents 10×10;

(f) *Standard form* occurs frequently in computing (see floating point) and is a representation which combines decimal numbers with indexed numbers:

$$7.5 \times 10^5, \ 3\cdot98 \times 10^{-5}$$

(g) *Real numbers.* In computer studies, sets of numbers are often given an overall classification depending on whether they are exclusively integer values or may contain fractional numbers. The latter are called *real* numbers. Thus the following numbers are all classed as *real* even though the list contains some integer values:

$$13\cdot62, \ -175\cdot3, \ 9\cdot0, 63\cdot01, \ -202\cdot00, 0\cdot1472$$

The following sections in this chapter will examine the ways in which arithmetic operations are performed on numbers represented in these various forms. It will be assumed that the reader is familiar with arithmetic operations on signed integers and fractions, so these will be given only a cursory treatment. Particular emphasis will be placed on those representations and operations relevant to computer studies and therefore most likely to be unfamiliar. However, it is important to understand the basis of the numbering system that we normally use and its relation to other numbering systems, and this will be discussed first.

The Denary Numbering System

The numbering system with which we are most familiar is the *denary* system which is based on the number ten. In common with other positional notations for representing numbers, the denary system uses only a small set of symbols for representing a number of any size; the positions of the symbols within the number determine their precise value. In the denary system, ten different symbols are used: 0, 1, 2, 3, 4, 5, 6, 7, 8, and 9. Thus a number such as 4293 is an abbreviated way of representing

	4 thousands +	2 hundreds	+	9 tens	+	3 units
or	4×10^3 +	2×10^2	+	9×10^1	+	3×10^0
or	4000 +	200	+	90	+	3

The number 10^3 is in *index notation* and represents $10 \times 10 \times 10$ or 1000; the number 10 is called the *base* and 3 is the *index*. This notation will be given further treatment later. Using index notation, the following table shows how the value of a digit is related to its position within the number:

Millions	Hundred Thousands	Ten Thousands	Thousands	Hundreds	Tens	Units
10^6	10^5	10^4	10^3	10^2	10^1	10^0
			4	2	9	3

(Note that any number raised to the power 0 is 1: $10^0 = 1$, $2^0 = 1$, $8^0 = 1$.)

A numbering system such as binary is based on the same principles except the base is 2 and the only symbols used are 0 and 1 (The binary and octal numbering systems are explained in chapter 19). Thus the binary number 1011 represents

$$1 \times 2^3 + 0 \times 2^2 + 1 \times 2^1 + 1 \times 2^0 = 8 + 0 + 2 + 1 = 11$$

Multiplication by the base results in the number being shifted one place to the left, with a zero filling the rightmost digit position:

4293	$\times$	10	=	42930	in denary;
1011_2	$\times$	10_2 (ie 2)	=	10110_2	in binary;
453_8	$\times$	10_8 (ie 8)	=	4530_8	in octal (base 8).

Division by the base shifts the number to the right:

430	$\div$	10	=	43	in denary;
1100_2	$\div$	10_2	=	110_2	in binary ;
330_8	$\div$	10_8	=	33_8	in octal;

Addition and Subtraction of Signed Integers

When two or more numbers are added together, the result is called the *sum* of the numbers; the *difference* of two numbers results when one is subtracted from the other. A list of numbers to be added are written one above the other with every digit in its correct column: 1234 + 567 + 82 + 307 is written

$$
\begin{array}{r}
1\ 2\ 3\ 4 \\
5\ 6\ 7 \\
8\ 2 \\
+\quad 3\ 0\ 7 \\
\hline
2\ 1\ 9\ 0
\end{array}
$$

The sum of the numbers is 2190.

The addition is performed by first adding the digits in the units column, followed by the tens column and so on.

Another way of performing the same addition is by splitting the addition into a number of stages as indicated by the brackets:

$$(((1234 + 567) + 82) + 307)$$

In other words, find the sum of the first two numbers, add it to the third number and then add the last number to this sum:

$$
\begin{array}{r}
1\ 2\ 3\ 4 \\
+\quad 5\ 6\ 7 \\
\hline
1\ 8\ 0\ 1 \\
+\quad 8\ 2 \\
\hline
1\ 8\ 8\ 3 \\
+\quad 3\ 0\ 7 \\
\hline
2\ 1\ 9\ 0
\end{array}
$$

Though this might seem like a rather laborious method for performing such a simple task, this is the way a computer would perform the calculation; it is easier for a computer to add complete numbers in pairs rather than adding the separate digits of several numbers as we do when performing such calculations manually. (This is explained in Chapter 21 on Computer Logic)

To find the difference of two numbers, again the numbers are written with the digits in each number aligned correctly. Starting at the units column, each pair of digits is subtracted. Thus the subtraction 397 − 245 is written

$$
\begin{array}{r}
3\ 9\ 7 \\
-\quad 2\ 4\ 5 \\
\hline
1\ 5\ 2
\end{array}
$$

The difference of the numbers is 152.

Where a digit in the second number exceeds the corresponding digit in the first number, as in 356 - 64, then the method used is to "borrow" 10 from the adjacent digit to the left:

$$
\begin{array}{r}
4\ 5\ 6 \\
-\quad 6\ 4 \\
\hline
3\ 9\ 2
\end{array}
\qquad
\begin{array}{rcl}
6 - 4 &=& 2 \\
15 - 6 &=& 9 \quad \text{borrow of 1} \\
3 - 0 &=& 3
\end{array}
$$

Another way of considering a subtraction is by regarding it as the addition of a negative quantity:

$$456 - 64 = 456 + (-64)$$

This has the merit of dispensing with the need to perform subtraction at all; but what is needed is a method of representing negative numbers which takes advantage of this. Such a representation exists and is called the *complement* of a positive number. Suppose that the magnitude of the numbers being considered is less than 1000. (This is called the *modulus*). To calculate the complement of a number in this range, it is subtracted from 1000, the modulus. For example, the complement of 420 is (1000 −

420) = 580. Thus in ten's complement form, modulus 1000, the number -420 is represented as 580. Similarly, the number -64 would be represented as $(1000 - 64)$ = 936.

Now suppose that the same subtraction, $456 - 64$, is to be performed using complement arithmetic. The subtraction now requires the addition of the complement of 64 as follows:

```
      4 5 6
  +   9 3 6
    1 3 9 2
```

The final answer is given by neglecting the leading 1 (representing 1000) from the answer. Thus, once negative numbers have been converted into their complement forms, arithmetic operations involving combinations of addition and subtraction need only use addition. For manual arithmetic this is not too much of an advantage, but for computer arithmetic it is very important for two reasons:

(i) It reduces the amount of circuitry required in the ALU and control unit; not only does it mean that a single type of circuit is required for addition and subtraction, but also, as will be shown shortly, the functions of multiplication and division often use addition circuits.

(ii) Calculation of the complement of a binary number is much simpler than that for a denary number. For example, to find the complement of the number 6 in binary(0110), assuming a 4-bit wordlength (in other words, the modulus is $2^4 = 16$), only two simple steps are required:

(a) invert each bit;

(b) add 1.

Thus the complement of 0110 is $1001 + 1 = 1010$.

This is now the 2's complement of 6 and represents -6. 2's complement arithmetic is explained in detail in Chapter 20.

Multiplication and Division of Signed Integers

The *product* of two numbers results when they are multiplied together. For example, the product of 432 and 102 would be calculated as follows:

```
        4 3 2      Multiplicand
    ×   1 0 2      Multiplier
        8 6 4      (2 × 4 3 2)          1st partial product
      0 0 0 0      (0 × 4 3 2 0)        2nd partial product
  + 4 3 2 0 0      (1 × 4 3 2 0 0)      3rd partial product
    4 4 0 6 4                           Complete product
```

Note that the multiplication does not take place in one step. Instead the process is broken down into a series of simpler procedures. Starting with the rightmost digit of the multiplier, the multiplicand is multiplied by each digit of the multiplier. Each multiplication results in a partial product. Successive partial products are written one place further to the left than the previous one to allow for the magnitude of the multiplying digit. Note that multiplication by 0 gives 0000 for the second partial product, and normally this would not be written down. The final product is the sum of the partial products.

Computers frequently perform the calculation in much the same way. The main difference between the scheme shown above and the way a computer might manage the same calculation is that the partial products would be accumulated as the calculation progressed, rather than leaving the addition of the partial products until they had all been calculated. Another difference lies in the nature of the binary system that the computer would be using for the calculation: since both numbers would be in binary form, consisting only of 1's and 0's, calculation of partial products is tremendously simplified. The example above illustrates this point. Where the multiplying digit is 0, the partial product is 0; where the digit is 1, the partial product is merely the multiplicand shifted the appropriate number of places left. Using the example above (remembering that the computer would be working in binary, of course) a computer's multiplication procedure might be:

(i) Determine the first partial product, p1.

$$p1 = 2 \times 432 = 864$$

(ii) Add the first partial product to a register, A (initially containing 0) to be used for accumulating the partial products.

$$A = 0 + p1 = 864$$

(iii) Shift the multiplicand, M, left.

$$M = 4320$$

(iv) Determine the second partial product, p2.

$$p2 = 0 \times 4320 = 0000$$

(v) Add this to the accumulator register.

$$A = 864 + p2 = 864$$

(vi) Shift the multiplicand left.

$$M = 43200$$

(vii) Determine the third partial product, p3.

$$p3 = 1 \times 43200 = 43200$$

(viii) Add this to the accumulator register.

$$A = 864 + 43200 = 44064$$

(ix) Stop

Then, using this type of process, there is no necessity for using multiplication at all: the only processes required are shifting and adding. Generally, though many microprocessors still use this scheme, most larger modern computers have special circuitry specifically for multiplication to improve processing speed.

A problem in division, such as 195 ÷ 15, is usually tackled as follows:

```
          1 3
1 5 ) 1 9 5     19 (5) ÷ 15(0)    =    1 remainder 4  ...... (1)
      1 5 0     150 × 1           =    150              ..... (2)
        4 5     45                =    195 − 150   ..... (3)
        4 5     45 ÷ 15           =    3 remainder 0 ..... (4)
        0 0
```

195 is called the dividend, 15 is the divisor and the result, 13, is called the quotient.

The process involves the following steps:

(1)   The leftmost digit of the divisor is aligned with the leftmost digit of the dividend. Thus the divisor in this case is being treated as if it were a

factor of ten greater, that is, 150.

(2)   Comparison of the dividend, 195, with the divisor, 150 gives the first quotient digit of 1, representing ten 15's.

(3)   The previous two steps have established that there are at least ten 15's in 195. The process is now repeated with the remainder after 150 has been subtracted from the dividend. This remainder is 45.

(4)   Since there are exactly three 15's in 45, and there are no more digits of the dividend to consider, the final quotient has been determined.

This familiar process is the basis for a method used by many computers for performing integer division. This process is summarised as follows:

(i) Align the leftmost digits of the divisor and dividend.

(ii) Subtract the divisor from the dividend: 195 − 150.

(iii) If the result is not negative, continue to subtract the divisor from the remainder. The current quotient digit is the number of successful subtractions performed. In the example above, the second subtraction, 45 − 150, would terminate this stage with a quotient digit of 1.

(iv) Shift the divisor right and use the remainder as the new dividend.

(v) Repeat stages (ii)-(iv) until all digits in the dividend have been used. In the example, 45 would be shifted left to give 450; three successful subtractions of 150 are possible, giving a second quotient digit of 3; all digits of the dividend will then have been used.

To illustrate the process further, suppose that a computer is required to perform the division 138 ÷ 6. The following annotated table shows the steps involved:

Action	Dividend	Divisor	Remainder	Quotient digit
	138	6	138	−
Align leftmost digits	138	600		
Subtract			−462	0
Restore remainder	138	600	138	
Shift divisor right	138	060	138	
Subtract divisor	138	060	78	
Subtract divisor	138	060	18	
Subtract divisor	138	060	−42	2
Restore remainder	138	060	18	
Shift divisor right	138	006	18	
Subtract divisor	138	006	12	
Subtract divisor	138	006	6	
Subtract divisor	138	006	0	
Subtract divisor	138	006	−6	3
Stop				

The final quotient is 023.

Note that the only operations required are those of subtraction and shifting. The multiple subtractions shown are not necessary when working in binary. Each subtraction will give either a quotient digit of 1 or 0, and the remainder will either be positive or negative respectively. Remember also that since subtraction may be performed by addition of the complement, division can also be performed by adding and shifting operations exclusively. Thus all the basic arithmetic operations of addition, subtraction, multiplication and division are possible using only adding and shifting functions.

Numbers in Standard Index Form

When a decimal number, whether an integer or a fraction, is represented as the product of a number between 1 and 10 and a power of 10, it is said to be in *standard index form.*

Numbers in standard index form having a magnitude greater than or equal to 1 have a positive integer index. For example, 7×10^2 and $3 \cdot 34 \times 10^3$ are both greater than 1.

Fractions, that is numbers with magnitude less than 1, have a negative integer index. Thus $2 \cdot 35 \times 10^{-1}$ and $4 \cdot 63 \times 10^{-5}$ represent fractions.

To convert a decimal number into standard index form,

(i) move the decimal point so that it is immediately to the right of the first non-zero digit;

(ii) count the number of places the decimal point has been moved;

(iii) use this number as the index, with the sign determined as follows: if the point was moved left, the index is positive; if the point was moved right, the sign is negative; if the point was not moved at all, then the index is zero.

The following examples illustrate the process:

Example

$289 \cdot 7$	$=$	$2 \cdot 897 \times 10^2$	point moved 2 places left.
$0 \cdot 00567$	$=$	$5 \cdot 67 \times 10^{-3}$	point moved 3 places right.
$8 \cdot 44$	$=$	$8 \cdot 44 \times 10^0$	point moved 0 places.

To convert a number from standard form into normal decimal representation,

(i) move the decimal point the number of places indicated by the index of the number in standard index form;

(ii) if the index is positive, move the point right; if the index is negative, move the point left; if the index is zero, the point is not moved.

Example

$3 \cdot 67 \times 10^1$	$=$	$36 \cdot 7$	point moved 1 place right.
$7 \cdot 025 \times 10^{-3}$	$=$	$0 \cdot 007025$	point moved 3 places left.
$9 \cdot 5 \times 10^0$	$=$	$9 \cdot 5$	point not moved.

Numbers output from computers are frequently presented in standard index form, but using the letter "E" to separate the decimal part of the number (usually called the *mantissa*) from the index (usually called the *exponent*). For instance, a computer might display the result of a calculation as

$$-4 \cdot 365982E+07$$

which means

$$-4 \cdot 365982 \times 10^7 = -43659820$$

This form of representation is used extensively in computers for the internal representation of numbers, usually when arithmetic operations are required to be performed on real numbers. (This is explained in the section on "floating point" in Chapter 20).

The procedures for performing arithmetic operations on standard index numbers are explained in the following sections.

Addition and Subtraction

To add two numbers expressed in mantissa and exponent form, the following steps are required:

(i) Adjust the position of the decimal point in the mantissa of one of the numbers(usually the smaller of the two) to make its exponent the same as that of the other number.

(ii) Add the mantissas of the two numbers.

(iii) If necessary, adjust the result to put it into standard index form.

As an illustration, consider the addition of $2 \cdot 365 \times 10^1$ and $9 \cdot 978 \times 10^2$.

(i) To make the exponent of $2 \cdot 365 \times 10^1$ the same as that of the other number, move the point one place to the left in the mantissa and add 1 to the exponent:

$$2 \cdot 365 \times 10^1 \ = \ 0 \cdot 2365 \times 10^2$$

(ii) Add the mantissa of the numbers:

$$
\begin{array}{r}
9 \cdot 9\,7\,8 \\
+ \quad 0 \cdot 2\,3\,6\,5 \\
\hline
1\,0 \cdot 2\,1\,4\,5 \\
\end{array}
$$

The answer is $10 \cdot 2145 \times 10^2$

(iii) The answer is no longer in standard index form. The answer in the required form is therefore

$$1 \cdot 02145 \ \times \ 10^3$$

The process of subtraction is identical to that of addition except for step (ii) in which the mantissas of the numbers are subtracted.

Multiplication and Division

The procedure for the multiplication of two numbers in standard index form is:

(i) Multiply the mantissas.

(ii) Add the exponents.

(iii) If necessary, put the result into standard form.

Thus, for the numbers $1 \cdot 42 \times 10^2$ and $8 \cdot 92 \times 10^3$ the product would be given by

$$
\begin{aligned}
(1 \cdot 42 \times 8 \cdot 92) \times 10^{(2+3)} \ &= \ 12 \cdot 6664 \times 10^5 \\
&= \ 1 \cdot 26664 \times 10^6
\end{aligned}
$$

Where the signs of the mantissas and/or the exponents of the numbers are mixed, the same rules apply:

$$
\begin{aligned}
(-1 \cdot 42 \times 10^2) \times (8 \cdot 92 \times 10^{-3}) \ &= (-1 \cdot 42 \times 8 \cdot 92) \times 10^{(2-3)} \\
&= -12 \cdot 6664 \times 10^{-1} \\
&= -1 \cdot 26664 \times 10^0
\end{aligned}
$$

With division, the mantissas are divided and the exponents are subtracted:

$$(3 \cdot 74 \times 10^4) \ \div \ (8 \cdot 32 \times 10^2) = (3 \cdot 74 \div 8 \cdot 32) \times 10^{(4-2)}$$

$$= 0\cdot495 \times 10^2$$
$$= 4\cdot495 \times 10^1$$

As a further example,

$$(5\cdot62 \times 10^{-3}) \div (-1\cdot45 \times 10^{-2}) = (5\cdot62 \div -1\cdot45) \times 10^{(-3-(-2))}$$
$$= -3\cdot876 \times 10^{-1}$$

Errors in Calculations

In real life the numbers that we deal with are always approximate to some degree. Any physical measurement depends on the accuracy of the measuring instrument, and it is important to be aware of the limitations of the measuring device being used. For example, the accuracy of a measurement obtained from a ruler is dependent on the accuracy with which the ruler was constructed and how accurately it can be read. A measurement of 234 millimetres implies that the measurement could have been anywhere between $233\cdot5$ and $234\cdot5$ millimetres, assuming that the millimetre scale itself is accurate.

Where calculations using approximate figures are cumulative, as in $23\cdot6 + 556\cdot25 - 99\cdot7$, errors in the individual numbers could conceivably accumulate to give an answer with an unacceptably large error component.

In order to exercise control over the accuracy of calculations, and to have confidence in the answers produced, it is necessary to know something about the errors implicit in individual numbers and how these errors combine during arithmetical operations. This is particularly relevant to computer arithmetic where it is not always possible to represent numbers exactly. The following sections show how the effects of errors in numbers used in computations can be analysed, and in particular how this is related to arithmetic operations in computers.

Absolute Errors

The absolute error in a number is the exact value of the error. For example, if the cost of a litre of petrol is 37p and a customer puts $16\cdot3$ litres into his car, the total cost should be $554\cdot2$p. If customer is charged £$5\cdot54$, the absolute error is $0\cdot2$p. In general, however, the absolute error is not known; instead the maximum value of the *absolute error modulus* is given or can be deduced. The absolute error modulus is the *magnitude* of the absolute error in a number. For example, given that the number $24\cdot63$ is correct to four significant digits (or two decimal places in this case) the exact number could have been anywhere in the range $24\cdot625$ to $24\cdot635$. The maximum absolute error modulus is therefore $\pm0\cdot005$ or $\pm0\cdot5 \times 10^{-2}$

Suppose that a certain computer is only capable of storing numbers to an accuracy equivalent(in binary) to seven places. Then it must be assumed when performing calculations that the maximum absolute error modulus for any number stored in this computer is $\pm 0\cdot5 \times 10^{-7.}$

Absolute error, a, may be defined mathematically as follows:

$$a = A^* - A$$

where A^* represents the exact value of a number,

A represents the approximate value of the number.

The absolute error modulus is shown as $|a|$, where the vertical bars indicate the magnitude of the enclosed symbol.

Relative Errors

Sometimes it is convenient to express the magnitude of an error in an approximate value as the ratio between the absolute error modulus and the magnitude of the number itself. This is called a relative error and is calculated by dividing the absolute error modulus by the magnitude of the exact value:

$$r = \frac{|a|}{|A^*|}$$

However, it frequently happens that the exact value is not known, only the approximate value, and so quite often the relative error is given by

$$r = \frac{|a|}{|A|} \quad \text{which is generally accurate enough for most purposes.}$$

For example, the maximum relative error in the number $239 \cdot 27$, assuming that the number is correct to two decimal places, is given by

$$r = \frac{0 \cdot 005}{239 \cdot 27} = 0 \cdot 0000208 \text{ or } 2 \times 10^{-5} \text{ approximately.}$$

Relative errors are useful in determining absolute errors in calculations involving multiplication and division.

Errors in Addition and Subtraction

When a number of numbers are added, the maximum absolute error modulus in the sum is found by adding the individual errors in the numbers. The same rule also applies when numbers are subtracted. If the absolute errors associated with numbers A, B, C, D are a, b, c, d respectively, then the maximum error in the sum of these numbers is $a + b + c + d$.

Example 1.

Suppose that the internal representation of numbers in a certain computer allows a maximum accuracy of the equivalent of four decimal places. The following calculation is to be performed on four numbers, A, B, C, D stored in memory: $A + B + C - D$. No matter what the value of these numbers, the absolute errors associated with each of them will have a maximum value of 0.5×10^{-4}. Thus, when the calculation is performed, the maximum absolute error in the result will be the sum of the individual errors in the numbers, that is,

$$0 \cdot 5 \times 10^{-4} + 0 \cdot 5 \times 10^{-4} + 0 \cdot 5 \times 10^{-4} + 0 \cdot 5 \times 10^{-4}$$
$$= 4 \times (0 \cdot 5 \times 10^{-4}) = 2 \times 10^{-4}$$

Example 2.

Suppose that the answer to a calculation involving the addition of 1000 numbers must be accurate to two decimal places. Given this condition, it is now possible to determine the minimum accuracy required for each of the numbers used in the calculation. The reasoning is as follows:

(i) The absolute error modulus in the individual numbers will be magnified by a factor of 1000 in the answer.

(ii) If the numbers were accurate to four decimal places, then the error in the answer would be

$$1000 \times (0 \cdot 5 \times 10^{-4}) = \frac{1000 \times 0 \cdot 5}{10000} = \frac{0 \cdot 5}{10} = 0 \cdot 5 \times 10^{-1}$$

Thus the maximum error modulus could be $0 \cdot 05$, and therefore unacceptably large.

(iii) Numbers accurate to 5 decimal places could combine to give a maximum error of

$$1000 \times (0 \cdot 5 \times 10^{-5}) = 0 \cdot 5 \times 10^{-2} = 0 \cdot 005 \text{ in the answer.}$$

This satisfies the accuracy requirements for the calculation.

Errors in Multiplication and Division

The relative error in the product of two approximate numbers is the sum of the relative errors in the numbers. For example, if $12 \cdot 36$ and $52 \cdot 2$ are to be multiplied, the accuracy of the product could be specified as follows:

$$\text{Relative error in } 12 \cdot 36 = \frac{0 \cdot 5 \times 10^{-2}}{12 \cdot 36} = 0 \cdot 4 \times 10^{-3}$$

$$\text{Relative error in } 52 \cdot 2 = \frac{0 \cdot 5 \times 10^{-1}}{52 \cdot 2} = 0 \cdot 95 \times 10^{-3}$$

$$\text{Relative error in product} =$$
$$0 \cdot 4 \times 10^{-3} + 0 \cdot 95 \times 10^{-3} = 1 \cdot 35 \times 10^{-3}$$

Using the relationship, $r = \dfrac{|a|}{|A|}$ for the relative error,

$$\text{where} \quad r = 1 \cdot 35 \times 10^{-3} \text{ and}$$
$$A = 12 \cdot 6 \times 52 \cdot 2,$$

$$\begin{aligned}
\text{Absolute error in product} &= (1 \cdot 35 \times 10^{-3}) \times (12 \cdot 36 \times 52 \cdot 2) \\
&= 1 \cdot 35 \times 10^{-3} \times 645 \cdot 192 \\
&= \cdot 871
\end{aligned}$$

Thus the answer could be expressed as $645 \cdot 192 \pm \cdot 871$ or, keeping the answer to 2 decimal places,

$$645 \cdot 19 \pm 0.88$$

This is equivalent to saying that the exact answer could be anywhere between $644 \cdot 31$ and $646 \cdot 07$. The relative error in a quotient is the sum of the relative errors in the numerator and denominator. With this final relationship it is now possible to determine the accuracy of any arithmetical process involving combinations of addition, subtraction, multiplication and division.

Example 3.

The following calculation is to be performed on numbers which are accurate to 3 decimal places:

$$\frac{(2 \cdot 603 + 19 \cdot 255)}{0 \cdot 376 \times 5 \cdot 123}$$

The accuracy of the answer is to be determined. The calculation is performed as follows:

Maximum absolute error in numerator $(2 \cdot 603 + 19 \cdot 255)$

$$= 0 \cdot 5 \times 10^{-3} + 0 \cdot 5 \times 10^{-3}$$

$$= 1 \times 10^{-3}$$

Relative error in numerator $= \dfrac{1 \times 10^{-3}}{(2 \cdot 603 + 19 \cdot 255)}$

$= \dfrac{1 \times 10^{-3}}{21 \cdot 858}$

$= 0 \cdot 00045$

Relative error in denominator $= \dfrac{0 \cdot 5 \times 10^{-3}}{0 \cdot 376} + \dfrac{0 \cdot 5 \times 10^{-3}}{5 \cdot 123}$

$= 0 \cdot 0014$

Relative error in quotient $= 0 \cdot 00045 + 0 \cdot 0014$

$= 0 \cdot 00185$

Approximate answer $= \dfrac{21 \cdot 858}{1 \cdot 9262}$

$= 11 \cdot 3477$

Absolute error in quotient $= 11 \cdot 3477 \times 0 \cdot 00185$

$= 0 \cdot 021$

Hence the answer is $11 \cdot 3477 \pm 0 \cdot 021$ or $11 \cdot 348 \pm 0 \cdot 022$

Exercises

Addition and Subtraction

1.   *Perform the following additions as they would be performed by a computer, that is, in stages adding only two numbers at each stage:*

    (a) $13 + 279 + 67$

    (b) $32 \cdot 7 + 169 \cdot 0 + 72 \cdot 350 + 0 \cdot 732$

    (c) $73 \cdot 88 + 96 \cdot 2312 + 3 \cdot 142 + 7 \cdot 79$

2.   *Convert the following numbers into ten's complement form:*

    12, 127, 3, 99, 100

3. *Perform the subtractions listed below using addition of the complement. Check your answers by performing the calculations in the normal way.*

    (a) $65 - 37$

    (b) $72 - 6$

    (c) $-19 + 123$

    (d) $35 - 74$

    (e) $-17 - 425$

(Note that if the answer is a negative number, its magnitude may be checked by taking its complement).

Multiplication and Division

1.   *Find the products of the pairs of denary numbers listed below by means of a sequence of shifting and adding operations. At each step in the calculations show the value of the partial product and the multiplicand.*

    (a) 318 *and* 72

    (b) 763 *and* 101

    (c) 11,011 *and* 110

(Notice that the last example does not require any multiplications at all, because the only digits used are 1's and 0's: this is the basis of binary multiplication).

2.   *Perform the following divisions using shifting and subtracting operations. Set each calculation out in the form of a table such as that shown in the text to illustrate the process.*

    (a) 144/24

    (b) 72/18

    (c) 255/15

    (d) 197/37

Standard Index Form

1. *Convert the following numbers into standard index form:*

    $$123, \ 733 \cdot 5, \ -33 \cdot 34, \ 0 \cdot 0012, \ 5 \cdot 34, \ -0 \cdot 2234$$

2. *Convert the following indexed numbers to standard index form. (Remember that the E in the numbers is read as "ten to the power".)*

    $$0 \cdot 2301E+03 \quad -22 \cdot 312E+05 \quad 123 \cdot 340E-02 \quad -0 \cdot 3124E-05$$

3. *Perform the following additions and subtractions using the numbers converted to standard index form. The answers should also be converted to standard index form.*

    (a) $234 + 1234$

    (b) $0 \cdot 0035 + 0 \cdot 1203$

    (c) $34 \cdot 22 + 0 \cdot 014$

    (d) $166 - 17 \cdot 2$

    (e) $-0 \cdot 0157 + 0 \cdot 349$

4. *Perform the following multiplications and divisions using the numbers converted to standard index form. Convert the answers to standard index form where necessary.*

    (a) $32 \cdot 7 \times 5 \cdot 91$ *(e)* $67/2 \cdot 2$

    (b) $176 \times 15 \cdot 3$ *(f)* $243/19$

    (c) $0 \cdot 003 \times 45 \cdot 2$ *(g)* $5 \cdot 03/0 \cdot 12$

    (d) $0 \cdot 123 \times 0 \cdot 00566$ *(h)* $0 \cdot 04/0 \cdot 00017$

Errors in Calculations

1. *State the maximum absolute error modulus for each of the numbers below. Assume that the numbers are accurate to the number of decimal places shown.*

    $$23 \cdot 34, \ 678 \cdot 1, \ 778, \ -0 \cdot 0023, \ 0 \cdot 112, \ -0 \cdot 3$$

2. *Determine the relative error for the numbers listed above and express the answer in standard index form.*

3. *Find the maximum absolute errors in the following calculations:*

    (a) $13 \cdot 2 + 177 \cdot 33 + 67 \cdot 41$

    (b) $193 \cdot 97 - 46 \cdot 66$

    (c) $220 \cdot 3 - 1089 \cdot 22 + 338 \cdot 4 - 18 \cdot 67$

4. *Determine the accuracy with which the calculations below may be performed.*

    (a) $321 \cdot 712 \times 63 \cdot 101$

    (b) $10 \cdot 22 - 18 \cdot 9 \times 0 \cdot 15$

    (c) $568 \cdot 44/18 \cdot 9$

    (d) $90 \cdot 8 + \dfrac{123 \cdot 5 \times 3}{32} - 32$

Chapter 25

Algebra

Introduction

In algebra the processes of arithmetic are described in general terms using letters to represent numbers. Algebra is invaluable in a great number of scientific disciplines, including physics, chemistry, electronics and computer science. Many computer languages contain instructions closely resembling algebraic expressions, and a knowledge of algebra is an essential prerequisite to understanding and constructing computer programs.

Algebraic Notation

An algebraic *expression* is a generalisation of an arithmetic expression

such as
$$15 \cdot 3 \times 6 \times (13 - 10) + \frac{17 \cdot 3}{9}$$

Letters are used in place of some or all of the numbers in the expression, but the normal rules of arithmetic still apply. An algebraic expression equivalent to the arithmetic

expression above might be
$$pq\,(13 - b) + \frac{c}{d}$$

This algebraic expression has the same form as the arithmetic expression, but the letters represent any set of numbers rather than specific values. The letters used are often termed *variables*. By *substituting* values for the variables, the expression can be *evaluated*, that is, its numeric equivalent can be determined.

An algebraic expression consists of a number of 'terms' separated by addition or subtraction operators, and each term contains a number of factors containing numbers and letters connected by multiplication and division operators. For example, the

expression
$$a + bc - \frac{e}{f} + 16$$

has four terms, a, bc, $\frac{e}{f}$ and 16.

The first term contains only the single factor, a; the second term contains factor b and c connected by a multiplication operator (not usually shown but assumed to be there); the third term has factor e divided by factor f;the final term consists of the *constant* 16. Variables and constants are particular instances of factors.

Most, if not all high level computer languages use variables to represent the contents of memory locations. In BASIC for instance, the statement

LET X = A + 3

uses the variables X and A. The statement requires the value represented by A to be added to the constant 3 and the result transferred to the memory location represented by X.

Indexed variables such as p^3 or c^{-2} with constants as indices, also appear in algebraic expressions. In addition, however, the index itself may be a variable, term or expression:

$$x^i, \quad p^{xy}, \quad c^{j+3k}$$

Operator Precedence

When numbers are assigned to the variables in an algebraic expression, so that it might be evaluated, there are rules of arithmetic operator precedence which determine how the evaluation should proceed. For example, in the expression

$$x + yz$$

the multiplication of y and z must precede the addition operation. If the requirement was for the sum of x and y to be multiplied by z then the expression would be written

$$(x + y)z \quad \text{or} \quad z(x+y)$$

The brackets indicate that the addition operation is to precede the multiplication. The order of operator precedence is as follows:

1. Brackets.

2. Exponentiation (raising to a power).

3. Negation (eg -3)

4. Multiplication and Division

5. Addition and Subtraction

To illustrate these rules, consider the following expression:

$$x(y + 3z)^{-3} - \frac{p}{qr}$$

Given values for all of the variables, the expression would be evaluated as follows:

(i) Evaluate $(y + 3z)$. The term $x(y + 3z)^{-3}$ contains an expression in brackets which must be evaluated first. Within this bracketed expression are two terms, y and $3z$; the latter term involves a multiplication and so $3z$ would be calculated first. The product of 3 and z would then be added to y.

(ii) Evaluate $(y + 3z)^{-3}$. Since exponentiation has a higher precedence than multiplication, the value of the bracketed expression would be raised to the power -3.

(iii) Evaluate $x(y + 3z)^{-3}$. Multiply result of last step by x to give the value of the first term.

(iv) The second term, $\frac{p}{qr}$, could be regarded in two different ways, both giving the same answer but requiring different arithmetic operations. The term could be written in the following two equivalent forms:

$$\frac{p}{(qr)} \quad \text{or} \quad \left(\frac{\left(\frac{p}{q}\right)}{r} \right)$$

In the first form the multiplication in the brackets would be performed before the division; the second form would involve the division of p by q first and this quotient would then be divided by r. Both methods would result in the same answer. The ambiguity results from the equal precedence attributed to multiplication and division in algebra.

(v) Evaluate

$$x(y + 3z)^{-3} - \frac{p}{qr}$$

Now that the two terms have been evaluated, the second can be subtracted from the first to give the final answer.

It is worth noting at this point that the order of operator precedence explained above generally applies also to arithmetic expressions in high level computer languages, but great care must be taken when writing such expressions. For instance, in BASIC in a statement such as

LET A = P/Q*R   (/ is used for divide and * for multiply)

the expression on the right hand side of the = sign would be interpreted as

$$\frac{P}{Q} \times R \text{ and not } \frac{P}{Q \times R}$$

This is because the expression is evaluated from left to right, causing the division to be performed before the multiplication. However, to ensure that the order of evaluation goes as expected, it is wise to include brackets; if the required expression was

$$\frac{P}{Q \times R}$$

the BASIC statement would be written

LET A = P/(Q*R)   or   LET A = (P/Q)/R

Subscripts in Algebra

The Greek letter Σ (pronounced sigma) is frequently used in algebraic notation to represent the sum of a number of numbers. Thus the notation

$$\sum_{i=1}^{i=5} x_i$$

represents the sum of the five variables

$$x_1, x_2, x_3, x_4, \text{ and } x_5$$

In other words, it is the sum of any five numbers represented by these five variables. The integer "subscripts" attached to the variables indicate that the variables have some link with each other, but apart from that they are like any other variables. A variable with a subscript that is itself a variable, such as x_i represents a range of variables, as illustrated above. The number of variables so represented is determined by the consecutive integer values that can be taken by the subscript; these subscript values are 1 to 5 in the example above.

Thus, for the numbers $12, 3 \cdot 3, -7, -9 \cdot 2, 21$, the notation

$$\sum_{i=1}^{i=5} x_i$$

would represent $12 + 3 \cdot 3 + (-7) + (-9 \cdot 2) + 21$ and the variables

$$x_1, x_2, x_3, x_4, x_5$$

would have, in this case, the values $12, 3 \cdot 3, -7, -9 \cdot 2, 21$ respectively.

Subscript notation is often used to define certain types of repetitive processes suited to computer processing. For example, the following algorithm (method of solution) uses subscript notation to define how to convert an 8-bit binary integer number to an equivalent denary integer. If the binary number is represented by the variables

$$a_7, \quad a_6, \quad a_5, \quad a_4, \quad a_3, \quad a_2, \quad a_1, \quad a_0,$$

then the denary number, N, is built up using an iterative (repetitive) process based on the relationship

$$N = a_i + 2N \quad \text{where i} = 6, 5,....., 0 \text{ and N} = a_7 \text{ initially}$$

Note that this relationship is not to be viewed as an equation; it merely represents that successive values of N are calculated, each new value depending on the previous one. The process is best explained by means of an example. Supose that the binary number to be converted to denary is 01010010 (82). Then

$$a_7 = 0;$$
$$a_6 = 1;$$
$$a_5 = 0;$$
$$a_4 = 1;$$
$$a_3 = 0;$$
$$a_2 = 0;$$
$$a_1 = 1;$$
$$a_0 = 0;$$

To start the process, N is set to the value of $a_7 = 0$. A new value of N is then calculated using its current value:

$$N = a_6 + 2N = 1 + 2 \times 0 \quad = 1$$

The process is repeated until all of the binary digits have been processed:

$$N = a_5 + 2N = 0 + 2 \times 1 \quad = 2$$
$$N = a_4 + 2N = 1 + 2 \times 2 \quad = 5$$
$$N = a_3 + 2N = 0 + 2 \times 5 \quad = 10$$
$$N = a_2 + 2N = 0 + 2 \times 10 \quad = 20$$
$$N = a_1 + 2N = 1 + 2 \times 20 \quad = 41$$
$$N = a_0 + 2N = 0 + 2 \times 41 \quad = 82$$

Thus the final answer is 82.

Subscript notation occurs frequently in high level programming languages. In BASIC, for instance, the statement

LET X = A(1) + 1

contains the subscripted variable A with subscript 1. This indicates that A represents a number of memory locations containing numbers, and these locations are called A(1), A(2), A(3), and so on. The statement makes reference to the first of these locations, A(1), the contents of which is to be added to the constant 1 and the result stored in the location called X. The variable, A, is called an *array* and such variables are extremely useful in allowing reference to be made to a number of variables in a general manner.

Again the subscript may itself be a variable having a (previously assigned) integer value. Thus the statement

LET A(I) = B*3 + D

refers to the particular element of the array, A, defined by the value of the subscript, I. Arrays are described in more detail in the next chapter.

Algebraic Equations

Placing an equals sign between two algebraic expressions indicates that they have the same numeric value:

$$5x - 6 = 3 \quad \text{and} \quad 3y + 5 = y - 3$$

are both equations involving a single unknown variable. In each case the value or values of the variable for which the equation holds true may be determined by making the unknown the subject of the equation. This is achieved by applying a sequence of arithmetic operations to both sides of the equation until the variable alone is on the left hand side of the equals sign. For example, to solve the first equation the following steps would be followed:

(i) add 6 to both sides: $5x - 6 + 6 = 3 + 6$

that is, $5x = 9$

(ii) divide both sides by 5:

$$\frac{5x}{5} = \frac{9}{5}$$

or, $x = 1 \cdot 8$ which is the solution.

The solution to the second example might proceed as follows:

(i) subtract 5 from both sides: $3y + 5 - 5 = y - 3 - 5$

that is, $3y = y - 8$

(ii) subtract y from both sides: $3y - y = y - y - 8$

that is, $2y = -8$

(iii) divide both sides by 2: $y = -4.$

The following examples illustrate the procedures required for solving a variety of different equations with a single unknown.

Example 1

Solve $3(p - 3) = p + 2$

(i)   Remove the brackets

$3p - 9 = p + 2$

(ii)   Add 9

$3p = p + 11$

(iii)   Subtract p

$2p = 11$

(iv)   Divide by 2

The solution is $p = 5 \cdot 5$

Example 2

Solve $\quad \frac{2t}{6} + 7 = \frac{t}{4}$

(i)   Subtract 7

$$\frac{2t}{6} = \frac{t}{4} - 7$$

(ii) Subtract $\frac{t}{4}$

$$\frac{2t}{6} - \frac{t}{4} = -7$$

(iii) Multiply by 6

$$2t - \frac{6t}{4} = -42$$

(iv) Multiply by 4

$$8t - 6t = -168$$

$$2t = -168$$

The solution is $t = -84$

Example 3

Solve for x, $3x + c = k(1 - 2x)$.

In this instance it will be impossible to determine a numeric value for x, but if x is made the subject of a formula containing c and k, when values for these are known, the value of x can be determined.

(i) Remove the brackets

$$3x + c = k - 2kx$$

(ii) Get all terms containing x to one side by adding 2kx

$$3x + 2kx + c = k$$

(iii) Subtract c

$$3x + 2kx = k - c$$

x is common to the terms 3x and 2kx

$$x(3 + 2k) = k - c$$

(iv) Divide by term in brackets

$$x = \frac{k-c}{(3+2k)}$$

This is the solution and it illustrates the way in which a variable may be made the 'subject' of a formula.

Transposition of Formulae

As illustrated above, the subject of a formula is the single variable on one side of the equation. *Transposing* a formula means rearranging it so that a different variable is the subject of the formula. For example, in the equation of motion,

$$s = \tfrac{1}{2}ft^2$$

the distance travelled, s, by an object is related to its acceleration, f, and the time duration, t. By making t the subject of the equation, the equation can be used to find how long it takes for an object to travel the distance:

$$2s = ft^2$$

$$\frac{2s}{f} = t^2$$

Thus $t = \pm \sqrt{\frac{2s}{f}}$, and now t is the subject of the formula.

In general, the following guidelines will enable the subject of a formula to be changed:

1. Remove any roots by raising to the appropriate power.

2. Remove any fractions by multiplying each term by the common denominator.

3. Remove any brackets by multiplying out.

4. Bring all terms containing the subject variable to one side.

5. Where the subject occurs in more than one term, take it out as a common factor.

6. Isolate the subject by multiplying or dividing by factors.

7. Take a root if necessary.

The following examples illustrate the process. The number of the rule being applied is given in brackets.

Example 1.

Make x the subject of the formula $y = a - bx^2$

$$y = a - bx^2$$

$$-bx^2 = y - a \tag{4}$$

$$x^2 = \frac{y - a}{-b} = \frac{a - y}{b} \tag{6}$$

$$x = \pm \sqrt{\frac{a - y}{b}} \tag{7}$$

Example 2.

Make E the subject of the formula

$$V = \sqrt{(2E/M)}$$

$$V = \sqrt{\frac{2E}{M}}$$

$$V^2 = \frac{2E}{M} \tag{1}$$

$$V^2 M = 2E \tag{6}$$

$$E = \frac{V^2 M}{2} \tag{6}$$

Example 3.

Make x the subject of the formula $y = (x + a)(x - a)$

$$y = (x + a)(x - a)$$

$$y = x^2 - xa + xa - a^2 = x^2 - a^2 \tag{3}$$

$$x^2 = y + a^2 \tag{4}$$

$$x = \pm \sqrt{(y + a^2)} \tag{7}$$

Assignment

Denary to Binary

An iterative technique for converting binary integers to denary was presented in this chapter as an illustration of the use of the subscript notation. There is a similar algorithm for the reverse process, that is, denary to binary conversion. The algorithm is as follows:

LET N be a positive integer. To find its binary representation ($a_n\ a_{n-1}.....a_1\ a_0$), let $b_0 = N$ and iteratively calculate,

$b_1 = (b_0 - a_0)/2$
$b_2 = (b_1 - a_1)/2$
This is, in geneal
$b_k = (b_{k-1} - a_{k-1})/2$
where $a_k = 1$ if b_k is an odd number, and
$a_k = 0$ *if b_k is an even number.*
The procedure terminates when $bk = 0$.

The algorithm produces the binary coefficients in reverse order, that is the least significant digit, a_0 is produced first and the most significant digit, a_n is produced last.

Tasks

1. Using a range of denary numbers investigate the operation of the algorithm; show how each digit of the binary number is produced.

2. Write a program, based on the algorithm, to accept a denary number and convert it to binary. The output from the program should be a binary number with its digits in the correct order (the algorithm above produces the digits in reverse order).

Developmental Task

A method of determining whether a number is odd or even is to divide it by 2 and if there is no remainder, the number is even. The problem is how to do this in a programming language. Here is the basis of one possibility using 13 as an example:

    (i) divide the number by 2: $13/2 = 6 \cdot 5$

    (ii) remove the fractional part: $6 \cdot 5 \rightarrow 6$

    (iii) multiply this by 2: $6 \times 2 = 12$

    (iv) since this is not the same as the original number, the original number must have been odd. If the result was the same as the original number, it would have been even.

The programming language that you use will determine the precise coding required for this, so you should investigate the facilities that your particular language provides. Look through the language manual for suitable instructions. (Some languages provide MOD and DIV functions for integer division; MOD gives the remainder and DIV the integer quotient of the division. Other languages allow conversion from real numbers to integers).

Exercises

Algebraic Equations

1. Solve the following equations:

   (i) $3x + 5 = 2$

   (ii) $10s - 7 = 2s + 9$

   (iii) $6x/3 = 9$

   (iv) $p - 3p/2 = 1/2$

   (v) $3/x + 2/x = 1/4$

   (vi) $0 \cdot 3(3x + 2) = 0 \cdot 1(5 - x)$

2. Make the variable in brackets the subject of the equation.

   (i $v = u + at$ (t)

   (ii) $1/u + 1/v = 1/f$ (f)

   (iii) $y = (x - a)(x + a)$ (x)

   (iv) $z = x - 3y$ (y)

   (v) $c = \sqrt{\dfrac{E}{m}}$ (E)

Subscripts

1. Use subscripts and the summation (sigma) notation to represent the following:

   (i) The sum of 100 numbers.

   (ii) The sum of the first 20 integers.

   (iii) The sum of the squares of 25 numbers.

   (iv) The sum of the squares of the integers from 25 to 35 inclusive.

2. Use the algorithm for binary to denary conversion to find the denary equivalents of the following binary numbers (denary value in brackets):

   (i) 01101010 (106)

   (ii) 00010101 (21)

   (iii) 01000111 (39)

   (iv) 11001101 (205)

Chapter 26

Tabular Data

Introduction

The idea of an *array* of data was introduced in the previous chapter, and it was shown that such a data structure is an important tool in computer programming. This chapter develops further the concept of an array and its relevance to data processing by computer.

One-dimensional Arrays

A data structure comprising a list of items of information, such as numbers, is termed an 'array'. Algebraically, an array is usually defined as follows:

$$L_i \qquad i = 1,.....,N$$

The array has the name, L, in this instance and the i subscript takes values from 1 to N, where N is an integer representing the number of values in the array. Thus, for the six values, 3,4,2,0,1,9, N=6 and

$$L_1 = 3; \quad L_2 = 4; \quad L_3 = 2; \quad L_4 = 0; \quad L_5 = 1; \quad L_6 = 9$$

This is called a one-dimensional array because it is a simple list of numbers in which any particular number can be referenced by a single subscript.

A one-dimensional array could be used to represent a list of student marks in a number of subjects, prices of a number of articles, heights of children, or in fact any collection of numbers which can be conveniently grouped together. For this reason, arrays are frequently used to represent data which is to be analysed statistically.

Arrays used in computer languages represent a set of consecutive memory locations. Array notation allows this area of memory to be referred to by a single variable. In a BASIC program, for instance, the declaration

DIM L(20)

reserves 20 storage locations (or areas of memory capable of storing a single number) which are named L. DIM is an abbreviation for dimension. A subscript in brackets is used to specify which one of these 20 is being referenced at any time. Thus the notation L(5) refers to the fifth element of the array, L, in memory. In programs, a variable used for the subscript greatly facilitates processing operations on arrays. For example, in order to add 20 numbers held in the array, A, in memory, the following section of BASIC code could be used:

```
100 LET S = 0
110 FOR I = 1 TO 20
120 LET S = S + A(I)
130 NEXT I
```

Here S is being used to accumulate the contents of the array elements. The FOR statement sets the subscript I to an initial value of 1, and every time the NEXT I statement is encountered, increments I by 1 and repeats line 120. The instruction on line 120 adds the specified array element to the running total, S, and stores the result back to S.

The sequence of processing is therefore

$$S = 0 + A(1)$$
$$S = A(1) + A(2)$$
$$S = (A(1) + A(2)) + A(3)$$
$$S = (A(1) + A(2) + A(3)) + A(4)$$

and so on until A(20) is finally referenced.

If arrays were not implemented in the language then the addition would be effected by writing

LET S = A1 + A2 + A3 + A4 + ... + A20

where each number now has its own individual variable name and the numbers must be treated as individuals. This is obviously very unwieldy, and unworkable for large numbers (say 100 or more) of values.

Other languages such as Pascal and COBOL have similar facilities for allowing the use of arrays.

Two-dimensional Arrays

A table of information is an example of a two-dimensional array. A particular item in a table is referenced by its row and position within the row (or column). For example, the following table of benchmark results for BASIC (timing comparisons for the execution of standard programs or instructions on different computers) comprises five rows of timings in seconds, each row containing entries for four different models of microcomputers:

	1	**2**	**3**	**4**
Benchmark	**HP series 200**	**IBM PC**	**Apple II Plus**	**TRS-80**
1. Empty DO loop	0·82	6·43	6·66	7·98
2. Division	3·61	23·8	29·0	19·4
3. Subroutine jump	1·50	12·4	13·9	17·1
4. Substring	2·55	23·0	32·3	24·8
5. Prime number prog.	18·64	190·0	241·0	189·0

The benchmark result for division on the IBM PC (23·8 secs) requires two 'co-ordinates': the row for division and the column for the IBM PC.

If the table contained only a single column for the IBM PC then it would be an example of a one-dimensional array. Thus a two-dimensional array may be viewed as a set of one-dimensional arrays.

In array notation, the table could be represented by a single variable, B, with two subscripts, i (for the rows) and j (for the columns):

$$B_{i,j} \qquad i \quad = 1,...,5$$
$$j \quad = 1,...,4$$

The array is of size 5 by 4 (written 5 × 4), the size of arrays being defined as row × column.

Thus,

$$B_{2,1} = 3 \cdot 61, \quad B_{4,1} = 2 \cdot 55, \quad B_{5,4} = 189 \cdot 0$$

High level programming languages which allow one-dimensional arrays will almost invariably cater for two-dimensional arrays too. Again using BASIC as an example, a two-dimensional array must be declared before use with a DIM (dimension) statement such as

DIM A(5,4)

which allocates storage space sufficient for the 20 elements (5 × 4) of array, A. Program statements which make reference to this array must use two subscripts to refer to a particular element. Thus A(3,2) makes reference to the second element in the third row.

Performing Calculations on Arrays

Suppose that a certain computer program for producing graphics on a monitor stores information about simple geometrical shapes in tabular form. Each point of a figure to be drawn is stored in a table of x-y co-ordinates. These co-ordinates give the displacement of the next point to be drawn from the current position of the cursor. A rectangle, for example, might be stored as follows:

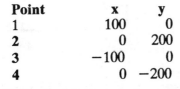

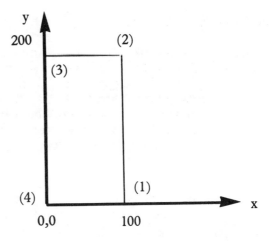

Point	x	y
1	100	0
2	0	200
3	−100	0
4	0	−200

A positive value indicates cursor movement right for x and up for y; negative values mean move left for x and down for y.

By performing various calculations on this array, the figure can be transformed in a number of different ways.

The following examples will assume that the co-ordinate values are stored in a two-dimensional array, A, of dimension 4 × 2:

j i	1	2
1	100	0
2	0	200
3	−100	0
4	0	−200

The transformed co-ordinates will be stored in the array B, also 4 × 2

(i) **Scaling.** Here the figure retains its shape but is drawn either larger or smaller depending on a scaling factor. The new co-ordinate values are calculated by multiplying each of them by a constant scaling factor. For example, to double the dimensions of the figure, each co-ordinate value would be multiplied by a scaling factor of 2:

$$B_{i,j} \;=\; 2 \times A_{i,j} \quad i = 1,...5 \\ j = 1,2$$

Thus B becomes

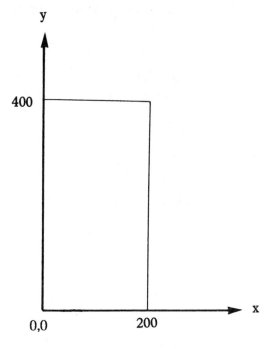

j	1	2
i		
1	200	0
2	0	400
3	−200	0
4	0	−400

Multiplication by a value smaller than 1 would reduce the size of the rectangle.

(ii) **Reflection about the x-axis.** The size and shape of the figure remains exactly the same but it is a mirror image. This transformation is effected by multiplying each x-ordinate by −1:

$$B_{i,1} \;=\; (-1) \times A_{i,1} \qquad i = 1,...,5$$

B becomes

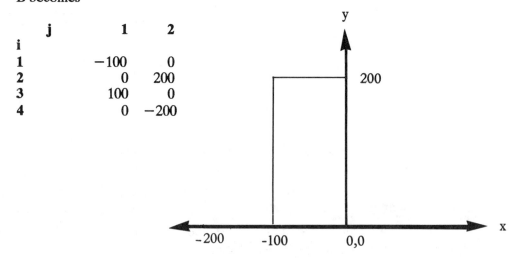

j	1	2
i		
1	−100	0
2	0	200
3	100	0
4	0	−200

(iii) **Reflection about the y-axis.** This has a similar effect to (ii), and is produced by multiplying each y-ordinate by −1:

$$B_{i,2} = (-1) \times A_{i,2} \qquad i=1,....,5$$

The x-ordinate is left as it is:

$$B_{i,1} \;=\; A_{i,1} \qquad i = 1,....,5$$

(iv) **x-shear.** Here the x-ordinate is formed from the sum of the x and y values, and the y value is unmodified. This distorts the shape of the figure:

$$B_{i,1} = A_{i,1} + A_{i,2} \qquad i = 1,...,5$$
$$B_{i,2} = A_{i,2} \qquad i = 1,...,5$$

B becomes

j	1	2
i		
1	100	0
2	200	200
3	−100	0
4	−200	−200

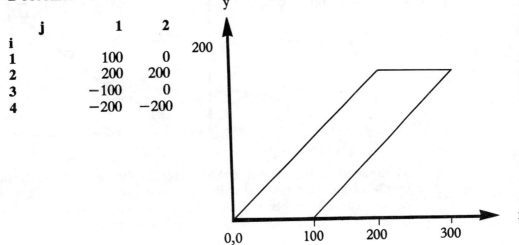

(v) **y-shear.** Similar to x-shear :

$$B_{i,2} = A_{i,1} + A_{i,2} \qquad i = 1,...,5$$
$$B_{i,1} = A_{i,1} \qquad i = 1,...,5$$

B becomes

j	1	2
i		
1	100	100
2	0	200
3	−100	−200
4	0	−200

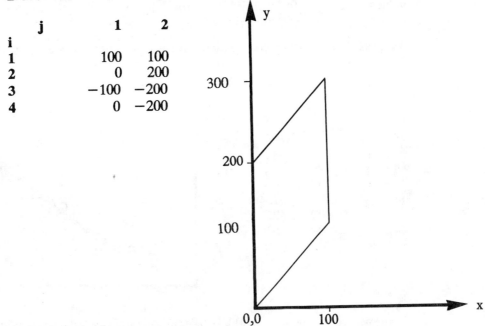

Linear Interpolation

Graphics animation effects on computers are frequently produced by plotting sequences of picture 'frames' in rapid succession. As a very simple example, suppose that a program is required to 'animate' a single dot by making it appear to follow a curved path. An array is to be used to store a number of co-ordinates of points on the path, but the amount of memory available for this purpose is severely restricted. The table of co-ordinates to be used might look as follows:

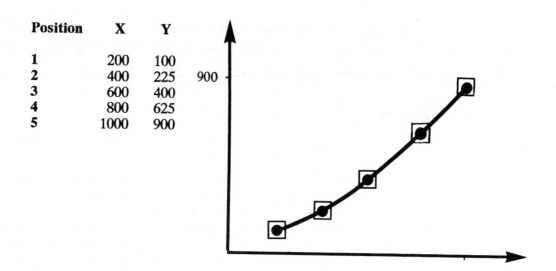

Position	X	Y
1	200	100
2	400	225
3	600	400
4	800	625
5	1000	900

The animation effect would be achieved by displaying the dot at the first point, pausing briefly, erasing it, displaying it at the second point, pausing briefly, erasing it, and so on until the dot had been displayed at every co-ordinate in turn. This same principle could be used to animate any figure by using this repetitive process of drawing, erasing and moving.

With so few points at which the dot is to be plotted, however, the movement would not be very convincing because the gaps between the points are too large to give the illusion of a smooth movement. The effect could be improved by defining more points on the path, but memory constraints may make this impossible. An alternative solution is to calculate intermediate points on the path using *linear interpolation*.

Interpolation is the process of calculating an intermediate value between two given values on a curve. In *linear* interpolation, the line joining the two points is assumed to be a straight line, and the interpolated point lies on this line.

Suppose that we decided to calculate a single intermediate point mid-way between each of the values given on the curve. The new table would become

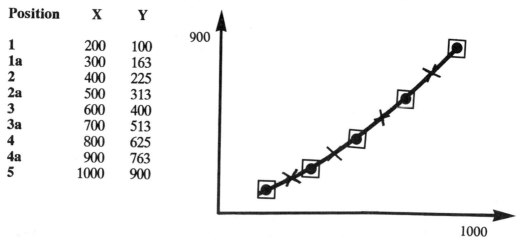

Position	X	Y
1	200	100
1a	300	163
2	400	225
2a	500	313
3	600	400
3a	700	513
4	800	625
4a	900	763
5	1000	900

Positions 1a, 2a, 3a, 4a, are the calculated values and are marked with an "x" on the graph. Each interpolated point has been calculated as follows:

> (i) Take the two x-ordinate values between which the intermediate point is to be found.

> (ii) Subtract these two values.

> (iii) Halve the difference.

> (iv) Add the difference to the first x value.

(v) Do the same with the y-ordinates.

So, to interpolate linearly between two points x2 = 400, y2 = 225 and x3 = 600, y3 = 400, the calculation would be:

$$x' = 400 + (600 - 400)/2 = 400 + 100 \quad = 500$$
$$y' = 225 + (400 - 225)/2 = 225 + 87.5 \quad = 313 \text{ approx.}$$

where x' and y' represent the co-ordinates of the calculated point between the points (400, 225) and (600, 400).

The interpolated point need not be mid-way between the other two. Perhaps it may be necessary to calculate several intermediate points in order to make the movement sufficiently smooth. Generally, with linear interpolation, one of the ordinates (the x-ordinate, for instance) is known, and the other ordinate is to be calculated. In our example, if three intermediate points were required then the x values would increase in steps of 50: 200 [250,300,350] 400 [450,500,550] 600 etc. Given a value for x' (that is, the x-ordinate of the intermediate point) y' could be calculated as follows, assuming that the two enclosing co-ordinates are represented by (x1,y1) and (x2,y2):

$$y' = y1 + (y2 - y1)\frac{(x' - x1)}{(x2 - x1)}$$

For example, if x' = 450 then

$$y' = 225 + (400 - 225) \times \frac{(450 - 400)}{(600 - 400)} = 225 + 175 \times \frac{50}{200} = 269 \text{ approx.}$$

The formula merely adds a proportion of the difference between the y-ordinates (y2 - y1) to the lower y-value (y1). The proportion added is determined by where x' is located relative to x1, that is the ratio (x' - x1)/(x2 - x1).

If we represent (x' - x1)/(x2 - x1) as the *interpolating factor, p*, then the formula becomes

$$y' = y1 + p(y2 - y1)$$

This is the standard formula for Linear Interpolation. Notice that p is always a value between 0 and 1. Though the concept of linear interpolation has been illustrated with a simple problem in computer graphics programming, it is not limited to this type of application. For example, given any table of information such as that shown below for logarithms, it is possible to determine (approximately) any intermediate value:

x	log x
80	1·9031
81	1·9085
82	1·9138
83	1·9191
84	1·9243
85	1·9294

For example, linear interpolation could be used to determine approximately the value of log 81·25:

$$\log 81{\cdot}25 = \log 81 \quad + 0{\cdot}25(1{\cdot}9138 - 1{\cdot}9085)$$
$$= 1{\cdot}9085 \quad + 0{\cdot}25(0{\cdot}0153)$$
$$= 1{\cdot}9113 \text{ approx.}$$

Assignment

Picture Shows

Earlier in this chapter some examples were presented to illustrate calculations on arrays using simple 2-dimensional graphics. Though it was not mentioned at the time, the examples were thinly disguised matrix multiplications. For the present purposes, a matrix may be regarded as a 2-dimensional array, and multiplying a co-ordinate pair by a 2 × 2   matrix has the effect of transforming the co-ordinates. This can be represented by the following notation

$$(xt, yt) = (x,y) \begin{pmatrix} a & c \\ b & d \end{pmatrix}$$

which states that the point (x,y) transforms to the point (xt, yt) when multiplied by the matrix (array)

$$\begin{pmatrix} a & c \\ b & d \end{pmatrix}$$

The matrix operation shown above produces the equations

$$xt = ax + by$$

$$yt = cx + dy$$

The choice of a,b,c and d determines the particular transformation to be performed on the point. The application of this process is that standard transformations of shapes may be performed by applying certain, standard types of transform matrices. Some of these matrices are shown below. A transformation of a shape is performed by applying the transform matrix to each point in the shape. Some interesting effects can result.

1. *Identity (no effect)* $\begin{pmatrix} 1 & 0 \\ 0 & 1 \end{pmatrix}$

2. *Scaling* $\begin{pmatrix} S1 & 0 \\ 0 & S2 \end{pmatrix}$ *(S1 is the x scaling factor and S2 is the y scaling factor)*

3. *Reflection about the x-axis* $\begin{pmatrix} 1 & 0 \\ 0 & -1 \end{pmatrix}$

4. *Reflection about the y-axis* $\begin{pmatrix} -1 & 0 \\ 0 & 1 \end{pmatrix}$

5. *Y shear* $\begin{pmatrix} 1 & S \\ 0 & 1 \end{pmatrix}$ *(S is the shear factor)*

6. *X shear* $\begin{pmatrix} 1 & 0 \\ S & 1 \end{pmatrix}$

Tasks

Using graph paper draw a simple (but interesting) geometrical shape consisting of straight lines and note the position of each point of the shape in x-y co-ordinates.

Apply a transform matrix to the points in your shape and draw the transformed points on graph paper. Repeat for different transforms.

Developmental Task

Most books on interactive computer graphics will explain the use of matrices in 2-dimensional transformations. Read up on the subject (such books are usually packed with good illustrations of the effects that can be achieved) and try to find out how to perform a rotation of a figure through a specified angle.

Chapter 27

Geometry and Graphics

Introduction

In Chapter 11, Categories of Software, a number of types of graphics packages were discussed. The main purpose of this chapter is to provide a basic grounding in the types of facilities offered by such graphics packages, and in particular those which facilitate the drawing of simple two and three-dimensional geometrical figures.

Software for Computer-aided Design (CAD) and Graphic Design in particular assume fundamental familiarity with simple geometrical principles and terminology. These too will be examined in this chapter.

Common Geometrical Figures

In this section a number of common geometrical figures will be described. Each will be defined, a guide to sketching the figure will be provided where necessary, and formulae will be given for calculating perimeters, areas and volumes where relevant. Symbols quoted in formulae or referred to in explanations are related to the diagrams provided for each figure.

2-Dimensional Figures

Triangle

Definition: A triangle is a closed figure having three sides and three included angles. Certain triangles have special names:

(i) A right-angled triangle - one of the enclosed angles is 90 degrees (that is, a right-angle).

(ii) An isosceles triangle - two sides and two angles are the same.

(iii) An equilateral triangle - all sides and angles are equal.

(iv) A scalene triangle - all its sides and angles unequal and does not contain a right-angle.

(i) 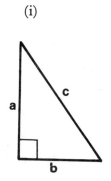   (ii) 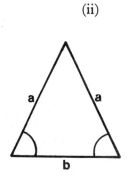   (iii) 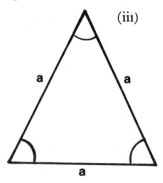   (iv)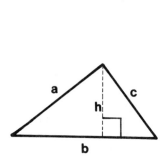

Types of Triangles

Perimeter: This is the sum of the sides, that is,

$$perimeter = a+b+c$$

Area: The name is given by the formula

$$area = \frac{b \times h}{2}$$

Rectangle

Definition: A rectangle is a quadrilateral (four sided figure) in which opposite sides are equal and parallel and adjacent sides are at right-angles to each other. A square is a special case of a rectangle in which all of the sides are of equal length.

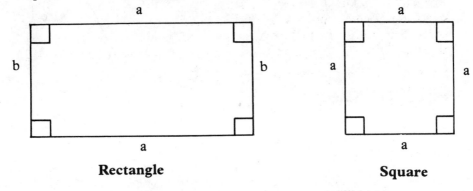

Rectangle   **Square**

Perimeter: This is twice the sum of two adjacent sides, that is,

$$perimeter = 2(a+b) \text{ and for a square} = 4a$$

Area: The area is the product of two adjacent sides:

$$area = a \times b \text{ and for a square} = a^2$$

Parallelogram

Definition: Parallelograms are quadrilaterals with opposite sides equal and parallel, but the included angles are not right-angles. A parallelogram with adjacent sides of different lengths is called a rhomboid, and when all four sides are of equal length, it is called a rhombus.

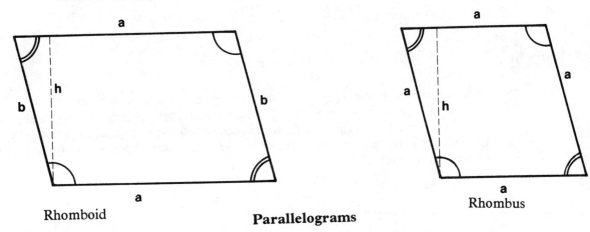

Rhomboid   Rhombus

Parallelograms

Perimeter: Calculated the same way as for a rectangle, that is by finding the sum of all the sides.

$$perimeter = 2(a+b) \text{ and for a rhombus} = 4a$$

Area: Choose one side and draw a perpendicular from it to the opposite side. The area is a product of the length of the side and the perpendicular.

area = a × h

Trapezium

Definition: A trapezium is a quadrilateral with no parallel sides. A trapezoid has two parallel sides.

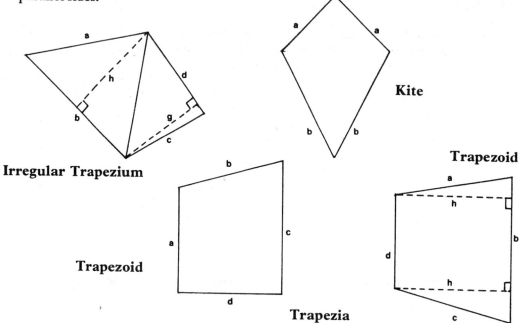

Irregular Trapezium

Kite

Trapezoid

Trapezoid

Trapezia

Perimeter: The sum of the sides:

perimeter = a+b+c+d

Area: In general, this is found by splitting the figure into two triangles and adding their area together. Thus

$$area\ of\ a\ trapezium\ \ = \ \frac{b \times h}{2} + \frac{d \times g}{2} = \ \text{½}\ (bh + dg)$$

For a trapezoid, the heights of the triangles are the same:

$$area\ of\ a\ trapezoid = \frac{h}{2}\ (b + d)$$

Polygon

Definition: Strictly speaking, polygons are figures having three or more sides. However, a polygon is usually regarded as a figure with more than four sides. If the sides are all the same length the figures are classed as regular polygons; irregular polygons have sides of unequal lengths. Regular polygons are named according to the number of sides they have:

5 sides: pentagon

6 sides: hexagon

7 sides: heptagon

8 sides: octagon

9 sides: nonagon

The accurate construction of a regular polygon can be quite difficult and depends on the particular polygon required, but for sketching purposes the easiest method, which will work for any polygon, is as follows:

    (i) draw a circle;

    (ii) using dividers or a compass, divide the circumference of the circle into an equal number of parts by trial and error;

    (iii) join the divisions with straight lines.

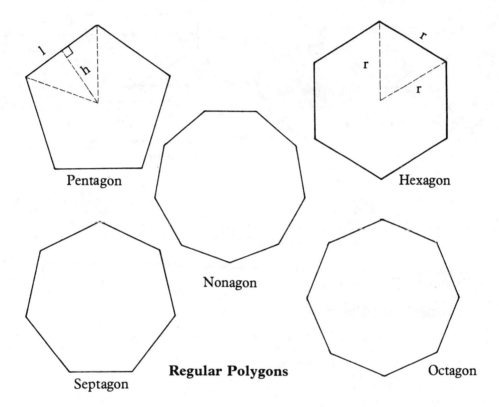

Perimeter: The sum of the sides. For a regular polygon having n sides of length, l, the perimeter is given by

    perimeter = nl

Area: The area of an irregular polygon is found by dividing it into triangles and calculating the sum of the areas.

For a regular polygon of n sides each of length, l, the area is given by

    area of regular polygon = ½ *(lh)* × *n*

where h is the perpendicular distance from one of the sides to the centre of the figure.

Circle

Definition: A circle is the path of a point passing round a given point (the centre of the circle) and keeping the same distance from it (the radius).

The figure below shows the characteristics of the circle in terms of lines and areas created by the lines.

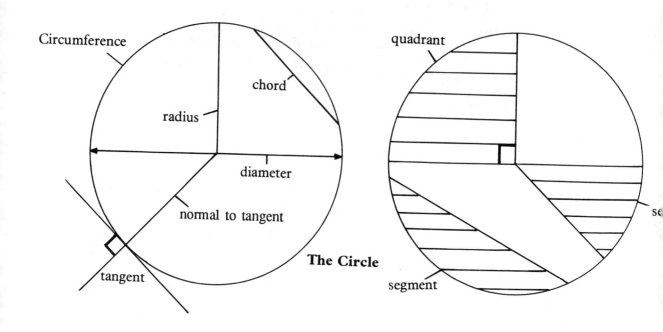

Circumference: This is given by

$$circumference = 2 \times \pi \times radius \quad \text{or} \quad \pi \times diameter$$

Area: If *r* is the radius of the circle,

$$area = \pi r^2$$

Ellipse

Definition: An ellipse is rather like a flattened circle. It has a major axis, which is the longest line that can be drawn through the centre of the ellipse, and a minor axis, which is the shortest line through its centre.

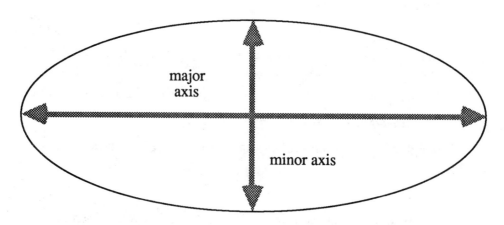

To sketch an ellipse, the following method, called the intersecting lines method, can be used:

(i) Draw the rectangle ABCD and the major and minor axis.

(ii) Divide EO into a number of equal parts, say 6.

(iii) Divide ED into the same number of equal parts.

(iv) Join the points on ED to H and draw lines from G through the points on EO.

(v) The points of intersection marked with the small square give points on the curve.

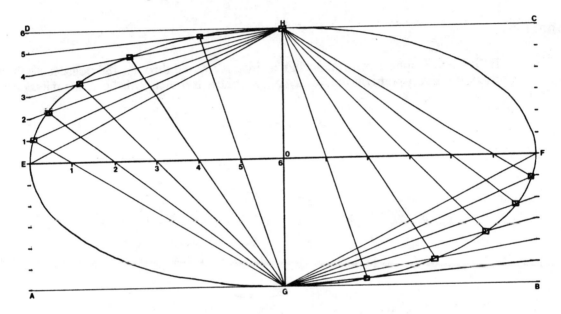

Sketching an ellipse

3-Dimensional Figures

Prism

Definition: A prism has a base which is a three or more sided figure and a uniform cross section. In right prisms the plane of the base is perpendicular to the height of the prism.

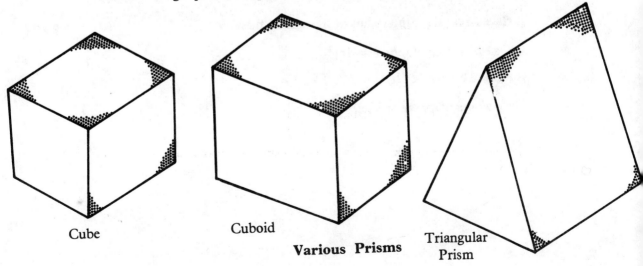

Cube

Cuboid

Various Prisms

Triangular Prism

A cube, or regular hexahedron, is a square prism with six square faces. A cuboid is a rectangular right prism.

Surface Area: This is the sum of the areas of the faces of the prism. The general formula for the surface area of a right prism of height h is given by

Surface area of right prism = Ph + 2A

where P is the perimeter and A the area of the base.

Volume: The volume of a right prism with cross sectional area A is given by

Volume of right prism = Ah

where h is the height of the prism.

Sphere

Definition: A sphere is formed when a circle is rotated through 180 degrees about its diameter. Every point on the surface of the sphere is the same distance from its centre.

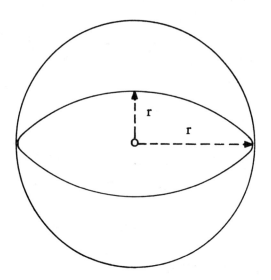

Surface Area: If r is the radius of the sphere then

surface area of sphere = $4\pi r^2$

Volume: This is given by

volume of sphere = $\frac{4}{3}\pi r^3$

Cylinder

Definition: A cylinder is a prism with a circular base.

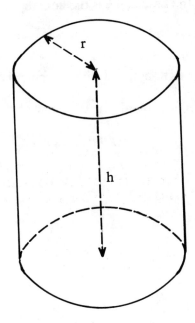

Surface Area: For a cylinder of radius r and height h,

surface area of cylinder $= 2\pi rh + 2\pi r^2 = 2\pi r(h + r)$

Volume: This is the area of the base times the height:

volume of cylinder $= \pi r^2 h$

Right Pyramid

Definition: In a right pyramid, the perpendicular from the apex to the base (the height of the pyramid) passes through the centre of the base. A rectangular pyramid has a rectangular base and a triangular pyramid has a triangular base. A triangular pyramid in which all four faces are equilateral triangles is called a tetrahedron.

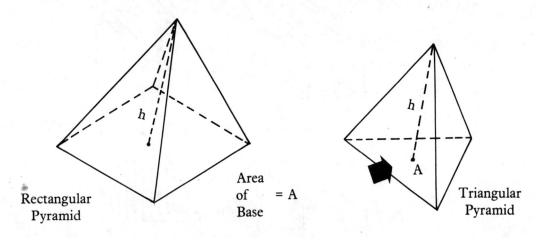

Right Pyramids

Surface Area: This is the sum of the areas of the faces.

Volume: The general formula for the volume of a right pyramid is given by

$$volume\ of\ right\ pyramid\ =\ \tfrac{1}{3}Ah$$

where A is the area of the base and h is the height perpendicular to the base.

Cone

Definition: A cone is a right pyramid with a circular base.

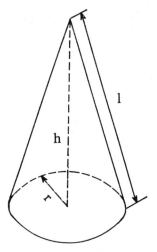

Surface Area: The curved surface of a cone has area πrl, where l is the slant height of the cone, and the base is a circle. Thus

$$surface\ area\ of\ cone\ =\ \pi r^2 + 2\pi rl = \pi r(r + 2l)$$

Volume: The volume of a cone is given by

$$volume\ of\ cone\ =\ \tfrac{1}{3}\pi r^2 h$$

Pictorial Drawings

There are various ways of presenting 3-dimensional objects pictorially, the commonest and most important of which is the *isometric projection*. This, and three other types of presentation are illustrated in the figure below.

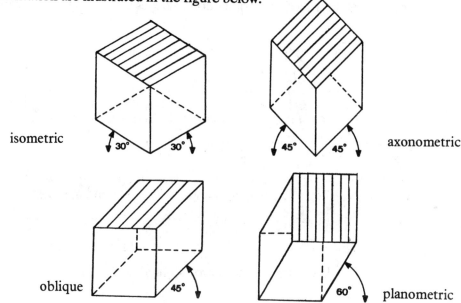

Isometric Projections

In an isometric drawing all horizontal lines are drawn at 30 degrees and all vertical lines remain vertical. The only slight difficulty with isometric projections is in dealing with curves such as circles. The technique for doing so is illustrated in the next figure.

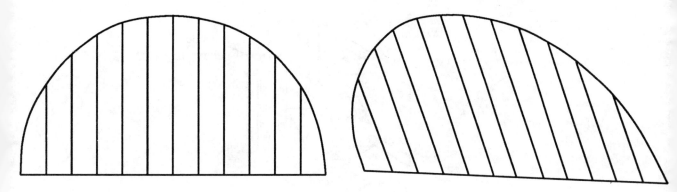

Isometric view of a semicircle

A base line is divided into a number of equal parts, and vertical lines are drawn from the base to the curve. These lines are transferred to the equivalent points on the isometric drawing and a freehand curve is drawn to join the ends. The next figure shows how a block with curved surfaces is drawn as an isometric projection.

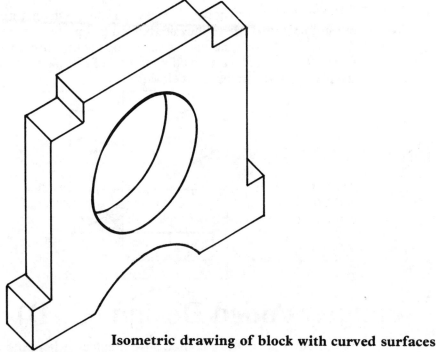

Isometric drawing of block with curved surfaces

Orthographic Projections

An orthographic projection is a representation of a solid object by showing it viewed from three different viewpoints, or *elevations*. The three elevations are:

    (i) Front elevation - the object viewed from the front.

    (ii) Side elevation - the object viewed from the side.

    (iii) Plan - the object viewed from directly above.

In each case, the view that an observer would have is translated as a 2-dimensional representation on the drawing paper. The next figure illustrates the process for an orthographic projection of a rectangular prism placed on one edge.

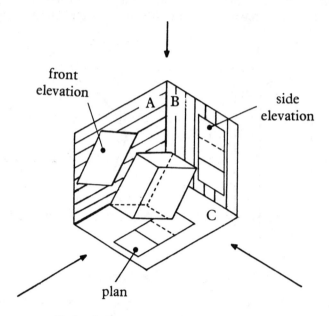

Principle of orthographic projections

The correspondences between edges and vertices in the three elevations are indicated by faint lines, and where they are hidden in a particular elevation, they are shown as dotted lines. Where the plan is shown below the front elevation, as in the previous figure, the projection is termed a 1st Angle Projection. A 3rd Angle Projection shows the plan view above the front elevation.

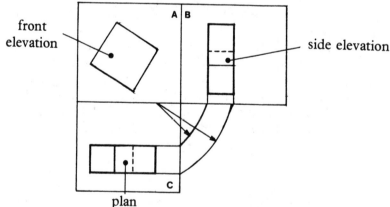

Computer-Aided Design (CAD)

In computer-aided design, interactive graphics (where the user has control over the operation of the graphics software) is used to design components and systems of mechanical, electrical and electronic devices. These applications include designing buildings, car body shapes, hulls of ships, machine components and electronic circuits. The emphasis is frequently on producing precise drawings for manufacturing or architectural purposes. Such graphics packages offer facilities for drawing and manipulating 2-dimensional or 3-dimensional geometrical figures. Typical facilities allow the user to:

-   draw standard shapes such as rectangles, triangles and circles;

- move shapes around the screen;

- enlarge or reduce figures;

- pattern fill areas of the screen;

- position text of various sizes at different angles;

- automatically dimension lines;

- rotate figures about specified axes;

- generate 3-D images from orthographic projections;

- magnify specified areas of the screen to allow fine detail editing;

- transfer the work to output devices such as plotters.

Communication with the computer is generally through such devices as light pens, mice and graphics tablets which give greater flexibility and ease of use than keyboards. Special high-resolution monitors are generally used so that drawings can be designed and edited with great accuracy.

Assignment *Desktop Publisher*

In a conversation with Paul Halligan, a friend of yours who runs a small publishing business, you discover, with some surprise, that he subcontracts to freelance artists all the technical drawings that go into his books. A great number of these drawings are of a very simple nature but they must be produced with high definition so that they can be photographed and reduced or enlarged. You mention to him that there are numerous packages on the market for producing such drawings on microcomputers and that you have one such package that you use for producing posters and advertising literature for a club that you run. You agree to show him examples of the types of drawings that can be produced and give him a demonstration of the package.

Tasks

1. Produce drawings of a range of geometrical shapes that can be produced on graphics packages to which you have access. Suitable packages are those for graphic design, CAD or desktop publishing.

2. Investigate the use of the package for the production of other types of illustrations, for example, statistical graphs.

3. Give a practical demonstration of the range of effects that can be achieved by the program.

Developmental Task

Identify from current computing magazines the range of graphics software available, and for which machines the packages are suitable.

Chapter 28

Graphs

Introduction

This chapter deals with Cartesian graphs of simple algebraic functions. An equation of the form

y = 3x + 2

is called a Cartesian equation, and a graph of the equation is called a Cartesian graph. The *dependent* variable, y (the value of y depends on x), is said to be a *function* of the *independent* variable, x, or

y = f(x)

When y is used as the vertical scale of a graph, and x is used for the horizontal scale, every point on the resulting grid can be represented by a pair of values, (x,y), called the Cartesian coordinates of the point. Cartesian coordinates are also referred to as *rectangular coordinates*. Henceforth, they will be referred to as just coordinates. The point at which the two axes meet is called the origin and has coordinates (0,0).

The next figure shows the coordinates of a number of points on a graph.

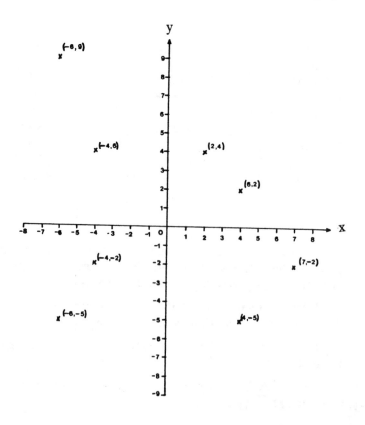

Examples of rectangular coordinates

In each case, the coordinates have been derived by counting the number of units the point is horizontally displaced from the origin for the x-ordinate, and the displacement vertically for the y-ordinate. The x-ordinate is negative for points to the left of the origin and the y-ordinate is negative for points below the origin.

Graphs of Linear Functions

A function of the form

$$y = mx + c$$

where m and c are constants (values which do not change), is called a *linear* function of x, since it defines a straight line with *slope* or *gradient*, m, and *intercept*,c.

The next table shows a number of coordinates on the line when m $= 2$ and c $= -4$.

Co-ordinates for y $= 2x - 4$

x	-5	-4	-3	-2	-1	0	1	2	3	4	5
y $= 2x - 4$	-14	-12	-10	-8	-6	-4	-2	0	2	4	6

The following figure shows the corresponding graph of the straight line.

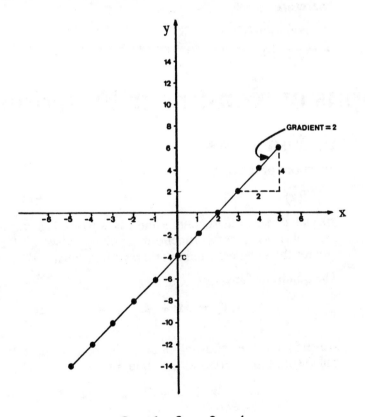

Graph of y = 2x - 4

Notice that the line intersects the y-axis at the point y $= -4$; this is called the intercept and is the value of c.

Though eleven points are given in the table above, in fact only two are absolutely necessary in order to draw the graph. However, it is best to use three points as a check that no mistake has been made in calculating the points.

Determination of the equation of a straight line

Given that a line can be drawn knowing only two coordinates on the line, it should be possible to find the equation of the line from these two coordinates.

First it is necessary to define what is meant by the slope or gradient of a line. Given two points on the line, the gradient is the ratio between the change in y to the change in x. So for the points (3,2) and (5,6) the gradient is given by

$$gradient = \frac{change\ in\ y}{change\ in\ x} = \frac{6-2}{5-3} = \frac{4}{2} = 2$$

In order to define a line, it is necessary to determine its gradient and intercept. Suppose it is required to find the equation of a line between the points (0,2) and (4,14). This is the type of problem which programs for graphic design must solve frequently. First the gradient of the line is determined:

$$gradient = \frac{14-2}{4-0} = 3$$

The equation of the line is therefore

y = 3x + c

Now the value of c, the intercept, is determined by substituting one pair of coordinates into the equation:

14 = 3(4) + c   or   2 = 3(0) + c

Therefore c = 2.

The equation of the line is

y = 3x + 2

Graphs of Non-linear Functions

Quadratic Functions

Functions of the form

f(x) = x^2 − 2   or   f(x) = x^2 − 3x + 2

are called *quadratic* functions and when plotted as graphs they produce curves called parabolas. In general, functions involving powers of the independent variable of greater than one are called *non-linear* functions.

The quadratic functions

$$y = x^2 - 3x + 2, \quad y = x^2 - 2x + 1 \quad and$$
$$y = x^2 + x + 1$$

are shown in the following figure. The points where the curves cross the x-axis are called solutions or *roots* of the equations

$$x^2 - 3x + 2 = 0, \quad x^2 - 2x + 1 = 0 \quad and \quad x^2 + x + 1 = 0$$
respectively.

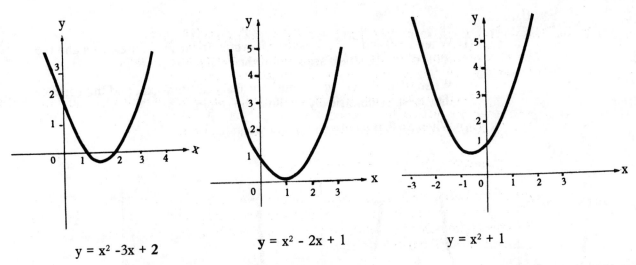

$$y = x^2 - 3x + 2 \qquad\qquad y = x^2 - 2x + 1 \qquad\qquad y = x^2 + 1$$

Quadratic functions

Notice that the graphs show three different possibilities for the number of roots of a quadratic equation:

    (i) Two different roots where the curve crosses the x-axis.

    (ii) A double root where the curve just touches the x-axis.

    (iii) No roots because the curve never crosses the x-axis.

Another point to note is that if the coefficient of the x^2 term is negative then the curve will have a single minimum point and if the coefficient of the x^2 term is positive the curve will have a single maximum point. These two cases are illustrated in the following figure.

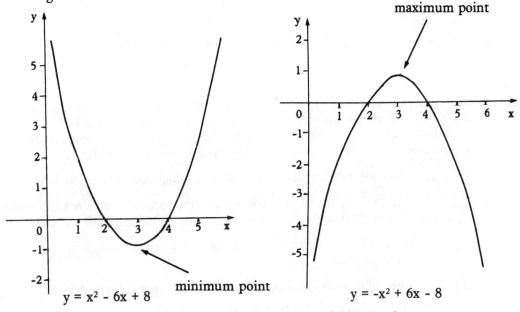

$$y = x^2 - 6x + 8 \qquad\qquad y = -x^2 + 6x - 8$$

Minimum and Maximum of Quadratic

Drawing Quadratics

A quadratic function has the general form

$$y = ax^2 + bx + c$$

The values that the coefficients a, b and c have determine the form of the quadratic curve. The effect of the sign of the coefficient, a, has been noted already; more useful observations for drawing quadratics are listed below and are illustrated in the next figure.

(i) When b=0 and c=0, the curve is symmetrical about the y-axis and the roots of the function are both at the origin.

(ii) When b=0, the curve is symmetrical about the y-axis, and the roots, if they exist, symmetrically straddle the origin.

(iii) When c=0, the curve passes through the origin.

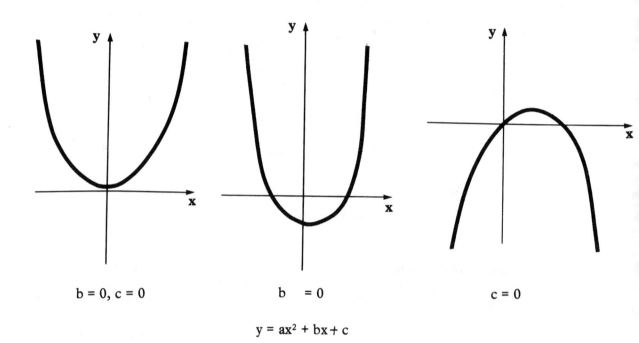

$$y = ax^2 + bx + c$$

Various Graphs of Quadratic Functions

To sketch the graph of a quadratic, use the observations above in conjunction with a table of at least six evenly spaced coordinates on the curve. The range of these coordinates should be such that it covers the roots of the function and the maximum or minimum point. The locations of these points may be identified as follows:

(a) Roots occur where the y values change sign for consecutive values of x.

(b) A maximum point occurs where, for consecutive increasing values of x, the magnitude of the y values change from increasing to decreasing.

(c) A minimum point occurs where the y values change from decreasing to increasing.

The following table shows the coordinates for the function $y = 2x^2 - x - 6$

Coordinates for $y = 2x^2 - x - 6$

x		−4	−3	−2	−1	0	1	2	3	4
y			30	15	4	−3	−6	−5	−0	9	22
				A	B	C	D	E		

The coordinates show that there is a root between points A and B (y changes sign), and that there is a minimum value between points C and D (y goes from decreasing to increasing). The second root is at point E. The graph is shown in the following figure.

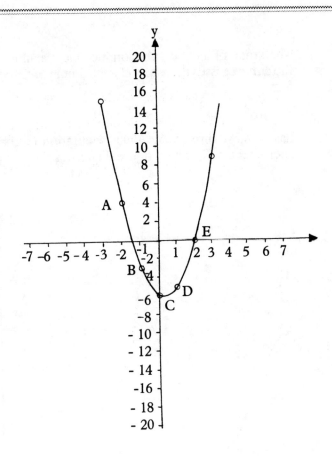

Graph of y = 2x² - x - 6

Cubic Functions

Functions of x of the form

$$f(x) = ax^3 + bx^2 + cx + d$$

are called *cubic* functions and, like quadratic functions, have characteristic curves. The cubic function

$$y = x^3 - 6x^2 + 11x - 6$$

is shown in the next figure.

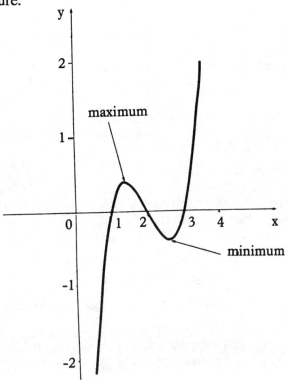

The cubic function y = x³ - 6x² + 11x - 6

The graph of a cubic function has one maximum point and one minimum point, and the curve crosses the x-axis at a maximum of three places. Thus a cubic equation of the form

$$ax^3 + bx^2 + cx + d = 0$$

has at most three roots. The orientation of the curve depends on the sign of the coefficient, a. The next figure illustrates the two possible cases.

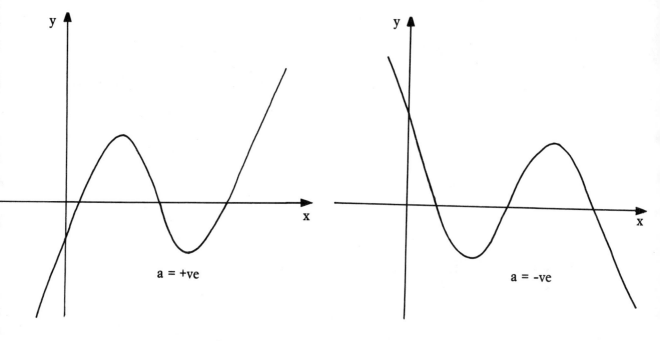

$$y = ax^3 + bx^2 + cx + d$$

Different Forms of Cubic Functions

Drawing Cubics

The procedure for sketching graphs of cubic functions is much the same as that for quadratics, that is, once the location of the roots and the maximum and minimum points have been identified from a table of xy values, drawing the graph is quite straightforward. Once more, the coefficients give a good indication of the character of the curve. Some consequences of the values of the coefficients are given below:

(i) When b, c and d are all zero, the curve passes through the origin which is the only root of the curve, that is, the only place at which $x = 0$.

(ii) When c and d are both zero, the curve has two roots, one of which is zero.

(iii) When d is zero, there will be at least one root at the origin, and a possibility of a further two roots elsewhere.

The following figure illustrates a number of these situations.

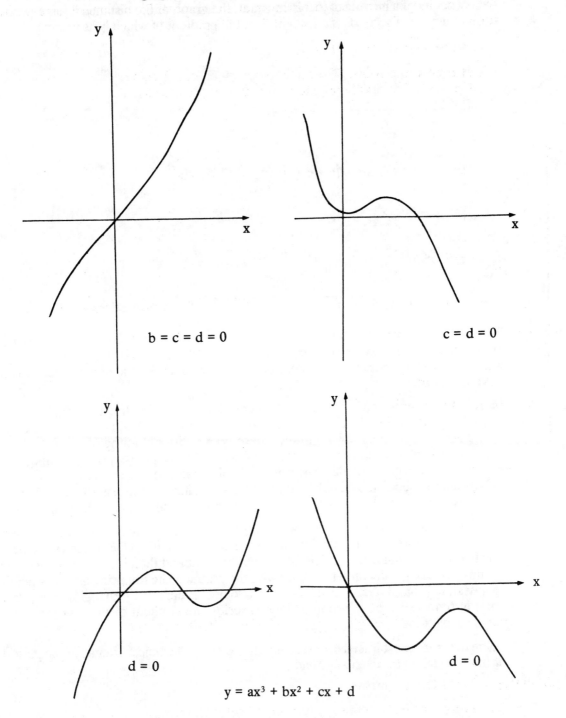

$b = c = d = 0$

$c = d = 0$

$d = 0$

$d = 0$

$$y = ax^3 + bx^2 + cx + d$$

Various graphs of cubic functions

Using Graphs

The types of graphs considered in this chapter, namely Cartesian graphs, are very convenient sources of reference. Other types of graphs, such as those considered in the next chapter, provide useful means of conveying statistical information in a visual manner but, unlike graphs in this chapter, they are not too useful for analytical purposes. A good example of the usefulness of Cartesian graphs is their application in kinematics, the study of the motions of bodies as a function of time.

Time and distance graphs

If the velocity of a moving object is constant, the graph of the distance it has travelled after a number of seconds is a straight line, the gradient of which is its velocity.

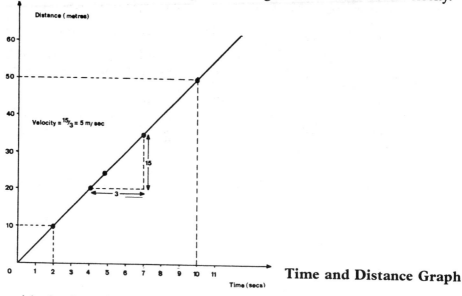

Time and Distance Graph

If we wished to know how far the object had travelled after, say, 10 seconds, we would merely read off the distance corresponding to 10 seconds, that is 50 metres. Similarly, we could easily determine from the graph that it would take the object 2 seconds to travel 10 metres.

Moreover, suppose that the graph had been determined by direct observation, for example by measuring the distance travelled by the object at fixed times (as indicated by the 5 points on the graph). Plotting these points shows that the object must have been travelling at a constant velocity (because the graph is a straight line) and consequently the graph could be used to interpolate between these fixed points to give us information about any time/distance combination, not just those marked. The graph could also be used to extrapolate values beyond the current limits of the graph's axes.

Another example of a time and distance graph is the graph of the motion of an object, such as a ball, thrown vertically into the air. The object initially has a certain velocity which gradually diminishes to zero at its highest point and then increases again under the influence of gravity until it collides with the ground. The following graph of height against time is parabolic. The velocity of the object is constantly changing but, at any point in time, it can be determined by measuring the gradient of the tangent to the curve at that time.

Again the graph can be used to determine the height of the object after any time period, or the time taken to reach any height.

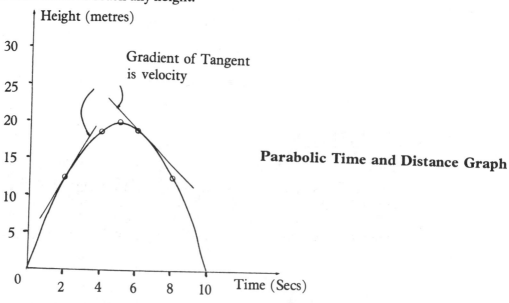

Parabolic Time and Distance Graph

Time and Velocity Graph

When the velocity of an accelerating object is plotted against time, the resulting graph is a straight line. This graph has two interesting properties:

(i) The gradient of the line represents the acceleration of the object.

(ii) The area under the graph between any two values of time represents the distance travelled by the object in that time.

For an object starting at rest and accelerating at 3 metres/second^2, the graph would appear as shown in the following figure. Thus the distance travelled in 4 seconds from rest is shown by the shaded area in the figure. The area, which is triangular, is calculated by applying the formula

$$area = \frac{base \times height}{2} = \frac{4 \times 12}{2} = 24 \; metres$$

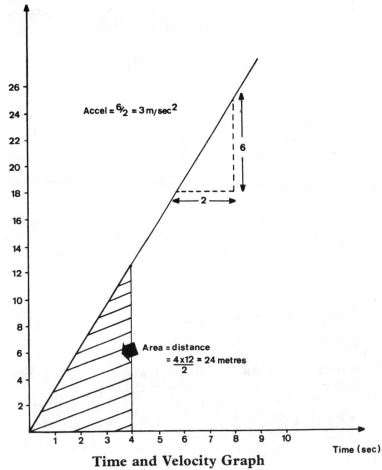

Time and Velocity Graph

The average speed of the object could be calculated by determining the total distance travelled (that is the total area under the graph) and dividing this by the total time taken.

Finding the distance travelled from a time and velocity graph is rather more difficult when the acceleration of the object is not constant; the resulting graph is no longer a single straight line, and may in fact be a curve as illustrated in the following Figure. Here the curve is a quadratic, representing a constant rate of change of acceleration.

The simplest method for determining the area under a curve is to plot the curve on squared graph paper and count the number of squares covered. Complete squares are counted first; part squares greater than a half are counted as whole squares; part squares less than half are ignored. The final count is multiplied by the number of distance units represented by a single square. The following figure illustrates the process.

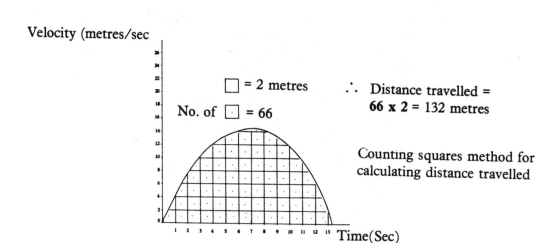

Velocity (metres/sec

☐ = 2 metres   ∴ Distance travelled =
No. of ☐ = 66   66 **x 2** = 132 metres

Counting squares method for
calculating distance travelled

Time(Sec)

Another method, which is more amenable to computer analysis, is called the *trapezoidal rule*. The area under the curve is considered to be a number of thin trapezoids, the area of each of which is found by applying the following formula:

$$area\ of\ strip = \frac{1}{2}d(y_i + y_{i+1})$$

where d is the width of the strip, and

y_i and y_{i+1}

are consecutive values of the function at a distance d apart. (See the following figure). The total area is the sum of all of the trapezoids:

$$A = \frac{1}{2}d(y_0 + y_1) + \frac{1}{2}d(y_1 + y_2) + \ldots + \frac{1}{2}d(y_{n-1} + y_n)$$

or

$$A = \frac{1}{2}d[(y_0 + y_n) + 2(y_1 + y_2 + \ldots + y_{n-1})]$$

Where there are assumed to be x_0 to x_n points on the horizontal axis.

The more trapezoidal strips used, the more accurate is the estimation of the area.

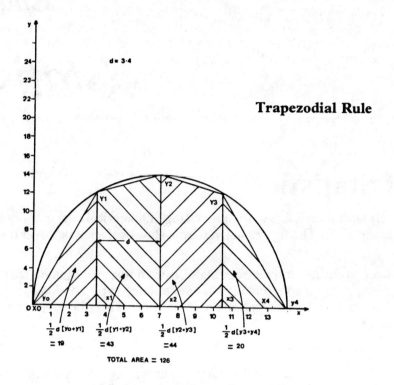

Trapezodial Rule

Chapter 29

Statistics

Types of Statistics

The term *statistics* refers to the processing of numerical data in order to make it more comprehensible. The figures derived from statistical analysis are also known as 'statistics'.

The word 'statistics' derives from 'state', since it was governments that first recognised the urgent need for coherent information relating to population densities, distribution of wealth, political trends, and so on. Broadly speaking, the subject can be divided into two areas:

(a) Descriptive statistics

These deal with methods of describing large amounts of data. Such data is summarised in a wide variety of different forms: as single numbers representing central values or measures of dispersion; as tables of figures; as pictorial representations; as graphs. Whatever the method employed, its function is to make a mass of figures easier to understand by organising it in a way which emphasises any trends within the figures.

(b) Analytical statistics

These deal with methods enabling conclusions to be drawn from the data.

This chapter will consider only descriptive statistics since analytical statistics generally involves mathematical techniques beyond the scope of this book.

Statistics are quoted in all manners of ways in everyday life:

"Megadent can reduce tooth decay by up to 30%"
"Smoking causes 200 deaths per day"
"Profits rose by 50% last year"
"The average salary of teachers is £8563·79"

The student of statistics must be able to consider critically, statements such as those above by asking such questions as:

"What is the source of this information?"
"What (if anything) is being left unsaid?"
"How has the data been obtained?"
"What evidence is there for making this statement?"
"Is it intended to be misleading?"
"What does it actually mean?"

Hopefully, this chapter provides a framework for producing and evaluating simple statistical quantities, so that they can be viewed intelligently and produced without ambiguity.

Pictorial Representations

Suppose that a certain college is divided into four faculties and it is necessary to show pictorially the relative number of students in each faculty for particular academic years. Table below shows the figures to be used.

Table of Students arranged by Faculty

FACULTY	NO. OF STUDENTS			
	1982	1983	1984	1985
Business Studies	889	913	1076	1253
Humanities	501	626	715	836
Science	416	481	263	352
Technology	387	412	448	479
TOTAL	2193	2435	2502	2920

This data could be represented diagrammatically in a number of forms,

- Pictogram
- Pie Chart
- Bar Chart
- Graph

Many software packages are available to take the hard work out of producing the last three types of diagrams; integrated packages (explained in Chapter 11) such as Framework, Lotus 123 and Supercalc 3 all will produce such diagrams from data stored in spreadsheet form. However, since such programs may not be available, the construction of these diagrams will be explained.

Pictograms

This form of presentation involves the use of pictures to represent a set of figures. For example, the student numbers in the four faculties for 1985 could be shown as follows:

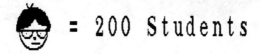

Here the same picture, representing a number of students, is shown repeatedly; the values of the figure for each faculty is indicated by the number of pictures shown.

An alternative method sometimes employed is to represent a number by the size of the picture used:

Growth of Business Studies

1982

1985

This second type of representation, however, can easily be very misleading. If the height of the picture is made approximately proportional to the quantity being represented, then the width of the picture will probably be increased by a corresponding amount to make it look right. However, this produces an increase in area and gives a false impression to the eye. For example, if the figure being represented doubles, then the area will look disproportionately large. Even if great care is taken in making the area of the pictures relatively accurate representations of the quantities, it is still quite difficult to interpret such diagrams, and they are best avoided altogether.

Pictograms which are drawn well and which are not misleading can be very effective in presenting data in a non-technical way. The pictures immediately arrest the attention of the observer and at the same time impart the required information.

Pie Charts

A pie chart is a circle divided into segments, looking rather like a pie or cake cut into slices - hence its name. The area of each segment is proportional to the size of the figure represented, and the complete 'pie' represents the overall total of all the component parts. It is therefore a convenient way of illustrating the sizes of component quantities in relation to each other and to the overall total. The student numbers for 1982 could be shown in pie chart form as follows:

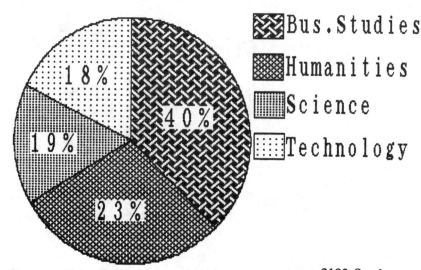

2193 Students
1982 Student numbers

The pie chart is constructed as follows:

(i) Find the overall figure to be represented by the full circle by totalling the component figures: $889 + 501 + 416 + 387 = 2193$.

(ii) Since the area of a segment depends on the angle that it makes at the centre of the circle, each figure is used to determine the angle required for its segment of the chart:

889 *requires an angle of* $\dfrac{889}{2193} \times 360 = 146°$ *approximately.*

501 *requires an angle of* $\dfrac{501}{2193} \times 360 = 82°$ *approximately.*

416 *requires an angle of* $\dfrac{416}{2193} \times 360 = 68°$ *approximately.*

387 *requires an angle of* $\dfrac{387}{2193} \times 360 = 64°$ *approximately.*

Total $= 360°$

(iii) Draw a circle and use a protractor to divide the circle into the appropriately sized segments.

(iv) Indicate the percentage contribution that each segment makes to the whole 'pie', label each sector and give the whole diagram a title.

(v) Where appropriate, state the source of the data.

In order to compare the student figures for the two years, 1982 and 1985 for instance, the relative size of the circles can be used to reflect the growth in numbers, as shown in the figure below.

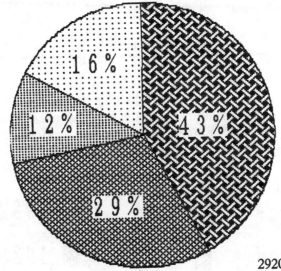

2920 Students
1985 Student Numbers

However, great care must be taken to ensure that the *areas* of the circles represent the total figures and not their radii or diameters. The figure shows the two circles correctly proportioned. If r1 represents the radius of the circle used for representing the student numbers for 1982, and r2 is used for the radius of the circle for 1985, then the relationship between r1 and r2 is given by

$$\frac{\pi r1^2}{\pi r2^2} = \frac{2193}{2920}$$

In other words, the ratio between the areas of the first circle of radius r1 and the second circle of radius r2 is the same as the ratio between student numbers for 1982 and 1985.

When r2 is made the subject of the formula, we have

$$r2 = r1\sqrt{\frac{2920}{2193}}$$

Thus, for r1 = 4 units,

$$r2 = 4 \times \sqrt{\frac{2920}{2193}} = 4 \times \sqrt{1\cdot33} = 4 \times 1\cdot15 = 4\cdot62 \text{ units}$$

Bar Charts

A basic bar chart, such as that shown in the figure below for 1982 student numbers, consists of a series of bars with lengths proportional to the quantities they represent. The scale of the vertical axis in the diagram is in units of number of students and the horizontal axis is labelled with abbreviations for the four faculties.

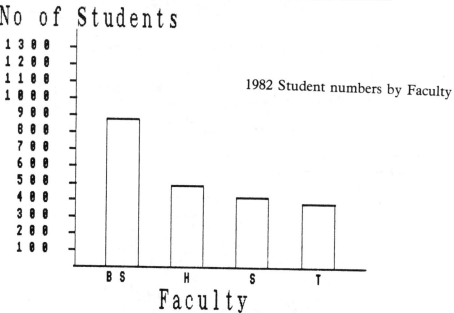

There are numerous variations of the basic bar chart, the commonest of which is the Multiple Bar Chart shown in the figure below. Here, the figures for two years are represented side by side for each faculty.

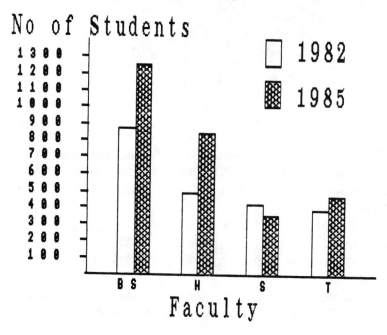

Bar charts are very useful for depicting a series of changes in the figures of interest. They are generally preferable to pictograms because they are easier to construct and they can represent data more accurately. Multiple bar charts are not recommended for more than four sets of figures. More than this number of adjacent components detracts from the clarity and usefulness of the diagram.

Graphs

Again referring to the student numbers given earlier, suppose it was required to compare the way that student numbers changed over the four years, for the faculties of Business Studies and Science. One possible way to do this would be to use a Multiple Bar Chart with the horizontal axis labelled with the four years 1982-85. Two adjacent bars could be used for the faculty figures for each year and the diagram would look much the same as in the previous figure.

However, the figures could be illustrated in a more striking manner by means of a graph such as that shown below.

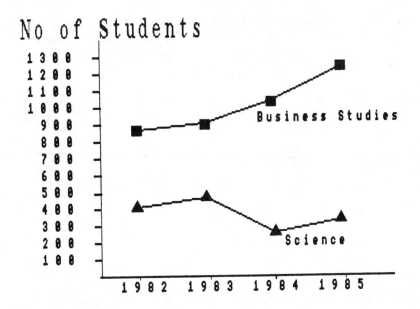

The lines joining the points marked with the square and triangle symbols help to emphasise trends, so that it is quite easy to see that Business Studies student numbers are increasing whereas those of Science are declining. It should be noted, however, with this particular type of diagram, that using the connecting lines to interpolate intermediate values is not possible: the horizontal scale does not represent a continuous quantity with meaningful values between those marked.

The construction and use of graphs in general have already been discussed in Chapter 28, but it is appropriate at this point to make some observations about the presentation of the type of graph used in this current context.

(i) The choice of horizontal scale can greatly affect the visual impression that is given. Though the next two figures represent the same data, by compressing the horizontal scale in the right hand figure the graph appears much more dramatic. The left hand figure conveys an accurate impression of the data whereas the right hand figure distorts it.

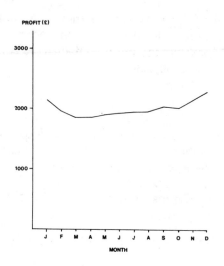

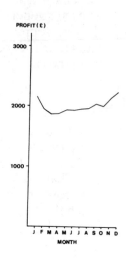

(ii) The vertical scale should always start at zero, again to avoid giving the wrong impression. In the next figure (below left) the vertical scale starts at a point close to the range covered by the figures, and the resulting graph further dramatises the data.

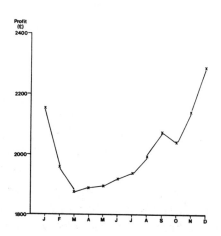

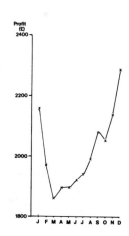

When the vertical scale covers only the range that the data spans and the horizontal scale is compressed, the data becomes totally distorted, as illustrated in the figure above right.

It is difficult to believe that all the four previous figures are based on exactly the same data.

(iii) Quote the source of the data so that the actual figures used can be checked if required.

Frequency Distributions

The table below shows the mileages recorded by a number of refuse disposal vehicles in one week.

Mileages Recorded by Refuse Disposal Vehicles

482	502	466	408	486	440	470	447	413	451	410	430
469	438	452	459	455	473	423	436	412	403	493	436
471	498	450	421	482	440	442	474	407	448	444	485
505	515	500	462	460	476	472	454	451	438	457	446
453	453	508	475	418	465	450	447	477	436	464	453
415	511	430	457	490	447	433	416	419	460	428	434
420	443	456	432	425	497	459	449	439	509	483	502
424	421	413	441	458	438	444	445	435	468	430	442
455	452	479	481	468	435	462	478	463	498	494	489
495	407	462	432	424	451	426	433	474	431	471	488

A casual examination of this set of figures is unlikely to reveal anything other than the fact that most of the figures are in the 400's with an occasional one in the 500's. From a table in this form it would be very difficult to determine any patterns present in the data. For instance, are the numbers evenly distributed, or is there a certain small range containing a preponderance of figures compared to other similar ranges?

The statistical techniques considered in this part of the chapter allow raw data such as that in the above table to be summarised and presented in a form which facilitates identification of trends and allows the significance of the figures to be grasped. It should be noted, however, that as the crude data is converted into more convenient forms of representation, the fine details within the data begin to be lost.

Ungrouped Frequency Distributions

A first step in the analysis of the data in the table could be to sort the figures into ascending order of magnitude and at the same time to note the number of times any figures are repeated. The next table has been produced in this manner and it is termed an *ungrouped frequency distribution*. The table consists of a list of every unique mileage with its *frequency* of occurrence, that is, the number of times it occurred in the original table.

Ungrouped Frequency Distribution

Mileage	Freq	Mileage	Freq	Mileage	Freq	Mileage	Freq
403	1	434	1	456	1	479	1
407	2	435	2	457	2	481	1
408	1	436	3	458	1	482	2
410	1	438	3	459	2	483	1
412	1	439	1	460	2	485	1
413	2	440	2	462	3	486	1
415	1	441	1	463	1	488	1
416	1	442	2	464	1	489	1
418	1	443	1	465	1	490	1
419	1	444	2	466	1	493	1
420	1	445	1	468	2	494	1
421	2	446	1	469	1	495	1
423	1	447	3	470	1	497	1
424	2	448	1	471	2	498	2
425	1	449	1	472	1	500	1
426	1	450	2	473	1	502	2
428	1	451	3	474	2	505	1
430	3	5	2	475	1	508	1
431	1	453	3	476	1	509	1
432	2	454	1	477	1	511	1
433	2	455	2	478	1	515	1

Notice that the sum of the frequencies is equal to the number of items in the original table, that is,

$$\sum f = 120$$

Grouped Frequency Distribution

Though the data has now been organised, there are still too many numbers for the mind to be able to grasp the information hidden within them. Therefore the next step is to simplify the presentation of the data even further. At this stage, in the production of a *grouped frequency distribution*, the crude data is replaced by a set of groups which split the mileages into a number of small ranges called *classes*. The following table is an example of a grouped frequency distribution based on the ungrouped frequency distribution shown in the previous table.

Grouped Frequency Distribution

Mileages	Frequency
400 to under 420	12
420 to under 440	27
440 to under 460	34
460 to under 480	24
480 to under 500	15
500 to under 520	8
	___
TOTAL	**120**
	___

The overall range of mileages, 403 to 515, has been split into six classes each covering an equal sub-range of the total range of values. Notice that the class limits, that is the boundary values of the classes, do not overlap, nor are there any gaps between them; these are important characteristics of grouped frequency distributions.

The effect of grouping data in this way is to allow patterns to be detected more easily. For instance, it is now clear that most of the figures cluster in and around the '440 to under 460' class. The cost of being able to extract this piece of information is loss of the exact details of the raw data; a grouped frequency distribution summarises the crude data. Thus any further information deduced or calculated from this grouped frequency distribution can only be approximate.

Choice of Classes

The construction of a grouped frequency distribution will always involve making decisions regarding the number and size of classes to be used. Though these choices will depend on individual circumstances to a large extent, the following guidelines should be noted:

(i) Class intervals should be equal wherever possible.

(ii) Restrict the number of classes to between ten and twenty; too many or too few classes will obscure information.

(iii) Classes should be chosen such that occurrences within the intervals are mainly grouped about the mid-point of the classes in order that calculations based on the distribution can be made as accurately as possible. Examination of the ungrouped frequency distribution should highlight any tendencies of figures to cluster at regular intervals over the range of values considered.

(iv) Class intervals of 5, 10 or multiples of 10 are easier to work with than intervals such as 7 or 11 (manually, that is: it is not a problem when using a computer package for statistical analysis).

Cumulative Frequency Distributions

The next table contains an additional two columns to the data in the previous table. The entries in the column labelled "Cumulative Frequency" have been calculated by keeping a running total of the frequencies given in the adjacent column. As expected, the final entry shows that the sum of all the frequencies is 120. The final column shows the same accumulated figures as percentages of the total number of figures.

This new table allows further observations to be made regarding the data being examined. For example, the table now shows that 80·8% of the vehicles travelled less than 480 miles; 6·7% (100 − 93·3) of the vehicles travelled more than 500 miles; 20% (80·8 − 60·8) of the vehicles travelled between 440 and 480 miles.

'LESS THAN' CUMULATIVE FREQUENCY DISTRIBUTION

Mileages	Frequency	Cumulative Frequency	Cumulative Percentage
400 to under 420	12	12	10.0
420 to under 440	27	39	32.5
440 to under 460	34	73	60.8
460 to under 480	24	97	80.8
480 to under 500	15	112	93.3
500 to under 520	8	120	100.0
TOTAL	120		

Because the figures have been accumulated from the lowest class to the highest, this table is called a 'less than' cumulative frequency distribution. The next table shows a 'more than' cumulative frequency distribution in which the frequencies have been accumulated in reverse order.

'MORE THAN' CUMULATIVE FREQUENCY DISTRIBUTION

Mileages	Frequency	Cumulative Frequency	Cumulative Percentage
400 to under 420	12	120	100.0
420 to under 440	27	108	90.0
440 to under 460	34	81	67.5
460 to under 480	24	47	39.2
480 to under 500	15	23	19.2
500 to under 520	8	8	6.7
TOTAL	120		

Hence, the table shows directly that 90% of the vehicles travelled more than 420 miles and 6·7% travelled more than 500 miles. Simple calculations also allow 'less than' figures to be derived, just as 'more than' figures can be calculated from the 'less than' cumulative frequency distribution.

Histograms

When the data in a grouped frequency distribution is presented diagrammatically, the resulting representation is called a *histogram*. The class groupings are used to label the horizontal axis, and the frequency (either as an actual figure or as a percentage of the total number of figures) is used for the vertical axis. The next figure shows the grouped frequency distribution.

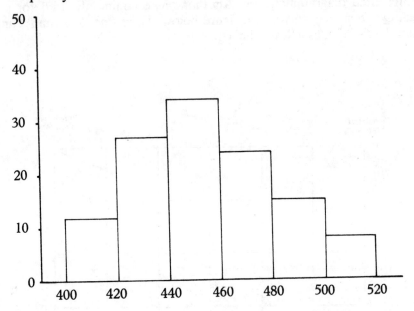

A histogram essentially consists of vertically aligned rectangles in which:

    (i) The widths represent the class intervals.

    (ii) The heights represent the frequencies.

The area of a rectangle in a histogram is directly proportional to the quantity that it represents. This is the distinction between a histogram and a bar chart which looks somewhat similar. Where a histogram has unequal class intervals, as illustrated in the next figure, great care must be taken to ensure that the areas under the rectangles are still proportioned correctly.

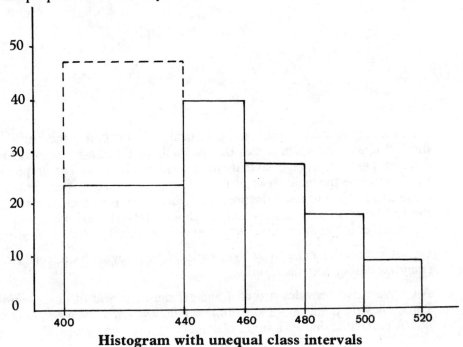

Histogram with unequal class intervals

Notice that the first class, representing 39 occurrences, being twice as wide as the other class intervals, is drawn half height. The dotted line shows the result of drawing it incorrectly: the diagram would be seriously in error.

Ogives

Ogive is the name given to the graph obtained when a cumulative frequency distribution is represented diagrammatically. Another name commonly used for an ogive is a *cumulative frequency curve*. The figure below shows one 'less than' cumulative frequency distribution as a 'less than' ogive.

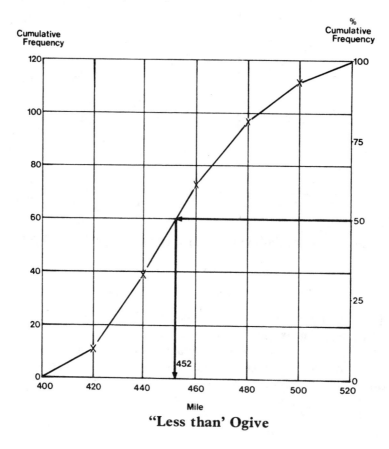

"Less than' Ogive

Note that ogives start at zero on the vertical scale and end at the outside class limit of the last class. The vertical axis on the right of the diagram gives the cumulative frequency as a percentage, so that either scale may be used. The graph may be used in the same way as the table on which it is based. Thus, approximately 50% of the mileages are less than 452 miles (see the previous figure). This is an approximate figure because the 50% point does not correspond exactly with a class boundary; it is not clear whether the mileages in the interval 440 to under 460 are evenly distributed over the interval.

Ogives may also be of the 'more than' variety when they are based on the corresponding cumulative frequency distribution.

An ogive curve provides a useful and efficient method of determining *percentiles*. Percentiles are points in the distribution below which a given percentage of the total lies. A percentile divides a set of observations into two groups. For example, using a 'less than' ogive, 25% of the mileages are below the 25 percentile (that is below 434 miles approximately). Commonly used percentiles are known as *quartiles*:

the 25th percentile is the first quartile;
the 50th percentile is the second quartile (also known as the *median*);
the 75th percentile is the third quartile.

Percentiles are a very useful way of expressing such statistics as "50% of the individual wealth of the U.K. is in the hands of 5% of the population".

Measures of Location

Measures of location, or measures of central value, are average values. The most common types of averages are

(i) The *Arithmetic Mean* (or just *mean*).

(ii) The *Median*.

(iii) The *Mode*.

Each one of these measures attempts to represent a collection of figures with one single figure, though in fact each really is only representative of one aspect of the figures. They all may be determined exactly from ungrouped data, or approximately from grouped data. The following sections summarise the methods of calculation and the significance of each average.

In the following pages reference will be made to the data in the ungrouped frequency distribution shown in the table below.

Children in Mean Street

House Number	1	2	3	4	5	6	7	8	9	10	11	12	13	14	15	16	17	18	19
Number of Children	0	0	0	0	0	0	1	1	1	1	2	2	2	2	3	3	4	5	6

The following notation will be used:

Σ = sum of

$\bar{x}$ = mean value

x_i = single value

n = number of values

f = frequency

Mean

Calculation of the mean

(a)   Ungrouped data.

(i) add together all the values;

(ii) divide by the number of values.

The mathematical notation for the calculation is

$$\bar{x} = \frac{\sum x_i}{n} \qquad i = 1,....,n$$

Using the values in the table above this gives

$$\bar{x} = \frac{33}{19} = 1 \cdot 74 \text{ approx.}$$

(b)   Grouped frequency distribution.

(i) multiply each class mid point by the class frequency;

(ii) add these values together;

(iii) divide by the sum of the frequencies.

The mathematical notation for the calculation is

$$\bar{x} = \frac{\sum (f \times Class\ mid-point)}{\sum f}$$

Using the values in the table on page 385 this gives

$$\bar{x} = \frac{12 \times 410 + 27 \times 430 + 34 \times 450 + 24 \times 470 + 15 \times 490 + 8 \times 510}{120}$$

$$\bar{x} = 454 \cdot 5$$

Significance of the mean

The arithmetic mean indicates what value each item would have if the total of all values were shared out equally. If it is wished to know the result that would follow from an equal distribution of something (consumption of beer per head, for instance) the mean is the most suitable measure.

Features of the mean

- makes use of every value in the distribution;
- can be distorted by extreme values;
- can be used for further mathematical processing;
- may result in an impossible figure (1 · 74 children);
- best known of all the averages.

Median

Calculation of the median

    (a)   Ungrouped Data.

        (i) arrange the data into ascending order of magnitude;

        (ii) locate the middle term - this is the median. (If there are an even number of numbers and there is no middle term then the nearest to the mid-point on either side will do)

The median item in the Mean Street example is the 10th one and the value of the median is therefore 1. In the mileages example, the middle item is the 60th and the median value is 452 miles.

    (b)   Grouped frequency distribution.

        (i) produce the equivalent ogive;

        (ii) read off the value of the 2nd quartile - this gives the median value. (See the 'less than' ogive on page 388)

Significance of the median

The median is merely the value of the middle term when the data is arranged into ascending order of magnitude. Consequently there will be as many terms above it as below it. If a person interested in a job with a firm wanted some idea of the salary to expect, he or she might use the median salary as a guide.

Features of the median.

- uses only one value in the distribution;
- cannot be used for further mathematical processing;
- it is always an actual value occurring in the distribution;
- it can be computed from incomplete data.

Mode

Calculation of the mode

The mode is usually derived from an ungrouped frequency distribution by determining the value which occurs most frequently. In Mean Street, the value occurring most frequently is 0 children. In the table on page 384 showing the ungrouped frequency distribution there are several modes: each mileage which occurs three times is a mode of the distribution of mileages.

Significance of the mode

As the mode is the value that occurs most frequently, it represents the typical item. It is this form of average that is implied by such expressions as 'the average person' or 'the average holiday'.

Features of the mode

- it is an actual value;
- it cannot be used for further mathematical processing.

Dispersion

Quoting an average value, such as the mean, is an attempt to describe a distribution figure by a single representative number. Such averages, however, suffer from the disadvantage that they give no indication of the spread, or *dispersion*, of the figures represented. For example, the following two sets of numbers have identical means but the range of values is much greater in the first case than the second:

$$10 \quad 20 \quad 30 \qquad \text{mean value} = 20$$
$$18 \quad 20 \quad 22 \qquad \text{mean value} = 20$$

The next figure further illustrates how two distributions with the same mean value can have greatly different distributions.

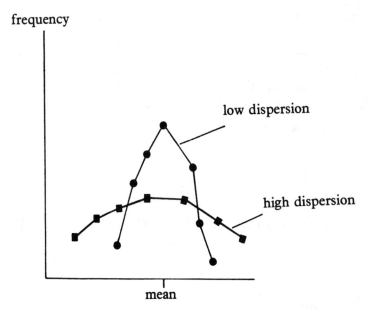

It is therefore also desirable to be able to describe the dispersion of data in a distribution with just a single figure. Four such measures will be described. They are

    (a) the *range*;

    (b) the *interquartile range*;

    (c) the *mean deviation*;

    (d) the *standard deviation.*

Range

The *range* is merely the difference between the highest and the lowest values:

Range = highest value − lowest value.

The range of the distribution of mileages given in the ungrouped frequency distribution table on page 384 is given by

Range = 515 − 403 = 112 miles.

Unfortunately the range, like the mean, is influenced by extreme values. If the majority of the figures in the distribution cluster around a certain value, but there are a small number having extreme values, then the range does not provide a very accurate measure of the dispersion of the majority of the distribution. For example, if in the ungrouped frequency distribution table one of the mileages had been 112 miles, then the range would be 515 − 112 = 403 miles, more than three times the previous figure, even though only one figure had changed.

Interquartile range

The disadvantage with the range as a measure of dispersion, as identified above, can be overcome to some degree by ignoring the extreme high and low values so that the measure of dispersion is representative of the majority of the distribution. One method of doing this is to use the values at the lower limit of the 3rd quartile and the upper limit of the 1st quartile as the values from which the range is calculated.

These figures give the *interquartile range*. For example, with reference to the 'less than' ogive, these figures are as follows:

Lower limit of 3rd Quartile (75th percentile) = 476
Upper limit of 1st Quartile (25th percentile) = 434
Interquartile range = 476 − 434 = 42 miles

Another measure of dispersion which is sometimes useful is the *semi-interquartile range* which is found by dividing the interquartile range by two. Another name for this latter measure of dispersion is the *quartile deviation*.

The chief disadvantages of these measures of dispersion are that they still are unable to take into account any degree of clustering in the distribution, and they do not use all of the values in the distribution.

Mean Deviation

Another method of measuring dispersion is to find the deviations of all the items from the average, ignore their signs, and find the arithmetic mean of their magnitude. This is known as the *mean deviation*.

As an example, suppose it is required to find the mean deviation of the following set of numbers:

27	33	36	37	39	39	40	44	50	55

(i) Sum of numbers = 400

(ii) Mean value

$$= \frac{400}{10} = 40$$

(iii) Deviation from mean :

−13	−7	−4	−3	−1	−1	0	4	10	15

(iv) Sum of deviations (ignoring sign) = 58

(v) Mean deviation

$$= \frac{58}{10} = 5 \cdot 8$$

The mean deviation of the numbers is $5 \cdot 8$.

Standard deviation

The Greek letter σ is universally adopted to represent standard deviation. The formula for standard deviation is as follows:

$$\text{Standard deviation } (\sigma) = \sqrt{\frac{\Sigma(x - \bar{x})^2}{n}}$$

or, where the figures come from an ungrouped frequency distribution,

$$\sigma = \sqrt{\frac{\Sigma f(x - \bar{x})^2}{\Sigma f}}$$

Setting out the calculation in the form of a table, and using the figures above for the mean deviation calculation, the calculation may be performed as follows:

x	$(x - \bar{x})$	$(x - \bar{x})^2$
27	-13	169
33	-7	49
36	-4	16
37	-3	9
39	-1	1
39	-1	1
40	0	0
44	4	16
50	10	100
55	15	225
$\Sigma x = 400$		$\Sigma(x - \bar{x})^2 = 586$

Difference from Average of 40 [handwritten annotation]

$$\text{Standard deviation } (\sigma) = \sqrt{\frac{(x - \bar{x})^2}{n}} = \sqrt{\frac{586}{10}} = 7 \cdot 655$$

Note that by squaring the difference between the mean and a value, the minus signs disappear.

To summarise, the steps involved in calculating the standard deviation of a distribution are as follows:

(i) Calculate the arithmetic mean.

(ii) Subtract the mean from each value.

(iii) Square each value in (ii).

(iv) Find the sum of all the values in (iii).

(v) Divide by the number of numbers.

(vi) Take the square root of the result of (v).

Where the standard deviation is to be calculated from an ungrouped frequency distribution, in step (ii) the result would be multiplied by the frequency of the value, and in step (v) the sum of the frequencies would be used as the divisor.

Reference is frequently made to the *variance* of a distribution. This is the square of the standard deviation. In the example immediately above, the variance of the distribution is given by

$$\text{Variance} = (\text{standard deviation})^2 = 58 \cdot 6$$

and conversely,

$$\text{Standard deviation} = \sqrt{\text{variance}} = \sqrt{58 \cdot 6} = 7 \cdot 655$$

Comparison of measures of dispersion

Of the measures of dispersion considered in this section, the *standard deviation* is the most important, but also the most difficult to comprehend. Basically, the standard deviation provides a measure of the likelihood of any random value from the distribution being close to the arithmetic mean of the distribution.

The greater the measure of deviation, the less likely it is that any value chosen at random will be the mean value.

Its importance lies chiefly in the considerable use made of it in analytical statistics, and a familiarity with it is crucial to making progress in more advanced statistical techniques.

The *range* is very easy to calculate but is sensitive to extreme values, and it does not take into account all of the figures or give any indication of the clustering of data. It is not generally a very reliable or accurate measure of dispersion.

The *interquartile range* also has the disadvantage that only two values from the distribution are used in its calculation, but it is less affected by extreme values. It is useful when the distribution is evenly distributed except for a number of extreme values.

The *mean deviation* has the advantage of using all of the figures in the distribution and is a measure of how far, on average, the values in the distribution are dispersed from the mean value. Its chief disadvantage is that it is not particularly well suited to algebraic treatment.

If the distribution of values is fairly symmetrical about the mean, bell shaped and the number of items is large, (that is, it is more or less what is known as a *normal distribution* as shown in the next figure), then the following relations are approximately true:

$$\text{Quartile deviation} = \frac{2}{3} \text{ standard deviation, and}$$

$$\text{Mean deviation} = \frac{4}{5} \text{ standard deviation.}$$

Thus, for approximately normal distributions (which are of great importance in analytical statistics), the quartile and mean deviations may be used to approximate the standard deviation.

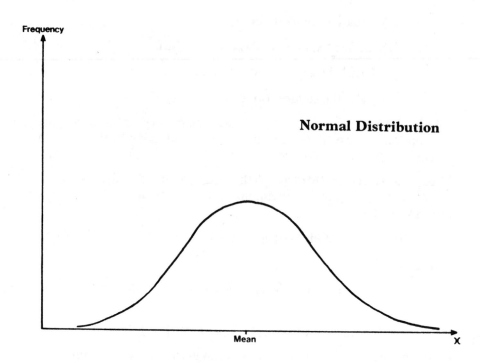

Statistics Packages

Because of the usefulness of statistical analysis in such a wide variety of disciplines - in business, medicine, social sciences and many others - there are now a great number of computer programs available to ease the amount of laborious (and error-prone) work involved in statistical analysis. Many of these packages are subject orientated (for example, SPSS - Statistical Package for Social Sciences) offering facilities relevant to the subject, while others are purely general purpose.

Many statistics packages will generate diagrams such as pie charts and bar charts automatically. Most of the well known integrated packages and spreadsheets contain functions to calculate means and standard deviations and also to produce statistical diagrams from data entered.

When using such packages, however, it is vital that the user is aware of the theory on which the package operates, particularly when the package is being used for analytical statistics. When considering the use or purchase of a program for statistical analysis, a vital factor is the quality and detail of the documentation provided; with good documentation the user can be confident about the interpretation of the statistical analysis undertaken.

Assignment

The Unix Explosion

Developed by Bell Laboratories of the USA around 1970 for use on minicomputers, the Unix operating system has evolved into a multi-user system for 16-bit business microcomputers. The developers of Unix pioneered the concept of operating system portability - the capability of operating on various types of computers - by writing the operating system in a high-level language called 'C', also developed by Bell Laboratories.

The Unix operating system is never actually sold to its users - they must buy a licence from Bell in order to use it. The table below of the predicted annual distribution of new Unix licences over six years shows how the popularity of Unix is rapidly increasing, particularly for microcomputers.

Annual Distribution of New Unix Licences

	1981	1982	1983	1984	1985	1986
Mainframes	9	20	115	248	325	370
Minicomputers	1310	2200	3375	5050	6710	7690
Microcomputers	1320	23,710	110,600	269,800	414,800	495,500

Source: BYTE October 1986

Tasks

1. By means of a pictogram, a bar chart and a pie chart, show the estimated relative usage of Unix on the different types of systems for 1986.

2. Use graphs to show the estimated increase in usage of Unix over the six years on the different types of systems.

3. Illustrate the cumulative use of Unix for each type of system over the six years, and for the total number of users irrespective of the type of computer system.

Developmental Task

Make sure that you understand what is meant by the term 'operating system' and try and find out what, if anything, makes the Unix system different from other operating systems for microcomputers (such as CP/M or MS-DOS).

Chapter 30

Accounting

This chapter will introduce a number of simple accounting concepts which are not only important in financial management of business organizations but which are also suitable for computerization. The chapter does not intend to be a 'crash' course in accountancy as this would be beyond the scope of this text. It does however seek to explain in simple terms the reasons why each process takes place and the procedural steps involved.

The Purpose of Accounting

Accountancy has three main functions:

1. The recording of financial information.

2. The provision of management information.

3. The 'stewardship' function.

Each of these will be briefly explained.

The Recording of Financial Information

The accountancy function has developed from the need of the organization to keep accurate records. This process is referred to quite simply as *book-keeping*. Such records must be kept in a suitable format so that they can be interpreted and analysed. (It is this stage of the process which is referred to as *accountancy*). The financial statements produced are the means by which the performance of the organization can be assessed by its management.

Other people will also wish to see that accurate financial records have been kept. The Inland Revenue, Customs and Excise (who administer the VAT system), bank managers and other providers of finance may require sight of the organization's records. Thus it is essential that the system used to maintain the records of the organisation is comprehensive, accurate and can be interpreted not only by the organization's own managers but also by outsiders. A computerized system which ensures that these requirements are met is therefore of tremendous benefit to an organization.

The Provision of Management Information

The second of the accounting functions is the provision of information for management. As a basic concept this is as true for the sole trader as it is for the multi-national corporation. Both must be managed and both require appropriate and accurate financial information which will guide them in their decision making. The information that they require must enable them to:

(a) establish and monitor the financial targets of the organisation;

(b) control income and expenditure within the organisation.

The type of accounting is usually known as cost and management accounting and is concerned with the preparation of budgets for each part of the organisation and the costing of its operations. As we see later in this chapter there is an increasing application of computerized systems in this area.

The Stewardship Function of Accounting

The final function of accounting is to allow an assessment of the 'stewardship' of an organization. By this it is meant that it should provide a method by which the owners of the organization can assess how effectively and efficiently the managers of the business are performing their task. Clearly this role is most important in organizations in which ownership (the shareholders) is separated from control (the management) for in such circumstances the individual shareholder will not wish to be involved or informed of the day-to-day operations of the business. it will be sufficient for the managers to provide an honest and accurate picture of the performance of the organization over a trading period such as six months or a year to satisfy the owners. This is provided in the form of a balance sheet, profit and loss account and other financial statements. Obviously it will be necessary to have such statements verified and it is at this stage that the accountancy function takes on the role of audit. Here an outside independent auditor will confirm the accounts and so ensure their accuracy.

Other individuals and organizations outside the business will also wish to be made aware of the organization's performance. Therefore the Inland Revenue and the Customs and Excise Department have the right to inspect an organization's financial records. Furthermore all limited companies must also provide sets of their accounts to the Companies Registrar which may then be examined by any member of the general public.

All three of these functions can be facilitated by the use of computerized systems. For such systems introduce accuracy, efficiency and the ability to handle vast amounts of data. The ease with which records can be compared, collated and analysed allows a considerable amount of information to be generated. No large organization in the country performs its financial management and accountancy function without the use of computers. Increasingly even the smallest business is recognising the same benefits.

Accountancy Applications

The remainder of this chapter will concentrate on the evaluation of a number of accountancy applications which are in widespread use in many organisations. These are:

1. Order Processing and Invoicing.

2. Sales Ledger Systems.

3. Purchases and Creditors Systems.

4. Purchase Ledger Systems.

5. Nominal or General Ledger Systems.

6. Stock Control.

7. Costing Systems.

8. Financial Planning Systems.

Order Processing and Invoicing

This procedure is fundamental to the operation of any business involved in trading operations. It involves two separate but inter-related activities. The first activity commences when the organization receives an order from a customer. It is essential that in whatever form the order is received whether it is by psot, telephone, verbally or by the use of a computer link, that all the relevant details are immediately recorded. These relevant details include:

  (i) the date that the order is received;

  (ii) the customer's name, address and reference;

  (iii) the customer's order number;

  (iv) a description of the goods required including any necessary reference numbers;

  (v) the quantity of goods ordered;

  (vi) the price per item excluding VAT;

  (vii) the total order value excluding VAT;

  (viii) any discount which is offered to the customer;

  (ix) the VAT which must be added to the price;

  (x) the total order value including VAT;

  (xi) the delivery date required.

This provides the organization with a complete record of each order received and allows the generation of an invoice number which will be the supplier's key reference. If this information is entered into a computerized system it will enable the creation of a database containing all orders identified by the customer and by the item to be supplied. It can also link to the sales ledger system discussed in the next section.

The second stage in the process is the production of an invoice. This is the supplier organization's bill to the customer. This may be sent with the goods when they are supplied or it may be sent separately to the customer. In addition to the details specified above the invoice will also include:

  (i) a date by which the payment should be made (usually 30, 60 or 90 days depending on the length of credit which is being extended to the customer);

  (ii) any other relevant details relating to payment conditions (such as provision for payment by instalments).

As there are many different ways in which organizations process orders and invoices it is important that the system employed suits the organization's particular requirements. There are many packages available for use on a variety of types of computer and different kinds of business may have specific requirements in this respect. If a suitable package cannot be purchased *off the shelf* the supplier may have to develop its own program which satisfies its needs and links to the other systems it operates.

Sales Ledger

This is the organization's record of its current trading position with its customers and clients. As an order is received and processed through the sales order system it is added to the sales ledger. This ledger will be updated daily and will indicate when payment has yet to be received for a completed order. As payments are received they should be checked against the relevant invoice and if they tally, the customer's outstanding account can be credited. As each outstanding invoice is paid it can be removed from the *live* file and placed on record for further analysis. This will indicate the level of sales in specific trading periods or the amount of business transacted with a particular customer.

The sales ledger if it is computerized should provide the following information:

  (i) a record of all outstanding unpaid invoices;

(ii) the total amount owing to the organization at any one time;

(iii) the amount owed by each customer;

(iv) the length of time each debt has been outstanding.

Such information is vital to any organization as only by being aware of how much it is owed can decisions be made regarding future expenditure plans.

The amount owed by individual customers is also important for each will normally be allocated a *credit limit* and once this has been exceeded the supplier must carefully consider whether or not future orders should be met until payment for previous orders has been made.

The organization also needs to be aware of the *age* of debtors. In other words how long the money has been owed. As was mentioned in the previous section it is normal to allow some period of business credit but it is necessary to remind customers that payment is now due by sending a statement which specifies how much is owed, the orders to which this relates and a request for payment.

A computerized sales ledger system is capable of providing all such information and is often able automatically to produce statements at appropriate intervals. Some systems even produce statements which are increasingly strongly worded if payment is

The sales ledger system should also be capable of dealing with credit notes which the organization may have to raise if the goods it has supplied are faulty or in some way unacceptable to the customer. The customer will be credited with the appropriate amount which may reduce its current level of debt or be set against the cost of future orders.

Purchases and Creditors Systems

These systems basically follow exactly the same procedures as the order processing system except that they relate to the organization's own purchase of goods and supplies. A computerized system will record all orders which the organization places and identify the following details:

(i) the purchase order number;

(ii) the supplier's name, address and reference;

(iii) a description of the goods ordered;

(iv) the quantity ordered;

(v) the price per item excluding VAT;

(vi) The total order price excluding VAT;

(vii) any discounts which are sought;

(viii) the amount of VAT included in the order price;

(ix) the total order value;

(x) the delivery date required.

Some systems will generate the actual purchase order, produce a remittance advice when payment for the order is sent to the supplier and even the cheque itself.

The system will develop a database which provides information about which suppliers have been used, their quality, reliability and price competitiveness. This allows the purchaser to make better informed decisions about which supplier to use in the future.

A computerized system may even be programmed to select the most appropriate supplier based on criteria such as prices, delivery dates and discounts offered.

Purchase Ledger Systems

This system is comparable to the sales ledger except that it contains records relating to the organisation's suppliers. As purchase orders are placed, the ledger is debited the appropriate amount against the specific supplier. When goods are received and a payment is made the outstanding amount is balanced and the supplier's account cleared.

The system will also have to cope with credit notes which the organization may receive if goods it has paid for are later found to be defective.

The purchase ledger should produce the following analysis:

(i) An overall total of the organization's outstanding debts;

(ii) A breakdown showing when each debt payment has to be made.

This not only allows the organization to analyse its overall financial position it also permits it to plan and monitor its cash flow. In other words when will it need specific amounts to pay its creditors.

The ledger should also be capable of identifying:

(i) the amount owing to each supplier;

(ii) the 'age' of each of these outstanding debts.

This permits the organization to maintain good trading relationships with its suppliers by not allowing substantial debts to build up over long periods of time. (This presupposes that the organization wishes to pay outstanding invoices promptly. Many large organizations have sufficient purchasing power that they can afford to keep suppliers waiting for payment. This allows the optimum use of its money as suppliers are unwilling to press too strongly for payment for fear of losing a large customer.)

Nominal or General Ledger Systems

This is an overall record of the organisation's expenditure and income and classifies each transaction according to its purpose or name (hence the title 'nominal ledger'). It brings together the information from the sales ledger and the purchase ledger (which are referred to as *primary ledgers*). Basically the keeping of any ledger is a means of analysing transactions on a daily basis. Thus the number of different accounts contained in a ledger (for instance the purchase ledger may include individual accounts for electricity, gas and oil or simply one account for heating) is determined by the degree of analysis required by the organisation. The nominal ledger will therefore contain accounts for Sales, Purchases, Heating, Wages, Rent, etc. To allow such classification each entry is normally coded with an appropriate account code when it is entered into the system. So, for example, the code for heating may be 015 and all transactions for this commodity will be entered with this code.

The nominal ledger will produce information which is used to draw up some of the organization's most important financial statements such as:

(i) the Profit and Loss Account (which is a record of the organization's trading performance during the year);

(ii) the Balance Sheet (which gives a statement of the organization's assets and liabilities at a particular point in time).

While such statements can be produced manually, it is far easier to use a computerized system because, if a full range of accountancy applications are being used, then all the necessary information to produce them is contained in different files within the overall system. The key to a successful overall system is the ability to assess each file and transfer the appropriate information from each to a separate program capable of combining the data to give the complete financial statements.

Stock Control System

Most organizations need to carry stock. If the organization is involved in manufacturing it must hold stocks of components and raw materials. A retail organization must hold stocks of goods to meet customer needs and even an organization in a service industry must keep stocks of the stationery it uses. Stock holding is an important concern of management. Holding too much stock is unnecessarily adding to the costs of the organization, while holding insufficient stock can result in production delays, loss of sales and other operational failures.

The organization needs therefore to keep appropriate stock records which monitor not only the movement of stock into and out of the organization but also helpt to maintain minimum and maximum stock levels.

This is an extremely obvious application for a computerized system and examples of stock control programs have been used extensively earlier in this book to illustrate programming and coding techniques.

The system must hold records for each stock item which hold the following information:

(i) maximum and minimum stock levels for each item. These are determined by the regularity of use of the particular item and the speed with which the stock can be replaced. So for example if the organization holds floppy disks as a stock item and finds that it uses approximately 30 floppy disks a week and that it takes a maximum of 7 working days to get new supplies then it may decide never to hold less than 50 disks in stock for if it did it might find itself out of stock before replacements are received from a supplier. Furthermore the organization has decided on a maximum stock of 250. It does not wish to hold more as it will simply be tying up cash in unproductive stock. Yet it has found that if it buys 150 disks at one time from its supplier it gains substantial discount.

(ii) Movements into and out of stock must be recorded as they occur. Receipts must be logged showing the date, the supplier and the invoice number. When stock is issued the appropriate requisition number and department or section which has received the goods must be recorded.

(iii) With each transaction the balance of stock is adjusted and the systems indicate that a reorder is necessary once the stocks are running close to the minimum stock level. The amount ordered should keep the stock below the maximum stock level.

Stock control systems allow management to control financial resources efficiently. Money is not wasted by being tied up in unproductive stock. Information from the stock control system can be fed into other systems. For example when goods are received into Stock from a supplier this can trigger the purchase ledger system into generating a payment. Similarly when reorder levels are reached a purchase order can be generated from that system. Finally details of the value of all stock transactions are transferred to the Nominal Ledger system for inclusion in the profit and loss account and the balance sheet.

Costing Systems

A costing system calculates the cost of production of a single item or a range of items. It combines the individual costs of each component part. These include the labour costs involved, raw materials used, energy needed in the production process and an apportionment of the overall administrative costs of the organizations. Added to this must be the organization's profit margin which may be calculated as a standard percentage added to the cost price or may be determined by reference to the price of competitors' products or what customers are willing to pay.

A computerized system is able to perform these tasks much more simply and effectively than can be achieved using manual means. If the costs of materials are entered into the computer a suitable program will divide the total by the number of units produced. Similarly the labour cost can be apportioned once the level of output per worker is determined. As individual costings change the program is able to adjust the cost per unit and suggest possible revisions in the selling price.

An extramely useful feature of such systems is the ability to determine in advance the likely effects of changes in the cost of individual component parts. This involves the use of a *what ... if* structure. So for example the organisation can assess the changes in the cost of its final product if its raw material suppliers increased their costs by 20% or wages rose by 6% or electricity charges were put up by 10%. Such information allows management to make decisions in advance of likely changes. This could involve a shift to a new supplier or a transfer of power source.

Financial Planning Systems

Most organizations have as a prime objective the achievement of profit. In order to make a profit the organization must earn sufficient revenue from the sale of its products to exceed the costs it has incurred in operating and producing. It is usually a relatively simple task to calculate revenue. Simply determine the number of goods which have been sold and multiply this quantity by the price per item. Unfortunately this becomes more complex as the range of goods sold increases.

The calculation of cost is a little more complex for the organization incurs a variety of different costs in producing its product. Some remain constant irrespective of the quantity which is produced. These are termed *fixed* costs. Examples include the rent on the premises or the rates paid to the local authority. Clearly as these do not vary as output increases they become a smaller proportion of the cost of an individual item as more is produced. The example below illustrates.

Quantity	Fixed Cost (Rent of Property per annum)	Fixed Cost per unit
£	£	£
10	500	50
50	500	10
100	500	5

As production rises the fixed cost per item falls. Other costs increase as output increases. These are called *variable* costs. Raw materials are an example of variable costs. Obviously the more an organization makes the more it will have to pay for its raw materials. (It may of course gain some cost advantage by buying in bulk as its demands rise).

Combining fixed and variable costs give the organization its total costs and it is these which must exceed its *total* revenue before it can make a profit. Clearly then, an organization may make a loss if its output is low but as it produces and sells more it will eventually move through a *break- even point* into profit. As the name suggests, the break-even point is where the organization neither makes a profit or a loss - it simply breaks even. Management obviously wish to know the levels of output at which they will make a loss and those at which they are operating profitably and so they combine the figures to produce what is referred to as a *break-even chart* or analysis. An example is given on the next page.

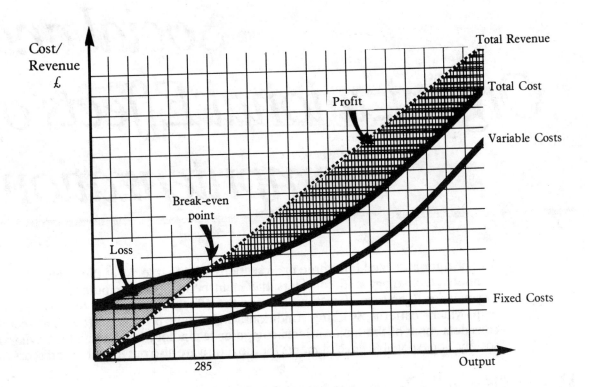

Break-even Analysis

It can be seen that the organization will make a loss until it produces 285 units at which point it *breaks even*. Output in excess of 285 is profitable.

As we noted earlier computer programs incorporating *what ... if* capabilities allow management to anticipate the consequences of changes in revenue or costs. The level at which profitable production can be achieved may rise if costs also rise. Alternatively if it is able to increase the price for which it sells each unit, revenue increases and the break-even point is achieved at a lower level of output. Such systems allow management to make decisions with a high degree of accuracy and to be able to respond quickly and effectively to changing conditions.

Chapter 31

Social and Organizational Effects of Computerization

This chapter is divided into three main sections. The first looks at the applications of computer technology and considers the main benefits of computerization for an organization. The second section looks at the effects of computer technologies on employment patterns, working conditions, and career prospects. The final section considers some of the major effects computer technology has had and is having on society. Some possible developments for the future are also put forward for discussion.

Benefits of Computerization

Business applications such as payroll and stock control were among the earliest to be computerized. Although increasing use is being made of computers in manufacturing industry, science and medicine, business applications still constitute the greatest usage. A number of categories of computer application can be identified:

(a) Accounting Systems

(b) Management Information Systems (MIS)

(c) Decision Support Systems (DSS)

(d) Electronic Office Systems

(e) Computer-aided Design and Manufacture (CAD-CAM)

(f) Computers in science and medicine

(g) Artificial Intelligence

Accounting Systems

Accounting systems include:

Payroll

Payroll systems are concerned with the production of payslips for employees and the maintenance of records required for taxation and other deductions. In a manual system, the preparation of payroll figures and the maintenance of payroll records is a labour intensive task. Although tedious and repetitive, it is a vitally important task. Most employees naturally regard pay as being the main reason for work and resent delays in payment or incorrect payments, unless of course it is in their favour! The weekly or monthly payroll run affects almost all employee records in the payroll master file, so batch processing is normally used. This processing method provides numerous opportunities to maintain the accuracy of the information. The repetitive nature of the task makes it a popular candidate for computerization, especially with organizations which employ large numbers of people. The automatic production of reports for taxation purposes also provides a valuable benefit. Smaller organizations with only several employees probably do not regard payroll as a high priority application for computerization. The benefits are not as great if the payroll task can be carried out by one or two employees who also carry out a number of other jobs.

Stock Control

Any organization which keeps stocks of raw materials or finished goods needs to operate a stock control system. Although stock constitutes an asset, it ties up cash resources which could be invested in other aspects of the business. Equally, a company must keep sufficient quantities of items to satisfy customer demand or manufacturing requirements. To maintain this balance a stock control system should provide up-to-date information on quantities, prices, minimum stock levels, and re-order quantities. It should also give warning of excessively high, or dangerously low levels of stock. In the latter case, orders may be produced automatically. A stock control system can also generate valuable management reports on, for example, sales patterns, slow-moving items, and overdue orders.

Sales Accounting

When credit sales are made to customers, a record needs to be kept of amounts owing and paid. Payment is normally requested with an invoice, which gives details of goods supplied, quantities, prices and VAT. Credit sales are usually made on for example, a 14, 21 or 28 day basis, which means that the customer has to pay within the specified period to obtain any discounts offered. Overdue payments need to be chased, so sales accounting systems normally produce reports analysing the indebtedness of different customers. Debt control is vital to business profitability and computerized systems can produce prompt and up-to-date reports as a by-product of the main application.

Purchase Accounting

These systems control the amounts owed and payments made to suppliers of services, goods or materials used in the main business of the company. For example, a car manufacturer will need to keep records of amounts owing to suppliers of car components and sheet steel manufacturers. Delayed payments to suppliers may help cash flow, but can harm an organization's image, or even cut off a source of supply when a supplier refuses to deliver any more goods until payment is made. A computerized system will not ensure payment, but it can provide the information that payment is due.

General Ledger

The general ledger keeps control of financial summaries, including those originating from payroll, sales and purchase accounting and acts as a balance in a double entry system. Reports are generally produced at the end of financial periods, including a balance sheet.

For many organizations, the systems described above can be computerized using packaged software.

Management Information Systems (MIS)

Although computers can perform routine processing tasks very efficiently, it is generally recognized that, for a business to make use of a computer solely for the processing of operational information, constitutes a waste of computer power. A MIS is designed to make use of the computer's power of selection and analysis to produce useful *management* information.

A MIS has a number of key features:

 (i) it produces information beyond that required for routine data processing;

 (ii) timing of information production is critical;

 (iii) the information it produces is an aid to decision-making;

 (iv) it is usually based on the database concept (explained in Chapter 6).

The information provided tends to be related to the different levels of management.

The claims for MIS are sometimes excessive. It is rarely the complete answer to all a company's information needs, but when successfully implemented, it provides a valuable information advantage over competitors.

Decision Support Systems (DSS)

A DSS aims to provide a more flexible decision tool than that supplied by a MIS. MIS tend to produce information in an anticipated, predefined form and as such, do not allow managers to make ad hoc requests for information. DSS tend to be narrower in scope than MIS, often making use of microcomputer systems and software packages. Examples of DSS are, electronic spreadsheets, for example, Lotus 123, file managers and relational database management systems such as Dbase IV. The main features of these and other packages are described in some detail in Chapter 11. In addition, financial modelling and statistical packages are considered to be DSS tools. A major benefit is the independence they allow for information control by individual managers and executives. When, for example, a sales manager requires a report on sales figures for the last three months, a microcomputer with database package may provide the report more quickly than the centralized Management Information Services (Chapter 2).

Electronic Office Systems

The automation of office procedures tends at present to be rather fragmented, some staff making extensive use of computers, whilst others rely almost completely on manual methods. The Electronic Office is a concept which views the office as an integrated whole, where many procedures are automated and much of the communication is by electronic means. The main components of the Electronic Office are described in Chapter 6, but briefly, may include the following:

 (i) Word processing;

 (ii) Decision Support Systems (DSS) - discussed above;

 (iii) Electronic messaging and electronic mail;

 (iv) Electronic diaries and calendars;

 (v) Electronic notice boards;

 (vi) Telecommuting.

The last component, *telecommuting* has the potential to revolutionize working habits. Basically, it means the use of a terminal or microcomputer workstation linked to a company's computer at another location. In many cases, this removes the need for attendance at the office for workers such as programmers and typists or even executive staff. The main disadvantage is the loss of personal contact between staff, which can require considerable cultural readjustment. Such a system also has consequences for employee supervision and security of information.

Computer-Aided Design and Manufacture (CAD-CAM)

Computer-Aided Design (CAD)

With the use of a graphics terminal and cross-hair cursor (described in Chapter 18), or similar device, a designer can produce and modify designs more rapidly than is possible with a conventional drawing board. Ideas can be sketched on the screen, stored, recalled and modified. The computer can also be instructed to analyse a design for comparison with some specified criteria. Drawings can be rotated and tilted on the screen to reveal different three-dimensional views. CAD is used in the design of ships, cars, buildings, microprocessor circuits, clothing and many other products. With the use of CAD a manufacturer has a distinct advantage over non-computerized competitors, in terms of speed and flexibility of design.

Computer-Aided Manufacture (CAM)

A number of areas of computer use can be identified in the manufacturing process.

    (i) Industrial robots;

    (ii) Computer numerical control (CNC) of machine tools;

    (iii) Integrated CAD-CAM;

    (iv) Automated materials handling;

    (v) Flexible manufacturing systems (FMS);

Industrial Robots. Basically, a robot replaces the actions of a human arm and consists of 3 main elements, a mechanical arm with 'wrist' joint, power unit and microprocessor or central controlling computer. To be called a robot, it must be able to react, albeit in a limited way, to external events and alter its course of action according to a stored program. Such sensitivity to the environment is provided by sensors, for example, to recognize stylized characters and differentiate between shapes. The main areas of use are in spot welding, paint spraying, die casting and to a lesser extent, assembly.

Computer Numerical Control (CNC). CNC operation of machine tools has been widespread for some years because the repetitive nature of machining tasks lends itself to simple programming. However, as is the case with robots, the use of microprocessors allows the machine tool to vary its actions according to external information. The actions of the machine can be compared with a design pattern held by the computer. Any significant variations from the pattern are signalled to the machine tool which, through the microprocessor, reacts appropriately (known as Computer Aided Quality Assessment - CAQ). Other information regarding tool wear or damage can be picked up by sensors and communicated to the human supervisor who takes remedial action.

Integrated CAD-CAM. In fully integrated CAD-CAM systems, the designs produced using CAD are fed straight through to the software which controls the CNC machine tools, which can then produce the design piece. The CAD software checks the compatibility of the design with a component specification already stored in the computer.

Automated Materials Handling. There are around 80 fully automated warehouses in Britain. A fully automated materials handling system consists of a number of sub-systems:

- stock control;

- part or pallet co-ordination;

- storage and retrieval;

- conveyor control.

Installation generally proceeds one sub-system at a time, each being fully tested before proceeding with the next sub-system. A materials handling system, controlled by a central computer, allocates storage locations in the warehouse, automatically re-orders when a predetermined minimum level is reached, retrieves parts as required by the factory and delivers them by conveyor belt to the waiting robots or CNC machines.

Flexible Manufacturing Systems (FMS).   Such systems are beneficial where production batches are small and necessitate frequent changes in the sequence and types of processes. The aim of FMS is to remove, as far as possible, the need for human intervention (other than a supervisor or 'machine minder') in the production process. The main elements of FMS are, CNC machine tools (with diagnostic facilities), robots, conveyor belt and central computer and controlling software. In simple terms, the computer has information on parts, machine tools and operations required. The robots serve the CNC machines by presenting them with parts to be machined and loading the correct machine tools from racks. In Crewkerne, Somerset, a factory uses FMS to produce bomb release mechanisms for military aircraft but the system is flexible enough to produce thousands of other components with the minimum of human intervention.

Computers in Science and Medicine

Science

To predict weather conditions accurately requires vast amounts of data regarding past conditions. Large supercomputers allow such volumes of data to be stored, recalled, updated, and analysed on a national and sometimes international basis. Computer graphics and computer enhanced satellite pictures are also used to provide interesting and informative weather forecasts for television viewers. Computer simulations can allow testing of product designs without, at least in the initial stages, the expense of building the actual product. Airline pilots are trained in computerized flight simulators which can simulate almost any event a pilot is likely to encounter.

Medicine

Computer-controlled life support systems can monitor a patient's condition via a number of sensor devices checking on, for example, pulse rate, body temperature and blood pressure. This frees nursing staff for other duties and has the benefit of providing a continuous monitoring facility. Computer-assisted diagnosis systems make use of artificial intelligence to assist a physician in diagnosing a patient's condition. This raises the question of how much reliance should be placed on computers with artificial intelligence. It seems reasonable that a doctor should use an expert system as an aid to diagnosis, but less reasonable that a treatment decision should be made on the basis of computer diagnosis alone. A particularly exciting development involves the use of computers to assist the plastic surgeon in the repair of facial injuries or deformities. The patient's face is scanned by a camera and the image digitized for display on a computer screen in three-dimensional form. This image can be rotated or tilted on screen by the surgeon and experimental 'cuts' made, the results of which can then be viewed on screen from any angle. In this way, a plastic surgeon can study the results of a variety of strategies before making a single mark on the patient.

Artificial Intelligence (AI)

Artificial intelligence is an attempt to model human thought processes and systems are evolving in the following areas:

(i) Expert or Knowledge-Based Systems (which are examined in Chapter 11);

(ii) Robotics (described earlier in this Chapter);

(iii) Natural Language (which is considered in Chapter 11).

Expert systems may, in the future, pose a threat to the autonomy at present held by doctors, lawyers and other professionals. It is not inconceivable that medical diagnosis and legal advice may be provided by machine. Such systems exist already but only provide limited support. The restraint, if any, on such developments may stem from ethical and moral forces, as well as the professions wish to protect their interests. It may be, of course, that humans will prefer to retain personal contact with their doctor or solicitor, even if a machine is making most of the decisions.

Computers and Employment

The rapid advances in computer and micro-electronic technologies have occurred in a period of erratic change in the Western economies and it is difficult to quantify the extent to which computerization has affected the levels of employment. Although computerization is far from being wholly responsible for increased unemployment, it has undoubtedly been a contributory factor. No attempt is made in this text to relate numbers of employed or unemployed to computerization. Instead, discussion will centre on the identifiable effects of computerization on employment patterns and prospects. The following effects may result from computerization:

(i) Retraining

(ii) Redeployment

(iii) De-skilling

(iv) Changes in working practices

(v) Regrading and changes in career prospects

(vi) Redundancy

(vii) Changes in working conditions (Health and safety).

Each of the above effects can be identified in different types of job.

Office Work

Computerization is common in most areas of office work, for example, word processing, electronic messaging, and accounting systems. Additionally in some specialized areas such as banking, automatic tellers are replacing humans for routine banking transactions.

Re-training

Generally, an organization will choose to make full use of their existing staff, rather than search for new staff who already have the skills required. Depending on the nature of the job, the retraining needed may be radical or quite minor. For example, a typist has keyboard skills which are quite readily transferrable to the task of word processing. The retraining needed centres on the concept of text editing, mailing lists, the use of floppy disks and printers. The aim is to give the operator the knowledge, skill and understanding to make maximum use of the facilities provided by a word processor. Word processing is a general skill which can be applied in different ways in different organizations. Similarly, the use of a software package for sales accounting or stock control needs knowledge and skills, some of which are transferrable to other packages. Familiarity with computers in general and expertise in the use of some packages, provides an individual with the confidence to quickly pick up skills for new applications as they arise.

Redeployment

Computerization generally reduces manpower requirements but increases the opportunities for business expansion. Redeployment means moving staff from one area of work or responsibility to another, generally with retraining. Redeployment is a common result of computerization in any area of work.

De-skilling

The judgement as to whether or not a job is de-skilled by computerization is a rather subjective one. For example, does a wages clerk using manual methods require a higher level of skill than a data entry operator? The answer is probably yes, although a trade union may argue otherwise in the interests of improved job regrading. On the other hand it is generally accepted that higher level skills are required to use a word processor than a typewriter.

Changes in Working Practices

Staff may be required to carry out a wider range of tasks as a result of computerisation. For example, in smaller offices a clerk may be required to answer customer enquiries and carry out data entry at a terminal. Flexibility rather than specialization is often the key to the introduction of new technology. The lines of demarcation in the newspaper industry had to disappear before computerization could take place.

Regrading and Career Prospects

Sometimes, improvements in job gradings are introduced in order to encourage staff to accept computerization. At the same time, career prospects in office work are generally diminished. In the banking industry, the prospects for managerial jobs have diminished drastically in the last two decades. Currently, few clerical staff who did not enter the job with a degree have prospects for managerial posts.

Redundancy

Computerization of office work inevitably reduces the manpower requirements for the existing level of work, but redundancy does not always result. This is usually because computers are introduced in response to an expansion in the business of an organization.

Health and Safety

Anxiety and stress could cause problems. Many staff, particularly older members, may feel anxious about the security of their job or possible redeployment. They may become unhappy about personal contact being replaced by a computer screen.

Most people, as they get older, prefer continuity rather than constant change and computerization usually means radical and frequent change. Anxiety can also result from a fear of 'falling behind'. This applies to many people working with computers, because the changes and advances are so rapid.

Ergonomics

Ergonomic design recognizes certain health and safety problems which can result from computer usage and attempts to design equipment and working environments which minimize the hazards. A number of health and safety concerns are recognized in relation to VDU screens:

- exposure to radiation;

- induction of epileptic fits;

- mental and physical fatigue;

- eyestrain, eye damage and visual fatigue;

- muscular strain.

Suitable working practices and well-designed equipment can largely avoid such dangers, for example, gentle lighting, lack of screen flicker and hourly breaks for VDU operators. Other concerns relate to the design of office furniture and the general office environment, including temperature and noise levels.

Manufacturing Industry

Most of the factors described in relation to office work apply equally in factory work, but the following additional points are worth mentioning.

Job Satisfaction. Shop floor workers who supervise and service the machines have a cleaner, less dangerous job than traditional skilled machinists. It may be surmised that young people, without the experience of the old skills, will look more favourably on such supervisory jobs than the older workers.

New Job Opportunities. If automated systems such as Flexible Manufacturing Systems (FMS) are to be successful, then the number of jobs in factories using FMS must inevitably decrease. Opportunities lie in the creation of a new range of jobs. Many such jobs are in software engineering and in the design of automated systems. The Japanese experience is that new, highly-skilled jobs are created in the development and design fields in companies which manufacture automated equipment and commercial machinery, whereas both skilled and unskilled jobs are lost in the companies using this equipment. The Japanese experience is being mirrored in the UK.

Increased Unemployment. Many older, skilled workers have been made redundant because of the loss or de-skilling of their jobs through automation. On the other hand, the redundancies may have occurred without automation because of loss of competitiveness.

Computers and Society

There is general agreement that computers and related technologies will bring great social changes, but there are wide differences of opinion about what they will be, the rate at which they will occur and the extent to which they are beneficial. It must be emphasized that many of the following points are highly subjective and open to debate.

Benefits

The benefits include:

- Increased productivity;

- Higher standard of living;

- Cleaner and safer working conditions;

- Shorter working hours;

- More leisure time.

Costs

The costs include:

- Polarization of people into two groups - the technologically advantaged and disadvantaged;

- Increasing crime and delinquency rates;

- The threat of a totalitarian state;

- Invasion of privacy.

The remainder of this section looks at two important areas of concern regarding the future impact of computers on society, namely *telecommuting* and *personal privacy*. Some of the effects are already apparent.

Telecommuting - The Office at Home

At present, millions of office workers travel by car or public transport to their respective places of work. Nearly all organizations carry out their business from centralized offices because information needs to be exchanged, usually on paper documents and decisions need to be made, which requires consultation between individuals. Through the use of telecommunications, and centrally available computer databases, office staff of the future may work from home via a computer terminal.

There are a number of advantages to be gained from home-based work:

- Savings in travel costs;

- No necessity to live within travelling distance;

- Flexible hours of work;

- Equality between men and women. Bringing up children can be a shared activity;

- Savings for the organization in terms of expensive city-centre offices.

There are also several potential drawbacks:

- Loss of social contact;

- Need for quiet workroom at home. This can be difficult in a small flat;

- The difficulty of 'office' accommodation is compounded when two or three members of a family all work from home;

– Loss of visible status for senior staff in terms of a 'plush' office and other staff to command.

Computers and Personal Privacy

Since the 1960s, there has been growing public concern about the threat that computers pose to personal privacy. Most countries, including the UK, have introduced legislation to safeguard the privacy of the individual. The Data Protection Act of 1984 was passed after a number of government commissioned reports on the subject. The Younger Report of 1972 identified ten principles which were intended as guidelines to computer users in the private sector. A government White Paper was published in 1975 in response to the Younger Report, but no legislation followed. The Lindop Report of 1978 was followed by a White Paper in 1982 and this resulted in the 1984 Data Protection Act. The principles detailed in the Younger Report formed the foundation for future reports and the Data Protection Act. They are listed below.

(i) Information should be regarded as being held for a specific purpose and should not be used, without appropriate authorization, for other purposes.

(ii) Access to information should be confined to those authorized to have it for the purpose for which it was supplied.

(iii) The amount of information collected and held should be the minimum necessary for the achievement of a specified purpose.

(iv) In computerized systems handling information for statistical purposes, adequate provision should be made in their design and programs for separating identities from the rest of the data.

(v) There should be arrangements whereby a subject could be told about the information held concerning him or her.

(vi) The level of security to be achieved by a system should be specified in advance by the user and should include precautions against the deliberate abuse or misuse of information.

(vii) A monitoring system should be provided to facilitate the detection of any violation of the security system.

(viii) In the design of information systems, periods should be specified beyond which information should not be retained.

(ix) Data held should be accurate. There should be machinery for the correction of inaccuracy and updating of information.

(x) Care should be taken in coding value judgements.

The White Paper which followed the Younger Report identified certain features of computerized information systems which could be a threat to personal privacy:

(i) The facility for storing vast quantities of data;

(ii) The speed and power of computers make it possible for data to be retrieved quickly and easily from many access points;

(iii)   Data can be rapidly transferred between interconnected systems;

(iv)   Computers make it possible for data to be combined in ways which might otherwise not be practicable;

(v)   Data is often transferred in a form not directly intelligible.

The 1984 Data Protection Act sets boundaries for the gathering and use of personal data. It requires all holders of computerized personal files to register with a Registrar appointed by the Home Secretary. The holder of personal data is required to keep to both the general terms of the Act, and to the specific purposes declared in the application for registration.

From the individual's point of view, the Act can be said to have a number of weaknesses:

(i)   Penalties for infringement of the rules are thought to be weak and ineffective;

(ii)   There are a number of exemptions from the Act. Some holders do not need to register and there are exceptions to the right of access to one's own file. There are also limits to confidentiality;

(iii)   The Registrar is appointed by the Home Secretary and cannot therefore, be wholly independent.

Assignment   *The Great Computer Debate*

The Student's Union at Bedlington College of Further Education is running a debate on the following motion.

"The tangible effects of computer technology on patterns and conditions of employment to date provide cause for pessimism with regard to the future of Western society."

Task

You have been offered the choice of speaking FOR or AGAINST the motion. Make your choice and prepare notes for a speech to last about ten minutes.

Chapter 32

Written and Verbal Communications

Communicating Effectively

The need to communicate effectively

There are three important reasons why it is essential for organisations to be effective in their communications:

(a) to aid decision making;

(b) to enhance the organisation's reputation;

(c) to ensure the effective operation of the organisation's systems.

To aid decision-making

Effective decision-making is founded upon obtaining and interpreting all appropriate information. Without such information decisions are likely to be the product of guesswork or speculation. Managers require accurate, relevant and up-to-date information to act rationally and competently. Imagine a large manufacturing company deciding to invest in expensive new manufacturing equipment without first identifying whether it can afford the equipment and physically accommodate it within the existing plant. The person taking the decision will need to know how much loss of production will result whilst it is installed, which personnel if any have the skills to operate it and whether the market can absorb the higher output of goods produced using the new machinery. It would be foolish to contemplate such a course of action without first obtaining information to provide the answers to these questions. A local authority would not attempt to raise its rates, close a school, or build council houses without its officers first seeking all the data necessary to advise the members of the alternative courses of action available, and the consequences of pursuing them.

Whether the decision-making takes place in a commercial company or a public body the decision-makers ultimately have to account to the people they represent, be they shareholders or ratepayers. It is essential that managers have access to all the information appropriate to their responsibilities. Nothing is as damaging to a manager's reputation as a public recognition that he was unaware of important information. You may have noticed how often in Parliament members try to embarrass their political opponents by revealing information that the opponent was unaware of.

To enhance the organisation's reputation

Effective external communications enhance the reputation and image of the organisation and result in good customer relations. When a customer contacts a business wanting to know whether the order has been processed yet, or a prospective buyer asks if the business can supply a specific product, at what price, and how soon, reputations can be made and lost depending upon the efficiency of the response. An organisation which unduly delays in responding to customers' enquiries or complaints, or where the telephone is never answered, will develop a poor standing in the eyes of its existing and potential customers.

To ensure the effective operation of the organisation's systems

If internal communications are effective, systems within the organisation operate smoothly, for example its financial system, stock control and personnel functions. As a result, deficiencies and problems can be identified quickly and remedial action taken, thus maintaining product and service standards and high staff morale. Take two simple examples. Firstly, a slack system of stock control can result in orders being lost and long delays in delivery occurring. Secondly, an ineffective personnel department that fails to recognise and act upon an employee's grievance could be responsible for an escalation of the problem into an industrial dispute.

To summarise, poor communications result in lack of information, disinformation, misunderstanding and confusion. To help overcome such undesirable consequences, an organisation should pay close attention to all forms of communication. In practice this means selecting, collating and presenting the data to be communicated in a suitable format. This may be a report, balance sheet, a letter or a chart. In fact, as we shall see, part of the skill of communicating is to choose the most suitable format to transfer the information. Once the format is selected, further skills are required of the communicator to use the format in the manner it demands. Usually accuracy will be important, but sometimes style and tone as well, for instance when writing a letter or sending a memorandum.

Your role as a communicator

In our daily lives and particularly in our jobs we must assume the role of a communicator. Because of the importance of communications we all need to be aware of the skills required. We should be aware of (a) sources of information; and (b) purpose and method.

Being aware of the sources of information

To obtain data you must be aware of the main sources that can be drawn upon, for instance within the organisation where records and files are kept and how they can be accessed. Outside the organisation you must be able to use the information facilities of libraries, government departments, local authorities and so on. Sometimes there are legal obligations to make available to the public specific types of information. The Companies Registry in Cardiff holds files on all registered companies. These can be examined on the payment of a small fee, and can provide a valuable source of information, such as a company's annual accounts. The Local Government (Access to Information) Act 1985 imposes upon all local authorities the obligation to provide details of meetings, agendas and minutes which are available for public inspection. It also requires a local authority to publish certain information including a register containing the names and addresses of all its elected members.

Being aware of the purpose and message of the communication

You must also be conscious of:

> (i) the contents of the message, for instance is it an order, a piece of advice or merely 'for information only'; and

> (ii) the method of communicating it, for instance should you write a letter or pass the message on by telephone.

Your decision will be influenced by the size of the target audience, whether the message is urgent, physical factors such as the design of the work place, and also cost.

The essential test of your ability as a communicator is whether you are understood. But we should remember that there are always two sides to communication, the person giving the message and the person receiving it. Just as it is important that your communications must be understood, you will also need the skills involved in receiving information and being able to take appropriate action on it.

The skills of communicating

We give, receive and exchange information all the time, whether in work or outside it. All this activity involves communication skills. It is a curious fact that most of us will only be vaguely aware of how successful we are at using your communication skills. Usually it is only when something goes wrong that we recognise the weakness of our communication, for instance when we are told "I am sorry but I don't follow you", or when we fall back on the expression "Know what I mean?". For most of us the only time our communication skills are specifically developed and formally assessed occurs during our education. Even then there may be significant areas of communication that are not a part of the curriculum. For most of us, using a telephone, speaking publicly and filling in forms are abilities acquired from personal experience. We seem to survive this lack of formal training, although how well we cope is sometimes more difficult to estimate.

The major activities of communicating are reading, writing, listening and speaking. Of these it tends to be the oral activities which receive least attention during our school careers. Perhaps this is because the nature of oral communication makes it more difficult to assess than a letter or essay which clearly has a more permanent form. The elements of communications are all essentially inter-connected. The writer expects his words to be read, whilst the reader will read to discover the writer's message. The speaker addresses his words to the listener intending that they be heard, whilst the listener tries to understand the speaker's message from the words he or she hears. Superficially it may appear that the skills of reading and listening are less demanding than those of writing and speaking. This is not so. Effective reading and listening can only be successfully achieved by high levels of concentration. As communication is a two-way process it is not realistic to divorce the skills of the person transmitting the information from those of the person receiving it. A person with good communication skills must be both a good speaker and a good listener, or a good writer and a good reader. Unfortunately, effective transmitting and receiving skills do not always coincide. You will probably have met someone who is an excellent listener, responsive and attentive, but who is unable to string more than a few words together themselves; or someone who is excellent at relating a story but does not concentrate on listening to others. Some of the most important aspects of good communicating are identified below.

Speaking and listening

A speaker should:

> (i) have a wide vocabulary and choose from it with care;

(ii) use the correct pronunciation of words;

(iii) deliver sentences at a reasonable speed;

(iv) vary the intonation of the delivery;

(v) maintain some eye contact with the listener, allowing the listener the opportunity to intervene whenever this is called for.

A listener should:

(i) concentrate on the words used by the speaker;

(ii) interject to clarify points of difficulty or confusion but in a way which does not break the speaker's flow;

(iii) maintain attention by looking at the speaker;

(iv) respond non-verbally to what is being said – nodding to signify understanding or approval, or smiling to provide encouragement.

Writing and reading

A writer should:

(i) express ideas and information in a form which is grammatically correct;

(ii) write legibly;

(iii) edit and correct the written material before issuing it;

(iv) employ sound vocabulary;

(v) ensure correct spelling.

A reader should:

(i) check words that he or she is not sure of by using a dictionary;

(ii) read at a reasonable speed so as not to lose the sense of the message;

(iii) try to summarise the main points mentally as they appear;

(iv) where necessary 'skim' material (Skimming is considered later).

Of course these points about communication skills are for general guidance only. For example, if you are engaged in taking down notes whilst a speaker is giving a lecture, you are simply providing yourself with a record of the major points that are being made. As long as the notes are only for your personal use any method you use to express them is acceptable if you understand it. Often people develop their own shorthand for note-taking purposes.

The conventions of communicating

So far we have concentrated on skills but we cannot ignore the importance played by convention when we are considering methods of communicating. Convention is concerned with generally accepted practice, and in the business world it plays a very important part in both verbal and written communication. Let us consider an example of a verbal convention. In many areas of employment it is still the convention for employees to use the formal methods of address when speaking to seniors – either 'Sir' or 'Mister', 'Mrs.' or 'Ms.'. It might not constitute insubordination to speak of a senior using his or her Christian name, but it would certainly be unfavourably received. In the same way, the use of slang expressions in a conversation with the managing director or chief executive will not generally improve one's career prospects. Convention is more significant in the written word, especially in business letters, notices and reports, that is in formal written communications. It would not, for example, present a very convincing picture of a well run organisation if the company decided to dispense with the use of punctuation in its business documents. It might also give rise to a great deal of confusion. As grammatical convention and construction is so important it is considered in more detail below.

Grammar

The most basic component of written language is the 'word'. We can talk of the words used in a language as its vocabulary. Whilst a single word can convey a meaning, in order to express complex ideas and the relationship of things to each other, we use sentences. Sentences are made by linking words together. A sentence should be complete in itself and convey a question, a statement or a command. To create a sentence the writer must follow certain rules which are referred to collectively as the rules of grammar.

The aim of grammar is to ensure that the words of a sentence are arranged so that together they convey a single meaning. If they are capable of bearing more than one meaning the sentence is ambiguous and accurate communication is lost. For example, consider the sentence, 'The sales manager told the production manager that his department was a disgrace to the company'. We do not know from this which department is 'a disgrace to the company'. A further example is the sentence, 'Applications are invited from men over twenty five years of age and women.' Can female applicants be under the age of twenty five? Slight changes in the construction of a sentence can completely alter the meaning of the sentence, so it is important to pay careful attention to the words being used. For instance, compare the sentences:

> 'Only I wrote to the company'.

> 'I only wrote to the company'.

> 'I wrote only to the company'.

> 'I wrote to the company only'.

By moving the word only through the sentence different meanings emerge. In addition a single word can be stressed by printing it in italic form in order to emphasise its meaning and, in doing so, possibly remove ambiguity as well. Using one of the examples above, 'I only wrote to the company', we do not really know whether the writer is emphasising the means by which he communicated with the company, or whether the writer is stressing the fact that he wrote but did nothing else.

The components of a sentence

There are eight different parts of speech which can be used to form sentences. These are:

> (a) verbs;

> (b) nouns;

> (c) pronouns;

> (d) adjectives;

> (e) adverbs;

(f) prepositions;

(g) conjunctions; and

(h) interjections.

Verbs

The words in a sentence each perform different functions. Verbs are words indicating the state or the action of a subject and are sometimes referred to as 'being' or 'doing' words. The most common verbs are to be and to have. Verbs can be used in different tenses to signify the time at which the event they describe occurs, thus 'I talked' (past tense), 'I am talking' (present tense) and 'I shall talk' (future tense). They can be used actively and passively to convey different emphasis, for instance 'The Government cuts civil servants' pay'. Here cuts is used actively and as it immediately follows Government it emphasises that word. This could alternatively be expressed as 'Civil servants' pay is cut by the Government'. This sentence now emphasises who has suffered the cut rather than those responsible for it.

Nouns

Nouns are words that name a person or place or thing. If the thing is tangible, with a shape and volume, such as a factory, an individual or a manufactured product then the noun is a concrete one. If the thing is intangible, such as a quality, a value or an attribute (for example justice or information) the noun is said to be abstract. Collective nouns are used to describe a group of things, for instance a 'firm' of accountants. It is important not to refer in the same sentence to a group as a single entity and then as a collection of individuals, thus, 'The management took their places and it then commenced its business'.

Pronouns

Pronouns are used instead of nouns to identify a person or thing already mentioned or known from the context of the sentence. There are personal pronouns (such as I, you and they), and interrogative pronouns (such as who, what and which). Interrogative pronouns are used to enquire or question.

Adjectives

Adjectives describe nouns; 'the large warehouse', 'the green folder', 'the main entrance'. An error to be avoided is the use of superfluous adjectives. Examples might include 'a major disaster' or 'a noisy disturbance'. In fact the use of adjectives as a complete contrast to the nouns they are describing can be used to humorous effect – 'a quiet disturbance'. (This figure of speech is known as an oxymoron.) Some adjectives are relied upon so extensively that it becomes difficult to know what they are really intended to mean. The adjective 'nice' is one of the most over used in our language.

Adverbs

Adverbs describe verbs, for instance 'the workforce is slowly learning the skills,' or 'she often calls'. or 'the shop is closed simply because of the power cut'. In these examples the adverbs are 'slowly', 'often' and 'simply'.

Prepositions, conjunctions and interjections

Prepositions describe directions or position (in, on, under etc.), conjunctions join words together (and,or) and interjections are exclamations (oh! and ah!).

Which of these eight parts of speech appear in a sentence obviously varies according to the message the writer is seeking to convey, and the tone and style which is being used. However, all sentences must consist of a subject and a verb. This can occur with just two words such as 'I called' or 'Richard paid'. In both cases there is a subject. the individual performing the action, and a verb, indicating the activity of the subject. Some verbs require an object as well as a subject to make proper sense. We are left wondering in the case of the caller whom, why and how he called.

A group of words without a verb is referred to as a phrase. A phrase may make sense even though it lacks a verb, for instance, 'Mr. J. Owen – Quality Control Supervisor'.

Punctuation

The purpose of punctuation is to provide tone and expression to the written word and provide pauses to help the reader grasp what has been said before moving on to the next idea or set of ideas.

Different types of punctuation provide the writer with alternatives for achieving these purposes. Although grammatical rules certainly exist for the use of correct punctuation, probably the best guide to punctuation is the writer's own sense of what feels right. This often becomes clear when reading back over the written material. In oral rather than written communications the speaker has greater control over punctuation using gestures, expressions, tone of voice and pauses. For example, pauses can be lengthened to heighten the emphasis on what has just been said.

The full stop

The full stop is the single most important component of punctuation. It is used to end the sentence. It also appears in some abbreviations, for instance Mr. Smith, and R. Smith J. P. When does a sentence end? Perhaps the most helpful advice is to think about how the writing would sound if it were being spoken. Where would the breaks come? Bear in mind that people often manage to produce longer sentences when they are speaking than would look or feel right if seen in written form.

The comma

A comma is used to make a short pause within the sentence. Short sentences are helpful to the reader. They are easy to follow. Used excessively, however, they restrict the writer's style and create an impression in the reader's mind like travelling in a jerky car. Whilst a straightforward writing style assists the reader's understanding, the longer sentence may be necessary to closely link related ideas. It is then that the comma becomes useful. It should be borne in mind that over enthusiastic use of commas may hinder the reader's understanding rather than help it.

The main uses of a comma are:

(i) in lists, as a means of separating items;

(ii) to report direct speech, as for instance in the following sentence. The secretary said, "The office has been busy all day".

(iii) to mark the end of a clause. 'In reply to your letter of 24th May, I have now spoken to the people concerned'.

   (iv) as a substitute for brackets. 'The clerical assistant, a man
        of fifty five, took early retirement'.

   (v) to enable adverbial phrases to appear in the middle of
       sentences. Words like 'however' and 'nevertheless' are
       adverbial phrases.

The semi-colon

Sometimes a writer needs to introduce a longer pause than a comma, but does not wish
the sentence to end. To achieve this the semi-colon is used. The three situations in
which it is usually employed are:

   (i) to stress the separate identity of listed items. "The file
       included: the clients name; his date of birth; his previous
       employment experience; and details about his state of
       health."

   (ii) to emphasise a conjunction. "We are not happy about
        your attitude to time-keeping; and we do not intend to
        alter your working hours."

   (iii) to act as a conjunction by joining two related sentences.
         'The word processor is a valuable asset; it has
         revolutionised our office procedures'.

The colon

The colon can be used in a number of ways. It is used:

   (i) to introduce a list, hence it appearance after the word
       'used' above;

   (ii) as a means of dividing a general idea from the
        explanation. 'Personal computers are valuable tools: they
        are quick, cost effective, and easy to operate'

   (iii) to contrast one idea with another. 'Economic expansion
         creates jobs: economic decline reduces them'.

Brackets

These are a method of providing additional information in the form of an aside. "Mrs.
Black (Company Secretary) spoke at the meeting." Often brackets (known technically
as parentheses) can be replaced by commas. Which method is the more appropriate in
the last sentence? As a means of introducing a note of confidentiality, however,
brackets can be most effective. "You may recall me telling you (when we met over
lunch last week) that the merger is likely to go ahead."

Dashes

The dash is another device for introducing a pause, and creating emphasis. Dashes lose
their impact if they are used too frequently. When a dash is introduced in a sentence
the phrase or clause following it should end with a dash – or a full stop.

The apostrophe

An apostrophe is used to indicate possession. Compare the following three sentences:

'The council's duty is a statutory one' (One council)

'The councils' duty is a statutory one' (More than one council)

'A statutory duty is imposed upon councils' (All councils, but no apostrophe is needed because there is no possession by the councils. It is a simple plural).

Note, however, that a possessive pronoun (its, hers, theirs, yours) does not require an apostrophe. An apostrophe is also used where one word is a contraction of two, for example, 'don't' (do not) and 'it's' (it is). The apostrophe is used in place of the missing letter or letters and not, as is often mistakenly believed, between the two words forming the contraction. For example, how would you contract 'does not'? The correct contraction is 'doesn't' not 'does'nt'. Note, also, the difference between 'its' (possessive pronoun) and 'it's' (contraction of it is). Although these contractions are used all the time in speech, it is usual to use them in writing only when reporting direct speech. For instance, in speech we might say "what's the difference?" whereas we would write 'what is the difference?'

Quotation marks

Double quotation marks are used to indicate directly reported speech: The supervisor said, "The morale of my staff is high." Single quotation marks are used for titles, for instance 'The Economist'. They are also used in written directly reported speech to indicate quotations used by the speaker. The supervisor said, "The morale of my staff is high and the foreman said to me yesterday 'its because of the recent government order'". There are two ways of reporting speech; directly, as in the example above, and indirectly. Indirectly reported speech involves describing past events. In indirect speech the statement above would read: The supervisor said the morale of his staff was high and that the foreman had told him the previous day it was due to the recent government order. Indirect speech is commonly used as a way of recording in minutes of meetings, the discussion that has taken place between the members present. It is an alternative to directly quoting them which is likely to be a tedious process and very demanding of the minute taker's skill.

Paragraphs

Just as words combine to form sentences, so sentences combine to form paragraphs. A paragraph contains a group of sentences related to the same idea or ideas. When the idea or topic changes a new paragraph should begin. The pause between one paragraph and the next signifies the change of content. The use of paragraphs involves care; whilst a paragraph that is too long can cause the reader difficulty in coping with larger blocks of information, paragraphs that are too short are disconcerting and confusing.

Internal and External Communication Methods and Formats

We have already examined methods of communication through the use of written, verbal and non-verbal means. In the case of written communications we have seen that an essential element to achieve effectiveness is an awareness of grammar. Now we need to consider the methods and formats that can be used to convey information. Before doing so, however, it is important to recognise that business communication has two different aspects to it. On the one hand there are the communications within an organisation – its internal communications – and on the other there are its external communications. In a sense it is artificial to split up the communication activity of an organisation in this way. The skills of communication are essentially the same whether a person is dealing with his fellow employees or his organisation's customers and clients. However, different needs are met by the use of different methods and the internal information demands of an organisation do not necessarily coincide with the external demands. For example, most external dealings tend to be formal, whereas internal information transfers, especially verbal exchanges, are often of a less formal kind. In addition, the formats used for the purpose of giving, receiving and exchanging information vary widely according to the nature and content of the information, who is providing it and who is receiving it. Thus the means used to arrange an interdepartmental football competition are unlikely to have much in common with those used in designing and implementing a feasibility study on company relocation. This is particularly so if the study has to be presented to the entire board in the form of a fully documented formal report, accompanied by an oral presentation. Similarly, the way in which an organisation communicates its response to a letter of complaint from a customer, is unlikely to be the same as the treatment given to a grievance raised by an employee concerning conditions of service.

Methods of internal communication

Conveying information involves making a number of decisions. It is of course necessary to know what the content of the information is. This may not always be as simple as it seems. If the communicator is part of the information chain it is possible that such a person may be confused about the message to be transferred, having failed to receive it clearly. If a senior issues you with a vague instruction to, "Tell the staff about the safety arrangements", you will need to ascertain the following points: (i) which safety arrangements?; (ii) which staff – all of them?; (iii) where are the safety arrangements described?; (iv) why is this communication necessary – perhaps a legal obligation or a policy decision?

Whatever the reason, it is difficult to place communication of information in context if there is no apparent purpose in transferring it; what precisely is it that the staff need to be told? When you are the initiator of the communication it will be easier to obtain answers to most of these questions; you will presumably know why you need to transfer the information, for instance!

Having ascertained what the information is, why it needs to be transmitted and who needs it, a choice must then be made as to how it should be transmitted, that is the method of delivery. In its simplest form this involves asking:

> (i) should the method be formal or informal?; and

> (ii) should the method be verbal or non-verbal?

Most of the physical means available to transmit information are capable of being used either formally or informally. Letters, reports, speeches and instructions can all be delivered in a style and tone which reflects strict conventions or alternatively a relaxed and more individual approach. However, many communications have to be fitted into prescribed formats allowing for no choice. All organisations rely on the use of forms to simplify and standardise information flows. A company may, for instance, use standard form contracts to trade under, accident report forms to detail accidents occurring at work, and invoice forms for billing customers. Sometimes such forms must comply with statutory requirements. For instance, information regarding the insurance of premises and the ownership of a business must be displayed publicly in a standard form. Thus a distinction needs to be drawn between circumstances where an organisation:

> (a) chooses to use a form as part of its internal communications system. An example is the use of forms to obtain and record employees personal details;

(b) is obliged by law to provide information, without a particular format being prescribed, for instance the requirement that employers provide employees with written details of the contract of employment that exists between them; and

(c) is obliged by law to provide information using a prescribed format, for instance, to register with the Data Protection Authority to store personal records on computer.

Among the most common means used to transmit information internally are: memoranda, notes, notices, reports, accounting statements, files, agendas, minutes, telephone conversations, meetings, public address systems and face to face contact. Evidence suggests that for the average employee involved in administrative or clerical duties, a breakdown of the working hours he or she spends using different methods of communication will reveal around three quarters of that time spent in oral communications (i.e. speaking and listening).

Forms of internal communication

The memorandum

The memorandum is a very common means of transferring information in written form within the organisation. Memoranda may be handwritten, although usually they are typed, and their main purpose is to convey a brief message. The layout of the memorandum is standardised, and most organisations will use memoranda that have pre-printed headings and carry their business name. The memorandum will indicate from whom it has come, to whom it is addressed, the date, a reference or heading, and who, if anyone, has received copies. The originator should keep a copy of the memorandum. If several copies are being sent a tick is placed against the names of each individual receiving one, to indicate that this is his/her copy. In addition to the addressee, copies should be sent to individuals who need to know the message being sent. It may, for example, be courteous to keep a superior informed of a matter which is being dealt with by a member of his or her staff. It also gives the superior an opportunity to intervene if he or she is concerned about the way the matter is being dealt with.

Clearly it is important for an employee who uses a memorandum to be familiar with the organisation's structure and so be aware of who within it ought to be given a sight of the communication. Whilst it is necessary to circulate all communications between staff, it should be recognised that key personnel within a section or department may be unable to perform their jobs satisfactorily if they are not provided with essential information, and 'kept in the picture'.

A memorandum does not need to be signed, although the originator may initial it. Nor does it needs compliments such as 'Dear Sir', or 'Yours sincerely'.

The main uses of memoranda are:

(i) to issue an instruction, for instance, "please attend the meeting to be held at....";

(ii) to record a fact or series of facts that the recipient should be aware of, thus, "I attended the meeting as you instructed";

(iii) to put forward suggestions. An example might be, "I would suggest that in future you deal with the clients in a more tolerant way," or, "I feel it would help the department if extra time were made available at the staff meetings";

(iv) to express a point of view, thus, "In response to your comments at the meeting last week, I take the view that the major priority of the department is cost cutting."

It has already been noted that the initiator should keep and file a copy of each memorandum. Like any written communication its great value is that it provides a permanent record for the initiator and it is valuable evidence of any action taken if a dispute arises. Indeed it is useful to follow up important oral exchanges by means of a confirmatory memorandum whenever possible.

Usually a memorandum form is small in size and this physically prevents messages from becoming too wordy.

Instructions

Whilst a memorandum may be used to pass on instructions, there are also other commonly used written methods. For instance, staff may receive an instruction manual. This might contain information on the operation of equipment used in the place work. It could also describe the action to be taken in the event of an accident at work, or the procedure to be adopted by a member of staff who is unable to report in for work.

Simple instructions may appear on equipment or in the office or plant to identify what action should be taken in the event of a fire. The method which is used is obviously largely determined by the specific context. For example, it would be appropriate to give to all new starters a plant diagram indicating the location of fire exits with general instructions on the action that should be taken in the event of a fire breaking out.

Instructions are used to:

(i) tell the recipient to act in a certain way, for example, "In the event of a generator failure you should report the matter to the plant manager immediately";

(ii) tell the recipient they are restrained from acting in a certain way, for example, "Under no circumstances should unauthorised staff enter the research and development unit";

(iii) simply tell a potential user how to use an item of equipment, for example, "To operate press button A, select the appropriate file and type your message".

In expressing instructions, style is very important. The imperative form should be used when the instruction must be complied with, for instance, "Enter all new client details on Form 5A" or "You must enter..." Since failure to observe an instruction may have serious consequences it is essential to use such expressions as "must", "ought" and "should". Such language will make the recipient fully aware of the nature of the obligation that is imposed when a written instruction is personal rather than directed towards the workforce generally. The use of imperative language may appear to be authoritarian. "Telephone the Sales Director and pass on my congratulations", as an instruction to an assistant,is likely to result in the Sales Director receiving a less enthusiastic message than if the assistant received the instruction prefixed with "please", although even with the addition "please" the instruction is still clearly a command.

As with all forms of communication, the method and the delivery should always reflect the context, and in the case of instructions it is essential that they be expressed both clearly and logically. This may involve sequencing the instructions as a list of numbered points, rather than combining them all , in no particular order, as a general statement. For instance, a set of instructions to a market researcher engaged in field work might read:

    (i) greet the interviewee with the time of day – "good morning" etc;

    (ii) introduce yourself and the name of your company;

    (iii) show evidence of your identity;

    (iv) briefly explain the nature and purpose of the survey;

    (v) explain that the survey will last only ten minutes, and the information obtained will be of great value.

Presented in this way the interviewer can learn the instruction sequence and consequently relate to the interviewee as an efficient professional, whereas a muddled set of instructions could result in a messy presentation and a refusal by the potential interviewee to be interviewed.

Internal publications

Large organisations find it helpful to regularly publish a bulletin or magazine for distribution to all members of the workforce. Bulletins are usually cheaply produced, whilst magazines are often glossy and attractive, reinforcing the reputation and status of the organisation. Such magazines are usually produced by very large companies, such as Shell and I.C.I. but, whether it is a magazine or a mere bulletin that is used, such a publication is a useful way of passing on information that is:

- purely personal – weddings, retirements, deaths of staff etc; or

- organisational – changes in personnel, company trading activity, new systems being introduced, and so on.

Notice boards

Notice boards are one way of communicating generally within an organisation. They are invariably split into sections dealing with a range of topics from sport to Union meetings.

Some organisations make use of a display board. This may be restricted to information on one topic, but may be placed strategically so as to gain maximum impact. For instance, a display board concentrating on health and safety matters might be located at the entrance to the staff canteen where employees queue up for meals.

The advantages of a notice board are in its:

- • – cheapness;

- • – ability to be kept up to date easily; and

- • – accessibility.

They do, however, suffer from certain drawbacks including:

- • – the possibility that some staff ignore them altogether;

- • – the likelihood that staff may be selective and examine only those sections of the board which are of interest to them;

- • – the fact that notices inevitably lack detail because of the physical limitations of the board;

- – the tendency for the board to become overcrowded which can cause people to ignore it because of the poor visual presentation of material.

Suggestion boxes

Suggestion boxes are used very successfully by some organisations as a method of encouraging employees to put forward their own ideas on all aspects of the organisation's business such as improvements to the company's products, or its systems. They have the advantage of improving employee involvement in the company affairs, and in the case of the best ideas may produce savings for the company. It is common to offer cash payments for ideas which are accepted. Despite appearing to be a relatively modern way of communicating within a large organisation where the individual's voice might not otherwise be heard, suggestion schemes have in fact been in existence for at least one hundred years.

Meetings

The experience of most employees, irrespective of whether they work in the public or the private sector, is that the further up the organisational ladder they climb the more meetings they are required to attend. They may have to prepare documents for meetings, attend and speak at meetings, and take notes at meetings. The fact is that 'the meeting' is generally regarded as one of the most appropriate ways of enabling views to be aired, shared and discussed and in this way provide a suitable forum for arriving at decisions. Those who have experienced meetings soon become aware that the efficient and effective use of a person's time is not always realised by attending a meeting.

A recent training film for business managers conveys this message humorously. The entire working day is spent attending meetings, which leaves no time to prepare for them, so this work has to be carried out at home. As a consequence most of the staff attending the meetings are so tired that they fall asleep.

Agendas

The success of a meeting often depends upon the way in which the chairperson conducts it, but it is more likely to be successful if every member knows in advance when and where the meeting is to be held, and the nature and order of the business. If reports or other written documents are to be considered at the meeting these should be issued in advance, rather than 'tabled' (that is, first presented at the meeting itself). The document used to inform staff of a meeting is called an agenda.

Minutes

It will be noticed that the second item on the specimen agenda refers to the minutes of a previous meeting. Minutes are records kept of the business of meetings. They include not only decisions made by the meeting, but also the discussions which lead to any decision. Minutes are in fact a type of report. It is usually the responsibility of a secretary appointed by the members of the meeting to keep a record of the proceedings as members discuss issues and reach decisions. It is then the Secretary's responsibility to prepare formal minutes from this record. The minutes will be typed and distributed to members of the meeting, usually accompanied by the next agenda. Minutes are of particular value when the meetings which they record are held regularly as, for example, in the case of a local authority committee which meets each month. Under such an arrangement the first proper business of the meeting is the approval of the minutes of the last meeting.

This process has the effect of reminding members what was previously discussed and decided, enabling them to check whether agreed action has been taken, and allowing them the opportunity to accept (or reject) the minutes as an accurate record of the previous meeting. As with other written records, minutes should be clear, precise, and as concise as possible, but without losing essential accuracy, if they are to be approved as a true account of the previous meeting. The style of writing appropriate to minutes is to keep sentences short. It is not necessary to link one point with another. Where reference is made to the statements of individuals speaking in the meeting indirect speech should be used. Finally, for reference purposes, a system of numerical recording is commonly used against each minuted item.

It should be noted that there is a statutory obligation for local authorities to keep minutes of their proceedings, and that these minutes are made available for public inspection. Consequently, local authority minutes are formally framed, sometimes providing full details of motions and amendments which were put to council meetings.

Abstracts or summaries

Anyone who has administrative and clerical responsibilities deals with written material constantly. In a managerial post, in order to cope efficiently, a person will find it necessary to reduce or condense much of the written material they are faced with. Letter, reports, memoranda and other communications are being generated on a daily basis and if every word has to be read the manager is likely to develop a steadily increasing backlog of incomplete or untouched work that fills the in-tray

Two ways in which this difficulty can be overcome are by improving personal reading techniques and by requiring subordinates to summarise material.

The manager may use techniques to improve his or her reading skill.

To do this it is necessary to become aware of the different levels of reading. These are skimming (or scanning), 'normal' reading and in-depth reading. Which level a person uses firstly depends upon having a proficiency in all three. Having acquired this it becomes possible to adopt whichever technique is best suited to the time available for reading the material, and the nature of the material itself. Most people read at the normal level without difficulty, for normal reading is reading for pleasure; reading a newspaper, a magazine or a novel. The rate at which material is understood at this level will generally not matter. If, however, the material being read is hard to understand because the ideas it expresses are difficult to grasp or the vocabulary used is largely unfamiliar, there is a tendency to read it superficially. In-depth reading involves spending time in working towards an understanding of difficult material. It is a valuable skill for the student! In the working environment constant change means that even experienced staff face reading challenges from time to time. A clear example of this is the effort made by people experiencing for the first time the language of computing. Thus in-depth reading is very much a part of working life. By its nature it is a slower process than normal reading and can consume large quantities of the manager's limited time.

Certainly there is a loss of efficiency when, after ploughing through a body of complex written material, it is realised that none of it was really relevant after all. To help avoid this problem, and to generally improve reading speeds, the technique of skimming is used. It is a technique with which most people are familiar, although success in using it does not automatically follow from knowing it. It involves glancing through material, paragraph by paragraph, to gain a feel for the content. Then the reader may return and re-read the material thoroughly if the content is relevant and time permits, or simply rely upon the general impression obtained. In the latter case this may be enough to enable the reader to participate effectively at a meeting, or telephone a customer, or perhaps interview applicants for new jobs.

A manager may instruct subordinates to abstract or summarise the material.

These two expressions are essentially the same. Summarising involves the process of writing a shorter version of a communication, whether the original is oral (for example the discussions of a meeting which are converted into minutes) or written (such as a lengthy report).

The task of summarising may become necessary at any time. A superior may call a member of staff into the office with the instruction, "Can you provide me with a written summary of the developments in our negotiations with the Council over the planning application for the new factory?" Or perhaps an internal telephone call may be received for the employee's superior from a senior member of the organisation who simply instructs, "Will you pass on the following details concerning the Bridgewater Contract?", and then narrates a sequence of events.

Three skills are vital for effective summarising:

- – A thorough understanding of the material. This is essential in order to produce an effective summary. You may recall having your ability to understand unfamiliar material assessed through comprehension exercises at school.

- – Selecting the essential points from the material. There must be no alteration to the factual content and no additions to the material made. The main theme and major factual components should emerge from the information selected and arguments that have been used.

- – Writing the summary clearly and, of course, concisely. If this is not achieved the whole purpose of the summary is defeated. Textual material can often be condensed by using a single word to replace a group of words, and by reducing sentence (and hence paragraph) length.

A summary should read as a whole, rather than as a collection of disconnected sentences. To achieve such unity involves maintaining a logical sequence to the ideas being expressed in the passage, and exercising care in linking sentences. A wide vocabulary will clearly help.

Papers

Though given different names, papers, documents or briefs are all contributions to debate, discussion and decision making. Their function is to assist someone to perform another task. The format of these 'papers' is usually looser than a report and subject to the licence of a writer. They will, however, usually have some of the features of a report: title, sub-headings, indications or policy options, etc.

A briefing paper/document, usually referred to as a 'brief', provides the essential background information on a topic that is necessary to guide another person charged with further development of that topic. Its function is not to offer conclusions, but to describe a situation and its boundaries, and indicate areas of decision.

A discussion paper/document, like a 'brief', provides the necessary background information but goes further either in indicating the areas to be resolved by further discussion and decision, or offering for further discussion or decision conclusions offered tentatively, with arguments organised for and against with an identified preference.

Notes

Notes are short pieces of writing intended to identify only key points or issues, in which discussion or contextual information is omitted. Notes for a talk, or speaker's notes, are a listing of the major points or issues identified without more information or argument than is necessary. In this it is akin to a summary report, but the intention is oral delivery and not written presentation. Notes can be seen as pieces of writing preceding either papers or reports.

One special sort of note that is sometimes used is to keep a record of a meeting or a set of decisions, akin to minutes, but recording much more fully the reasoning and arguments that were used than a 'minute' might do.

Reports

Reports may be made verbally, but are usually written. A report is a document which examines a specific topic or topics in order to: convey information; report findings; put forward ideas and suggestions. In addition, a report will usually make recommendations upon which action can be taken. There are many ways of classifying reports. This is a reflection of the variety of activities that they are used to consider and the differing contexts in which they are used. The most common distinctions are between formal and informal, and between routine and special reports.

Formal and Informal reports

Formal reports are detailed and require structure and subdivision. Informal reports are usually shorter, less structured and more generally used. The more structured nature of a formal report reflects the greater detail of the information contained in it, and it is likely to consist of:

    (a) a title page;

    (b) a contents page;

    (c) a summary of the recommendations;

    (d) an introduction (containing the terms of reference);

    (e) the information on which the report is based;

    (f) conclusions;

    (g) recommendations;

    (h) appendices;

    (i) references to information sources relied upon, for example the use of books, papers and other reports which are listed in the reference section of the report with their titles, their author and where they can be located.

It should be stressed that even the so called 'informal report' is essentially a formal document for it must observe certain conventions of layout. Representing a work of research, argument and recommendation, a report provides its author with a significant test of his or her communication skills. It is certainly possible that an individual's reputation may be enhanced or seriously damaged by the quality of the report they produce. The report may circulate amongst a range of senior staff throughout the organisation, be discussed at meetings, and be filed for public reference. Whatever its progress it will carry the author's name.

Routine and special reports

Routine reports are a common feature of most industrial, commercial and public organisations. As their name suggests, they are produced as a matter of internal routine as part of the information system of the organisation. For example, a routine report would be a report on sales figures produced by the sales department, or an annual report dealing with trading activity for each fiscal year. Routine reports are generally standardised. A special report is a 'one-off', dealing with a non-routine matter. This could be an evaluation of the performance of a group of employees, a report of a conference attended, or an enquiry into the restructuring of the entire organisation. Because a special report is not concerned with a routine issue its structure will not be standardised. It will, however, be based upon terms of reference. These are simply the set of instructions given to its author(s). Furthermore, the format of the report is likely to follow the sequence identified below:

- (a) a statement of the terms of reference of the report. These will specify its objective or objectives;

- (b) a statement of facts or arguments, set out logically, regarding the subject being investigated;

- (c) the identification of viable solutions to the problem, giving the respective strengths and weaknesses of each course of action. This stage is usually referred to as the 'findings';

- (d) the recommendation, supported by appropriate reasons.

In addition, detailed information may be contained in appendices included at the back of the report. The body of the report will contain references to the appendices, but the text will be prevented from becoming too detailed by including the appendix material separately.

Different stages of reports

Before a full report is given, a variety of reports which fall short of a full report may be requested:

- an **interim report** is either a review of general progress and indication of future lines of enquiry or a report concerned with one topic of particular urgency which cannot await the full report;

- a **field report** indicates the evidence on which a full report may be used; it is thus raw material for the conclusion and thus rarely indicates the nature of the conclusion;

- a **summary report** is entirely dominated by its conclusions, giving only such argument and evidence as is necessary to give a context to these conclusions.

The qualifying verbs customarily used in requests for reports (and other forms of communication) indicate the stage at which the communication is being made:

- to 'draft' is to produce a report in a form with a certain roughness of presentation and tentativeness of conclusion, but as a preliminary to a final, more polished version;

- to 'prepare' is a slightly more advanced stage of drafting but still subject to a final revision and reassessment;

- to 'write' or 'provide' is to produce the final version or one in which only minor textual amendment will be necessary.

Writing reports

Report writing is an important skill for administrators in all organisations.

What, then are the skills needed by the report writer? There are essentially three of them: the skills of preparation, construction and writing.

Skills of preparation

It is impossible to proceed without being entirely clear as to the reasons for the report. Having established these reasons it is then necessary to identify all the recipients of the report. There may in fact be a distribution list already in existence. Sources of information need to be identified and relevant information gathered from them, which must be evaluated, so that it can be classified. Since information makes up the core of any report, it is helpful to remember that the way in which it is used will depend upon the purpose of the report. The information may simply need re-presenting. For example, if the report is to provide a list of the highways which the local authority must repair, once the basic information has been gathered, the task is then to express it in a clear , concise way.

It may be that an explanation is required, thus a report upon the implications of the latest Finance Act or DTI survey could not stop short at simply regurgitating the content of these documents once they have been obtained. The report would also need to comment upon their effect, or implications, or meaning, in other words it will have to do something with the material – to process it in some way.

Finally a report may involve original thought by its author where he or she is obliged to make proposals, for example, to report on possible designs for a new stock control system. Here objectivity is called for in weighing up the pros and cons of the alternatives.

There are many points to bear in mind in preparing the report, but above all the report should read as a document which is clear, concise and relevant. It is also useful to be aware of the broader implications of the report, for instance is its content an issue that is the subject of conflict between your senior and another member of the organisation?

Constructing the report

Having obtained all the raw data considered necessary for inclusion within the report, the next step is to consider how the report should be constructed.

Layout is particularly important in formal reports, since these will contain a considerable body of detailed material which needs to be carefully structured to avoid repetition and satisfy the need for clarity and coherence. It should be remembered when writing a report that, as with any form of written communication, a permanent record is being created. Whether a written communication is filed depends upon its importance as a record for the organisation, but reports will invariably be filed as they represent research which may prove valuable to the organisation in the future.

The report should clearly indicate the arrangement of material within it, using headings and numbering where appropriate. Patterns used for reports may vary according to their subject matter and purpose but as a general guide the arrangement will be likely to adopt the following order:

- introduction;
- background;
- data;
- analysis;
- conclusion;
- appendices.

The introduction

This will seek to establish not only the purpose of the report and the authority under which the author is acting, but also the author's name, for whom the report has been prepared, and what its subject matter is, if this is not apparent from the statement of its purpose. It should, or course, also be dated.

In a long report the introduction could usefully include a list of the main section headings, as a form of index.

Background

Sometimes it is necessary to trace the background or history of events which have led to the preparation of the report. In doing so the writer is providing the reader with a perspective that helps to set the report in context. If the background information is not essential to obtain a proper understanding, but is still felt to be of value, it can be inserted as an appendix.

Data

It is upon the data or facts which the report contains that the writer will be seeking to present the alternative arguments concerning the report's proposals. It is essential, therefore, that this information is accurate, and preferably supported by a reference to its source. If data is of a detailed or technical kind it should be contained in an appendix or appendices, and simply be summarised in the body of the report. If this is not done the reader may find it difficult to grasp the salient features of the data or factual material being presented. The types of detailed and technical data referred to above could include statistical information, specialised material such as an economic model or statutory regulations, and financial data. Indeed most reports will inevitably examine the cost implications of any proposals they contain, unless these attract no additional costs.

Analysis

This is likely to be the most intellectually demanding aspect for the writer, for it involves presenting arguments for and against the proposal(s) of the report, in an objective way. It requires the writer to perform a critical analysis of the data set against the context of the purpose for which the report has been prepared.

Conclusion

The conclusion may include a summary of the main aspects of the report. It will certainly present the recommendations of the writer, and if these are detailed they should be individually listed.

Appendices

It has already been suggested that in the interests of producing a readable report which flows, appendices are an invaluable way of incorporating important data which would otherwise get in the way. If appendix material is used it is essential that it is accurately referenced and cross-referenced in the body of the report to offer the reader a layout which makes access to the information as straightforward as possible. It is most frustrating for a person who is discussing a report in a meeting to spend unnecessary time thumbing through it to locate a particular section or statement, on which he or she wishes to comment. To help overcome this, headings and numbering should be used.

Headings

These should be as simple and as brief as possible. A general heading or title will be given to the report as a whole, and the remainder of the report will carry main headings, for instance, 'Conclusions', with the text under these main headings broken up by sub headings, such as, 'Financial implications', 'Personnel implications', and so on.

Numbering

Not only should each page be numbered, but also the paragraphs of the text, unless the report is very short. Thus each main heading might be given a prefix letter, 'A', 'B', 'C', etc., each sub heading within it a prefix number '1', '2', '3', and each paragraph an additional number. In this way any paragraph within the report can be located quickly with the existence of an index, cross referencing page number to paragraph references. Thus an individual paragraph might appear as 'B.1.7'

Writing the report

The usual style to adopt is one which aims to be clear and brief. It should also be straightforward, although the writer should be conscious of the political implications of the report within the organisation, choosing words with care so as to avoid unnecessary friction. The text must also be relevant. Readers of the report will lose patience if they have to wade through material which is superfluous.

Report writers should avoid using jargon or cliches. For instance avoid, 'At the present point in time', and use 'now' or 'at present'; 'An all-time high', is better expressed as 'a peak'; and 'Insofar as it concerns this company higher productivity would be occasioned by maximising employer/employee participation levels,' would be more understandable if it read 'Higher company productivity would result from effective industrial relations.'

Before producing a final version of the report it is often useful to seek the comments of colleagues, especially superiors, on its style, presentation and content.

External Written Communications

Since organisations exist to meet the needs of customers and clients they spend a significant proportion of their time communicating with them. But external communications do not stop there. Whether an organisation likes it or not it has to deal with outside bodies and individuals who impose demands upon it. For instance, it must deal with the Inland Revenue when its corporation tax is assessed, the Department of Social Security in making national insurance contributions and the local authority when paying its rates. It also enters into relationships with: its suppliers, from the local electricity board for its power supplies to printers for its stationery; its advisers, including accountants and lawyers; its bank; the landlord from whom it may rent its property; and the trade union, whose members it employs.

Obviously communication between the organisation and this diverse range of outsiders takes place in many different ways. Often communications will be oral. These take place over the phone or by meeting face to face. For the moment, however, we are concerned with the methods used to communicate in writing, whether the organisation is the initiator or at the receiving end of the process. The major form of external written communication is the official letter.

Official/business letters

There are a number of reasons why it is essential for such official letters to meet high standards of communication. For instance:

(i)   outsiders invariably judge an organisation by the letters it writes, especially if they have not dealt with it in any other way, thus a business letter performs a public relations role;

(ii)   the letter may be designed to convey an instruction, for instance to a bank, and it could be financially harmful if it is misinterpreted;

(iii) a letter may give rise to legal ability, for instance if it is defamatory or where it constitutes an offer or an acceptance in contractual negotiations.

It should also be borne in mind that the contents of a letter may be widely circulated, for example, if it is a letter to a newspaper editor explaining a company's reasons for closing a local plant or perhaps responding to a specific public criticism. In such circumstances the construction of the letter is particularly important. Not only are there public relations to be maintained (or perhaps restored) but also the tort of defamation to be considered, for unjustifiable statements that harm the reputation of an individual or an organisation may be actionable and result in the writer paying substantial damages as compensation.

The purpose of the official letter

In commerce and industry business letters are used for many different purposes. The writer needs to be quite clear about the purpose of the letters he or she is writing, for what it says and how it says it reflects who the recipient is and why the communication is being made. It is not difficult to appreciate that the letter a company writes to another company apologising for a delay in supplying goods will be in a very different tone from that it writes to its bank complaining that the bank has wrongfully dishonoured a cheque drawn by the company. Similarly, a local authority housing department might be expected to respond by letter to a request for information about the availability of a council house somewhat differently than it would to a council tenant's statement that unless a different rent collector is appointed the tenant will assault the existing rent collector the next time he appears.

The type of letter that an organisation writes in terms of its content, style (formal or informal) and tone (friendly or restrained) reflects the purpose of the communication. Whatever the purpose is, however, it should always be borne in mind that the use of business correspondence is a means of avoiding a time-consuming and unnecessary face to face meeting. It also provides both parties with a permanent record of the arguments that they have made, and matters they have agreed.

Writing official letters

The layout

The general layout of a business letter says something of the organisation which has written it. If the layout is pleasing to the eye and contains at a glance the major information the recipient requires – who the sender is, when it was sent, and what it is concerned with – the recipient is encouraged to regard the organisation sending it as efficiently run. Thus, it is not just a case of satisfying standard conventions when writing an official letter. It also has to do with providing a communication in a form which advertises a chosen image for the organisation. The point has already been made that the content of a letter should always be presented courteously.

Regarding content, it is sometimes said that the 'ABC' of efficient and effective official letters is:

- accuracy;
- brevity;
- clarity.

But looking beyond content, there are other features of a letter which make an impact on the reader:

- the design of the printed letter head;
- the quality of the paper;
- the style and quality of the typewriter or printer head used;
- the positioning of the text within the space available; and
- the use of margins.

A well written letter that meets the requirements of accuracy, brevity and clarity may nevertheless be let down if the letterhead is out of date and has to have typed amendments made to it, the paper is thin, and the text is cramped on to a page that is too small, or located at the top of the page leaving a large gap below it.

Having made the observation that a business letter should be regarded in its totality, covering content, style and layout, we can now go on to identify the conventions that a business letter should observe. These include:

The sender's address

If the letter does not contain a printed letter head, the sender's address should be included in the top right hand corner of the first page.

The date

This appears after the sender's address, and is usually inserted on the right hand of the page. The month should be written in full to distinguish clearly the date from the reference included in the letter.

The salutation or greeting

It is usual now to use the recipient's name whenever possible, for example, 'Dear Mr. Green'. When the recipient is named in this way the letter should be ended,'Yours sincerely'. If the greeting, 'Dear Sir' or, 'Dear Madam' is used the letter should close 'Yours faithfully'. If the letter is written to someone the writer knows well it will begin, 'Dear Paul' and may end, 'With best wishes'. Letters to a newspaper editor begin simply, 'Sir'.

Title or subject line

This is an underlined heading which briefly indicates the subject of the letter. Although not essential it can be very helpful for the addressee. For example, it allows the appropriate file to be found quickly. It is a particularly useful device, therefore, when dealing with accounts and policies, when the number or reference can be inserted as a heading.

The sender's name

This appears after the close, and usually in the form of a signature. It is common practice to print the name beneath the signature, and to indicate the status of the writer, for example, 'Senior Housing Officer', or, 'Company Secretary'. Sometimes the letters 'p.p.' are used against the signature. This carries a specific legal meaning and indicates that the signatory is empowered to sign on behalf of another person or the organisation itself.

It is common for less senior staff to be allowed to sign letters, and in this case the indication of the signatory's status will include who he or she is acting on behalf of, thus 'Assistant Marketing Manager, for Marketing Manager'. Sometimes a personal assistant may sign a letter under specific authority. If so, the following forms of words would appear, 'Dictated by Mrs. Pearce and signed in her absence'. It is sometimes the practice to send all letters in the name of a senior manager, leaving the writer to add the manager's signature on items of routine correspondence.

References

The purpose of using references in business letters is to link subsequent correspondence on the same subject matter with the file, and also to ensure that a reply can be directed to the right department or individual. It is therefore a means of ensuring that correspondence is dealt with promptly, and that the author of the letter can, if necessary be traced. This is obviously more important in larger organisations than smaller ones. Usually two references are provided. They appear as 'Your Ref:' and 'Our Ref:' enabling both the sender and the recipient to link the letter to their respective filing systems. The normal practice is for the initials of the person signing the letter to appear first, followed by an oblique and then the initials of the secretary/typist. Longer references may refer to the file number or the department.

Enclosures

Very often the enclosure is of more value than the covering letter which accompanies it. It is vital to indicate that a letter includes enclosures, as a reminder to whoever prepares the letter for posting. Common devices are asterisks and stickers, but the most common method is to type 'Enclosure', 'Encl' or 'Enc.' at the bottom left hand side of the letter.

The recipient's name and address

This may appear either at the top left hand side of the letter beside the date, or alternatively at the bottom left hand side, below the sender's signature.

Types of official letter

The main types of letters are:

- letters requesting and providing information;
- letters of complaint;
- circulars and standard letters;
- references and testimonials.

Letters requesting or providing information

For many organisations these types of letters make up a substantial proportion of their business correspondence. This is perhaps even more the case for public sector organisations, such as local authorities, than for private sector ones. Local authorities receive many requests for information relating to the services they provide. If the letter is requesting information it is essential that the writer has first clearly established in his or her mind precisely what he or she wants to know. For example, suppose a company was to write to a local authority in the following way: 'Please let us know of the grants that you offer." Such a request is most unhelpful. The council needs to know what specific need the enquiry is related to. The company may be interested in grants for setting up a new business, or for taking on additional staff, and so on. Presumably the company is clear about the purpose for which the grant is being sought, so this should be clearly expressed in the letter.

When a letter supplies information, the writer should seek to ensure that it is written in a form which is understandable to the recipient. This may seem a very obvious requirement, but often staff who have worked in a particular department for a long time are so familiar with procedures and technical expressions that they forget that outsiders do not share this knowledge. Equally, it may be obvious from the content of the letter of request that the writer faces particular difficulties which should be recognised when responding to it. Many examples can be given. The letter may indicate that the writer has great difficulty in communicating and so very simple language should be used in writing a reply. It may be evident that the writer is distressed, for instance a pensioner worried about his inability to meet the rates demand, or a single parent anxious about the housing conditions for his or her family. In such circumstances whatever information is provided should be accompanied by some general words of support, although of course one should beware of making promises that it may not be possible to keep.

In business situations perhaps the most common type of written enquiry is that from one of the parties in the chain of distribution to another (for example retailer to wholesale, or wholesaler to manufacturer) requesting information on prices, and specifications of goods, availability, trade discounts and so on. The reply to such an enquiry will usually be a letter of quotation. As with any letter of enquiry the writer should be courteous, set out questions clearly and in sufficient detail, and include any information that is relevant to the enquiry, for instance that the matter is urgent.

The reply should deal with each question raised accurately and completely and should reflect a tone and style which indicates a genuine desire to be of service. This may, for instance, involve providing additional information which was not requested but which will clearly be helpful to the enquirer. Finally, it is in the interests of the organisation sending the reply to do so as soon as possible. In the case of a commercial organisation this can only enhance its reputation, and it may well result in an order being placed. An example of a letter of enquiry is given below.

Letters of complaint

A letter of complaint will invariably be based upon a grievance held by the complainant. An organisation may receive such letters; it may also need to write them itself. Often when the complaint comes from an individual the letter will reflect strong emotions. These may be quite justified yet be most unhelpful in constructing a letter which is appropriate to its purpose. Thus, such a letter should not be abusive, threatening (if it is the first letter that has been written) or contain allegations which it may not be possible to substantiate. Rather it should set out the facts as the writer understands them, avoid irrelevancies, and be polite. For instance, it is good practice to make it clear in the letter that the writer anticipates a favourable response to the complaint if it is found to be established after enquiry. These observations are of particular importance when an organisation is making the complaint. Compare the following examples of letters of complaint sent by an organisation to a customer:

```
Dear Sir,

We refer to the as yet unpaid sum of £378 owed to us by
you. We find it intolerable that we should have to write to
you demanding payment of your bill. It is our policy to
vigorously pursue claims against our debtors, and since you
have chosen to ignore this debt we shall have no
alternative but to commence legal proceedings unless
payment is made forthwith.

We should point out to you that this company is not run as
a charity, even though you obviously believe that it is.

Yours faithfully,
```

Dear Mr. Smith

We are sure that there must be some good cause for your delay in settling payment of your account Number 876413. If we can assist in any way in overcoming any difficulties you may have we should be glad to do so. If so, would you either call in, or give us a ring as soon as possible.

It may be that you have already made payment, in which case we apologise for inconveniencing you.

Yours sincerely,

Dear Mr. Smith,

We have received no reply to our reminder of the non-payment of your account. We must now regretfully point out to you that unless we hear from you as to the position within the next seven days, we shall have to consider taking steps to recover the amount.

Yours sincerely,

If it is discovered that the complaints made in the letter received from as customer or client are justified, it will be necessary to write a letter of apology, offering to make amends. This may involve financial compensation or adjustment, the replacement of goods, or an indication that an employee in the organisation has been disciplined. Of course, the examination of the complaint may reveal that it is totally without foundation, or there is some real doubt about its justification. In this case it will not be appropriate to make an offer of amends, unless in circumstances of genuine doubt the organisation chooses to maintain goodwill, by making perhaps a token gesture. Whatever the circumstances, letters responding to criticisms must be very carefully constructed. If the criticism is well founded the response should admit the error using restrained language, thus, "upon immediate enquiry it became clear that an administrative error resulted in your goods being misdirected. Please accept the company's apologies for the inconvenience you have been caused". It would be excessive for example, to add, "You may be assured that this will never happen again", for even in the most efficient organisations errors can and do occur and there can be no guarantee that a similar problem might not arise in the future.

Even if the organisation does not believe the complaint to have any foundation, it is still necessary to provide a response, and the question arises as to how this should be framed. Since the organisation will doubtless wish to maintain goodwill, as future orders may depend upon maintaining a sound relationship with the customer, it is vital that the customer is not made to feel foolish. It may help if the response is sent out under the signature of a senior member of staff, to signify the importance the organisation attaches to the criticism. This is especially true where the organisation is a service provider, particularly in the public sector, where because of the size of organisations it is easy to fall into the trap of responding to correspondence of all kinds by means of standardised letters which appear as cold, bureaucratic and impersonal.

An example of a reply to an unfounded complaint is given below.

Dear Mrs. Taylor,

Thank you for your letter of 20 April 19xx. I am sorry that you felt you received discourteous treatment when our accounts department contacted you by telephone regarding your bill. I have spoken to the member of staff you dealt with and put your complaint to him.

I am satisfied that he dealt with the matter correctly. However, I am glad you drew my attention to your concern, since we value good customer relations, and are always prepared to investigate customers' criticisms or complaints.

I hope the matter is now satisfactorily cleared up, and that we can remain of service to you in future.

Yours sincerely

When there is doubt about the substance of the complaint there is clearly no need to provide an admission of responsibility or an apology. Nevertheless, in the interests of goodwill, which in turn reflects upon the reputation and good name of the organisation, it is important that the response reflects the concern of the organisation and recognises that the writer of the letter of complaint is genuinely upset or annoyed.

The reply might read as follows:

Dear Mr. Jones,

I am sorry to learn of your annoyance at the refusal of the department's collectors to remove your kitchen units that are in your rear yard. The refuse collection teams are under instruction to collect all refuse on their weekly visit which in their opinion can be physically lifted and safely carried on their vehicles.

It is, however, sometimes necessary to arrange for a larger refuse vehicle to collect specific items. Such an arrangement will need to be made in this case.

If you would kindly contact this office (extension 225) letting us know when it would be convenient to remove your kitchen units, immediate arrangements will be made to do so.

Yours sincerely,

Finally it should be noted that letters of complaint should be dealt with promptly. This, of course, is true of all business correspondence but in the case of complaints it may take time to carry out an enquiry. Thus it is essential to notify the complainant as soon as the letter of complaint is received that the matter is being dealt with, for example:

```
Thank you for your letter indicating that you account has
been overcharged by £874. The matter is being urgently
investigated and we should be able to give you a full reply
within five days.
```

To summarise, complaints are an inevitable outcome of administrative, commercial and industrial activity. Complaints may or may not be justified, but the manner in which organisations respond in writing (and indeed orally) to them may, in the view of the customer or rate-payer, be as important as the product or service itself.

Circulars and standard letters

Circulars are used more commonly for advertising purposes, whereas standard letters may fulfil a variety of purposes, for example, inviting job applicants to attend for interviews or inviting customers to a company presentation. In the case of a standard letter, whilst the bulk of the information it conveys is standard, some provision will need to be made for the non-standard aspects of it.

Thus a standard letter inviting applicants to attend for interview might read:

```
You are invited to attend an interview for the post of
......
The interview will be held on ... 19xx, at Crown House,
High Row, Carlington, commencing at ...am/pm.
If you are unable to attend would you please contact the
Personnel Department as soon as possible.
```

Such letters can be stored on a word processor and the blanks completed as appropriate for each separate occasion.

Circulars are addressed, 'Dear Sir or Madam', 'Dear Elector' and so on, whereas most standard letters will contain the salutation, 'Dear Mr. Jones', 'Dear Ms., Peters', etc. Referring to the recipient's name creates a more personal impression than using 'Sir' or 'Madam' but it will not usually be possible to personalise a circular because of the large number of copies involved.

Since a circular is aimed at selling a product, a service or, as in the case of an election, a person and party, it should be designed to:

(i)   create an instant impact – perhaps through the use of a headline, or photograph, or the dramatic use of colour;

(ii)   encourage the recipient to read it – a 'lightweight' text using simple language and a style appropriate to the message should achieve this. A prospective local government candidate, for example, will not try to sell him or herself in the same way as a double glazing business will be marketing new windows;

(iii)   be memorable – very often achievable by using a slogan or some striking advertising 'copy', for instance "can you afford not to read this?".

References and testimonials

All organisations are called upon from time to time to write references and, to a lesser extent, testimonials. A reference is a statement, commonly given on a standard form provided by the prospective employer but sometimes produced as a letter, which is provided for a future employer (company, college etc.), by someone who has knowledge of the applicant; and contains a statement of the applicant's qualities and abilities. These may be qualities of character, or abilities related to work performance.

A testimonial is a letter of commendation, written either by the employer or by some other person or body with whom the applicant has had dealings. A major distinction between a testimonial and reference is that a reference is sent direct from the person providing it to the person requiring it, whereas a testimonial is held in the possession of the applicant who sends a copy of it in support of a job application. Not surprisingly, prospective employers value references more highly than testimonials, for a testimonial can be easily forged and tends to highlight the strengths of the applicant and ignore his or her weaknesses.

When an organisation, or indeed an individual, is required to provide a reference it may recognise a moral obligation to be as open and honest in its assessment as possible. In consequence, it may quite genuinely make statements which it believes to be true, but which in fact are not true. The law recognises that a person has a right to protect his or her reputation, and an action can be brought for damages under the tort of defamation where such reputation has been harmed by an untrue statement of a defamatory kind.

The defence of privilege exists to strike a balance between the need to protect reputations and allow freedom of expression in a communication made between a person acting under a moral obligation to provide a reference and a person having a professional interest in receiving it.

If an organisation writes a letter of reference containing untrue statements about the applicant, providing the reference was issued without malice, the existence of privilege will provide a complete defence to the organisation.

A letter of reference usually follows a traditional layout, and an example is included below:

Anne Clark: 6 South Green, Stainmore, Essex.

I have known the above for over five years, and I am very happy to write in support of her application for the position of clerical officer.

Anne joined this company as a sales clerk, and after three years was promoted to her present position as sales assistant.

She has shown a conscientious and mature attitude to her job and can work well with others, although recently she has found difficulty in working with one of her colleagues with whom she has had a number of disagreements. She is an ambitious young woman whose career prospects are limited in this organisation by the lack of promotional posts available.

I have every confidence that if her application is successful you will find Anne to be a valuable addition to your staff. I will certainly be sorry to lose her. Please contact me if you require any further details.

Yours faithfully,

A final note on references.

Firstly there is no legal obligation upon an organisation to provide a reference.

Secondly the permission of the referee should be sought before his or her name and address are included on the application form. In cases where an appointment needs to be made rapidly, it is possible that the referee will be telephoned to provide an oral reference, and it does not assist the applicant if the referee is not prepared. In any case there may be reasons why a referee will decline the invitation to act in this capacity.

The Curriculum Vitae, and Letters of Application

So far this section on external written communication has stressed the organisation as the communication initiator. It is also, of course, a recipient. Staying with the theme of organisation as an employer we can note that references and testimonials are associated with outgoing staff. As far as potential new staff are concerned, when a business is seeking to fill a vacancy it will short-list candidates for interview based on its assessment of the written material they will have sent it, often in the shape of a completed application form. There are two other documents commonly associated with job seeking, and it is these that we now consider. They are

    (i) the Curriculum Vitae

    (ii) the Letter of Application.

A Curriculum Vitae

A curriculum vitae, often shortened to 'C.V.' is a document which provides a brief summary of a person's career and personal development. It is like an abbreviated life story. A C.V. is useful when applying for jobs which do not require completion of an application from. They are also useful in support of a general letter of enquiry about job availability sent to a particular organisation. A well constructed C.V. is a valuable asset to you in seeking a job interview, for when a potential employer is drawing up a short-list of applicants for interview the main source of data available will be information contained in C.V. documents. It is usual practice to divide a curriculum vitae into a number of sections, each dealing with a separate aspect of the subject's background. These are likely to include:

    (i) personal details;

    (ii) education;

    (iii) qualifications;

    (iv) work experience;

    (v)   interests, hobbies;

    (vi) general information.

On the next two pages we give an example of a completed curriculum vitae.

Since some of the details contained in a curriculum vitae need to be amended or added from time to time, it is useful to record the curriculum vitae on disk, so that these changes can be easily accommodated.

Curriculum Vitae

Name: Paul Michael O'Grady

Age: 19 Date of Birth: 20.4.70
Marital Status: Single
Nationality: British
Home Address
11, Conway Steet,
Alberton, 2AL 3DD
Telephone Number: Alberton (0833) 60330

Education

1981 - 1983 Greenlane Comprehensive School, Woodfield,
London N6. Member of school soccer team. Member of school
cricket team.

1983 - 1986   Cardinal Newman RC Comprehensive School
Alberton. Member of school soccer team (Captain 1985).
Member of school cricket team. Winner of the school
Challenge Cup for best all round sportsman or woman (1984).
Formed school rock band in 1984.

1986 - 1988   Alberton College of Further Education,
Alberton. Organised regional college football competition
(1986).

Qualifications

1986

GCE 'O' Level English Literature Grade B

GCE 'O' Level Mathematics Grade C

GCE 'O' Level Geography Grade C

GCE 'O' Level Art Grade D

CSE History

CSE Woodwork

('O' levels with Midland Universities Examining Board; CSE
with Southern Board)

1988 BTEC National Diploma in Business Studies:

Subjects taken (with grades): Organisation in its
Environment I and II Pass Merit; People in Organisations I
and II Merit Merit; Finance Distinction; Accounts
Distinction; Information Processing I and II Merit
Distinction; Business Law Pass; Human Resource Management
Merit; Marketing Pass; Statistics Merit.

Work Experience

1987 Work experience placement for 5 weeks as part of
college course, with Heavy Metals Engineering Plc.,
Longbridge Works, Alberton, involved in clerical duties in
the sales and accounts departments.

1988 Work experience placement for 5 weeks as part of
college course, with Charmleigh Plastics Ltd., New Road,

West Burrington, working in the finance and accounts office.

1988 - to date. Accounts clerk with Charmleigh Plastics Ltd. (from August 1987) dealing with salaries and wages. (Present salary £6,850 pa)

Interests

I have a keen interest in all outdoor sports, particularly football. I am a regular first team player for Alberton FC which plays in the local league. I also play bass guitar in the band I formed at school in 1984, and enjoy all kinds of music. I follow the music press closely.

General Information

Career opportunities with my present employer are limited, and I am seeking an opportunity to develop my career in accounts work. I am intending to enrol on the 'A' level accounts evening class course at college in September. Although I have family ties in Alberton I am fully prepared to work outside the area. I hold a full driving licence.

I became engaged in April, and my fiancee and I are getting married next May.

I have to give 1 month's notice to terminate my present job.

Referees

The following persons will act as referees:

Mr. Peter Parker,

Personnel Officer, Charmleigh Plastics Ltd., New Road, West Burrington, Tel: (0706) 46368

Mrs. Susan Blake,

BTEC National Course Co-ordinator, Alberton College of Further Education, Great Barton Street, Alberton, Tel: (0442) 292911

Fr. Shaun Tomelty,

Church of St Johns, Albany Avenue, Alberton, Tel: (0442) 215981

Letters of Application

From time to time it is necessary to construct letters in which the writer is seeking a post with a potential employer. The image conveyed by such a letter is clearly of importance if the applicant is to stand a chance of being called for interview. Two letters of application are included below. They illustrate the do's and don'ts of producing such letters, and help to show how essential it is for any letter, whatever its purpose, to be properly constructed.

```
(i) Mr. D Greensmith                        5 Beach Drive
Personnel Manager                           Tilney-on-Sea
Arrow Financial Services Ltd.               Southshire
Arrow House                                 15 September 19xx
Barborough
Southshire

(ii) Your ref:DG/PP

(iii) Dear Sir,

(iv) I wish to apply for the post of administrative trainee
which was recently advertised by your company in the
Barborough Recorder.

(v) I have enclosed my curriculum vitae in support of the
application.

(vi) Since completing a business studies course at
Barborough College in June, I have been working for
Dicksons Supermarkets engaged in storeroom duties. At the
same time I have been looking for a post to enable me to
use and develop my business studies skills. The advertised
post seems ideal since you require someone with a knowledge
of information technology and basic accounting procedures
and both these areas I studied for two years on my course.

(vii) I have to give a fortnights notice to terminate my
present job, and can arrange to be available for interview
at any time convenient to you.

Yours faithfully,
```

Kate Smythe

```
Kate Smythe
```

Kate Smythe's letter is clearly written and well presented. Her letter contains the following points:

  (i) the name, status and address of the recipient;

  (ii) the company reference;

  (iii) the formal salutations "Dear Sir" with its appropriate close "Yours faithfully" which are appropriate to the formality of a letter of application;

(iv) a formal application for the job in the first paragraph, identifying which post is involved and where she heard about it;

(v) reference to enclosures, in this case her C.V.;

(vi) a brief account of her background educational and employment experience, emphasising the suitability of her college work for the advertised post. Note how she introduces a positive statement that she wishes to use and develop her business skills;

(vii) a concluding paragraph which indicates her availability for interview and suggests her keenness to be considered for the post.

Compare this letter of application with Susan Wilson's letter which is included below:

> 10 Parkside
> Medford
> Southshire
>
> 22 September
>
> Dear Mr. Greensmith,
>
> I saw the advert about the trainee, me mum and me think it might be the sort of job I would like, seeing as how I've done some bookkeeping in the past and I enjoy it. I am 19 and I left school at 16. I've got 3 GCSE's, and I've worked in two shops but I am fed up with my present job because I don't like the people. If you want to get hold of me quick you can phone Mrs. Johnson next door who will take a message.
>
> Yours faithfully,
>
> *Susan Wilson*
>
> Susan Wilson

By the way of contrast this letter is badly written, containing a number of major flaws. Among them are the following:

(i) no company reference is given, nor the name and title of the recipient or his company;

(ii) the close to the letter, "Yours faithfully" is inappropriate to the salutation "Dear Mr. Greensmith";

(iii) the job is not clearly identified, and since it is Susan who is applying for the job it is hard to see why her mother should be involved. It suggests Susan is someone who cannot make up her own mind;

(iv) she refers to bookkeeping, but does not elaborate and consequently we do not know how much bookkeeping she has done and at what level;

(v) it would be helpful if she indicated the subjects in which she obtained her GCSE's;

(vi) we are left wondering whether the difficulties she has in her present job are due to faults in her own character;

(vii) referring to Mrs. Johnson without giving her telephone number is simply making work for Mr. Greensmith or his secretary in the event that the company does wish to contact Susan urgently;

(viii) the letter contains a number of grammatical errors, and it is not supported by any further information about the applicant in the form of curriculum vitae.

Telex

Telex is a system of written communication used primarily by industry and commerce. The message is transmitted using a teleprinter, and the telex user is given a Telex number, which acts like a telephone number. A telex directory is also provided. Telex facilities are operated by British Telecom.

The advantages of using telex are that:

(a) the message can be transferred virtually instantaneously;

(b) a written record is kept of the communication;

(c) messages can be sent at any time so, provided the recipient's teleprinter has been left on, it is possible, for example, to pass a message from the United Kingdom during working hours to New Zealand while the staff of the organisation are at home because of the different time zone.

(d) errors typed out on the teleprinter can be easily identified by inserting the word "error" and then retyping the correct message.

Because the use of telex facilities is costly (charges are based upon time rather than the number of words) the message should be terse but understandable. Normally, grammatical rules are dispensed with. An example of a telex message would be:

> "MANAGING DIRECTOR VANDOR P.L.C.
> ARRIVING 17:30 FRIDAY 31ST OCTOBER. PLEASE
> MEET. ARRANGE BOARD MEETING FOR 20:00
> SAME DAY. MAIN AGENDA ITEM JORDANIAN.
> CIRCULATE FINANCIAL REPORT 89/S/2 IN
> ADVANCE. BOOK HOTEL ACCOMMODATION
> ONE NIGHT"

Fax

Fax is an electronic system which uses telephone lines to transfer documents from a sender to a recipient. The document is printed out on the recipient's Fax machine, saving the time that would otherwise be taken up in sending material through the post.

Forms

The nature and scope of forms

We live in an environment of forms. The major social events of our existence such as births, marriages and deaths are recorded on them. We complete them for licences, insurance policies, job applications, property purchases, credit transactions, membership of organisations, and so on. They encroach on most aspects of our lives and, if we work in an administrative job, the likelihood is that processing of forms will be a main aspect of our jobs.

What is a form and why is it necessary? A form is simply a document of a standardised type, prepared in advance and used as a means of eliciting information from the person completing it. This is achieved by including instructions indicating the nature of the information being required and leaving spaces or blocks where it can be inserted. As with any type of information gathering mechanism, the skill in obtaining an accurate and comprehensive response lies in designing appropriate questions and presenting them in a suitable layout. Nevertheless, it should be remembered that there may be considerable skill involved in effectively completing a form as well.

Individuals and organisations alike are constantly exposed to a bombardment of forms to be completed. Nevertheless, many organisations find it useful and necessary to produce their own forms. They may be used as part of an internal system of communication, such as stock records and computer input forms, or as an aspect of external communications, for instance application forms, market research surveys, and questionnaires used to test consumer satisfaction with products and services. A local authority will use many types of forms to obtain relevant information ranging from grant applications for loft insulation to planning applications and forms dealing with council house applications. You may have had to complete a form to apply for assistance with this course from your employer, you certainly had to complete a registration form to commence the course, and later on you may have to complete an examination entry form. In addition you have to complete a form to: tax a car; obtain insurance; join a trade union; obtain credit; apply for a passport; take out a mortgage; record your income for tax purposes, to name but a few examples.

The advantages of using forms to obtain and record information are:

- the information obtained can be precisely tailored to the needs of the organisation by the use of suitable questions;

- the information is provided in a standard order which assists the processing of it;

- unnecessary correspondence can be avoided; and

- detailed information can be rapidly accessed.

It might also be added that the effective use of forms in an organisation can save time and money. However, these benefits can be offset by the over enthusiastic use of forms generating irrelevant and unnecessary information. Thus the first question to be asked before designing a form is whether it is really necessary. Perhaps there is a simpler way of obtaining the information. Even if this is so the fact remains that the form is a major tool of communication for all types of organisations. It is an indispensable mechanism for obtaining information, and monitoring processes and activities.

The design and layout of forms

The design and layout of forms is a skilled task, often carried out by specialists. Essentially it involves constructing questions appropriate to the information being sought and ordering them in a suitable way.

The following should be considered in designing a form:

(i)   Instructions to the recipient

It helps to remember that a form involves two-way communication. The recipient should be clear how the form should be completed, to whom it should be returned, when it should be returned by and, perhaps, what purpose it serves the organisation seeking to obtain the data. A valuable general instruction is to indicate that no part of the form should be left unanswered, and that questions that do not apply to the recipient should be answered, "Not applicable".

(ii)   The questions

Questions can be framed in different ways, but as long as they are clear and precise it is simply a matter of design preference as to the method used. An example of different approaches is the use of direct and indirect questions, thus "What is your reason for seeking the job?" (direct), "Is there anything you are dissatisfied about in your present post" (indirect) and open and closed quotations thus " Have you ever bought one of our products? Please answer yes or no (closed), "if you have ever bought one of our products what did you like about it?" (open). The language of each question should be kept as simple as accuracy permits, and it should never be necessary for the recipient to spend time working out what a question means. If a question inevitably involves the use of technical expressions, a note of explanation should be provided, preferably as close to the question as possible. The designer should be aware of the types of reader who will complete the form, to ensure that its language reflects the most basic level of literacy that any reader may possess. A questionnaire for completion by accountants would probably use a wider range of vocabulary than would be desirable in a form to be completed by nine year old school children!

(iii)   The responses

It should be absolutely clear how the recipient is required to respond to the questions. Common methods of response include: "Please place a tick in the appropriate box", "Please answer 'yes' or 'no'", and "Please state briefly your reasons". If the recipient is confused it is possible for the answer given to be the opposite of the correct one. When a written or typed response is asked for, sufficient space should be made available.

(iv)   Question sequence

This should be logical. An application form for a job might commence with a section dealing with the applicant's personal details: name; age; marital status; number of dependants. It would then require information on qualifications and work experience. This would be followed by a section identifying the applicant's interests and hobbies, a section specifying referees, and finally a section enabling the applicant to identify the qualities which make him or her suitable for the post.

(v)   Processing considerations

Sometimes the information obtained needs to be collated for the preparation of statistical or survey reports. It may be that the organisation is seeking to identify trends and general patterns rather than use information obtained on an individual basis. If this is so it is vital that the information is presented in a way which is as easy as possible to process. If the information is to be processed electronically then the capacities of the data processing equipment will need to be considered. In such cases instructions may be of vital importance: the machine may be unable to pick up and 'read' anything other than black ink or print.

(vi)   Legal implications

Many forms are the direct product of statutory provisions. Applications to renew business leases, to provide information for the Registrar of Companies, to register as an elector, to complete an income tax return, and to tax and insure a motor vehicle all involve the completion of forms that are required by statute. Often criminal penalties can be imposed if the information provided is known to be false. In the case of insurance proposals, the proposer (the applicant) is under a positive legal obligation to provide information materially relevant to the risk to be insured, even if this is not asked for on the form. An organisation insuring its premises against fire is likely to find the insurance company avoiding the policy if it discovers that the organisation is knowingly employing a convicted arsonist. It will be no defence for the organisation to say that the policy did not ask "Do you have in your employment any convicted arsonists? If so please give details."!

Specific types of forms

The variety of forms in common use is so vast that it is impossible to give anything other than a very general description of what they include. It may, however, help to identify the broad categories into which they fall. These categories relate to the purpose of the form and, clearly, the content of the form will usually reflect the purpose or objective the organisation has in using it.

Thus the forms are used:

- to keep records –financial, personnel, statistical, and so on;
- for applications – for jobs, grants, hearings before an industrial tribunal;
- for making orders or bookings – goods from a supplier, a package holiday, a credit transaction, internal requisitions;
- to monitor processes and make assessments – stock records, the evaluation of product quality, work sheets, income tax returns;
- for carrying out surveys (usually by means of questionnaires) – consumer reaction to a new product, the Census.

Oral communication

Having examined in some detail the written methods used by organisations in the communication process, we must conclude by looking at the methods of oral communication that organisations use. These include: the use of the telephone; dictation; verbal presentation of reports; interviewing; and meetings. It should be recalled that oral communication involves not only the skills speaking but of listening as well. A communication system is ineffective if its staff are poor listeners; poor listening can result in letters having to be redrafted and/or retyped, orders being misdirected and meetings needing to be rearranged.

The larger and more complex an organisation becomes the more important it is for those operating the communications system to guard against it becoming too unwieldy. When oral messages are being transferred, the larger the number of employees involved in the chain of communication, the greater the danger of the message becoming distorted. The story is told of the message being sent along the trenches during the First World War which began its life as "3000 Germans advancing on the West flank. Send reinforcements" but ended up as "3000 Germans dancing on a wet plank. Send three and four pence"!

A good listener is someone who:

- concentrates on the speaker's delivery without being distracted by external or internal factors (noise and daydreaming, for example, or the speaker's mannerisms);
- is not emotionally affected by the statements the speaker makes;
- listens to everything that is being said, rather than concentrating on main points, or homing in only when the speaker sounds more interesting;
- recognises that people are able to take in words much faster than they can be spoken, and develops a strategy for overcoming the spare time this

disparity provides. Note taking is a useful device for doing so. Obviously, the nature of the subject matter is a significant factor. If the speaker is using complex language and sophisticated concepts the spare time for thoughts the listener may have is likely to be very limited.

Styles of oral communication

As a general proposition oral communications are either formal or informal. Informal speech is used largely in our social and domestic relationships. The language used is abbreviated for we know each other well, and lengthy explanations are not called for. Compare a chat you might have with a close friend with the casual conversation you might have with a stranger at a business function, and assess how much the language you use varies according to the recipient.

Formal speech is appropriate to the work environment where the speaker represents the organisation and should, therefore, deliver his or her words with more care and precision, in a carefully structured way. Clearly, a telephone conversation with a business customer does not warrant a style or tone which is over familiar or excessively casual. A personal telephone call to a friend, however, is quite a different matter.

The nature of oral communication is affected not only by the purpose of the statements being made, the formal/informal distinction, but also by the physical proximity of the parties. Face to face communication enables much closer awareness to develop through the uses of forms of non-verbal communication such as facial expressions and other forms of body language, whereas more distant communication, for example the use of the telephone, effectively eliminates the use of non-verbal signs and emphasises the importance of the language being used.

The significance of these elements of formality/informality, and physical distance lies in the different social rules which govern oral communications. For instance, in face to face communication we tend to respond in different ways to the people we are dealing with, according to our perceptions of what they expect of us. You might feel it quite out of order to crack a joke with your Head of Department, whereas you do this all the time with colleagues of the same grade as yourself. Status then is an important factor in the determination of what we say to others. If the Head of Department leads the conversation by telling a joke we may feel this is a suitable opening for a humorous anecdote that it would not otherwise have seemed appropriate to tell.

Thus, it is not true to say that being physically close necessarily produces a less formal approach to oral communication, nor that it is impossible to communicate informally over a distance (for instance phoning a friend).

Methods of oral communication

The telephone

Within most organisations the telephone is a vital tool in the business of communicating. It is important not just as a link with customers and clients, but also as a means of communicating internally throughout the organisation if it is equipped with a PABX system.

It is often necessary to think out what needs to be said before making a telephone call. If information to be imparted over the phone is complex it is especially important to make sure it has been understood and correctly recorded by the person at the receiving end. Asking for imparted information to be repeated may be useful in identifying any confusion that may arise.

The following guidelines should be followed when using the telephone:

- when making or receiving a call the identity of the parties should be established at the outset;

- a pad and pen or pencil should be immediately to hand in order to avoid keeping the other person waiting;

- the parties should speak as clearly as possible; often telephone conversations are conducted in very noisy environments which makes it difficult to distinguish the voice on the telephone from other extraneous sounds;

- avoid keeping a caller waiting for long periods whilst information is being sought: it is far better to arrange to call back;

- when the call is completed make a note of the details of the conversation and take appropriate action (pass the message on, or place the note in the relevant file).

Dictation

Dictation is used as a means of conveying a message orally which is to be transposed into writing – usually into a letter. If the dictation is face to face it provides the secretary taking down the message with an opportunity to clarify any problems straightaway. If, however a tape is made, the person dictating the message should ensure that it is delivered clearly, that punctuation is identified and that difficult words or expressions such as unusual surnames are spelt out.

Interviews

Probably the most important factor in conducting an interview is to be properly prepared. The interview room should be laid out so that the interviewer and the interviewee are close enough to be able to hear each other properly. The interviewer (or the panel) should have examined the application prior to the interview and have identified a systematic approach to the questioning of the applicant. Of course, not all interviews are concerned with appointing new staff; they may be disciplinary or involve dealing with a complaint from a customer. Whatever the case, the interviewer should have carefully examined the background details before the interview is conducted.

The following points should be observed during an interview:

- the interviewee should be welcomed and the chairperson of the interview panel should introduce him or herself and other members;

- the purpose of the interview should be explained and the interviewee encouraged to feel at ease;

- the responses of the interviewee to questions should be carefully listened to. It is important not to disturb the interviewee's train of though or to monopolise the conversation;

- the questions themselves should be pertinent, and a note should be kept of the points that need to be remembered as the interview proceeds;

- the interview should be concluded when the interviewers have received the information they need.

The situation should be summarised. If it is possible to do so any decision which has been reached should be communicated immediately. Alternatively, it should be explained that a decision will be communicated at a later stage, and an indication given as to when this is likely to be. It is courteous to thank the interviewee for attending and, in the case of a job application for which a decision can be made after the interviews have been completed, it may be thought appropriate to provide the unsuccessful applicants with some brief words of reassurance.

Assignment *The Computer Company Merger*

Following the merger of Macro Computers with the Business Software Group, the first board meeting of the new company, Business Computers and Software Ltd. resulted in a number of important changes being implemented. One of them was the establishment of a personnel department. Previously neither company had operated a personnel department, but had left personnel matters to individual departments to sort out for themselves.

You have been transferred to this new department, where your job involves you working as a senior assistant to the Personnel Officer Anne Robinson. After your initial meeting with Ms Robinson, at which a variety of issues were discussed, you received the following internal memorandum from her:

From: Personnel Officer

To: Senior Personnel Assistant

Date: 9 June 19xx

Re: Establishment of Standardised Materials

I have given thought to our conversation on the need for standardised letters and forms to meet the functions of the new department. I am satisfied that we cannot standardise job adverts, however please provide me with drafts of the following:

Forms:

- a job application form that all job applicants would have to complete (I would want it to contain sufficient information to enable me to use it as an employee record form)

- a staff appraisal form to record job performance

Letters to fulfil the following tasks:

- invite applicants for job interviews;

- inform an applicant that he/she is not being called for interview;

- inform an interviewee that he/she is not being offered the job;

- offer the job to the successful interviewee;

- issue a formal warning to an employee guilty of misconduct stating that dismissal will result from a repetition of the conduct complained of;

- issue a dismissal;

- inform an employee that he/she is being made redundant.

I am aware that this is a substantial task but would ask you to complete it as a matter of urgency.

Tasks

1.   Draft the forms and letters requested in the memorandum, using a content, tone and style appropriate to each of them.

2.   Write a memorandum to the Personnel Officer indicating that you expect the work to take considerable time to complete.

Developmental Task

Obtain examples of some of the above documents, letters and forms used by public and private sector organisations in your area. Compare these in order to produce a dossier containing a single example of each document, letter or form which combines the examples of best practice in each.

Chapter 33

Persuasion, Argument and Co-operation

Appropriate methods of communication

We have already discussed the different methods of communication in some depth in Chapter 32. Here we can note that the decision as to a suitable method of communication to meet the needs of the particular occasion is one which can easily overlooked by a person who is overworked, or simply not appreciated, and in consequence great damage can be done.

Consider the following examples:

(i) an assistant in a Management Information Services Department has been given the task of producing a formal report on some aspect of the work of her department. She spends a considerable amount of time researching and writing up the report, including a number of evenings working at home. Her superior indicated when she gave her the task that if she performed it thoroughly it could mean a promotion. The day after she completes the report she receives an internal memorandum from her superior which simply states, "I acknowledge receipt of your report, which due to recent management rethinking is no longer needed";

(ii) at the office Christmas party the Manager gives a speech before all the office staff. One of the staff present is 62 and has urged the company to let him continue working until the age of 65. After discussion the company has agreed his request. However at the end of his speech the Manager concludes, "and I am pleased to say that Harry is being given early retirement. Quite a Christmas present, eh, Harry!";

(iii) one of the senior staff of a company comes bursting into the typing pool where there are ten typists at work. In his hand is a letter typed by one of the typists who has only just started working for the company. "This is a disgrace, and you are a disgrace. You are not fit to work here. Type it again!" he shouts across the room to the typist, at the same time screwing up the letter and throwing it on the floor.

In the first example above, the tactless communication of her superior is likely to produce a reaction in the assistant which at best sees her superior as insensitive and unreliable and at worst leads her to look for a new job. In the second example the

Manager's public address is clearly inappropriate, for at least two reasons. Firstly it indicates a possible weakness in the channels of communication in the organisation, and secondly it demonstrates a lack of sensitivity on the part of the Manager regarding the time and place for a statement of this kind to be made. Let us consider these two issues in turn. To begin with the Manager appears to have received misinformation from the company, since Harry has negotiated to stay on. Alternatively the company may have changed its mind about the early retirement, without telling Harry, which is inexcusable. But quite apart from the question of how well informed the Manager actually is, and even assuming the information is correct, it is doubtful whether the speech at the office party is, in the circumstances, a suitable occasion to reveal that Harry is leaving. He may regard the matter as confidential; something which he would want to tell colleagues about in his own time. He may be sensitive about his age. At very least it would be wise to alert him in advance of what is going to be said, so that he is given an opportunity to give or refuse his consent to it. In matters of a personal nature it is most important to guard against making them public, certainly at an inappropriate time and place. This holds true whether the information is revealed expressly, as in this case, or if it is allowed to leak out. In organisations where other staff are 'in the know' about a personal matter before the individual who is directly affected (promotion, disciplinary matters, redundancy and so on), not only does the individual concerned feel angry, hurt and possibly humiliated, fellow staff are also likely to sympathise with that person, and perhaps see their organisation as one which is insensitive to the feelings of its staff. The lack of trust and confidence this can create is harmful to the type of relationship between employee and organisation that is needed if the employee is to give of his or her best.

In the last example the criticisms that can be levelled at the senior member of staff are that: (i) he has publicly humiliated the typist; (ii) he has made no allowance for the fact that she is a new starter; (iii) he has revealed himself in the eyes of a member of staff to be someone totally lacking in manners and grace in an ill-tempered response to an incident to which he seems to have totally over-reacted. It is unlikely that either the typist in question or the others in the typing pool will give of their best to this member of staff in the future. Indeed as someone lacking in self control it may have been purely by chance that his outburst did not include a sexist comment such as "You women are all the same!" (assuming the typist to be female!), resulting in them refusing to work any further until an apology has been given. Unnecessary oral confrontations of this sort are usually counterproductive and should be avoided.

Reasons for communicating

It is not possible to gauge the appropriateness of the method used to communicate without considering what reason or function the communication is seeking to fulfil. Since communicating is a two way process it is necessary to examine not only the aim or intention of the person initiating the communication, but also the perception of the person receiving it. For instance when a senior member of staff says to a junior employee, "You're looking rough today. I doubt whether you are fit for anything," the employee may take this to be a way of issuing a rebuke, whilst the intention of the senior was simply to be sociable and sympathetic. It is easy for messages to be misinterpreted. It is possible to classify the reasons for communicating as seen from the initiator's standpoint, into four separate categories of intention:

    (a) to give or obtain information;

    (b) to encourage or persuade;

    (c) to indicate sociability; or

    (d) to provide psychological support.

Clearly these categories can and do overlap. For instance when one colleague says to another, "There is a quicker way of working out your figures, if you would like me to show you," the statement falls under (a) and (c) above, whilst when a supervisor tells a junior employee, "Although you did not receive the promotion you performed very well in the interview, and you should apply for Mrs. Wilkins position when she leaves next month," categories (a), (b) and (d) are each involved.

Persuasion - an important management skill

Each of the categories referred to demands different skills on the part of the initiator to be effective. For example giving information requires precision of presentation, whilst persuasion, which is a skill in itself, will usually involve the communicator in using a wide repertoire of devices to achieve the desired effect such as a change in belief or attitude. Persuasive powers are valuable to all those in positions of power and authority, such as managers and politicians, whilst they are equally necessary to anyone engaged in the business of selling goods or services, such as advertisers, sales staff and so on. Some of the issues associated with persuasive powers are:

The choice between 'hard sell' and 'soft sell'

This is the choice whether to put pressure on people, or whether to create an impression of unbiased neutrality. The door to door salesman is traditionally associated with the 'hard sell' approach. Advertising companies using television commercials to increase the sales of products often rely upon subtle techniques to persuade. Within an organisation persuasive tactics used on staff are likely to rely on both methods.

The use of argument

The construction and delivery of an effective argument is a highly developed skill, which may involve using legal, economic, financial, political or moral principles in support of the argument or perhaps relying on expert opinions. Thus an employer may attempt to convince the staff of the need for individual economies or greater output by arguing a financial case, or by presenting the findings of an investigative body into the work of the organisation, such as the report of a systems analyst.

Style of presentation

Whether the approach is hard sell or soft sell, and whatever argument is being relied upon by the persuader, the style of presentation must be carefully considered. This involves identifying the character of the audience or individual and tailoring the approach accordingly. It is really a case of adapting the approach to meet the needs of requirements of the recipient. For example is humour likely to be a successful device; what is the social background of the individual or group; is the audience partisan? It may not be felt that in communicating with the intention of being purely sociable, very heavy demands of skill are placed upon the communicator. In an organisation the status hierarchy can sometimes have the effect of stifling this form of communication, for a superior will sometimes feel that fraternising with junior staff is a recipe for future discipline problems, and may also erode his or her status. As between staff at the same level, sociability usually helps to create close bonds of group identity with the result that individuals will be more prepared to work together as a team.

Finally a word about psychological support. Whilst it is appropriate to provide words of comfort and assistance to those who have experienced a personal trauma, there are clearly occasions when specialist advice and help is needed. A large organisation which seeks to meet its obligations towards the staff by providing them not only with a source of income, but also with an environment that is emotionally and socially supportive, will operate a personnel department to cope with such issues as family bereavement, illness and related personal problems.

The needs of the individual and the group

Under this heading we can consider some of the points that the manager should bear in mind when dealing with the management of the workforce:

(i) the workforce is a group, and will perform most effectively when its individual members are encouraged to see themselves as a cohesive self supporting team. Teamwork relies heavily upon leadership, and a good leader is someone whom the group can respect;

(ii) individuals working for the organisation have particular needs which should be identified and recognised. An employee will usually be seeking both personal and career development and a system for enabling this development to be monitored through regular employer/employee dialogue is valuable;

(iii) adequate physical and psychological rewards both to groups and individuals should be given to mark achievement and encourage further development;

(iv) the climate of the organisation should be carefully monitored. For instance, organisations in which there are group rivalries, or where excessive competition is encouraged or the rewards system is considered to operate unfairly will possess a climate of disharmony that is not compatible with an efficient and effective business unit.

In practical terms the manager can introduce systems to assist in the task of managing human resources. These generally include machinery for staff consultation, grievance procedures, and induction programmes. The working timetable should be designed to enable staff to meet together as groups to discuss problems and issues. Ideally the communications network should be structured so as not only to meet the direct resource requirements of the organisation, but also to meet the needs of the staff as people. Thus events such as anniversaries, births, and promotions should be 'picked up' within the system and celebrated. For most people such rituals are part of the culture of our society and there is no reason why the working environment should not encourage them. It has been said that a good manager is a person who has a clear picture of the organisation in his or her mind. Such a mental picture is one which needs to be heavily focussed on the staff of the organisation, the resource that makes the organisation work. Management has considerable control over the social environment of the workplace, and must always be mindful that a workforce which operates as a socially cohesive unit will work far more effectively for the organisation than will one in which there is division and conflict.

Groups and their characteristics

Ideally an organisation should be structured in such a way that it is able to achieve the objectives it has set for itself. In order that the organisation may carry out all the necessary tasks to achieve this, authority is delegated to various levels of management. Such authority allows them to plan and take appropriate action. The organisation's operations are broken down and divided between various departments. This will allow staff to specialise and develop expertise in particular jobs or functions. Usually to complete a complex task a group of individuals are required to work together. There must be co-ordination and co-operation between the individuals making up the group, as well as between the separate groups themselves.

It is possible to identify the following characteristics which are common to most work groups.

The sharing of common goals

All of the group's members wish to achieve a common purpose. They believe this can be most successfully accomplished collectively. However individuals may have a variety of goals and of course may be members of several groups. Thus they may work closely with their boss (who is a member of management) while at the same time being a member of a trade union. Sometimes the goals of unions and management groups are the same, such as creating a stable organisation with security of employment. Sometimes they may be in conflict, such as a disagreement over wage demands.

Influencing each other

Social interaction means that people in a group influence the values, ideas, beliefs or attitudes of other members. This influence may be a result of discussion between the various members, for example at a committee meeting where people may be encouraged or persuaded to adopt the beliefs of the majority.

Non-verbal communication may also play a part in influencing a member of a group to conform to group thinking. For example the social rejection of a member by 'sending him to Coventry' that is refusing to speak to him represents considerable pressure upon an individual to conform to the group will. Thus a trade union may decide that some form of industrial action is necessary. A complete ban on overtime is called for. If one individual member defies the ban, 'being sent to Coventry' may make him feel that the long term displeasure of his fellow workers is not worth the short term gain of overtime payment.

Group structure

A group will normally have some form of structure or set of rules, however informal, so that members can relate more easily to one another. Group names, or the values that a group shares, may be stable and consistent over a long period and may well outlast the original group members for instance where a number of employees form a football team which lasts for long after the founders of it have stopped playing, or no longer work for the organisation.

Often an unofficial leader emerges as the person most likely to act as group spokesperson on any issue. In unofficial industrial disputes, or where local residents are angry over some community matter it is common to find a vocal member of the group who will speak to the media as the group's representative.

Recognition of members

Members of a group must recognise fellow members in some way and also know who does not belong to their group. Football teams and their fans, as well as the military, depend upon uniforms, slogans or songs. If there is also some form of emotional tie between the group this will exaggerate these outward signs. Work groups which are cohesive or closely bound together are generally more productive. Groups can also provide social status, security and social satisfaction particularly if the members are encouraged to participate in the decision making process and enjoy social events together.

Types of Groups

In work organisations there are three main types of groups. These can be referred to as:

    (a) executive or command groups;

    (b) committees and project (or task force) groups;

    (c) informal groups.

In any organisation there may well be variations of work groups under each of these main headings. This can be expected where the purpose of the organisation and its associated groups differ markedly. The first two types of groups are formal in that it is for management to decide the make-up of the group and its assigned tasks. The third type of group is often seen as an alternative to a formal grouping, and forms out of the natural affinity that people have for each other in certain situations. Let us consider these groups in more detail.

Executive or command groups

Such groups are composed of managers and their staff. They will be engaged in a wide variety of tasks including planning, organising, motivating and co-ordinating the different groupings within the organisation. Each of these groupings or departments will have its own specialism and must co-ordinate with other groups. Thus the manager of a group, for example a production planning manager, will be head of a group providing plans to guide the production of goods manufactured on the shop floor.

At the same time the production planning manager is part of a unit headed by the production director and this group must meet regularly to discuss production problems relating to such matters as quality and quantity.

The manager of each group can thus be seen as the link between fellow members of the work group and the executive or command group. So, while each formal work group has the responsibility to carry out specific tasks in the organisation, such as work study, they must co-ordinate with other groups, such as production, to provide a service that will benefit the organisation as a whole rather than simply to perform their own tasks in isolation. Thus the work study department should be seeking improvements in efficiency in areas of greatest priority to the organisation. Clearly it would not benefit the organisation if this department sought only to evaluate those areas which the department's members regard as being of greatest personal interest.

Committees or project groups

Formal groupings into committee or project groups may be established on a long term basis, for instance, a committee which meets every week to discuss a particular area of responsibility, such as the safety committee. Alternatively they may be short term and established to perform a specific limited project. Such a project group might be asked to design a package for a particular product or have the task, say of surveying a specific piece of development land. The project group would be disbanded at the end of the project but could be reconvened for the next task. A long term committee, such as the housing committee of a local authority, will have defined objectives and a structure that will endure beyond the participation of the original members.

The more formal the committee, the greater is the need for elected officers, such as a secretary and a chairman. Rules and procedures, such as standing orders will help to reinforce the status of the committee and enable individual members to define their roles more clearly. Project or task groups draw people from various departments and therefore cut across the normal structure of the organisation. Such groupings may assist communications and co-operation throughout the organisation by enhancing lateral integration.

Informal groups

Informal groups will vary in the degree of informality they possess. They can range from semi-formal groups such as casual meetings called by managers to discuss current problems to the informal group which congregates at the drinks machine during breaktimes and discusses a variety of subjects including the latest rumours, the short comings of management and the state of the world.

Informal groups have certain advantages:

(i) they provide psychological security for most people feel that there is 'safety in numbers'. People feel more assured when they know that there are others in the same position as they themselves;

(ii) they allow people to establish their own identity or status something more easily achieved in a small group. In a large organisation individual workers commonly feel themselves to be an inconsequential part of an enormous structure, or as it is said, a small cog in a large wheel!

(iii) they help to satisfy people's needs for friendship and support. Members can share jokes and grumbles with friends and so improve social relationships;

(iv) they provide the opportunity for people with similar ideas and values to meet together and reinforce their attitudes. This is common with people of a similar political persuasion;

(v) they provide an informal communication network which supplements the formal channels, the 'grapevine', by which one group can pass messages to each other and so rumour can spread rapidly. The grapevine is sometimes used by managers as an unofficial channel to pass on information;

(vi) they may provide solutions to problems for a group. For instance if a member is experiencing difficulties, the rest of the group may recognise this and so work harder to 'carry' the less productive member.

Informal groups may also display disadvantages:

(i) the group could show considerable resistance to change despite management's concern to improve group working. It can be easier to 'sell' changes to individuals than to groups. Such inflexibility may mean that managers will develop a reluctance to introduce innovations;

(ii) members may be reluctant to 'step out of line' and so may suppress their own feelings if these differ radically from the group's attitudes. Such conformity could lead to less innovation or creativity;

(iii) the 'grapevine' is often the source of rumours which may have no foundation in truth but nevertheless can cause serious disharmony in an organisation. The vacuum created by the lack of positive information from management will be quickly filled by rumours created by the mischievous or the ill-informed;

(iv) the group may test its strength against the rules laid down by management. For example members may finish work early or expand tea and lunch breaks. This could lead to conflict with a 'them and us' situation developing with management which will not improve industrial relations or efficiency. You may also have noted how people often behave quite differently when they are acting in a group rather than individually. This is a striking and important psychological characteristic of the group. For instance a manager may well find that an employee who is amenable and easy to get on with face to face, behaves obstructively and anti-socially when in a work group. The explanation is not always easy to pin point. It may have to do with the individual's perception of the peer group expectation of his or her behaviour. It may also be a result of genuinely assuming the cultural values of the group even when these values conflict with individual values.

The Purpose of Groups

Groups may evolve or be formed for various purposes. They can evolve out of a random association of individuals who find themselves bonded together by some common interest, such as the threat of redundancy. If the reason for membership of a group becomes obsolete then members will lose interest in it and it will die.

An individual's need for group membership

Individuals join groups for the following reasons:

(i) **as a means of achieving goals or targets.** Personal or organisational objectives may be more easily attained in a group. A singer joining a band is an example demonstrating how both personal and group ambitions may be enhanced by providing a more versatile combination;

(ii) **in order to satisfy their social needs.** People are naturally sociable and need to be with others and share common ideas, values and pleasures. They may join clubs or societies simply to enjoy the company of others;

(iii) **in order to share or help in a process that requires others.** This may be giving a service, producing goods or for recreational purposes such as a football team;

(iv) **as a method of establishing and displaying their own stance in society.** A person may join a political party with the intention of becoming a future candidate at a local election or perhaps to help and encourage others to do so.

An organisation's need for groups

Organisations use groups for various purposes:

(i) **to carry out tasks which are not easily carried out by an individual alone.** Thus to take a simple illustration, to run a successful racing car team needs skills and talents which are brought together in harmony. Each member of the team has his own duties and responsibilities and the work is distributed amongst the team, according to their individual skills;

(ii) **to ensure that important aspects of the work are well managed and controlled.** The group could have a specific responsibility within the organisation, such as work study measurement, and would be expected to ensure that this was carried out effectively and efficiently. This is an example of how groups evolve to deal with the specialism demanded by the organisation;

(iii) **to make decisions and solve problems.** Pooling the knowledge and experience of a number of people may result in better quality decisions. Local authorities make extensive use of committees to decide both policy and the priority of objectives. The operation of the organisation is then delegated to the full-time employees of the appropriate department;

(iv) **for arbitration, conciliation and negotiation processes.** Often a group provides a variety of personnel with a wide spread of values, ideas and beliefs which will give a more objective view or solving disputes of various kinds. There is also a legal requirement to have a wide representation on bodies such as industrial and administrative tribunals;

(v) **to seek to involve workers in decision making and so encourage commitment which facilitates the effective implementation of the decision.** If people are allowed to put forward their own ideas and these are thoroughly discussed, then whether or not they are adopted, there will be a stronger commitment to seek a successful outcome than if the decisions for change were made elsewhere and thrust upon them;

(vi) **for gathering, processing and distributing information.** A committee may be formed to undertake these functions and so provide a vital co-ordinating link between departments. The role of the Safety Committee in an organisation, composed of members from each department, is a useful example;

(vii) **to evaluate and analyse past decisions or events.** A committee may be set up to evaluate past decisions and to initiate inquiries.

Overlap or conflict of purposes

Individual and organisational purposes may overlap. They may combine and confirm each other, such as the ambitious executive's desire to be part of a successful company. In some cases, however, individual and organisational purposes will conflict. Some of the social activities of informal work groups, such as a long chat during tea breaks, may well stand in the way of higher production and so conflict with organisational objectives. Work groups may informally agree to lower outputs per man than those expected by management. Sometimes an individual's needs are lost in conforming to group decisions. For example a group decision to ban overtime may reduce an individual's earning capacity and so conflict with his desire to maximise earnings.

Chapter 34

Data Structures

Introduction

A sound knowledge of basic data structures is essential for any computer programmer. A programming task will almost invariably involve the manipulation of a set of data which normally will be organised according to some coherent structure. It could be that the data is to be read in and processed, in which case a detailed knowledge of its structure is obviously essential. Furthermore, processing the data might involve organising it in a way that facilitates its subsequent retrieval, as in information retrieval applications. Output from the program might require that the data is presented in yet another form. So a single program might be required to handle a number of data structures; only by having a thorough knowledge of basic data structures can the programmer choose, or design, the structures most appropriate to the problems being addressed.

From a programming viewpoint, the study of data structures involves two aspects, namely, the theoretical principles upon which the structures are founded, and the practicalities of implementing them using a computer. This chapter addresses both of these considerations by describing a number of important data structures and their applications to programming tasks.

Fundamental principles

A data structure is essentially a number of data *items*, also called *elements* or *nodes*, with some relationship linking them together. Each item consists of one or more named parts called *fields* occupying one or more memory locations in the computer. In its simplest form, an element can be a single field occupying a single word of memory.

A list of numbers occupying consecutive memory locations in a computer is a simple data structure:

Memory Location	Contents
1000	56
1001	34
1002	123
1003	11
1004	77

The relationship linking the individual elements is merely the order in which they are stored in memory. In order to access the next element in the list (that is, an element's *successor*) it is necessary only to increment the memory address; the previous element at any point in the list (that is an element's *predecessor*) is found by decrementing the current memory address. This simple structural relationship allows the list to be accessed in sequential order.

Data structures such as *linked lists* provide pointers linking elements together. So, for example, to access the above numeric list in ascending order of magnitude, an extra field could be added to each element to point to the next element in the sequence:

Memory Location	Contents	
	Link	Value
1000	1004	56
1001	1000	34
1002	0000	123
1003	1001	11
1004	1002	77

Now, starting with location 1003 and following the links, the list can be accessed in ascending order: the link contained in location 1003 indicates that the number succeeding 11 is in location 1001; location 1001 contains the number 34 plus a pointer showing that the next number in the sequence is to be found at location 1000; the list terminates at location 1002 which contains the final number, 123, and a zero link indicating that there are no more elements in the list.

Linked lists make it easier to insert or delete elements at any position in the sequence of items, at the cost of increased complexity and increased memory demands.

Other data structures such as stacks and queues restrict access to elements to certain points of a sequential data structure, normally the start or end. With stacks, elements may only be added or deleted at one end of the list; queues allow items to be added at one end and deleted at the other.

One common method of implementing on a computer all of the data structures outlined above is by means of an *array,* a concept introduced in Chapter 26, Tabular Data, and discussed in more detail in the next section.

Arrays

Storage of arrays

High-level procedural languages such as BASIC, COBOL and Pascal allow programmers to manipulate tabular data stored in *arrays.* The programmer merely declares the name, size and dimension of the array and the language processor takes care of allocating memory for it.

The immediate access store (memory) of a computer consists of a large number of memory locations, each with its own unique address (see Chapter 22). Memory locations have addresses ranging from 0 to $n-1$, where n represents the total number of memory locations available in the computer. For example, in a computer which has 640K bytes of user memory, byte addresses will range from 0 to $(640 \times 1024) - 1$, that is, 0 to 655359.

If a programmer defines a one-dimensional array of, say, twenty integers each occupying a single word, then the language processor must assign sufficient storage space for the array in user RAM and be able to find any array element as quickly as possible. Locating an array element requires a small calculation involving the starting address of the array, which is termed the *base address,* and the number of bytes per array element.

For example, suppose we have a one-dimensional array A_k of single byte words, where k is over the range 0 to 20, with base address b. Then element A_0 will have address

$$b + 0 = b$$

Element A_1 will have address

$$b + 1$$

and, in general, element A_k will have address

$$b + k.$$

The following diagram shows the relationship between array elements and memory locations:

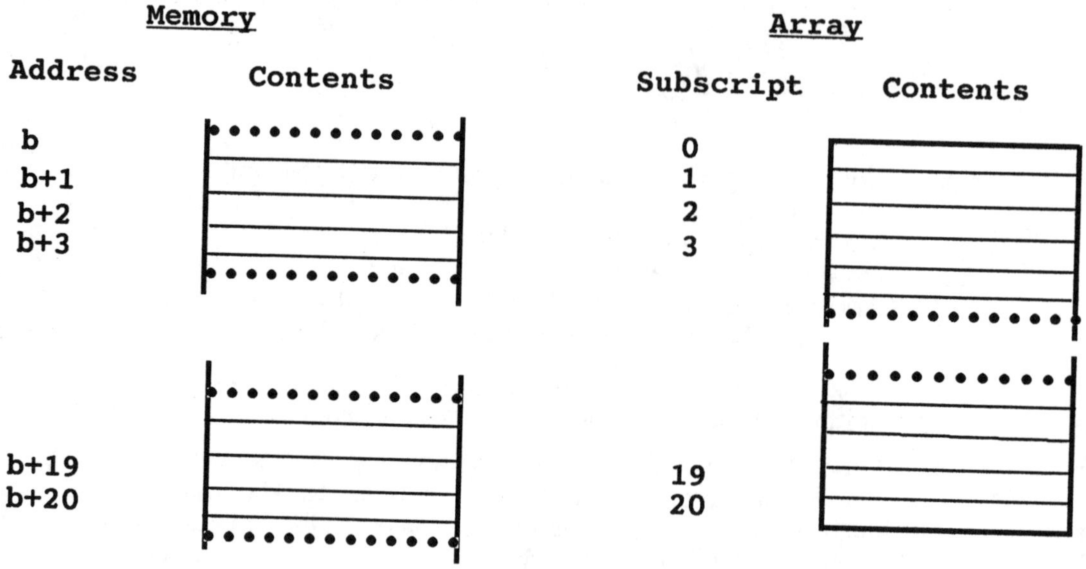

1-D Array

Because the memory of a computer is essentially a one-dimensional array of memory locations, when it is required to represent a two-dimensional table, a slightly more complicated calculation is necessary: the language processor must convert a two-dimensional array element into a one-dimensional physical memory address.

Suppose now that we are considering the storage requirements of a two-dimensional array, $T_{j,k}$, single word integers and size 10 × 6 that is, a table with 10 rows ($j=0$ to 9) and 6 columns ($k=0$ to 5) as shown below.

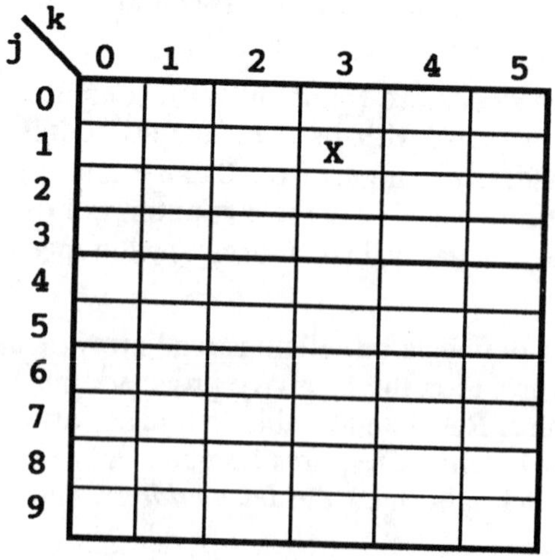

10x6   Array

If the base address is at location b, and the array is stored row by row, then the elements of the array might be stored in memory as follows:

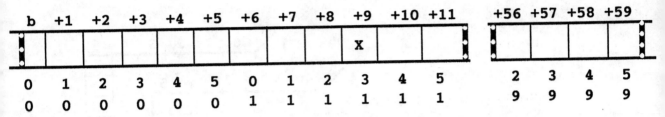

b	+1	+2	+3	+4	+5	+6	+7	+8	+9	+10	+11		+56	+57	+58	+59
								X								
0	1	2	3	4	5	0	1	2	3	4	5		2	3	4	5
0	0	0	0	0	0	1	1	1	1	1	1		9	9	9	9

Storage of 2-D Array

The calculation required to convert from a two-dimensional array element $T_{j,k}$ to a memory location, M, is

$$M = b + j \times 6 + k$$

For example, element $T_{0,3}$ would occupy the location

$$M = b + 0 \times 6 + 3 = b + 3,$$

and element $T_{3,2}$ would be at location

$$M = b + 3 \times 6 + 2 = b + 20$$

The calculations above assume that the array is of size 10×6. In general, if the array is of size $m \times n$, then an element $T_{j,k}$ would translate to the location

$$M = b + j \times n + k$$

This is called a *mapping function,* a formula which uses the array size and the element subscripts to calculate the memory address at which that element is located.

Note that if the array is stored column by column rather than row by row, the mapping function becomes

$$M = b + k \times m + j$$

Extending this scheme to an array, $D_{i,j,k}$, of three dimensions and size $l \times m \times n$, the conversion calculation becomes,

$$M = b + i \times m \times n + j \times n + k$$

The diagram on the next page illustrates the correspondence between array elements and memory locations for a three-dimensional table of size $3 \times 5 \times 6$.

Here, i can be considered to be the subscript which specifies a number of tables, each of size $j \times k$. Thus, $D_{2,3,5}$ references element (3,5) of the third table (for which i=2). This corresponds to the location

$$M = b + 2 \times 5 \times 6 + 3 \times 6 + 5 = b + 83$$

Further application of the principles explained above allow arrays of any number of dimensions to be handled.

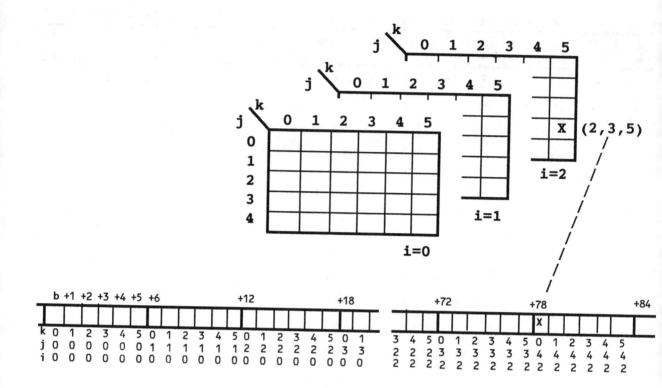

3-D Array vs Memory vector

Iliffe vectors

When speed has a higher priority than memory requirements, a table look-up scheme is sometimes adopted for accessing array elements. The main drawback of using a mapping function is the time taken to perform the address calculation, which will generally involve one or more relatively slow multiplication operations. The number of calculations can be significantly reduced by pre-calculating row or column addresses and storing them in another table.

For example, suppose that we have a 3×5 array as illustrated below:

j \ k	0	1	2	3	4
0	b	b+1	b+2	b+3	b+4
1	b+5	b+6	b+7	b+8	b+9
2	b+10	b+11	b+12	b+13	b+14

3x5 Array

We first calculate, and then store in three consecutive memory locations, the starting address for each of the three rows. This is called an *Iliffe vector* (see diagram below).

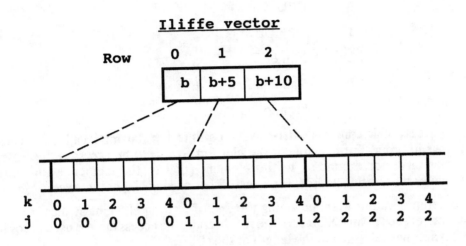

Use of Iliffe Vector

So, given the row subscript for the array element to be accessed, the Iliffe vector is consulted for the starting address of that row, and the location of the required element is found by using the column subscript as an offset to be added to this row address. When implemented in assembly language or machine code using appropriate addressing modes, this scheme virtually eliminates the necessity for any address calculations.

Access tables

The principle of using a table containing the starting addresses of data items is particularly useful for accessing elements of string arrays. The diagram below shows how an access table is used to point to the starting locations of string array elements stored in memory.

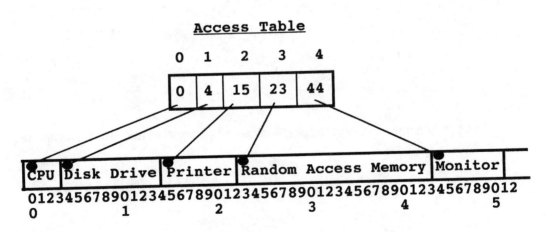

Access Table for String Arrays

The array S_k (k= 0 to 4) to be represented consists of a number of string elements of variable sizes, each terminated by a special character indicating the end of the string. In this instance, the strings, with their subscripts, are:

0	CPU
1	Disk Drive
2	Printer
3	Random Access Memory
4	Monitor

The access table contains entries which point to the starting locations of each of the strings in order. For example, if the element S_3 was to be accessed, the entry in the access table corresponding to this element (that is, the element with subscript 3) provides the starting address for S_3 which has a value "Random Access Memory".

Sometimes, rather than indicating the end of a string element by means of a special character such as an ASCII carriage return code, the access table is used in conjunction with another table giving the length of the string:

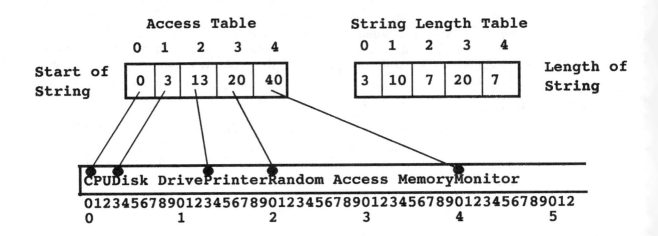

Access Table and String Length Table

This scheme improves access speed but at the expense of additional storage requirements.

Search strategies

Having stored a number of data items in an array, it is more than likely that it will at some time be necessary to search the data structure for the occurrence of specific items of data. For example, suppose that an array A_k (k=0 to 9999) is being used to store stolen credit card numbers, and it is to be searched in order to ascertain whether a shop customer is using a stolen credit card. The search algorithm might be as follows:

```
k = 0
pos = -1
card_found = FALSE
while k <=array_size and not card_found
        if S(k) = Card_number
                then    card_found = TRUE;
        pos = k
        endif
        k = k  +  1
endwhile
if card_found
        then    card number is located in S(pos)
        else    card number is not in stolen cards list
endif
```

Each element in the list is compared with the number of the customer's card; if a match is found, the iteration is terminated by setting the boolean variable *card_found* to *True*, and the position of the value in the array is stored in the variable *pos*; if the loop ends and the variable *card_found* still has a value of *False*, then the customer's card is not in the list of stolen credit cards. This technique is called a *sequential search*.

Though very straightforward, a sequential search can be very time consuming, since it could necessitate the complete list of 10,000 elements being searched. A faster method is possible if the list of card numbers is in ascending or descending numerical order. This alternative method is called *binary search*, or sometimes *binary chop*.

For example, suppose that the list of stolen card numbers is in ascending numerical order, then a binary search proceeds as follows:

1. Set the array subscript to *mid*, middle value. In this case *mid* is 9999/2, which is 5000 to the nearest integer.

2. Compare required *card_number* with S(*mid*).

3. (a) If *card_number* < S(*mid*) then *card_number* can only be in the first half of the array.
   (b) If *card_number* > S(*mid*) then *card_number* can only be somewhere in the latter half of the array.
   (c) If *card_number* = S(*mid*) then the card number has been found.

4. If the card number has not yet been found, repeat from step 1 using *mid* as the size of the array.

The procedure successively reduces the size of the array to be searched by a factor of two. For an array of size 10,000, this means that only a maximum of 14 elements need to be examined in order to determine whether a particular element is a member of the list. Thus, for 10,000 elements, the search size reduces as follows:

Number of comparisons	Array size to be searched
0	10,000
1	5,000
2	2,500
3	1,250
4	625
5	313
6	157
7	79
8	40
9	20
10	10
11	5
12	3
13	2
14	1

Notice that 2^{14} is the smallest power of 2 which exceeds the maximum array size of 10,000:

$$2^{13} = 8,192 \text{ which is less than 10,000;}$$

$$2^{14} = 16,384 \text{ which is greater than 10,000.}$$

This is how the maximum figure of 14 comparisons has been derived.

A more formal version of the binary search algorithm can be stated as follows:

```
low = 0
high = array_size
pos = -1
card_found = FALSE
while low < high and not card_found
mid = int((low + high))/2
case TRUE of
        when S(mid) = card_number : card_found = TRUE;
                pos = mid
        when S(mid) > card_number : high = mid
        when S(mid) < card_number : low = mid
endcase
endwhile
if card_found
        then    stolen card number is located in S(pos)
        else    card number is not in list
endif
```

In order to select the appropriate part of the array to be searched, the algorithm uses two variables, *low* and *high*, to store the lower and upper bounds of that part of the array. They are used to calculate the mid point, *mid*, (rounded to the nearest integer value using the *int* function), so that the value stored there can be compared with the value required (the card number, in this example). Each time the comparison fails, the lower or upper bound is adjusted and the procedure is repeated. The process continues until either the value is located or the lower and upper bounds coincide, in which case the value does not exist in the array. The variable *pos* is used to store the position of the value if it exists in the array; a negative value for *pos* indicates that the search was unsuccessful.

The binary search method will usually be employed when the array size is large, otherwise the processing overheads caused by the algorithm's increased complexity make it unsuitable.

Linear Lists

Stacks

A stack is a data structure characterised by the expression "Last In First Out" (LIFO), meaning that the most recent item added to the stack is the only one which can be removed from the stack. A *stack pointer* is used to keep track of the last item added to the stack, that is, the current top of the stack.

Suppose that we wish to implement a stack using a one-dimensional array, S_i where $i=1$ to 5. A special register, sp, must be reserved as the stack pointer, and this will have an initial value of 0 indicating that the stack is empty.

To add, or *push*, an item to the stack, the following steps are required:

1. Check that there is room in the stack to add another item. In this case, the stack is full when sp has a value of 5, that is, when all of the elements in the array S_i have been used to store items. When the stack pointer is at its maximum value, and another item is required to be stored on the stack, a *stack overflow* condition has occurred, and it will not be possible to push the item onto the stack.

2. If an overflow condition does not exist, the stack pointer is incremented and the item is transferred to the array element pointed to by the stack pointer.

For example, suppose that the number 15 is to be pushed to the stack. After completing the operation the stack will look like this:

```
i       S i
1       15<─────────────sp=1
2       -
3       -
4       -
5       -
```

After adding two more numbers the stack will contain three elements and the stack pointer will have a value of 3:

```
i       S i
1       15
2       6
3       21 <───────────  sp=3
4       -
5       -
```

The algorithm for pushing a value to a stack can be summarised as follows:

```
if       sp < maximum size of stack        {test for overflow}
   then  sp  = sp + 1;                      {increment stack ptr}
         S_sp = item                        {push item}
   else  Stack overflow
endif
```

To remove an item from the stack, often called *pulling* or *popping* a value, requires the reverse procedure:

1. Check that the stack is not empty, that is, sp is greater than zero. If the stack is empty, an attempt to pull a non-existent value causes a *stack underflow* condition to arise.

2. If the stack is not empty, the item on the top of the stack, as

shown by the stack pointer, is transferred to its destination and the stack pointer is decremented.

Thus, after pulling a value from the stack S_i, it would be in the state shown below:

i	S_i	
1	15	
2	6 <─────────── sp=2	
3	21	
4	-	
5	-	

Notice that the value pulled from the stack, 21 in this instance, still exists in the stack: it is not necessary to actually remove a value from the stack since, by decrementing the stack pointer, this is effectively what has happened. Pulling a value from a stack is effected by copying the value to its destination before decrementing the stack pointer. The top of the stack is now the second element of the array which contains the value 6.

To summarise, the algorithm for pulling a value from a stack is:

> **if**   sp > 0   {that is, stack is not empty}
>   **then** item = S_{sp};   {transfer item to destination}
>   sp = sp − 1   {decrement stack pointer}
>   **else** stack underflow
> **endif**

Application of Stacks

The stack is used frequently in programming languages for control structures. In Acorn's BASIC, for example, GOSUB, FOR...NEXT, REPEAT...UNTIL and procedure/function calls all use stacks in their implementation. The GOSUB instruction causes control to be transferred to the line specified in the instruction. Subroutine instructions are executed as normal until a RETURN instruction is encountered, whereupon control returns to the instruction following the last GOSUB instruction executed. Thus, with the fragments of BASIC code illustrated below, the subroutine starting at line 1000 is called at line 100 by the GOSUB 1000 instruction. The BASIC interpreter must store its current position in the program so that after executing the subroutine it can return control to this same position when a RETURN instruction is encountered. This is accomplished by pushing the return address to a stack prior to jumping to the start of the subroutine.

```
10    REM *** Mainline program ***
. . . . . . . . . . . .
. . . . . . . . . . . .
90    REM Call subroutine starting at line 1000
100   GOSUB 1000
105   REM Program continues here after completing subroutine
110   LET a = x + 1
120
. . . . . . . . . . . .
etc
. . . . . . . . . . . .
990   STOP
999   REM *** End of Mainline program ***


1000 REM *** Subroutine code goes here ***
1010
. . . . . . . . . . . .
etc
. . . . . . . . . . . .
1490 RETURN
```

When a RETURN instruction is executed, the top of the stack is pulled and the interpreter continues from that address. In this way the same subroutine can be called from different parts of the program and control will always return to the instruction following the GOSUB instruction.

Another reason for using a stack is that it facilitates the use of nested control structures. In the example above, it is in order to have another GOSUB instruction in the subroutine at line 1000:

```
10      REM *** Mainline program ***
............
............
90      REM Call subroutine starting at line 1000
100     GOSUB 1000
105     REM Program continues here after completing subroutine
110     LET a = x + 1
120
............
etc
............
990     STOP

999     REM *** End of Mainline program ***
1000    REM *** Subroutine code goes here ***
1010
............
1100    GOSUB 2000
1200
............
1490    RETURN
2000    REM *** Code for second subroutine goes here ***
2010
............
etc
............
2490    RETURN
```

In this instance the stack is used twice: the return address appropriate to the subroutine call at line 100 is pushed to the stack, then the return address for the second, nested, subroutine call is pushed to the stack during execution of the first subroutine at line 1100.

When the RETURN statement at line 2490 is executed, BASIC pulls the top of the GOSUB stack causing control to return to line 1200, the line following the most recent GOSUB instruction. The RETURN statement at line 1490 causes BASIC to pull the new top of the stack which provides the return address for the first GOSUB call at line 100. This technique allows subroutines to be nested to any depth, subject to the size of the GOSUB stack.

The same principle applies to the management of FOR..NEXT loops in BASIC. A separate stack is used to store information regarding the FOR..NEXT control variables. The BASIC interpreter stores on the stack five pieces of information when it encounters a FOR statement:

- the address of the control variable

- the type of the control variable

- STEP size

- TO limit

- the address of the next statement following FOR

The stack pointer is incremented by the number of words occupied by this information, and then the statement following the FOR instruction is executed.

A NEXT instruction will cause BASIC to use the information on the top of the stack to either repeat the statements between the FOR and NEXT instructions, or to exit the loop if the control variable has exceeded its maximum value. If the latter is the case, the FOR..NEXT stack pointer will be decremented to remove the top of the stack thus terminating this loop.

The use of a stack again allows nesting of FOR..NEXT loops, subject to a depth governed by the size of the FOR..NEXT stack.

A REPEAT..UNTIL stack is used in a similar way to that of the FOR..NEXT stack, though the procedures for managing REPEAT..UNTIL loops are simpler.

Procedures and functions in BASIC are handled in a similar manner to the GOSUB structure, but the BASIC interpreter has to cope with additional problems associated with passing parameters and saving the values of local variables so that they can be subsequently restored. These extra problems are once again overcome by the use of stacks.

Another application of a stack will be described in a later section dealing with the *tree* data structure.

Queues

The data structure known as a *queue* has the same characteristics as the queues we encounter in everyday life. For instance, a queue at the checkout counter of a supermarket increases at its rear as customers join the queue to have their purchases totalled, and only reduces in size when a customer is served at the head of the queue, the checkout counter. A queue of cars at traffic lights behaves in a similar manner, with cars exiting the queue only at its head and joining the queue only at its rear.

A *queue* is a data structure in which elements are added only at the rear of a linear list and removed only from the front, or head, of the list. A queue is often given the name FIFO list, from the initial letters of the words in the phrase "First In First Out" which describes the order of processing the elements of the list.

Suppose that an array, Q_k (k=0 to 30), is to be used as a queue. *Head* will be used to keep track of the front of the queue and *Rear*, the end of the queue:

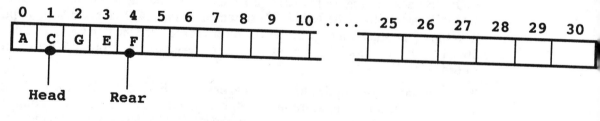

Simple Queue

Initially, the queue is empty so that *Head* = *Rear* = 0. When an item is added to the queue, *Rear* is incremented; when an item is removed from the list, *Head* is incremented. Assuming that the queue is simply storing single alphabetic characters, the table on the next page illustrates the operation of the queue for ten queue operations:

Operation	Item	Head	Rear	State of queue
		0	0	Empty
1. Add item	A	0	1	A
2. Add item	C	0	2	AC
3. Add item	G	0	3	ACG
4. Add item	E	0	4	ACGE
5. Remove item	A	1	4	CGE
6. Add item	F	1	5	CGEF
7. Remove item	C	2	5	GEF
8. Remove item	G	3	5	EF
9. Remove item	E	4	5	F
10. Remove item	F	5	5	Empty

The following algorithms show how items are added to a queue and removed from a queue, assuming *array_size* is the maximum size of the array *Q* used for storing the queue.

```
{Add item to stack}
if Rear <= array_size
        then Q (Rear) = item;
                Rear = Rear + 1
        else Queue is full
endif
{Remove item from stack}
if Rear <> Head
        then item = Q (Head);
        Head = Head + 1
        else Queue is empty
endif
```

Notice that the queue is empty when the head pointer has the same value as the rear pointer. Notice also that, unlike a queue in real life, as items are added and removed, the queue moves through the array since both the head and rear pointers are incremented. This means that eventually the queue will run out of space, at which time an overflow condition will occur. The solution to this problem is to implement a circular queue which re-uses array elements that are empty

Circular Queues

The diagram below illustrates the principles of a circular queue:

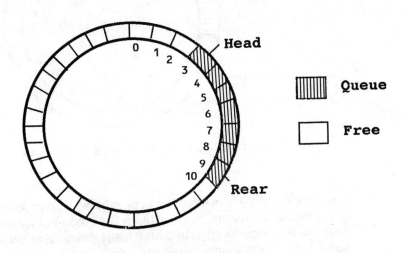

Circular Queue (m=30)

The circular arrangement of the array elements is merely a means of illustrating the principles of operation of a circular queue; the data structure used to store the queue is physically the same as before, that is, a one-dimensional array.

Head and *Rear* are again used, but this time when either of them reach a value equal to m, the maximum size of the array, they start again at the beginning, using up elements which previously have been removed from the queue. The diagram shows the queue in a state where ten items have been added to the queue and three items have been removed. The next diagram shows that the queue has completely traversed the array such that *Rear* is equal to m, and there are five items in the queue.

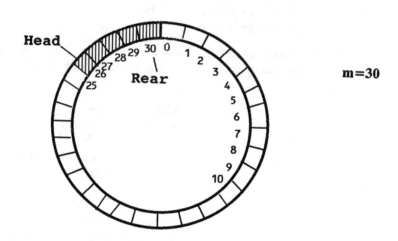

Circular Queue with Rear at Upper Bound

The next item to be added to the queue will be inserted at position 1, so that *Rear* has a value of 0 rather than $m + 1$. In other words, when *Rear* exceeds the upper bound reserved for the queue, it takes the value of the lower bound. The same thing applies to the *Head* of the queue. The next diagram shows the queue, having traversed all the elements of the array, starting to re-use unoccupied positions at the beginning of the array.

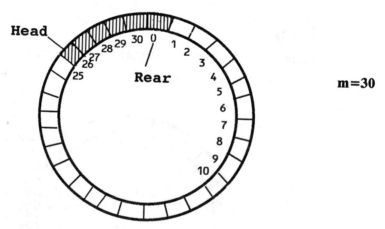

Circular Queue Re-using Deleted Elements

A slight difficulty with a circular queue is being able to differentiate between an empty queue and a full queue; the condition for a non-empty queue can no longer be that *Rear* <*Head* since, depending how many items have been added and removed, it is possible for a non-empty queue to be such that *Rear* has larger value than *Head*. The previous two diagrams above illustrate both queue states, the first where *Head* < *Rear* and the second where *Head* > *Rear*.

One solution to this problem is to adopt the convention that *Head* always points to the array element immediately preceding the first item in the queue rather pointing to the first item itself; since *Rear* points to the last item in the queue, the condition that *Head* = *Rear* indicates an empty queue. *Head* and *Rear* are initialised to be equal to the array's upper bound rather than zero. Thus, initially, the queue is empty.

The queue becomes full only when the rear pointer catches up with the head pointer. The fragments of pseudocode below define the processes of adding an item to a circular queue and removing an item from a circular queue:

```
{Add item to circular queue}
if Rear = Upper_bound                          {check for upper limit}
            then Rear = Lower_bound            {start at beginning or..
            else Rear = Rear + 1               .. increment rear pointer}
endif
if Rear <>Head                                 {check for queue full}
            then Q(Rear) = item                {add item to queue}
            else Queue is full                 {overflow condition}
endif
{Remove item from circular queue}
if Head <>Rear                                 {check for queue not empty}
      then if Head = Upper_bound               {check for upper limit}
                  then Head = Lower_bound       {start at beginning or..
                  else Head = Head + 1          .. increment head pointer}
         endif;
         item = Q(Head)                        {remove item from queue}
      else Queue is empty                      {underflow condition}
endif
```

Applications of queues

Most printers in common use today contain a quantity of RAM for the purpose of temporarily storing (or *buffering*) data transmitted from a computer. The buffer allows the computer to transmit, for example, a few kilobytes of data to the printer very quickly and allow the printer to print it autonomously, (that is, without further intervention from the computer). This allows the computer to continue processing other tasks while the relatively slow printer deals with the data it has received.

The printer buffer must operate as a queue, because the data must be printed in the same order as it was transmitted from the computer. As data is received by the printer, it is added to the buffer queue until either the computer stops transmitting data or the queue is full. The printer then commences to process the data in the queue, starting at the head of the queue and ending when the queue is empty. This process of filling up the buffer quickly and then emptying it at the speed of the printer continues until the computer ceases to transmit data. Buffers may range in size from a few kilobytes to several megabytes of RAM. A microprocessor in the printer itself deals with the way the data queue is processed.

Circular queues are frequently used by operating systems for spooling operations. For example, in a multi-user system in which a printer is shared between a number of users, print jobs may be spooled to a disk drive. The queue thus formed on the disk will be processed by the printer in the order the jobs were received (unless a priority system is in operation). As one job is printed, room will be available on the disk area allocated to the printer for another job; the circular queue principle applied to spooling will allow optimum use of the disk area allocated to print jobs. The operating system keeps track of the appropriate queue head and rear pointers required to operate the circular queue.

Linked Lists

Suppose that we are using an array to store a number of alphabetic items in alphabetical order as shown below:

Element	Data
0	Aaron
1	Abelson
2	Bateman
3	Craddock
4	Dunfy
5	Eastman
6	
7	
8	
9	

Adding a new item such as "Gregory", while maintaining the alphabetic ordering, is easy:

Element	Data
0	Aaron
1	Abelson
2	Bateman
3	Craddock
4	Dunfy
5	Eastman
6	Gregory
7	
8	
9	

The item is merely added to the end of the list. However, to insert "Crawford" requires rather more effort: all of those entries after "Craddock" must be moved down the array so that "Crawford" may be inserted immediately after "Craddock". The list becomes:

Element	Data
0	Aaron
1	Abelson
2	Bateman
3	Craddock
4	Crawford
5	Dunfy
6	Eastman
7	Gregory
8	
9	

For a list containing hundreds or thousands of entries, this process could be considerably time-consuming.

An alternative approach is to introduce a second array containing pointers which link the elements together in the required order. Now an element, or *node*, contains a pointer in addition to the data. So, returning to the original list, it would be represented as follows:

	Node	Data	Pointer
Start——>0		Aaron	1
	1	Abelson	2
	2	Bateman	3
	3	Craddock	4
	4	Dunfy	5
	5	Eastman	−1
Free——>6			
	7		
	8		
	9		

The original list is now in *linked list* form. Given the start position of the list, stored in *Start*, the pointers link the items together in the correct alphabetical order. The end of the list is indicated by a *null pointer*, in this case −1. Another pointer, *Free*, keeps track of the next free location for storing new items, and it is incremented whenever a new item is inserted or added to the list. Adding "Gregory" to the list would entail changing the "Eastman" pointer from -1 to 6 (that is, the value currently given by *Free*) and putting "Gregory" at the position indicated by *Free*:

	Node	Data	Pointer
Start——>0		Aaron	1
	1	Abelson	2
	2	Bateman	3
	3	Craddock	4
	4	Dunfy	5
	5	Eastman	6
	6	Gregory	−1
Free——>7			
	8		
	9		

"Gregory" is given a null pointer to indicate that it is the last item in the list, and *Free* is incremented.

In pseudocode form, the steps illustrated above to add an item to the end of a linked list are as shown below.

```
begin
        i = Start;              {copy start pointer}
        while ptr(i)<>null      {follow pointers until null pointer found}
               i = ptr(i)
        endwhile
        ptr(i) = Free;          {link new item to current last node}
        data(Free) = item;      {store new data in next free node}
        ptr(Free) = null;       {store null pointer in next free node}
        Free = Free + 1         {increment next free pointer}
end
```

The notation *ptr(i)* is used for the pointer located at node *i*, and *data(i)* represents the data at node *i*. For example, in the alphabetical list above, *ptr(2)* = 3 and *data(2)* = "Bateman".

Now, to add "Crawford" only one pointer is altered, rather than re-arranging the items in the array, and the new node is added to the end of the list:

	Node	Data	Pointer	
Start———>	0	Aaron	1	
	1	Abelson	2	
	2	Bateman	3	
	3	Craddock	7	
	4	Dunfy	5	
	5	Eastman	6	
	6	Gregory	−1	
	7	Crawford	4<——— inserted node	
Free———>	8			
	9			

Thus, the order of accessing the array in alphabetical order is

$$0 - 1 - 2 - 3 - 7 - 4 - 5 - 6$$

In pseudocode, the algorithm for inserting a node to maintain the alphabetic ordering, is shown below:

```
begin
  i = Start;                                {copy start pointer}
  found = FALSE
    repeat
      if data(i) >item                      {ie alphabetically }
        or Start = null                     {allow for empty list}
        then found = TRUE                   {insertion position found}
        else p = i;                         {save current node}
          i = ptr(p)                        {next node in list}
    endif
    until found                             {insertion position located}
      or i = null                           {reached end of list}
  if i = start
    then data(Free) = item;                 {insert at head of list}
      ptr(Free) = Start;
      Start = Free
    else ptr(p) = Free;                      {insert in body of list}
      data(Free) = item;
      ptr(Free) = i
  endif
  Free = Free + 1                           {increment next-free pointer}
  end.
```

The increased complexity of this algorithm arises partially from the necessity to allow for the list being initially empty, this state being recognised by Start containing a null pointer. If the list is empty initially, then Start is set equal to Free which contains a pointer to the first available node, and the new data together with a null pointer are stored in this node. To delete a node merely entails ensuring that its predecessor's pointer links the node following it. For example, to delete "Bateman", the pointers would be adjusted as follows:

	Node	Data	Pointer	
Start———>	0	Aaron	1	
	1	Abelson	3	
	2	*Bateman*	3<——— deleted node	
	3	Craddock	7	
	4	Dunfy	5	
	5	Eastman	6	
	6	Gregory	−1	
	7	Crawford	4	
Free———>	8			
	9			

The pointer order is now

0 - 1 - 3 - 7 - 4 - 5 - 6

which misses out the third item in the array containing "Bateman".

The pseudocode algorithm is as follows:

```
begin
    i =Start;                        {copy start pointer}
        found = FALSE
        repeat
          if data(i) = item or Start = null  {ie found node or empty list}
             then found = TRUE        {deletion position found}
             else p = i;              {save current node}
                  i = ptr(p)          {next node in list}
          endif
          until found or i = null     {deletion position located
                                      or reached end of list}
        if Start = null or i = null   {ie empty list or reached end
                                      of list without finding node}

          then node does not exist!   {not possible to delete node}
        else if i = start
             then  Start = ptr(i)     {delete head of list}
             else  ptr(p) = ptr(i)    {skip node in body of list}
             endif
        endif
end.
```

The algorithm allows for three special cases:

   (i)   The list is empty - this means that it is not possible to delete an element.

   (ii)   The item to be deleted is not in the list - again, it is not possible to delete this item.

   (iii)   The item to be deleted is the first one in the list - this requires that Start must be set to point to the second node in the linked list.

With a linked list it is possible to locate any element by following the pointers, irrespective of the physical location of the item. Rather than storing the list in consecutive elements of an array, confined to a certain range of memory locations, it is perfectly feasible to store the elements of the linked list anywhere in the memory space allocated to a user program. For this reason, an alternative, and more general, diagrammatic form is often used for linked lists, in which each node contains one or more pointers and one or more words of data. For example, the linked list immediately above might be represented as follows:

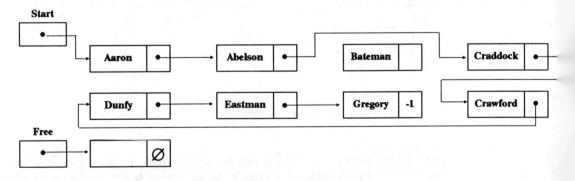

Alternative diagram of linked list

Arrowed lines are used to show the order in which nodes are linked together, and special nodes indicate the start point of the list and the next free node.

Linked lists have a number of advantages over arrays :

1. Greater flexibility for the location of nodes in memory (it is even possible for nodes to be located on auxiliary storage, such as magnetic disks, rather than in main memory).

2. The ease with which nodes may be added or deleted from the list.

3. By adding more pointers, the list may be traversed in a number of different orders.

On the debit side for linked lists:

1. Locating specific items necessitates searching the list from the start node, whereas arrays allow direct access to elements.

2. Linked lists require more memory because of the need for pointers.

3. Linked lists involve more "housekeeping" operations because of the necessity to change pointers when adding or deleting nodes.

Applications of linked lists

With an interpreted language such as BASIC, variables must be accessed as quickly as possible so that program processing speed is acceptably fast. One method of ensuring this is by the use of linked lists.

In one such scheme, used by Acorn BASIC, variables starting with the same character are given their own linked list, so that there is a linked list for each possible starting character. Though the lists are quite separate, each with its own start pointer, they occupy a common area of memory and link around each other. Each node in the linked lists contains the name and value of the variable, plus a pointer to the next variable with the same starting letter. The diagram below illustrates this scheme at the stage where a number of variables with starting letters A, B or C have been created.

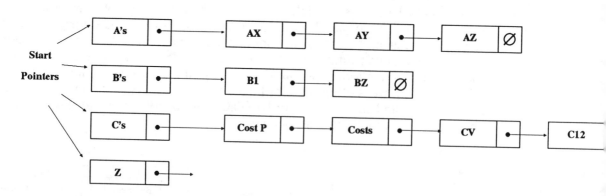

Linked lists of BASIC variables

The start pointers for the linked lists are stored in a table in a specific area of memory. The first pointer in the table contains the address of node for the first variable starting with the letter *A* to be created in the current program, in this case *AX*. This node contains a pointer to the second variable created, *AY*, and its node contains a pointer to *AZ*, the last variable created starting with the letter *A*. Similar lists occur for the variables starting with *B* (*B1* and *B2*) and *C* (*CostP*, *CostS*, *CV* and *C12*). Because the lists link around each other, there is a common free-space pointer for all the lists.

To find a particular variable's node, the starting letter of the variable is converted into an address giving the start pointer for its linked list, and the nodes of this list are traversed in pointer order until the variable is located. For example, suppose that the table of start pointers was at memory location 1000, and the variable *B2* is to be accessed. The letter *B* is first converted into a number indicating its position in the alphabet, that is 2, and this is added to the start address of the table.

Thus, 1000 + 2 = 1002 is the location of the start pointer for the linked list of variables beginning with *B*. The first node in the list is for variable *B1*, which is not the one required, so its pointer is used to access the next node in the list. This time the variable found is *B2* as required.

For a program containing many variables, this scheme can dramatically reduce the time required to locate a certain variable, provided variable names are chosen with different starting letters. It is worth noting that in this instance, a knowledge of the internal organisation of an interpreter can help the programmer to write more efficient programs.

Linked lists are also used for procedures and functions so that they can be located as quickly as possible no matter where in the program they are referenced. Otherwise, a program would have to be searched sequentially from the beginning every time a procedure or function was invoked.

Trees

Tree terminology

The term *tree* refers to a non-linear data structure in which nodes have two or more pointers to other nodes, forming a hierarchical structure as illustrated below:

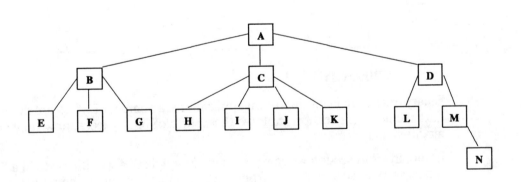

Tree(1)

Node A is the *root* node of the entire tree with pointers to three *subtrees*. B, C and D are known as *children* of the *parent* node A. Similarly, E, F and G are children of B. Nodes B to N are all *descendants* of A, just as nodes L to N are all descendants of D. Nodes such as H, I and L, which have no children, are known as *leaves* or *terminal nodes*.

Trees are useful for representing hierarchical relationships between data items, such as those found in databases. For example, a record in an employee file might have the following structure:

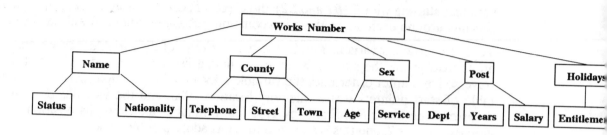

Tree(2)

Stored as a tree, the data can be accessed in a number of ways. For example, extracting the first level of the tree provides a summary of the employee, giving Name, Home county, Sex, Post and Holidays taken; accessing only the fourth subtree provides details of the employees current position; accessing the tree in order of the five subtrees provides all the employees details.

A binary tree is a particular type of tree which has more uses than a general tree as described above, and is also much easier to implement. Binary trees are described in the following two sections.

Binary Trees

A binary tree is a special type of tree in which each parent has a maximum of two children which are linked to the parent node using a left pointer and a right pointer. The general form of a binary tree is shown below:

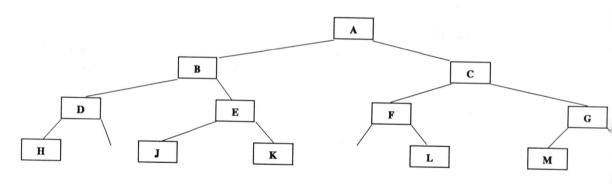

Binary Tree

Binary trees have many important applications, a number of which are described in the next section. This section explores the nature of binary trees, how they are created, modified and accessed.

In the previous section we saw that in order to locate a specific node in a linked list it is necessary to search the list from the beginning, following the pointers linking the nodes together in the appropriate order. For a list containing a large number of elements, this process could be very time consuming. The solution to the same problem with an array structure was to use the binary search technique (see section on Search Strategies); the same principle can be applied to a linked list if the list is in the form of a *Binary Tree*. Consider the alphabetically ordered linked list described earlier in the section on linked lists.

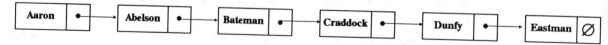

Diagrammatic form of alphabetic names table

Now suppose that the same list is represented as a binary tree with two pointers in each node, one pointing to an element alphabetically less than the node data (a *left pointer*) and the other pointing to an element alphabetically greater than the node data (a *right pointer*):

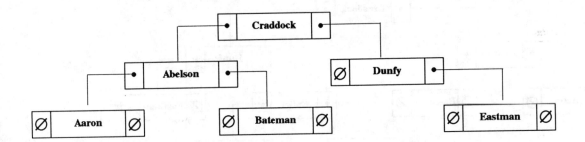

Binary tree form of alphabetic names table.

If we were looking for Eastman, the procedure would be as follows:

(i) Compare Eastman with the *root node*, Craddock.

(ii) Because Craddock is alphabetically less than Eastman, follow the right pointer to Dunfy.

(iii) Compare Eastman with Dunfy.

(iv) Dunfy is alphabetically less than Eastman so again follow the right pointer to Eastman.

(v) The next comparison shows that the required node has been located.

Each comparison confines the search to either the upper or lower part of the alphabetic list, thus significantly reducing the number of comparisons needed to locate the element required.

To add an element, Crawford for example, to the configuration shown above, whilst retaining the alphabetic ordering, is merely a matter of searching for the new item until a null pointer is encountered. In this example, a null pointer occurs when attempting to go left at Dunfy. Crawford is installed in the next free node and Dunfy's left pointer points to it. The new tree is shown below:

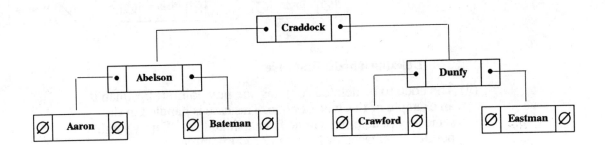

Binary tree with new item inserted

Unfortunately, deleting a node is not quite so simple. Three cases can arise, and these are described with reference to the diagram below which is an extended form of the binary tree shown above.

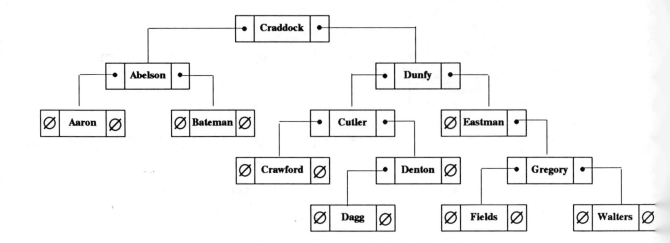

Tree used to illustrate how to delete nodes

(i) The node to be deleted is a terminal node, or *leaf*, having null left and right pointers. Bateman is an example of such a node. Deleting it is simply a matter of setting Abelson's right pointer to the null pointer:

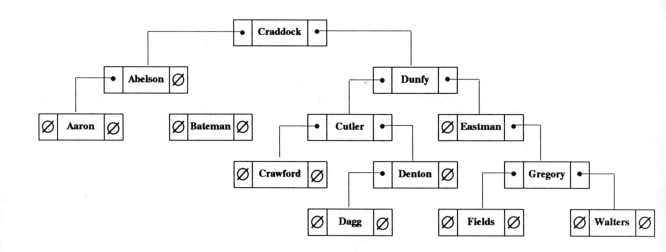

Deleting a node: first case

(ii) The node to be deleted contains one null pointer. Eastman is an example of this type of node. This case is handled in the same way as deleting a node from a linked list - Dunfy's right pointer is replaced by Eastman's right pointer:

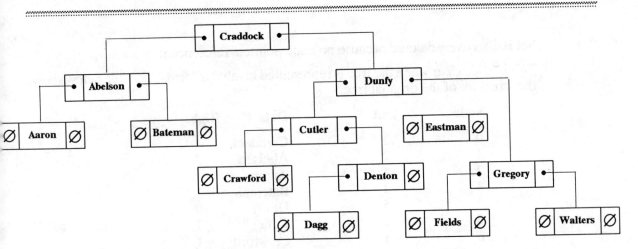

Deleting a node : second case

(iii)   The node to be deleted contains no null pointers. There are
two possibilities here: replace the deleted entry with an entry
from its right subtree, or an entry from its left subtree. We will
consider both of these using Dunfy as the item to be deleted
from the original tree.

Taking the left subtree first, the procedure is to search the left subtree for the largest
entry by following the right pointers at each node until a null pointer is found. The left
subtree of Dunfy is

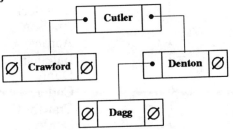

Left subtree

and the largest value is Denton. In order that Dunfy can be deleted whilst still retaining
the correct ordering, it is replaced by Denton and a number of pointers are adjusted
as shown below:

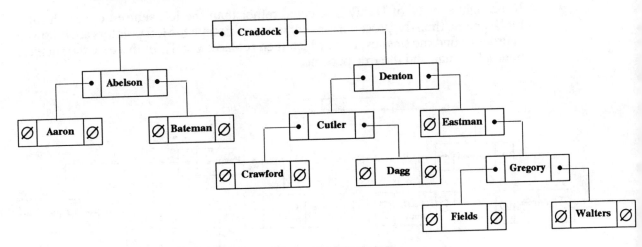

Adjusting pointers for node deletion

Denton's pointers are replaced by Dunfy's pointers; Craddock's right pointer now
points to Denton; Cutler's right pointer now points to Dagg.

Note that for clarity the diagram above gives the impression that nodes have been
moved around, but all that occurs in practice is that pointers are changed to alter the
nodes that are to be linked together or deleted; the Dunfy node still exists in the tree

but is effectively deleted because no node pointers reference it.

This is made clear when the tree is represented in tabular form. The table below shows the structure of the original tree.

Node	Left	Data	Right
0	1	Craddock	4
1	2	Abelson	3
2	−1	Aaron	−1
3	−1	Bateman	−1
4	5	Dunfy	9
5	6	Cutler	7
6	−1	Crawford	−1
7	8	Denton	−1
8	−1	Dagg	−1
9	−1	Eastman	10
10	11	Gregory	12
11	−1	Fields	−1
12	−1	Walters	−1

With the node Dunfy deleted, the table becomes

Node	Left	Data	Right	
0	1	Craddock	7	
1	2	Abelson	3	
2	−1	Aaron	−1	
3	−1	Bateman	−1	
4	5	Dunfy	9< ——————— deleted node	
5	6	Cutler	−1	
6	−1	Crawford	−1	
7	5	Denton	9	
8	−1	Dagg	−1	
9	−1	Eastman	10	
10	11	Gregory	12	
11	−1	Fields	−1	
12	−1	Walters	−1	

If the right subtree of Dunfy is selected rather than the left subtree to search for a replacement, then the procedure is very similar: this time the left pointers are followed in order to find the smallest item, which then replaces Dunfy. In this case the smallest item is Eastman and the tree becomes

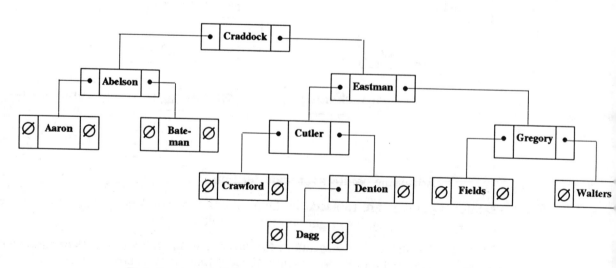

Deleting a node(3)

Methods of tree traversal

Having created a binary tree, it is likely that it will need to be accessed in some particular order, alphabetically for example. The algorithm for visiting the data items of a binary tree in alphabetical order is an example of *in-order* traversal and can be stated quite simply:

In-order traversal:

visit the left subtree in in-order then
visit the root node then
visit the right subtree in in-order.

Notice that the algorithm makes reference to itself. In other words, the algorithm for visiting a subtree is exactly the same as that for visiting a tree. The seemingly endless process of visiting trees within trees within trees etc. continues until a null pointer is encountered, allowing the process to terminate, or *bottom out*. The operation of the algorithm is best illustrated by means of an example. Consider the tree shown below:

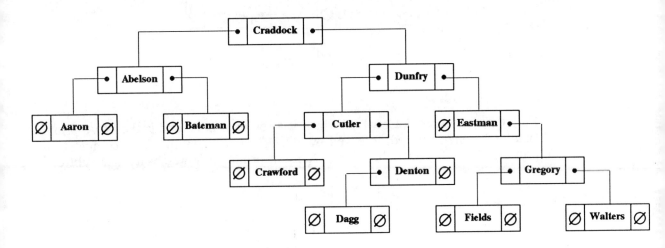

Tree traversal

Suppose that we wish to print this tree in alphabetical order, that is perform an in-order traversal. Then the procedure would be as follows.

The left subtree of the *root node,* Craddock is

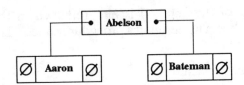

Subtree

To print this subtree, we must first print its left subtree, which is just the entry Aaron which has no descendants. We therefore print "Aaron". Now we can print the node data, "Abelson" and turn to the right subtree of Abelson. This right subtree is simply Bateman, which is then printed.

This completes the printing of the left subtree of Craddock, so now "Craddock" can be printed. Now the right subtree of Craddock is to be printed. The right subtree of Craddock has as its root node Dunfy:

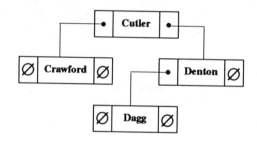

We must first print Dunfy's left subtree, which is

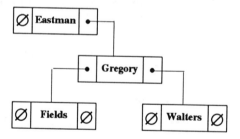

Subtree

Cutler's left subtree is Crawford which is a terminal node and is therefore printed. "Cutler" is then printed, followed by "Dagg" then "Denton". This completes the printing of Dunfy's left subtree, so "Dunfy" is printed followed by its right subtree.

In order, this subtree would be printed:

"Eastman" - "Fields" - "Gregory" - "Walters"

which completes the process.

The simplicity of this method is also reflected in the pseudocode version of the algorithm. We begin by defining a procedure called "Tree" which prints a tree starting at a specified node:

```
procedure Tree(node)
begin
  l = lptr(node)              {get this node's left pointer}
  if l <> null               {if there is a left subtree, print it}
      then Tree(l)
  endif
  print(node)                {print the data at this node}
  r = rptr(node)             {get this node's right pointer}
  if r <>null                {if there is a right subtree, print it}
    then Tree(r)
  endif
end.
```

Notice that this procedure calls itself; this is termed *recursion*, a very useful programming device. The procedure *Tree* is invoked to print the left subtree at a particular node
by passing the left pointer as a *procedure parameter*, or to print the right subtree by
passing the right pointer as a procedure parameter. A procedure parameter allows
values to be transmitted to the procedure which are local to the procedure, having no
existence outside the procedure.

In the example above, *node* is a parameter which initially points to the root node. By
making the procedure call, *Tree(root)*, the procedure is invoked with the value of *root*
passed to the parameter *node*. In the procedure, *node* is used to get the value of the
left pointer using *l = lptr(node)*. If it is not a null pointer, *l* is now passed to the
procedure recursively using *Tree(l)*, and now node has the value of the pointer for the
left subtree. In this way, the procedure *Tree* is used recursively to process subtrees,
only printing a node and going on to the right subtree when a null pointer is encountered.

To illustrate the operation of the pseudocode, consider the following binary tree which
is to be processed in alphabetical order:

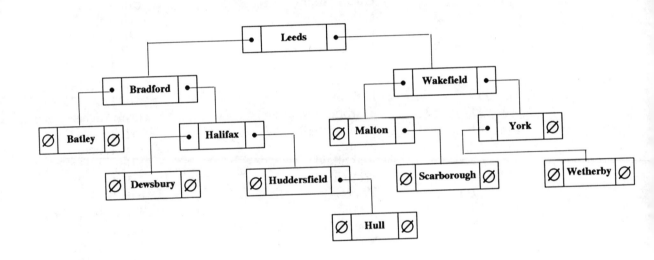

The equivalent table is as follows:

Node	Left	Data	Right
0	1	Leeds	6
1	4	Bradford	2
2	5	Halifax	3
3	−1	Huddersfield	9
4	−1	Batley	−1
5	−1	Dewsbury	−1
6	10	Wakefield	7
7	8	York	−1
8	−1	Wetherby	−1
9	−1	Hull	−1
10	−1	Malton	11
11	−1	Scarborough	−1

The next table traces the pseudocode, indicating the action taken at each invocation
of *Tree*. Only the pointer currently relevant is indicated in the two pointer columns.

The process is started by the call *Tree(0)*.

Node	Left	Data	Right	Action
0	1	Leeds		call Tree(1)
1	4	Bradford		call Tree(4)
4	−1	Batley		print "Batley"
4		Batley	−1	exit Tree(4)
1		Bradford		print "Bradford"
1		Bradford	2	call Tree(2)
2	5	Halifax		call Tree(5)
5	−1	Dewsbury		print "Dewsbury"
5		Dewsbury	−1	exit Tree(5)
2		Halifax		print "Halifax"
2		Halifax	3	call Tree(3)
3	−1	Huddersfield		print "Huddersfield"
3		Huddersfield	9	call Tree(9)
9	−1	Hull		print "Hull"
9		Hull	−1	exit Tree(9)
3		Huddersfield		exit Tree(3)
2		Halifax		exit Tree(2)
1		Bradford		exit Tree(1)
0		Leeds	6	call Tree(6)
6	10	Wakefield		call Tree(10)
10	−1	Malton		print "Malton"
10		Malton	11	call Tree(11)
11	−1	Scarborough		print "Scarborough"
11		Scarborough	−1	exit Tree(11)
10		Malton		exit Tree(10)
6		Wakefield		print "Wakefield"
6		Wakefield	7	call Tree(7)
7	8	York		call Tree(8)
8	−1	Wetherby		print "Wetherby"
8		Wetherby	−1	exit Tree(8)
7		York		print "York"
7		York	−1	exit Tree(7)
6		Wakefield		exit Tree(6)
0		Leeds		exit Tree(0)

As each invocation of *Tree* is completed, control is returned to the point where the procedure was called. For example, if currently the root node of a subtree is node 7, York, then *exit Tree(7)* returns control to the instruction following *call Tree(7)* which happens to be the end of Tree(6), Wakefield; similarly, exit Tree(6) returns control to the point where Tree(6) was called, the end of Tree(0). Successively returning to parent nodes is the bottoming out process referred to above, and it relies heavily on the use of a stack (see the section on applications of stacks earlier).

Using the recursive procedure, *Tree*, hides the use of the stack because of the way that procedure parameters are handled. On entering a procedure, the current values of its parameters are pushed to a stack and are replaced by the values passed to the procedure; the original values of the parameters are restored only when the procedure is exited. For example, the procedure call *Tree(2)* passes the value 2 to the parameter *node*. At this point, *Tree(1)* is being processed with *node* having a value of 1. So before *node* takes the value 2, its current value, that is 1, is pushed onto the stack. Then *node* is given the value 2 and the procedure is executed. When control returns to the point following the call *Tree(2)*, the top of the stack, the value 1, is pulled and copied to *node* thus restoring it to its local value.

The tree traversal algorithm given above is called in-order tree traversal, one of three main methods of accessing trees. The other two methods are called *pre-order* and *post-order* traversal. These are defined as follows:

Pre-order traversal:
visit the root node, then
visit all the nodes in the left subtree in pre-order, then
visit all the nodes in the right subtree in pre-order

With reference to the tree above, pre-order traversal would produce the list

Leeds Bradford Batley Halifax Dewsbury Huddersfield
Hull Wakefield Malton Scarborough York Wetherby

Post-order traversal:
visit all the nodes of the left subtree in post-order, then
visit all the nodes in the right subtree in post-order, then
visit the root node

This would produce the list

Batley Dewsbury Hull Huddersfield Halifax Bradford
Scarborough Malton Wetherby York Wakefield Leeds

Notice that the definitions of pre-order and post-order traversals again are recursive, allowing them to be handled in the same way as the in-order traversal.

Applications of binary trees

Sorting

A binary tree can be used to order a set of integers using the following algorithm:

```
begin
repeat
    read num                    {get next number}
    addnode(0)                  {call procedure}
until no_more_numbers           {continue until all numbers read}
end
procedure addnode(node)
begin
  if data(node) >num
    then if lptr(node) = null
            then createnode (num)
            else addnode(lptr(node))      {recurse using lptr}
         endif
       else if rptr(node) = null
            then createnode (num)
            else addnode(rptr(node))      {recurse using rptr}
          endif
    endif
end
```

Initially, the first number in the list is stored in the root node. Then, in turn, each of the remaining numbers is compared with the current root node (ie *data(node)*) to determine whether the number should be in the left subtree or the right subtree. If the number is greater, then it must go somewhere in the right subtree, otherwise it must go somewhere in the left subtree. If the appropriate subtree pointer is null, a new node is created containing the number and the subtree pointer links it to the tree; when the subtree pointer is not null, the process calls itself (recurses) using the pointer as the new root node. The procedure *createnode(num)*, referred to in the algorithm merely allocates space for new nodes, stores the number in the new node and links it to the tree by adjusting the parent's left or right pointer.

As an example, suppose the following list of numbers is to be used to created an ordered tree as described above:

57   10   26   13   85   2   30   63   120

The tree would assume the form

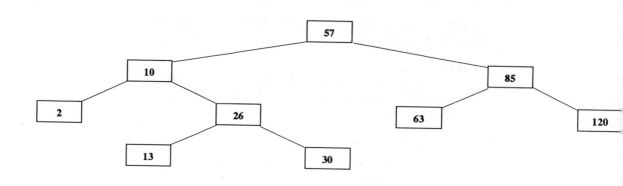

Sorting using a binary tree

The numbers could be visited in ascending order using in-order traversal, as described in the previous section, to give the list

2   10   13   26   30   57   63   85   120

Representing arithmetic expressions

Compilers often transform arithmetic expressions into more manageable forms prior to generating object code. A binary tree representation of an arithmetic expression is one such transformation. Consider the expression

$$B + C*D$$

The equivalent binary tree representation is

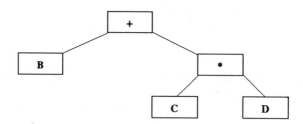

Transforming arithmetic expressions

An in-order traversal of the tree produces the original expression. This type of representation is relatively easy to handle by a compiler: if a node contains an operator, the left subtree is evaluated, the right subtree is evaluated and the two values obtained are the operands for the operator at that node. If a subtree also contains an operator node, the same procedure is used recursively to produce the intermediate result. In the example above, + at the root node causes the left subtree to be evaluated, resulting in the value assigned to B; however, the right subtree contains the operator node * (multiplication) causing a recursive call to its left and right subtrees before the multiplication, $C*D$, can be evaluated.

Here are some further examples of expressions represented as binary trees:

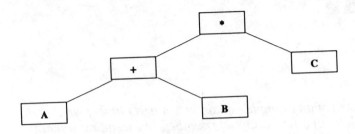

Example tree : (A+B)*C

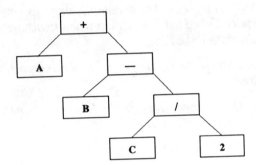

Example tree: A + B − C/2

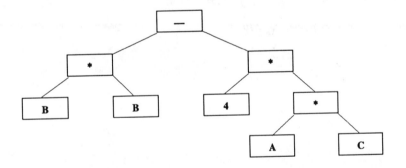

Example Tree: B*B − 4*A*C

All of the expressions provided above are in *infix notation*, that is, with the arithmetic operators positioned between the operands. Thus, to add two numbers, *A* and *B*, using infix notation we would write *A* + *B*. There are two other standard notations for arithmetic expressions, namely, *postfix* and *prefix* notations. In postfix notation, A + B is written *AB*+ and in prefix, +*AB*. By traversing the binary tree in in-order we saw that the infix expression resulted. Perhaps unsurprisingly, traversing the tree in post-order gives the postfix expression, and traversing the tree in pre-order gives the prefix expression. The table below shows the same expressions in the three different forms:

Infix	Postfix	Prefix
B+C*D	BCD*+	+B*CD
(A+B)*C	AB+C*	*+ABC
A+B−C/2	ABC2/−+	+A−B/C2
B*B−4*A*C	BB*4AC**−	−*BB*4*AC

Postfix notation is also known by the name *Reverse Polish* notation, extensively used in the programming language Forth and of general importance in computing.

Exercises

1. *By means of an example explain how a new number would be inserted into an array containing numbers in ascending order of magnitude. Write a pseudocode algorithm for the procedure.*

2. *When an item is deleted from a linked list, the storage space released can be reclaimed by using a linked list of free space. Suggest a method of accomplishing this, explaining how the free space linked list is modified when items are added and deleted from the data linked list.*

3. *Write pseudocode for pre-order and post-order traversal of binary trees.*

4. *Draw binary trees for the following expressions and hence convert them to postfix and prefix notation:*

   (i)   *(A+B)*(A−B)*

   (ii) *B^(C+D) - C*D*

   (iii) *A*(B−C/D)+E*

   (iv) *(−b + SQRT(D))/(2*a)*

   (v)   *(x+N/x)/2*

Assignment   *Links with the past*

A large furniture retailer with a number of outlets sells stock which is classified according to three broad categories:

    (i) Kitchen furniture

    (ii) Bedroom furniture

    (iii) Living room furniture

Over a period of a month, each item sold is stored on a central computer file as a record containing the following information:

        Item category

        Stock number

        Description

        Retail price

        Salesperson

        Date of sale

        Customer name

        Customer address

Task

Assuming that the file is extensive and queries require a fast response time, suggest data structures appropriate to the following processing tasks, justifying your choices:

    (i) Calculating the total sales for a particular salesperson in order to determine the amount of commission to be paid.

    (ii) Printing the details of sales for a particular category of furniture in reverse chronological order, ie most recent sales first.

    (iii) Searching for a sale made to a particular customer.

    (iv) Locating all items with a particular stock number.

    (v) Calculating the total sales for the month.

Chapter 35

Sorting Techniques

Introduction

For computing purposes, a distinction has to be made between *internal* and *external* sorting. Where large volumes of data have to be sorted, such as entire files held on magnetic tape or disk, an external sort is used; this involves repeated transfers of data between memory and backing storage media. Internal sorting, which is the subject of study in this section, involves the sorting of items entirely within memory into a strict ascending or descending order. For programming purposes, the items to be sorted are held in a one-dimensional array. The purpose of the data items will vary according to the application, but they may serve, for example, as keys to logical records. Direct access files frequently make use of indexes to identify the locations of individual records on a storage medium. Searching such an index for a particular record key value is often more efficient if the index is sorted into a particular sequence.

The study of sorting algorithms is a long standing area of research in computer science and many highly efficient but complex methods have been developed. In order that the main principles of sorting can be understood, this text provides a detailed description of three relatively simple sorting techniques, namely the:

- exchange or 'bubble' sort;

- selection sort;

- insertion sort.

Each narrative description is followed by:

- an outline of the main programming requirements needed to implement the sort in a high level language;

- a pseudocode algorithm with detailed annotation of the main processes;

- annotated sample programs implemented in Microsoft BASIC and Turbo Pascal.

Exchange Sort or Bubble Sort

If it is assumed, for example, that items are to be sorted into ascending sequence, then the idea of the bubble sort is that, firstly the smallest value 'bubbles' to the top or beginning of the list, followed by the second smallest into the second position, the third smallest into third position and so on. The process can best be illustrated by a practical example as follows.

Consider a one-dimensional array of 5 elements, each containing an integer value. The array is known by the symbol M and each element in the array is identified by its subscript. The array elements and their contents are shown below.

```
Array elements  M(1) M(2) M(3) M(4) M(5)
Contents         3    6    2    1    5
```

The bubble sort requires that the array of values be scanned repeatedly and that with each scan, or more properly, *pass,* adjacent pairs of numbers are compared to see if they are in the required order; if necessary they exchange positions. In the above example, the first pair, 3 and 6, are compared and found to be in the correct order; no exchange is necessary. Then the second and third items, 6 and 2, are compared, found to be in the incorrect order and are exchanged. The array now appears as follows:

```
Array elements  M(1) M(2) M(3) M(4) M(5)
Contents         3    2    6    1    5
```

The first pass continues with the comparison of the third and fourth items, 6 and 1; these require exchanging and the list becomes:

```
Array elements  M(1) M(2) M(3) M(4) M(5)
Contents         3    2    1    6    5
```

The first pass ends with a comparison of the fourth and fifth items, now 6 and 5 respectively; again, an exchange is required. At the end of this first pass, the sequence appears as:

```
Array elements  M(1) M(2) M(3) M(4) M(5)
Contents         3    2    1    5    6
```

The sort is not yet complete and further passes are needed. The complete process is illustrated below. Underlining indicates those values currently being compared and, if necessary, exchanged.

Array elements	M(1)	M(2)	M(3)	M(4)	M(5)	
Pass 1	3	6	2	1	5	
	3	6	2	1	5	exchange
	3	2	6	1	5	exchange
	3	2	1	6	5	exchange
End of Pass 1	3	2	1	5	6	
Pass 2	3	2	1	5	6	exchange
	2	3	1	5	6	exchange
	2	1	3	5	6	
	2	1	3	5	6	
End of Pass 2	2	1	3	5	6	
Pass 3	2	1	3	5	6	exchange
	1	2	3	5	6	
	1	2	3	5	6	
	1	2	3	5	6	
End of Pass 3	1	2	3	5	6	
Pass 4	1	2	3	5	6	
	1	2	3	5	6	
	1	2	3	5	6	
	1	2	3	5	6	
End of Pass 4	1	2	3	5	6	

A number of features can be identified in the above process:

- with each pass, the smallest value moves one position towards the beginning (the left) of the array;

- after the first pass, the largest value is at the end of the array. At the end of each subsequent pass, the next largest number moves to its correct position;

- the sort has been completed before the final pass.

Referring to this last feature, the sort is complete by the end of Pass 3. Why then is a further pass necessary? The answer is that the first comparison in Pass 3 results in an exchange between the values 2 and 1. If it is assumed that the occurrence of an exchange indicates that the sort is not complete, then a further pass is needed to determine that the array is sorted; that is, there have been no exchanges. The maximum number of passes required is always *n-1*, n being the number of items in the array. Frequently, the sort is complete well before this maximum is reached and any further passes are wasted. Consider the following sequence.

```
Array elements   M(1) M(2) M(3) M(4) M(5) M(6)

Contents          3    1    2    6    7    9

Pass 1            3    1    2    6    7    9   exchange
                  1    3    2    6    7    9   exchange
                  1    2    3    6    7    9
                  1    2    3    6    7    9
                  1    2    3    6    7    9

End of Pass 1     1    2    3    6    7    9

Pass 2            1    2    3    6    7    9
                  1    2    3    6    7    9
                  1    2    3    6    7    9
                  1    2    3    6    7    9
                  1    2    3    6    7    9

End of Pass 2     1    2    3    6    7    9
```

The maximum number of passes necessary should be *n-1*, that is, 5. Instead, the sort is completed by the end of the first pass and confirmed by the lack of exchanges in the second pass.

Program Requirements

(i)   Comparison of adjacent values in an array

Assuming that the values are held in a one-dimensional array, reference is made to elements within the array by subscript. For example, the 4th element in an array called *list*, is addressed by *list*(4). To carry out a pass of all the elements in an array requires the use of a program loop to increment the subscript from 1 to n, the variable being the size of the array. This can reduce by 1 after each complete pass, because the largest number 'sinks' to the bottom of the list and therefore need not be considered in subsequent passes; the efficiency of the algorithm is thus improved. For the sake of simplicity, this particular feature is not used in the illustrative algorithm or programs.

(ii)   Exchanging the positions of adjacent values

Assuming that the programming language in use does not provide an 'exchange' or 'swap' instruction, then a temporary store is required to allow the exchange to take place, For example, to exchange the contents of two variables, *first* and *second,* using a temporary store, *hold,* requires the following processes:

1. Copy contents of *first* into *hold;*

2. Copy contents of *second* into *first*;

3. Copy contents of *hold* into *second.*

This can be illustrated as follows with some example values:

Location	first	second	hold
Initial contents	6	3	
After process 1	6	3	6
After process 2	3	3	6
After process 3	3	6	6

(iii)   Detecting completion of the sort

A *flag* or *sentinel* variable, initialized for example, to 0 at the beginning of each pass and set to 1 if any exchanges take place during a pass, can be used to detect the completion of the sort before the maximum number of passes has been completed. For simplicity, the following algorithm does not include this feature, although it is used in the sample BASIC and Pascal programs;

A Bubble Sort Algorithm in pseudocode of array *M*, containing *n* elements

```
prog bubble sort
  number := n {number of values and subscript of last item}
  while passes <= number - 1 do {control number of passes}
   item := 1 {initialize array subscript}
   while item <= number - 1 do {loop for one pass}
    if M(item) > M(item - 1) then swap
                              {swap if necessary}

    endif
    item := item + 1 {increment subscript}
   endwhile {end of single pass}
   passes := passes + 1 {increment number of passes}
  endwhile {end of all passes}
endprog
```

Bubble Sort in Microsoft BASIC of 20 numeric values in array M

```
10   dim M(20)    {declare array}
20   for item = 1 to 20
30     input M(item)   {fill array}
40   next item
50   number = 20 {number of items}
60   passes = 1 {initialize passes}
70   exchange = 1
80   while passes <= number - 1 and exchange <> 0 {while not sorted}
90     item = 1      {initialize subscript}
100    exchange = 0 {flag for swap}
110    while item <= number - 1 {n-1 comparisons}
120      if M(item) > M(item + 1) then gosub 210 {swap elements}
130      item = item + 1
140    wend  {single pass}
150    passes = passes + 1 {increment passes}
160 wend {completion of all passes}
170 for item = 1 to 20
180    print M(item);   {print sorted items}
190 next item
200 end
210 rem subroutine to swap array element positions
220 spare = M(item) {temporary location}
230 M(item) = M(item + 1) {I+1 element into Ith element}
240 M(item + 1) = spare {Ith element from temporary location}
                        {into I+1 element}
250 exchange = 1 {set flag for swap}
260 return {end of swap routine}
```

Some versions of BASIC, including the Microsoft version, provide a *swap* command, so the subroutine in the above listing could be removed and line 120 amended to read:

```
if M(item) > M(item + 1) then swap M(item), M(item + 1)
```

Bubble sort in Turbo Pascal to sort 20 integer items in array *M*

```
program bubble (input, output);
const
 number = 20;   {number of values to sort}
var
 M :array[1..number] of integer; {declare array}
 exchange :boolean;   {flag for swap}
 item, passes, spare :integer;
begin
 for item := 1 to number do   {fill array M}
  begin
   writeln('number');
   readln(M[item]);
  end;
 passes := 1;            {initialize to first pass}
 exchange := true;
 while (passes <= number - 1) and (exchange) do   {control passes}
  begin
   item := 1;   {initialize element pointer}
   exchange := false; {initialize swap flag before each pass}
   while item <= number - 1 do {control number of comparisons}
    begin
     if M[item] > M[item +1] then {compare adjacent values}
      begin                        {swap elements}
       spare := M[item];
       M[item]  := M[item + 1];
       M[item + 1] := spare;
       exchange := true;   {set flag to indicate swap}
      end;
     item := item + 1; {move pointer to next element}
    end;
   passes := passes + 1; {increment pass counter}
  end;
 for item := 1 to number do   {display sorted array}
  begin
   writeln(M[item]);
  end;
end.
```

Selection Sort

This method also requires the comparison and exchange of elements in a list. It is based on the principal that the item with the lowest value is exchanged with the item at the beginning or *head* of the list and that the process is repeated with *n-1* items, *n-2* items and so on, until only the largest item is left.

Consider an array M which contains six integer values as follows:

```
M(1) M(2) M(3) M(4) M(5) M(6)
 15    8   -3   62   24   12
```

The list is to be sorted into strict ascending sequence to become:

```
M(1) M(2) M(3) M(4) M(5) M(6)
 -3    8   12   15   24   62
```

The underlined values indicate the length of the list to be examined in each scan.

```
15 8 -3 62 24 12      Starting sequence
```

```
-3  8  15  62  24  12      -3 exchanged with 15 at head of list
-3  8  15  62  24  12      no exchange needed
-3  8  12  62  24  15      12 exchanged with 15 at head of list
-3  8  12  15  24  62      15 exchanged with 62 at head of list
-3  8  12  15  24  62      no exchange needed
```

The first pass of n items returns the value of -3 as being the smallest value in the list; this value moves to the head of the list and the previous head, 15, is moved to the position formerly occupied by -3. The list to be scanned is now *n-1* items and has the value 8 at its head. The next pass reveals 8 as the smallest value, but no exchange is made because it already heads the shortened list. The next pass examines *n-2* items and returns 12 as the lowest value, which is exchanged with 15 at the head of the shortened list. The process continues until only two items remain, 24 at the head and 62 at the rear; no exchange is needed and the list is sorted.

Program Requirements

Certain features are similar to those of the bubble sort described earlier.

(i) Comparison of values in different locations in an array.

(ii) Exchange of values in different, although not necessarily adjacent, positions in the array.

(iii) The use of a pointer to allow element positions to be stored and incremented and also to be used as a subscript to refer to the contents of an individual location.

(iv) The use of a temporary store to enable an exchange of element positions.

A Selection Sort Algorithm in Pseudocode of array *M* containing *n* elements

```
prog selection
 number := n {number of values to sort}
 for head := 1 to n - 1 {increment head}
  present_value := M(head)    {value of current head}
  present_pointer := head     {position of current head}
  for next_one := present_pointer + 1 to n {increment}
                                        {search pointer}

  if M(next_one) > present_value then
    present_value := M(next_one) {store smaller value and
    present_pointer := next_one {its position in the list}
  endif
  endfor
  if present_pointer <> head then {check smallest value not already
                                  {at head}
    temp := M(head)   {temp is a temporary store for the swap}
    M(head) := M(present_pointer)  {exchange smallest/head values}
    M(present_pointer) := temp
  endif
 endfor
endprog
```

The use of a temporary location *temp* in the above algorithm is not strictly necessary, since the smallest value is assigned to *present_value* at the end of a scan and as the following program implementations illustrate, the swap could be implemented with:

```
M(present_pointer) := M(head);
M(head) := present_value.
```

Selection Sort in Microsoft BASIC for 20 items in array *M*

```
10  dim M(20)   {declare array}
20  for item = 1 to 20
30   input M(item)   {fill array}
40  next item
50  number = 20 {length of array}
60  for head = 1 to number - 1 {increment head}
70    present.value = M(head) {store head value}
80    present.pointer = head {and its position}
90    for next.one = present.pointer + 1 to number {step through list}
100    if M(next.one) < present.value then
            present.value = M(next.one): {store smaller value}
            present.pointer = next.one   {and its position}
110   next next.one
120   if present.pointer <> head then gosub 180 {check smallest value}
                                              {not already at head}
130 next head
140 for item = 1 to 20
150  print M(item);
160 next item
170 end
180 rem swap routine
190 M(present.pointer) = M(head){exchange smallest value}
200 M(head) = present.value     {with head value}
210 return
```

Turbo Pascal selection sort of 20 integer values in array *M*

```
program selection (input, output);
 const
  number = 20;
 var
  M :array[1..number] of integer; {declare array}
  head, next_one, present_value,
  present_pointer :integer;

begin
 for next_one := 1 to number do
  begin
   write ('number');
   readln (M[next_one]);   {fill array}
  end;
 for head := 1 to number - 1 do   {increment head}
  begin
   present_value := M[head];   {store head value}
   present_pointer := head;    {and its position}
  for next_one := present_pointer + 1 to number do   {step through list}
   begin
    if M[next_one] < present_value then
     begin
      present_value := M[next_one];   {store smaller value}
      present_pointer := next_one;    {and its position}
     end;
   end;
   if present_pointer <> head then   {check smallest value}
                                     {not already at head}
    begin
     M[present_pointer] := M[head];  {exchange smallest value}
     M[head] := present_value;       {with head value}
    end;
  end;
```

```
  for next_one := 1 to number do
    begin
     writeln(M[next_one]);
    end;
 end.
```

Insertion Sort

This method can best be illustrated with the example of an unsorted pack of playing cards. Assuming that the cards are to be put into a row of ascending sequence (the least value on the left), the procedure may be as follows:

> take the first card from the *source* pile and begin the *destination* row;
>
> continuing with the rest of the source pile, pick one card at a time and place it in the correct sequence in the destination row.

The process of finding the correct point of insertion requires repeated comparisons and where an insertion requires it, movement of cards to make space in the sequence. Thus, the card to be inserted, *x*, is compared with successive cards in the destination row (beginning from the largest value at the right hand end of the destination row) and where *x* is less than the card under comparison, the latter is moved to the right; otherwise *x* is inserted in the next position to the right.

Program Requirements

The procedures are fairly simple, although a practical exercise with a pack of cards should help to clarify them.

(i) As with previous sorts, reference to array subscripts is required to allow comparison with different elements in the array;

(ii) Nested loops are needed; the outer one for selecting successive values to be inserted into a destination sequence and the inner for allowing the insertion value to be compared with those already in sequence;

(iii) Control of the outer loop does not present a problem as it simply ensures that all values are inserted, starting with the second; the first obviously needs no comparison as it is the first to be inserted.

(iv) The inner loop controls the movement of values through the destination list to allow insertion of new values at the appropriate points. This loop may be terminated under two distinct conditions:

– a value in the destination sequence is less than the value to be inserted;

– there are no further items to the left in the destination sequence.

To ensure termination under these conditions, a *flag* or *sentinel* is used. In the algorithm and the program implementations, array element (0) is used to store the value to be inserted, thus ensuring that when the left hand end is reached, no further comparisons are made.

The following algorithm illustrates the procedure; the analogy of a pack of cards is continued.

Insertion Sort Algorithm in Pseudocode of *n* elements in array M

```
prog insertion;
 for pick_card = 2 to num_in_pack {pick cards singly, starting with sec
   in_hand := M(pick_card) {store value of card to insert}
   m(0) := in_hand {to prevent insertion beyond left}
                           {end of destination sequence}
   j := pick_card - 1 {ensures comparison with first card}
   while in_hand < M(j) do {card to insert < next card to the left in}
                           {destination sequence}
     M(j + 1) := M(j) {move card > card to insert, to the right}
     j := j - 1  {pointer to next card}
                 {compared with card to insert}
   endwhile
     M(j + 1) := in_hand {insert card into destination sequence}
 endfor
endprog
```

Insertion sort in Microsoft BASIC of 20 numeric values in array M

```
10   dim M(20)
20   for card = 1 to 20
30     input M(card)   {fill array}
40   next card
50   num.in.pack = 20   {number of cards to be sorted}
60   for pick.card = 2 to num.in.pack   {pick cards singly, starting with}
                                        {second}
70    in.hand = M(pick.card) {store value of card to insert}
80    M(0) = in.hand {prevent insertion beyond left end of}
                     {destination sequence}
90    j = pick.card - 1 {ensures comparison with first card}
100   while in.hand < M(j) {card to insert < next card to left}
                           {in destination sequence}
110     M(j + 1) = M(j) {move card > card to insert to the right}
120     j = j - 1 {pointer to next card compared with card}
                  {to insert}
130   wend
140   M(j + 1) = in.hand   {insert card into destination sequence}
150 next pick.card
160 for card = 1 to 20
170   print M(card);  {display sorted card values}
180 next card
190 end
```

Turbo Pascal insertion sort of 20 integer values in array M

```
program insertion (input, output);
 const
  num_in_pack = 20;   {number of items to sort}
 var
  M :array[0..num_in_pack] of integer; {declare array}
  card, pick_card, in_hand, j :integer;
begin
 for card := 1 to num_in_pack do   {fill array}
  begin
   write ('number');
   readln (M[card]);
  end;
 for pick_card := 2 to num_in_pack do {pick cards singly, starting with}
                                      {second}
  begin
   in_hand := M[pick_card];   {store value of card to insert}
```

```
  M[0] := in_hand; {prevent insertion beyond left end of}
                   {destination sequence}
  j := pick_card - 1; {ensures comparison with first card}
  while in_hand < M[j] do  {card to insert < card to left}
                           {in destination sequence}
    begin
      M[j + 1] := M[j];  {move card > card to insert to right}
      j := j - 1;  {pointer to next card compared with card}
                   {to insert}
    end;
    M[j + 1] := in_hand; {insert card into destination sequence}
  end;
  for card := 1 to num_in_pack do
    begin
      writeln (M[card]);  {display sorted list}
    end;
end.
```

Comparative efficiency of sorting methods

The sorts described so far are not the most sophisticated, and in many cases, are not very quick. They are, however, relatively simple to understand and they have been chosen for this reason. More efficient, and consequently more complex, sorting algorithms include the:

Shell Sort

Named after its designer, D.L. Shell in 1959, it is a refinement of the insertion sort and divides the list into groups which are sorted separately. For example, with an array of eight items, those which are four positions apart are sorted first; the four groups will each contain two items. A second pass groups and sorts afresh the items which are two positions apart; this involves two groups, each with 4 items. Finally, all items (only one position apart) are sorted in a final pass. With each pass, the *distance* between the keys is *halved*, effectively changing the contents of each group. Successive passes continue until the distance between the elements in a group is one. The idea of the Shell sort is that the early passes compare items which are widely separated and thus remove the main disorders in the array. Later passes may then require fewer movements of items.

Quicksort

This *partition* sort was invented by C.A.R Hoare, who called it 'Quicksort' because of its remarkable speed. It is based on the exchange principle used in the bubble sort described earlier and is one of the fastest array sorting techniques, for large numbers of items, currently available. Quicksort is based on the general principle that exchanges should preferably be made between items which are located a large *distance* apart in an array. Initially, the array is divided into two *partitions,* using the mid-point. Beginning at the left-most position in the array, the item in this position is compared with the item at the mid-point position. If the former is less than the latter, the next item in the partition is compared with the mid-point element. The comparisons with the mid-point item are repeated with successive items in the partition until one is found which is greater than or equal to the mid-point item. The same process is used on the right-hand partition until an item is found which is less than or equal to that at the mid-point position. Once items are found in both partitions which satisfy these respective conditions, they are swapped. Successive comparisons and swaps are carried out until each item in each partition has been compared with the mid-point item. The whole process continues *recursively* (it calls itself repeatedly), further sub-dividing the partitions, until each sub-partition contains only one item, when the array is sorted. The topic of recursion is dealt with in Chapter 34 on Data Structures.

Quicksort's speed stems from the fact that the early passes bring items close to their final sequence, leaving the last few passes to make only minor changes.

Tree Sort

This is a *selection* sort and is described in the chapter on Data Structures. Like Quicksort, the binary tree sort uses the technique of recursion.

Comparing the efficiency of various sorting algorithms with one another requires careful use of 'bench test' data to ensure that comparisons are fair and specialists in the subject of sorting have spent a great deal of time analysing the various methods. It is beyond the scope of this text to pursue such analysis in detail, but some broad comparisons can be made of the relative efficiency of the simple sorts described so far. It must be said that where only a few items are to be sorted, little tangible benefit will be gained from using a sophisticated sort, as opposed to a simple one. With a larger number of items, the limitations of simple sorting algorithms, such as the bubble sort, soon become apparent. Another factor which may affect a sort's performance is the degree to which items are out of order to begin with.

The *bubble sort* is probably the least efficient and is rarely used by experienced programmers. It is, however, a simple sort to understand and provides a good introduction to any programmer wishing to develop their skill in this area. The *selection sort* generally performs better than the *insertion sort*, except when the items are almost in order to begin with.

Assignment   *Sort it out*

Task

Compare the efficiency of three sorting techniques: use pre-written programs, suitably amended to include a timing mechanism to measure the speed of sorting.

Test each sorting technique with

> (i) **10 values**
>
> (ii) **100 values**
>
> (iii) **1000 values**
>
> > a) **randomly presented,**
>
> then   b) **almost sorted**

Comment on your results and give a presentation to the rest of the class on one sorting technique.

Chapter 36

COBOL

Scope of the Chapter

COBOL is a very complex language intended to facilitate the development and implementation of full scale data processing applications in the business environment. Consequently, mastering COBOL in its entirety takes a great deal of time and effort even with the help of one of the dozens of books currently on the market aimed at facilitating this process. Our intention is merely to provide a sound basis for further study. To this end, the material presented covers a small subset of the full language, enough to be able to understand and construct fairly simple application programs.

The chapter is divided into four main sections. The first section provides an overview of the COBOL language, including a complete program described in detail to give you a 'feel' for the language. The second section describes the function and structure of COBOL more thoroughly, giving numerous examples of COBOL code. The third section contains a number of complete example programs based on a common theme, with suggestions for programming exercises. The final section contains ideas for programming projects.

If you work through the example programs provided, and spend time on the exercises, you should be in a strong position to undertake a more thorough study of COBOL. It cannot be emphasised strongly enough, however, that learning a programming language requires *practice* in writing programs and learning from mistakes; reading about COBOL will never make you a COBOL programmer.

There are many COBOL compilers on the market, each with its own minor variations and extensions aimed at getting the best out of the computer on which the programs are to be run. Though the programs provided in this book were written using UTAH COBOL on an IBM PC, every attempt has been made to avoid the use of non-standard program constructs so that the programs are as transportable as possible to other machines/compilers.

Concerning the compilation of the programs, it is not possible to provide detailed instructions since this is a compiler-dependent process; you must consult the reference manual provided with the COBOL compiler that you are using for the precise manner in which this is accomplished.

The Structure of a COBOL Program

The four divisions

A COBOL program is divided into four areas termed DIVISIONS which appear in the order IDENTIFICATION division, ENVIRONMENT division, DATA division and PROCEDURE division. The contents of each of these divisions is dependent on the requirements of the program, but generally a division will contain a number of SECTIONS subdivided into PARAGRAPHS. Within each paragraph there will be a number of SENTENCES containing CLAUSES. This structure deliberately follows the organisation of ordinary English text such as that found in a report. Many of the possible entries are optional; the program below contains just about the absolute minimum for a COBOL program:

```
000010  IDENTIFICATION DIVISION.
000020   PROGRAM-ID. MinProg.

000030  ENVIRONMENT DIVISION.

000040  DATA DIVISION.

000050  PROCEDURE DIVISION.
000060  BEGIN.
000070     DISPLAY "This is all I do!".
000080     STOP RUN.
000090  END PROGRAM MINPROG.
```

A COBOL program must have its name declared in the IDENTIFICATION division, but both the ENVIRONMENT and DATA divisions have no compulsory entries. The PROCEDURE division contains a single paragraph, "BEGIN", containing just two statements. This program merely displays the message "This is all I do!" on the monitor screen and then terminates. The final line of the program marks the physical end of the program, though not all COBOL compilers have this requirement.

IDENTIFICATION DIVISION

The IDENTIFICATION DIVISION allows the programmer to describe the whole program in general terms by supplying, under appropriate headings, such information as the name of the program, its author, when it was written and what it does. Some of this information is optional and none of it has a direct effect on the program's operation.

ENVIRONMENT DIVISION

In the CONFIGURATION SECTION of the ENVIRONMENT DIVISION are details of the computers on which the program was developed and is intended to be run, and the INPUT-OUTPUT SECTION specifies the peripheral devices to be used for reading or writing the files which will be defined later in the program.

DATA DIVISION

The DATA DIVISION contains a FILE SECTION in which each file named in the INPUT-OUTPUT SECTION is given a File Description (FD). The FD contains the file name and one or more record names. The structure of a record is defined hierarchically using LEVEL numbers starting at 01 and getting progressively bigger for finer definitions.

The WORKING-STORAGE SECTION of the DATA DIVISION contains definitions of other data items specifically referenced in the PROCEDURE DIVISION of the program but which are not part of any file.

PROCEDURE DIVISION

Finally, the PROCEDURE DIVISION defines precisely how the processing is to be performed. The programmer may give PARAGRAPH names to groups of SENTEN-CES to which reference may be made from other parts of the program, and these paragraphs may be grouped together into SECTIONS.

Each SENTENCE, terminated with a full stop, defines one or more operations to be performed; in keeping with the general philosophy of making a COBOL program easily readable, the instructions often read like ordinary English sentences. As an example, the SENTENCE

```
PERFORM PARA-1 UNTIL ENDFILE IS EQUAL TO "YES".
```

specifies that control is to be transferred to the paragraph named PARA-1, the paragraph is to be executed and this is to be repeated until a certain condition obtains. This condition is that the identifier (variable) *ENDFILE* contains the letters "YES"; when this condition is true, the loop will end and the next sentence will be executed.

Example Program

Program specification

The program shown in Listing 1 has been provided to give you an idea of the form of a COBOL program and the purpose of each of its main constituent parts. It is described in great detail so that you can use it for reference purposes when writing your own programs.

The program is designed to search a file of book titles and print those which deal with a certain subject. Each record in the file contains the title of the book, its author and three numeric codes related to its subject matter. The user enters one such subject code and the program prints out a list of books dealing with that subject.

Here is a sample of typical subject codes:

Subject	Code
Artificial Intelligence	10
BASIC	11
Boolean Algebra	12
C	13
COBOL	14
Computer Science	15
Data Structures	16
Databases	17
Fortran	18
Graphics	19
Hardware	20
Information Technology	21
Pascal	22
Program design	23
Programming	24
Robotics	25
Software	26
Spreadsheets	27
Wordprocessing	28

The Category Codes

So a book such as "Pascal" by Findlay and Watt would be stored in the file as the record

```
Pascal          Findlay & Watt          222415
```

with the numeric code indicating that the book concerns Pascal(22), Programming(24) and Computer Science(15).

This record would be selected, therefore, if the file was being searched for any one of these three codes.

The program first asks the user to enter the code to be used for the search, and then searches the file printing out records that contain the code as they are located. The program structure diagram is shown below:

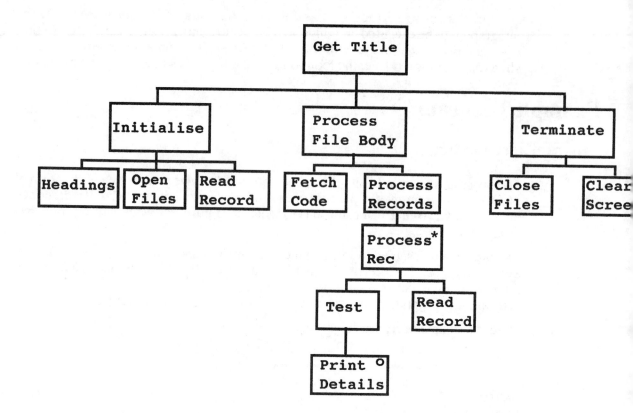

Structure diagram for Titles program

The data file accessed by the program contains the following records:

Title	Author(s)	Categories
Artificial Intelligence	Charniak	001510
Computer Architecture	Wilks & Kerridge	001520
Computer Graphics	Hearn & Baker	152619
Data Structures for Micros	Langsam & Augenstein	001516
Digital Computer Fundamentals	Bartree	152024
Educational Computing	Scanlon & O'Shea	152624
Foundations of Robotics	Siegler	102520
High Resolution Graphics	Angel & Griffith	152619
Hitch-hikers Guide to AI	Forsyth & Naylor	261024
Information Technology	Zorkoczy	212024
Introduction to Robotics	Critchlow	102520
Logo Programming	IBM	262410
Mastering Computers	Wright	152026
Microcomputer Graphics	McGregor & Watt	152619
Microcomputer Primer	Waite	152619
Pascal	Findlay & Watt	222423
Pascal for Students	Kemp	222423
Principles of Program Design	Jackson	232616
Problem Solving with Prolog	Conlon	241017
Programming for Poets	Conway & Archer	242618
Programming in C	Kochan	132426
Structured Programming in COBOL	Boettcher	142426
The AI Business	Winston & Prendergast	102615
The Intelligent Micro	Williams	102511
Turbo C	Borland	132426
Utah COBOL	Ellis Computing	142426

For a category code of 24(Programming), the output from the program is a listing on the printer containing the following details:

Title	Author(s)
Digital Computer Fundamentals	Bartree
Educational Computing	Scanlon & O'Shea
Hitch-hikers Guide to AI	Forsyth & Naylor
Information Technology	Zorkoczy
Logo Programming	IBM
Pascal	Findlay & Watt
Pascal for Students	Kemp
Problem Solving with Prolog	Conlon
Programming for Poets	Conway & Archer
Programming in C	Kochan
Structured Programming in COBOL	Boettcher
The Intelligent Micro	Williams
Turbo C	Borland
Utah COBOL	Ellis Computing

Program Listing

```
000010 IDENTIFICATION DIVISION.
000020 PROGRAM-ID.        GET-TITLE.
000030 AUTHOR.            Nick Waites and David Turnbull.
000040 DATE-WRITTEN.      OCTOBER 1988.
000050*REMARKS.           A program to extract titles and authors
000060                    of books corresponding to a particular
000070                    category code.
000080
000090
000100 ENVIRONMENT DIVISION.
000110 INPUT-OUTPUT SECTION.
000120 FILE-CONTROL.
000130     SELECT TITLE-FILE ASSIGN TO DISK
000140          ACCESS IS SEQUENTIAL
000150          ORGANIZATION IS LINE SEQUENTIAL.
000160     SELECT PRINT-FILE ASSIGN TO PRINTER.
000170
000180 DATA DIVISION.
000190 FILE SECTION.
000200 FD TITLE-FILE
000210     LABEL RECORDS ARE STANDARD
000220     VALUE OF FILE-ID "B:TITLES.TXT".
000230 01 DETAILS.
000240     03 TITLE            PIC X(30).
000250     03 AUTHORS          PIC A(20).
000260     03 CATEGORIES.
000270        05 CAT1          PIC 99.
000280        05 CAT2          PIC 99.
000290        05 CAT3          PIC 99.
000300
000310 FD PRINT-FILE
000320     LABEL RECORD IS OMITTED.
000330 01 PRINT-REC           PIC X(80).
000340
000350
000360 WORKING-STORAGE SECTION.
000370 01 PAGE-HEADING.
000380     03 FILLER          PIC A(27) VALUE SPACES.
000390     03 FILLER          PIC A(26) VALUE
000400          "TITLES FOR CHOSEN CATEGORY".
000410     03 FILLER          PIC A(27) VALUE SPACES.
000420 01 COLUMN-HEADINGS.
000430     03 FILLER          PIC A(12) VALUE SPACES.
000440     03 FILLER          PIC A(5)  VALUE "Title".
```

```
000450      03 FILLER          PIC A(30) VALUE SPACES.
000460      03 FILLER          PIC A(9)  VALUE "Author(s)".
000470      03 FILLER          PIC A(24) VALUE SPACES.
000480 01 TITLE-LINE.
000490      03 FILLER          PIC A(6) VALUE SPACES.
000500      03 TITLE1          PIC X(35).
000510      03 FILLER          PIC A(6) VALUE SPACES.
000520      03 AUTHORS1        PIC A(20).
000530      03 FILLER          PIC A(13) VALUE SPACES.
000540 01 END-FLAG            PIC X.
000550      88 END-OF-FILE     VALUE IS "Y".
000560 77 SUB-CODE            PIC 99.
000570
000580 PROCEDURE DIVISION.
000590 INITIALISE.
000600      OPEN INPUT TITLE-FILE
000610           OUTPUT PRINT-FILE.
000620      PERFORM HEADINGS.
000630      PERFORM READ-RECORD.
000640
000650 PROCESS-FILE-BODY.
000660      PERFORM FETCH-CODE.
000670      PERFORM PROCESS-REC UNTIL END-OF-FILE.
000680
000690 TERMINATE.
000700      CLOSE TITLE-FILE
000710            PRINT-FILE.
000720      DISPLAY ERASE.
000730      STOP RUN.
000740
000750 HEADINGS.
000760      WRITE PRINT-REC FROM PAGE-HEADING
000770           AFTER ADVANCING PAGE.
000780      WRITE PRINT-REC FROM COLUMN-HEADINGS
000790           AFTER ADVANCING 4 LINES.
000800      MOVE SPACES TO PRINT-REC.
000810      WRITE PRINT-REC
000820           AFTER ADVANCING 1 LINE.
000830
000840 FETCH-CODE.
000850      DISPLAY ERASE.
000860      DISPLAY (9, 20) "ENTER CATEGORY CODE  :".
000870      DISPLAY (11, 20) "A 2 digit number please".
000880      ACCEPT  (9, 42) SUB-CODE.
000890      DISPLAY ERASE.
000900      DISPLAY (9, 24) "PROCESSING RECORDS - Please wait".
000910
000920
000930 PROCESS-REC.
000940      IF   (CAT1 EQUAL TO SUB-CODE)
000950        OR (CAT2 EQUAL TO SUB-CODE)
000960        OR (CAT3 EQUAL TO SUB-CODE)
000970           PERFORM PRINT-DETAILS.
000980      PERFORM READ-RECORD.
000990
001000
001010 PRINT-DETAILS.
001020      MOVE TITLE TO TITLE1.
001030      MOVE AUTHORS TO AUTHORS1.
001040      WRITE PRINT-REC FROM TITLE-LINE
001050           AFTER ADVANCING 1 LINE.
001060
001070
001080 READ-RECORD.
```

```
001090        READ TITLE-FILE
001100             AT END MOVE "Y" TO END-FLAG.
001110
001120 END PROGRAM GET-TITLE
```

Description of program

Lines 10-60

This is the IDENTIFICATION DIVISION in which the program is identified in terms of its name, "GET-TITLE", its author(s), when it was written and a brief description of its function. The REMARKS declaration is preceded by the "*" in column 7 to identify it as a comment; some compilers accept the word REMARKS as a valid entry in the IDENTIFICATION division. The PROGRAM-ID entry is the only compulsory entry in this division.

Lines 100-160

The ENVIRONMENT DIVISION contains the INPUT-OUTPUT SECTION in which the programmer defines the peripheral devices associated with any files accessed in the program. In this instance, two files are used: TITLE-FILE which is the data file stored on floppy disk, and PRINT-FILE which is a file used for transferring output to the printer.

Line 180

This is the start of the DATA DIVISION in which each file and identifier referenced in the PROCEDURE DIVISION is specified in terms of structure and format. The DATA division comprises two sections in this program, namely the FILE SECTION in which the files named in the INPUT-OUTPUT SECTION are defined, and the WORKING-STORAGE SECTION containing declarations of all the other identifiers used in the program.

Line 190

This is the start of the FILE SECTION.

Lines 200-290

This block of lines contains the FD (File Description) of TITLE-FILE.

The sentence "LABEL RECORDS ARE STANDARD" is required for some compilers when defining disk files; label records are special internally generated records which provide information about the file.

Line 220 tells the compiler that this file is to be located on floppy-disk drive B under the name "TITLES.TXT".

The *level number* 01 is used to identify the name assigned to the records of the file, in this case "DETAILS". Other level numbers, from 02 to 49 are used to define the hierarchical structure of the records. Each field within the record is assigned a name and, providing it is not followed by a higher level number, its size and character is specified by means of a PIC (PICture) clause. For example, "TITLE" has a PICture of X(30) which means that the field will contain exactly 30 alphanumeric(X) characters. A 9 in the picture clause indicates a numeric field and an *A* means an alphabetic field.

The field called "CATEGORIES" is termed a *Group Item* because it is a name given to a group of sub-fields. Only *elementary items,* that is fields not further subdivided, are given pictures. The structure of a group item is defined by the pictures of its constituent items, so "CATEGORIES" comprises six numeric characters since each of its three sub-fields contains two numeric characters.

Lines 310 to 330 define the structure of the file assigned to the printer. Again, the sentence "LABEL RECORD IS OMITTED" is required by some compilers when specifying files that are assigned to a printer. This time the record definition indicates that the record merely contains 80 alphanumeric characters, the width of a line on an 80-column printer; this program will be transferring data to the printer a line at a time.

Lines 360-560

This is the WORKING-STORAGE SECTION of the DATA DIVISION in which identifiers not directly associated with files are defined. Lines 370-410, for example, define a group item called "PAGE-HEADING" which will be used to print a heading for the printout. The word "FILLER" is recognised by the compiler as an elementary item having no function other than to reserve an area of memory. FILLERS can be used as frequently as required in the DATA division but may only be given values using the VALUE clause in the WORKING-STORAGE section, not in the FILE section. Though a FILLER has the form of an identifier, it cannot be referenced in the PROCEDURE division. The three FILLERS constituting "PAGE-HEADING" together define a line of text having the form

```
←——27 spaces——→TITLES FOR CHOSEN CATEGORY←————27 spaces————→
```

Similarly, the fillers in "COLUMN-HEADINGS" define a line of text of the form

```
←—12—→Title←————————30————————→Author(s)←——24——→
```

In the PROCEDURE division, "PAGE-HEADING" and "COLUMN-HEADINGS" are transferred to PRINT-REC, the record description associated with the file assigned to the printer. By this means, a variety of different lines of text can be printed without the need to define lots of different files, each with a different record description, all assigned to the printer.

The group item "TITLE-LINE" contains the identifiers "TITLE1" and "AUTHORS1". In the PROCEDURE division, when a record is to be printed, the book title and authors given in the record will be transferred to these two fields prior to "TITLE-LINE" being printed. This would not be possible if "TITLE-LINE" consisted entirely of FILLERS. Note also that using the identifier names "TITLE" and "AUTHORS" rather than "TITLE1" and "AUTHORS1" here would cause ambiguity because the former two identifier names are used as field names within the record description "DETAILS" in the FILE section.

Lines 540 and 550

The level number 88 is reserved for the definition of "Condition Names". A condition name is used in place of a condition to make it more readable. Thus at line 670, where the statement reads

```
PERFORM PROCESS-REC UNTIL END-OF-FILE.
```

without the use of the condition name "END-OF-FILE" the statement would be of the form

```
PERFORM PROCESS-REC UNTIL END-FLAG EQUAL TO "Y".
```

The first form of the statement is much more readable than that of the latter. Condition names are discussed further in the description of the operation of the PROCEDURE division below.

Line 560

Level 77's are often used for those identifiers which cannot be logically associated with any other identifiers. They define *non-contiguous,* that is independent, identifiers. In this instance, "SUB-CODE" is used to store the subject code of interest.

Lines 580-1120

This constitutes the PROCEDURE division which specifies all the processing tasks to be performed by the program and closely corresponds to the program structure diagram. The very last instruction is required to be the "END PROGRAM" statement in some COBOL compilers.

Lines 580-730

This section of the program defines its logical structure by grouping together in paragraphs its main procedures. Line 590 is a *paragraph name* which labels a section of the program. A paragraph name may be used merely to clarify the structure of a program, as in this instance, or as a means of transferring control to a section of the program. Examples of the latter function occur later on in the program.

The "INITIALISE" paragraph comprises three *sentences*. The first of these, the "OPEN" statement causes channels to the two files "TITLE-FILE" and "PRINT-FILE" to be opened. This is necessary before any records can be accessed. The statement tells the compiler that records are to be read sequentially from "TITLE-FILE" and written sequentially to "PRINT-FILE".

The word "PERFORM" is recognised by the compiler as a command to

      (i) branch to the section of the program located at the label specified in the statement,

     (ii) execute all of the sentences in this paragraph,

    (iii) return control to the statement immediately following the PERFORM statement.

In other words, a PERFORM statement allows the programmer to modularise a program by using subroutine-like constructs.

The paragraph "HEADINGS" prints the page and column headings for the printout, and "READ-RECORD" reads the first record in the data file. Both of these procedures are explained in more detail later.

Lines 650-670

This section invokes two procedures and performs the main processing tasks. "FETCH-CODE" requests the user to enter the required category code and "PROCESS-REC" searches the category codes of the current record for the presence of that code, prints the details of title and author if a match is found and, finally, reads the next record in the data file. The PERFORM..UNTIL construct used in line 670 causes the paragraph "PROCESS-REC" to be repeatedly executed until the condition represented by the condition name "END-OF-FILE" is true; this occurs only when an attempt is made to read past the last record in the file.

Lines 690-730

This is the final paragraph in the mainline program. The two active files are closed using the CLOSE statement, the monitor screen is cleared with "DISPLAY ERASE", and the program's execution is terminated with "STOP RUN". Note that the DISPLAY verb, which is used exclusively for controlling output to the VDU, can be used in a variety of ways to display literal text or the value of variables as well as performing such functions as clearing the screen or producing inverse characters. The DISPLAY verb is further described below.

Lines 750-820

The "HEADINGS" paragraph deals with producing the page and column headings on the printer by writing a sequence of records to the file "PRINTER-FILE" which is assigned to the printer.

The WRITE verb is followed by a record name, "PRINT-REC" in this instance, and two optional clauses. The first clause, starting with the word "FROM" allows data to be transferred from an identifier to the record before the record is written to the appropriate file. On line 760, the data stored in "PAGE-HEADING" is copied to

"PRINT-REC" before being transmitted to the printer. The second optional clause, "AFTER ADVANCING PAGE" sends a form feed character to the printer prior to printing the data held in "PRINT-REC". The same format allows a number of line feed characters to be sent to the printer before printing a line of text; this is illustrated in the next sentence starting on line 780. Here the data in "COLUMN-HEADINGS" is transferred to "PRINT-REC" and the printer is caused to skip four lines before printing the line of column headings.

In line 800, blanks or "SPACES" are transferred to the record "PRINT-REC" (the MOVE verb is used for data transfer in COBOL) prior to the record being printed, and has the effect of printing a blank line after the heading. This instruction is necessary because COBOL does not allow you merely to say "ADVANCE 1 LINE"; the AFTER ADVANCING clause must accompany a WRITE statement.

Lines 840-900

This paragraph, labelled "FETCH-CODE", displays a prompt for the user to type a two-digit, numeric category code which is to be the focus of the data file search. The DISPLAY verb in line 850 clears the screen and the following line causes the literal "ENTER CATEGORY CODE :" to be displayed at row 9 column 20 on the VDU. Similarly, line 870 displays "A 2 digit number please" 11 lines down from the top of the screen and 20 character positions in from the left margin.

The ACCEPT verb transfers characters typed in at the keyboard to the named identifier ("SUB-CODE", for example, in line 880) after first positioning the cursor at the row and column specified.

The screen produced by "FETCH-CODE" looks like this:

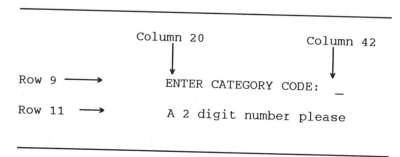

Lines 930-980

This paragraph processes the current record by comparing the code typed in by the user with the three category codes stored in the record. The function of the IF statement should be quite clear: if one of the codes in the record matches matches the code stored in "SUB-CODE" then the program invokes the paragraph "PRINT-DE-TAILS" which causes the title and author(s) of the current record to be printed, otherwise, if a match has not been found, control merely passes to the next sentence in line 980.

"READ-RECORD" does exactly that - it reads the next record in the data file so that it is ready for processing by this paragraph if the end of the file has not been reached.

Lines 1010-1050

This paragraph is performed when a record match has been obtained and the details of the record are to be printed. The two MOVE statements cause the title and author(s) stored in the data record to be copied to the corresponding fields in "TITLE-LINE" in WORKING-STORAGE. This allows the output sent to the printer to be presented in a clear manner, aligned with the appropriate column headings.

The formatted line is then transferred to "PRINT-REC" and then printed.

Lines 1080-1100

This paragraph, containing a single sentence, reads the next available record from the data file and transfers its contents to the appropriate record in the FILE section of the DATA DIVISION. The appropriate record in this instance is called "DETAILS". If there are no more records available, that is, the end of the file has been reached, the letter "Y" is moved to "END-FLAG" making the condition name "END-OF-FILE" true; this terminates the processing loop and causes program control to progress to the final "TERMINATE" paragraph which ends the program execution.

Fundamental Concepts

Though the preceding section described an example COBOL program at some length, a number of important details were either omitted or mentioned only briefly. This section will cover these points more thoroughly and prepare you for the task of writing your own programs.

Punctuation

Punctuation marks in COBOL serve much the same function as those in ordinary English prose. Commas and semicolons are interchangeably used to separate words and phrases so that statements are clearly presented. Full stops in COBOL indicate the end of sentences just as they do in English. Certain things, like division declarations such as "DATA DIVISION." and paragraph names such as "READ-RECORD." must be terminated with a full stop, but commas and semicolons are entirely optional. A sentence may span more than one line.

Here are some rules governing the use of punctuation characters in COBOL:

(i) Full stops, commas and semicolons must immediately follow the last letter of a word and be followed by a space.
Example:

```
MOVE 0 TO TOTAL, COUNT.
```

(ii) The left parenthesis, "(", must not be followed by a space and the right parenthesis, ")", must not be preceded by a space.
Example:

```
DISPLAY (10, 20) "Enter stock number".
```

Coding Format

Each line of a COBOL program contains 80 columns split into 5 regions:

(i) a sequence (line) number occupying columns 1-6;

(ii) an indicator (typically a "-" or "*") occupying column 7;

(iii) area A occupying columns 8-11;

(iv) area B occupying columns 12-72;

(v) an identification code occupying columns 72-80.

The use of the identification code dates back to the days when programs were punched onto cards (which could be easily mixed up with those of other programs); the identification code is usually left blank these days.

The "-" indicator is used to continue a broken word or literal from one line to the next, otherwise there is no need to show that a line spans more than one line. For example, the following literal requiring a continuation indicator would be written as follows:

```
         1         2         3         4         5         6         7
1234567890123456789012345678901234567890123456789012345678901234567890123456789012
A...B...........................................................................
  01 Column-headings               PIC X(80) VALUE
       "    Name                    Number          District           Item Co
     "de  No.Sold     Value".
```

Notice that the literal stops at column 72 on the first line and continues on the next line after the quotation marks in column 12.

Generally speaking, it is not good programming style to split a word or a clause; the readability of a COBOL program is very important, so choose convenient places to break sentences. For example, it would be bad programming style to do this:

```
         1         2         3         4         5         6         7
1234567890123456789012345678901234567890123456789012345678901234567890123456789012
A...B...........................................................................
       WRITE PRINT-LINE FROM COLUMN-HEADINGS AFTER ADVANCING 2
       LINES.
```

Instead, split the line at the beginning of the last clause and indent the second line:

```
         1         2         3         4         5         6         7
1234567890123456789012345678901234567890123456789012345678901234567890123456789012
A...B...........................................................................
       WRITE PRINT-LINE FROM COLUMN-HEADINGS
            AFTER ADVANCING 2 LINES.
```

The "*" indicator in column 7 causes the compiler to completely ignore the whole of the line, allowing the programmer to add comments to the program. Another good way to make a program readable is to insert blank lines at suitable places; the compiler will just ignore them. Area A is used to identify *headers*. Headers are division names, section names and paragraph names and must start somewhere in area A, though they are allowed to extend as far as necessary into area B. Examples of headers are

```
       PROCEDURE DIVISION.
       INPUT-OUTPUT SECTION.
       PROGRAM-ID.
       PROCESS-RECORD-PARA.
```

In addition, file descriptions (FD) and 01 levels must start in area A. Anything else is confined to area B.

Data item descriptions

Entries in the DATA DIVISION to describe data items have the following general format:

1) Level number

2) Item name

These two must be present for all data items.

3) PICTURE clause

This must be present for all elementary data items.

4) VALUE clause

5) OCCURS clause

6) REDEFINES clause

These are three optional entries (note that there are a number of others which are not discussed here).

Here is an example of a simple DATA DIVISION entry:

```
         1         2         3         4         5         6         7
1234567890123456789012345678901234567890123456789012345678901234567890 12
A...B.................................................................  .
    05 Surname                    PICTURE IS A(20).
     |    |                         |
   Level  Item name               PICTURE
   number                         clause
```

In the remainder of this chapter, and where relevant, statements will be defined by format specifications showing their general structures using a standard form of notation. For example, the format of the MOVE statement is given as

```
              { literal-1  }
      MOVE {identifier-1}  TO  identifier-2 [identifier-3] .....
```

and it is interpreted as follows:

1. The underlined words must be present.

2. One of the items in the curly brackets must be present.

3. Items in square brackets may or may not be present.

Here are a number of possible MOVE statements together with the appropriate format statements:

```
      MOVE Account-num-A  TO Account-num-B
ie    MOVE identifier-1   TO identifier-2


      MOVE "Non-numeric value"  TO  Error-message
ie    MOVE literal-1            TO  identifier-2


      MOVE 0          TO  Count       Total       Flag
ie    MOVE literal-1  TO  identifier-2 identifier-3 identifier-4
```

Some statements, such as the DISPLAY statement, have a number of different formats; in such cases each format is listed.

The IDENTIFICATION DIVISION

The function of the IDENTIFICATION DIVISION is to identify the source program for documentation purposes. It has the following format:

```
IDENTIFICATION DIVISION.
PROGRAM-ID. program-name.
[AUTHOR. comment entry.]
[INSTALLATION. comment entry.]
[DATE-WRITTEN. comment entry.]
[DATE-COMPILED. comment entry.]
[SECURITY. comment entry.]
```

Although this division is treated as comments by the compiler, any reserved words present are checked and must therefore be in upper case and follow the COBOL rules. Here is an example using all of the possible entries:

```
000010 IDENTIFICATION DIVISION.
000020 PROGRAM-ID. EXAMPLE-PROG.
000030 AUTHOR. NICK WAITES
000040 INSTALLATION. OWN PC.
000050 DATE-WRITTEN. MAY 31ST, 1990.
000060 DATE-COMPILED. MAY 31ST, 1990.
000070 SECURITY. COPYRIGHT F.N.WAITES 1990.
000080* comment lines have an asterisk in column 7.
```

The ENVIRONMENT DIVISION

The general format of the ENVIRONMENT DIVISION is as follows:

```
          1         2         3         4         5         6         7
1234567890123456789012345678901234567890123456789012345678901234567890123456789012
    A...B.........................................................................

    ENVIRONMENT DIVISION.

    [CONFIGURATION SECTION.
      SOURCE-COMPUTER. comment [WITH DEBUGGING MODE].
      OBJECT-COMPUTER. comment.]

    [INPUT-OUTPUT SECTION.
      FILE-CONTROL.
        SELECT .........
        SELECT .......
        ...............
        SELECT ......... ]
```

Both of the sections within the ENVIRONMENT DIVISION considered here are optional; it is permissible to have the ENVIRONMENT DIVISION header by itself with no other entries in this division.

The CONFIGURATION SECTION allows you to identify the computer on which the source code was compiled and on which the compiled program is to be executed; the two are often exactly the same. These entries are treated as comments by the compiler but when the WITH DEBUGGING MODE clause is included, lines with "D" in column 7 are compiled; otherwise, when this clause is omitted, lines with "D" in column 7 are ignored. This allows you to include code solely for the purpose of debugging the program and which can be treated as comments when the program has been fully tested and the final version is compiled.

The INPUT-OUTPUT SECTION is used to link the names of files used in the program with physical devices such as disk drives and printers, and to specify the type of each file defined. Each such entry in this section is included under a SELECT statement of which there may be several, as illustrated above. Every SELECTED file must be described in the FILE SECTION of the DATA DIVISION. (See "File descriptions" in the section on the DATA DIVISION). The next section deals with the different ways that files may be organised and accessed.

Types of files in COBOL

COBOL provides three types of file organisation:

       (i) SEQUENTIAL;

       (ii) RELATIVE;

       (iii) INDEXED.

Sequential files must be processed in a fixed order but relative and indexed files allow random file processing idependently of the physical order in which the records are stored in the file.

Sequential files are always provided by COBOL compilers but the latter two types, which both allow random file processing, may or may not be supported. Since Utah COBOL does not directly support indexed organisation (a companion program called "Btrieve" is required) but does support relative file organisation, which is a little simpler to use, it is this form of file organisation which is used where relevant here. However, for completeness, the principles governing the use of indexed files are also discussed in this section.

The later section on the PROCEDURE DIVISION contains details concerning the use and format of file-handling statements for each type of file discussed here.

Sequential files

The records of a sequential file must be processed in a fixed sequence which is determined by the order in which the records were initially created. So, to process a particular record of a sequential file, a program must start at the beginning of the file and read each record in turn into memory until the required record is located. Unlike a record within a random file, there is no means by which a certain record within a sequential file can be directly located and read into memory independently of the preceding records in the file.

File organisation and method of access is defined for each file used in the program in the FILE-CONTROL paragraph of the INPUT-OUTPUT SECTION. For sequential files, the following format is used:

```
          1         2         3         4         5         6         7
1234567890123456789012345678901234567890123456789012345678901234567890 12
A...B....................................................................

ENVIRONMENT DIVISION.
INPUT-OUTPUT SECTION.
FILE-CONTROL.
                                        {PRINTER}
    SELECT file-name-1 ASSIGN TO {DISK    }

                          {LINE SEQUENTIAL}
    [, ORGANIZATION IS {SEQUENTIAL      }]

    [, ACCESS MODE IS SEQUENTIAL].
```

Notice the spelling of ORGANIZATION: a common error, and one sometimes difficult to detect, is spelling it with an "S" instead of the "Z".

Examples of SELECT statements for sequential files, and how they relate to the general format of the SELECT statement, are provided below.

Examples:

```
1.    SELECT Customers ASSIGN TO DISK.
      SELECT file-name-1 ASSIGN TO DISK.
```

This is the simplest form of a SELECT clause. If, as illustrated here, the ORGANIZATION and ACCESS clauses are omitted, sequential organization and access are assumed. Thus the select statement

```
    SELECT CUSTOMERS ASSIGN TO DISK,
       ORGANIZATION IS SEQUENTIAL,
       ACCESS MODE IS SEQUENTIAL.
```

is exactly equivalent to example 1.

```
2. SELECT data-file ASSIGN TO DISK,
      ORGANIZATION IS LINE SEQUENTIAL.
```

The LINE SEQUENTIAL option is used for text files, that is, files of records which have been produced using a text editor and which are separated from one another by a line feed and carriage return character.

```
3. SELECT Report-1    ASSIGN TO PRINTER.
   SELECT file-name-1 ASSIGN TO PRINTER.
```

Relative files

When a *relative* file is created, the relative position of each record within the file must be specified before the record is written to the file. This is achieved by storing the required position in a *relative key* field associated with the file prior to storing the record. The relative key is a numeric item defined in the WORKING-STORAGE SECTION of the DATA DIVISION. Each record must have a unique integer value, or *key*, which is used to identify its position in the file. For example, in a stock file consisting of stock item records, each item of stock will have a code to identify it uniquely, and part of this stock code might specify a record's position within the file: the four numeric digits of the code GRA0105 could be used to specify that this item occupies position 105 in the file. Thus, if the relative key was called "Stock-number" the value 105 would be transferred to it prior to reading or writing the record. (See example 1 below for the format of the appropriate SELECT statement).

This is the general format for the SELECT statement of a relative file:

```
          1         2         3         4         5         6         7
1234567890123456789012345678901234567890123456789012345678901234567890123456789012
   A...B.........................................................................

      ENVIRONMENT DIVISION.
      INPUT-OUTPUT SECTION.
      FILE-CONTROL.
          SELECT file-name-1 ASSIGN TO DISK

          ORGANIZATION IS RELATIVE

                              {DYNAMIC   }
                              {SEQUENTIAL}
          ACCESS MODE IS      {RANDOM    }

          RELATIVE KEY IS data-name-1.
```

Examples of SELECT statements for relative files are provided below.

Examples:

```
1.    SELECT Stock-file ASSIGN TO DISK
          ORGANIZATION IS RELATIVE
          ACCESS MODE IS RANDOM
          RELATIVE KEY IS Stock-number.
```

Using the ACCESS MODE IS RANDOM clause allows you to read or write the file randomly and requires that in the PROCEDURE DIVISION you OPEN the file for I-O (Input-Output) and READ/WRITE/REWRITE/DELETE statements must use the INVALID KEY format. (See "File handling" in the section on the PROCEDURE DIVISION).

The field containing the relative position of a record to be read or written is "Stock-number" which must be defined in the WORKING-STORAGE SECTION as a numeric field of no more than seven digits.

```
2.    SELECT Customer-file ASSIGN TO DISK
          ORGANIZATION IS RELATIVE
          ACCESS MODE IS SEQUENTIAL.
```

Relative files may be accessed sequentially as well as randomly if the ACCESS MODE IS SEQUENTIAL clause is used. This is useful when all the records of a randomly organised file are to be processed, for printing out for instance. In this instance, the relative key is not used and the records are accessed as if the file was sequential.

In this instance, in the PROCEDURE DIVISION the file can be opened for INPUT, OUTPUT or I-O and READ/WRITE/REWRITE statements use the AT END format. (See "File handling" in the section on the PROCEDURE DIVISION).

```
3.    SELECT Customer-file ASSIGN TO DISK
      ORGANIZATION IS RELATIVE
      ACCESS IS DYNAMIC
      RELATIVE KEY IS Cust-acc-no.
```

The ACCESS IS DYNAMIC clause allows the file to be accessed randomly and/or sequentially in the same program. Thus, for a relative file OPENed for I-O in the PROCEDURE DIVISION, the sequential file access statements or random file access statements may both be used. (See "File handling" in the section on the PROCEDURE DIVISION).

Indexed files

Indexed files are associated with indexes which store the positions of records according to designated key fields. When a record within an indexed file is to be accessed, the index is first searched for the location of the required record and then the record is accessed. This allows the use of non-numeric keys.

The general format of the SELECT statement for an indexed file is shown below:

```
         1         2         3         4         5         6         7
1234567890123456789012345678901234567890123456789012345678901234567890123456789012
   A...B....................................................................

ENVIRONMENT DIVISION.
INPUT-OUTPUT SECTION.
FILE-CONTROL.
      SELECT file-name-1 ASSIGN TO DISK

         ORGANIZATION IS INDEXED

                              {DYNAMIC   }
                              {SEQUENTIAL}
         ACCESS MODE IS       {RANDOM    }

         RECORD KEY IS data-name-1.
```

This time, *data-name-1* must be an alphanumeric field within the record definition of *file-name-1*. It is the *prime record key* which must have a unique value for each record in the file. As with relative files, when a record is to be accessed, the key value must be moved to the record key field before a READ/WRITE/REWRITE/DELETE instruction is issued.

Indexed files, like relative files, may be processed either sequentially or randomly. (See previous section on relative files). Some versions of COBOL allow alternate record keys to be specified so that files may be processed more flexibly.

The examples for relative file SELECT statements are applicable to indexed files, the only difference being the use of the RECORD KEY IS ... instead of RELATIVE KEY IS ... clause.

The DATA DIVISION

The DATA DIVISION comprises a number of SECTIONS, including the FILE SECTION and the WORKING-STORAGE SECTION to be considered here. You must define the structure of all the files used by the program in the FILE SECTION, and all other identifiers referenced in the PROCEDURE DIVISION must be defined in the WORKING-STORAGE SECTION. This is a simplified explanation of the structure and function of the DATA DIVISION, but it is perfectly adequate for the purpose of presenting an easy introduction to COBOL.

The FILE section contains complete descriptions of all the files included under the

heading FILE-CONTROL in the INPUT-OUTPUT SECTION of the ENVIRON-
MENT DIVISION. Each file is described in terms of its record structure. COBOL
allows you to define this record structure very flexibly using a number of useful
language facilities, and the following example file description will be used to illustrate
a number of these facilities.

```
          1         2         3         4         5         6         7
1234567890123456789012345678901234567890123456789012345678901234567890123456789012
A...B.............................................................................
FD Employee-file
      LABEL RECORDS ARE STANDARD
      VALUE OF FILE-ID IS "B:Payroll.DAT"
      DATA RECORD IS Employee.
   01 Employee.
      03 Full-name.
         05 First-names        PIC A(20).
         05 Surname            PIC A(15).
      03 Sex                   PIC A.
         88 Male                        VALUE IS "M".
      03 Categories            PIC A.
         88 Valid-employee-type    VALUES ARE "C", "H", "S", "D".
      03 Hourly-rates.
         05 Normal-rate        PIC 9(3)V99.
         05 Overtime-rate      PIC 9(3)V99.
      03 Salary1 REDEFINES Hourly-rates.
         05 Salary             PIC 9(6)V99.
         05 FILLER             PIC 99.
      03 Tax OCCURS 12 TIMES   PIC 9(4)V99.
      03 Rest-of-info          PIC X(60).
```

Level Numbers

The possible level numbers are:

01 :	indicates that the item is a *record*;
02 through 49 :	indicates that this item is a *field*, that is, part of a record;
77 :	indicates that this item is independent of any other item, a *non-contiguous* item;
88 :	used to define a *condition name*.

Items which are followed by one or more items with higher level numbers (in the range
02 to 49) are called *group items* and allow a number of items to be grouped together
under one name. *Elementary items* are not further subdivided. Below, for instance, the
group item "Full-name" is subdivided into the two elementary items "Surname" and
"Initials":

```
   03 Full-name.
      05 Surname    PICTURE IS A(15).
      05 Initials   PICTURE IS A(4).
```

Elementary items are always followed by a PICTURE clause; group items are never
followed by a picture clause.

Item names

An identifier (field) name, such as "TITLE" or "END-OF-FILE" must be formed
according to the following rules:

    (i) it must not contain more than 30 characters;

    (ii) it must not contain any characters other than the letters(upper
and/or lower case) A-Z, the numeric characters 0-9 and the
hyphen("-");

(iii) it must not start or end with a hyphen.

(iv) it must not be a *reserved word*, that is, a word such as WRITE or MOVE or DISPLAY, which is part of the COBOL language. A list of COBOL reserved words are given in Appendix A of this chapter.

(v) The word FILLER may be used to define a field name which is not required to be referenced in the PROCEDURE DIVISION.

Examples of valid identifier names are

```
Cost-Price, EOF, RUNNING-TOTAL-1
```

Invalid identifiers are

```
RUNNING-TOT.   (because of the "."),
END-FLAG-      (ends with a "-"),
DATE           (reserved word)
```

Note that UTAH COBOL requires all identifiers to be in upper case.

PICTURE clause

The PICTURE IS clause (often abbreviated to PIC) is used in the DATA DIVISION to define the format of elementary items. Certain characters are used to indicate the type of field being defined, the three most important being:

```
9    numeric
A    alphabetic
X    alphanumeric
```

The length of a field, that is the maximum number of characters it contains, may be defined by the repeated occurrence of one of these symbols or by the use of a number enclosed in parentheses. For instance,

```
PIC XXXXXX  is the same as PIC X(6)
```

and means that the field being defined is composed of a combination of six alphabetic, numeric or special characters (such as ?, *, or &).

In addition, the symbol "V" is used to indicate the position of the decimal point in a numeric field and the symbol "S" means that the number is signed (that is, it can be positive or negative). Here are some examples of PICTURES containing these symbols:

A(20)	an alphabetic field containing a maximum of 20 letters or spaces
999V99	a number with three figures before the decimal point and two figures after
X(15)	an alphanumeric field of 15 characters
99	a two-digit integer number
S9(6)V99	a signed number with six figures to the left of the decimal point and two figures after

All of these types of field definitions may be used anywhere in the DATA DIVISION. Another set of characters are reserved for data items defined in the WORKING-STORAGE SECTION. They are used for items which are to be output and are called *editing characters* and are of two forms: *insertion characters* and *floating characters*.

Insertion characters, such as "." and "," are used to insert the relevant symbol into a numeric field which is to be printed. For instance, to show a decimal point in a field you might write

```
PICTURE IS     9999.99
```

Floating characters like +, − and $ are used to display the relevant sign and the same
time suppress the printing of zeroes. The two characters * and Z also suppress zeroes
but leave the overall size of the field the same. The examples in the table following
should clarify the effects of these editing characters. The examples assume that data is
being transferred from a sending field to a receiving field, the second containing editing
characters. The result is how the data would appear when printed.

Sending PICTURE	Sending Data	Receiving PICTURE	Result
9(5)	12345	ZZZ99	12345
9(5)	00123	ZZZ99	123
9(5)	04000	ZZZ99	4000
9(3)	123	$999	$123
9(3)	012	$999	$012
9(3)	123	$$99	$123
9(3)	012	$$99	$12
S99	-12	-99	-12
S99	-12	+99	-12
S99	12	+99	+12
S99	12	-99	12
S99	-12	99	12
9(5)	12345	***99	12345
9(5)	00123	***99	**123
9(5)	12345	$ZZ,ZZ9.99	$12,345.00
9(5)	00123	$ZZ,ZZ9.99	$ 123.00
9(5)	12345	$$$,$$9.99	$12,345.00
9(5)	00123	$$$,$$9.99	$123.00
9999V9	12345	$$$,$$9.99	$1,234.50
999V99	12345	$**,**9.99	$***123.45
99V999	12345	$**,**9.99	$****12.34

VALUE clauses

In the WORKING-STORAGE SECTION, the PICTURE clause may be followed by
an optional VALUE clause which allows a value to be assigned to a field at the time
the program is compiled. Fields cannot be given VALUES in the FILE SECTION.
Here are some typical examples of fields which have been assigned initial values:

```
         1         2         3         4         5         6         7
1234567890123456789012345678901234567890123456789012345678901234567890123456789012
    A...B..................................................................

    WORKING-STORAGE SECTION.

    01 Valid-codes              PIC X(26)    VALUE IS
          "ABCDEFGHIJKLMNOPQRSTUVWXYZ".

    77 Total                    PIC 9(5)V99  VALUE 0.

    77 Total                    PIC 9(5)V99  VALUE ZERO.

    77 Number-one               PIC 9        VALUE 1.

       03 Answer                PIC AAA      VALUE "YES".

       05 Empty-string          PIC X(20)    VALUE SPACES.

       03 FILLER                PIC A(10)    VALUE ALL "-".
```

VALUES such as 1, 2.6, −3 are called *numeric literals*, or *constants. Non-numeric
literals* are such VALUES as "YES" or "-". The words "ZERO" and "SPACES" are

called *figurative constants* and may also be used in the PROCEDURE DIVISION in conjunction with the MOVE statement. The reserved word "ALL" can be used in front of literals to construct figurative literals.

File descriptions

The file name is "Employee-file" and the three clauses in the file description (FD) state that it is a disk file, to be found on drive B under the name "Payroll.DAT", and the records within the file are called "Employee".

The clause, LABEL RECORDS ARE STANDARD, is always used for a file assigned to a disk drive. If a file is assigned to a printer rather than to a disk in the INPUT-OUTPUT SECTION, then the clause LABEL RECORD IS OMITTED is used instead.

The clause, VALUE OF FILE-ID, is always used to connect the logical file name used in the program with the actual file on the disk; there is no necessity for the two names to be the same.

Records

A record description in the file section is indicated by an 01 level entry after the file description (FD). When a read-file instruction is encountered in the PROCEDURE DIVISION, a single record is transferred into a section of memory which has been allocated to the file. The contents of this section of memory are referenced according to a record description. This means that record descriptions must be devised to make it easy to extract data from a record. The example given previously shows a record called "Employee" which has been defined using a variety of data structures.

Group items

The first 03 level, the group item "03 Full-name.", has two components. In the PROCEDURE DIVISION, you could use either the group item or the elementary items "First-names" and "Surname". For instance, the complete name could be moved using a statement such as

```
MOVE Full-name TO Name-field,
```
or the surname alone could be transferred using

```
MOVE Surname TO Surname-field.
```

Notice that a group item does not have a PICTURE clause; only elementary items which do not contain sub-fields are given PICTURES.

Group items are always regarded by the COBOL compiler as having an alphanumeric picture. The implication of this is that in the PROCEDURE DIVISION you cannot perform arithmetic operations on group items, though it is permissible to transfer group items. Thus, in the example record description provided earlier, it would generate an error if you tried to use the group item "Salary1" in a calculation even though its two components are entirely numeric. However, the elementary item "Salary" could be used in a calculation.

Condition names

A condition name is used to either simplify a conditional statement used in the PROCEDURE DIVISION, or to make such a statement more readable. In the example, it is used in two instances, both to simpify and to clarify the use of codes. The lines

```
03 Sex            PIC A.
   88 Male            VALUE IS "M".
```

are used to associate the code "M" with the identifier "Male", allowing a PROCE-DURE DIVISION statement such as

```
IF Male PERFORM M-para,
```

to be written in preference to

```
IF Sex = "M" PERFORM M-para.
```

The first conditional statement is easier to read than the second though they both perform exactly the same function: to PERFORM the paragraph labelled M-para if the employee is male.

The second example of the use of a condition name associates four possible values with the condition name "Employee-type". This considerably simplifies a code validation check. To check that the code in the field "Category" is only one of the four possible, namely C, H, S, or D, we could write

```
IF Category = "C" OR
   Category = "H" OR
   Category = "S" OR
   Category = "D"
   NEXT SENTENCE
ELSE    PERFORM Invalid-type-code.
```

This would perform the paragraph labelled Invalid-type-code if the field Category did not contain one of the permissible codes, otherwise it would skip to the next sentence.

Compare this with the same test using the condition name Employee-type:

```
IF Valid-employee-type   NEXT SENTENCE
ELSE  PERFORM Invalid-type-code.
```

The second form is much easier to understand and to maintain if more categories are to be included at some later date.

The REDEFINES clause

There are occasions when it is useful to store data with different formats in the same storage area. This is the case in the example record description where the same storage locations are used to store the rates of pay for hourly paid employees or, if the record is for a salaried employee, the monthly salary. The REDEFINES clause is used for this purpose:

```
          1         2         3         4         5         6         7
123456789012345678901234567890123456789012345678901234567890123456789012
   A...B....................................................................
       03 Hourly-rates.
          05 Normal-rate         PIC 9(3)V99.
          05 Overtime-rate       PIC 9(3)V99.
       03 Salary1 REDEFINES Hourly-rates.
          05 Salary              PIC 9(6)V99.
          05 FILLER              PIC 99.
```

The group item, "Hourly-rates", consists of two elementary items each comprising five numeric digits (the "V" in 9(3)V99 is an *implied decimal point* which does not occupy a character position in the number - see the section on picture clauses). Because the group item, "Salary1", REDEFINES "Hourly-rates", they both occupy the same storage area, but their component items are different; this allows the programmer to reduce very easily the amount of storage space required for data whilst still retaining the convenience of being able to use an appropriate data structure.

The REDEFINES clause is often used in conjunction with the OCCURS clause described in the next section.

Defining arrays using the OCCURS clause

The OCCURS clause is used to define arrays of one or more dimensions. In the example record description, it is used to reserve space for twelve numeric fields, each containing six numeric digits:

```
          1         2         3         4         5         6         7
1234567890123456789012345678901234567890123456789012345678901234567890 12
    A...B...............................................................
          03 Tax OCCURS 12 TIMES    PIC 9(4)V99.
```

The twelve elements of the array thus defined are referenced in the PROCEDURE DIVISION with the aid of a subscript. For example, the first element is Tax (1), the second is Tax (2), and so on to Tax (12). As to be expected, a suitably defined variable can be used as the subscript, as in Tax (K), where K would be defined as a two-digit integer in the WORKING-STORAGE SECTION:

```
          77 K                     PIC 99.
```

Here is another example of the OCCURS clause, this time used in conjunction with the REDEFINES clause:

```
          01 Days-of-week       PIC A(21) VALUE
                "MonTueWedThuFriSatSun".
          01 Day-table REDEFINES Days-of-week.
             03 Week-day OCCURS 7 TIMES PIC A(3).
```

Now, because the elements of the array "Day-table" occupy the same storage area as "Days-of-week", Week-day (1) contains "Mon", Week-day (2) contains "Tue", and so on.

Though the examples of the OCCURS clause provided so far have involved the repeated occurrence of elementary items, this is not a restriction of the language, as illustrated by the next example:

```
          01 Item-details OCCURS 100 TIMES.
             03 Item-code     PIC 9(6).
             03 In-stock      PIC 9(5).
             03 Unit-cost     PIC 9(5)V99.
```

In this instance, "Item-details" is a group item occurring 100 times. It can be subscripted in the usual manner, in which case it can only be treated as an alphanumeric field, or its components can be subscripted and treated as elementary items. Thus it is allowable in the PROCEDURE DIVISION to use the following notations:

```
          Item-details (I); Item-code (I); In-stock (I); Unit-cost (I)
```

where the elementary item, "I", has been defined as an integer in the WORKING-STORAGE SECTION.

Note that, when using subscripts in COBOL, the left parenthesis, "(", is always preceded by a space.

The PROCEDURE DIVISION

The PROCEDURE DIVISION is used to specify the processing that is to be performed by the program. The processing instructions are written in a form closely resembling ordinary English, in a deliberate attempt to make a COBOL program easy to understand by non-specialists. A typical procedure division is composed of a number of *sentences*, the basic unit of the procedure division. Each sentence, containing one or more *statements* specifying a processing operation, is terminated with a full-stop. Sentences may be combined to form *paragraphs* which in turn can be grouped into *sections*. Paragraphs and sections, being headers, must be given names. The following sections describe some of the most commonly used COBOL statements.

Data transfer (MOVE)

One of the most common tasks performed in the PROCEDURE DIVISION is the transfer of data from one memory location to another. In such a process the source of the transfer is often called the sending field or sender, and the destination is called the receiving field or receiver. A MOVE statement is used to perform this type of operation. Its format is shown below:

```
           { literal-1  }
    MOVE {identifier-1}   TO   identifier-2 [identifier-3] .....
```

A MOVE statement is frequently used to transfer data from one field to another in preparation for producing output on a printer. The receiving field will often contain editing characters to improve the quality of the printout. Whatever the reason for the transfer, there are a number of rules which govern it:

(i)   The data is copied from the sending field to the receiving field(s), so that the data is still intact in the sending field.

(ii)   When the receiving field is alphanumeric or alphabetic, it is filled from left to   right. If the sending field width is smaller than that of the receiving field, vacant   character positions in the receiving field are filled with spaces:

```
[ABCDEF]  ──────→  [ABCDEF    ]
 X(6)               X(9)
```

If the sending field is wider than the receiving field, the receiving field is filled from left to right, truncation of the data occurring at the right-hand side:

```
[ABCDEFGHI]  ──────→  [ABCDE]
 X(9)                  X(5)
```

(iii)   With numeric moves the positions of the decimal points (implied or otherwise) in the sending and receiving fields determine the effect of the move on the receiving field:

```
[123.45]   ──────→  [0123.450]
 999.99              9999.999
[123V45]   ──────→  [0123V4500]
 999V99              9999V9999
[1234.56]  ──────→  [34.5]
 9999.99             99.9
[1234]     ──────→  [34.0]
 9(4)                99.9
```

In each case the decimal points are aligned first, and then the transfer of the digits from the sending field to the receiving field is effected. Any vacant positions are filled with zeroes.

(iv)   All group moves are treated as alphanumeric.

(v)   Figurative constants are allowed in MOVE statements:

```
MOVE SPACES TO Blank-line.
MOVE ALL "-" TO Underline.
MOVE ZEROS TO Total, Tax.
```

Screen Handling (DISPLAY, ACCEPT)

The DISPLAY statement allows information to be displayed on the VDU of the computer system. Two formats are commonly used:

```
                        {literal-1   }   {literal-2    }
(1)   DISPLAY {identifier-1} [{identifier-2}] ...

                                        {literal-1   }   {literal-2   }
(2)   DISPLAY (line, column)  {identifier-1} [{identifier-2}] ...
```

Format (1) will cause the specified literals and/or contents of identifiers to be displayed at the current cursor position. Examples of DISPLAY statements and their general formats are shown below:

```
DISPLAY "The account number is: "   Cust-ac-no.
DISPLAY  {literal-1}                 {identifier-2}

DISPLAY Stock-num,      Current-level,   Min-level.
DISPLAY {identifier-1} {identifier-2}   {identifier-3}
```

Format (2) is similar to the other format except that the cursor position at which the data is to be displayed may be specified in terms of line and column. The line and column may be numeric literals or numeric data items:

```
DISPLAY (5, 10) "Reading file ....."
DISPLAY (I, J) Item(I, J)
```

Often used in conjunction with DISPLAY, the ACCEPT statement allows data to be entered at the system keyboard during program execution and stored in a data item. Three formats are commonly employed:

```
(1)   ACCEPT identifier.
(2)   ACCEPT (line, column) identifier.
(3)   ACCEPT identifier FROM DATE
```

The first two formats are equivalent to the DISPLAY statement formats; the cursor position can be specified, or not, prior to capturing data from the keyboard and transferring it to the designated identifier. Examples:

```
ACCEPT Yes-No-Answer.
ACCEPT (20, 8) Number-of-Sales.
```

The third format allows the program to access data, in the form of the current date, already available in the system. The date is usually provided in the form YYMMDD, that is, the year of the century, the month of the year, and the day of the month. For example, 15th January 1990 would be represented as 900115. This six-digit, unsigned, numeric elementary item would be transferred to the named identifier. Example:

```
ACCEPT Todays-date FROM DATE.
```

Arithmetic operations (ADD, SUBTRACT, MULTIPLY, DIVIDE)

Most business calculations can be performed using the arithmetic operations of addition, subtraction, multiplication and division. In COBOL these four operations are available in the form of the ADD, SUBTRACT, MULTIPLY and DIVIDE statements. The formats of these statements are all very similar:

```
              {literal-1   }    {literal-2   }
(a)   ADD {identifier-1} [TO] {identifier-2} [GIVING identifier-3]
```

Examples:

```
ADD 3 TO Line-Counter
ADD Tax TO Cost GIVING Total-price
```

```
                {literal-1   }     {literal-2    }
(b)   SUBTRACT {identifier-1} FROM {identifier-2} [GIVING identifier-3
```

Examples:

```
SUBTRACT 1 FROM Counter-down
SUBTRACT DisCounter FROM Price GIVING Selling-price
```

(c) <u>MULTIPLY</u> {literal-1   } <u>BY</u> {literal-2   } [<u>GIVING</u> identifier-3]
              {identifier-1}   {identifier-2}

Examples:

```
MULTIPLY 1.5 BY OT-hours
MULTIPLY Hours BY Rate GIVING Pay
```

(d) <u>DIVIDE</u> {literal-1   } {<u>BY</u>}   {literal-2   } [<u>GIVING</u> identifier-3
              {identifier-1} {<u>INTO</u>} {identifier-2}

Examples:

```
DIVIDE 11 INTO Stock-num
DIVIDE Stock-num BY 11 GIVING Int-result
```

The following remarks apply to all four arithmetic statements defined above:

1. Identifier-1 and identifier-2 must be elementary numeric items.

2. If the optional GIVING clause is used, the result of the calculation is stored in identifier-3, otherwise the result of the calculation replaces identifier-2. For example, the statement

```
ADD 1 TO Counter
```

is equivalent to

```
Counter = Counter + 1
```

that is, the value stored in Counter is increased by 1. However, the statement

```
ADD 1 TO Counter GIVING New-counter
```

would leave Counter unchanged and give New-counter the value Counter + 1.

3. Identifier-3 may be a numeric item containing editing characters such as *, +, Z etc.

Control Structures (GO TO, IF, PERFORM)

These statements allow you to alter the order in which the program instructions are performed.

The **GO TO** statement is an unconditional branch instruction causing program control to transfer to a specified position in the program (normally a paragraph header). For example,

```
GO TO Process-error
```

would cause the computer immediately to commence processing the statements following the paragraph header "Process-error".

The use of the GO TO statement is discouraged in structured programming because of its tendency to produce programs which are difficult to understand and maintain. Its use can almost invariably be avoided, as is illustrated by the complete lack of GO TO statements in the example programs presented in this chapter.

The **IF** statement allows a selection to be made between alternative courses of action.

It has the following format:

```
     {condition      } {statement-1  }           {statement-2   }
  IF {condition-name} {NEXT SENTENCE} [ELSE {NEXT SENTENCE}]
```

The condition can take the two forms shown below:

```
                                    {EQUAL TO     }
                                    {LESS THAN    }  {literal      }
  (i)  identifier-1 IS [NOT]  {GREATER THAN}  {identifier-2}
```

The symbols =, < and > may be used in place of EQUAL, LESS THAN and GREATER THAN respectively.

```
                              {NUMERIC   }
  (ii) identifier-3 IS [NOT]  {ALPHABETIC}
```

The different forms of the IF statement are best explained with examples.

Examples:

```
1. IF   Pay-rate IS LESS THAN 3.50    PERFORM Err-rtn.
   IF   {condition}                    {statement-1}
```

If the condition is true, statement-1 is executed, otherwise statement-1 is ignored and control passes to the next sentence.

```
2. IF   Line-count = 60 MOVE 0 TO Line-count ELSE ADD 1 TO Line-count.
   IF   {condition}       {statement-1}       ELSE {statement-2}
```

If the condition is true, statement-1 is executed, otherwise statement-2 is executed before control passes to the next sentence.

```
3. IF   Ok-to-store        PERFORM Write-record.
   IF   {condition-name}   {statement-1}
```

If the condition name is true, statement-1 is executed, otherwise control passes to the next sentence.

```
4. IF   Surname IS ALPHABETIC   NEXT SENTENCE   ELSE    PERFORM Err-rtn.
   IF   {condition}             NEXT SENTENCE   ELSE    {statement-2}
```

If the condition is true, that is, the class test "Surname IS ALPHABETIC" is true, control passes to the next sentence following the IF statement, otherwise statement-2 is executed before control passes to the next sentence.

The ALPHABETIC and NUMERIC class tests are often used in validation checks to ensure that fields are of the correct format. For example, if the elementary item Number-sold has been defined as X(6), then a statement such as

```
  ACCEPT Number-sold
```

will allow the user to enter any sequence of alphanumeric characters, not just numeric characters. Before the contents of this item could be processed numerically, it would be necessary to confirm that only numeric characters had been entered, otherwise a runtime error might occur; a statement such as

```
  IF Number-sold IS NOT NUMERIC PERFORM Error-rtn
```

could be used to prevent this from happening.

```
5. IF   Valid-response    NEXT SENTENCE
        ELSE DISPLAY (20, 10) "Invalid input"
             DISPLAY (21, 10) "Acceptable inputs are Y or   ".
   IF   {condition-name} NEXT SENTENCE
        ELSE {statement-2}
```

If the condition name is true, control passes to the next sentence, otherwise the two DISPLAY statements constituting statement-2 are executed. A multiple statement such as that above, containing a number of instructions, may be used for statement-1 or statement-2.

```
6. IF    (CAT1 EQUAL TO SUB-CODE)
      OR (CAT2 EQUAL TO SUB-CODE)
      OR (CAT3 EQUAL TO SUB-CODE)        PERFORM PRINT-DETAILS.
    IF {condition}                       {statement-1}
```

A condition may be a compound condition connected by the AND and OR logical operators.

```
7. IF   Rec-type = 1   PERFORM Add-record
      ELSE IF Rec-type = 2 PERFORM Delete-record
      ELSE PERFORM Invalid-code-rtn.
    IF   {condition}     {statement-1}
      ELSE {statement-2}
```

Here, statement-2 is itself an IF statement. This nesting of IF statements is a useful way of dealing with a field which has a number of known values, each of which requires processing in a different manner.

The function of the PERFORM statement is to allow one or more sentences within a program to be executed out of sequence by transferring control to a part of the program labelled with a paragraph name. For instance, the statement

```
PERFORM  Check-digit-calc
```

would cause the computer to branch to the paragraph called "Check-digit-calc" and execute all the statements within this paragraph before returning to the statement immediately following the PERFORM. PERFORM has three commonly used formats:

```
(1)  PERFORM  paragraph-1
```

This is the simplest form of the PERFORM statement as described above. It is also pssible to specify a range of paragraphs to be PERFORMed by using the word THROUGH or THRU:

```
PERFORM paragraph-1 THROUGH paragraph-2
```

Here *paragraph-1* is the start of the range of paragraphs and *paragraph-2* is the last paragraph in the range to be performed.

Example:

```
PERFORM Validation-check-1 THRU Validation-check-5
```

The same option of specifying a range of paragraphs is possible in the next two formats also.

```
                              {integer-1  }
(2)  PERFORM  paragraph-1 {identifier-1} TIMES
```

The paragraph, or range of paragraphs, named are executed the number of times specified. If *identifier-1* initially has a negative or zero value, the control will pass immediately to the next statement after the PERFORM.

Examples:

```
1.    PERFORM Process-table 10         TIMES.
      PERFORM paragraph-1    integer-1 TIMES

2.    PERFORM Print-rtn     I                TIMES.
      PERFORM paragraph-1 identifier-1 TIMES

3.    PERFORM P1            THRU P3          J         TIMES.
      PERFORM paragraph-1 THRU paragraph-2 identifer-1 TIMES
```

```
                              {condition-name-1}
(3)  PERFORM  paragraph-1  UNTIL  {condition-1      }
```

Here the named paragraph or range of paragraphs will be executed until the specified condition is true. The condition may also be a compound condition using AND and

OR operators. If the condition is initially true, control will pass immediately to the next statement after the PERFORM.

Examples:

```
1.   PERFORM  Process-file UNTIL  End-of-file.
     PERFORM  paragraph-1  UNTIL  condition-name-1

2.   PERFORM  P6           THRU P8           UNTIL  Flag = 1.
     PERFORM  paragraph-1 THRU paragraph-2 UNTIL  condition-1

3.   PERFORM  Proc-list UNTIL No-swaps OR Counter   List-length
     PERFORM  paragraph-1 UNTIL condition-1
```

In this example, *condition-1* is a compound condition consisting of a condition name, *No-swaps*, connected by the OR operator to the condition *Counter > List-length*.

File handling (OPEN, CLOSE, READ, WRITE, DELETE, REWRITE)

Sequential files

Statements that are appropriate to the processing of sequential files are:

```
OPEN
READ
WRITE
REWRITE
CLOSE
```

(i)   OPEN - initialises file input and output operations. The OPEN statement must precede any file processing statements. Sequential files may be OPENed according to the following format:

```
          {EXTEND}
          {I-O   }
          {INPUT }
     OPEN {OUTPUT} file-name-1 [,filename-2] ...
```

Examples:

1.   `OPEN OUTPUT Son-payroll-file.`

OPENing a file for output prepares the computer system for transferring records to a backing storage medium (a disk, for example) or a printer from the memory of the computer. If the file has been assigned to a disk drive, a new file will be created or, if it already exists, it will be overwritten. This statement would precede the issuing of a WRITE instruction.

2.   `OPEN INPUT Father-payroll-file.`

This prepares the computer for transferring records from a backing storage device to the area of memory reserved for the file. This statement would precede the issuing of a READ instruction.

3.   `OPEN I-O Updated-customer-file.`

This allows records to be read and then rewritten (usually after being modified) to the file. This allows a sequential file to be updated without the necessity of creating a new file. This statement would normally precede the issuing of READ and REWRITE instructions.

4.   `OPEN EXTEND Transaction-file.`

This prepares the computer for outputting records to the end of a file, that is, extending the number of records in the file without destroying existing records. This statement would precede the issuing of a WRITE instruction.

(ii)   WRITE - transfers a record from memory to an output device. The general format of the WRITE statement contains clauses relevant to vertical positioning for files assigned to a printer:

```
WRITE record-name [FROM identifier-1]

        {BEFORE}              {identifier-2}
      [ {AFTER } ADVANCING    {integer     } LINES ]
                             {PAGE         }
```

Examples:

1.   WRITE Customer-rec.

This transfers the data currently contained in the specified record area to the output device (eg disk file, printer) assigned to the relevant file.

2.   WRITE Validated-rec FROM WS-rec.

The FROM clause is the equivalent of executing a MOVE statement prior to writing the record. Thus the statement above is equivalent to the two statements:

```
MOVE WS-rec TO Validated-rec.
WRITE Validated-rec.
```

3.   WRITE Detail-line AFTER ADVANCING 2 LINES.

This is appropriate to printer output, causing two carriage returns and line-feeds to be sent to the printer prior to printing the contents of the specified record ("Detail-line" in this instance). The BEFORE option causes the control characters to be sent to the printer after the record has been printed.

4.   WRITE Page-heading AFTER ADVANCING PAGE.

This causes a form feed control character to be sent to the printer before printing the contents of the specified record.

(iii)   READ - transfers the next available record from the assigned backing storage device to the area of memory allocated to the relevant file. The general format is shown below:

```
READ file-name RECORD [ INTO identifier-1 ]
     AT END imperative-statement.
```

Examples:

1.   READ Club-members RECORD AT END MOVE 1 TO End-flag.
      READ file-name   RECORD AT END imperative-statement.

This causes the next available record of the specified file to be transferred to the area of memory allocated to the file. Only if the end of the file is encountered when attempting to read another record is the statement following AT END executed. This imperative-statement may comprise a number of statements terminated by a full stop.

2.   READ Trans-file INTO Temp-rec AT END PERFORM Finish-off.

The INTO option causes the record read to be copied into the specified identifier. The statement above is equivalent to the two statements:

```
READ Trans-file AT END PERFORM Finish-off.
MOVE Trans-rec TO Temp-rec.
```

This assumes that "Trans-rec" is the record description of "Trans-file".

(iv)   REWRITE - replaces the last record read from the file with the current contents of the record area assigned to the file. It assumes that the file has been OPENed for I-O. The format of the statement is:

```
REWRITE record-name [ FROM identifier-1 ].
```

The FROM option has the same effect as that in the WRITE statement described above.

Examples:

1.   `REWRITE Employee-rec.`

This overwrites the last record read from the file by the current contents of the area of memory allocated to the file, that is, the current contents of the record held in memory.

2.   `REWRITE Stock-rec FROM Temp-area.`

This issues a MOVE statement to transfer the contents of <u>Temp-area</u> to <u>Stock-rec</u> prior to writing *Stock-rec* to the file.

(v)   CLOSE - this is used to terminate the processing of input and output files. The format of the CLOSE statement is shown below:

```
CLOSE file-name-1 [, file-name-2 ] ....
```

A file must be OPEN before it can be CLOSEd.

In order to start reading an OPENed sequential file from the beginning, first CLOSE the file and the reOPEN the file for INPUT.

Examples:

1.   `CLOSE Members-file.`
2.   `CLOSE Trans-file, Master-file.`

Relative files

Relative files allow either random access or sequential access, depending on the form of the SELECT statement used in the INPUT-OUTPUT SECTION of the ENVIRONMENT DIVISION (see "Relative files" in the earlier section on the ENVIRONMENT DIVISION). When a relative file is to be accessed as if it were a sequential file, then the input-ouput statements are the same as those appropriate to sequential files as described in the preceding section; these will not, therefore, be described again.

Statements that are appropriate to the processing of relative files are:

```
OPEN
READ
WRITE
REWRITE
DELETE
CLOSE
```

(i)   OPEN - as for sequential files.

(ii)   WRITE - transfers a record from memory to an output device.

There are two general formats for relative files, the appropriate format depending on the access mode required.

The first format is used for relative files which are to be accessed as sequential files. Format (2) is appropriate to relative files accessed randomly.

```
(1)   WRITE record-name [FROM identifier-1]

              {BEFORE}                  {identifier-2}
            [ {AFTER } ADVANCING        {integer     } LINES ]
                                        {PAGE        }
```

Examples: as for sequential files.

```
(2)   WRITE record-name [FROM identifier-1]
            [INVALID KEY imperative-statement].
```

When this format is used, the requested record number must be transferred to the RELATIVE KEY identifier associated with the file prior to issuing the WRITE statement. This identifier must be defined in WORKING-STORAGE as a numeric field. The INVALID KEY clause is invoked if the record to be written already exists in the file, in which case the imperative statement is executed. The REWRITE statement (see later) is used if a record is to be overwritten.

In addition, the file must have been OPENed for I-O (input-output) prior to executing the WRITE statement.

Note that it is necessary to have a full stop after the imperative-statement, otherwise the statement(s) following the WRITE will only be executed when an INVALID KEY condition arises. This is a frequent cause of run-time errors in COBOL programs.

Examples:

```
1.    MOVE rec-pos TO rel-key-1.
      WRITE customer-record
            INVALID KEY DISPLAY "This customer already exists".
```

Here, *rel-key-1* is the field which has been identified as that containing the RELATIVE KEY for the file. The record *customer-record* will be released to the output device if the record position identified by *rel-key-1* is unoccupied, otherwise the message "This customer already exists" will be displayed on the screen. The DISPLAY statement is the imperative-statement in this instance.

```
2.    WRITE summary-rec FROM ws-summary
            INVALID KEY MOVE 4 TO ERROR-NUM, PERFORM ERROR-ROUTINE.
```

The FROM clause causes the contents of *ws-summary* to be transferred to *summary-rec* prior to attempting to write this record. This time, if the INVALID KEY claused is invoked, the MOVE statement is executed followed by the PERFORM statement.

(iii)   REWRITE - this is identical to WRITE except that the specified record position must *exist* in the file, irrespective of whether or not it is empty. Thus REWRITE is usually used when an existing record is to be updated or modified in some way.

The general format for REWRITE is:

```
REWRITE record-name [FROM identifier-1]
        [INVALID KEY imperative-statement].
```

When a relative file is being accessed sequentially, the INVALID KEY clause is not used. (See the description of REWRITE for sequential files)

As with the WRITE statement, in order to use this statement, the file must previously have been OPENed for I-O.

Example:

```
      MOVE stock-num TO rel-key-2.
      REWRITE stock-rec
            INVALID KEY DISPLAY "No such stock item on file".
```

The stock file has a RELATIVE KEY called *rel-key-2* to which has been MOVEd the stock item's position in the file. IF the REWRITE fails because this position is outside the limits of the file, the message "No such stock item on file" is DISPLAYed.

(iv)   READ - This transfers a record from the file medium to the file record area in memory, making it available for processing. The two possible formats allow a relative file to be read either sequentiqlly or randomly.

```
(1)       READ file-name RECORD [ INTO identifier-1 ]
            AT END imperative-statement.
```

This format is used when the file is to be read sequentially and has been OPENed for INPUT or I-O.

Examples: see sequential files.

```
(2)          READ record-name [INTO identifier-1]
                  [INVALID KEY imperative-statement].
```

This format is used only when the file has been OPENed for I-O, that is, for random access. The position of the required record must previously have been transferred to the RELATIVE KEY assigned to the file. The INVALID KEY clause is invoked if the record position specified is outside the bounds of the file, that is, the record specified does not exist in the file.

Example:

```
MOVE id-num TO rel-key-3.
READ Master-file
     INVALID KEY DISPLAY "Record number ", rel-key-3,
                " does not exist",
          MOVE 3 TO err-flag.
```

The record in position *id-num* is to be read from the backing storage device assigned to file *Master-file*. If this record does not exist, the INVALID KEY clause is invoked causing the two statements in this clause to be executed. The field *rel-key-3* is the RELATIVE KEY field for the file as defined in the SELECT statement for the file.

(v)   DELETE - this is used to remove a record from a random disk file.

The format is:

```
DELETE file-name RECORD
          INVALID KEY imperative-statement.
```

The file must have previously been OPENed in the I-O mode, and must not be a sequential file. In addition, the DELETE statement must have been preceded by a successful READ statement for it to be successful. The INVALID KEY clause must be used.

Example:

```
MOVE member-code TO rel-key-5.
READ Members-file INVALID KEY DISPLAY "No such member".
DELETE Members-file RECORD
     INVALID KEY DISPLAY "No such member - can't delete".
```

(vi)   CLOSE - as for sequential files.

Indexed files

Indexed files are very similar to relative files in that they also allow both sequential and random access. The main difference between the two types of file is that an indexed file has a separate index file associated with it. This index allows you to assign non-numeric keys to files and, as explained in "Indexed files" in the section on the ENVIRONMENT DIVISION, the RECORD KEY must form part of the record description for the file. Because of the close similarities between relative files and indexed files, the statements appropriate to them are also almost identical. The main difference between relative and indexed file processing for random access is that before accessing a record:

(i) for relative files the record position must be contained in the RELATIVE KEY field defined in the

WORKING-STORAGE SECTION and,

(ii) for indexed files the record identifier (key) must be contained in the RECORD KEY defined in the record description of the file.

Thus, all of the statements described for relative files are identical for indexed files, except for a small addition required for the READ statement, and this is explained below.

Statements that are appropriate to the processing of indexed files are:

```
OPEN
READ
WRITE
REWRITE
DELETE
CLOSE
```

(i)   OPEN - as for sequential/relative files.

(ii)   WRITE - as for relative files.

(iii)   REWRITE - as for relative files.

(iv)   READ - This transfers a record from the file medium to the file record area in memory, making it available for processing. The two possible formats allow an indexed file to be read either sequentially or randomly.

(1)   <u>READ</u> file-name NEXT RECORD [INTO identifier-1]
                <u>AT END</u> imperative-statement.

This format, with the inclusion of the word NEXT, is used when the file is to be read sequentially in the DYNAMIC access mode and has been OPENed for I-O.

Example:

```
READ Customer-file NEXT RECORD AT END MOVE "Y" TO E-O-F.
```

This reads the next available record of the indexed file "Customer-file" as if it were a sequential file.

(2).   <u>READ</u> record-name [<u>INTO</u> identifier-1]
                [<u>INVALID</u> KEY imperative-statement].

This format is the same as that for relative files.

(v)   DELETE - as for relative files.

(vi)   CLOSE - as for sequential/relative files.

Summary of permissible statements

The table below summarises permissible file-handling statements for each type of file, its organisation, access mode and open mode. The abbreviations used in the table have the following meanings:

```
I     Input
O     Output
I-O   Input-Output
E     Extend
X     Operation is possible
```

So, for example, the table shows that for a sequential file opened for I-O, the READ and REWRITE statements are permitted, but the WRITE and DELETE statements are not.

Organisation

		SEQUENTIAL				RELATIVE				INDEXED			
Access mode	OPEN mode-	I	O	I-O	E	I	O	I-O	E	I	O	I-O	E
SEQUENTIAL	READ	X		X		X		X		X		X	
	WRITE		X		X		X		X		X		X
	REWRITE			X				X				X	
	DELETE							X				X	
RANDOM	READ					X		X		X		X	
	WRITE						X	X			X	X	
	REWRITE							X				X	
	DELETE							X				X	
INDEXED	READ					X		X		X		X	
	WRITE						X	X			X	X	
	REWRITE							X				X	
	DELETE							X				X	

Stages in the development of a COBOL program

In general terms, the stages involved in producing an executable COBOL program are as follows:

1. Write the source code using a program/text editor. The documentation that accompanies a COBOL compiler will specify the type of text file that the compiler requires as input. Some compilers, of which UTAH COBOL is an example, will supply a program editor as part of the COBOL system; others will recommend suitable editors.

2. Compile the program. The compiler will check the source code and issue an error report if it detects any syntactic or semantic errors. An example of a typical error report is shown below.

```
Line#   Col# Err#  Lvl  Messages
=================================================================

000310  19   0003   F   Syntax error or period missing from prior line.
000420  26   0004   F   File not selected in the INPUT-OUTPUT SECTION.
000590  1    0057   W   Warning Line numbers out of sequence.
000600  43   0005   F   OCCURS limited to one level.
000740  34   0006   F   Subscripted items cannot be REDEFINED.
000750  27   0051   W   Warning more than 30 characters in a word.
000810  54   0007   F   PICTURE items must be elementary.
000820  36   0017   F   VALUE OF FILE-ID missing.
000840  20   0018   F   Subscript literal contains illegal character.
000950  22   0020   F   OCCURS clause is illegal at 01 level.
000980  60   0021   F   VALUE is illegal with OCCURS.
000990  28   0050   W   Warning LITERAL truncated right end.
001030                  Last line read by the compiler .
                 F = > 'FATAL'. OBJ file won't run.
                    Try again!
           Correct errors and recompile.
```

Each line of the report supplies a number of pieces of information relating to an error that has been detected. The first piece of information is the number of the line containing the error; next is the position within the line (col#) at which the error was detected; then there is a code number assigned to the error; following this is the type, or level, of error - F (fatal) means that the compiler has been unable to produce the object code and the program must be corrected and recompiled, and W (warning) indicates that the error is not as serious, has not prevented object code generation and the program may still function correctly when run; finally there is a short explanation of the cause of the error.

3. Identify and correct compilation errors. The source code must be corrected and the program recompiled. Steps 2 and 3 may have to be repeated a number of times until the program compiles successfully.

4. Link the program. This is the process of linking subroutines required by the program into the object code. These subroutines form part of a library of procedures which are referenced by the compiler at compile time. Some compilers may not require this stage to be performed as a stage separate from compilation.

5. Run the program. This stage may produce run-time errors, that is errors which only become apparent when the program is first executed or at some later date during the testing phase. Detection of the cause of a run-time error might again necessitate correction of the source code and recompilation of the program.

Example Programs

Outline descriptions of example programs

The example programs in this section are based on a small business employing a number of sales representatives who periodically present details of their sales. The programs are not intended to represent an authentic sales recording system; rather, each program illustrates one or more important programming techniques or principles as succinctly as possible.

Program documentation is kept brief to encourage study of the commented source code, though the structure of each program is fully described with a JSP chart. It is recommended that you type in and compile each program, and attempt the exercises suggested at the end of the chapter.

The purpose of each program is as follows:

The first program uses the sales details to produce a sequential sales file. This program illustrates screen handling and the creation of sequential files.

The second program sorts this sales file into ascending order of salesman number, producing a sorted sales file which is also sequentially organised. This program illustrates sequential file processing, the use of an array and a simple sorting technique.

The third program produces a tabulated report of the sales file on a printer or a disk file. This program illustrates the process of producing a printed report.

The fourth program is used to create disk space for the random file used in the final program.

The fifth and final program uses the sorted sales file to update a summary file keeping a month by month record of total sales for each salesman in the current financial year. This program illustrates random file handling.

Example program #1 - Creating a sequential file

Program specification

This program is used to record each sale made by the sales representatives as a separate record in a sequential file.

The user is required to enter the sales data by responding to prompts on the screen. Each prompt for data is accompanied by a short help message displayed at the bottom of the screen.

After entering a complete sales record, the user has the opportunity of saving the record to the file or not if it has been transcribed incorrectly. In either case the user then has the opportunity of enetering another record or terminating the program.

The screen mask displays the current date as obtained from the system, and a count of the number of sales records saved to the sales file.

Program structure diagram

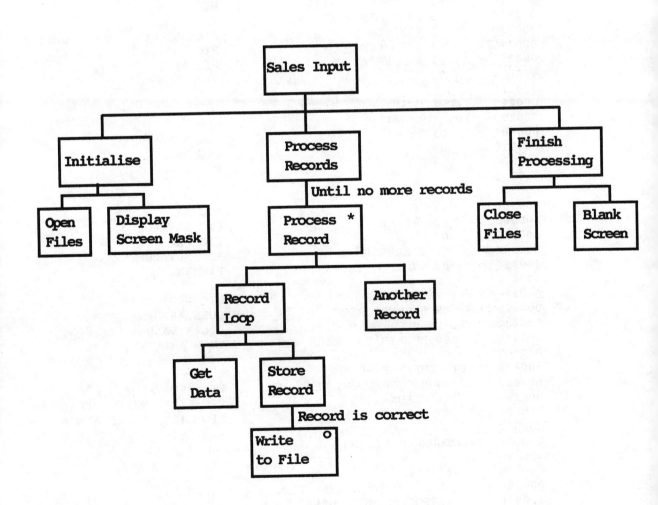

Source code

```
000010 IDENTIFICATION DIVISION.
000020    PROGRAM-ID.            SALES-INPUT.
000030    AUTHOR.               NICK WAITES AND DAVID TURNBULL.
000040    DATE-WRITTEN.         OCTOBER 1988.
000050*   REMARKS.              A program written in COBOL
000060*                         to create sales records.
000070
000080 ENVIRONMENT DIVISION.
000090    CONFIGURATION SECTION.
000100    INPUT-OUTPUT SECTION.
000110    FILE-CONTROL.
000120        SELECT SALES-FILE ASSIGN TO DISK,
000130        ORGANIZATION IS LINE SEQUENTIAL.
000140
000150 DATA DIVISION.
000160    FILE SECTION.
000170    FD SALES-FILE
000180          LABEL RECORDS ARE STANDARD
000190          VALUE OF FILE-ID "B:SALES.DAT".
000200    01 SALES-REC.
000210       03 SALESMAN-NUMBER             PIC 9999.
000220       03 SALESMAN-NAME               PIC A(25).
000230       03 TAX-MONTH                   PIC 99.
000240       03 ITEM-CODE                   PIC 9(5).
000250       03 NUMBER-SOLD                 PIC 9(5).
000260       03 SALES-VALUE                 PIC 999V99.
000270
000280    WORKING-STORAGE SECTION.
000290    01 RUN-DATE.
000300       03 YY                          PIC 99.
000310       03 MM                          PIC 99.
000320       03 DD                          PIC 99.
000330
000340    01 TDATE.
000350       03 TD                          PIC XX.
000360       03 FILLER                      PIC X VALUE "/".
000370       03 TM                          PIC XX.
000380       03 FILLER                      PIC X VALUE "/".
000390       03 TY                          PIC XX.
000410
000420    01 INPUT-COND                     PIC A VALUE "Y".
000430       88 NO-MORE-RECS         VALUES ARE "N", "n".
000440    01 CORRECT-COND                   PIC A VALUE "N".
000450       88 REC-IS-CORRECT       VALUES ARE "Y", "y".
000460
000470    01 TEMP-VARIABLES.
000480       03 RECORD-COUNT                PIC 999 VALUE 0.
000490       03 BLANK-LINE                  PIC X(30) VALUE SPACES.
000500       03 DASHED-LINE                 PIC X(58) VALUE ALL "-".
000510
000520 PROCEDURE DIVISION.
000525
000530    INITIALISE.
000540      OPEN OUTPUT SALES-FILE.
000550      PERFORM SCREEN-MASK.
000560
000570    PROCESS-RECORDS.
000580      PERFORM RECORD-LOOP THRU ANOTHER-RECORD
000590          UNTIL NO-MORE-RECS.
000595
000600    FINISH-PROCESSING.
```

```
000610        CLOSE SALES-FILE.
000620        DISPLAY ERASE.
000625
000630        STOP RUN.
000635
000640*---------PERFORMed Paragraphs start here ------------
000645
000650     SCREEN-MASK.
000660        DISPLAY ERASE.
000670        DISPLAY (6, 11) DASHED-LINE.
000680        DISPLAY (20, 11) DASHED-LINE.
000690        DISPLAY (22, 11) DASHED-LINE.
000700        DISPLAY (2, 33) "SALES RECORD".
000710        DISPLAY (3, 32) "DATA INPUT SCREEN".
000720        DISPLAY (2, 64) "DATE : ".
000730        DISPLAY (8, 19) "Salesman Name    :".
000740        DISPLAY (10, 19) "Salesman Number  :".
000750        DISPLAY (12, 19) "Tax Month        :".
000760        DISPLAY (14, 19) "Item Code        :".
000770        DISPLAY (16, 19) "Number Sold      :".
000780        DISPLAY (18, 19) "Sales Value      :".
000790        DISPLAY (24, 2) "HELP        : ".
000800        DISPLAY (24, 67) "RECORDS : ".
000810        ACCEPT RUN-DATE FROM DATE.
000820        MOVE DD TO TD.
000830        MOVE MM TO TM.
000840        MOVE YY TO TY.
000850        DISPLAY (2, 71)  TDATE.
000860        DISPLAY (24, 77) RECORD-COUNT.
000870*-----------------------------------------
000880     RECORD-LOOP.
000890        DISPLAY (24, 13)
000900         "Salesman Name   -  Surname followed by Initial.".
000910        ACCEPT (8, 37)          SALESMAN-NAME.
000920        DISPLAY (24, 13)
000930         "Salesman Number -  District(1/2/3) + 3 digits  ".
000940        ACCEPT (10, 37)         SALESMAN-NUMBER.
000950        DISPLAY (24, 13)
000960         "Tax Month   -  MAXIMUM 2 Digits.              ".
000970        ACCEPT (12, 37)         TAX-MONTH.
000980        DISPLAY (24, 13)
000990         "Item Code   -  MAXIMUM 5 Digits.              ".
001000        ACCEPT (14, 37)         ITEM-CODE.
001010        DISPLAY (24, 13)
001020         "Number Sold  -  MAXIMUM 5 Digits.             ".
001030        ACCEPT (16, 37)         NUMBER-SOLD.
001040        DISPLAY (24, 13)
001050         "Sales Value -  FORMAT 999.99                  ".
001060        ACCEPT (18, 37)         SALES-VALUE.
001070        DISPLAY (21, 30) "SAVE RECORD (Y/N)? : ".
001080        ACCEPT (21, 53) CORRECT-COND.
001090        DISPLAY (21, 30) BLANK-LINE.
001100        IF REC-IS-CORRECT
001110           WRITE SALES-REC
001120           ADD 1 TO RECORD-COUNT.
001130*        ENDIF
001140*-----------------------------------------
001150     ANOTHER-RECORD.
001160        DISPLAY (24, 77) RECORD-COUNT.
001170        MOVE "N" TO CORRECT-COND.
001180        MOVE SPACES TO SALES-REC.
001190        DISPLAY (21, 28) "ANOTHER RECORD (Y/N)? : ".
```

```
001200          ACCEPT  (21, 54) INPUT-COND.
001210          DISPLAY (21, 28) BLANK-LINE.
001220          DISPLAY (8,  37) BLANK-LINE.
001230          DISPLAY (10, 37) BLANK-LINE.
001240          DISPLAY (12, 37) BLANK-LINE.
001250          DISPLAY (14, 37) BLANK-LINE.
001260          DISPLAY (16, 37) BLANK-LINE.
001270          DISPLAY (18, 37) BLANK-LINE.
001280*----------------------------------
001290          END PROGRAM SALES-INPUT.
```

Program output

```
2001Brady  S            09555530000550050
1011Johnson B           09234560000645634
1011Johnson B           09540340002232450
3017Jobling F           09111010000303430
3018Aaron  P            09120900006222000
1003Abelson K           09122120000523130
2001Brady  S            09343450000407650
2006Peters A            09222010000334560
2012Denham M            09222010000545450
1015Taylor M            09347890001212345
1015Taylor M            09778690000105030
3017Jobling F           09458900000466670
2005Adams  R            09565450000444500
2001Brady  S            09111010001212000
1003Abelson K           09222030000404560
2005Adams  R            09666010000540050
2012Denham M            09220130000434256
3017Jobling F           09600020000632100
```

Example program #2 - Sorting a sequential file

Program specification

The sales file produced by the first program is sorted by this program into ascending order of salesman number.

The sort is performed internally by first reading the file into an array and then applying a simple bubble sort on the array.

Finally, a new sequential file is created containing the sorted sales records.

The program reports its progress by displaying messages on the screen at various stages of its operation.

Program structure diagram

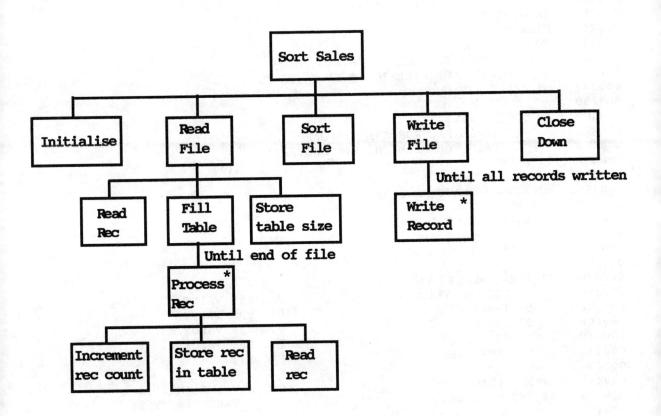

Source code

```
000010 IDENTIFICATION DIVISION.
000020    PROGRAM-ID.          SORT-SALES.
000030    AUTHOR.              NICK WAITES.
000040    DATE-WRITTEN.        MARCH 1990.
000050*   REMARKS.             A PROGRAM WRITTEN IN COBOL
000060*                        TO SORT A SALES RECORDS.
000070
000080 ENVIRONMENT DIVISION.
000090    CONFIGURATION SECTION.
000100     SOURCE-COMPUTER. IBM-PC.
000110     OBJECT-COMPUTER. IBM-PC.
000120    INPUT-OUTPUT SECTION.
000130    FILE-CONTROL.
000140         SELECT UNSORTED-FILE ASSIGN TO DISK,
000150             ORGANIZATION IS LINE SEQUENTIAL.
000160         SELECT SORTED-FILE ASSIGN TO DISK,
000170             ORGANIZATION IS LINE SEQUENTIAL.
000180
000190 DATA DIVISION.
000200    FILE SECTION.
000210    FD UNSORTED-FILE
000220         LABEL RECORDS ARE STANDARD
000230         VALUE OF FILE-ID "B:SALES.DAT".
000240    01 SALES-REC-U               PIC X(46).
000250
000260    FD SORTED-FILE
000270         LABEL RECORDS ARE STANDARD
000280         VALUE OF FILE-ID "B:SALES.SRT".
000290    01 SALES-REC-S               PIC X(46).
000300
000310    WORKING-STORAGE SECTION.
000320     01 SORT-TABLE.
000330        03 ITEM OCCURS 50 TIMES.
000340          05 CODE-NUM-T          PIC 9999.
000350          05 REST-OF-REC         PIC X(42).
000360
000370     01 TEMP-VALUES.
000380        03 RECORD-COUNT          PIC 999 VALUE 0.
000390        03 TABLE-SIZE            PIC 999 VALUE 0.
000400        03 I1                    PIC 999 VALUE 0.
000410        03 I2                    PIC 999 VALUE 0.
000420        03 TEMP-ITEM             PIC X(47).
000430
000440     01 END-FLAG                 PIC X VALUE "N".
000450     88 END-OF-FILE                    VALUE IS "Y".
000460
000470     01 SORT-FLAG                PIC X VALUE "N".
000480     88 TABLE-SORTED                   VALUE IS "Y".
000490
000500     01 BLANK-LINE               PIC X(80) VALUE SPACES.
000510
000520 PROCEDURE DIVISION.
000525
000530    INITIALISE.
000540      OPEN INPUT    UNSORTED-FILE
000550            OUTPUT  SORTED-FILE.
000560
000570    READ-FILE.
000580      PERFORM READ-UNSORTED-FILE.
000590
000600    SORT-FILE.
```

```
000610        PERFORM SORT-RTN UNTIL TABLE-SORTED.
000620
000630     WRITE-FILE.
000640        PERFORM PROCESS-SORTED-FILE.
000650
000660     CLOSE-DOWN.
000670        CLOSE  UNSORTED-FILE,
000680               SORTED-FILE.
000690
000700        STOP RUN.
000710*———— PERFORMed Paragraphs start here ————·
000720     READ-UNSORTED-FILE.
000730        DISPLAY ERASE.
000740        DISPLAY (10, 10) "Reading unsorted file...".
000750        MOVE ZERO TO RECORD-COUNT.
000760        READ UNSORTED-FILE
000770              AT END MOVE "Y" TO END-FLAG.
000780        PERFORM FILL-TABLE UNTIL END-OF-FILE.
000790        MOVE RECORD-COUNT TO TABLE-SIZE.
000800*————————————————————————————--
000810     FILL-TABLE.
000820        ADD 1 TO RECORD-COUNT.
000830        DISPLAY (12, 10) RECORD-COUNT, " records in file".
000840        MOVE SALES-REC-U TO ITEM (RECORD-COUNT).
000850        READ UNSORTED-FILE
000860              AT END MOVE "Y" TO END-FLAG.
000870*_____
000880     SORT-RTN.
000890        DISPLAY (10, 1) BLANK-LINE.
000900        DISPLAY (10, 10) "Sorting file....".
000910        MOVE "Y" TO SORT-FLAG.
000920        SUBTRACT 1 FROM RECORD-COUNT.
000930        MOVE 1 TO I1.
000940        ADD 1 TO I1 GIVING I2.
000950        PERFORM EXCHANGES RECORD-COUNT TIMES.
000960*————————————————————————————-
000970     EXCHANGES.
000980        IF CODE-NUM-T (I1) IS GREATER THAN CODE-NUM-T (I2)
000990              MOVE ITEM (I1) TO TEMP-ITEM
001000              MOVE ITEM (I2) TO ITEM (I1)
001010              MOVE TEMP-ITEM TO ITEM (I2)
001020              MOVE "N" TO SORT-FLAG.
001030*     ENDIF
001040        ADD 1 TO I1.
001050        ADD 1 TO I2.
001060*————————————————————————————--
001070     PROCESS-SORTED-FILE.
001080        DISPLAY (10, 10) BLANK-LINE.
001090        DISPLAY (10, 10)
001100           "Sort complete: Writing sorted file...".
001110        MOVE 0 TO I1.
001120        PERFORM WRITE-RECORD TABLE-SIZE TIMES.
001130        DISPLAY (10, 10) BLANK-LINE.
001140        DISPLAY (10, 10) "Program Terminated".
001150*————————————————————————————--
001160     WRITE-RECORD.
001170        ADD 1 TO I1.
001180        WRITE SALES-REC-S FROM ITEM (I1).
001190
001200     END PROGRAM SORT-SALES.
```

Program output

```
1003Abelson K              09122120000523130
1003Abelson K              09222030000404560
1011Johnson  B             09234560000645634
1011Johnson  B             09540340002232450
1015Taylor   M             09347890001212345
1015Taylor   M             09778690000105030
2001Brady    S             09555530000550050
2001Brady    S             09343450000407650
2001Brady    S             09111010001212000
2005Adams    R             09565450000444500
2005Adams    R             09666010000540050
2006Peters   A             09222010000334560
2012Denham   M             09222010000545450
2012Denham   M             09220130000434256
3017Jobling  F             09111010000303430
3017Jobling  F             09458900000466670
3017Jobling  F             09600020000632100
3018Aaron    P             09120900006222000
```

Example program #3 - Printing a sequential file

Program specification

This is a report program designed to produce a tabulated printout of the sales file.

The user is allowed to enter the name of the file to be printed (either the unsorted file SALES.DAT, or the sorted file SALES.SRT) and the output device to be used (either a file name so that the output may be stored on disk, or the word "PRINTER" so that the report is printed immediately).

The format of the report is illustrated after the program listing.

Program structure diagram

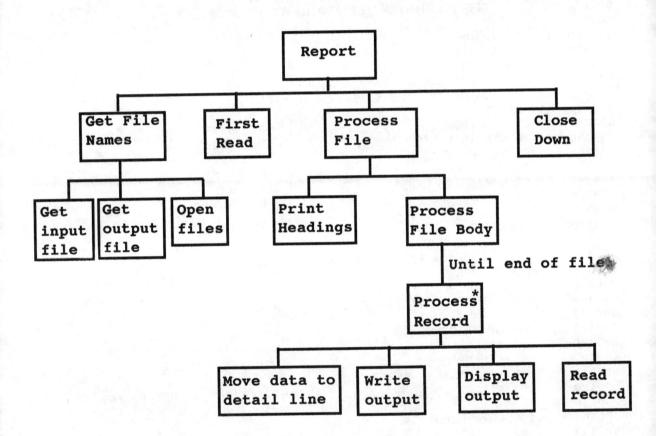

Source code

```
000010 IDENTIFICATION DIVISION.
000020    PROGRAM-ID.          PRINT-SALES.
000030    AUTHOR.              NICK WAITES.
000040    DATE-WRITTEN.        MARCH 1990.
000050*   REMARKS.             A PROGRAM WRITTEN IN COBOL TO
000060*                        PRINT A FILE OF SALES RECORDS.
000070
000080 ENVIRONMENT DIVISION.
000090    CONFIGURATION SECTION.
000100     SOURCE-COMPUTER. IBM-PC.
000110     OBJECT-COMPUTER. IBM-PC.
000120    INPUT-OUTPUT SECTION.
000130    FILE-CONTROL.
000140        SELECT SALES-FILE ASSIGN TO DISK,
000150            ORGANIZATION IS LINE SEQUENTIAL.
000160        SELECT PRINTER-FILE ASSIGN TO PRINTER.
000170
000180 DATA DIVISION.
000190    FILE SECTION.
000200    FD SALES-FILE
000210        LABEL RECORDS ARE STANDARD
000220        VALUE OF FILE-ID IS INPUT-FILE.
000230    01 SALES-REC.
000240       03 CODE-NUM-I              PIC 9(4).
000250       03 SALESMAN-NAME-I         PIC A(25).
000260       03 TAX-MONTH-I             PIC 99.
000270       03 ITEM-CODE-I             PIC 9(5).
000280       03 NUMBER-SOLD-I           PIC 9(5).
000290       03 SALE-VALUE-I            PIC 999V99.
000300
000310    FD PRINTER-FILE
000320        LABEL RECORDS ARE STANDARD
000330        VALUE OF FILE-ID IS OUTPUT-FILE.
000340    01 PRINTER-REC                PIC X(80).
000350
000360    WORKING-STORAGE SECTION.
000370
000380     01 PAGE-HEADING.
000390        03 FILLER                 PIC X(34) VALUE SPACES.
000400        03 FILLER                 PIC X(12) VALUE
000410            "SALES REPORT".
000420        03 FILLER                 PIC X(34) VALUE SPACES.
000430
000440     01 COLUMN-HEADINGS.
000450        03 FILLER                 PIC X(13) VALUE
000460            "CODE NUMBER  ".
000470        03 FILLER                 PIC X(25) VALUE
000480            "SALESMAN NAME            ".
000490        03 FILLER                 PIC X(10) VALUE
000500            "TAX MONTH ".
000510        03 FILLER                 PIC X(7) VALUE
000520             "ITEM   ".
000530        03 FILLER                 PIC X(13) VALUE
000540            "NUMBER SOLD  ".
000550        03 FILLER                 PIC X(11) VALUE
000560            "SALES VALUE".
000570
000580     01 UNDERLINE                 PIC X(80) VALUE
000590            ALL   "-".
000600
000610     01 BLANK-LINE                PIC X(80) VALUE SPACES.
```

```
000620
000630    01 DETAIL-LINE.
000640         03 CODE-NUM-P                     PIC X(13).
000650         03 SALESMAN-NAME-P                PIC X(25).
000660         03 TAX-MONTH-P                    PIC X(10).
000670         03 ITEM-CODE-P                    PIC X(7).
000680         03 NUMBER-SOLD-P                  PIC X(13).
000690         03 SALE-VALUE-P                   PIC 999.99.
000700
000710    01 END-FLAG                           PIC X VALUE "N".
000720    88 END-OF-FILE                              VALUE IS "Y".
000740    01 I-O-FILENAMES.
000750         03 INPUT-FILE                  PIC X(14) VALUE SPACES.
000760         03 OUTPUT-FILE                 PIC X(14) VALUE SPACES.
000770
000780    PROCEDURE DIVISION.
000820
000830       GET-FILE-NAMES.
000840          DISPLAY ERASE.
000850          DISPLAY (10, 10) "Enter name of INPUT file :"
000860          ACCEPT INPUT-FILE.
000870          DISPLAY (12, 10) "Enter name of OUTPUT file..."
000880          DISPLAY (13, 10) "...or        'PRINTER'        :"
000890          ACCEPT OUTPUT-FILE.
                 OPEN INPUT  SALES-FILE,
                      OUTPUT PRINTER-FILE.
000910
000920       FIRST-READ.
000930          READ SALES-FILE
000940              AT END MOVE "Y" TO END-FLAG.
000950
000960       PROCESS-FILE.
000970          PERFORM PRINT-HEADINGS.
000980          PERFORM PROCESS-RECORD UNTIL END-OF-FILE.
000990
001000       CLOSE-DOWN.
001010          CLOSE  SALES-FILE,
001020                 PRINTER-FILE.



001030
001040          STOP RUN.
001050*------ PERFORMed Paragraphs start here -----------
001055
001060       PROCESS-RECORD.
001070          MOVE CODE-NUM-I       TO CODE-NUM-P.
001080          MOVE SALESMAN-NAME-I  TO SALESMAN-NAME-P.
001090          MOVE TAX-MONTH-I      TO TAX-MONTH-P.
001100          MOVE ITEM-CODE-I      TO ITEM-CODE-P.
001110          MOVE NUMBER-SOLD-I    TO NUMBER-SOLD-P.
001120          MOVE SALE-VALUE-I     TO SALE-VALUE-P.
001130
001140          WRITE PRINTER-REC FROM DETAIL-LINE.
001150          DISPLAY DETAIL-LINE.
001160
001170          READ SALES-FILE
001180              AT END MOVE "Y" TO END-FLAG.
001190*-------------------------------------
001200       PRINT-HEADINGS.
001210          WRITE PRINTER-REC FROM PAGE-HEADING
001220                  AFTER ADVANCING PAGE.
001230          WRITE PRINTER-REC FROM COLUMN-HEADINGS
001240                  AFTER ADVANCING 3 LINES.
001250          WRITE PRINTER-REC FROM UNDERLINE.
```

```
001260
001270          DISPLAY ERASE.
001280          DISPLAY PAGE-HEADING.
001290          DISPLAY (4, 1) COLUMN-HEADINGS.
001300          DISPLAY UNDERLINE.
001310
001320      END PROGRAM PRINT-SALES.
```

Program output

SALES REPORT

Code Number	Salesman Name	Tax Month	Item Number	Sold	Sales Value
1003	Abelson K	09	12212	00005	231.30
1003	Abelson K	09	22203	00004	045.60
1011	Johnson B	09	23456	00006	456.34
1011	Johnson B	09	54034	00022	324.50
1015	Taylor M	09	34789	00012	123.45
1015	Taylor M	09	77869	00001	050.30
2001	Brady S	09	55553	00005	500.50
2001	Brady S	09	34345	00004	076.50
2001	Brady S	09	11101	00012	120.00
2005	Adams R	09	56545	00004	445.00
2005	Adams R	09	66601	00005	400.50
2006	Peters A	09	22201	00003	345.60
2012	Denham M	09	22201	00005	454.50
2012	Denham M	09	22013	00004	342.56
3017	Jobling F	09	11101	00003	034.30
3017	Jobling F	09	45890	00004	666.70
3017	Jobling F	09	60002	00006	321.00
3018	Aaron P	09	12090	00062	220.00

Example program #4 - Creating space for a random file

Program specification

This program reserves disk space for the relative file used in the next program. It does so by creating a sequential file of the maximum number of fixed length records required by the relative file.

The program reports its progress at various stages, finally displaying the number of records created.

Each 'dummy' record in the file consists entirely of spaces.

Program structure diagram

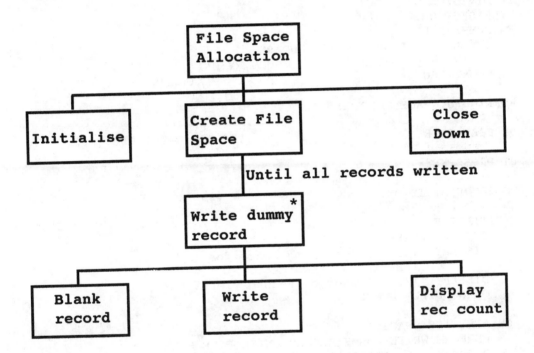

Source code

```
000010 IDENTIFICATION DIVISION.
000020    PROGRAM-ID.          ALLOCATE-SPACE.
000030    AUTHOR.              NICK WAITES.
000040    DATE-WRITTEN.        MARCH 1990.
000050*   REMARKS.             A PROGRAM WRITTEN IN COBOL TO
000060*                        ALLOCATE SPACE FOR A RANDOM FILE.
000070
000080 ENVIRONMENT DIVISION.
000090    CONFIGURATION SECTION.
000100     SOURCE-COMPUTER. IBM-PC.
000110     OBJECT-COMPUTER. IBM-PC.
000120    INPUT-OUTPUT SECTION.
000130    FILE-CONTROL.
000140        SELECT DUMMY-FILE ASSIGN TO DISK,
000150            ORGANIZATION IS SEQUENTIAL,
000160            ACCESS MODE IS SEQUENTIAL.
000170
000180 DATA DIVISION.
000190    FILE SECTION.
000200    FD DUMMY-FILE
000210        LABEL RECORDS ARE STANDARD
000220        VALUE OF FILE-ID IS "B:SUMMARY.DAT".
000230    01 DUMMY-REC                    PIC X(121).
000240
000250    WORKING-STORAGE SECTION.
000260
000270    01 FILE-SIZE                    PIC 999 VALUE 100.
000280
000290    01 PRESS-KEY                    PIC X.
000300
000310    PROCEDURE DIVISION.
000320
000330      INITIALISE.
000340        DISPLAY ERASE.
000350        DISPLAY (10, 10) "Creating space for ",
000360            FILE-SIZE, " records".
000370        DISPLAY (12, 10) "No. of records left: ".
000380        OPEN OUTPUT DUMMY-FILE.
000390
000400      CREATE-FILE-SPACE.
000410        PERFORM WRITE-DUMMY-RECORD UNTIL FILE-SIZE = 0.
000420        DISPLAY (16, 10) "File allocation complete".
000430        DISPLAY (18, 10) "Press <Return>/<Enter> to continue..."
000440        ACCEPT PRESS-KEY.
000450
000460      CLOSE-DOWN.
000470        CLOSE  DUMMY-FILE.
000480
000490        STOP RUN.
000500
000505*----- PERFORMed Paragraphs start here -------
000506
000510      WRITE-DUMMY-RECORD.
000520        MOVE SPACES TO DUMMY-REC.
000530        WRITE DUMMY-REC FROM SPACES.
000540        SUBTRACT 1 FROM FILE-SIZE.
000550        DISPLAY (12, 32) FILE-SIZE.
000560
000570      END PROGRAM PRINT-SALES.
```

Example program #5 - Updating a relative file

Program specification

This final example program updates a random file containing a month-by-month summary of sales made by each sales representative.

The summary contains entries for each month's sales in the current financial year, and the accumulated total todate for the whole year.

The sorted sales file is read and the sales value of all the items accredited to the current salesman are totalled. The total sales are then added to the appropriate month's total and to the year total of the sales representative's summary record before the new record is rewritten to the summary file.

The summary file is a relative file, the relative key being the last three digits of the salesman number, which must be in the range 1 to 100. (This is because the number of records in the summary file is restricted to an arbitrary maximum of 100 records).

It is assumed that the sales file used for updating the summary file contains sales for a single month, and that it has been sorted into sales representative number order, that is, all the sales made by a particular representative are grouped together.

Program structure diagram

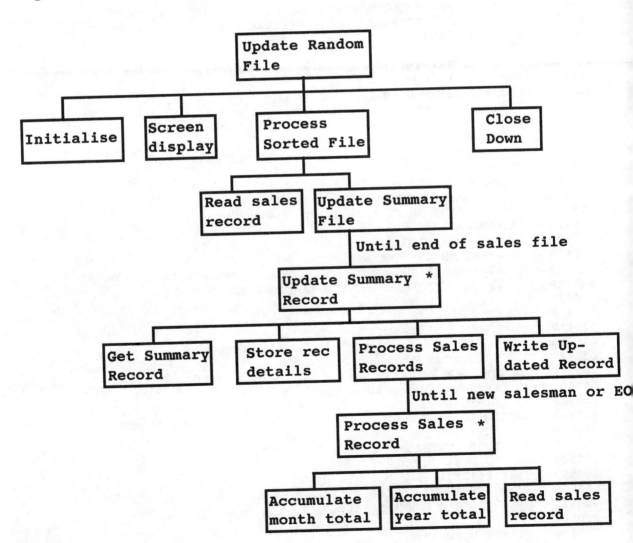

Source code

```
000010   IDENTIFICATION DIVISION.
000020      PROGRAM-ID.          UPDATE-SUMMARY.
000030      AUTHOR.              NICK WAITES.
000040      DATE-WRITTEN.        MARCH 1990.
000050*    REMARKS.             A PROGRAM WRITTEN IN COBOL TO
000060*                         UPDATE A RANDOM FILE.
000070
000080   ENVIRONMENT DIVISION.
000090      CONFIGURATION SECTION.
000100       SOURCE-COMPUTER. IBM-PC.
000110       OBJECT-COMPUTER. IBM-PC.
000120      INPUT-OUTPUT SECTION.
000130      FILE-CONTROL.
000140          SELECT SALES-FILE ASSIGN TO DISK,
000150              ORGANIZATION IS LINE SEQUENTIAL.
000160          SELECT SUMMARY-FILE ASSIGN TO DISK,
000170              ORGANIZATION IS RELATIVE,
000180              ACCESS MODE IS RANDOM,
000190              RELATIVE KEY IS REL-KEY.
000200
000210   DATA DIVISION.
000220      FILE SECTION.
000230      FD SALES-FILE
000240          LABEL RECORDS ARE STANDARD
000250          VALUE OF FILE-ID IS "B:SALES.SRT".
000260      01 SALES-REC.
000270         03 CODE-NUM-I.
000280            05 DISTRICT-I              PIC 9.
000290            05 KEY-NUM-I               PIC 999.
000300         03 SALESMAN-NAME-I            PIC A(25).
000310         03 TAX-MONTH-I                PIC 99.
000320         03 ITEM-CODE-I                PIC 9(5).
000330         03 NUMBER-SOLD-I              PIC 9(5).
000340         03 SALE-VALUE-I               PIC 999V99.
000350
000360      FD SUMMARY-FILE
000370          . LABEL RECORDS ARE STANDARD
000380            VALUE OF FILE-ID IS "B:SUMMARY.DAT".
000390      01 SUMMARY-REC.
000400         03 CODE-NUM-S                 PIC 9(4).
000410         03 SALESMAN-NAME-S            PIC A(25).
000420         03 YEAR-TOTAL-S               PIC 9(6)V99.
000430         03 MONTH-TOTAL-S OCCURS 12 TIMES PIC 9(5)V99.
000440
000450   WORKING-STORAGE SECTION.
000460
000470   01 REL-KEY                          PIC 999.
000480
000490   01 TEMP-NUM                         PIC 9(4).
000500
000510   01 END-FLAG                         PIC X VALUE "N".
000520   88 END-OF-FILE                            VALUE IS "Y".
000530
000540   PROCEDURE DIVISION.
000546
000550   INITIALISE.
000560       OPEN INPUT  SALES-FILE,
000570            I-O SUMMARY-FILE.
000580
000590   SCREEN-DISPLAY.
000600       DISPLAY ERASE.
```

```
000610          DISPLAY (4, 30) "Summary file update".
000620          DISPLAY (10, 10) "Updating record number: ".
000630
000640     PROCESS-SORTED-FILE.
000650          READ SALES-FILE
000660              AT END MOVE "Y" TO END-FLAG.
000670          PERFORM UPDATE-SUMMARY UNTIL END-OF-FILE.
000680
000690     CLOSE-DOWN.
000700          CLOSE  SALES-FILE,
000710               SUMMARY-FILE.
000720
000730          STOP RUN.
000740
000745*---- PERFORMed Paragraphs start here --------
000747
000750     UPDATE-SUMMARY.
000760          MOVE CODE-NUM-I TO TEMP-NUM.
000770          MOVE KEY-NUM-I TO REL-KEY.
000772          READ SUMMARY-FILE INVALID KEY PERFORM I-K-RTN1.
000774          MOVE CODE-NUM-I TO CODE-NUM-S.
000780          MOVE SALESMAN-NAME-I TO SALESMAN-NAME-S.
000790          DISPLAY (10, 35) KEY-NUM-I.
000810          PERFORM PROCESS-SALES-REC UNTIL
000820               CODE-NUM-I IS NOT EQUAL TO TEMP-NUM
                         OR END-OF-FILE.
000830          REWRITE SUMMARY-REC INVALID KEY PERFORM I-K-RTN2.
000840
000844*-----------------------------------
000850     PROCESS-SALES-REC.
000860          ADD SALE-VALUE-I TO MONTH-TOTAL-S (TAX-MONTH-I).
000870          ADD SALE-VALUE-I TO YEAR-TOTAL-S.
000880          READ SALES-FILE
000890              AT END MOVE "Y" TO END-FLAG.
000900*------------------------------------
000905
000910     I-K-RTN1.
000920          DISPLAY CODE-NUM-I, "NO SUCH RECORD".
000930*------------------------------------
000935
000940     I-K-RTN2.
000950          DISPLAY CODE-NUM-I, "CAN'T WRITE TO THIS RECORD".
000960
000970     END PROGRAM UPDATE-SUMMARY.
```

Reserved Words

COBOL contains a large number of words which are recognised by the compiler as key words having special meanings. These reserved words must be spelled correctly and used in the correct context according to the syntax of the language. They are listed here so that you know which combinations of characters to avoid when deciding on your program identifiers, and also to give you an idea of the true complexity of the full COBOL language.

The list of reserved words includes the additions introduced in COBOL 85 (the successor to COBOL 74) which attempts to bring COBOL more in line with the current trend towards structured programming.

ACCEPT	AREA	COMMUNICATION
ACCESS	AREAS	COMP
ADD	ASCENDING	COMP-0
ADVANCING	ASCII	COMP-1
AFTER	ASSIGN	COMP-3
ALL	AT	COMPUTATIONAL
ALPHABET	ATTRIBUTE	COMPUTATIONAL-3
ALPHABETIC	AUTHOR	COMPUTE
ACCEPT	AUTO-SKIP	CONFIGURATION
ACCESS	BEEP	CONTAINS
ADD	BEFORE	CONTENT
ADVANCING	BEGINNING	COMP-1
AFTER	BINARY	COMP-3
ALL	BLANK	COMPUTATIONAL
ALPHABET	BLOCK	COMPUTATIONAL-3
ALPHABETIC	BOTTOM	COMPUTE
ALPHABETIC-LOWER	BY	CONFIGURATION
ALPHABETIC-UPPER	CALL	CONTAINS
ALPHANUMERIC	CANCEL	CONTENT
ALPHANUMERIC-EDITED	CD	CONTINUE
ALSO	CF	CONTROL
ALTER	CH	CONTROLS
ALTERNATE	CHARACTER	CONVERTING
AND	CHARACTERS	COPY
ALPHABETIC-LOWER	CLASS	CORR
ALPHABETIC-UPPER	CLOCK-UNITS	CORRESPONDING
ALPHANUMERIC	CLOSE	COUNT
ALPHANUMERIC-EDITED	COBOL	CSEG-MEMORY
ALSO	CODE	CURRENCY
ALTER	CODE-SET	DATA
ALTERNATE	COLLATING	DATE
AND	COLUMN	DATE-COMPILED
ANY	COMMA	DATE-WRITTEN
ARE	COMMON	DAY

DAY-OF-WEEK	EXTEND	MODULES
DE	EXTERNAL	MOVE
DEBUG-CONTENTS	FALSE	MULTIPLE
DEBUG-ITEM	FD	MULTIPLY
DEBUG-LINE	FILE	NATIVE
DEBUG-NAME	FILE-CONTROL	NEGATIVE
DEBUG-SUB-1	FILE-ID	NEXT
DEBUG-SUB-2	FILLER	NO
DEBUG-SUB-3	FINAL	NOT
DEBUGGING	FIRST	NUMBER
DECIMAL-POINT	FOOTING	NUMERIC
DECLARATIVES	FOR	NUMERIC-EDITED
DELETE	FROM	OBJECT-COMPUTER
DELIMITED	GENERATE	OCCURS
DELIMITER	GIVING	OF
DEPENDING	GLOBAL	OFF
DESCENDING	GO	OMITTED
DESTINATION	GREATER	ON
DETAIL	GROUP	OPEN
DISABLE	HEADING	OPTIONAL
DISK	HIGH-VALUE	OR
DISPLAY	HIGH-VALUES	ORDER
DIVIDE	I-O	ORGANIZATION
DIVISION	I-O-CONTROL	OTHER
DOWN	IDENTIFICATION	OUTPUT
DSEG-MEMORY	IF	OVERFLOW
DUPLICATES	IN	PACKED-DECIMAL
DYNAMIC	INDEX	PADDING
EGI	INDEXED	PAGE
ELSE	INDICATE	PAGE-COUNTER
EMPTY-CHECK	INITIAL	PERFORM
ENABLE	INITIALIZE	PF
END	INITIATE	PH
END-ADD	INPUT	PIC
END-CALL	INPUT-OUTPUT	PICTURE
END-COMPUTE	INSPECT	PLUS
END-DELETE	INSTALLATION	POINTER
END-DIVIDE	INTO	POSITION
END-EVALUATE	INVALID	POSITIVE
END-IF	IS	PRINTER
END-MULTIPLY	JUST	PRINTING
END-OF-PAGE	JUSTIFIED	PROCEDURE
END-PERFORM	KEY	PROCEDURES
END-READ	LABEL	PROCEED
END-RECEIVE	LAST	PROGRAM
END-RETURN	LEADING	PROGRAM-ID
END-REWRITE	LEFT	PURGE
END-SEARCH	LENGTH	QUEUE
END-START	LENGTH-CHECK	QUOTE
END-STRING	LESS	QUOTES
END-SUBTRACT	LIMIT	RANDOM
END-UNSTRING	LIMITS	RD
END-WRITE	LINAGE	READ
ENTER	LINAGE-COUNTER	RECEIVE
ENVIRONMENT	LINE	RECORD
EOP	LINE-COUNTER	RECORDS
EQUAL	LINES	REDEFINES
ERASE	LINKAGE	REEL
ERROR	LOCK	REFERENCE
ESCAPE	LOW-VALUE	REFERENCES
ESI	LOW-VALUES	RELATIVE
EVALUATE	MEMORY	
EVERY	MERGE	
EXCEPTION	MESSAGE	
EXIT	MODE	

RELEASE
REMAINDER
REMOVAL
RENAMES
REPLACE
REPLACING
REPORT
REPORTING
REPORTS
RERUN
RESERVE
RESET
RETURN
REVERSED
REWIND
REWRITE
RF
RH
RIGHT
ROUND
ROUNDED
RUN
SAME
SCREEN
SD
SEARCH
SECTION
SECURITY
SEGMENT
SEGMENT-LIMIT
SELECT
SEND
SENTENCE
SEPARATE

SEQUENCE
SEQUENTIAL
SET
SHELL
SIGN
SIZE
SORT
SORT-MERGE
SOURCE
SOURCE-COMPUTER
SPACE
SPACES
SPECIAL-NAMES
STANDARD
STANDARD-1
START
STATUS
STOP
STRING
SUB-QUEUE-1
SUB-QUEUE-2
SUB-QUEUE-3
SUBTRACT
SUM
SUPPRESS
SYMBOLIC
SYNC
SYNCHRONIZED
TABLE
TALLYING
TAPE
TERMINAL
TERMINATE
TEST

TEXT
THAN
THEN
THROUGH
THRU
TIME
TIMES
TO
TOP
TRAILING
TRUE
TYPE
UNIT
UNSTRING
UNTIL
UP
UPON
USAGE
USE
USING
VALUE
VALUES
VARYING
WHEN
WINDOW
WITH
WORDS
WORKING-STORAGE
WRITE
ZERO
ZEROES
ZEROS

Exercises

Example Program #1

1. Using program #1 as a model, write a data entry program for a file that you have designed. Plan the appearance of the screen mask on squared paper before writing the program so that you can calculate the coordinates for each prompt and input.

2. Modify example program #1 such that when a field is to be entered, the corresponding field of the previous record is displayed, allowing the user to just press <ENTER> to accept this data rather than enter new data; this can save time when certain fields do not change from record to record, or when only certain fields of an incorrect record are to be changed.

Sometimes the COBOL compiler will facilitate this type of operation by providing special options in the ACCEPT statement, otherwise you must provide your own code. A possible approach to programming this facility is to reserve an area of WORKING-STORAGE for a copy of the input record to be used as a buffer for each field to be entered. Each field of the new record, in turn, is read into its buffer; if the buffer contains one or more characters constituting new data, its contents are transferred to the corresponding field of the actual record description in the FILE SECTION; if the buffer is empty because the user has pressed <ENTER> without entering any data, no action is taken, thus allowing the previous contents of that field to remain.

3. Write a program to validate a sequential file such as that created by example program #1. Each record should be subjected to as many checks as possible to ensure that the data has been entered correctly. Here is a list of possible validation checks with brief descriptions of their purposes:

(i) *Alphabetic/Numeric class test* to ensure that fields do not contain invalid characters.

(ii) *Range check* to ensure that numeric data is within certain prescribed limits.

(iii) *Code check* to determine whether a code field contains one of a limited number of special codes.

(iv) *Presence check* to ensure that a field's contents are present, that is, the field has been entered and is not empty.

(v) *Control totals* which are pre-calculated totals of numeric fields (typically monetary fields); these are compared with the same totals calculated during computer processing. For example, in the example sales file, the sale value field for all the source records could be totalled prior to entry to the computer - this would be the control total. The validation program would then keep a running total of this field as the records are processed. When the whole file has been validated, the control total would be compared with the calculated total as a check that no mistake had been made during the data entry phase.

Example Program #2

1. Use example program #2 as a model for sorting the data file you designed and created in the previous exercise.

2. Implement a selection sort or an insertion sort in COBOL using either your own file or the one provided for example program #2. Sorts are described in detail in Chapter 35

Example Program #3

1. Write a program to print a report of one of your own files, using example program #3 as a guide.

2. In the sales file used for the example programs the first digit of the salesman code number represents the district in which the salesman operates. Modify example program #3 so that the report will show district subtotals and a grand total for sales as illustrated below:

SALES REPORT

CODE NUMBER	SALESMAN NAME	TAX MONTH	ITEM	NUMBER SOLD	SALES VALUE	DISTRICT TOTAL	GRAND TOTAL
1003	Abelson K	09	12212	00005	231.30		
1003	Abelson K	09	22203	00004	045.60		
1011	Johnson B	09	23456	00006	456.34		
1011	Johnson B	09	54034	00022	324.50		
1015	Taylor M	09	34789	00012	123.45		
1015	Taylor M	09	77869	00001	050.30		
						1231.49	
2001	Brady S	09	55553	00005	500.50		
2001	Brady S	09	34345	00004	076.50		
2001	Brady S	09	11101	00012	120.00		
2005	Adams R	09	56545	00004	445.00		
2005	Adams R	09	66601	00005	400.50		
2006	Peters A	09	22201	00003	345.60		
2012	Denham M	09	22201	00005	454.50		
2012	Denham M	09	22013	00004	342.56		
						2685.16	
3017	Jobling F	09	11101	00003	034.30		
3017	Jobling F	09	45890	00004	666.70		
3017	Jobling F	09	60002	00006	321.00		
3018	Aaron P	09	12090	00062	220.00		
						1242.00	
							5158.65

3. Modify example program #3 to allow for the report spanning more than one page. You should arrange that the page number appears at the bottom of each page and that the page column headings are printed at the top of each new page.

Example Program #5

1. Write a program to produce an end of year report from the summary file updated in example program #5. The report should print out the following information:

(i) The total sales for each month for each district.

(ii) The year total for each district.

(iii) The year total for the whole company.

(iv) The total sales for each month for each salesman.

(v) The year total for each salesman.

You will probably need to sort the summary file prior to producing this report and base the program structure on the structure of the sorted file. Design your own output format, attempting to make it as clear as possible.

Project

The Video Rental Company

A video rental company wishes to put a microcomputer system into all of its outlets. The software is required to perform the following functions for each outlet:

1. Record the details of each video tape title in stock.
2. Record the details of each of its customers.
3. Keep track of the current videos on loan.
4. Calculate the charge to be made to customers returning video tapes.

The structure of each file is as follows:

Video Tape File.

Field	*Purpose*
Tape identifier code:	Numeric code which uniquely identifies each tape
Charge code:	Charge for one day's hire
Title:	Full name of video
Category:	Comedy/Thriller/Horror etc
Certificate:	PG/Universal/15/18 etc
Hire count:	Number of times tape has been hired
Cost price:	Purchase price
Current return:	Running total of income from tape
Status:	Whether the video is currently on hire or on the shelves
Membership number:	The membership number of the current/last customer to hire the video
Hire Date:	When the video was hired

Customer File.

Field	*Purpose*
Membership number:	Unique identifier
Address:	
Telephone number:	
Date:	When customer joined club

Programs Required.

1. Update Customer File: Add new customer
                                         Modify customer details

2. Update Video Tape File: Add video to file
                                         Delete video from file
                                         Modify video details

3. Record Loan: Set video status flag to
                                           indicate that video is on loan

4. Acknowledge return of video(s) and calculate hire charge.

5. List details of videos that have been on hire for more than two days.

6. Display list of all videos in stock.

The system works as follows:

Customers are given a membership card when they join the club. This card has the customer's membership number on it and must be produced when hiring videos.

The details of each hired video are entered through the keyboard before the customer leaves the shop. These details comprise the customer's membership number (entered only once no matter how many videos are hired) and the video identifier code. The customer record is retrieved first in order to confirm that the membership number and address match (the customer is asked to give his/her address so that the assistant can check it against the computer display). The video title is retrieved from the Video Tape File using the identification code and displayed on the screen for visual confirmation that the code and title match, and the hire date is automatically retrieved from the system. The details of the hire are displayed on the screen and the assistant checks them before storing the record. The status field is set to indicate that the video is on hire.

When a video is returned, its code number is entered and the video record is retrieved and the relevant data is displayed. The assistant checks that the details are correct before confirming that the video has been returned. The computer then calculates the hire charge based on the return date and the hire date. This charge is accumulated for each video returned. The video record is written back to the Video file with the Status field set to a code representing that the video is available for hire. The customer then pays the appropriate fee.

Every morning the Video File is processed so that all videos that have been on loan for more than two days are printed out, together with the customer details retrieved from the customer file. The shop assistant will then take appropriate action.

If a customer enquires about a video, the complete list of videos currently in stock is displayed in alphabetical order. The display shows the video title, its status, category, certificate and charge code.

The same principles described here could also be adapted to a CD hire club.

Project

Computer Literacy

Design a system which will allow you to store the titles and authors of articles on computing. (The first program described in this chapter is a rudimentary information retrieval program based on this idea). Your system will be required to perform the following functions:

(i)   Store details of the articles.
(ii) Retrieve details of all articles relating to a certain topic, or by a certain author, or containing a certain keyword.
(iii) Print a report of the above records.
(iv) Browse through the whole file.

The articles file will need to store the following details for each article:

Field	Purpose
Title	The full title of the article
Author(s)	The author or authors
Publication	The periodical in which the article appeared
Date	When the article was published
Categories	A list of codes indicating the areas that the article covers

You will need to design a menu program to allow the user to decide how to use the system. It should give the user the opportunity of:

Displaying the possible category codes
Entering one or more codes and obtaining a list of articles on the screen
Printing this list
Entering an author and obtaining a list of articles by that author
Printing this list
Entering a keyword and obtaining a list of articles whose titles contain the keyword
Printing this list
Browsing through the file record by record
Printing the displayed record

In addition, you will need a program to allow you to enter article details to create and add to the file.

A similar system to this could de devised for Estate Agents, the file being based on house details instead.

Project

The Club's Records

Design a system for use by clubs to keep track of their membership. The system will need to perform the following functions:

(i)   Store members' details.
(ii)   Modify members' details.
(iii) Record payment of annual subscriptions.
(iv)   Send reminders to members whose subscriptions are overdue.

The members file will need to contain the following details:

Field	*Purpose*
Name	Member's name
Title	Mr/Mrs/Miss etc
Address	Member's address
Telephone no.	
Date of birth	
Date of joining club	
Membership number	To keep track of how many members there have been since it started
Sex	Whether male or female
Status	Senior or junior member
Subscription	Amount paid in the current year
Other information	Special details relating to type of club

Your system will allow authorised users (access should be restricted by using ID codes) to retrieve a member's record and modify it if, for instance, there has been a change of address. You should be able to use the file as a mailing list so that reminders can be generated automatically when subscriptions are overdue. A report program will provide a list of all current members. A further program will allow the recording of subscriptions.

Absolute address. The actual machine address of a memory location.

Access. The process of seeking, reading or writing on a storage device.

Access mechanism. A mechanism for moving the read-write heads to a position at which data can be read or written, for example, the moveable head mechanism in a magnetic disk unit.

Access method. The method used to retrieve data from a storage system, for example, serial, sequential or random access.

Access time. The time taken to retrieve data from a storage device, that is, from the moment the instruction is executed to the moment when the data is placed in memory.

Access table. A table look-up method used for accessing elements of string arrays.

Accumulator. A storage location, sometimes a special register in the arithmetic-logic unit of the processor, in which arithmetic operations are performed on numbers and where results are temporarily stored.

Acoustic coupler. A type of modem which allows computer data to be received or transmitted as audio tones using a telephone handset.

Addend. The addend constitutes one of the operands in an addition and is added to the augend.

ADA. A high level programming language used for programming real-time applications.

Adder. Electronic circuitry in a computer capable of carrying out addition. It accepts three inputs, the addend, augend and carry to produce two outputs, the sum and carry.

Address. An identifier for a memory location in which data is stored. It may also be that part of an instruction which specifies the location of an operand.

Addressing. The means of assigning data to storage locations and subsequently retrieving them according to a key.

ALGOL. ALGOrithmic Language; a high level programming language suited to mathematical and scientific applications.

Algorithm. A computational procedure or series of instructions for the solution of a particular problem.

ALU. An acronym for arithmetic-logic unit, a component part of the CPU or processor; used for arithmetic operations and logical comparisons of, stored data.

Analogue signal. A signal, such as that produced by the human voice, which is transmitted along a channel of, for example, the telephone network.

Analogue/digital converter (ADC). A device for converting analogue signals to the digital form useable by a digital computer. For example, the temperature measurements taken from a furnace can be digitized by an ADC and monitored by computer.

AND operation. A Boolean logical operation applied to two operands. If both are equal to 1 (TRUE) then the result or output is 1 (TRUE).

Applications software (programs). Programs to deal with user applications, for example, stock control or word processing. They may be packaged or specially written.

Arithmetic shift. A shift of the digits in a location or register to affect a multiplication or division of the number. For example, in binary notation, a left shift of 'n' places is equivalent to dividing the number by 2 to the power 'n'.

Array. A block of storage locations occupying a known area of memory and accessed using a base address and offset from the base.

Artificial intelligence (AI). The ability of a computer to take on some attributes of intelligence, for example, learning and improving its performance through the use of repeated experience.

ASCII code. A set of character codes standardized under the American Standard Code for Information Interchange.

Assembler. Translator program to convert assembly language instructions into their machine code equivalents.

Assembly language. A machine-orientated programming language which uses mnemonic codes (memory aids) to identify instructions. Programs written in assembly language must be translated into machine code by an assembler program before execution.

Asynchronous transmission. The transmission of characters along a channel at irregular intervals, for example, those produced by keyboard operation.

Audit trail. A mechanism, usually built into the applications software, to allow the tracing of a transaction's history from input through to output. Auditing is an essential part of any accounting application as a guard against accidental or deliberate misuse of data.

Augend. One of the operands used in addition which is replaced by the result of the addition.

Auxiliary storage. Synonymous with backing store, for example, magnetic tape or disk.

Base address. An address in a program instruction which forms the starting point for relative addresses and allows the calculation of the absolute or machine address.

Base address. The starting location for an array.

BASIC. A high level programming language suitable for on-line program development and popularly used to introduce beginners to programming techniques. Acronym for Beginner's All-purpose Symbolic Instruction Code.

Batch. A collection of transactions awaiting processing as a single unit.

Batch file. A facility available with the MS-DOS operating system for the automatic execution of regularly used sequences of commands.

Batch processing. A method of processing transactions which allows accuracy control totals to be associated with each batch. Each batch is dealt with as an entity, so that one error causes the rejection of the whole batch for correction and re-submission. Used where delay in updating is acceptable to users. Contrast with real-time.

Batch total. A total produced from selected values in a batch, for example, invoice quantities. Used to control the progress of a batch of transactions through each stage of processing. Totals are checked at each stage.

BCD. Abbreviation for binary coded decimal notation. Each decimal digit is coded with four binary digits.

Binary number system. A number system with the base or radix of 2 and in which only two digits are used, one and zero.

Binary search or chop. A method of searching a sequenced table or file. The procedure selects the upper or lower half based upon an examination of its midpoint value. The selected part is then similarly halved, and so on until the required item is detected.

Binary tree. A form of tree data structure in which each node has a left pointer and a right pointer to other nodes in the tree.

Bit. Contraction of binary digit (0 or 1). A bit is the smallest element of data or instruction representation in a computer. Bits are usually handled in groups of, say, 8, 16 or 32, depending on the architecture of the computer.

Block. A group of logical records transferred between memory and peripherals as a unit. Also known as a 'physical' record.

Blockingfactor. The maximum number of logical records which can be fitted into a block.

Block marking. A function in word processing packages, for marking sections of text for special attention, such as moving, deleting or copying.

Blow. The process of writing onto a 'chip' memory such as EPROM (Erasable Programmable Read Only Memory.

Board. A rectangular circuit board which can be slotted inside the casing of a computer to give added memory or program facilities.

Boolean algebra. A system of algebra developed by the mathematician George Boole. Its application to computers lies in its facility for expressing the logical operations carried out by a computer.

Branch instruction. An instruction which specifies the address of the next instruction, normally out of program sequence. A branch may be conditional or unconditional. Also known as a jump instruction.

Bubble memory. A non-volatile memory device which uses magnetized 'bubbles' to represent binary data.

Bucket. An area of direct access storage such as disk which may consist of a number of blocks of data and can be addressed as a unit.

Buffer. A temporary storage area for data being transmitted between devices and components of a computer system. Buffers are used in terminals, storage and other peripherals and in the CPU. They can compensate for speed differences between relatively slow peripheral devices and the CPU.

Bug. A defect or malfunction in a computer program or system.

Bus. An electrical connection within a computer system and along which data is passed.

Byte. A group of bits handled as a unit by a computer system. Generally, a byte is formed from eight bits.

CAD. An acronym for Computer-Aided Design. A designer makes use of a computer, screen and lightpen or similar device as aids to design.

Cambridge ring. A network configuration developed at Cambridge University and used in local area networks.

Ceefax. A broadcast system transmitting text information from central computer databases. Text is transmitted in 'frames' with television pictures for display on a television set with special adapter. One-way transmission only.

Cell. In relation to spreadsheets, a single location identifiable by co-ordinate references.

Central processing unit (CPU). The components of a computer system with the functions for control and processing, namely the control unit and the arithmetic/logic unit. Often known as the 'processor'.

Centralized processing. All computer processing is carried out centrally. Contrast with distributed processing.

CGA. Acronym for Colour Graphics Adaptor.

Chain printer. A line printer where characters are linked into a chain which rotates at high speed and characters are printed at the appropriate positions as they traverse the paper.

Character codes. A code use to represent characters, for example, ASCII.

Character printer. Prints a single character at a time, as do, for example, the dot matrix and daisy wheel printer.

Check digit. An additional digit appended to a number to provide a self-checking device for transcription errors, for example, the modulus 11 check digit.

Chip. A slang term for a small piece of silicon with etched integrated circuits. They may have different functions, for example, memory or processor chips.

Circular or cyclic shift. The shifting of bits from one end of a location to reappear at the other, for example, a right shift of 2 moves the two bit values from the two rightmost positions to the two leftmost positions.

Closed User Group (CUG). Reserved pages in a viewdata system such as Prestel, which are only accessible by a restricted group of users.

Cluster. In relation to the MS-DOS operating system, a cluster is a group of disk sectors which can be identified in the File Allocation Table (FAT) as relating to a particular file. Thus, a file may occupy a number of non-contiguous clusters.

COBOL. A high level programming language used for programming business and file processing applications. Acronym for COmmon Business Orientated Language.

CODASYL. An acronym for COnference on DAta SYstems Languages. Responsible for standards in Codasyl database management systems.

Coding sheet. A pre-printed sheet of paper used by programmers to record their program source code. The sheets are tabulated for a particular programming language.

COM. An acronym for Computer Output on Microforms. Data is recorded in a physically condensed form and can be viewed with a special projector.

Compiler. A program which translates high level source code into the object or machine code of the target machine.

Concentrator. A device for concentrating transmission from a number of low speed lines into a high speed line.

Conditional branch instruction. Program control is 'branched' out of its normal sequence when specified conditions occur.

Constant or literal. A value which is set at compilation time and does not change during program execution.

Control characters. Perform special functions, for example, carriage return on a printer.

Control total. A total accumulated on a batch of data to be processed. The computer accumulates the same total during data entry and checks its consistency. Used in batch processing.

Control unit. The functional component within the Central Processing Unit (CPU) of a computer which fetches instructions one by one, interprets them and 'triggers' the appropriate action.

Controlled redundancy. Used in connection with relational databases and refers to the duplication of certain key data items which allow connections to be made between different relations or files in a database.

Conversational mode. The user is in direct communication with the computer via a series of prompts and responses, usually via a visual display unit. Also known as interactive mode.

CP/M (Control Program Microcomputers). An operating system for microcomputers.

cps. Acronym for characters per second.

CPU. Acronym for Central Processing Unit. It is the 'brain' of the computer, incorporating the control unit and the arithmetic-logic unit (ALU).

Credit note. A document which signifies that a customer's account is to be credited by a given amount, thus reducing the customer's indebtedness to the supplier.

Creditor. A person or organization which owes money to a business for goods or services supplied on credit.

CSMA/CD. Acronym for Carrier Sense Multiple Access with Collision Detector. A method of access control used on broadcast computer networks such as the 'bus' network.

Current instruction register (CIR). A register in the CPU for the storage of the current instruction for decoding and execution.

Cylinder. A grouping of tracks in the same vertical plane, as for example, in a disk pack. Synonymous with seek area - all the tracks available whilst the read-write heads are in one position. The concept of the cylinder is used in addressing indexed sequential files.

Daisy wheel printer. A rather slow, high quality output character printer which uses a print wheel with each character font on a 'petal' on its periphery.

Database. A collection of inter-related data stored together on a direct access storage medium to serve one or more applications.

Database Management System (DBMS). The programs required to control the use of a database. For example, Relational DBMS and Codasyl DBMS.

Data capture. The collection of data at the source point by automated means, for example, optical mark reading, point-of-sale (POS) terminals.

Data collection. The process of gathering raw data for preparation and computer processing, for example, the collection of timesheets for a payroll run.

Data control. The process of controlling the accuracy and completeness of data during the data processing cycle. In batch processing, for example, this includes verification and validation (batch totals etc.). The responsibility for day-to-day control lies with the data control staff in the Data Processing Department or Management Information Services.

Data description language (DDL). A language for describing data, generally the logical data, during database construction.

Data format. A description of the length and form of data values.

Data independence. The property of a database which allows the alteration of its overall logical or physical structure without changing the applications' views of the data.

Data item. The smallest unit of data that has meaning as information, for example, name, date of birth in a personnel record. Synonymous with 'field'.

Data manipulation language (DML). The language used by the programmer to process and manipulate data in a database.

Data transmission. The electronic transmission of data via a telecommunications link.

Data word. A unit of computer storage containing an item of data.

Debug. To remove errors from a computer system, for example, syntax or logic errors in a computer program. The process is usually supported by software utilities such as a trace or debugger.

Desktop publishing (DTP). A computer system with facilities for combined text and graphics presentation, 'cut and paste' and font selection, which are necessary for publishing.

Digitizer. A device to convert analogue signals into a sequence of digital values. For example, maps or pictures can be digitized for computer storage and processing.

Direct access storage. A facility which allows data to be retrieved directly from a storage device without reference to the rest of the file, for example, magnetic disk.

Directory. Used by the operating system to record the names of files, their size and the date they were created or last updated.

Disk pack. A set of disks mounted on a central spindle and accessible as a unit by read-write arms.

Diskette. A small, flexible disk or 'floppy' disk, particularly popular with microcomputer systems.

Distributed processing. A system where computer power is not centralized, but is distributed to geographically separate branches of an organization, or amongst user systems within the same branch. This can be facilitated through the use of networked computers.

Documentation. The written description necessary for the testing, implementation and maintenance of a system. The documentation broadly falls into three categories, program, user and operator documentation.

DOS. Acronym for Disk Operating System - MS(Microsoft)-DOS.

Double buffering. Where the input-output buffers are used in tandem to speed data throughput.

Double density disks. Floppy disks with track density of 48 tracks per inch (tpi). The actual number of tracks used is 40.

Double-precision arithmetic. Computer arithmetic using storage locations double the usual length to increase accuracy.

Drivers. Files which enable a package to make use of the particular capabilities of different peripherals, for example, screen and printer drivers.

Dry running. A process of checking the logic of a computer program by hand and off-line.

Dumb terminal. A terminal without any processing power of its own, that is, with no 'intelligence'.

Duplex or full duplex. Simultaneous transmissions of data in both directions with the use of two channels.

EBCDIC. An acronym for Extended Binary Coded Decimal Interchange Code. It is an 8-bit code used mainly on IBM equipment.

EGA. Acronym for Enhanced Graphics Adaptor. Used as a standard for the resolution of colour graphics screens.

Electronic Mail. The transmission of mail by electronic means via a computer network. There is usually a 'mailbox' facility for the storage of messages awaiting collection.

Electrostatic printer. A printer which uses electrostatic charges to 'fix' characters to the paper.

Encryption. The transformation of data passing through a communications link into an encoded form which prevents its interpretation by unauthorized persons 'tapping' the line.

Exchangeable disk. Hard disk storage which is removable.

Execute phase. The part of the 'fetch-execute' cycle in which the instruction is executed.

Expert system. A computer system programmed using artificial intelligence techniques to provide information or decisions relating to some narrow area of human expertise, for example, house conveyancing, house plant care, medical diagnosis. Also known as 'knowledge-based' systems.

Exponent. The power to which a base is raised. Relevant to floating point arithmetic.

Expression. A logical or mathematical statement represented symbolically.

Facsimile Transmission (FAX). The transmission of a copy of a document via a telecommunications link. Usually, it is transmitted in digital form.

Feasibility study. A study carried out by systems analysts and interested parties to ascertain possible solutions to an information processing problem.

Fetch-execute cycle. The activity of the CPU in fetching, decoding and executing program instruction one by one in a cycle.

Fibre optics. A means of transmitting data in light form.

Field. A subdivision of a record containing an item of information. Synonymous with data item.

Fifth generation computers. A combination of advanced hardware and software; characteristics include, faster processors, the use of multiple processors for 'parallel' processing, natural language processing and more human-orientated input-output devices, such as speech synthesizers, voice recognition devices and 'mice'.

File. A collection of logically related records, for example, a stock file or a personnel file.

File allocation table (FAT). A table used by the MS-DOS operating system and stored on disk to record the allocation of disk clusters to individual files.

File organization. Methods of organization records in a file, for example, serially, sequentially or randomly.

File server. A local area network node which handles workstation access to shared storage and controls the exchange of files between network users.

Fixed head disk. A disk unit with one read-write head per track. No head movement is necessary.

Fixed length record. A record with a fixed physical length in terms of the number of bit positions it occupies.

Fixed point arithmetic. Arithmetic without taking account of the radix point position. Numbers are treated as whole numbers for the purposes of calculation. The programmer has to keep track of the radix point to control calculations.

Floating point arithmetic. Arithmetic using floating point numbers, the absolute value of which are determined by a mantissa and an exponent.

Flowchart. A diagrammatic representation showing the flow of control in a

computer system.

Footer. In relation to word processing, a standard line of print, defined to appear at the bottom of each page in a multi-page document.

Footprint. The physical desk or floor space needed by a computer system or peripheral.

Format - disk. A process which establishes the sector size on a disk for a particular operating system and establishes a file allocation table (FAT) and root directory.

Format - text. A word processing function to arrange text in a particular way, for example, with a straight or ragged right hand margin.

FORTRAN (FORmula TRANslator). A high level programming language particularly useful for programming scientific and mathematical applications.

Fourth generation languages (4GLs). Higher level languages which allow applications to be generated with the minimum of procedural programming; includes Applications Generators.

Frequency division multiplexing (FDM). The separation of different data streams with the use of different frequency bands for each.

Front-end processor (FEP). Usually a minicomputer handling incoming and outgoing communications traffic for a mainframe computer, which is left free to carry out the main processing tasks.

Functional area. A section or department within an organization with a particular function, for example, sales or accounts.

Function key. A programmable key on a keyboard. There are usually ten or twelve and they are used by different software packages for different functions.

Gate. An electronic circuit which accepts a number of inputs and provides the requisite output. The output will depend on the function of the gate. Synonymous with logic gates, for example AND and OR gates.

Gateway software. Software to allow access from a network to external computers and their databases.

Generation. May relate to the version of a file. In file security, historical copies can be kept, which are identified by generation according to relative age - 'grandfather, father, son'. Generally associated with tape file processing.

Gigabyte. One thousand million bytes.

Golf ball. Spherical print head with character fonts in relief on the surface.

Graph plotter. A computer output device which produces graphical material under computer control. There are two main types, the flat bed and the drum plotter.

Half-duplex. Data transmission in both directions, but not simultaneously.

Hard sectoring. Small index holes determine the beginning of sectors on a disk. The sector size cannot be altered.

Hashing. A technique using an algorithm to generate disk addresses for records within a random file. The technique aims to achieve an even distribution of records and to minimize overflow.

Hash total. A control total used in batch processing. Totals are derived from values such as account numbers and are thus meaningless apart from their control function. Also known as nonsense totals.

Head crash. A collision between the read-write head and the surface of the disk, which usually results in severe disk damage. May be caused by dust or other impurities on the disk surface.

Header. In relation to word processing, a defined heading which is to appear at the top of every page in a multi-page document.

Hexadecimal ('Hex'). Number system with the base 16. Uses digits 0 to 9 and then A, B, C, D, E and F. Often used as shorthand for binary codes in technical manuals for computer systems and by programmers who make use of assembly language.

High level language. A language remote from any particular machine code. Each instruction in a high level language usually equates with a number of machine code instructions.

Hit rate. A percentage figure expressing the proportion of records in a file 'hit' during a processing run.

$$Hit\ rate = \frac{Number\ of\ records\ 'hit'}{Number\ of\ records\ in\ file} \times 100$$

Host computer. A computer providing a central service to a number of other computers in a network.

Icon. A symbol on a screen menu representing a program option.

Iliffe vector. A table look-up method for accessing array elements.

Immediate address. The operand is held in the address portion of an instruction word, so no further access to memory is needed.

Impact printer. A printer which uses an impact mechanism, usually against an ink ribbon to produce characters on paper.

Indexed sequential. A method of organizing a file on a direct access storage device such as disk, where records are organized in sequence according to a primary record key and indexes provide a means of referring to records directly.

Indirect address. An instruction word contains an address, not of the operand but of another address which itself contains the address of the operand. This process can be repeated so that the actual operand is obtained through several levels of indirect addresses.

Infix notation. An expression places the operator between the operands, for example X + Y.

Information flow diagram. A diagram which identifies the flows of information between different functional areas of a business.

Initialize. To set variables to an initial value at the beginning of program execution.

Input device. Any peripheral device which transfers data from an external source into the memory of the computer.

Instruction address register (IAR). Keeps track of locations where instructions are stored. It is incremented each time an instruction is received, so that it has the address of the next instruction. Also known as Program Counter (PC) and Sequence Control Register (SCR).

Instruction format. The layout of an instruction word - the number of bits allocated to each part.

Instruction set. The set of all machine instructions available with a particular computer.

Instruction word. A memory word containing an instruction.

Intelligent terminal. A computer terminal with some processing power and storage capacity.

Integrated package. A package which provides several general-purpose packages in one, for example, spreadsheet, word processor, database and communications.

Inter-block gap (IBG). The physical gap between blocks of data on magnetic tape to allow the starting and stopping of the tape between block transfers.

Interpreter. A translator program which interprets and directly executes program statements. Contrast with compiler.

Interrupt. A break in the activity of the central processor caused by an external event. For example, the completion of an input/output operation by a peripheral results in an interrupt to the processor to return to the original routine. During the input/output operation, the processor can be occupied with other processing until interrupted.

Iterate. Commonly, to undertake a series of steps repeatedly, usually until a certain condition or result is achieved. More correctly, a process of calculating a result through a repeated series of steps, in which successive approximations are made until the desired result is achieved.

Jump instruction. Synonymous with branch instruction.

Karnaugh map. A method of representing logical relationships in table form.

Key-to-disk. A method of encoding source data onto magnetic disk prior to input and processing.

Kilobyte (kb). A unit of computer storage - 1024 bytes.

Latency. The rotational delay which occurs as the read-write head waits for a revolving magnetic disk to bring the required block of data into the read-write position.

Least significant bit (LSB). The rightmost digit in a group of bits.

Light pen. A 'pen-like' input device which uses a photo-electric cell to indicate positions on a screen, for example, to select items from a menu on screen.

Line printer. A printer which effectively prints a line of text at a time. Contrast with character printer.

Linked list. A data structure in which nodes have pointers to other nodes in some sequential order.

Linker. A program which incorporates any necessary machine code routines, from a library of standard routines, into an object program after compilation.

LISP (LISt Processing). A programming language where data elements are used in 'lists'. Its main application is in the field of artificial intelligence.

List. A simple data structure consisting of a sequence of elements.

Local area network (LAN). A network of connected computers confined to a small area, say to a group of buildings on one site.

Logical operator. One of the logical functions, AND, or OR, NOT etc. used on variables.

Logical shift. A shift of bits in a location which takes no account of numeric value. Contrast with arithmetic shift.

Logo. A high level language designed by Seymour Papert to encourage an 'active' approach to computer-aided learning through the use of 'turtle' graphics. Shares many of the features of LISP.

Low-level language. A machine-orientated programming language as opposed to a problem-orientated high level language. Generally, each low level language instruction has a single machine code equivalent.

Machine code or language. The pattern of bits directly executable by a computer.

Macro-instruction. An instruction in a source language (high level or low level) which, when compiled, produces a number of machine code instructions.

Magnetic disk. A disk-shaped backing storage medium which provides direct access. Each magnetizable surface is divided into tracks and sectors addressable by the computer. Each addressable location may contain one or more logical records.

Magnetic tape. A serial access backing storage medium. It consists of a reel of plastic tape with a magnetizable coating to allow the representation of data. Generally, records are stored and accessed sequentially because the medium is non-addressable.

Magnetic ink character recognition (MICR). An input method whereby a reading device 'recognizes' stylized characters printed in magnetizable ink. Used almost exclusively by the banking industry to read coded data from cheques.

Main memory. The primary memory of a computer system which stores programs and data currently being processed by the CPU. Contents are lost when the power is switched off and so is supplemented by backing storage.

Mantissa. The fractional part of a floating point number. The absolute value is determined by the value of the exponent.

Masking. The extraction of specified bits from a group of bits with the use of a 'mask'.

Master file. A file which contains permanent or semi-permanent information on a subject. Usually affected by transactions during the updating process.

Megabyte (mb). Roughly one million bytes - a measurement of computer storage.

Memory address register (MAR). Provides the location address of the specific memory word to be read from or written to via the memory buffer register (MBR).

Memory buffer register (MBR). Whenever the contents of a memory word are to be transferred in or out of memory, they pass through the MBR. This applies to data and instructions.

Message switching. A technique of switching messages between nodes in a network. Usually carried out by a mainframe or minicomputer at the 'hub' of the network.

Micro Channel Architecture (MCA). A computer system architecture pioneered and patented by IBM. Forms the basis of IBM's PS-2 range of microcomputers.

Microprocessor. A central processor (control unit and arithmetic-logic unit) on a single chip.

Millisecond (ms). One thousandth of a second.

Minuend. In subtraction, the number from which another number (subtrahend) is extracted is known as the minuend.

Mnemonic. A memory aid generally used for representing machine code operations in assembly language, for example, LDA for LoaD Accumulator.

Modem (MOdulator-DEModulator). A device for converting the digital signal produced by a computer into an analogue form suitable for transmission along a telephone line. Also capable of carrying out the reverse process for incoming data.

Most significant bit (MSB). The leftmost bit in a group of bits.

Mouse. A hand-held cursor-control device.

Multiplexer (MUX). A device which transmits data arriving from several sources along a single transmission medium, by modulating the carrier wave for each data stream. Two major methods of producing separately identifiable signals are time division and frequency division multiplexing.

Multi-processing. The use of multiple processors for executing programs.

Multi-programming. The processing of several jobs apparently at the same time. Programs and data relating to jobs are partitioned in memory and the CPU makes use of its high speed to switch control between them. This is possible because when a job is occupied with input or output, the CPU is free to carry out other tasks.

Multi-tasking. The concurrent processing of several tasks, relating to a single user, in memory at the same time.

Multi-user. A facility to allow more than one user to use a computer at the same time. Requires that the operating system can share the computer's resources and protect users' files from other users.

NAND gate. A logic gate with two or more inputs and whose output is 0 if all inputs are 1 and 1 if any inputs are 0.

Nanosecond. One thousand millionth of a second.

Natural language processing. Allows a user to use 'free-form' English as a means of communicating with a computer. May be typed or spoken.

Network. A number of computers connected together for the purposes of communication and processing.

NLQ. Near Letter Quality. A standard of printing by some dot matrix printers, which attempts to approach that of daisy wheel printers.

Node. An element of a data structure containing data and pointers to other nodes.

Node. A component in a computer network, for example, one microcomputer station in a local area network.

Non-volatile memory. A storage medium which continues to hold data after the power is removed, for example, ROM, EPROM and PROM. Contrast with RAM which is volatile.

NOR gate. A logic gate with two or more inputs whose output is 0 if any input is 1 and 1 if all input values are 0.

Normalize. In floating point arithmetic the representation uses a mantissa and exponent. A normalized number is one conforming to this representation (standard form).

NOT gate. A logic gate with a single input and a single output. The input is inverted so that if the input is 0 the output is 1 and vice-versa.

Object program. The machine code or object program produced after compilation of the source program. The object program is executable on the target machine.

Octal. A number system using the base eight. The octal system uses the digits 0 to 7 and each digit position represents a power of eight.

Off-line. Not under the control of the CPU or processor.

Offset. The displacement required from a base address in order to access a particular element of an array.

On-line. Under the control of the CPU or processor.

One address instruction. The instruction word only allows reference to one operand address.

Opcode. The part of an instruction word which defines the operation to be performed.

Operand. A data item to be operated upon. The instruction word may contain the actual operand or an address which refers to the operand directly or indirectly.

Operating system. The basic suite of programs which supervise and control the general running of a computer system.

Optical character recognition (OCR).

The recognition by an OCR device of characters (usually stylized) by measuring their optical reflectance.

Optical disk. A high capacity storage device (measured in gigabytes) which makes use of laser technology to record and read data on the disk.

Optical mark reading (OMR). Process whereby an OMR device identifies values on a pre-printed document by the position of pencil marks. Usually, boxes on the document are indicated as representing particular values and each can be indicated by a pencil mark in the relevant box.

OS/2. Acronym for IBM's multi-tasking, multi-user Operating System 2.

OSI model. Open Systems Interconnection model. Developed by the International Standards Organization, it lays down standards for network systems.

Output device. Any peripheral which transfers data from the internal memory of the computer to the outside world.

Parallel processing. The technique of executing a number of computer instructions in parallel. A number of interconnected processors called transputers are needed to do this. Most computers only have one processor and carry out instructions one after the other.

Parallel running. When a new system is implemented, the old system is continued until the users are satisfied that the new system is functioning correctly and reliably.

Parallel transmission. The transmission of bit groupings in parallel.

Parity. A minimal form of error checking in data transmission, whereby an extra bit is added to a group of bits to make the total number of bit 1s even (even parity) or odd (odd parity). The parity is checked after each transmission.

Partition. A division of memory, either disk or RAM.

Pascal. A high level, block-structured programming language named after Emile Pascal, a French mathematician.

Peripheral device. Any computer device under the control of the central processor, but external to it.

Picosecond. One million-millionth of a second.

Pilot testing. A method of system implementation which only applies a new system to a portion of the live data. The remainder is processed by the old method until the users of the pilot data are satisfied concerning the system's accuracy and reliability.

Plotter. Flat bed or drum graph plotter.

Pointer. An arrow or 'finger' in the cursor position which allows the selection of menu options on screen, possibly with a 'mouse'.

Port. A place of entry to or exit from a central processor, dedicated to a single channel, for example, a printer port.

Prestel. A public viewdata system accessible by telephone line and Prestel adapter. It provides pages of information on a wide variety of general and specialist information.

Primary key. A data item which ensures unique identification of an individual record.

Print server. A local area network node which shares its printer facility amongst all users on the network. Print jobs are queued and may be executed in turn or according to assigned priorities.

Processor. See central processing unit.

Program counter (PC). A register which contains the address of the next instruction to be executed. Synonymous with sequence control register (SCR) and instruction address register (IAR).

Program specification. A specification produced by a systems analyst as part of a system specification and detailing all the requirements of the related applications software.

Program testing. The process of running a program with test data to check the correctness and completeness of output.

Prolog. A programming language based on mathematical logic. It is used extensively in artificial intelligence (AI) applications and is particularly suitable for database applications. Adapted by the Japanese for programming their 'fifth generation' computers.

PROM (Programmable Read Only Memory). A chip which can be 'blown' or programmed by the user to produce non-volatile memory store (ROM).

Protocol. A set of rules governing the format of messages transmitted in computer networks. Compatibility needs to be established between communicating devices so that they can 'talk' to each other.

Pull-down menu. A facility commonly available in integrated software such as Framework, whereby the user can 'pull' a menu onto the screen by selecting an icon or symbol on screen, or a word from a range at the top of the screen.

Quad-density disks. Floppy disks with a track density of 96 tracks per inch (tpi) and double the number of sectors used on double-density disks.

Query language. A language designed for users to make ad hoc enquiries of a database.

Queue. A linear list data structure in which elements are added at one end and removed from the other end.

Radix. The base of a number system, for example, the radix for the binary number system is 2, for the decimal system, 10.

RAM. Random access memory - the main memory of the computer.

Random access. A facility for accessing a storage medium for any record or data item, without reference to the rest of the file. Also known as direct access. Main memory and disk storage provide this facility.

Read only memory (ROM). Storage medium which allows only 'reading' and not 'writing'.

Record. A group of related data items forming an entity. A subdivision of a file.

Register. A storage location, usually within the CPU with special (for example Program Counter) or general purpose functions (storage of intermediate values during processing).

Relation. A two-dimensional array or table forming a 'flat' file. Terminology associated with relational databases.

Relational algebra. A language providing a set of logical operators for manipulating 'relations' (files) in a relational database.

Relational database. A database made up of relations or two-dimensional tables.

Relative addressing. A method of addressing where each address is relative to a 'base' address. Each address is given a 'displacement' value to relate its position to the base address. By altering the 'base', a program can be relocated in memory. If the base address is taken as the address of the current instruction, this is known as self-relative addressing.

Remote job entry (RJE). The transmission of a batch job via a telecommunications link to a central computer for processing.

Repeater. A signal amplifier, which passes packets of data onto the next node in a network.

Response time. Generally refers to interactive systems (via VDUs or other terminals) and indicates the time which elapses from the entry of a query or command at the keyboard and the receipt of the computer's response on screen.

Reverse polish (postfix notation). A form of expression where the operators succeed the operands. For example, the expression (W + X) * Y + Z in infix notation, becomes WX + Y * Z +.

Reverse video. A reversing of background and foreground colours on a VDU screen to highlight selected characters.

Rewrite. To overwrite an existing record with an updated version of it. This is only possible with direct access storage.

Ring network. A network topology where computers are connected in a ring structure. Evolved in Cambridge and known as the Cambridge ring.

RISC. An acronym for Reduced Instruction Set Computer in which the decoding circuitry is limited to the most frequently used instructions, thus producing smaller, faster processors.

RPG (Report Program Generator). A high level programming language designed to allow trained users (as opposed to specialist programmers) to generate reports from computer files.

Schema. The overall logical definition of a database.

Search. The scanning of data items for those in accord with specified criteria, for example, salaries in excess of 10,000 in a Personnel file.

Sector. A subdivision of a track on a magnetic disk. Constitutes the smallest addressable unit on a disk.

Seek time. The time taken for moveable read-write heads to move to the selected track or cylinder on a magnetic disk.

Self-relative address. An address calculated by adding a 'displacement' value to the address of the current instruction. That is, the address is in a position relative to the address of the current instruction. See also relative address.

Sequence control register (SCR). See program counter.

Sequential access. The retrieval of records according to the sequence of their organization, for example, a customer file stored in Customer Account number order.

Sequential organization. A method of storing a file so that records are sequenced according to a primary record key, for example, a Stock Code.

Serial access. Retrieving records in the order that they are physically stored, in other words, as they come.

Serial organization. Simply, records stored one after the other, not necessarily in sequence, for example, an unsorted tape file.

Serial transmission. Transmission of data, usually via a telecommunications link, whereby the 'bits' follow one another in a serial fashion. Contrast with parallel transmission.

Set (Codasyl definition) A set is a named collection of record types. Each set specified in a scheme (logical database definition) must have one record type declared as its OWNER and one or more record types declared as MEMBER records. For example, a Customer record may 'own' a number of Order records.

Sign and magnitude. Integer numbers represented in a computer with the most significant bit as the sign (0 for positive and 1 for negative).

Simplex. Transmission of data in one direction only.

Soft sectored. Sectors are marked on magnetic disk by means of software rather than physical markers.

Source program. A program written in a programming language (high or low level). It must be translated into machine code before execution.

Spooling (Simultaneous Peripheral Operation On Line). Making more efficient use of hardware during input-output operations by using faster peripheral devices in parallel with normal job processing, as a temporary substitute for slower devices. For example, output destined for printing may be spooled to an area of disk and dumped from there to the printer while the processor is left to carry on with other tasks.

SQL. Structured query language. A nonprocedural 4th generation programming language.

Stack. A linear list data structure allowing access to elements only at one end of the list.

Star network. A network topology, whereby a main 'host' computer at the 'hub' services a number of peripheral systems.

Stop bit. A bit used to indicate the end of a character in asynchronous transmission.

Structured programming. A programming design technique which makes use of control structures such as 'IF ... THEN ... ELSE' and 'DO ... WHILE ...' to combine and control separate functions within a program. Only three basic control structures are used; sequence of operations, selection of alternative operations and repetition or iteration.

Subroutine. A self-contained routine, coded once within a program, which may be 'called' at any point during the main program. After execution of the subroutine, control is returned to the instruction immediately following the call.

Subschema. A limited logical view of a database derived from the schema (overall logical database view) to be used by an applications program.

Subtrahend. One of the two operands in a subtraction which is subtracted from the 'minuend' to give a result.

Synchronous transmission. The transmission of data in 'streams'. The sender and the receiver devices are synchronized so that individual characters are identified within the stream. No start or stop bits are needed. Special 'SYN' characters are transmitted periodically to maintain the synchronization. Contrast with asynchronous transmission.

Syntax. The formal rules of grammar and structure governing the use of a programming language.

Syntax error. Where the syntax rules are broken in program coding. Generally, such errors are indicated by a compiler or interpreter.

Systems analysis. The study of an activity with a view to its computerization.

Systems analyst. A person specializing in systems analysis.

Systems software. Program purchased as part of a computer system and which are concerned with the general running of the hardware and not with specific applications. Examples include, operating systems, utilities and compilers.

Tape deck/drive/transport. An operational device for the processing of magnetic tape files.

Teleconferencing. The conducting of a conference through the use of computers and telecommunications links.

Telecommuting. Working from home with the use of a computer link to the actual office.

Teletext. Systems such as Oracle and Ceefax which use spare bandwidth on television transmissions to send 'pages' of information from a computer database to television sets fitted with special adapters. The database provides information on a variety of subjects of general and specialist interest.

Test data. Data specially prepared for the testing of program output for accuracy and consistency with the requirements of the program specification.

Three address instruction. An instruction format which allows for three addresses.

Timesharing. The technique, often used with interactive systems, whereby the CPU shares out its time amongst a number of users, with the aim of giving good response times to each. The allocation of time is known as 'time slicing'.

Token ring network. A local area network industry standard. Its main proponent is IBM.

Top-down design. Designing a program according to its overall logic, in terms of its identifiable components and then defining those components in further detail and so on, until the required level of detail is obtained.

Trace. A software facility which traces the path of a program's execution. Useful in the detection of logic errors.

Transaction file. A file containing transactions to be used in the updating of a master file.

Transaction logging. The recording of transactions on a separate serial file at the same time as they update the relevant master files.

Translator. A program for the translation of source code into object or machine code, for example, a compiler, an interpreter or an assembler.

Transputer. A processor with serial links to allow communication with other transputers. The basis of parallel processing computers.

Tree. A non-linear list in which each node has a number of pointers to other nodes in a hierarchical structure.

Two address instruction. An instruction format which allows for two addresses.

Update. A process whereby a master record is amended by a transaction to reflect the current position.

Utility. A program which performs a common task such as sorting a file or copying a disk.

Validation. A process, usually carried out by a validation or 'data vet' program, to check that data falls within specified valid criteria, for example, that hours of overtime worked fall within a range from 0 to 20.

Verification. The process of checking the accuracy of data transcription, usually in a data encoding operation such as key-to-disk, prior to batch data input. Commonly, verification involves the re-keying of the data by another operator and the verifier machine compares keys depressed with data already stored.

Viewdata. Generic term for database systems which provide two-way communication with users via telecommunications links and terminals. The database may be public (e.g. Prestel) or private. Information is provided in 'pages' which can be accessed either by page number or through hierarchical indexes.

Virtual memory. An extension of main memory to include on line disk storage, such that a programmer can regard the total memory space as being available for a program. Programs are written in segments or pages and are called into main memory as required.

VDU. Acronym for visual display unit and comprising screen and keyboard.

VGA. Video graphics array. A resolution standard for colour graphics displays.

Voice output. The technique of simulating the human voice by computer means.

Voice recognition. A technique to allow computer input to be supplied directly by a human voice.

Volatile. A property associated with computer memory, whereby it loses its data when power is removed.

Wide area network (WAN). A network which makes use of the telecommunications network to link computer systems over a wide geographical area.

WIMP. Acronym for Windows, Icons, Mice and Pull-down menus, all of which are commonly used in user-friendly, menu driven packages.

Winchester disk. A high density, hermetically sealed disk originally developed by IBM in the early 1970s. The technology is now extensively used for hard disk microcomputer systems.

Window. An area of screen dedicated to a particular function. The user may have several 'windows' on screen at one time.

Word. A unit of memory storage addressed as a single unit.

Word processor. A computer system used for generating documentary material. May be dedicated to the task or may be a computer system with word processing package. The essential components are screen, keyboard, disk store and printer.

Word wrap. A feature of word processing. As text is typed, words move automatically to the start of a new line if there is insufficient room for them at the right hand margin.

Write. To transfer data from main memory to a storage device such as disk. If the transfer is to an output device it is known as printing.

Write protect. A mechanism to prevent accidental or deliberate overwriting of a disk's contents.

WYSIWYG. Acronym for What You See Is What You Get. Used to describe word processors which allow the screen to show text exactly as it is printed.

Index